Teaching and Learning Mathe

MATHEMATICS TEACHING AND LEARNING

Volume 2

Mathematics Teaching and Learning is an international book series that aims to provide an important outlet for sharing the research, policy, and practice of mathematics education to promote the teaching and learning of mathematics at all school levels as well as teacher education around the world. The book series strives to address different aspects, forms, and stages in mathematics teaching and learning both in and out of classrooms, their interactions throughout the process of mathematics instruction and teacher education from various theoretical, historical, policy, psychological, socio-cultural, or cross-cultural perspectives. The series features books that are contributed by researchers, curriculum developers, teacher educators, and practitioners from different education systems.

For further information:
https://www.sensepublishers.com/catalogs/bookseries/mathematics-teaching-and-learning/

Teaching and Learning Mathematics through Variation

Confucian Heritage Meets Western Theories

Edited by

Rongjin Huang
Middle Tennessee State University, USA

and

Yeping Li
Texas A&M University, USA
Shanghai Normal University, China

SENSE PUBLISHERS
ROTTERDAM/BOSTON/TAIPEI

A C.I.P. record for this book is available from the Library of Congress.

ISBN: 978-94-6300-780-1 (paperback)
ISBN: 978-94-6300-781-8 (hardback)
ISBN: 978-94-6300-782-5 (e-book)

Published by: Sense Publishers,
P.O. Box 21858,
3001 AW Rotterdam,
The Netherlands
https://www.sensepublishers.com/

All chapters in this book have undergone peer review.

Printed on acid-free paper

ADVANCE PRAISE FOR
TEACHING AND LEARNING MATHEMATICS THROUGH VARIATION

"This book paints a richly detailed and elaborated picture of both teaching mathematics and learning to teach mathematics with variation. Teaching with variation and variation as a theory of learning are brought together to be theorized and exemplified through analysis of teaching in a wide variety of classrooms and targeting both the content and processes of mathematical thinking. Twenty diverse chapters from leading scholars provide a uniquely comprehensive view into this fundamental pillar of Chinese teaching, and demonstrate how the lens of variation reveals underlying connections between effective teaching practices around the world. Highly recommended."
– Kaye Stacey, Emeritus Professor of Mathematics Education, University of Melbourne, Australia

"Many teachers in England are excited by the concept of teaching with variation and devising variation exercises to support their pupils' mastery of mathematics. However, fully understanding and becoming proficient in its use takes time. This book provides a valuable resource to deepen understanding through the experiences of other teachers shared within the book and the insightful reflections of those who have researched this important area. Variation is central to a national programme to improve mathematics achievement in England and many teachers have asked the question *"why didn't I think of teaching like this before? It makes perfect sense!"*
– Debbie Morgan, Director for Primary Mathematics, National Centre for Excellence in the Teaching of Mathematics, United Kingdom

TABLE OF CONTENTS

vii

Part V: Commentary and Conclusion

JILL ADLER

FOREWORD

In the recent past, I have included engagement with the notion of variation in the Masters course I teach focused on Teaching and Learning Algebra. Most of the students are practicing teachers. Their responses to the literature they read were interesting. For example, "this is common sense", "this is what we do", they said. They protested the need to theorize the idea, unconvinced of the value of making these 'common sense', 'obvious' elements of their teaching visible and explicit. Over time the course matured. At the same time, my own research describing and interpreting shifts in mathematics teaching in South African classrooms drew substantively on the notion of variation as significant for exemplification in mathematics pedagogy (Adler & Ronda, 2015, 2017b; Adler & Venkat, 2014). And the teachers, both Masters students and others I work with in our professional development project, have come to appreciate the worth of deliberate attention to what and how they exemplify mathematical ideas, processes, and practices in their teaching. They further appreciate how this critical work of teaching is strengthened by attention to "variation amidst invariance" (Watson & Mason, 2006), to "contrast" and "similarity" (Marton & Tsui, 2004), to building generality and appreciating underlying structure in mathematics. Deliberate attention to selecting and sequencing examples enables them to teach more coherently; or more 'powerfully' as some have said; and having a language with which to talk about these aspects of teaching ignites and supports collaborative practice.

It was thus with enthusiasm that I accepted the invitation to write the foreword for this book. I was delighted by the opportunity of being able to read all its chapters in advance of others, and to pre-view their contents.

In the introductory chapter, the editors, Rongjin Huang and Yeping Li, provide an overview of the book, how and why it emerged in this form, and what they as editors and chapter authors hope can be learned. Indeed, there are numerous places in the book with review and reflective comments. There are introductory comments prefacing each part of the book, and two reflective and review chapters in the last part. Therefore, I will not go down that path here, but rather focus on what has stood out for me as I traversed the various chapters and contributions, for it is in these that I see its value and encourage its wide and critical reading.

What stands out first is the profound respect for the complex work of mathematics teaching, and the teachers who carry out this work. The pioneering work of Lingyuan Gu in Gu, Huang, and Marton (2004) has inspired a number of studies on mathematics teaching through principles of variation. And that is the key – it is mathematics teaching that is studied, and then described, so as to make visible and explicit what it is that this work entails. Of course what is taught is not synonymous with what is learned, but what is taught – made available to learn – is critical. The mostly Chinese, but also other teachers who are the 'subjects' of the studies reported in various chapters in the book, are the leading actors in the story of variation that is developed. In his introduction to Section III, Konrad Krainer notes this too, and describes the positioning of teachers in the chapters in that section as key 'stakeholders' in mathematics education research and practice. Teachers are key participants in developing knowledge and understanding of the learning and teaching of mathematics in school. There is much to learn across the chapters in this book, both from the ways in which research has been carried out on specific classroom practices, and the induction of new mathematics teachers – and so learning as both researcher and new teacher from experienced teachers and teaching.

This is not the first book that foregrounds mathematics teaching practices in China, and it will not be the last. Its uniqueness, in the words of the editors, is its foregrounding and focus on variation. This includes a meta analysis of a 'pedagogy of variation' as it emerged in China and was described initially by Gu; explorations of such pedagogy in algebra and geometry lessons, and different types of lessons (review, problem-solving), as well as textbooks and other curricula texts; and engagement with research and writings on how ideas and theories of variation have been used in mathematics education research elsewhere. Its broad goal is to advance systematic examination of the teaching and learning of mathematics across contexts, through variation.

And this leads to what stands out next for me in the book: the language that has been developed to describe a pedagogy of variation as it is used in China and then elsewhere. Elaboration of terms like *Bianshi,* the distinction made between conceptual variation and procedural variation, *Pudian* (scaffolding), and related concepts of anchoring knowledge, chains of knowledge, make it possible for readers to interpret and engage with the research on these practices, and then relate these to their own research and teaching. The stand out for me is (and perhaps this is a function of translation into English) is the similarity of word use in mathematics education research elsewhere. Yet, the use often has different nuanced meanings, provoking reflection on what we mean when we name constructs as we must do in furthering conversations about our work. Key chapters in this book tease out similarities and differences in approaches and theories using variation, making it further possible for readers to grapple too with systematic examination across contexts and uses.

I will focus here only on the distinction between conceptual and procedural variation, as these words (conceptual, procedural) abound in the literature in mathematics education, referring sometimes to knowledge, sometimes to understanding, and sometimes to proficiency. In my current lesson study work with teachers (see Adler & Ronda, 2017a), the first task in planning a research lesson is to decide on the 'lesson goal.' We also refer to this goal, following Marton et al (op cit) as the 'object of learning.' We have found it useful and important to distinguish whether the 'object' is a mathematical concept (e.g., the notion of equality or the meaning of 'solution' or 'solve') or a mathematical procedure (e.g., algorithms or methods/strategies for finding the solution to an equation). Both the notions of equality and solution, and the methods and strategies for solving problems with equations are important in our curriculum, and introduced in the early secondary years. Then, depending on what is intended to be in focus, the examples, tasks, representations, and related meditational talk in the lesson would need to differ substantively. The research reported in many chapters in this book use the distinction between procedural and conceptual variation to analyze lessons and what is made available to learn. As I interpreted and learned from these studies, I appreciated the strong link here to pedagogic work: to elements, perhaps, of pedagogic content knowing, to when and how to transform a figure and so make available a new concept, to selecting a problem with multiple solution strategies, and to selecting many problems calling on the same underlying strategy. For sure, the use of 'procedural' here is in no way pejorative, without any relation to the notion of rules without reasons (knowing how without why), it is in alignment with procedural fluency in teaching as elaborated in Kilpatrick, Swafford, and Findell (2001). Yet, I believe there is still work to do, across uses of these constructs, to define more clearly what we mean when we use them, how we 'see' these in teaching and learning mathematics practices, and how they work analytically.

My third take away, is the question 'why now?' Why is it that variation in pedagogy is capturing attention now, or recapturing attention now? I first came across the notion of 'variation' in the mid-1980s as a pre-service primary mathematics teacher educator. I used Dienes' (1973) perceptual variation productively in that work. It was interesting to see the influence of Dienes' work in the early research in China. Yet, as I shifted my attention to language practices in multilingual mathematics classrooms, and teachers' knowledge and practice, 'variation' did not feature. A short answer would be that my work lies within the social turn (Lerman, 2000), shaped also by social justice interests away from the cognitive or perceptive. But this trivializes the depth and breadth of Vygotskian theory. Yet it is now, some two decades later, that the value of the notion of variation for research and practice is in focus. And it has become important for a mathematics teacher professional development and research project in a context of deep inequality and poverty in South Africa.

A tentative suggestion, and this is how the chapters in this book resonate for me, is that variation is a productive metaphor/construct/tool (depending on how it is used) in our work, as we become more attuned to the complex work of mathematics teaching and the core practices of mathematics teaching within and across diverse classroom contexts. Pedagogic variation is perhaps one such core practice. The contribution of this book at this juncture is not only that it provides the field access in English to an important strand of mathematics education research in China, but it also positions this work in curriculum and pedagogy elsewhere – it offers a view and stimulates further work into pedagogy of variation around the world.

REFERENCES

Adler, J., & Ronda, E. (2015). A framework for describing mathematics discourse in instruction and interpreting differences in teaching. *African Journal of Research in Mathematics, Science and Technology Education, 19*(3), 237–254.

Adler, J., & Ronda, E. (2017a). A lesson to learn from: From research insights to teaching a lesson. In J. Adler & A. Sfard (Eds.), *Research for educational change: Transforming researchers' insights into improvement in mathematics teaching and learning* (pp. 133–143). London: Routledge.

Adler, J., & Ronda, E. (2017b). Mathematical discourse in instruction matters. In J. Adler & A. Sfard (Eds.), *Research for educational change: Transforming researchers' insights into improvement in mathematics teaching and learning* (pp. 64–81). Abingdon: Routledge

Adler, J., & Venkat, H. (2014). Teachers' mathematical discourse in instruction: Focus on examples and explanations. In M. Rollnick, H. Venkat, J. Loughran, & M. Askew (Eds.), *Exploring content knowledge for teaching science and mathematics* (pp. 132–146). London: Routledge.

Dienes, Z. P. (1973). A theory of mathematics learning. In F. J., Crosswhite, J. L. Highins, A. R. Osborne, & R. J. Shunway (Eds.), *Teaching mathematics: Psychological foundations* (pp. 137–148). Ohio, OH: Charles A. Jones Publishing.

Gu, L., Huang, R., & Marton, F. (2004). Teaching with variation: An effective way of mathematics teaching in China. In L. Fan, N. Y. Wong, J. Cai, & S. Li (Eds.), *In How Chinese learn mathematics: Perspectives from insiders* (pp. 309–348). Singapore: World Scientific.

Kilpatrick, J., Swafford, J., & Findell, B. (2001). *Adding it up: Helping children learn mathematics.* Washington, DC: National Academy Press.

Lerman, S. (2000). The social turn in mathematics education research. In J. Boaler (Ed.), *Multiple perspectives on mathematics teaching and learning* (pp. 19–44). Westport, CT: Ablex.

Marton, F., & Tsui, A. B. M. (2004). *Classroom discourse and the space of learning.* Mahwah, NJ: Lawrence Erlbaum Associates.

Watson, A., & Mason, J. (2006). Seeing an exercise as a single mathematical object: Using variation to structure sense-making. *Mathematical Thinking and Learning, 8*(2), 91–111.

Jill Adler
School of Education
University of the Witwatersrand
Johannesburg, South Africa

ACKNOWLEDGEMENTS

We would like to take this opportunity to thank our 45 contributors for their commitment and contribution. It has been a great learning and collaboration opportunity for everyone involved. Indeed, the chapters have been revised multiple rounds based peer reviews over the past two years. Our contributors have made great efforts to ensure the high quality of their chapters. We also want to thank external reviewers for their help in reading and commenting on the manuscripts. It would not be possible to have such a high quality collection of chapters without their constructive inputs. These reviewers include:

Afl Coles (Bristol University, UK);
Akihiko Takahashi (Depaul University, USA);
Andrzej Sokolowski (Lone Star College, USA)
Arthur B. Powell (Rutgers University Newark, USA)
Qian Chen (Sichuan Normal University, China);
Chunlian Jiang (University of Macau, Macao);
Glenda Anthony (Massey University, New Zealand);
Jeremy Strayer (Middle Tennessee State University, USA);
Ke Wang (Texas A&M University, USA)
Ko Po Yuk (Hong Kong institute of Education, Hong Kong);
Sarah K. Bleiler-Baxter (Middle Tennessee State University, USA)
Sasha Wang (Boise State University, USA)
Wenjun Li (Southern Illinois State University, USA);
Xianwei Y. Van Harpen (University of Wisconsin–Milwaukee, USA).

We are grateful to Middle Tennessee State University and Texas A&M University for various support during the process of editing and publishing the book. In particular, we thank a Faculty Research and Creative Activity Grant from Middle Tennessee State University for funding the publication of the book. Last, but not least, we extend our gratitude to Dr. Kyle Prince for his throughout and professional edits of the entire book manuscript and Mr. Michael Rugh for his assistance in proofreading book chapters.

PART I

THEORETICAL PERSPECTIVES

RONGJIN HUANG AND YEPING LI

1. INTRODUCTION

A PERSONAL JOURNEY TOWARD UNDERSTANDING
THE PEDAGOGY OF VARIATION

Both editors grew up in China and became high school mathematics teachers there. They learned about mathematics teaching in China not only as students, but also as teachers. *Bianshi* (i.e., changing or varying) teaching, or *Bianshi* exercise, viewed as a basic approach, has been used regularly in mathematics classroom instruction. Seeking multiple solutions to a problem, applying a mathematical method or strategy to solve a set of interconnected problems, and varying a problem into multiple problems are basic skills valued by all mathematics teachers in China. A variety of related books, journal articles, and teaching materials have been available for mathematics teachers to adapt such mathematics problems and methods in class. In 1990's, *Bianshi* teaching, was clearly recognized and promoted as one of the most important teaching approaches nationwide due to Gu's successful teaching experiment, which increased students' mathematics achievement on a large scale in Qingpu County, Shanghai (Experimenting Group of Teaching Reform in maths in Qingpu, 1991). In his dissertation, Gu (1994) summarized four instructional principles including: emotional principle, accumulation step by step principle, activity principle, and feedback principle. To implement these principles, Gu (1994) further proposed different variation strategies for learning different types of mathematics knowledge such as concepts and facts, principles and theorems, and problem solving. He coined the strategies as concept-oriented variation and process-oriented variation.

As a graduate student at the University of Hong Kong in late 1990s, the first editor also had an opportunity to learn about the theory of variation, written by Marton and his colleagues (Marton & Booth, 1997; Marton, 2015). The theory presumes that learning is about developing new ways of seeing or experiencing the object of learning, it is necessary to experience certain patterns of variation and invariance in order to discern critical features of the object of learning. Teaching then means to construct appropriate spaces of variation (Marton & Booth, 1997). Pondering on the Chinese practice in mathematics instruction and Marton's variation theory of learning in general, the first editor developed his initial desire to explore the characteristics of mathematics instruction in Shanghai and Hong Kong from the perspective of variation (Huang, 2002). Based on a fine-grained analysis of eight Hong Kong lesson videos from TIMSS 1999 Video Study and 11 Shanghai lesson videos, he

R. Huang & Y. Li (Eds.), Teaching and Learning Mathematics through Variation, 3–11.

provided a new description of Chinese mathematics classroom instruction where the teacher emphasized exploring and constructing knowledge, provided exercise with systematic variation, and scaffolded students' engagement in the process of learning (Huang & Leung, 2004). Building on Huang's (2002) dissertation and Gu's (1994) research, Gu, Huang and Marton (2004) further interpreted and theorized the Chinese *Bianshi* teaching practice in mathematics by building connections with Western theories, including Dinese' theory (Dienes, 1973), Marton's theory of variation of learning (Marton & Booth, 1997), notions of scaffoldings (Wood, Brunner, & Ross, 1976) and the concept of Vygotsky's (1962) "Zone of proximal development" (Gu et al., 2004). They argued that *Bianshi* teaching is an effective way for promoting meaningful learning in large size classrooms.

The idea of developing this book grew directly from our previous publication on mathematics teaching in China (see, Li & Huang, 2013). As the previous book provided the first comprehensive account of how the Chinese teach mathematics and improve teaching, it has become clear to us that readers want to learn more about mathematics teaching in China. Existing research documented many important features of Chinese teachers' practices, such as Teaching Research Group (e.g., Ma, 1999; Yang & Ricks, 2013), teaching contest (e.g., Li & Li, 2009), instructional coherence (e.g., Chen & Li, 2010), and teaching and learning through variation (e.g., Gu, Huang, & Marton, 2004). In the spirit of making a focused account of specific features one at a time, this book was designed to focus on teaching and learning mathematics through variation.

Clearly, the book differs from previously published books on mathematics teaching in China, as all contributors were asked to focus on this specific feature. The book is unique, as it provides readers with both comprehensive and in-depth accounts of this important feature practiced in mathematics classrooms in China.

The book also differs from many previous books through the inclusion of chapters that document similar practices in other education systems. The initial thought was to find out if similar practices were available in other education systems, and if so, provide a venue for us to learn about these practices from an international perspective. Such a thought was soon confirmed through our on-going work with mathematics teachers in the USA. We noticed that some teachers used mathematical tasks in their instructional designs and classroom instruction that reflected several principles of variation pedagogy, but they could not articulate the rationale for such tasks when asked. To examine U.S. teachers' capacity in adapting variation pedagogy, a group of U.S. mathematics teachers was asked to implement a Chinese lesson plan that is designed according to *Bianshi* teaching principles. This exploratory study led to an exemplary lesson that implements mathematical practice effectively through using the patterns of variation (Huang, Prince, & Schmidt, 2014). Such an initial success also led us to believe that this effective teaching practice in China could be adapted in mathematics classroom teaching in other education systems. This book should be an important and valuable read for those who seek ways of improving their teaching practice in order to advance student learning.

WHAT THIS BOOK IS ABOUT

Improving the quality of mathematics teaching and learning has been the focus of mathematics education for years. One method has been to identify and examine specific approaches and practices that prove to be effective in high-achieving education systems, including China (e.g., Fan, Wang, Cai, & Li, 2004; Leung, 1995; Li & Huang, 2013; Stevenson & Lee, 1997; Stigler & Stevenson, 1991). Existing studies (e.g., Gu, Huang, & Marton, 2004; Wong, 2008) have documented that *Bianshi (i.e. teaching with variation)* is a commonly used and effective approach in mathematics teaching and learning in China. Meanwhile, researchers in the West have also emphasized the use of variation to improve mathematics teaching and learning, such as deliberately varying mathematical tasks to facilitate students' learning of mathematics (Rowland, 2008; Watson & Mason, 2008). Specifically, Learning Study, a combination of lesson study and design experiment guided by Marton's theory of variations for learning (e.g., Cheung & Wong, 2014; Lo & Marton, 2012; Marton & Pang, 2006), has demonstrated its potential importance in prompting students' learning and participating teachers' professional development. The use of pedagogy of variation seems to be effective for promoting students' learning in mathematics in different contexts. However, there is a lack of systematic examination of the pedagogy of variation for learning, *teaching and learning mathematics through variation in particular*, which could go well beyond what we know has been valued in China. Possible questions that can be examined include: What are the theoretical foundations and interpretations of *Bianshi* teaching that has been proven to be effective in China? What are possible similarities and differences among various notions of teaching and learning mathematics through variation globally? How may a theory of teaching and learning mathematics through variation be related to curriculum development? How may such a theory be used in mathematics teacher preparation and teacher professional development? Are the notion of teaching and learning through variation culturally specific or universal? A systematic examination of these questions will not only help us better understand the characteristics of mathematics teaching in China, but it will also connect with what are perceived as effective practices in other education systems.

STRUCTURE OF THE BOOK

This book is organized into five parts to provide both general and specific accounts of teaching and learning through variation. The first part presents various notions about teaching and learning through variation (Gu, Huang, & Gu, 2017; Pang, Bao, & Ki, 2017), an extension of using variation in a dynamitic learning environment (Leung, 2017), and a synthesis of the pedagogy of variation (Watson, 2017). The second part provides various examples about the pedagogy of variation that has been used to guide mathematics teaching in China. The vivid lesson cases include different topics such as algebra and geometry, which were enacted in different types of lessons, such as the introduction of new concepts (Huang & Leung, 2017; Mok, 2017), exploration of new propositions (Qi, Wang, Mok, & Huang, 2011), problem solving (Peng, Li, Nie, & Li, 2017), and review of knowledge (Huang, Huang, & Zhang, 2017). The third part extends to other aspects that can contribute to the success of classroom instruction through variation, including textbooks (Zhang, Wang, Huang, & Kimmins, 2017) and teacher professional development approaches (Ding, Jones, & Sikko, 2017; Han, Gong, & Huang, 2017). The fourth part demonstrates how the pedagogy of variation has been widely used in mathematics teaching and task design in selected countries including Japan, Israel, Sweden, and the U.S. Finally, the fifth part contains three commentary chapters to provide specific accounts of the pedagogy of variation and its implications for mathematics instruction from different lenses such as East Asian perspective (Wong, 2017), European perspective (Marton & Häggström, 2017), and Western perspective (Mason, 2017). In addition to these chapters, each of parts 2–4 includes preface for readers as a guide for reading and reflecting upon that part. The preface for the entire book helps highlight some important ideas that the reader can attend to.

Collectively, the book provides a rich picture about what the theories of variation pedagogy look like and how the theories have been implemented in teaching various topics and lessons in China. In addition, a focus on the use of variation pedagogy in textbooks, novice teachers' mentoring, and implementing innovative ideas of new curriculum through professional development programs at system levels may be crucial for implementation of the variation pedagogy in classrooms. Finally, the book provides evidence that the pedagogy of variation can be utilized in selected educational systems.

WHAT READERS CAN EXPECT TO LEARN

The reader may find that each chapter tells a story about the theory of variation pedagogy and its application in mathematics classroom instruction. Some big ideas can emerge when comparing and contrasting different chapters within and across parts. In this session, we attempt to highlight some of these big ideas.

What is variation pedagogy? Four chapters in Part I illustrate major notions of teaching and learning through variation. In Chapter 2, Gu et al. (2017) discuss the historical and cultural origin of *Bianshi* teaching (i.e., *teaching with variation)*, describe experimental studies on synthesizing the concepts and mechanism of *Bianshi* teaching, present theorization of *Bianshi* teaching over the past decades, and report the latest attempts to develop the *Bianshi* teaching theory by incorporating western notion of learning trajectory. Pang et al. (2017) juxtapose and compare the major claims of *Bianshi* teaching and *Variation Theory of Learning* (Marton, 2015) through examining a mathematics lesson from the two theoretical lenses. They conclude that both theories appreciate the importance and necessity of experiencing certain patterns of variation and invariance for student learning. Although the priorities of sameness and differences when constructing patterns of variation differ, they are complementary, and thus essential. Leung (2017) discusses how variation can be used as a pedagogical tool in the context of mathematics teaching and learning when a dynamic virtual tool is employed. He proposes a set of Principles of Acquiring Invariant that is complementary to the patterns of variation in Marton (2015)'s *Theory of Variation of Learning* and is further explored under a tool-based teaching and learning environment. Finally, Watson (2017), building on comparing various notions of variation, argues that the use of variation in mathematics teaching should draw on leaners' attention to "dependency relationships" that are invariant in mathematics, and illustrates how a careful use of variation can lead to abstraction of new ideas. The notion of "dependency relationships" echoes the notion of "core connection" articulated by Gu et al. (2017).

How can variation pedagogy be effectively implemented in mathematics classrooms? Part II includes five chapters demonstrating various examples in Chinese classrooms. Chapter 6 (Peng et al., 2017) focuses on the teaching of problem solving by examining a well-structured lesson on solving right triangles in contextual situations from the perspective of variation. Two major patterns of variation are used to develop student problem-solving ability and generalization. They are varying the conditions or contexts of the problems and seeking various methods of solving the problem. Chapter 7 (Qi et al., 2017) reports an experimental study on teaching an algebraic proposition guided by *Bianshi* teaching principles and features of student learning. Their data analysis revealed that a vibrant application of the Chinese pedagogy of variation in tandem with a mathematical thinking dimension enhanced student-learning outcomes. Chapter 8 (Huang & Leung, 2017) provides a fine-grained analysis of a geometry lesson based on Gu et al. (2004)'s framework. It reveals that the dimensions of conceptual variation focus on contrasting concept and non-concept images, and juxtaposing prototypical and non-prototypical figures, while dimensions of procedural variation demonstrate competence in setting and implementing deliberate tasks for students' development of reconfiguration processing ability. Systemic use of variation could help students to develop conceptual understanding and problem solving ability in geometry. Chapter 9 (Huang et al., 2017) discusses the challenges when an experienced teacher adopted procedural variation in a review lesson. Chapter 10 (Mok, 2017) examines algebraic lessons in Shanghai and Hong Kong *from the perspectives of variation theory of learning*. In the application of these ideas to learning experiences in lessons, discernment is made possible when variation of the critical aspects of the object of learning is embedded in the design of the instructional tasks or in the interaction between teacher and students and between students. This chapter illustrates key skills in creating useful patterns of variation in teaching and learning, including contrast, generalization, fusion, and separation.

How to support the implementation of variation pedagogy? Part III includes three chapters focusing on closely related aspects of implementing variation pedagogy.

In Chapter 11, Zhang et al. (2017) examine the features of variation in mathematics textbooks. Analyses of selected textbooks reveal that multiple strategies of presenting variation tasks are used to introduce concepts. Both conceptual and procedural variation tasks are used to develop mathematical concepts. To develop mathematics skills, the textbooks first present problem situations progressively with an increasing complexity. In addition, procedural variations are used to guide students to experience mathematical thinking methods through the process of concept development and problem solving. In Chapter 12 (Ding et al., 2017), the authors examine the dynamic between an expert teacher and a junior teacher within school-based teaching research activities. They found the expert teacher's mentoring to be effective in two distinct ways: (1) the use of the commonly shared teaching notions to help the junior teacher understand the theoretical elements of teaching with variation; (2) the use of commonly shared teaching frameworks and language to help the junior teacher to understand the deliberate focus on the fundamental 'chains' in learning mathematics and the dynamic teaching process of *Pudian* (akin to 'scaffolding'). The contribution of the study is that it expands knowledge of how teacher learning takes place through the support of an expert practitioner. Han et al. (2017), in Chapter 13, report a study on how a combination of theoretical perspectives informed lesson study, which helped the teachers, with the support from knowledgeable others, to shift their focus toward student learning. The data analysis further revealed that the students could get ample opportunities to experience critical aspects of object of learning when the teacher enacts appropriate dimensions of conceptual and procedural variations in the classroom and develops their conceptual understanding of the concepts.

Is the teaching through variation culture specific?   Part IV includes four chapters demonstrating how variation pedagogy is utilized in selected countries in various ways. In Chapter 14, Hino (2017) carefully re-examines the well-documented Japanese structured problem solving approach from the perspective of variation. She identifies three types of variation embedded in the Japanese approach. Two lessons are used to illustrate these three patterns of variation: presenting problems with variation, providing opportunities for students to construct variation themselves, and promoting students' reflection on variation toward the intended object of learning. This chapter highlights the importance of purposeful use of variation to promote students' learning cross-culturally. Barlow et al. (2017), in Chapter 15, present a sequence of four-day lessons that aimed at developing students' capacity of generalizing a pattern for the purpose of developing functional relationships. The development of the featured tasks was informed by a theory of variation. Data analysis suggests that these lessons promoted students' algebraic reasoning aligned with the vision established in U.S. curriculum documents. In Chapter 16, Peled and Leikin (2017) extend a dimension of variation about the multiplicity of mathematics problems. Two types of mathematical problems are used to illustrate different purposes. One involves a "regular" problem that allows for multiple approaches to solving the problem. Another is modelling situations, where problem solvers are encouraged to interpret the situation from various perspectives and establish different models that lead to different solutions. The chapter opens a dialogue about the usefulness of each type of problem for different objects of learning. Runesson and Kullberg (2017), in Chapter 17, presents a longitudinal study in Sweden on learning study, which is a modified lesson study, enhanced by using variation pedagogy as an instructional design principle. Through iterative cycles of teaching and revising, the lesson on division with a denominator between zero and one has been improved to draw students' attention to the intended object of learning. Moreover, Runesson and Kullberg attempt to address a crucial issue of sustainability of learning from the learning study by comparing a following up teaching of a different topic by the same teacher that did the learning study.

CONTRIBUTION AND FUTHER SUGGESTIONS

This book is designed to make important contributions in four ways. First, by inviting internationally well-known scholars who are interested in teaching and learning mathematics through variations to contribute their insights, we aim to build toward a solid foundation for theorizing this perspective. Second, a collection of chapters contributed by scholars in China provides lesson cases on the development and application of this pedagogy in teaching specific topics and lessons (e.g., concept, problem solving, exercise or review, etc.). Meanwhile, the factors influencing teachers' utilization of variation pedagogy such as curriculum development and teacher professional development are explored. Third, some cases on adopting variation pedagogy in selected countries are presented. Fourth, commentary chapters on the original studies in the book from Eastern, Western, and European perspectives provide thoughtful insights into the theories of teaching and learning through variation and the application of these theories. Taken collectively, the book aims to theorize this pedagogical perspective and to provide cases showing how this pedagogical perspective can be used and implemented in mathematics teaching and learning, curriculum development, and teacher education.

Although the book has made important contribution to mathematics education as aforementioned, studies on the theories and application of variation pedagogy could be further developed in many ways. First, empirical studies on the effectiveness of implementing variation pedagogy to increase student achievement on a large scale should be conducted. Second, since effective implementation of variation pedagogy is related to curriculum and teacher professional development, developing relevant teaching materials based on variation pedagogy will be essential.

REFERENCES

Chen, X., & Li, Y. (2010). Instructional coherence in Chinese mathematics classroom – a case study of lessons on fraction division. *International Journal of Science and Mathematics Education, 8,* 711–735.

Cheung, W. M., & Wong, W. Y. (2014). Does lesson study work? A systematic review on the effects of lesson study and learning study on teachers and students. *International Journal for Lesson and Learning Studies, 3*(2), 2–32.

Common Core State Standards Initiative. (2010). *Common core state standards for mathematics.* Washington, DC: National Governors Association Center for Best Practices and Council of Chief State School Officers. Retrieved from http://www.corestandards.org

Dienes, Z. P. (1973). A theory of mathematics learning. In F. J. Crosswhite, J. L. Highins, A. R. Osborne, & R. J. Shunway (Eds.), *Teaching mathematics: Psychological foundation* (pp. 137–148). Ohio, OH: Charles A. Jones Publishing Company.

Experimenting Group of Teaching Reform in Mathematics in Qingpu County, Shanghai. (1991). *Xuehui Jiaoxue* (Learning to teach). Beijing, China: People Education Publishers. (In Chinese)

Fan, L., Wong, N. Y., Cai, J., & Li, S. (2004). *How Chinese learn mathematics: Perspectives from insiders.* Singapore: World Scientific.

Gu, L. (1994). *Theory of teaching experiment: The methodology and teaching principles of Qingpu* [In Chinese]. Beijing: Educational Science Press.

Gu, L., Huang, R., & Marton, F. (2004). Teaching with variation: An effective way of mathematics teaching in China. In L. Fan, N. Y. Wong, J. Cai, & S. Li (Eds.), *How Chinese learn mathematics: Perspectives from insiders* (pp. 309–348). Singapore: World Scientific.

Huang, R. (2002). *Mathematics teaching in Hong Kong and Shanghai: A classroom analysis from the perspective of variation* (Unpublished doctoral dissertation). The University of Hong Kong, Hong Kong.

Huang, R., Prince, K., & Schmidt, T. (2014). Developing algebraic reasoning in classrooms: Variation and comparison. *Mathematics Teacher, 108*, 336–342.

Leung, F. K. S. (1995). The mathematics classroom in Beijing, Hong Kong and London. *Educational Studies in Mathematics, 29*, 297–325.

Li, Y., & Huang, R. (2013). *How Chinese teach mathematics and improve teaching.* New York, NY: Routledge.

Li, Y., & Li, J. (2009). Mathematics classroom instruction excellence through the platform of teaching contests. *ZDM-The International Journal on Mathematics Education, 41*, 263–277.

Lo, M. L., & Marton, F. (2012). Toward a science of the art of teaching: Using variation theory as a guiding principle of pedagogical design. *International Journal for Lesson and Learning Studies, 1*(1), 7–22.

Ma, L. (1999). *Knowing and teaching elementary mathematics.* Mahwah, NJ: Lawrence Erlbaum Associates.

Marton, F. (2015). *Necessary conditions of learning.* New York, NY: Routledge.

Marton, F., & Booth, S. (1997). *Learning and awareness.* Mahwah, NJ: Lawrence Erlbaum.

Marton, F., & Pang, M. F. (2006). On some necessary conditions of learning. *The Journal of the Learning Science, 15*, 193–220.

Marton, F., Runesson, U., & Tsui, A. B. M. (2003). The space of learning. In F. Marton, A. B. M. Tsui, P. Chik, P. Y. Ko, M. L. Lo, I. A. C. Mok, D. Ng, M. F. Pang, W. Y. Pong, & U. Runesson (Eds.), *Classroom discourse and the space of learning* (pp. 3–40). Mahwah, NJ: Lawrence Erlbaum.

Rowland, T. (2008). The purpose, design, and use of examples in the teaching of elementary mathematics. *Educational Studies in Mathematics, 69*, 149–163.

Stevenson, H. W., & Lee, S. (1997). The East Asian version of whole-class teaching. In W. K. Cummings & P. G. Altbach (Eds.), *The challenge of Eastern Asian education* (pp. 33–49). Albany, NY: State University of New York.

Stevenson, H. W., & Stigler, J. W. (1992). *The learning gap: Why our schools are failing and what we can learn from Japanese and Chinese education.* New York, NY: Summit Books.

Stigler, J. W., & Stevenson, H. W. (1991). How Asian teachers polish each lesson to perfection. *American Educator, 15*(1), 12–20, 43–47.

Vygotsky, L. S. (1978). *Mind in society.* Cambridge, MA: Harvard University Press.

Watson, A., & Mason, J. (2006). Seeing an exercise as a single mathematical object: Using variation to structure sense- making. *Mathematical Thinking and Learning, 8*(2), 91–111.

Wong, N. Y. (2008). Confucian heritage, culture leaners' phenomenon: From exploration middle zone" to "constructing bridge". *ZDM-The International Journal on Mathematics Education, 40*, 973–981.

Wood, D., Brunner, J. S., & Ross, G. (1976). The role of tutoring in problems solving. *Journal of Child Psychology and Psychiatry, 17*, 89–100.

Yang, Y., & Ricks, T. E. (2013). Chinese lesson study – Developing classroom instruction through collaborations in school-based teaching research group activities. In Y. Li & R. Huang (Eds.), *How Chinese teach mathematics and improve teaching* (pp. 51–65). New York, NY: Routledge.

Rongjin Huang
Department of Mathematics Sciences
Middle Tennessee State University, USA

Yeping Li
Department of Teaching, Learning and Culture
Texas A&M University, USA
Shanghai Normal University, China

FEISHI GU, RONGJIN HUANG AND LINGYUAN GU

2. THEORY AND DEVELOPMENT OF TEACHING THROUGH VARIATION IN MATHEMATICS IN CHINA

INTRODUCTION

Chinese students' strong performance in mathematics in various international comparative studies has been noticed for decades (Fan & Zhu, 2004). In particular, Shanghai students' outstanding performances in PISA (OECD, 2010, 2014) have stunned educators and policy makers around the world. Researchers have investigated Chinese students' excellent performance in mathematics from different perspectives (Biggs & Watkins, 2001; Fan, Wang, Cai, & Li, 2004), including societal, socio-cultural perspectives (Stevenson & Stigler, 1992; Sriraman et al., 2015; Wong, 2008), student behaviors (Fan et al., 2004), teacher knowledge, and teacher professional development perspectives (An, Kulum, & Wu, 2004; Fan, Wong, Cai, & Li, 2015; Huang, 2014; Ma, 1999), and classroom instruction perspectives (Huang & Leung, 2004; Leung, 1995, 2005; Li & Huang, 2013).

A close examination of mathematics instruction in China may help better understand why Chinese students can succeed in large class-size classrooms. Typically, Chinese mathematics classrooms have been described as large and teacher dominated, with students who are well disciplined, passive learners (Leung, 2005; Stevenson & Lee, 1995). Classroom teaching in China is polished (Paine, 1990), fluent and coherent (Chen & Li, 2010; Wang & Murphy, 2004), with a focus on the development of important content, problem solving, and proof (Huang & Leung, 2004; Huang, Mok, & Leung, 2006; Leung, 2005). Furthermore, from a cultural and historical perspective, Chinese mathematics instruction has been identified with two fundamental characteristics: (1) two-basics-oriented (basic knowledge and basic skills) teaching, and (2) direct explanation and extensive practices with variation (Li, Li, & Zhang, 2015; Shao, Fan, Huang, Ding, & Li, 2013). Particularly, Gu, Huang and Marton (2004) theorized teaching through variation[1] and argued that teaching through variation is an effective way to promote meaningful learning in mathematics for classes of large size. In this chapter the authors further examine the practice of teaching through variation from a cultural perspective and provide state-of-the-art studies on teaching through variation in China. Finally, the authors discuss how teaching through variation can be implemented to promote deep learning of mathematics in classrooms.

R. Huang & Y. Li (Eds.), Teaching and Learning Mathematics through Variation, 13–41.

TEACHING THROUGH VARIATION: A CULTURALLY INDIGENOUS PRACTICES

Teaching and learning mathematics through variation is a widespread idea in China as reflected in the old Chinese maxim, "Only by comparing can one distinguish" (有比较才有鉴别). There are different opinions about using variation in mathematics education. Some focus on using problems with variation in textbooks or curriculum (Cai & Nie, 2007; Sun, 2011; Wong, Lam, Sun, & Chan, 2009) while others emphasize using tasks with variation in classrooms for promoting student learning (Gu et al., 2004; Huang & Leung, 2004, 2005). Teaching through variation in this chapter is aligned with the following definition:

> To illustrate essential features of a concept by demonstrating various visual materials and instances, or to highlight essential characteristics of a concept by varying non-essential features. The goal of using variation is to help students understand the essential features of a concept by differentiating them from non-essential features and further develop a scientific concept. (Gu, 1999, p. 186)

In her study, Sun (2011) argued that the concept of conducting a lesson or practice with variation problems is an "indigenous" feature in China. First, the major traditional philosophical systems such as Confucianism (儒家) imply the variation notion. For example, Confucius said, "I do not open up the truth to one who is not eager to get knowledge, nor help out any one who is not anxious to explain himself. When I have presented one corner of a subject to any one, and he cannot from it learn the other three, I do not repeat my lesson." (The Analects, 7: 8) (举一隅不以三隅反, 则不复也) This principle emphasizes the importance of self-motivated inquiry for understanding invariant patterns within different situations. Second, many ancient Chinese mathematics treatises such as *Nine Chapter of Arithmetic Arts*《九章算术》have been organized in a similar structure: concrete examples (stereotype problem) – invariant methods – application (variation problems). In this way, the invariant principles (general methods) were developed through the exploration of the variation of concrete examples and further consolidated by application in a variety of novel problems.

When discussing learning and teaching mathematics, ancient mathematicians also emphasized heuristic strategies through making use of variation. For example, in *Shuan Fa Tong Bian Ben Mo*《算法通变本末》, Yanghui (杨辉, no details) pointed out that "good learners can grasp the whole category from typical examples; they don't need to teach them all in detail" (Song, 2006). It means that teachers should adopt analyzing typical cases or instances, illustration with diagrams, and drawing inferences about other cases from one instance to help learners to broaden their knowledge from concrete instances. Another example, in *Zhoubi Suanjin*《周髀算经》, a classic mathematics treatise, the following conversation between the teacher (Chenzi) and a student (Rongfang) revealed the teaching philosophy:

Rongfang: *I do not master the Dao (way). Can you teach me?*
Chenzi: *[...] Now in the methods of the Way [that I teach], illuminating knowledge of categories [is shown] when words are simple but their application is wide-ranging. When you ask about one category and are thus able to comprehend a myriad matters, I call that understanding the Dao. Now, what you are studying is the methods of reckoning (the principles of learning mathematics), and this is what you are using your understanding for. [...]. So similar methods are studied comparatively, and similar problems are comparatively considered. This is what sorts the stupid scholar from the clever one, and the worthy from the worthless. So, being able to categorize in order to unite categories-this is the substance of how the worthy will devote themselves to refining practice and understanding (Cullen, 1996, pp. 175–178, cited from Sun (2011)).*

The above discussions about learning mathematics focus on using concrete examples to make sense of a category (a concept), grasping ways (generalization) across categories, and developing a hierarchical system of categories. All of these ideas reflect the key notion of using variation problems in learning mathematics.

In addition to the aforementioned traditional cultural values, ancient mathematics treatises and the strategies of mathematics learning, a civil service examination system associated with "educational attainment, career goals, social status, and political ambitions" (Li, Li, & Zhang, 2015, p. 72) has been established since Qin Dynasty (605–1905) in China. In modern China, mathematics examinations exist at all grade levels. In particular, the entrance examination for high schools and colleges are high-stakes and competitive. The high-stakes examination system has contributed to the origin of forming two-basics–oriented mathematics teaching, supported with teaching through variation (Li et al., 2015). Since mathematics teaching and examination focus on basic knowledge and skills that are defined by curriculum standards and the two "basics" are relatively invariant, the exam items have to be designed differently every time, although they have to adhere to standards and textbooks. So, examination items have to be created based on prototype problems in textbooks with varying forms (i.e., many variations while maintaining the same essence, 万变不离其宗). Thus, practices with variation problems surrounding standards and textbooks have been proved in practice to be an effective way to prepare students to succeed in their examinations (i.e., practice makes perfect, 熟练生巧) (Li, 1999).

In addition to the traces of the roots in the ancient Chinese philosophy and mathematics treaties, teaching through variation has been promoted by the examination-oriented education system. Teaching through variation exists in many places without individuals' purposeful awareness.

EARLIER STUDIES ON TEACHING THROUGH VARIATION: CATEGORIZATION OF
VARIATION AND MECHANISM OF USING VARIATION

Teaching and learning through variation problems has been practiced for centuries in China. Yet, the practice has only been examined empirically over the last three decades. Gu and his colleagues have explored how to use and theorize teaching through variation (e.g., *Bianshi* Teaching 变式教学) to increase student achievement in mathematics since the 1980s (Bao, Huang, Yi, & Gu, 2003a,b,c; Gu, 1981, 1994; Gu et al., 2004; Qingpu experiment group, 1991). This section describes the major concepts of teaching through variation. First, the authors introduce two essentially different types of variation in mathematics classroom teaching: conceptual variation and procedural variation, based on effective teaching experiences (Gu, 1981). Then, a key concept of potential distance featuring the procedural variation based on empirical studies is discussed (Gu, 1994).

Conceptual Variation

Conceptual variation refers to the strategies that are used to discern essential features of a concept and to experience connotation of the concept by exploring varying embodiments of the concept (i.e., instances, contexts) (Gu et al., 2004). It aims to help students develop a profound understanding of a concept from multiple perspectives. The sections that follow illustrate the critical features of conceptual variation.

Highlighting essential features through variations and comparisons. Students' learning of geometrical concepts is closely related to the following major factors: experience with visual figures that represent the concept and verbal description of the concept. Previous teaching experience in geometrical concepts in middle schools demonstrates that directly defining a concept by describing essential features of the concept may help students memorize the concept. For example, the concept of altitudes of a triangle includes two critical features: perpendicular to one side and passing through the vertex at the intersection of the other two sides. However, the observation and experiment in Qingpu (Gu, 1994) revealed that if a teacher only told students the definition precisely and asked students to memorize the definition, then students were likely to have superficial and rigid understanding. Yet, if a teacher provided opportunities for students to observe and compare deliberately designed variation concept figures such as standard or non-standard position figures, or counterexamples, and then highlighted the essential features of the concept, students are more likely to synthesize the critical features of a concept based on observation of concrete instances. One example of variation figures used for developing the concept of altitude of a triangle is shown in Figure 1.

As shown in Figure 1, a standard figure is used to introduce the concept of altitudes of a triangle that is aligned with daily life experience. But the concept of altitudes in geometry is not equivalent to the perceived meaning of daily life

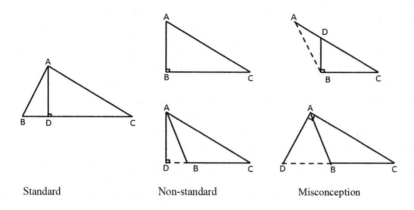

Figure 1. Altitudes of triangle

experience. Thus, identifying altitudes in various triangles (positions and types of triangles) helps students abstract the essential features of the concept. Finally, by contrasting some common misconception figures, the critical features of altitude: "perpendicular to a side and passing through the opposite vertex of the side" are further consolidated.

Eliminating the distraction of complex background through transformation and reconfiguration of basic figures. Geometrical figures usually consist of combinations of basic figures through separation, overlapping, and intersection. Sometimes basic figures are embedded in complex situations. The complex background figures often distract, distort, and mask students' perception of embedded basic figures. Thus, essential features of a geometrical concept embedded in complex backgrounds are often hidden and difficult to identify or even subject to being perceived inappropriately. To address this learning difficulty, a traditional strategy was to purposefully isolate geometrical objects explicitly (such as using colors) from complex background figures (including real contexts), which has been proven in practice to be effective. However, the experiment in Qingpu (Gu, 1994) demonstrated that such a strategy might resolve the problem that inappropriate perception of figures constrains appropriate recognition of a geometrical concept. How logical reasoning activities may influence the comprehension of a complex figure is an important issue. These strategies include: analyzing the structure of complex figures or generating a complex figure through transformation (i.e., translation, rotation, reflection, and shrinking and expanding) of basic figures. Through these decompositions and compositions, the focused figures can be separated from complex background figures (See Gu et al., 2004 for details).

Examining the effectiveness of using these variations through quasi-experiments. Since 1980, the Qingpu experiment team has examined the

17

effectiveness of these variation strategies through "identifying effective methods based on implementation", a Chinese version of "design-experiment" (Brown, 1992): repeated within a short period (once a week), which includes an entire cycle of planning – implementation – evaluation – improvement. The effectiveness of these variation strategies has been testified through more than 50 cycles of studies within one year. In particular, quasi-experiment methods (numbers of students in experimental class and control class are similar) were adopted. The experimental studies aimed to examine the effectiveness of using variation strategies. The results of one experiment are discussed below.

In the first experiment, the instructional content is the concept of perpendicular lines. The experimental group is class A (50 students); the concept of perpendicular lines was briefly explained, and then students were provided a set of variation practices. After that, students' errors were identified and discussed based on essential features of the concept. The control group is class B (51 students); the concept (definition of perpendicular lines) was repeatedly explained to students based on textbooks, then simple and repeated problems were provided for students to practice. After the class, a post-lesson evaluation test was conducted. To answer to the question, "What is the distance from a point to a straight line?", the students from the control class mainly recited the definition from the textbook, yet the students from the experimental class explained the definition based on their understanding. The average correct rates on a basic problem of constructing a perpendicular line in both groups were about 70%. However, with the answers to non-routine problems (constructing a perpendicular line in non-standard position triangles, see below), there were significant differences between the two classes as follows:

Item 1, in the figure (on the right), asked students to construct a line DE containing D and perpendicular to AD. There was a significant difference ($t = 2.13$, $p < .05$) between experimental class A (mean = 5.80 (out of 10 points)) and control class B (mean = 4.76).

Item 2, in the figure (on the right), asked students to construct the distance segments from B or C to line AD respectively. There was a significant difference ($t = 4.91$, $p < .01$) between experimental class A (mean = 6.04) and control class B (mean = 3.97).

Thus, this study revealed that teaching through deliberate variation problems appears to be more effective than teaching through repeated explanations of a definition.

The second experiment was conducted one month later. The instructional content was the SAS Postulate (Side-Angle-Side): If two sides and the included angle of one triangle are congruent to the corresponding parts of another triangle, then the triangles are congruent. The teaching strategy was swapped: class B was the experimental group and class A was the control group. In experimental class B, the theorem of SAS was briefly explained to students, and then variation problems (with variation figures) were provided for students to practice on. After that, students' errors were discussed and corrected, with particular attention to identifying hidden conditions within a complex figure or context. In the control class A, the teacher explained the theorem (SAS), students restated the theorem, and then students were given several variation problems (without figures, which consist of overlapping or separating basic figures) to practice on. A post-lesson test showed that the answers to two slight variation problems had mixed results; the means in the experimental class were 85% and 67% while those in the control class were 79% and 70%. However, the answers to another two proof problems that included complex variations showed significant difference between the two classes as follows:

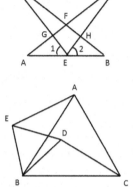

Item 3: in the figures (on the right), AE = BE, CE = DE, $\angle 1 = \angle 2$. Prove AD = BC. There was a significant difference ($t = 3.18$, $p < .01$) between experimental class B (mean = 8.66) and control class A (mean = 7.12).

Item 4: In the figure (on the right), $\triangle ABC \cong \triangle BDE$ are equilateral triangles. Prove: $\triangle BCD \cong \triangle BAE$.

There was a significant difference ($t = 2.11$, $p < .05$) between experimental class B (mean = 5.21) and control class A (mean = 3.50).

On item 3, students had to recognize the symmetrical structure of $\triangle ADE$ and $\triangle BCE$ On item 4, the students had to recognize that $\triangle BAE$ is rotated left 60° from $\triangle BCD$. These results show the effectiveness of using variation figures to help students identify target figures from a complex background figure.

In summary, the experimental studies in Qingpu (Gu, 1994) demonstrated that (1) designing variation problems based on essential features of a concept, and comparing and contrasting concept images and non-concept images could help students clarify connotations and extensions of a concept; and (2) reconfiguring the structure of a complex figure and forming a figure through transformation of basic figures could help students reduce cognitive load and promote their understanding of a concept in depth. Use of these strategies in teaching in a large class could promote more active learning.

Procedural Variation

Mathematical concepts are defined clearly and statically. Yet, obtaining mathematical activity experience and understanding of mathematical thinking methods are a dynamic process. Gu (1981) explored another variation, known as procedural variation. Procedural variation refers to creating variation problems or situations for students to explore in order to find solutions to problems or develop connections among different concepts step by step or from multiple approaches. Based on extensive teaching experience and reflection, Gu (1994) synthesized two critical features of procedural variation as follows (see Gu et al., 2004 for details).

19

Solving problems through transferring figures.   Transferring is one of most important methods of solving problems in mathematics instruction in China. It means to break down a complex problem into simpler problems. The simpler problems provide the foundation for solving the original complex problem. Or reversely, based on a basic problem, through adding constraints, complicated problems can be created. Figure 2 is an example of how transferring methods could help prove a geometrical theorem.

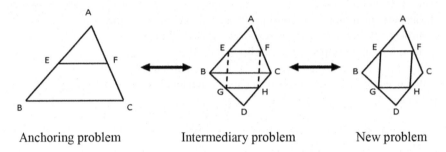

Anchoring problem   Intermediary problem   New problem

Figure 2. An example of transferring problems

Figure 2 shows how the mid-point quadrilateral that connects four midpoints of a quadrilateral is a parallelogram can be proven based on a simple "anchoring property", which states that the mid-segment of triangle (connecting two midpoints) is parallel and equal to half of the third side.

Building connections among different types of knowledge through categorization and building a hierarchical system of categories.   Categorization is an important mathematical thinking method. The key is to ensure that a categorization includes all instances without missing and overlapping. For example, the categorizations of triangles, the categorizations of special quadrilaterals, and the categorization of angles in a circle are typical examples of categorization activities. Another important issue is to build connections among various concepts and various concept figures, and to clarify logical relationships between different concepts. Figure 3 is a typical example of a concept map of angles in circles.

In Figure 3, there are three situations of inscribed angles in circles: the center of the circle is on one chord, between the two chords, or outside the two chords. In addition, there are: relevant angles formed between a tangent and a chord, angles formed inside of a circle by two intersecting chords, and angles formed outside of a circle by two intersecting tangents, two secants, or a tangent and a secant. However, Figure 3, which was presented by a teacher in a unit review lesson, presents the relationships among different angles clearly by adding critical auxiliary lines, both connecting relevant concepts and consolidating these concepts.

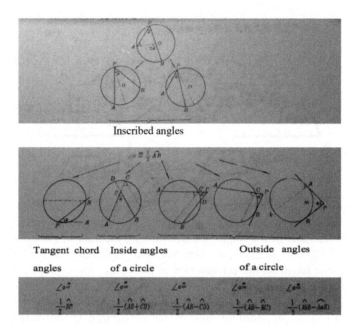

Figure 3. The measurement of angles in circles

Illustration of procedural variation with the analysis of an exemplary lesson. Procedural variation relates to different mathematical thinking, either converging transformation or diverging transformation. Procedural variation is also derived from a prototypical problem, or combination and transformation of representations, or re-recognition or discovering, and so on. Different ways of thinking and multiple representations when creating procedural variations are beyond being dealt with by any conceptual variation. However, making a problem more difficult and complex through extensively varying problems is contrary to the goals of teaching through variation. Varying problems must serve for instruction processes and purposes. In addition to the quantitative results shown previously, we illustrate how to appropriately use variation problems by analyzing an exemplary lesson developed during the Qingpu experiment. The lesson focused on the theorem for determining isosceles triangles. Here, we just describe two segments of the lesson.

Segment 1: Multiple constructions and multiple proofs. In Figure 4: in an isosceles triangle, given the base BC and the angle ∠B formed by a leg and the base, construct the isosceles triangle.

Students provided a variety of constructing methods. Some constructed ∠C = ∠B and extended the sides of the angles so that they intersect at A. Some constructed

21

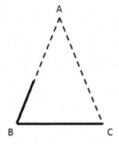 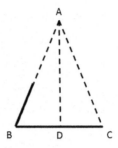

Figure 4. An incomplete isosceles triangle

the perpendicular bisector of base BC and intersect one leg at A. In addition, some students folded BC in half and found the vertex A and constructed the triangle. Based on the constructions of a triangle, the determining theorem of isosceles could be discovered: In $\triangle$ABC, if $\angle$B = $\angle$C, then AB = AC. Different proofs of this theorem could be found based on the construction of the figure. For example, the altitude of base BC can be constructed, or the bisector of angle A can be constructed, then prove $\triangle$ABD $\cong$ $\triangle$ACD; then, AB=AC can be obtained based on the properties of congruent triangles. In addition, students are encouraged to find various proofs: for example, if AB > (*or* <) AC, then $\angle$B > (*or* <) $\angle$C based on the property that in a triangle, the longer sides correspond to bigger angles. This is contradictory to the given of $\angle$B = $\angle$C. So, it is impossible that AB $\neq$ AC. This is *Reductio ad absurdum* (indirect reasoning). Moreover, if $\triangle$ABC and $\triangle$ACB are regarded as two overlapping triangles, then, because $\angle$B = $\angle$C, $\angle$C = $\angle$B, and BC=CB; thus, the two triangles are congruent (e.g., ASA) and therefore AB=AC. Based on different ways of constructing the figure, varying proofs were derived which are complementary to a single proof.

Segment 2: Varying the problems hierarchically. Based on previous teaching experience, exploration of multiple solutions to a problem and a set of problems which could be solved by the same method, should be better than seeking a solution to a problem regarding promoting students' flexibility and profoundness of mathematical thinking (Cai & Nie, 2007). However, the Qingpu experiment (Gu, 1994) indicated that exploring hierarchical-progressive variation problems could achieve a much better effect on student learning. The following is an exemplar for illustrating the feature of hierarchical-progressive variation problems. The initial problem is simple: In Figure 5(1), the bisectors of two base angles of an isosceles triangle $\triangle$ABC intersect at D, determine whether the $\triangle$DBC is an isosceles triangle.

The answer to the first problem (Figure 5(1)) is obvious. It aims to help students understand how to use judgment theorem and property theorem of isosceles triangles that are the basic knowledge of the content. In Figure 5(2), a segment EF passing through D is parallel to BC (EF$\parallel$BC). Students were asked to find all isosceles

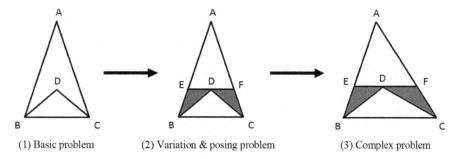

| (1) Basic problem | (2) Variation & posing problem | (3) Complex problem |

Figure 5. Hierarchical-progressive variation problems

triangles in the figure. ΔDBC and ΔAEF are obviously isosceles triangles, which is easy to prove. Then, students should focus on determining whether ΔEDB and ΔFDC are isosceles triangles. If they are, prove that they must be. In this case, students have to use judgment theorem and identify the common relationships among the bisectors of an angle, parallel lines, and isosceles triangles. Immediately, students were asked to create their own problems based on the relationships and solve them by themselves. Students found the following results: D is the middle point of EF; EF = EB + FC and so on. This procedural variation was used to pose and explore subsequent challenging problems. In Figure 5(3), ΔABC is not an isosceles triangle, but the bisectors of the base angles and parallel lines remain. Students are asked to individually think: among the statements posed in the previous problem, which ones are still tenable and which ones may be not true? This is a relatively complex problem. Repeated experiments showed that about 80% of the students who had experience with hierarchical-progressive variation problems could solve the complex problem, while only about 20% of the students who did not experience this process could solve the problem. Although, all students had similar academic backgrounds at preliminary stage of learning geometry.

In summary, the authors came to the following conclusions: (1) during mathematical activities, careful dealing with hierarchical levels of transferring from a related basic problem to a higher cognitive demand problem, and practicing with relevantly hierarchical-progressive variation problems could advance students' capacity in solving problems step by step; (2) synthesizing common experiences and features during different hierarchical-progressive variation processes, and classifying and connecting these relevant variations could promote students' development of hierarchical and systemic experiences. These strategies have evolved based on a great amount of effective teaching experiences. Actually, dynamic mathematics activities include an important characteristic, namely, the progression of knowledge and skills. This progression could be represented in the forms of hierarchical levels of knowledge or a series of strategies for, or experiences in, doing mathematics activities. Certainly, teaching through hierarchical-progressive variation problems is not the same as rote practice.

23

Mechanism of Procedural Variation

To understand the principles and mechanisms of procedural variation, the Qingpu experiment group (Gu, 1994) conducted a series of studies on student mathematical thinking processes between 1987 and 1988. These studies focused on psychological characteristics of learning through variation and describing progression of knowledge development and essential connections between what students have and what they are supposed to learn. The sections that follow describe the major findings of those studies (Gu, 1994) based on original data analysis (see Gu et al., 2004 for additional examples).

Anchoring knowledge point and new problems. Students' existing knowledge structure is the key factor influencing students' learning of new knowledge. The *anchoring knowledge point* is critical for the success of exploration of a new problem (Ausubel, 1978). *Anchoring knowledge point* refers to the previous knowledge point that underpins learning of the new knowledge.

There were 180 middle school students participating in this experiment. Seventh, eighth, and ninth grade students occupied one-third of the participants equally; male and female averaged half; and the ratio among high, average, and low achieving students is 3:4:3. Using stratified samplings, 60 students participated in the experiment: teaching through variation; another 60 students participated in dissemination of the experiment; yet another 60 students participated in a control group: direct teaching the concept. Activity cards are used as a research tool. One example is shown in Figure 6. There were 6 groups of 5 items, 30 items in total. Groups 1, 3, and 5 included items that can be solved based on visual perceptions (constructing figures based on given data and then making judgments based on visual perceptions) while groups 2, 4, and 6 included items that can be solved based on logical reasoning (Making conjectures based on the given and providing justification).

Regarding the problem in Figure 6, *the anchoring knowledge point* of students of different grade levels were different and therefore, the knowledge distance between the problem and anchoring knowledge point of different grade levels was different. Seventh graders knew about segment diagrams, but had the largest knowledge distance; eighth graders knew about translations of figures (such as two triangles) and had a shorter knowledge distance; and ninth graders knew about the relationship between a line and a circle and had the shortest knowledge distance. The test results showed that the correct rate of students increased as the knowledge distance decreases. This finding reveals that learning new knowledge or solving new problems not only relies on the anchoring knowledge point but also relies on the knowledge distance. This finding also indicates the mechanism of teaching and learning with progression and provides implications for teaching through progressive variation problems.

In addition, students could develop their mathematics cognition as they grow up across grades; how might the cognitive maturity influence students' ability in

Positional relationship between two circles A and B		Given conditions
⊙ ⊙	External	Big circle A, Radius R: Small circle B, Radius r:
⊙◦	External tangent	The distance between two centers of circles. AB=d
⊙◦	Secant	Exploratory problem
⊙	Internal tangent	Determine the positional relationship between circles A and B based on the given
⊙	Internal	quantitative relationship among R, r and d.

Figure 6. Example of activity cards (visual perception oriented judgment)

exploring a novel problem? To address this concern, another problem was posed: exploration of Pick's theorem was given to students of three grades (e.g., seventh, eighth, and ninth). The theorem is expressed as follows:

Given a simple polygon constructed on a grid of equal-distanced points (i.e., points with integer coordinates) such that all the polygon's vertices are grid points, Pick's theorem provides a simple formula for calculating the area A of this polygon in terms of the number N of *lattice points in the interior* located in the polygon and the number L of *lattice points on the boundary* placed on the polygon's perimeter:

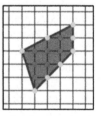

Although this theorem is totally new to all students, the knowledge needed for exploring this theorem is basic: area of triangle and counting, making the anchoring knowledge

$$A = N + \frac{L}{2} - 1$$

point quite similar for students in all grades. Thus, the knowledge distance is quite comparable as well. The incorrect rates (vertical axis) of solving these two problems across grades are displayed in Figure 7.

In Figure 7, the dash-line reveals that, even with the similar anchoring knowledge point for all students in all grades, the correct rate increased as the grade increased; this implies students' mathematical cognition maturity matters. The bold-line

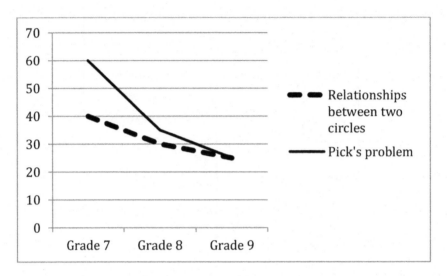

Figure 7. Incorrect rates of solving problems regarding different knowledge

indicates that with different anchoring knowledge point, the correct rate increased tremendously as the grade increased. The gains of correct rate of the two problems across grades are obviously different. This difference may reflect the co-impact of mathematical knowledge distance and cognitive level maturity. The "potential distance" between anchoring knowledge point and a new problem is determined by two factors: mathematical knowledge distance between anchoring knowledge point and the new problem, and cognitive maturity.

Measurability of potential distance.   As discussed previously, both the anchoring knowledge point and new problems are related to mathematical content. Thus, the potential distance could be measured through designing appropriate instruments (e.g., mathematical problems) and analyzing test results quantitatively. For instance, in the aforementioned examples (in Figure 7), the potential distance could be indicated by incorrect rate when exploring new knowledge or new problems. The lower the incorrect rate, the lower the potential distance. This is a kind of primary characterization/representation. Of course, further studies could be done through testing different content topics with larger samples and conducting advanced psychometric analysis to build standardized norms. Thus, potential distance is measurable, although more studies are needed in the area.

Differentiation of potential distance.   The potential distance between anchoring knowledge point and a new problem could influence the difficulties and achievements of students' exploration of the problem. If the potential distance between new knowledge and anchoring knowledge point is shorter (short distance

26

connection), it is easy for students to understand and master the new knowledge. If the potential distance is longer (long distance connection), the problem can support the development of students' exploratory ability. A teacher could adopt different orientations of instruction: direct, exploratory, or combination according to different potential distances and learning goals.

RECENT STUDIES ON PROCEDURAL VARIATION: CORE CONNECTION AND LEARNING TRAJECTORY

In addition to the definition and features of potential distance described in the previous section, it was noticed that when the potential distance is too long, a majority of students have difficulties in approaching the new knowledge, which we conjectured was due to heavy cognitive load (Gu, 1994). The key questions that need to be addressed include: how can teachers help students build bridges between anchoring knowledge point and new knowledge? How can teachers provide effective scaffolding activities? How can teachers use variation problems to shorten the potential distance, if possible? A second analysis of data taken from the Qingpu experiment (Gu, 1994) reveals partial answers to these questions. The major findings include identifying *core connection* and setting appropriate *Pudian* (i.e., scaffoldings). In addition, based on an attempt to incorporate the western notion of learning trajectory (Simon, 1995) with teaching through variation in Chinese mathematics classroom, it was found that the teaching guided by the combination of learning trajectory and teaching through variation could promote students' understanding of concepts.

Concept of Core Connection

In the Qingpu experiment (Gu, 1994), the teachers in the experiment group had emphasized the integration of numerical and geometrical representations, and invariant features within varying transformations after seventh grade. For instance, in the experimental class, the students were introduced to analyzing the positional relationship between two segments on a line using "segment diagrams" in algebraic lessons as shown in Figure 8.

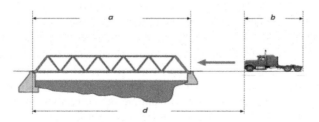

Figure 8. Positional relationships between two segments on a line

27

In Figure 8, a truck is shown travelling toward a bridge from East to West. The length of the bridge is a, the length of the truck is b, and the distance between the West end of the bridge and the front of the truck is d. To explore the quantitative relationship among d, a, and b, students need to determine the following relationships between the truck and the bridge: (1) when is the truck not on the bridge? (2) When is a portion of the truck driving on the bridge? (3) When is the truck entirely on the bridge? If students understand these problems clearly, then they can answer the relationship between two circles successfully (see Figure 6). Seventh graders know about segment diagrams and can apply the above process of variation problems to explore relationship between two circles. The longer potential distance of the seventh graders could be *shortened greatly*. Actually, the positional relationship of two circles can be transferred into the positional relationship between two segments (i.e., the distance between two centers of circles, radii). If students understand the positional relationship between two segments, then, they can easily grasp the positional relationship between two circles. It is critical to find the most essential and transferable connections between the anchoring knowledge point and the new problem. We define this type of crucial connection as "*core connection.*" Teaching through variation based on "*core connection*" could result in two unique effects.

Effects of Using Core Connection

The experiment data shows that there are important effects of using *core connection*. First, it could shorten the distance between anchoring knowledge point and a new problem. Second, it could mature cognitive thinking and advance thinking levels.

Shortening potential distance. Based on the experiment of potential distance, a deep analysis of the data shows that using *core connection* could shorten potential distance. Students' explorations of the five relationships between two circles between the experimental group and the control group (around 50 students) were examined and compared. In the experimental group, the teacher emphasized *core connection* by exploring problems with a truck and a bridge (Figure 8). Figure 9 shows students' correct rates in exploring these relationships in the experimental and control group in seventh grade, and control groups in seventh and eighth grades. The results indicated that students' correct rates from the experimental group was much higher than the control groups in seventh grade, and even higher than the control groups in eighth and ninth grades. These results imply that the use of *core connection* could shorten the potential distance significantly, and reduce the students' cognitive load.

Advancing thinking ability. Two types of test items, visual judgment and abstract logical reasoning, are used to examine the correlations between different mathematical thinking levels. The correlations between visual judgment and abstract logical reasoning in seventh, eighth, and ninth grades respectively are 0.390, 0.686, and 0.696. The data appears to imply that seventh grade is a transformative period

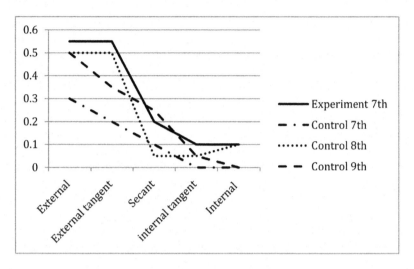

Figure 9. Correct rates of exploring new problems across different groups

from visual to logical reasoning. The scatterplots in Figure 10 further illustrate that students from the experimental group in seventh grade moved toward logical reasoning levels from visual perceptions. This means the transformation from visual judgment to logical reasoning occurred one year earlier (from eighth grade to seventh grade). Thus, variation problem focusing on *core connection* could promote students' transformation from visual judgment to logical reasoning significantly.

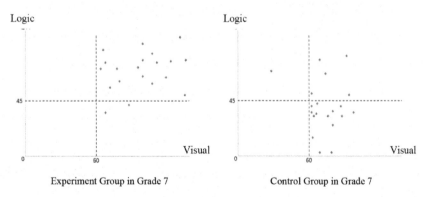

Figure 10. Scatterplots of students' thinking tests in seventh grade

Instructional Pudian

Building on the concept of *core connection* and its importance in procedural variation, this section further discusses another closely related concept of "*Pudian*"

(铺垫). According to Gu et al. (2004), *Pudian* is commonly used in Chinese classroom teaching, which is metaphorically described as "by putting blocks or stones together as a *Pudian*, a person can pick fruit from a tree which cannot be reached without the *Pudian*" (p. 340). Similar to the notion of scaffolding in the West (Wood, 1976), by establishing "*Pudian*", the students can complete the tasks that cannot be done without the "*Pudian*." In contrast, the *Pudian* emphasizes "the process and hierarchy" of learning (Gu et al., 2004, p. 340). In classroom instruction, *Pudian* could be appropriately applied to instructional design and implementation as follows: Teachers and students move from their existing knowledge and cognitive level toward obtaining new knowledge and solving new problems through effective instructional design (or *Pudian*). The segment diagram in Figure 8 is an appropriate example of how *Pudian* can help students move from existing knowledge toward exploring positional relationships between two circles.

There are multiple strategies to help students move toward higher levels of learning. By utilizing the terminology of scaffolding in the West (*Pudian*, in China), it is crucial to construct appropriate scaffolding when necessary, and remove the scaffolding when unnecessary. In particular, when designing discovering or exploratory learning, appropriateness of constructing and removing scaffoldings is essential. The researchers (Bao, Wang, & Gu, 2005; Huang & Bao, 2006) explored teaching of Pythagoras' theorem by using scaffolding notions (see Figure 11).

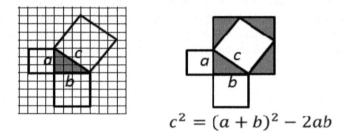

$$c^2 = (a + b)^2 - 2ab$$

Figure 11. Constructing and removing scaffoldings

In the left figure, when a, b, c given various integer values (Pythagoras' number triples), then various data sets of a^2, b^2, $2ab$ and c^2 could be collected; based on this data, many conjectures about the quantitative relationships among a^2, b^2, $2ab$, and c^2 could be made (including Pythagoras theorem, and other conditional equations). After making conjectures, the role of the scaffolding (left grid in Figure 11) is complete, and thus, scaffolding must be removed. The right figure in Figure 11, the sides are labeled as letters a, b, and c, and calculating the area of the square extending on the hypotenuse is the key. The *core connection* is: Formula of completing square of sum used to calculate the area of a combination figure. From the anchoring knowledge point (area of triangle and square), students can use the scaffolding in the right figure to prove the theorem. This is a creative strategy that has evolved over decades.

This strategy has derived from one of the traditional features of learning: learning and teaching progressively. Teachers usually identify several hierarchical-progressive levels of subject topics, and then employ procedural variation problems (*Pudian*) supporting students to transcend their existing knowledge (anchoring knowledge point) to higher levels of knowledge. In Figure 11, the right figure is a simple and effective scaffolding (i.e., procedural variation) to support students to find proofs. These scaffoldings are interconnected progressively, which is a major strategy in Chinese classrooms. The scaffoldings or *Pudian* are instructional artifacts, which are designed for prompting student learning. Appropriate design and use of scaffoldings requires teachers to be creative designers, supporters, and guiders of student learning. An effective design of scaffoldings in China usually focuses on the progression of mathematical knowledge development and the "*core connection*" of different levels of mathematical knowledge.

Variation, Learning Trajectory, and Student Learning

Traditionally, teaching through variation mainly focuses on subject knowledge structure and teaching strategies from a teachers' perspective. Recently, some researchers explored how teaching through variation could help focus attention on student learning (Huang, Miller, & Tzur, 2015; Huang, Gong, & Han, 2016).

Huang and colleagues (Huang et al., 2015) proposed a hybrid-model for analyzing students' learning opportunities in the classroom. This model includes three hierarchical layers of principles for guiding mathematical instruction in Chinese mathematical classrooms. Teaching through variation (with bridging) is located at a meso-level. A macro-level is *Hypothetical Learning Trajectory* (HLT) and micro-level is known as reflection on activity-effect relationship (Ref*AER). At macro-level, HLT (Simon, 1995; Simon & Tzur, 2004) focuses on three key aspects: (a) *goals* teachers set for student learning in terms of conceptions (activity-effect relationships) they are expected to construct, (b) *sequences of mental activities* (and reflections on them) hypothesized to promote students' transformation of their extant conceptions into the intended ones, and (c) *tasks* designed and implemented to fit with and promote hypothetical reorganization processes from available to intended mathematics. At a meso-level, based on teaching through variation, six components are proposed as being important for effective mathematics instruction. They are (1) tailoring old-to-new; (2) specifying intended mathematics; (3) articulating mental activity sequences; (4) designing variation tasks; (5) engaging students in tasks; and (6) examining students' progress through variation practice. At a micro-level, teachers could monitor students' learning through systemic reflections on activity-effect relationships that include: (1) continually and automatically comparing the effects of the activity with the learner's goal and (2) comparing a variety of situations in which the recorded activity-effect dyads are called upon, which can bring about abstraction of the activity-effect relationship as a reasoned, invariant anticipation. Based on a fine-grained analysis of 10 consecutive lessons taught by a competent teacher in middle school in Shanghai (Clarke et al., 2006) using this framework, the authors concluded that: "our analysis of learning opportunities indicates the power of teaching through variation to deepen and consolidate conceptual understanding and procedural fluency concurrently" (Huang et al., 2015, p. 104).

Moreover, Huang, Gong and Han (2016) explored how teaching through variation and incorporating the notion of learning trajectory could be used as a principle for designing and reflecting upon teaching to promote students' understanding of division of fractions. In their study, a lesson study approach (Huang & Han, 2015) was adopted: a group of teacher educators (practice-based teaching research specialist and University-based mathematics educators) and mathematics teachers worked together to develop lessons on division of fractions based on variation pedagogy and learning trajectory through three cycles of lesson planning, delivering/observing lessons, and post-lesson debriefings. Based on a literature review, a hypothetical learning trajectory on division of fractions was proposed as a foundation for the design of the lessons. Data consisted of lesson plans, videotaped lessons, post-lesson quizzes, post-lesson discussions, and teachers' reflection reports. This study revealed that by building on the learning trajectory and by strategically using variation tasks, the lesson was improved in terms of students' understanding, proficiency, and mathematical reasoning.

Combined, these studies indicate that teaching through variation and incorporating learning trajectory (reflection on activity-effect relationship of student learning) could provide students with opportunities to develop conceptual understanding and procedural fluency concurrently.

INTERPRETATION, IMPLICATIONS AND SUGGESTIONS

In previous sections, we discussed major concepts and principles of teaching through variation that included two types of variations, potential distance, core connection, and *Pudian* (scaffolding). All of these ideas envision a core conception of learning through exploring a series of hierarchical-progressive tasks. This section interprets teaching through variation from other theoretical perspectives and discusses implications for classroom instruction.

Theoretical Interpretations

Gu et al. (2004) explored theoretical interpretations of teaching through variation from multiple theoretical perspectives. First, from the perspective of *meaningful learning* (Ausubel, 1978) that emphasizes establishing the non-arbitrary and substantive relationship between learners' prior knowledge and the new knowledge, they argued that conceptual variation could help students understand the essence of a concept and develop substantial relationships. Meanwhile, procedural variation could help students develop well-structured knowledge and non-arbitrary connections between different types of knowledge. Second, the notion of duality of mathematics learning (Sfard, 1991) proposes that mathematical concepts can be conceived in two fundamentally different ways: structurally (as objects), and operationally (as processes). Gu et al. (2004) claimed that by creating these two types of variation, it would enhance students' understanding of two aspects of a mathematical object: operational process and structural object (these two aspects of a mathematical object are complementary). Third, Gu et al. (2004) also discussed the similarities and differences between scaffolding (Wood et al., 1976) and *Pudian* (i.e., a strategy of procedural variation). Although both scaffolding and *Pudian* emphasize the support for students to achieve higher learning goals within zone of proximal development (Vygotsky, 1978), *Pudian* devotes more attention to core connection and hierarchical progression. Fourth, Gu and colleagues also discussed the relationships among Dienes' theory (Dienes, 1973), Marton's variation pedagogy (Marton & Tsui, 2004; Marton, 2015), and teaching through variation (Gu et al., 2004). Dienes emphasizes "mathematical variability" and "perceptual variability", while Marton stresses the patterns of what varies and what is invariant. Both of them mainly focus on *conceptual variation*. Thus, Gu et al.'s (2004) theory of teaching through variation developed the concept of variation pedagogy by illustrating procedural variation that focuses on developing problem solving ability and building a well-structured knowledge base. In the following section, an additional dimension of teaching through variation, namely, *dimensions of variation*, will be discussed.

Dimensions of variation.   Mathematical instruction has often been criticized in the past. For example, in the 1940s, famous mathematicians Courant and Robbins (1941) critiqued mathematics instruction that focused on simple procedural practice, which may develop students' formal operation ability but has nothing to do with profound understanding of mathematics. In fact, precise understanding of mathematical concepts is the foundation of mastering mathematics, and effective problem solving is at the heart of all mathematics. Teaching through variation in China focuses on two fundamental aspects: understanding of concepts from multiple perspectives through conceptual variations and developing problem-solving ability and well-structured knowledge base through purposefully selected procedural variation.

The mechanisms and principles of teaching through variation (hierarchical-progressive learning) include: (1) a measurable, plausibly potential distance between existing knowledge (anchoring knowledge point) and the new knowledge or new problems; adjusting the potential distance based on instructional goals and student learning readiness is critical; (2) both conceptual variation and procedural variation should reflect the core connection between existing knowledge and new knowledge to be learned, and design variation problems should surround the *core connection*. By using appropriate procedural variation problems surrounding the *core connection*, the potential distance could be shortened and learners' thinking ability could be advanced.

Based on the research on classroom instruction reforms and practices over the past three decades, researchers have identified the following three critical aspects of "*core connection*": (1) Situation and application. This aspect is concerned with background and meaning of discovery and development of mathematics. It should be pointed out that background and application should not be treated as simply additional information. Rather they should be carefully considered from the perspectives of mathematical necessity and promoting learners' understanding. For example, the segment diagram in Figure 8 presenting the relationships between a truck and a bridge seem simple, but it reflects the essential quantitative relationship that could be used to present the positional relationship between the truck and the bridge and could be further transferred to present the positional relationship between two circles. (2) Computation and reasoning. These are two basic and fundamental mathematical thinking methods that form a system of mathematical thinking. Mathematical thinking methods reflect the simplicity and convenience of logical connections within variant contexts or situations. For example, in Figure 5, the variation practices regarding isosceles triangles provide an example demonstrating *core connection* in a logical system from a problem-solving perspective. (3) Cognition of learners. Most importantly, student learning should be the focus of all decisions. When designing applications or contexts, it is critical to consider if they could motivate student learning and are conducive to developing students' cognition and thinking. In Figure 11, the scaffolding (left figure) is designed for discovering Pythagoras' theorem by creating several sets of Pythagoras triples; the other scaffolding (right figure) is designed for discovering proofs of Pythagoras' theorem by calculating areas by completing square of sum. These are typical examples on how scaffoldings (*Pudian*) could be designed based on *core connection* between existing knowledge and new knowledge.

In summary, situation and application, computation and reasoning, and cognition level are three relatively independent dimensions, which form a comprehensive space of variation. Of course, when designing a particular lesson, we may focus on one or several dimensions and design greatly meticulous variation in those selected dimensions. Although constructing variation problems should be open, it should focus on essential goals: contexts of knowledge and development of new knowledge; transformation between complex and simple problems; and eliminating rote learning and mastering general and powerful methods.

Implications for Reform of Classroom Instruction

The tradition of teaching through variation has evolved for a long time in China. For further development, attention should be focused on the following two issues.

Variation surrounding core connection. Variation does imply neither "the more, the better", nor "the more difficult, the better." There is an old saying, "ten thousand variation problems remains the same principle (万变不离其宗)". The principle is promoting students' learning of mathematics. Teaching through variation effectively requires addressing students' learning differences. In order to implement differentiated instruction, multiple formative assessments could help teachers understand student learning, and adopt appropriate strategies of teaching through variation. These formative assessments include student-learning worksheets and post-lesson homework sheets, which are developed, based on instruction objectives of units or lessons and used for diagnosing and removing learning obstacles, discussing major problems in class, and designing and making use of post-lesson homework.

In addition, when designing procedural variation, it is crucial to identify and make use of *core connection* about different content. Take one released item on 2012 PISA test, for example (Figure 12).

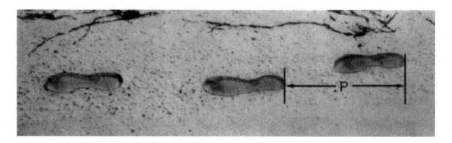

Figure 12. Walking problem on 2012 PISA test

The picture shows the footprints of a man walking. The pace length *p* is the distance between the rear of two consecutive footprints.

For men, the formula $p/n = 140$, gives an approximate relationship between *n* and *p* where, *n* = number of steps per minute, and *p* = pace length in meters.

Question 1: If the formula applies to Heiko's walking and Heiko takes 70 steps per minute, what is Heiko's pace length? Show your work.

Question 2: Bernard knows his pace length is 0.80-meters. The formula above applies to Bernard's walking. Calculate Bernard's walking speed in meters per minute and in kilometers per hour. Show your work.

Question 1 is used to test whether participants understand the formula, which acts as scaffolding for solving question 2. Question 2 is used to examine flexibility in using the formula and application of the relationship among distance, time, and velocity in daily situations. Each question demonstrates clear core connection between anchoring knowledge point and a new problem.

Core connection in algebra is abounding. For example, regarding operations with polynomials: the basic concept and skills include factors and like terms. Yet, like terms could be combined or split for different purposes. The purpose of using variation problem practice is not mainly for deriving a specific multiplication formula, or splitting, adding or factorizing formula. Rather it serves for understanding the core thinking methods: applications of operational principles of polynomials through transformation. For instance, first, transformation between multiplication and factorization, namely, $(x - 1)(x - 12) = x^2 - 13x + 12$: from left to right means multiplications (combination of like terms); inversely, it is factorization (including splitting like terms). Second, when discussing quadratic equations through the comparison of two equations: $x^2 + px + q = 0$ and $(x - a)(x - b) = 0$, where a and b are roots of the equation, then, the relationships between roots could be presented as follows: $a + b = -p$, $ab = q$ (Vieta's Theorem): $x^2 + px + q = 0$ can be transformed as $\left(x + \dfrac{p}{2}\right)^2 = A$ (where $A = \dfrac{p^2 - 4q}{4}$), thus, the quadratic formula can be derived. Third, when studying the quadratic function $y = x^2 + px + q$, the function can be transformed as: $y = \left(x + \dfrac{p}{2}\right)^2 - A$, thus, when $x = -\dfrac{p}{2}$, y = maximum value of the function; Moreover, the monotone and symmetry properties of functions can be analyzed easily. In this way, the operations of multiplication, factorization, and completing the square can lead to the discussion of relationships between roots and coefficients of quadratic equations, monotonous properties, and symmetric features, maximum or minimum value of quadratic functions. This is a typical example in school mathematics of how new concepts can be derived through making use of core connection.

Variation promoting self-exploratory exploration. One possible derivation of using variation in teaching is direct telling. Superficially, using variation knowledge eventually leads to telling rigid and cumbersome formulas. The ultimate goal of improving mathematics instruction is to develop students' self-exploratory learning ability and their ability to learn how to learn by themselves without teaching in the future. Thus, it is necessary to establish a new classroom ecology of harmony in relationships between teachers and students. For example, teaching Pythagoras' theorem for illustrating an ideal classroom ecology. Rigorous proofs of Pythagoras' theorem are difficult for students to understand; "measurement and calculation", or "cutting and pasting" methods are visual and interesting, but the teacher normally provides the results. The following is an example of self-exploratory learning of Pythagoras's theorem (Bao et al., 2005).

As shown in Figure 11, students are asked to make conjectures based on calculating the area of squares in several situations (Figure 13).

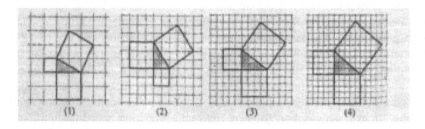

Figure 13. Make conjectures through calculating area of squares

In class, by using calculations on several diagrams (1)–(4) in grids, students created a set of data (see Figure 14).

Area	Diagram (1)	Diagram (2)	Diagram (3)	Diagram (4)	
a^2	1	4	9	16	......
b^2	4	9	16	25	......
$2ab$	4	12	24	40	......
c^2	5	13	25	41	......

Figure 14. Data collected based on selected diagrams

Based on these data, students are encouraged to make conjectures (correct and unexpected conjectures). The following is an excerpt focusing on proving and refuting:

1. S1: Based on the data in the table [Figure 14], I find that $c^2 = 2ab + 1$.
2. T: [Surprise! Unbelievable] how can you make this conjecture? Is it possible?
3. S2: I investigated when $a = 2$, $b = 4$, $2ab = 16$, $c^2 = 20$, $c^2 \neq 2ab + 1$.
4. T: Student 2 used a counterexample to refute your conjecture. It disproves $c^2 = 2ab + 1$.
5. S3: Mr. I found that when the difference between a and b is 1, the result is tenable.
6. T: [Thinking in brain: $c^2 = (a - b)^2 + 2ab$, when $b - a = 1$, $c^2 = 2ab + 1$] This suggestion is correct. This is a conditional equation. Good, let us examine the other equation that many of you suggested: $a^2 + b^2 = c^2$.
7. S4: This equation is tenable regarding the given four figures and numbers. But, I think that even if I examine 100 examples and the result is true, I cannot be sure that the equation is true when examining the next situation. So, we have to prove that this is true for all situations.
8. T: Whether $a^2 + b^2 = c^2$ is a theorem? Examining more cases cannot prove it. What do we need to do?
9. Ss: We have to prove.

The previous discourse illustrated that students were actively involving mathematical reasoning activities such as making conjectures ((1)), disproving and refuting ((3)~(5)), and developing proofs ((7)~(9)). The teacher was a facilitator to guide and solicit students' explorations.

Variation and learning trajectory. As discussed throughout this chapter, the core idea of teaching through variation can help students develop profound understanding of mathematical concepts and flexibility in problem solving through forming a well-structured knowledge system using hierarchical-progressive variation problems which surround the core connection between different types of knowledge. Paying attention to student cognitive readiness and development is also one key dimension of core connection. Yet, there are no concrete suggestions about how teachers can pay attention to student thinking and solicit student thinking. To this end, the exploratory studies by Huang et al. (2016) revealed an alternative. That is, to incorporate notions of learning trajectory with teaching through variation. Huang et al. (2016) found that through the combination of two theoretical perspectives, teachers were able to shift their focus on student thinking and solutions during lessons and post-lesson reflections, which eventually resulted in students' development of deep understandings. They further argued that the notion of teaching through variation emphasizes specific strategies in using systematic tasks progressively (content-focused), but it has not paid explicit attention to the route of children's learning. Thus, the incorporation of these two perspectives may provide a useful tool for designing and delivering lessons: Teaching through variation could help teachers strategically design and implement tasks in line with students' learning trajectory.

CONCLUSIONS

This chapter discussed the cultural and historical origin of teaching through variation. The traditional culture value and ancient mathematical learning ideas have afforded mathematical teaching and learning through variation, and the exam-oriented education system has further strengthened this practice. Based on experiences and empirical studies, the core concepts and major mechanisms of teaching through variation have been developed. Two types of variation include conceptual variation and procedural variation. The former focuses on building the essential connections between existing knowledge and new knowledge, developing profound understanding of a concept from multiple perspectives. The latter intends to develop students' problem-solving ability and develop an interconnected knowledge structure. By considering potential distance and *Pudian*, which are associated with core connection between existing knowledge (anchoring knowledge point) and the new knowledge or new problems, teachers are expected to design and implement hierarchical-progressive variation problems to achieve mathematical instructional goals. Appropriate implementation of teaching through variation is likely to develop students' conceptual understanding and procedural fluency concurrently. However, theoretically, more empirical studies on defining and measuring potential distance, and defining and identifying core connection among different types of knowledge are needed. In addition, how to develop teaching through variation by incorporating relevant theoretical perspectives such as learning trajectory (Simon, 1995) and mathematical teaching practices (NCTM, 2014) is a new endeavor worthy of exploring. Practically, implementing teaching through variation effectively requires teachers to possess a profound understanding of content knowledge and rich instructional expertise. It calls for pertinent teacher professional development programs.

NOTE

[1] Teaching through variation is exchangeable with teaching with variation, or *Bianshi* teaching, 变式教学, in this chapter.

REFERENCES

An, S., Kulm, G., & Wu, Z. (2004). The pedagogical content knowledge of middle school mathematics teachers in China and the U.S. *Journal of Mathematics Teacher Education, 7*, 145–172.

Ausubel, D. P. (1978). *Educational psychology: A cognitive view* (2nd ed.). New York, NY: Holt McDougal.

Bao, J., Huang, R., Yi, L., & Gu, L. (2003a). Study in bianshi teaching [In Chinese]. *Mathematics Teaching [Shuxue Jiaoxue], 1*, 11–12.

Bao, J., Huang, R., Yi, L., & Gu, L. (2003b). Study in bianshi teaching [In Chinese]. *Mathematics Teaching [Shuxue Jiaoxue], 2*, 6–10.

Bao, J., Huang, R., Yi, L., & Gu, L. (2003c). Study in bianshi teaching [In Chinese]. *Mathematics Teaching [Shuxue Jiaoxue], 3*, 6–12.

Bao, J., Wang, H., & Gu, L. (2005). *Focusing on the classroom: The research and production of video cases of classroom teaching* [In Chinese]. Shanghai: Shanghai Education Press.

Biggs, J. B., & Watkins, D. A. (2001). Insight into teaching the Chinese learner. In D. A. Watkins & J. B. Biggs (Eds.), *Teaching the Chinese learner: Psychological and pedagogical perspectives* (pp. 277–300). Hong Kong/Melbourne: Comparative Education Research Centre, the University of Hong Kong/ Australian Council for Education Research.

Brown, A. L. (1992). Design experiments: Theoretical and methodological challenges in creating complex interventions in classroom settings. *Journal of the Learning Sciences, 2*(2), 141–178.

Cai, J., & Nie, B. (2007). Problem solving in Chinese mathematics education: Research and practice. *ZDM-The International Journal on Mathematics Education, 39*, 459–473.

Chen, X., & Li, Y. (2010). Instructional coherence in Chinese mathematics classroom – A case study of lessons on fraction division. *International Journal of Science and Mathematics Education, 8*, 711–735.

Clarke, D. J., Keitel, C., & Shimizu, Y. (2006). *Mathematics classrooms in twelve countries: The insider's perspective*. Rotterdam, The Netherlands: Sense Publishers.

Courant, R., & Robbins, H. (1941). *What is mathematics?* New York, NY: Oxford University Press.

Doenes, Z. P. (1973). A theory of mathematics learning. In F. J. Crosswhite, J. L. Highins, A. R. Osborne, & R. J. Shunway (Eds.), *Teaching mathematics: Psychological foundations* (pp. 137–148). Ohio, OH: Charles A. Jones Publishing.

Fan, L., & Zhu, Y. (2004). How have Chinese students performed in mathematics? A perspective from large-scale international comparisons. In L. Fan, N. Y. Wong, J. Cai, & S. Li (Eds.), *How Chinese learn mathematics: Perspectives from insiders* (pp. 3–26). Singapore: World Scientific.

Fan, L., Wong, N. Y., Cai, J., & Li, S. (2004). *How Chinese learn mathematics: Perspectives from insiders*. Singapore: World Scientific.

Fan, L., Wong, N. Y., Cai, J., & Li, S. (2015). *How Chinese teach mathematics: Perspectives of insiders*. Singapore: World Scientific.

Gu, L. (1981). *The visual effect and psychological implications of transformation of figures on teaching geometry* [In Chinese]. Paper presented at annual conference of Shanghai Mathematics Association, Shanghai, China.

Gu, L. (1994). *Theory of teaching experiment: The methodology and teaching principles of Qingpu* [In Chinese]. Beijing: Educational Science Press.

Gu, L., Huang, R., & Marton, F. (2004). Teaching with variation: An effective way of mathematics teaching in China. In L. Fan, N. Y. Wong, J. Cai, & S. Li (Eds.), *How Chinese learn mathematics: Perspectives from insiders* (pp. 309–348). Singapore: World Scientific.

Gu, M. (1999). *Education directory* [In Chinese]. Shanghai: Shanghai Education Press.

Huang, R. (2014). *Prospective mathematics teachers' knowledge of algebra: A comparative study in China and the United States of America*. Wiesbaden: Springer Spectrum.

Huang, R., & Bao, J. (2006). Towards a model for teacher's professional development in China: Introducing keli. *Journal of Mathematics Teacher Education, 9*, 279–298.

Huang, R., & Han, X. (2015). Developing mathematics teachers' competence through parallel Lesson study. *International Journal for Lesson and Learning Studies, 4*(2), 100–117.

Huang, R., & Leung, F. K. S. (2004). Cracking the paradox of the Chinese learners: Looking into the mathematics classrooms in Hong Kong and Shanghai. In L. Fan, N. Y. Wong, J. Cai, & S. Li (Eds.), *How Chinese learn mathematics: Perspectives from insiders* (pp. 348–381). Singapore: World Scientific.

Huang, R., & Leung, F. K. S. (2005). Deconstructing teacher-centeredness and student-centeredness dichotomy: A case study of a Shanghai mathematics lesson. *The Mathematics Educators, 15*(2), 35–41.

Huang, R., Mok, I., & Leung, F. K. S. (2006). Repetition or variation: "Practice" in the mathematics classrooms in China. In D. J. Clarke, C. Keitel, & Y. Shimizu (Eds.), *Mathematics classrooms in twelve countries: The insider's perspective* (pp. 263–274). Rotterdam, The Netherlands: Sense Publishers.

Huang, R., Miller, D., & Tzur, R. (2015). Mathematics teaching in Chinese classroom: A hybrid-model analysis of opportunities for students' learning. In L. Fan, N. Y. Wong, J. Cai, & S. Li (Eds.), *How Chinese teach mathematics: Perspectives from insiders* (pp. 73–110). Singapore: World Scientific.

Huang, R., Gong, Z., & Han, X. (2016). Implementing mathematics teaching that promotes students' understanding through theory-driven lesson study. *ZDM-The International Journal on Mathematics Education, 48*(3).

Leung, F. K. S. (1995). The Mathematics classroom in Beijing, Hong Kong and London. *Educational Studies in Mathematics, 29*, 197–325.

Leung, F. K. S. (2005). Some characteristics of East Asian mathematics classrooms based on data from the TIMSS 1999 video study. *Educational Studies in Mathematics, 60*, 199–215.

Li, S. (1999). Does practice make perfect? *For the Learning of Mathematics, 19*(3), 33–35.

Li, X., Li, S., & Zhang, D. (2015). Cultural roots, traditions, and characteristics of contemporary mathematic education in China. In B. Sriraman, J. Cai, K. H. Lee, L. Fan, Y. Shimizu, C. S. Lim, & K. Subramaniam (Eds.), *The first sourcebook on Asian research in mathematics education: China, Korea, Singapore, Japan, Malaysia, and India (China and Korea sections)* (pp. 67–90). Charlotte, NC: Information Age.

Li, Y., & Huang, R. (2013). *How Chinese teach mathematics and improve teaching*. New York, NY: Routledge.

Ma, L. (1999). *Knowing and teaching elementary mathematics: Teachers' understanding of fundamental mathematics in China and the United States*. Mahwah, NJ: Erlbaum.

Marton, F. (2015). *Necessary conditions of learning*. New York, NY: Routledge.

Marton, F., & Pang, M. F. (2006). On some necessary conditions of learning. The *Journal of the Learning Sciences, 15*, 193–220.

Marton, F., & Tsui, A. B. M. (2004). *Classroom discourse and the space of learning*. Mahwah, NJ: Erlbaum.

National Council of Teachers of Mathematics. (2014). *Principles to actions: Ensuring mathematical success for all*. Reston, VA: Author.

OECD. (2010). *PISA 2009 Results: What students know and can do: Student performance in reading, mathematics and science* (Vol. I). Paris: OECD Publishing.

OECD. (2014). *PISA 2012 Results in focus: What 15-year-olds know and what they can do with what they know*. Paris: OECD Publishing.

Paine, L. W. (1990). The teacher as virtuoso: A Chinese model for teaching. *Teachers College Record, 92*(1), 49–81.

Qingpu Experiment Group. (1991). *Learn to teaching* [In Chinese]. Beijing: Peoples' Education Press.

Sfard, A. (1991). On the dual nature of mathematical conceptions: Reflections on processes and objects as different sides of the same coin. *Educational Studies in Mathematics, 26*, 114–145.

Shao, G., Fan, Y., Huang, R., Li, Y., & Ding, E. (2013). Examining Chinese mathematics classroom instruction from a historical perspective. In Y. Li & R. Huang (Eds.), *How Chinese teach mathematics and improve teaching* (pp. 11–28). New York, NY: Routledge.

Simon, M. A. (1995). Reconstructing mathematics pedagogy from a constructivist perspective. *Journal for Research in Mathematics Education, 26*, 114–145.

Simon, M. A., & Tzur, R. (2004). Explicating the role of mathematical tasks in conceptual learning: An elaboration of the hypothetical learning trajectory. *Mathematical Thinking and Learning, 6*(2), 91–104.

Song, X. (2006). The Confucian education thinking and Chinese mathematical education tradition [In Chinese]. *Journal of Gansu Normal College, 2*, 65–68.

Sriraman, B., Cai, J., Lee, K. H., Fan, L., Shimizu, Y., Lim C. S., & Subramaniam, K. (Eds.). (2015). *The first sourcebook on Asian research in mathematics education: China, Korea, Singapore, Japan, Malaysia, and India (China and Korea sections).* Charlotte, NC: Information Age.

Stevenson, H. W., & Lee, S. (1995). The East Asian version of whole class teaching. *Educational Policy, 9*, 152–168.

Stevenson, H. W., & Stigler, J. W. (1992). *The learning gap: Why our schools are failing and what we can learn from Japanese and Chinese education.* New York, NY: Summit Books.

Sun, X. (2011). "Variation problems" and their roles in the topic of fraction division in Chinese mathematics textbook examples. *Educational Studies in Mathematics, 76*, 65–85.

Wang, T., & Murphy, J. (2004). An examination of coherence in a Chinese mathematics classroom. In L. Fan, N. Y. Wong, J. Cai, & S. Li (Eds.), *How Chinese learn mathematics: Perspectives from insiders* (pp. 107–123). Singapore: World Scientific.

Wong, N. Y. (2008). Confucian heritage culture learner's phenomenon: From "exploring the middle zone" to "constructing a bridge". *ZDM-The International Journal on Mathematics Education, 40*, 973–981.

Wong, N. Y., Lam, C. C., Sun, X., & Chan, A. M. Y. (2009). From "exploring the middle zone" to "constructing a bridge": Experimenting in the Spiral *bianshi* mathematics curriculum. *International Journal of Science and Mathematics Education, 7*, 363–382.

Wood, D., Bruner, J. S., & Ross, G. (1976). The role of tutoring in problem solving. *Journal of Child Psychology and Psychiatry, 17*, 89–100.

Feishi Gu
East China Normal University
Shanghai, China

Rongjin Huang
Middle Tennessee State University
Murfreesboro, USA

Lingyuan Gu
Shanghai Educational Science Academy
Shanghai, China

41

MING FAI PANG, JIANSHENG BAO AND WING WAH KI

3. *'BIANSHI'* AND THE VARIATION THEORY OF LEARNING

Illustrating Two Frameworks of Variation and Invariance in the Teaching of Mathematics

INTRODUCTION

In the past two decades of cross-cultural research on mathematics education, a key element that has gained popularity is the use of variation and invariance in the teaching and learning of mathematics (e.g., Häggström, 2008; Sun, 2011; Watson & Mason, 2005; Wong et al., 2009). According to Gu, Huang and Marton (2004), Chinese teachers have been found to systematically juxtapose examples, tasks, and problems that differ in important respects to help students develop a deep understanding of the mathematical content to be learned. Two groups of researchers, one in Sweden and Hong Kong led by Ference Marton, and the other in Shanghai headed by Gu Ling-yuan, arrived separately at a similar insight on the use of variation and invariance in their analysis of mathematics classroom practices. The former, developed by Marton's group, is known as the variation theory of learning (Marton & Booth, 1997; Marton & Tsui, 2004; Marton & Pang, 2006; Marton, 2015; Pang & Ki, 2016), and the latter, developed by Gu's team, is known as *bianshi* jiaoxue (teaching with variation; e.g., Bao, Huang, Yi, & Gu, 2003; Gu, 1991; Gu, Huang, & Marton, 2004). These two theories are referred to as VT and BS in the following sections.

The aim of this study was to develop a better understanding of the differences between the two theories, both of which focus on the importance of differences and sameness (or variation and invariance) in teaching and learning; to explore whether the two are contradictory, independent, or complementary; and to compare the static descriptions of the two theories. We closely examined the classroom practices of an experienced mathematics teacher in Shanghai, who was inspired by the BS framework and made systematic use of variation and invariance. We invited the researchers of the two above-mentioned research groups to analyze and comment on the patterns of variation and invariance in the same lesson in terms of their respective theories.

Obviously we cannot treat the lesson as a direct and complete enactive representation of the BS framework. Nonetheless, by comparing the interpretations of the same lesson by researchers of the two theories, some useful comparisons

R. Huang & Y. Li (Eds.), Teaching and Learning Mathematics through Variation, 43–67.

and connections between the two theoretical lenses can be achieved, and some methodological issues concerning the relation between educational theory and practice can be made explicit.

THEORETICAL FRAMEWORK

The point of departure of this paper is a conjecture embodied in the two independently developed frameworks mentioned above. The conjecture suggests that the pattern of variation and invariance within and between units of teaching, such as problems, tasks, examples, or illustrations, in the interactions between the teacher and students has a great influence on what students might learn from participation in that interaction. The first framework, VT, is intended for learning and teaching powerful ways of seeing in different subject domains; it was developed in particular by Ference Marton and his colleagues in Hong Kong and Sweden (Marton & Booth, 1997; Marton & Tsui, 2004; Marton & Pang, 2006; Marton, 2015; Pang & Ki, 2016). The second framework, BS, is intended to capture and make explicit good practices in mathematics teaching in China; it was named and codified by Gu Ling-yuan (Bao et al., 2003; Gu, 1991; Gu et al., 2004). We begin by very briefly describing these two frameworks.

With its origins in phenomenography, VT posits that we identify novel meanings and make them our own by discerning the ways in which things differ in certain respects but are otherwise the same (as opposed to discerning how things are the same in certain respects, but differ otherwise). This means, for instance, that multiplication can be better understood if we see how it differs from division, rather than if we *only* see how different multiplication tasks resemble each other. Similarly, we understand addition better if we see how it differs from subtraction (e.g., Marton & Pang, 2013; Pang & Marton, 2013).

According to Marton and Pang (2006), VT is concerned with how to enable learners to handle novel situations in powerful ways. Above all, learners need to develop the capability to discern which aspects or features must be taken into account when deciding how to achieve the goal in a novel situation. Discerning those critical aspects or features involves noticing the ways in which one specific situation (a problem, task, or instance of the phenomenon) differs from others. For example, the ability to use appropriate tones in writing is a function of the ability to distinguish between situations or instances that necessitate the use of different tones; the ability of a financial analyst to make good judgments is a function of the ability to discern different patterns of economic data and indicators; and a child's ability to solve simple arithmetic word problems is a function of the ability to discern the parts and wholes and the relations between them in the specific problem situation. In this respect, VT differs from other learning theories because it focuses on the learning affordance of differences.

Interestingly, VT also highlights the important role of invariance (similarity) in affording the discernment of differences. According to Marton and Tsui (2004), to discern and focus upon the critical aspects (or dimensions of variation) of a phenomenon, the learner must experience variation in these aspects against a background of invariance. They suggest the use of four patterns of variation and invariance, 'contrast', 'separation', 'fusion', and 'generalization', for organising the learning instances. As explained in Pang and Ki (2016), when one critical aspect varies while the other aspects are kept invariant, the pattern is called 'separation.' The aspect to be varied is perceptually separated from the other aspects of the phenomenon and becomes salient to the learner. In contrast, when two or more critical aspects of the phenomenon vary simultaneously and are thus brought to the learner's awareness at the same time, this pattern is called 'fusion.' It helps the learner to discern and attend to the connections between or the joint and/or independent working of the changes in multiple critical aspects. The two other patterns of variation and invariance are more concerned with noticing the sameness and differences across different instances and non-instances of the phenomenon. For example, to grasp the concept of a square, one must 'contrast' it against something that is not a square. If every shape one has ever experienced is a square, then 'square' will be synonymous with shape and will carry no unique meaning of its own, not to mention the discernment and attention to its necessary aspects. Furthermore, to 'generalize' the idea of a square, one must see sameness, such as the same set of features (necessary values in its aspects and relations between them), across the various squares that one has experienced.

Out of these four patterns, Marton (2015) further proposed a new logical structure in which only three patterns of variation and invariance exist as the basic ones seen by the learners (i.e., contrast, generalization, and fusion) (see Figure 1). According to Marton (2015), "Both contrast and generalization separate aspects from what they are aspects of and from each other. Through contrast, we are trying to find necessary aspects of the objects of learning, those that define it. Through generalization, we want to separate the optional aspects from the necessary aspects" (p. 51). Here the 'necessary aspects' refer to the aspects that are necessary for the targeted learning of a particular way of seeing the phenomenon.

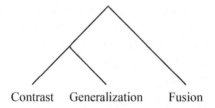

Contrast   Generalization   Fusion

Figure 1. The patterns of variation and invariance
(adopted from Marton, 2015)

Accordingly, there are two kinds of patterns: 'separation' and 'fusion', whereas 'separation' is of two kinds as well: 'contrast' and 'generalization.' Hence logically, this implies that 'separation' is on a higher level than the observational categories of 'contrast' and 'generalization.' Here 'observational' mainly refers to the ways in which instances are juxtaposed 'objectively' as seen from the observer's perspective (Marton, 2015). What makes the whole thing a bit convoluted is that 'fusion' belongs both to the lower, observational level, just as 'contrast 'and 'generalization' and to the higher level, along with 'separation' (*private communication* with Ference Marton, 2016). With due respect to how 'separation' relates to 'contrast' and 'generalization' and the differences in the hierarchical level of these patterns, Figure 2 can be used to illustrate the logical relationships between the four patterns originally stated in Marton and Tsui (2004).

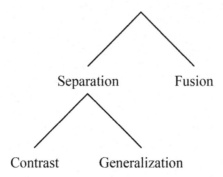

Figure 2. An extended interpretation of the logical relationships between the four patterns of variation and invariance

VT is intended to be a general theory about how people experience and learn to handle certain phenomena. It has been applied to many specific topics of learning across different subject disciplines and educational levels (e.g., Pang & Marton, 2003, 2005, 2007, 2013 in economics; Lo, Chik, & Pang, 2006 in science; Ko, 2013 in language; Kullberg, Martensson, & Runesson, 2016 in mathematics). In contrast, the BS framework, as Gu (1991) explains, attempts to theorize effective mathematics teaching practices in Chinese classrooms and extend the Chinese theory of *bianshi*.

Bao, Huang, Yi and Gu (2003) mention that the traditional *bianshi* in Chinese classrooms is used for learning concepts, and *bianshi jaioxue* (*jaioxue* means teaching and learning, and *bianshi* means variation in the form or move), making reference to the Education Dictionary (Gu, 1999), refers to the use of intuitive materials or example cases with different forms, or the change to the non-defining features of things to highlight the defining ones, so that learners can distinguish which features relate to the nature of the things concerned. In the development of the BS framework, Gu (1994) identified descriptive categories and systematized the instructional principles of such variations in mathematics classroom practices, including the use of standard examples, non-standard examples, and non-examples. This part of the BS framework is called 'conceptual variation.' Gu et al. (2004) also pointed out that by using conceptual variation, students can learn mathematical concepts from multiple examples – from concrete to abstract, from special to general – highlighting the essential features and clarifying the connotation of concepts by initially excluding (and later including) the interference of background and non-essential features of objects. Thus, conceptual variation could help students to understand the essence of concepts, and establish the substantive relationship between them.

Bao et al. (2003) also suggested that the BS framework extends the traditional concept of *bianshi*, which follows the idea of 'procedural variation.' They mention that while conceptual variation is concerned with the static aspects of mathematical objects, grasping the different meanings that they carry and their interrelationships, procedural variation is concerned with the objects' dynamic aspects, such as understanding the manner in which the concepts have evolved historically for humankind and psychologically for individuals, and the manner in which problems are solved and solutions are developed. It should be noted that Gu uses the terms conceptual and procedural in a somewhat different way than Hiebert and Lefevre (1986, p. 3ff). Hiebert and Lefevre use the words to distinguish between conceptual knowledge and procedural knowledge, with the former more concerned with conceptual understanding and explanation and the latter with the use of rules and algorithms for solving problems in mathematics, and the connection between the two. However, Gu's concept of procedural variation emphasizes the dynamic nature of concepts, and how they evolve and can be applied to new situations. Procedural variation can help students to understand where the knowledge came from and where it can be applied, thus allowing well-structured knowledge to be constructed. It can help students to form concepts, solve problems, construct a system of activity experience and comprehend different components of knowledge as a structure with non-arbitrary relationships between new and prior knowledge.

According to Gu et al. (2004), the idea of procedural variation in BS can be encapsulated as the means to 'progressively unfold the mathematical activities', which involves (1) scaffolding the formation of concepts from operations on concrete things to operations on symbols; (2) scaffolding the solution of a new problem through progressively transferring the new problem back to known problems and then deducing the new solution based on the known solutions; and (3) building 'a system of mathematics activities experience' by increasing the diverse pathways and hierarchical (multi-level) connections within and between the activities, which can be achieved by expanding problem-solving activities to include (a) variation on the problem, (b) different solutions to a problem, and (c) one solution applied to different problems.

Point (3) above indicates that procedural variation in BS is based on the idea that the cognitive structure of the learner is made up of two parts. The first is a reflection of the objective logical structure of concepts and propositions in mathematics, and the second are the specific, subjective problem-solving experiences of the learner. The two are integrated to form the overall mathematical cognitive structure of the learner.

Other important BS concepts proposed by Gu (1994) include 'potential distance' and '*Pudian.*' The potential difference is the difference between what the learner already knows and the new situation to which he or she can (or needs to) transfer and apply the knowledge. Procedural variation can be regarded as introducing a physical or conceptual artifact that the learner can use to bridge that distance (Gu et al., 2004, p. 126), which may include learning materials, activities, tasks, or problems. This kind of procedural variation is called *Pudian* (鋪墊) in Chinese, and the word has often been translated as 'scaffold' in English (such as in point (1) and (2) in the paragraph above). However, in Chinese, the word literally means 'padding', which means raising something to a higher level that is closer to the target level. No doubt, the concepts of potential distance and *Pudian* carry an unmistakable flavor of the writings of Vygotsky and Davydov (see, for instance, Davydov, 1990; Vygotsky, 1986). Davydov's approach is grounded firmly in rich, real-world experiences, which lead learners to understand mathematical concepts in a scientific fashion. Scientific concepts do not emerge spontaneously out of experiences, yet learners can be guided to think scientifically by reviewing sufficiently rich, preparatory experiences.

THE STUDY

Having described the concepts of VT and BS, both of which emphasize the importance of using variation and invariance in teaching and learning, one question remains: how are the two theoretical lenses similar to and different from each other when used to analyze or improve classroom practices? We believe that by juxtaposing them in the context of the same lesson, we can gain a better understanding of the patterns of variation and invariance within and between units of teaching and learning activity, and how the problems, examples, and concepts used in the interactions between the teacher and students affect what students experience and learn from such interactions. The research questions to be addressed are (1) can we distinguish the practices of teachers according to the two theories of VT and BS? and (2) can we distinguish the perspectives of the two theories of VT and BS when they are used to interpret a lesson? The first research question was addressed in the study by Pang, Marton, Bao, and Ki (2016), which found that the two frameworks did not distinguish between the practices that they are supposed to. Despite their shared emphasis on the importance of variation and invariance, the two frameworks do not imply what should be kept invariant and what should vary with regard to specific objects of learning.

In this study, we focused on the second research question. To this end, a mathematics lesson carried out in Shanghai was planned in accordance with the *bianshi* framework and analyzed in accordance with both frameworks. The comparison between the analyses thus focused on the aspects of the specific Grade Two lesson (on the addition of 3-digit numbers) that were made visible by the two frameworks. By illuminating similarities and differences between these two frameworks of variation and invariance, we aim to open up ways of combining the two.

Methods

Participating teacher.   The teacher conducting the lesson was a Level 1 teacher in Shanghai who was considered to be competent in teaching mathematics. She had 14 years of experience in mathematics teaching at primary school level and obtained her Master's degree in the area of mathematics education.

The teacher was invited to plan the lesson, based on her understanding of the mathematical topic chosen and of the BS framework. She learned the framework from a 'coach', an experienced mathematics teacher educator and expert in the BS framework. In the course of lesson planning, the coach simply acted as a consultant or source of help, and did not actively influence the pedagogical design or try to ensure that the lesson was designed specifically to follow the BS framework. If the teacher had any questions or enquiries regarding the BS framework and its application, she could ask for theoretical and pedagogical support from the coach. The coach considered the teacher to have a good level of understanding of the BS framework.

Participating school and students.   The school involved in this study had been open for only two years when the data were collected. It was situated in a newly developed suburb area of Shanghai, where two prestigious universities and a technology park are located. The students of the school were mainly from the families of the staff of these three giant institutions. The students' academic ability was considered to be above average in Shanghai.

The mathematical topic chosen.   The topic, '3-digit addition', was chosen for the research lesson with the following considerations: (1) it is one of the prescribed mathematical topics in the Grade Two mathematics curriculum of Shanghai; (2) the participating teacher believed that the topic was moderately difficult for most of her students; and (3) the date for teaching the topic in the school fit well with the data collection schedule of the study.

Analysis.   The systematic use of variation and invariance in the lesson was analyzed with reference to the two theories (BS and VT) simultaneously. It is noteworthy that the lesson to be analyzed was not intended to be an exemplary lesson that provided a direct and complete enactive representation of the BS framework.

Researchers of the two theories observed the lesson in Shanghai together. Based on the video recording, the researchers conducted the first round of analysis separately, using the respective theories of variation, and then met to exchange their views. They discussed questions concerning the similarities or differences they perceived in certain teaching episodes of the lesson, and their explanations of how the theory of variation was used.

In the following section, as the lesson was based on the BS framework, it is first described and analyzed in terms of teaching episodes with the use of the

BS framework. This will allow a good understanding of the rationale behind the instructional design and also provide a clear account of what really happened in the classroom. However, to make the text less repetitious, the same lesson is then analyzed in terms of topics with the VT framework. Conclusions are then drawn regarding the two theories and practices.

RESULTS AND FINDINGS

Analysis of the Shanghai Lesson on 3-digit addition based on the BS framework

Episode 1. The teacher began the lesson with some 2-digit addition tasks (see Figure 3). The students performed them very fluently with mental or oral calculation (i.e., saying aloud what they calculated in their minds).

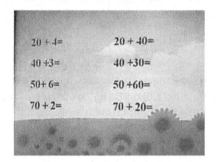

20 + 4=	20 + 40=
40 +3=	40 +30=
50+ 6=	50 +60=
70 + 2=	70 + 20=

Figure 3. The addition tasks given in Episode 1

The teacher asked the students what differences they could see between the tasks in the two columns. The students responded that the first column was about *joining the numerals for the whole tens with the numerals for the units* (整十数加上一位数) and the second column was about *adding whole tens to whole tens* (整十数加整十数); the numerals in the tens column needed to be added together. Based on that, she asked what other *more general patterns of addition* they had come across. One student gave the example of $35 + 35$ and explained that it involved the addition of both tens and units; to obtain the result, one would need to add the tens $(3 + 3)$ to get 6 tens, and add the units $(5 + 5)$ to get 10, and hence the total was 7 tens, i.e., 70.

Two kinds of variation were involved in the above interaction. (1) Having the same number appear at different locations consolidated the concept of place value; e.g., in $20 + 4$, the 4 is in the units place, but in $20 + 40$, the 4 is in the tens place. This is a type of conceptual variation. The teacher also introduced a procedural variation, a *Pudian* (scaffold), which paved the way for 3-digit addition in which they also needed to pay attention to the place values associated with the numerals. (2) In 2-digit addition, which the students had learned previously, there were cases where they needed to carry from the units to the tens, or the tens to the hundreds, as in the addition of 50 + 60. Later in the lesson, there were more examples of carrying from the tens to the hundreds, and further extending the idea by carrying from the hundreds to the thousands.

Episode 2. After finishing the review of 2-digit addition, the teacher began the main topic of the lesson, i.e., 3-digit addition. Before teaching the procedure for 3-digit addition, the teacher gave the students some problems (Figure 4) to solve by mental or oral calculation.

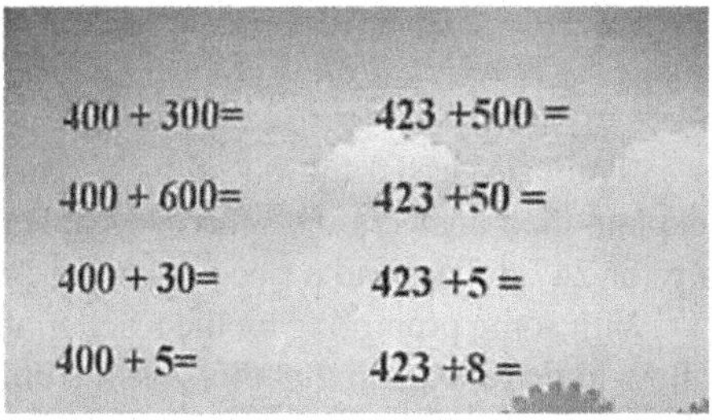

400 + 300=	423 +500 =
400 + 600=	423 +50 =
400 + 30=	423 +5 =
400 + 5=	423 +8 =

Figure 4. The addition tasks given in Episode 2

These tasks can be seen as special cases of 3-digit number addition. The second addends were *whole hundreds, whole tens or just units; the first addend in the left-hand column* was always the same whole hundred number (400), and in the right-hand column a slightly more complicated number (423). As the second addends were relatively simple, the students were able to get the answers fairly quickly, but needed more time when they came to the last question (423 + 8), in which they needed to carry-over. As in Episode 1, the teacher asked the students *what other general patterns of 3-digit number addition* they would expect to see in the future, and the students responded that there could be a case of addition that involved hundreds, tens, and units at the same time, and it might involve carrying.

These tasks also served as *Pudian* for the more general 3-digit addition. Almost all of them could be solved according to the rule that numerals must be added according to their place value, which the students had learned in 2-digit addition. The same basic operation is used in multiple-digit addition, no matter how many digits there are: pairs of numerals with the same place value are added to each other. Almost all of the items applied this idea directly, except for 423 + 8, which led to the next issue of carrying.

Episode 3. Before the teacher introduced the procedure for more complex 3-digit addition, she invited the students to recall daily experiences that involved the occurrence of 3-digit numbers and their addition. The teacher then posed an estimation task based on a possible real-life situation (see Figure 5).

She said, 'I saw a promotion in a new supermarket. They awarded gift coupons if the purchase was over 500 dollars. Which two of the three items in the slides should

Figure 5. The estimation task given in Episode 3

I buy?' The students actively discussed the question in pairs, and some students were then invited to explain their answers. The class was able to identify the correct answer (buying a lamp for 247 dollars and a rice cooker for 335 dollars would cost more than 500 dollars). With some prompting by the teacher, the students also came up with an easy-to-follow logic to explain that this was the only answer: they could consider the sum of the hundreds to obtain the first estimation and then look at the remaining 2-digit parts of the numbers to see whether they could possibly 'spill over 100'. In the case of $161 + 335$, the hundred digits only added up to 4, and 61 and 35 did not add up to a hundred, and hence $161 + 335$ could not be the correct choice.

This task also served as a *Pudian* for learning 3-digit addition in the following way: (1) it gave the students a preliminary experience of 3-digit addition; and (2) it gave the students some preliminary awareness that although the sum of over 500 depended on the value in the hundreds place, the result was not just related to the two numerals in the hundreds place; it was also related to the numerals in the tens place (as their sum might produce a carry-over) and also to the numerals in the units place. This problem therefore served as a *Pudian* for the focus later in the teaching unit that when doing column addition, it is better to start with the units column.

This task was also in close accordance with the procedural variation concept of transferring a new complex problem to a simpler problem that students have already solved. Through the discussion in this class, *the new question on 3-digit addition was transferred back to a previous simpler question on 2-digit addition.* By taking the addition of whole hundreds separately (to see whether the hundred digits added up to 5), what remained was in fact the problem the students had learned before, namely, the addition of 2-digit numbers and whether it would carry over to the hundreds column.

Episode 4. Next, the teacher asked the class, 'Can you help me to calculate exactly how much I actually paid (i.e., $247 + 335$)?' The students had not yet been formally taught how to do 3-digit addition. The teacher asked the students to discuss and write their ideas in their exercise books, and then on the blackboard to share with the whole class. Many representations of the calculation soon appeared on the blackboard. There was a place-value chart (Figure 6), but more examples showed

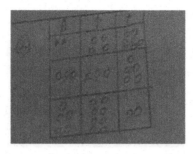

Figure 6. A student used place-value chart method to calculate

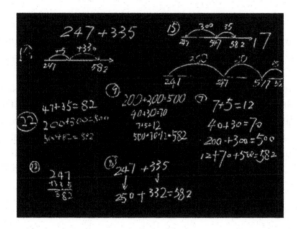

Figure 7. Various methods used by the other students

numerical or arrow expressions representing different ways of breaking down the addition into mentally easy-to-handle parts and processes (Figure 7).

In Figure 6, the student used a tool analogous to an abacus to represent 'concretely' the computational process of the 3-digit number addition. This was a conceptual variation, but can also be regarded as a procedural variation because computing is itself procedural. One can refer to the idea of 'procept' proposed by David Tall (1991). As a conceptual variation, it allowed students to see the different representations of 3-digit number addition; as a procedural variation, its purpose was to provide a more concrete mode, which could be used as a *Pudian* for establishing the more abstract method. The different representations and operations in Figure 7 served the same purposes of conceptual and procedural variation.

The students were given time to discuss with their neighbors to determine whether they understood the methods on the board and to group similar methods together. The teacher asked whether their own methods belonged to any of these groups. Through class discussion among the whole class, three major approaches were identified.

1. Jumps on number line

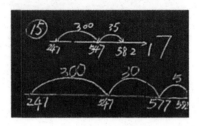

Figure 8. Using jumps on the number line to calculate

The two methods in Figure 8 were essentially the same; that is, they involved adding on from the first addend. Interestingly, the class used a range of different methods, such as the use of two jumps (+300 then + 35), (+5 then + 330), and (+330 then + 5); three jumps (+300 then + 5 then + 30), (+300 then + 30 then + 5), and so on. After some discussion, all were regarded as the same idea of splitting the addition into easier, more manageable parts; the order was not important, but (+35) was a bit clumsy to handle mentally and hence was divided further. Some students were then also able to recognize that a similar idea was used in some methods that use numerical expressions (e.g., 247 + 300 = 547, then 547 + 30 = 577, and then 577 + 5 = 582) and that these methods should also be included in this group.

2. Numerical addition of the same units

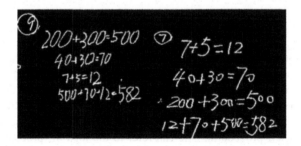

Figure 9. Adding the like units of 100, or 10, or 1

The students saw the two solutions in Figure 9 as the same because, although the order was reversed, they both added 'the same units' together and then combined the results. This approach was judged to be different from the previous approach because here both addends were split up. Some students pointed out that this was the same idea as the vertical column addition method (Figure 10) and the place-value chart method (Figure 6). The teacher then guided the students to see how carrying was handled in the two cases of horizontal and vertical calculation. The purpose here was to allow the students to understand the processes of the two methods. It was a *Pudian* for future further development on column calculation.

3 .Transformation of the numbers (into complete tens or hundreds)

Figure 10. Adding numbers in the like columns

The class also noticed another clever method (Figure 11) that gave the same correct result. The teacher guided the student who produced the method to explain it.

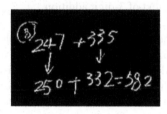

Figure 11. Transforming the numbers into complete 10s or 100s

Student: I first turn 247 into 250. Here 3 is added. Then 335 minus 3 equals 332. They add up to 582 together.

Teacher: Students, why do you think he made this change? Why does this change help?

Student: It rounds the number to tens.

Teacher: Is it like taking things from my left pocket and putting them into my right?

Student: Add 3 and minus 3.

Teacher: Yes. Has the sum of my little pockets changed?

Student: No.

Teacher: This method is very clever. You (the class) have shown so many clever approaches.

The activity above, besides guiding students towards the first two purposes of procedural variation in Gu et al. (2004) (namely as a *Pudian* for the formation of concepts from concrete things to symbols, and the solution of new problem through transferring of the new problem back to old problem), also achieved the third purpose, namely 'variation for extension', by increasing the diverse pathways and hierarchical (multi-level) connections through presenting different solutions to a problem. However, opening up different solutions also required the teacher to bring effective convergence or closure based on the variations. Here, the third method (with smart calculation), although interesting, could have led the less able students to lose focus on the main purpose of the lesson, which was to provide the progression from 2-digit to 3-digit addition, particularly, the use of column addition and starting by adding the units.

After this discussion, the teacher provided two more 3-digit number addition problems to consolidate what had been discussed. The problems were (a) 534 + 321 and (b) 259 + 198, both of which could be handled by certain approaches better than others. From (b), one can see that the teacher actually included the transfer of the smart calculation as an objective in her teaching, from the previous context of 2-digit addition to the present context of 3-digit addition.

Episode 5. The teacher then posed some challenging problems for further exploration (as shown in Figures 12, 13, and 14). Some of the digits in these problems were hidden, so the students needed to discern the dependency relationship in the addition process, namely, how the values of the different parts might influence the final result. The students needed to consider the possible values of the digits and the carry-overs they might generate, and to reason forward and backward along those lines to solve the problems.

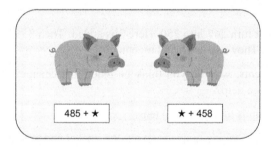

Figure 12. An exploration problem given in Episode 5

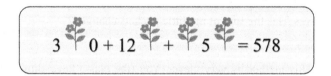

Figure 13. Another exploration problem given in Episode 5

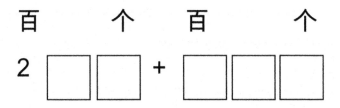

Figure 14. The last exploration problem given in Episode 5

The last problem (Figure 14) was used to conclude the lesson. The problem was as follows: 'Here are two 3-digit numbers. Some of the digits are covered with cards. To decide whether the result will be a 4-digit number, do I need to uncover some or all of the covered digits? And what would the digit have to be to cause such a difference?'

The purpose of this problem was 'variation for extension'; it added mathematical reasoning to the computing process. This extension activity enabled the students to understand the concept of place-value and the carry-over procedure in a more integrated and dynamic manner. The students also learned to adapt to variation and to recognize its invariant property. Looking for such invariance within variation situations is a fundamental way of thinking in mathematics. There are more than 7000 different answers to the problem in Figure 14. Various thought paths could be followed to work out the conditions under which the sum of the addition must be a 4-digit number: (1) if the 100-digit of the second number is 8 or 9, then the sum of the three numbers must be a 4-digit number; (2) if the hundreds digit of the second number is 7 and the sum of the two tens digits of the two 3-digit numbers exceeds or equals 10 (e.g., in the cases of 2<u>8</u>□+7<u>3</u>□, 2<u>4</u>□+7<u>6</u> and so on), then the sum of the two 3-digit numbers must be a 4-digit number; and (3) if the hundreds digit of the second number is 7, and the sum of the two tens digits of the two 3-digit numbers is only 9, then we need the sum of the two unit digits of the two 3-digit numbers to exceed 10, such that the sum of the 3-digit numbers will be a 4-digit number. The class discussion of this problem was as follows.

Teacher: So far today, the addition problems with 3-digit numbers have not exceeded 1000. Do you think it is impossible for the addition of two 3-digit numbers to produce a 4-digit number?

Student: No.

Student: For example, 999 + 100 will exceed...

Teacher: Very good. (Showing the problem in Figure 14) I would like to ask, if I want to judge whether the sum can get to 1000, which card should I take away first? Should it be one from the units place or the hundreds place?

Student: Hundreds place.

Teacher: Okay, suppose I follow your instruction. Now this (the hundreds digit of the first addend) is 2. To get to 1000, what could this hundreds digit (of the second addend) be?

Student: 8.

Student: 9.

Teacher: 8 and 9, any smaller value? Is it impossible to have a smaller value here?

Student: It's possible. 7 can also …

Student: There can be a carry.

Teacher: There can be a carry from where?

Student: The tens.

Teacher: So if the tens get full, there will be a carry-over to the hundreds place, right?

Teacher: So the fate of this 2 here (the hundreds digit of the first addend) may also rest on a possible carry of 1 (from the addition of the tens and units). So what can this digit (the hundreds digit of the second addend) be?

Student: 7.

Teacher: Is it only tens that can produce this carry to the hundreds?

Student: Units can also do so.

Teacher: Sometimes, unit digits also can, right?

Student: Imagine it is 299, and we can add 1 … or add …

As the lesson was running out of time, based on the last problem, the teacher gave the students a take-home task: 'Create some 3-digit number additions in which a change in one digit in a certain place of the addend might generate an effect on the final result in the hundreds place or even require a result in the thousands place'.

The idea of procedural variation was once again present in the take-home tasks, The students were asked to extend their imagination to other possible problem scenarios that could be solved using the principles or methods they had learned. The tasks also paved the way for the noticing of the possible direction of propagation of carrying, and hence the reason that in doing column addition, it is generally more convenient to start by adding the unit digits, then the 10-digits, and so on in the ascending sequence. While the tasks were procedural variation, they also involved conceptual variation and worked in accordance with the principle of conceptual variation: the problems were based initially on situations that would be more familiar and within the students' own imagination, before going onto familiar and not-so-familiar tasks and examples to be introduced in the next lesson.

Overall remarks. The Shanghai lesson was designed according to the teacher's understanding of the BS framework, particularly the ideas of conceptual and procedural variation. In the first and second episodes, students identified the relevant concepts in the familiar context of 2-digit number addition, and then in the new context of 3-digit number addition using relatively simple examples, followed by more general examples later in the lesson. This can be considered as conceptual variation, and also as the procedural variation of Pudian. By highlighting the anchoring knowledge (certain features in 2-digit addition), the teacher used scaffolding to extend the students' use of these concepts to novel problems (3-digit addition tasks that were more complex and distant from those that the students had previously encountered).

The use of procedural variation in the lesson was very explicit. The tasks were designed to provide increasing levels of challenge when moving from one task to the next, extending the use of the concepts further and further from the original examples, and with each task acting as a *Pudian* for later tasks. Another kind of procedural variation was used to get the students to share the different ways of performing the same addition and to make connections between them, enabling them to develop a deeper and more integrated understanding of the concepts and procedures involved, and the common principle underlying the various methods that appeared to be different on the surface. The third procedural variation, in contrast to *Pudian*, seemed to be the 'variation for extension' at the end of the lesson. To handle the more open situation, the students also needed to use inductive-deductive and hypothetical reasoning based on what they had learned.

Interpretation of the Same Lesson from the VT Perspective

In the previous section, the lesson on 3-digit addition was described and interpreted according to the BS framework. We invited researchers of the VT theory to analyze and comment on the variation and invariance in the same lesson. This allowed us to:

1. observe whether any of the practices using variation and invariance in one theory were contrary to the other theory, and
2. note any differences in how the two theories described or interpreted the same teaching and learning.

Object of learning. Both BS and VT share a similar goal of enhancing students' understanding, so that learning does not just involve the specific things that are taught, but the general principles embedded in them, which can be extended to future novel situations that the students will encounter. From the VT perspective, the object of learning of the Shanghai lesson (i.e., what the students were expected to learn) was obviously targeted at such a level, as it focused not only on the correct performance of an algorithm for 3-digit addition, but also on different methods. The indirect object of learning was the extension of the different methods for handling 2-digit addition to 3-digit addition with the use of certain principles that could be discerned in the 2-digit additions.

The critical aspects (dimensions of variation) made salient in the lesson went beyond basic issues such as the variation in value and place and in carrying-over according to an algorithm. The lesson looked at the differences between the methods, such as the different ways of seeking possible methods or sequences of splitting and regrouping the quantities in the computation process, and the different conditions under which the carry-over value in one place may affect the carry-over value in another. By opening up such a rich set of dimensions of variation, the breadth of learning in this lesson was much wider than that in lessons that only focus on a particular algorithm and its application.

When teaching the topic of 3-digit addition, a teacher can be aiming at quite different critical aspects, such as the most basic properties of the mathematical objects and methods, or big mathematical ideas behind the formation and transformation of these mathematical objects and methods. Of course, teachers should choose an object of learning appropriate to the characteristics of the target groups of learners to create an optimal learning space. In this lesson, the interaction in the class indicated that the object of learning was very well pitched to the level of the students, and they actively participated in the lesson.

Having mentioned that the students' ability level appeared to be good, one thing to note is the broad range of tasks of differing levels of difficulty used in the lesson. Some of the tasks were very easy for the students, very much against the folk belief that good students can be challenged by presenting them with more, and more difficult, problems. By bringing the students' attention to some seemingly very simple tasks in a familiar domain (2-digit addition), they were afforded to see the dynamic variation and invariance between them by enacting their existing concept and skills, and hence were more prepared to view the new domain (3-digit addition) in that light. Some of the tasks were challenging, such as the invitation to estimate whether the sum of two numbers reached or exceeded 500 before teaching the students 3-digit addition, and the last problem, which asked the students which of the unknown digits would make a difference to whether the sum of the 3-digit numbers became a 4-digit number. In solving these problems, the students used the aspects they could discern simultaneously to further explore their relationships through reasoning and trial and error. Therefore, the students' ability level was one factor. Yet, how to decide specific tasks and examples and stage the co-constitution of the learning space so that the general mathematics ideas could be discerned in order was another decisive factor for the success of the lesson.

Sameness, difference and Pudian. Both BS and VT emphasize the systematic use of variation and invariance in teaching and learning. However, BS seems to put more emphasis on the function of sameness and VT on the function of difference. The previous section makes it quite obvious that a lot of the teaching moves could be explained in terms of *Pudian* in the BS framework, which is concerned with bringing students closer to the target level so that they can generalize the underlying mathematical principle(s); in other words, so that they can see the *similarity between what they have learned and what is new*. The teaching design is led by the core connections among different mathematical objects and situations, i.e., their sameness or invariant mathematical structure. It is through this sameness that we see the transcending power of mathematics. In what ways does VT offer a different interpretation?

VT posits that experiencing difference is a necessary and basic condition for powerful learning, as it opens up new ways of seeing meaning, and enables learners to handle future novel situations more effectively. From the VT perspective, transfer occurs only when the learner experiences difference against a background of sameness. This lesson illustrated this point, in which the difference between the old and the new demanded the transfer in the first place. If the learner experienced no difference (or gap) between the 3-digit addition (the new) and the 2-digit addition (the old), then there would be no transfer, and in fact there would be no need to teach the lesson. Without this lesson, in which the difference (or gap) between 2-digit and 3-digit addition was dealt with seriously, the students would be less likely to see the transcending property of what they had learned.

Second, VT considers that what is transferred is often the difference that the learner has experienced in the original situation, or the contrast or changes she has made in the original situation (and hence the sensitivity to such critical aspects or dimensions of variation). Such experiences of difference, contrast or change, and the sensitivity to the relevant dimension(s) of variation help in exploring similar ways of differentiating, contrasting, or changing in the new situation. Thus, sensitivity towards the difference within a domain becomes the basis of sensitivity towards the sameness across domains. Looking closely at the *Pudian* of the lesson, it is not difficult to see that the teacher brought up contrast in the learned domain to strengthen students' discernment of the critical aspects before transferring them to the new domain.

Figure 3 provides a good example of how such contrast can be used for *Pudian*. The example was clearly too easy to be called a revision or practice exercise of 2-digit addition; it was an example of 2-digit addition purposely chosen for contrast. The first row contrasts two additions, drawing attention to the different ways the sum can be done. Both additions used the numeral 4 in the second addend, but in a different place (tens or units), and the method of doing the sum differed accordingly. The pattern of variation and invariance (the use of 40 versus 4 while other parts remained the same) acted as (1) a separation in which the place aspect was made salient, (2) a fusion of the place aspect to the value of the second addend (4 tens or 4 units) and (3) a fusion of the kinds of quantity of the second addend (whether whole tens or only units) to which the right part (or place) in the first addend the second addend should be added. To summarize, the contrast helped to make salient the meaning of place-value and the meaning of adding values in the correct place (adding tens to tens, but not tens to units). Then the same contrast was repeated row by row, with the numeral changing to 5, then 6, then 2. The pattern of variation and invariance helped the generalization of the pattern beyond the specific numerals used in the different rows.

Figure 4 also provides an interesting example of *Pudian*. It shows a particular set of 3-digit addition tasks. In relation to the 2-digit addition tasks in Figure 3, they were new tasks that the students had not done before; but, in relation to the later 3-digit addition tasks, they were *Pudian*. Comparing the left-hand column of Figure 4 with the tasks in Figure 3 reveals a clear difference: the first addends all change from whole tens to whole hundreds (i.e., from 2-digit numbers to 3-digit numbers). However, there is also a clear similarity: in both cases, the second addends are either all hundreds, all tens, or all units, but never a mix of the different kinds. The clear similarity and difference helped the transfer, or, in BS terminology, made the potential psychological distance between Figure 3 and the left-hand side of Figure 4 very small.

Looking across the two columns of Figure 4, one can see another contrast – a small move from a more salient case to a more obscure case (with the distracting details entered into the tens place and units place of the first addend). In BS terminology, the variation of some irrelevant attributes can train the learner to focus on the critical attributes and object of interest. In VT terminology, this is called 'generalization' (learners make a distinction between the essential and non-essential aspects of a concept). Although Figure 4 is only a small subset of the huge set of possible 3-digit addition tasks, its pattern of variation and invariance makes salient the same critical aspects and relationships mentioned earlier for 2-digit addition, and prepares the learner to handle more 3-digit addition tasks in the future.

Hence, to summarize, the direction of *Pudian* is driven by the sameness from a mathematical perspective, but the actual learning transfer (or the discovery of the sameness across different examples) only occurs through a very skillful use of differences. For the learner to discern and focus on the important aspects for the transfer, the learner needs to experience (1) the difference (or gap) between the old and the new tasks that calls for the transfer, (2) the difference in the original tasks that makes salient the critical aspects and relations that are useful and (3) the difference within a 'landing and test bed' set of new tasks that help in checking whether the transfer is actually valid. Both sameness and differences are therefore necessary.

Separation and fusion.   From the VT perspective, this lesson also made use of the variation-invariance patterns of separation and fusion to explore the cumulative effect of carrying that can originate from multiple places (hundreds, tens, and units). First there was the separation (in Figures 9 and 10), involving the adding of only multiples of hundreds, tens, or units. The students only had to focus on the addition in a single place, and to follow the consequence of carrying from that place forward, if necessary. At the end of the lesson, however, when the students came to the last problem (Figure 14), they needed to decide whether the sum would reach 1000, with many digits unknown and hence open to carrying. The students needed to attend to the possible variation of values in different places, find a way to handle it in order, and notice how carrying from one place could be affected not just by the sum at that location, but also by the sums in the lower places.

62

In this lesson, VT may further consider that effective fusion often requires more support in addition to the simultaneous variation of the aspects concerned. First, it probably demands a meaningful problem or purpose that calls for such fusion, and is understandable to the learners; second, it probably demands active problem solving processes or the assistance of conceptual tools to cope with the complex situation; and third, certain constraining patterns of variation and invariance may be required to create intermediate levels of less complex fusion so that the openness can be kept manageable. In this lesson, the problem was very well set, which fulfilled the first demand; the teacher also guided the students using forward and backward hypothetical mathematical reasoning, which fulfilled the second demand. The teacher also valued this learning situation because it facilitated mathematical thinking. To help the learners achieve fusion, the teacher made a certain part of the example invariant. For example, fixing the hundred digit of the first addend to '2' helped to reduce the openness. Subsequently, the teacher invited temporary assumptions from the students, such as making the hundred digit of the second addend 9, 8, or 7, and explored the reduced set of possible scenarios separately under each assumption. This addressed the third demand.

DISCUSSION AND CONCLUSION

It is quite obvious that there are some critical differences between the BS and VT frameworks. To begin with, the distinction that BS makes between conceptual and procedural variation is not made in VT. This has to do with VT's phenomenological origin in attempting to understand people's experiences and the meaning they make out of them: everything is described from a certain perspective (this is an inherent aspect of any description): the researcher's, the teacher's, or the learner's. The viewer's way of acting is always related to his or her way of seeing. Moreover, nothing is classified as inherently static or dynamic. While viewing a certain instance of the phenomenon, what is intended to be varying (dynamic) according to one viewer may be taken as invariant (static) by another. However, the analysis of this issue by the BS researcher clarified that a teaching move can involve both conceptual variation and procedural variation; BS does not draw a hard boundary between the two.

Another difference between the two frameworks is that VT often places the comparison of examples and non-examples early in teaching and learning, to facilitate the acquisition of the overall meaning of the concept. In contrast, BS often begins with standard examples, then introduces non-standard examples and finally non-examples. How the two views can be juxtaposed in the analysis of this lesson is not particularly clear because the lesson does not introduce new concepts or meanings; rather, it refines and extends existing concepts. Nonetheless, the teacher obviously contrasts alternative views to facilitate learning. With the opening tasks in Figures 9 and 10, students were invited to give multiple responses. Similarly, the students were invited to give their views on how to find the sum of 247 + 335. Therefore, the teacher did not simply transmit her ideas to the students; instead, she allowed space for alternative ideas to be contrasted or errors to be discussed (incidentally, no erroneous responses came up in the lesson, although the space was provided). For instance, in the last challenging problem of the lesson, the teacher actually made an implicit contrast between the hundreds digit being 8, 9 or, 7 in the second addend, and highlighted the interesting features in the case of 7.

More fundamentally, while both VT and BS researchers agree that new meanings can be generated when one discovers similarities among things that are conventionally taken as different, or differences among things that are conventionally taken as the same, if we scrutinize the two frameworks, it is clear that they differ in the relative emphasis on sameness and difference. It seems that the VT framework puts more emphasis on the value of seeing differences over sameness, and the BS framework puts more emphasis on the value of seeing sameness over differences. This difference is probably due to the difference in the context and point of departure between the two frameworks, and in the context in which the terms 'sameness' and 'difference' are used in the two frameworks in the lesson analysis.

The BS framework was developed by mathematics educators, aiming to lead students to develop a mathematical understanding of the world, in which the same concepts and relationships can be used across different situations. As students' mathematical knowledge develops, they also need to understand the connections between different mathematical representations and relationships, and hence, develop a parsimonious view of the knowledge concerned and an agile command of the various mathematical objects. In this sense, seeing the sameness among the vast number of instances in this knowledge space is especially important. Grasping the core concepts and the core connections between them will help to remediate the current trend of over-cramming substance into students, with the folk belief that giving them more, and more difficult, problems will naturally make them learn better and perform better in examinations.

However, similar to VT, BS scholars also believe in the use of differences, which is why the term *Bianshi* is used. This pedagogical framework does not stop at the point of offering 'big ideas', but tries to go beyond the Chinese tradition that emphasizes sameness to develop a teaching theory that asserts the need to use variation. BS is thus an especially valuable thought stimulator for VT researchers. At the same time, BS researchers are interested in using VT as a conceptual tool for conducting more close-up and scientific analyses of their variation-oriented practice.

VT was developed by researchers in the areas of education and psychology, who did not belong to a particular school subject discipline. VT originated from phenomenographic research, and the first objective was to make education more effective by challenging the taken-for-granted view of knowledge. People (including teachers) typically believe that the way they see the world is the true and only way to see it and that other people (including students) see it in the same way. However, phenomenographic studies comparing the different ways that people view the same phenomenon show that there are actually critical differences in terms of what aspects of the phenomenon people attend to at the same time. VT researchers argue logically that if an aspect of a phenomenon, as far as it has been experienced by the person, has never varied, why should the person be concerned about it? This conjecture has been supported empirically: the critical aspects that students are able to see at the end, but not the beginning, of a lesson are commensurate with those critical aspects that are varied in the teaching and learning process. The change in the critical aspects and their connections to the change in the overall situation, or vice versa, has thus become a key to developing targeted ways of seeing the phenomenon.

Hence, VT always focuses on difference. Yet at the same time, sameness has always been there in VT. To discover a certain difference, other things need to be kept invariant. In phenomenography, the same phenomenon has to be used to reveal the differences in people's way of seeing. In a classroom, varying all aspects at the same time throughout a lesson will obviously create more confusion than learning. The other aspects need to be invariant to make the varied aspect salient. Moreover, when comparing things to identify their differences, some logically implicit assumptions are made: (1) that it is somehow meaningful to make that comparison (i.e., they are comparable); and (2) that there is some common dimension(s) along which the things can exhibit their different values in relation to each other (i.e., they are different in a certain way).

Although BS and VT place different emphases on sameness and difference, the analysis of the lesson with the use of the two frameworks actually shows that they are highly compatible. The lesson inspired by BS is also regarded as a high quality lesson from the perspective of VT; it included both sameness and difference, and also afforded discernment, attention, and transfer in the way that VT sees as instrumental. It seems quite obvious that sameness or difference can be analytically separated, but in reality, they co-exist and are mutually dependent. The analysis of this lesson indicates that the two frameworks are compatible rather than mutually exclusive.

To conclude, a complementary relationship seems to exist between the two frameworks discussed here. The BS theory is more elaborate and explicit as far as the design of learning activities (tasks) is concerned in mathematics. Variation and invariance are closely related to the inherent structure of mathematical understanding. Furthermore, fine steps of variation and invariance are used as *Pudian* for students to reach that understanding. VT, a framework for learning in general, can help to explain how teaching can be designed to bring about learning, with a particular focus on patterns of variation and invariance as a way of directing students' discernment and attention, and thus the formulation of new meanings and relationships, and their transfer.

The procedural variation of BS seems to emphasize the *Pudian from one task or situation to another* and their connections so as to make the distance of proximal development manageable to students in constituting their space of learning and thinking. On the other hand, the contrast and separation of VT emphasizes the differences *within a task or situation*, so that critical aspects and alternative meanings people see in the task or situation can be made discernible and thus preparing the way of seeing for transfer. They are like working in complementary ways along to orthogonal directions.

The method of analyzing the same lesson with the two variation frameworks has been shown to be very useful for developing collective understanding between VT and BS researchers. While acknowledging the potential power of an integrated framework that synthesizes the two variation frameworks, it is useful to iterate that practice and theory are not direct products of each other, and more studies are needed to demonstrate more clearly how joint analysis using the two theoretical frameworks can provide the best contribution to the improvement of practice.

ACKNOWLEDGMENTS

The study reported in this chapter was made possible by the funding support from the University of Hong Kong.

REFERENCES

Bao, J., Huang, R., Yi, L., & Gu, L. (2003). Study of 'Bianshi Jiaoxue' [Teaching with variation]. *Mathematics Teaching*, 1–3.

Davydov, V. V. (1990). *Types of generalization in instruction*. Reston, VA: National Council of Teachers of Mathematics.

Gu, L. (1991). *Xuehui Jiaoxue* [Learning to teach]. Beijing, China: People's Education Press.

Gu, L., Huang, R., & Marton, F. (2004). Teaching with variation: A Chinese way of promoting effective mathematics learning. In L. Fan, N. Y. Wong, J. Cai, & S. Li (Eds.), *How Chinese learn mathematics: Perspectives from insiders* (pp. 309–347). Singapore: World Scientific.

Gu, M. Y. (1999). *Education directory* [In Chinese 教育大辭典]. Shanghai: Shanghai Education Press.

Häggström, J. (2008). *Teaching systems of linear equations in Sweden and China: What is made possible to learn?* Göteborg: Acta Universitatis Gothoburgensis.

Hiebert, J., & Lefevre, P. (1986). Conceptual and procedural knowledge in Mathematics: An introductory analysis. In J. Hiebert (Ed.), *Conceptual and procedural knowledge: The case of mathematics* (pp. 1–28). Hillsdale, NJ: Lawrence Erlbaum.

Ko, P. Y. (2013). Using variation theory to enhance English language teaching. *Transacademia, 1*(2), 31–42.

Kullberg, A., Martensson, P., & Runesson, U. (2016). What is to be learned? Teachers' collective inquiry into the object of learning. *Scandinavian Journal of Educational Research, 60*(3), 309–322. doi:10.1080/00313831.2015.1119725

Lo, M. L., Chik, P. M. P., & Pang, M. F. (2006). Patterns of variation in teaching the colour of light to primary 3 students. *Instructional Science, 34*(1), 1–19.

Marton, F. (2015). *Necessary conditions of learning*. London: Routledge.

Marton, F., & Booth, S. (1997). *Learning and awareness*. Mahwah, NJ: Lawrence Erlbaum.

Marton, F., & Pang, M. F. (2006). On some necessary conditions of learning. *Journal of the Learning Sciences, 15*(2), 193–220.

Marton, F., & Pang, M. F. (2008). The idea of phenomenography and the pedagogy for conceptual change. In S. Vosniadou (Ed.), *International handbook of research on conceptual change* (pp. 533–559). London: Routledge.

Marton, F., & Pang, M. F. (2013). Meanings are acquired from experiencing differences against a background of sameness, rather than from experiencing sameness against a background of difference: Putting a conjecture to the test by embedding it in a pedagogical tool. *Frontier Learning Research, 1*(1), 24–41.

Marton, F., Tsui, A. B. M., Chik, P. M., Ko, P. Y., Lo, M. L., Mok, I. A. C., Ng, F. P., Pang, M. F., Pong, W. Y., & Runesson, U. (2004). *Classroom discourse and the space of learning*. Mahwah, NJ: Lawrence Erlbaum.

Pang, M. F., & Ki, W. W. (2016). Revisiting the idea of 'critical aspects'. *Scandinavian Journal of Educational Research, 60*(3), 323–336.

Pang, M. F., & Marton, F. (2003). Beyond "lesson study" – Comparing two ways of facilitating the grasp of economic concepts. *Instructional Science, 31*(3), 175–194.

Pang, M. F., & Marton, F. (2005). Learning theory as teaching resource: Another example of radical enhancement of students' understanding of economic aspects of the world around them. *Instructional Science, 33*(2), 159–191.

Pang, M. F., & Marton F. (2007). The paradox of pedagogy. The relative contribution of teachers and learners to learning. *Iskolakultura, 1*(1), 1–29.

Pang, M. F., & Marton, F. (2013). Interaction between the learners' initial grasp of the object of learning and the learning resource afforded. *Instructional Science, 41*, 1065–1082.

Pang, M. F., Marton, F., Bao, J., & Ki, W. W. (2016). Teaching to add three digit numbers in Kong Kong and Shanghai: An illustration of differences in the systematic use of variation and invariance. *ZDM-The International Journal on Mathematics Education, 48*, 455–470.

Sun, X. (2011). 'Variation problems' and their roles in the topic of fraction division in Chinese mathematics textbook examples. *Educational Studies in Mathematics, 76*(1), 65–85.

Tall, D. O. (1991). The psychology of advanced mathematical thinking. In D. O. Tall (Ed.), *Advanced mathematical thinking* (pp. 3–21). New York, NY: Springer.

Vygotsky, L. S. (1986). *Language and thought*. Cambridge, MA: MIT Press.

Watson, A., & Mason, J. (2005). *Mathematics as a constructive activity: Learners generating examples*. Mahwah, NJ: Lawrence Erlbaum.

Wong, N. Y., Lam, C. C., Sun, X., & Chan, A. M. Y. (2009). From "exploring the middle zone" to "constructing a bridge": Experimenting the spiral *bianshi* mathematics curriculum. *International Journal of Science and Mathematics Education, 7*, 363–382.

Ming Fai Pang
Faculty of Education
The University of Hong Kong
Hong Kong SAR, China

Jiansheng Bao
Department of mathematics
East China Normal University, China

Wing Wah Ki
Faculty of Education
The University of Hong Kong
Hong Kong SAR, China

ALLEN LEUNG

4. VARIATION IN TOOL-BASED MATHEMATICS PEDAGOGY

The Case of Dynamic Virtual Tool[1]

INTRODUCTION

A characteristic in the process of acquiring mathematical knowledge is a dual relationship between variation and invariance. Mathematics activities can be seen as either seeking invariants while varying aspects that define/describe a mathematical situation or seeking to apply invariant mathematical concepts in various situations. Another way to posit this duality is through two realms where one can experience mathematical knowledge: a realm of perceptive observable variable phenomena generated by cultural artifacts (e.g. mathematical tools like an abacus or dynamic geometry software) and a realm of cognitive invariant mathematical patterns (e.g. abstract mathematical formulas or theories). Strategic use of variation can serve as transitory means to connect the two realms. This chapter discusses how variation can be used as a pedagogical tool in the context of mathematics teaching and learning, in particular when the use of a dynamic virtual tool is employed, to make this epistemological connection. The set of Principles of Acquiring Invariant proposed by Leung (2014) that is complementary to the patterns of variation in Marton's Theory of Variation will be further discussed and explored under a tool-based teaching and learning environment.

BACKGROUND

The Theory of Variation

Marton's Theory of Variation is a theory of learning and awareness that asks the question: what are powerful ways to discern and to learn? (cf. Lo & Marton, 2012; Marton, 2015; Marton & Booth, 1997) The Theory of Variation starts with a taken-for-granted observation: nothing is one thing only, and each thing has many features. In this theory, discernment is about how to go from a holistic experience of a phenomenon (e.g. seeing a forest) to separating out different features (e.g. seeing a tree) in the phenomenon. It concerns with how to pick up meaningful experiences through our senses, and how meaning comes about from relationships between similarity and difference derived under simultaneous attention. In particular, there is

R. Huang & Y. Li (Eds.), Teaching and Learning Mathematics through Variation, 69–84.
© *2017 Sense Publishers. All rights reserved.*

a discernment ordering from difference to similarity. That is, learning and awareness begins with noticing difference before observing similarity. Suppose I can only perceive "grey" in certain situations, then "grey" has no meaning for me even if you show me a grey chair, a grey car, or a grey cup, "Greyness" becomes meaningful to me only if I can perceive something else other than "grey". Thus in discernment, contrast (finding counter-examples focusing on difference) should come before generalization (which can be regarded as an inductive process focusing on similarity). A fundamental idea in the Theory of Variation is simultaneity. When we are simultaneously aware of (intentional focusing our attention on) different aspects of a phenomenon, we notice differences and similarities. By strategically observing variations of differences, similarities and their relationships, critical features of the phenomenon may be brought out. Morton proposed four patterns of variation as such strategic means: contrast, separation, generalization and fusion (Marton et al., 2004; see Figure 1 for descriptions of these patterns). A major undertaking of the Theory of Variation is to study how to organize and interpret a pedagogical event in powerful ways in terms of these patterns of variation (Lo & Marton, 2012).

Applications of the Theory of Variation in Mathematics Knowledge Acquisition

The first application of the four patterns of variation in the Theory of Variation to mathematics pedagogy was discussed in the context of a dynamic geometry dragging exploration (Leung, 2003). There, the four patterns of variation were used to interpret dragging modalities in a dynamic geometry construction problem to explore experimental reasoning and theoretical reasoning. This began a long programme of study by Leung, where in subsequent work; the four patterns were used as epistemic functions to analyses the developmental processes of mathematical proof and mathematical concept (see for example, Leung, 2008; Leung, 2012; Leung et al., 2013). An epistemic activity in doing mathematics is to discern critical features (or patterns) in a mathematical situation. When these critical features are given interpretations, they may become invariants that can be used to conceptualize the mathematical situation. In Leung (2012), classification of plane figures was used as an example to develop a variation-based pedagogic model. The model consists of a sequence of discernment units in which different variation strategies are used to unveil different feature types of a plane figure: intuitive visual type, geometrical property type, and equivalent geometrical properties type. Each discernment unit contains a process of mathematical concept development that is fused together by contrast and generalization driven by separation. The sequence represents a continuous process of refinement of a mathematical concept, from primitive to progressively formal and mathematical. Mhlolo (2013) later used this model as an analytical framework to interpret a sequence of richly designed mathematics lessons teaching the conceptual development of number sequence. The upshot is, from a variation perspective, mathematical concepts can be developed by strategic observation and variation interaction in terms of contrasting and comparing, separating out critical features, shifting focus of attention (cf. Mason, 1989) and varying features together to seek emergence of invariant patterns. A *variation interaction* is "a strategic use of variation to interact with a mathematics learning environment in order to bring about discernment of mathematical structure" (Leung, 2012). It is also a strategic way to observe a phenomenon focusing on variation and simultaneity. "Interaction" here is interpreted in the sense that the acts of observing may involve direct or indirect manipulation of the "mathematical object" (which may be a tool) under study.

PRINCIPLES OF ACQUIRING INVARIANCE

Simultaneity is the epistemic crux of variation. The four patterns in Marton's Theory of Variation are different types of simultaneous focus used to perceive differences and similarities which lead to the unveiling of critical features of what is being observed. Looking for an invariant in variation and using an invariant to cope with variation are essences of mathematical concept development. A mathematical concept is in fact an invariant. For example, the basic concept of the number "three" is an invariant cognized out of myriad representations of "three-ness". Thus in acquiring mathematical knowledge, to perceive and to understand an invariant amidst variation is a central epistemic goal. Leung (2014) proposed a set of four *Principles of Acquiring Invariance* that is complementary to Marton's (Marton et al., 2004) four patterns of variation in the context of mathematics concept development.

Difference and Similarity Principle

Contrasting differences and comparing similarities in order to perceive or generalize possible invariant features

Sieving Principle

Separating under prescribed constraints or conditions in order to reveal or be aware of critical invariant features or relationships

Shifting Principle

Shifting attention to focus on different or similar features of a phenomenon at different times or situations in order to discern generalized invariance

Co-Variation Principle

Co-varying or fusing together multiple features at the same time in order to perceive possible emergent pattern or invariant relationship between the features

These four principles work with the four patterns of variation in a concerted way. All four principles, just like the four patterns, are different aspects of simultaneity and contrast. They are "perceptual-cognitive" activities looking for mathematical invariants leading to development of mathematical concepts. In particular, they have the following predominant functions. Difference and Similarity Principle is about contrast and generalization leading to awareness of a perceptual invariant feature. Sieving Principle is about awareness of hidden invariant features that can be separated out under variation when only selected aspects of the phenomenon are allowed to vary. Shifting Principle is about diachronic (across time) simultaneity leading to possible generalization, particularly in the mathematics conjecture making process. Co-variation Principle is about synchronic (same time) simultaneity leading to fusing together of critical features in the mathematical concept formation process. These four principles are learner driven which can be cognitively mingled and nested together. During a variation interaction, a learner can apply these principles with different weight and transparency. Figure 1 is a summary of the relations between the Principles of Acquiring Invariance (PAI) and the patterns of variation.

Marton's Patterns of Variation (Marton, Runesson & Tsui, 2004):

Contrast In order to experience something, a person must experience something else to compare it with.
Separation In order to experience a certain aspect of something, and in order to separate this aspect from other aspects, it must vary while other aspects remain invariant.
Generalization In order to fully understand what 'three' is, we must also experience varying appearances of 'three'.
Fusion If there are several critical aspects that the learner has to take into consideration at the same time, they must all be experienced simultaneously (synchronic or diachronic).

Principles of Acquiring Invariance (PAI)	Main Relation to Patterns of Variation
Difference and Similarity	Contrast, Generalization
Sieving	Separation
Shifting	Fusion (Diachronic Simultaneity)
Co-variation	Fusion (Synchronic Simultaneity)

Figure 1. Relations between the principles of acquiring invariance and the patterns of variation

TOOL-BASED MATHEMATICS PEDGOGY

Tools/Artifacts mediate the representations and discourses of mathematical knowledge and expand the space of inquiry for students to discern and experience mathematics (cf. Leung & Bolite-Frant, 2015). In fact, "artifacts do much more than mediate: they are a constitutive part of thinking and sensing" (Radford, 2013, p. 8). There are two pedagogical perspectives to view tools/artifacts. The theory of instrumental genesis (Rabardel, 1995) explicates on how a learner develops a utilization scheme for a particular tool for problem solving and these schemes can be attached to the tool to make it into a pedagogical instrument. The Vygotskian approach regards artifacts as internalized psychological tools in the context of social and cultural interaction through a socio-semiotic process (Vygotsky, 1978, 1981).

Mathematical task is an important component in the teaching and learning of mathematics in the classroom. With the presence of a tool, the design of a mathematical task should capitalize the epistemic potentiality of the tool. A *tool-based mathematics task* is:

> A teacher/researcher design aiming to be a thing to do or act on in order for students to activate an interactive tool-based environment where teacher, students, and resources mutually enrich each other in producing mathematical experiences. In this connection, this type of task design rests heavily on a complex relationship between tool mediation, teaching and learning, and mathematical knowledge. (Leung & Bolite-Frant, 2015, p. 192)

Resources include the tool, physical or virtual manipulatives, and means associated with it in the mathematical knowledge construction process. Tools have affordance and constraint and they give potentials for variation interactions to happen in the mathematics classroom. Affordance means a relation between a tool-enriched environment and a learner that affords the opportunity for the learner to perform an action (cf. Gibson, 1977). Constraint of a tool is interpreted here as the boundary between the utilization of the tool and the intended mathematical content to be learned. It also provides opportunity for the learner to compromise problematic situations arise from using the tool.

Tool-Based Task Design Features

Leung and Bolite-Frant (2015) discussed in-depth tool-based task design under the following considerations:

1. Use strategic feedback from a tool-based environment to create learning opportunities for student.
2. Design activities to mediate between the phenomena created by a tool and the intended mathematical concept to be learned.
3. Make use of the affordances and constraints of a tool to design learning opportunities.
4. Switch between different mathematical representations or tools.

These *tool-based design features* are generic inter-related tool-based task design features that have pedagogical potential to create opportunities for learner actions and to reshape the boundary between tool usage and mathematics concept formation. Variation in tool-based mathematics pedagogy explores how these features and the Principles of Acquiring Invariance pedagogically mesh together in a tool-based environment for learners to acquire mathematical knowledge. In particular, what variation strategies based on the Principles of Acquiring Invariance can be designed to take advantage of the features of a specific chosen tool?

Tool-Based Task Design Epistemic Model

Exploring, constructing and explaining are three important aspects in mathematics knowledge acquisition. These shall form the core of the guiding principles for tool-based task design. Learners should engage in activities that blend these aspects in a progressive epistemic sequence that is conducive to the purpose and utility of the tool-based task. In this connection, Leung (2011) proposed a nested epistemic model for tool-based task design consisting of a nested sequence of three epistemic modes of activities. This model was conceived as a prototype for tool-based pedagogical design.

Practices Mode: Interact with the feedback from acting on the tool to develop skill-based routines, modalities of behavior and modes of situated dialogue.

Critical Discernment Mode: Observe, record, recognize and re-present (re-construct) invariance perceived from acting on the tool.

Situated Discourse Mode: Develop tool-based discourses to reason about the invariant perceived leading to making generalized mathematical ideas (e.g. a mathematical conjecture) and seek further to explain the ideas in formal mathematical ways.

These modes are nested in the sense that Critical Discernment Mode is a cognitive extension of Practices Mode, and Situated Discourse Mode is a cognitive extension of Critical Discernment Mode. An exploration space opens up for the learners as the sequence progresses where practices evolve into discernment followed by discernment evolving into discourses. Within each mode, cognitive activities can be organized by variation interactions and tool heuristics. Thus a tool-based pedagogical sequence can be designed through combining the epistemic modes, tool-based design features, and the Principles of Acquiring Invariance. The sequence presents an evolving process (not necessarily linear) that merges gradually from mainly perceptive experiential "thinking" while using a tool to mainly conceptual theoretical "thinking".

To summarize: *variation in tool-based mathematics pedagogy is a pedagogy that strategically organizes Principles of Acquiring Invariance and tool-based design features under the nested epistemic modes to create a tool-based environment for learners to acquire mathematical knowledge* (Figure 2).

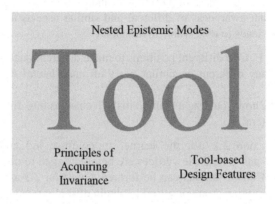

Figure 2. Variation in tool-based mathematics pedagogy

A DYNAMIC GEOMETRY EXAMPLE

The following is an example of a task sequence using the epistemic model and the Principles of Acquiring Invariance in tool-based mathematics pedagogy. It is conceptualized and designed by using a student DGE (Dynamic Geometry Environment) exploration studied in Leung, Baccaglini-Frank and Mariotti (2013).

TASK 1: Construction

Practice Mode: DGE Construction
Construct three points A, B, and C on the screen, the line through A and B, and the line through A and C. Construct a line *l* parallel to AC through B, and a line perpendicular to *l* through C. Label the point of intersection of these two lines D. Consider the quadrilateral ABCD (see Figure 3).

In this first task, the learner practices how to use DGE to do geometrical construction and begin to develop a personal routine to familiarize oneself with DGE. Affordances and constraints of the DG software are used are explored.

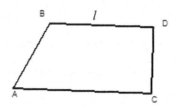

Figure 3. The DGE construction

75

TASK 2: Contrast and Comparison

Practice Mode and Principle of Difference and Similarity: Variation tasks are used to bring about awareness of different and similar aspects/features in a DGE phenomenon that leads to observable invariants.

2.1   Drag A, B, C to different positions to make different quadrilaterals
2.2   How many different or similar types of quadrilateral ABCD can you make?
2.3   Describe how you drag a point to make it changes into different types of quadrilateral

Questions 2.1 and 2.2 ask the learner to contrast and compare different positions of A, B and C as these vertices are being dragged to observe how many different types of quadrilaterals can be formed. Question 2.3 asks the learner to think about the dragging strategies used to obtain different types of quadrilaterals, thus motivating the learner to develop dragging skills and strategies, to relate strategic feedback and dragging action, and to begin a DGE-based reasoning about perceiving a DGE invariant. Figure 4 shows two snapshots for different positions of A where B and C are fixed. There are only two types of possible quadrilaterals: right-angled trapezium and rectangles. This is making use of the Difference and Similarity Principle.

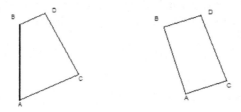

Figure 4. Snapshots for different positions of A where B and C are fixed

TASK 3: Separation of Critical Features

Critical Discernment Mode and Principles of Sieving and Shifting: Variation tasks are used to bring about awareness of critical (causal) relationships among the observed invariants.

3.1   Activate the Trace function for point A. Drag A while keeping B and C fixed to maintain ABCD to look like a rectangle.
3.2   Describe your experience and what you observe.
3.3   Make a guess on the geometrical shape of the path that A follows while restricting BCD to look like a rectangle. How do you make this guess? Call this guess a maintained-path (cf. Leung et al., 2013)

Question 3.1 asks the learner to use a special function in DGE to record the trace of point A as it is being dragged to keep ABCD looking like a rectangle. Using a rectangle as a perceptual invariant to constrain the dragging control makes visible the emergence of another perceptual invariant: the trace-mark of A which appears to take on a geometrical shape (see Figure 5). This gives rise to an uncertainty created by the dragging and tracing tools. Guessing and naming the trace motivates the learner to engage into a DGE discourse thus making use of the Sieving Principle.

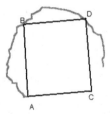

Figure 5. The trace-mark of A which appears to take on a geometrical shape

In questions 3.2 and 3.3, by asking the learner to describe his/her dragging experience and to make a guess on the geometrical shape of the traced path, the learner's cognitive mode is transiting from observation of DGE phenomena to discernment of critical features that could lead to concept formation. In particular, while the learner shifts his/her attention to the two perceptual invariants (the rectangular-like ABCD and the maintained-path) during dragging, attention to discern possible causal relationships between the two invariants may come about. This is Shifting Principle focusing on the pragmatic-epistemic continuum.

TASK 4: Simultaneous Focus

Situated Discourse Mode and Principles of Shifting and Co-variation: Variation tasks are used to bring about awareness of a connection between critical relationships observed and possible mathematical discourses (causal condition, formal/informal conjecture, concept, pattern, mathematical proof, etc.).

4.1   When A is being dragged to vary, vertices B, C and D either vary or not vary as a consequence. Observe the behavior of B, C and D while A is varying to and at the same time restricting ABCD looks like a rectangle.

4.2   Find a possible condition to relate the trace-path of A and the varying configuration of B, C and D.

4.3   Use the condition found in 4.2 to construct the maintained path

Questions 4.1 and 4.2 are a continuation of questions 3.3. The Shifting Principle continues with added attention to the consequential movements of the vertices A, B, C and D, and the Co-variation Principle comes into effect. In the process, the learner develops a DGE discourse for geometrical reasoning and construction. Question 4.3 is a consummation of the exploration in the form of a DGE soft construction (cf. Healy, 2000). The maintained-path takes the form of a circle centred at the midpoint of segment BC. The construction of this circle ensures D lies on the circle and when A is being dragged along this circle, ABCD becomes a rectangle (Figure 6). A DGE soft construction makes use of discrepancy to explore properties and relationships of geometrical objects.

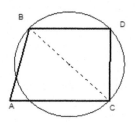 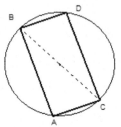

Figure 6. A circle is constructed to ensure when A is on it, ABCD becomes a rectangle

TASK 5: Conjecture and Proof (Development of Theoretical Reasoning)

Situated Discourse Mode and Principles of Co-variation: Development of DGE discourse to connect experimental reasoning and theoretical reasoning

- 5.1 Write a conjecture on what you have discovered in the form
  GIVEN A DGE construction
  IF (certain condition being maintained during dragging)
  THEN (certain configuration appears to be maintained during dragging)
- 5.2 Drag A along the constructed trace-path. Observe how different aspects of the figure vary together. Explain what you observe and formulate a logical argument to explain/prove your conjecture

Question 4.3 (Figure 6) is a DGE representation of a conjecture, question 5.1 asks the learner to write this in the form of a DGE-situated conditional statement, for example,

GIVEN Quadrilateral ABCD as constructed in TASK 1
IF A is being dragged along the circle centered at the midpoint of segment BC
THEN ABCD is always a rectangle

Question 5.2 challenges the learner to formulate an explanation (or even a proof) for the conjecture just formed. The reader can explore this discourse and to see how the Principles of Acquiring Invariance are embedded in the reasoning process.

A DESIGN EXAMPLE

A powerful aspect of integrating ICT into mathematics teaching and learning is ICT's ability to construct and present visual-numeric information in a continuous dynamic form that allows learners to capture invariant relationships (as was shown in the dynamic geometry example above). Another powerful ICT aspect is the possibility of designing and constructing synchronized multi-representations. When designing an ICT tool capitalizing on these two features, the Principles of Acquiring Invariance are helpful when organizing and conceptualizing the design. The possibilities of dynamic variation under constraints and synchronic co-variation given by ICT are potentially promising pre-conditions for applying the Principles of Acquiring Invariance. In the following paragraphs, an example of designing a GeoGebra applet is used to illustrate a Principles of Acquiring Invariance design that incorporates appropriate tool-based task design features.

Suppose we want to design an ICT applet for an Upper Primary (Grades 4 to 6) mathematics classroom to explore the relationship between the area and the perimeter of a rectangle. An objective for this exploration is to find out for a given perimeter, which rectangle gives the largest area. The following two features, with their Principles of Acquiring Invariance implications, are assumed to frame the design of the applet:

1. The perimeter is an independent variable. The two sides of the rectangles are variables that depend on the perimeter, and an area variable depends on the sides of the rectangle. These variables will be used for discerning difference and similarity, and the dependency among the (free and dependent) variables is used to design sieving (separating) out invariants.
2. Three dynamic interactive windows: 2D graphic, spreadsheet numeric table, 3D graphic. The elements/objects in these three windows should co-vary together according to the variables in 1. Shifting of attention and co-variation are the main variation interactions for these windows which have geometrical, numerical and graphical representations.

This interactive GeoGebra applet consists of three dynamic visual windows. On the left is a 2D graphic window that contains the main geometrical problem. The middle window is a dynamic numeric window that links with the 2D graphic window, and the right window is a 3D graphic window that also links with the 2D graphic window. Figure 7 is a snapshot of an example of such an applet.

The 2D Graphic Window

The upper slider fixes/adjusts the perimeter (10 to 40 units) of the rectangle. The slider below it adjusts one of the sides (side A) of the rectangle (start from 1 unit and increment by 1) for the chosen perimeter. Integral values are used only. The rectangle is constructed out of the numerical information from the two sliders and it varies accordingly as the sliders' values vary. The colour of the Side A slider and the colour of the corresponding sides of the rectangle match for visual identification.

The Dynamic Numeric Window

As the rectangle in the 2D graphic window varies when a slider's value is dragged to change, the values of the lengths of the two sides of the rectangle and its area (Side A, Side B, Area) are recorded in a Spreadsheet. When the rectangle moves, the Spreadsheet will update correspondingly to record the numerical changes of the three variables. The recording of any one of the variables can be stopped any time by pressing the recording button of that variable located at the top of the column of the spreadsheet.

The 3D Graphic Window

The 3D graphic window automatically embeds the rectangle in the 2D graphic window in a 2D plane, and the 3D perspective can be changed easily by a dragging motion. The point showing the relationship between Side A, Side B, and area is plotted in 3D with the trace function turned on. As the rectangle in the 2D graphic window varies, the point traces out a path that shows the relationship between the three variables.

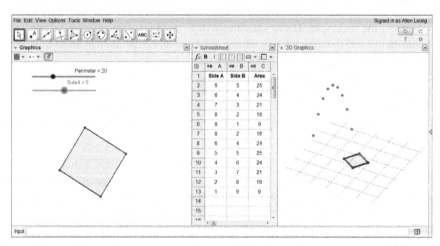

Figure 7. A GeoGebra Applet to explore the relationship between the area and the perimeter of a rectangle

What and how would students learn using this applet? Activity tasks can be designed where the tool-based design features work together with Principles of Acquiring Invariance. For example:

Task 1

1. Fix a perimeter value (say 16).
2. Drag Side A to different values.
3. Observe how objects in the three windows vary together.
4. Are there number patterns appear in the Spreadsheet window?
5. Write down what you discover.

Task 1 starts with Sieving (fixing a value and observe how other things vary) and the visual feedback thus generated begins a cognitive process for the learner connecting the phenomenal world created by the applet and the mathematical ideas embedded in the applet. The learner is in the Practice Mode experiencing how to Shift Attention among the different visual dynamic representations which co-vary together.

Task 2

1. Change the perimeter to other values like 20, 24, 36 and 40 (all divisible by 4).
2. Observe similar features in all these cases.
3. Write down what you discovered and make a conjecture.

Task 2 repeats and enriches the variation experiences obtained in Task 1. The learner enters the Critical Discernment Mode to relate Similarity and Difference that lead to generalization.

Task 3

1. Set the perimeter to 34.
2. Observe what happens in the spreadsheet window. Something should seem not right compared to what you have observed in Task 1 and Task 2. What is it?
3. Explain why and make some mathematical sense out of it.
4. Write down a conclusion on the mathematical idea/concept behind the three tasks.

The maximum value for the area appears (in pairs) in the spreadsheet window does not correspond to a square. This is not consistent with what are observed in Task 1 and Task 2. The learner needs to explain what happens based on what s/he experienced using this applet (Situated Discourse Mode). This discrepancy was intentionally designed in the applet (by allowing only integer input) resulting in an uncertainty which requires the learner to bridge from a conflict he/she sees on the screen to a mathematical concept behind the phenomenon.

From this design example, the Principles of Acquiring Invariance acts as a design guide for an ICT applet to mediate and represent mathematical knowledge, for an explorative pedagogy to create an uncertainty that requires leaners to reason mathematically, and for organizing the doing of mathematics. Indeed, these three realms are connected together under the same Principle of Acquiring Invariance lens (Figure 8). Thus, Principles of Acquiring Invariance manages and maintains the boundary between mathematical and pedagogical fidelities.

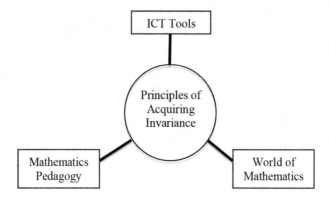

Figure 8. Principles of acquiring invariance as a meta-lens to maintain connections among three knowledge realms: tool, pedagogy and mathematics

DISCUSSION

In the above two examples, Principles of Acquiring Invariance, epistemic modes and tool-based design features are meshed together to explore the mathematical concept formation process from experimental observation to discernment of abstraction in the ICT context. The meshing is a complex design process that depends on multiple factors like the choice of tool(s), teachers' knowledge, choices of task design approach and pedagogy, and classroom cultures. A first remark on this meshing is that these different frameworks form a nested network rather than follow a linear hierarchy. At any one instance during an exploration, any one of the principles, modes and tool-based design features can take dominance. These cognitive activities are pretty much learner driven, but when designing a mathematical task, the designer can guide the learners to pay more attention to particular features while other features can be put in the cognitive background. A second remark is that the pedagogical approach discussed in this chapter is an attempt to crystalize a possible process bridging the experimental-theoretical gap in the ICT context. Specifically, the upshot of using variation and invariance is to drive an epistemic sequence that may look like:

Constraint → Pattern Observation → Predictability → Emergence of Causal Relationship → Concept Formation→Explanation/Proof

This chapter is an attempt to enrich the current research literature on the use of variation in mathematics education and to propose a perspective focusing on invariance that is pertinent to mathematics knowledge acquisition.

NOTE

[1]   This chapter is an expansion of the PME38 Research Report *Principles of acquiring invariant in mathematics task design: a dynamic geometry example* (Leung, 2014).

REFERENCES

Gibson, J. J. (1977). The theory of affordances. In R. Shaw & J. Bransford (Eds.), *Perceiving, acting, and knowing: Toward an ecological psychology* (pp. 67–82). Hillsdale, NJ: Lawrence Erlbaum.

Healy, L. (2000). Identifying and explaining geometrical relationship: Interactions with robust and soft Cabri constructions. In T. Nakahara & M. Koyama (Eds.), *Proceedings Of 24th Conference of the International Group for the Psychology of Mathematics Education* (Vol. 2, pp. 103–117). Hiroshima: Hiroshima University.

Leung, A. (2003). Dynamic geometry and the theory of variation. In N. A. Pateman, B. J. Doherty, & J. Zilliox (Eds.), *Proceedings Of 27th Conference of the International. Group for the Psychology of Mathematics Education* (Vol. 3, pp. 197–204). Honolulu, HI: PME.

Leung, A. (2008). Dragging in a dynamic geometry environment through the lens of variation. *International Journal of Computers for Mathematical Learning, 13*, 135–157.

Leung, A. (2011). An epistemic model of task design in dynamic geometry environment. *ZDM Mathematics Education, 43*, 325–336.

Leung, A. (2012). Variation and mathematics pedagogy. In J. Dindyal, L. P. Cheng, & S. F. Ng (Eds.), *Proceedings of the 35th Annual Conference of the Mathematics Education Research Group of Australasia* (pp. 433–440). Singapore: MERGA.

Leung, A. (2014). Principles of acquiring invariant in mathematics task design: A dynamic geometry example. In P. Liljedahl, C. Nical, S. Oesterle, & D. Allan (Eds.), *Proceedings of the 38th Conference the International Group for the Psychology of Education and the 36th Conference of the North American Chapter of the Psychology of Mathematics Education* (Vol. 4, pp. 89–96). Vancouver, Canada.

Leung, A., Baccaglini-Frank, A., & Mariotti, M. A. (2013). Discernment in dynamic geometry environments. *Educational Studies in Mathematics, 84*, 439–460.

Leung, A., & Bolite-Frant, J. (2015). Designing mathematics tasks: The role of tools. In A. Watson & M. Ohtani (Eds.), *Task design in mathematics education: The 22nd ICMI study* (pp. 191–225). New York, NY: Springer.

Lo, M. L., & Marton, F. (2012). Towards a science of the art of teaching: Using variation theory as a guiding principle of pedagogical design. *International Journal for Lesson and Learning Studies, 1*(1), 7–22.

Marton, F. (2015). *Necessary conditions of learning.* New York, NY: Routledge.

Marton, F., & Booth, S. (1997). *Learning and awareness.* Mahwah, NJ: Lawrence Erlbaum Associates, INC, Publishers.

Marton, F., Runesson, U., & Tsui, A. B. M. (2004). The space of learning. In F. Marton & A. B. M. Tsui (Eds.), *Classroom discourse and the space of learning* (pp. 3–40). Mahwah, NJ: Lawrence Erlbaum Associates, INC, Publishers.

Mason, J. (1989). Mathematical abstraction as the result of a delicate shift of attention. *For the Learning of Mathematics, 9*(2), 2–8.

Mhlolo, M. (2013). The merit of teaching mathematics with variation. *Pythagoras, 34*(2), 8. doi:10.4102/pythagoras.v34i2.233

Rabardel, P. (1995). *Les homes et les technologies, une approche cognitive des instruments contemporains.* Paris: Armand Colin.

Radford, L. (2013). Sensuous cognition. In D. Martinovic, V. Freiman, & Z. Karadag (Eds.), *Visual mathematics and cyberlearning* (pp. 141–162). New York, NY: Springer.

Vygotsky, L. S. (1978). *Mind and society.* Cambridge, MA: Harvard University Press.

Vygotsky, L. S. (1981). The instrumental method in psychology. In J. V. Wertsch (Ed.), *The concept of activity in Soviet psychology* (pp. 134–144). Armonk, NY: M.E. Sharpe.

Allen Leung
Department of Education Studies
Hong Kong Baptist University
Hong Kong SAR, China

ANNE WATSON

5. PEDAGOGY OF VARIATIONS

Synthesis of Various Notions of Variation Pedagogy

INTRODUCTION

In the last decade there has been a gradual increase in publications about the potential of variation theory for mathematics education. Mathematical concepts are often encountered by learners through examples, and the variation they experience through examples that have some similarity in structure leads them to generalise either about the properties of mathematical objects or about relations between them (Michener, 1978). The word 'variation' therefore elicits consideration of the possible variables that can be manipulated in teaching mathematics and designing tasks.

Task design always has with it, either explicitly or implicitly, assumptions about pedagogy, a fundamental belief being that learners will notice and generalize from patterns and relationships between what aspects vary and what aspects are invariant (e.g. Mason, 2000). By using historical examples, and examples presented at the 2013 ICMI Study Conference on Task Design in Mathematics Education (Margolinas, 2013), I reflect on the contribution that variation theory makes to our understanding of pedagogy in mathematics education. Through these examples I explore how variation is manifested in mathematics teaching, and identify a notion of 'dependency relationships' that are invariant in mathematics and which are often the intended object of learning. I look at various ways in which people draw attention to these invariants through use of variation and I compile statements that expand variation theory within mathematics education. Finally, I illustrate how careful use of variation can lead beyond generalization to abstraction of new ideas. The ICMI Study provides a snapshot of current practice in task design, and included a panel of presentations about the current use of variation to design tasks and pedagogy. However, I shall start with some observations from earlier examples of pedagogy.

MATHEMATICS PEDAGOGY OF VARIATION FROM SOME PAST TEXTBOOKS

I start with the beginning of a set of questions from a typical algebra textbook published in English in the early 20th century, chosen at random from a collection (Paterson, 1911, p. 120):

| 1. $(2x)^3$ | 2. $(-2x)^3$ | 3. $(-2x)^6$ | 4. $(2x)^6$ |
| 5. $(2x^2)^3$ | 6. $(-2x^2)^3$ | 7. $(-2x^2)^6$ | 8. $(2x^2)^6$ |

R. Huang & Y. Li (Eds.), Teaching and Learning Mathematics through Variation, 85–103.

The exercise goes on with more variation of letters, powers and structures, but these first eight questions provide raw material for more than mere practice of using algebraic notation. The examples have been constructed with care to draw attention to what varies and what stays the same, and to possible misconceptions a student may have, or mistakes they may make. The author goes on to say:

> The student will now have found out the following rules: (i) an even power of a negative quantity is positive, an odd power of a negative quantity is negative; (ii) $(x^p)^q = x^{pq}$ ... (p. 120)

This is followed by several other 'rules' which were to be 'found out' by reasoning inductively from the answers to the exercise. Paterson is explicit about the assumptions of his task construction: namely that learners will be led experimentally to a difficulty that has to be overcome, such as meeting '3 − 5' before negative numbers are formally introduced (p. A2) and noticing the difference between this and other examples. This visually obvious use of variation is not replicated very often in his book. More usually, Paterson uses varied collections of questions in which one subsequence of questions holds a particular similarity that is then disrupted in a new subsequence. Both of these uses of variation – with and without visual similarity – are used in most algebra textbooks of that era.

Knowledge of the value of careful variation also appears in some mid-twentieth century texts produced in England by teacher teams. The Midlands Mathematics Experiment, which was a syllabus based on New Mathematics, introduces straight lines by varying $L_1 = \{x,y: y = x\}$ to give:

$$L_2 = \{x,y: y = x + 1\} \qquad L_4 = \{x,y: y = x - 1\}$$
$$L_3 = \{x,y: y = x + 2\} \qquad L_5 = \{x,y: y = x - 2\}$$

and then asks: 'What do you notice about the lines L_1, L_2, L_3, L_4, L_5?' (MME, 1970, p. 53). Again, the purpose is to provide variation against an invariant background and the implied pedagogical intention is that learners will conjecture about the relationship between the variations in the algebraic expression and the differences in the graphical depiction of the sets of points. In this case, the chosen set of lines implies an understanding of the effects of near-simultaneous variation between examples but, unlike Paterson's era, such use of variation, whether visually obvious or not, is not easy to find in textbooks during the later part of the 20th century, nor currently.

Both of the above textbooks assume that teachers will encourage appropriate reflection in learners, and not merely rush on to the next idea or technique and the next set of questions to do. Variation, in the examples I have given, is not random but relates closely to the concepts or conventions being introduced. In each of the examples above, variation is also indicated visually by using similar notations so that the difference in outcomes can be related to the visual difference as well as to differences in mathematical meaning. However, other exercises from Paterson's book have an underlying attention to variations in structure and complexity *without* a visually invariant background. For example (p. 125):

Find the square of each of the following expressions
$a + b - c$ $x - y - z$ $-x - y - z$
$2a + 3b + 1$ $2x + 3y - 4z$ $3y - 4z + 2x$

Obviously there are opportunities here for an astute teacher or student to make comparisons, but the use of a, b, c and x, y, z among the examples introduces a further variation that, while necessary for becoming fluent and competent with algebra, makes comparison across all examples less likely without teacher intervention. Marton would describe this as 'fusion' (2015, p. 51) in which a learner has to appreciate the underlying mathematical idea (squaring trinomials) by fusing variations in notation, in coefficients and in signs so that they can recognize the idea whatever the combination of letters, numbers and signs. Such variations might have been met separately and are then brought together, fused. We could argue that if every mathematical idea were to be broken down so that learners had to work on each possible dimension of variation separately the whole business of learning mathematics would take decades. Nevertheless a reliance on generalizing from varied examples is evident in some early algebra textbooks. For example Godfrey and Siddons (1915, p. vi) suggest 'rough induction' as a 'sound' way to approach algebraic laws.

CURRENT 'TRADITIONS' IN VARIATION THEORY

Having shown that variation was used purposefully in mathematics pedagogy before recent theoretical articulations, I now present two examples from the 2013 ICMI Task Design Study Conference to illustrate some current thinking. These use the two main approaches to variation theory in the literature that are now well-established, a Swedish approach represented in this paper by Kullberg (2013) and a Chinese approach represented in this paper by Sun (2013).

The Swedish 'Tradition'

The Swedish approach originated in phenomenographic analysis of learning, which enables the researcher/developer/teacher to identify a critical aspect of the concept being learnt. These aspects are found in the variety of students' responses, rather than in analysis of the concept. The theory propounded by Marton (e.g. Marton & Pang, 2004; Marton, 2015) is that unless this critical aspect is varied against an invariant background, students will not notice it, so therefore its variation becomes a design imperative for teachers. However, application of this idea in classroom settings suggests that students experience variation not only through the task as written, but also through pedagogical acts that draw attention to the variation (Al-Murani, 2006; Kullberg, Runesson, & Mátensson, 2013).

Three full learning study cycles were carried out collaboratively with a small group of teachers by Kullberg and her colleagues (Kullberg et al., 2013). The part of the study I am going to look at focuses narrowly on the critical aspect of division that when the denominator, or divisor, is smaller than one (but still positive) the quotient will be greater than the dividend. This is the intended object of learning. For some understandings of division this idea is counterintuitive, since division in everyday life tends to involve reducing things in size, or sharing quantities between people. In this study the 'critical aspect' for division was chosen from the teachers' knowledge of students' difficulties. However, this same critical aspect could have been chosen as a result of analysing students' work on a particular task, or from clinical psychological research into children's understanding. The proposed variation is therefore the divisor, and its effect on the quotient, to draw attention to what happens when it is smaller than one by contrasting with what happens when it is greater than one.

Learning is described as 'seeing something in a new way by experiencing aspects that you have not experienced previously' (Kullberg et al., 2013, p. 616) and this is achieved by varying a critical aspect of the object of learning against a background of invariance thus producing something to notice – in this case the behaviour of a relationship. The teachers therefore co-planned the following collections of examples that would be used in the lesson (see Figure 1).

$$100 \cdot 20 = 2000 \qquad \frac{100}{20} = 5$$

$$100 \cdot 4 = 400 \qquad \frac{100}{4} = 25$$

$$100 \cdot 2 = 200 \qquad \frac{100}{2} = 50$$

$$100 \cdot 1 = 100 \qquad \frac{100}{1} = 100$$

$$100 \cdot 0.5 = 50 \qquad \frac{100}{0.5} = 200$$

$$100 \cdot 0.1 = 25 \qquad \frac{100}{0.1} = 1000$$

Figure 1. Examples used in a lesson on division
(adapted from Kullberg et al., 2013, p. 617)

I have subsequently presented this collection to a range of teacher or student audiences to understand reactions to the visual layout. The first thing that most people notice, through visual perception, is that 'there are lots of hundreds' or every line starts with 100. A little while later they may say that along each line there is a fraction with 100 at the top. The first column of equations shows multiples, and answers get smaller; the second column shows divisions, and answers get larger. The reason these similarities and differences are easily noticeable is because of the layout, so if you were responding visually to the spatial structure you could say that there were similarities in the lines and columns of the layout. These similarities match exactly the abstract mathematical similarities that are instantiated by the numbers and represented by the numerical symbols. By this I mean that extending the sequences of equations downwards or upwards using superficial similarities and number sequences, the horizontal relationship between multiplication and division would also be preserved. The form and structure of the visual representation matches the form and structure of the underlying mathematics. Mathematically, the division examples aim to hold the dividend (100) invariant while varying the divisor so that the intended object of learning appears as the varied behavior of the division. When the intended object of learning is the behavior of a dependency relationship, as it is here, there has to be variation in at least two features: at least one input feature and, hence, the output feature. The relationship itself has to be inferred through discerning the effects of its behavior, so showing the possible differences in behavior is clearly a sensible thing to do. Kullberg et al. (2013) refer to this as using 'contrast' after the four possible patterns of variation: *contrast, generalization, fusion,* and *separation* put forward by Marton, Runesson, and Tsui (2004).

Variation theory, as well as being used at the design phase, can also be used to analyze what is made available to be learnt through the pedagogy that accompanies the designed task. The lessons from this shared plan were analyzed by looking for variations in the way the plan was used, that is the ways in which teachers drew learners' attention to the embedded relationships. The study shows how many aspects of the learning environment, such as teachers' and students' verbal interactions and gestures made a difference to what was available to be learnt by drawing attention to the possible relationships between elements in the examples. The authors drew mappings to show how different teachers pointed to different connections in the examples (Figure 2).

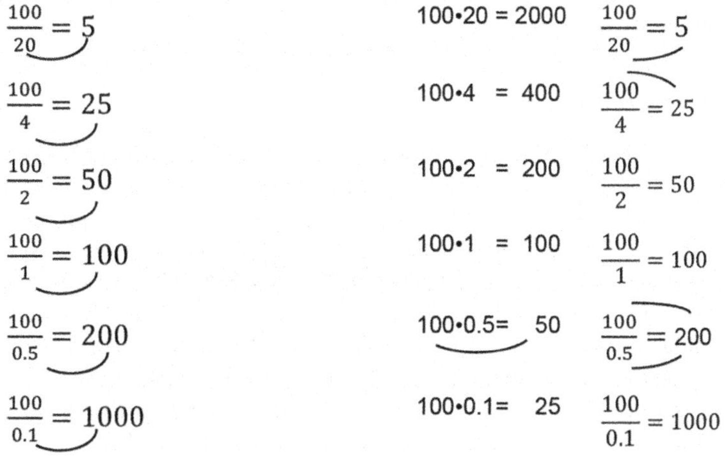

$$\frac{100}{20} = 5 \qquad 100 \cdot 20 = 2000 \qquad \frac{100}{20} = 5$$

$$\frac{100}{4} = 25 \qquad 100 \cdot 4 = 400 \qquad \frac{100}{4} = 25$$

$$\frac{100}{2} = 50 \qquad 100 \cdot 2 = 200 \qquad \frac{100}{2} = 50$$

$$\frac{100}{1} = 100 \qquad 100 \cdot 1 = 100 \qquad \frac{100}{1} = 100$$

$$\frac{100}{0.5} = 200 \qquad 100 \cdot 0.5 = 50 \qquad \frac{100}{0.5} = 200$$

$$\frac{100}{0.1} = 1000 \qquad 100 \cdot 0.1 = 25 \qquad \frac{100}{0.1} = 1000$$

Figure 2. Teachers' gestures to explain examples (from Kullberg et al., 2013, p. 618)

In the partial version on the left the teacher is connecting the divisor to the quotient, which could emphasize that as the divisor gets smaller the quotient gets bigger; however, it is also possible to focus on the fact that their product is always 100, which is what the teacher talked about. In the example of the right the teacher is less systematic about the relationship between multiplication and division, but points instead to illustrations of various aspects of the fundamental relationship, contrasting an example with divisor>1 with one where divisor<1, and was also talking about this contrast. This is important for the way that variation theory is seen within the mathematics education field, because a superficial look at it might suggest that the theory as applied to design is purely cognitive and concerned only with what is presented to learners in order for them to construct meaning individually through inductive reasoning. The addition of teachers' gestures and speech to the mix indicates a need to think also about attention and the disposition of learners to discern what is intended.

Kullberg's use of variation in this paper focuses only on what is *available* to be learnt, but we can surmise what students focus on. It could be argued that the same (not varied) gestures in different cases might help children learn about essential structure because it provides another representation; repetitive action, gesture, rhythm and speech is seen by some authors as an important aspect of learning structured knowledge (Hewitt, 2006). The gestures indicated in the leftmost example, together with the speech, emphasized the complementarity of division and multiplication through invariant gestures; the rightmost example gestures selected two contrasting examples that, with the speech, drew attention to the intended object of learning.

From this study we can see the value of varying the critical aspect, so it can be noticed by learners, and also the value of layout, speech and gestures that draw attention to the background invariant structure. In some of the textbook examples above, the 'drawing attention to' was intended through reflective questions and comments by the authors.

The Chinese 'Tradition'

I now exemplify the Chinese tradition of focusing on change. Sun (2013) points to two key features of task design: OPMS (one problem multiple methods of solution) and OPMC (one problem multiple changes). My interpretation of 'multiple changes' in the examples that she gives is that these can be transformations of layout and different representations. Also at the bottom of the page the numbers are changed, but the underlying structure of the problems is the same, that is similarly structured and hence similarly cognitive. Comparison and connection of these varying experiences is understood to be a fundamental mental activity. Sun uses variation as an analytical lens to describe the way that the official Chinese textbook presents the additive relationship as an object of learning (see also Marton, 2015, p. 249).

The page of the Chinese textbook (Figure 3) first shows four symbolic transformations of the relationship between 10, 3, and 13. It also shows physical materials that can be used, and some number facts between 11, 2, and 13 that can then be derived. It draws attention to symbolic notation by offering varied transformations of the relationships in which certain numbers have to be inserted. This illustrates two uses of OPMC. Firstly, Sun shows 'one problem with multiple representations' with each representation leading to a different solution method (OPMS). Secondly, she shows 'one problem with different parameters' which requires the same solution methods as above, but instantiated with different numbers. Contrasting this approach to the Swedish approach, we can ask: is the learner supposed to learn about the representations, because those are the things that vary? and: is the learner supposed to learn about the different solution methods because those are the things that vary? The variation is being used to support a variety of ways in which learners can enact and record the basic part-part-whole relationship, the additive relationship, which includes addition and subtraction as the relationship between 10, 3, and 13. Rather than learning about one varying critical aspect, the learner has to learn about the relationship. Is the learner supposed to learn only about $10 + 3$ equals 13, because that is the thing that does not change? Well not that either, even though this specific relationship is the invariant. The underlying principles are more complex and sustained than these questions would imply.

Figure 3. Page from Chinese textbook (Mathematics textbook developer group for elementary school, 2005)

On the page the actions and the notations are specific enactments of a fundamental relationship which will appear again and again throughout children's early learning of number. Deliberate and planned variation is obvious, but the core idea – the relationship between addition and subtraction – is constant throughout several pages of the book. It is the *invariant* nature of the additive *relationship* that is the intended object of learning, together with the varying ways in which we might recognize it. Sun describes and demonstrates that the space of learning is about blending patterns of variation and invariance by juxtaposing problems, examples, illustrations that resemble each other in some respects but differ in others so that learners have something to discern.

My understanding of what is presented by both Kullberg and Sun is that the variations presented visually in mathematics give a direct access to important variations around a core conceptual idea: in the example I have given from Kullberg, the visual layout can be used to draw attention to the mathematical structure that causes the variations in output, as well as drawing attention to the variation in outputs themselves; in the example I have given from Sun, the visual layout also gives access to actions with materials that embody various perspectives on the mathematical structure, and notations that record the relations embedded in those actions. In Sun's case, the intended object of learning is an invariant relation, whereas in Kullberg's case, the intended object of learning is a particular varying feature of the underlying relation.

However, mathematics is not merely the product of inductive reasoning from examples, so the provision of carefully varied examples and hoping that, or directing attention so that, learners may generalize inductively from experience cannot provide a full mathematical learning experience. In Sun's work, it is not only inductive generalization that leads to insight, nor is it only contrast and fusion (to use Marton's words) but some kind of cognitive work that abstracts the additive relationship from those processes. The cognitive work involved in using the experience of working with examples to identify implicit relationships is described by Gu, Huang and Marton as 'conceptual' and by Leung, Baccaglini-Frank and Mariotti (2013) as the identification of *level-2 invariants*, that is invariants that have to be discerned through experiencing an invariant relationship underlying variation. Cai and Nie (2007) talk about MPOS, multiple problems with one common method of solution, as also indicating that different problems might be manifestations of the same dependency relationship.

Learners have to be able to discern, to read, what is presented visually as a collection of parts – what Marton calls 'separation' (2015, p. 53) and we might also call 'analysis' (Huang, Mok, & Leung, 2006). The more mathematics we know, the more possible ways of reading a page of mathematics, or one mathematical expression, we have. We can go beyond the visual similarities and differences, especially with pedagogic help and direction. We can also go beyond induction, which enables us to build conjectures about objects and relations we have not yet met; but the more mathematics we know, the more capable we are of *de*duction by seeing a particular example as an instance of something we know about more generally, and being able to reason about its properties. Many textbooks tend to confuse these by offering collections of very varied examples from which little can be either induced or deduced, the purpose being to rehearse procedures. Difficulty is ramped by varying numbers, signs and arrangements rather than by scaffolding progress towards conceptual understanding, as is indicated in the Chinese example.

Variation in Dynamic Geometry

Having set up a contrast between learning the feature that is varied, and discerning an underlying invariant relationship, I now move to a geometrical example presented at the ICMI Study from a body of work by Leung and Lee (2008). In geometry we would expect visual representation to relate very closely to the relationships being represented and Leung has done extensive work to connect dynamic actions to underlying relationships. Tasks are presented in a dynamic geometry environment. This allows students to use the action of 'dragging' to vary particular features of a diagram while shifting their attention between parts and the whole of the object of exploration, consistent with a perspective of discernment of a concept through variation. The invariant patterns of a configuration can then be 'separated-out' by observing patterns of change.

It is this kind of use of controlled variation in mathematics that initially attracted me to variation theory, since it provides a connection between structures inherent in mathematics, the components of the learning environment, and plausible variation in students' learning.

In several of Leung's studies a digital record is kept of the work undertaken by a large number of students in a geometrical context (e.g. Leung, 2008, 2011, 2013). In the example I use here (Leung & Lee, 2008) students have been asked to vary a given quadrilateral ABCD by dragging point D so that the quadrilateral then has at least one pair of parallel sides. There are several possible correct answers which would be achieved by applying full geometrical reasoning, and a digital record of variation among students' answers provides an instant 'phenomenograph ' of the outcomes (Figure 4). From this picture it can be deduced what subset of appropriate geometrical properties is being used by students.

What has happened is that students have digitally dragged point D and left it somewhere new. The clusters of points show two distinct patterns: one pattern makes AD parallel to BC and the other pattern makes CD parallel to AB. Where these cross there is a further cluster that makes both pairs of lines parallel. There are also several points that show possible misunderstandings or alternative interpretations of the task. Thus the digital record gives a window into the relationships between the diagram, the task and their knowledge and capabilities. We observe this by, in Leung's words, "strategically *contrasting* and *comparing*, *separating* out critical features, *shifting focus of attention* and *varying features together* to see whether invariant patterns emerge" (2013, p. 7). Dynamic digital software makes it possible to use what he calls a 'sieving' principle, that is to sieve out and display certain critical invariant features of a dependency relationship.

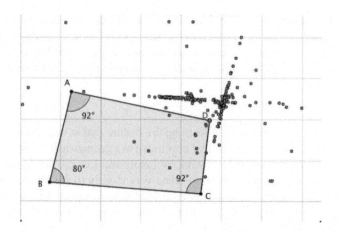

Figure 4. Graphical record of students' 'dragging' solutions (from Leung & Lee, 2008)

Direct perception is used in this task in two ways: firstly for the student who is trying to enact their understanding of 'parallel' and secondly by the researcher who is trying to map the range of possible understandings. Both of these perceptual acts lead to classical geometrical properties which can be seen and described visually, for example the properties of a parallelogram where both pairs of opposite sides are parallel. Leung's use of the phrase 'invariant patterns' is not referring to optical patterns, but to dependency relationships as level-2 invariants that are manifested through the behaviour of variables. By contrast the examples from Kullberg and Sun are both about mathematical properties that cannot be seen directly, but only experienced as the invariant connection between features of varying examples.

Although Leung and Lee's work described here is concerned with finding out what students do, a key aspect of good mathematics pedagogy, these insights are also relevant for thinking about teaching geometrical relations. Dynamic geometry software provides an immediate, accurate, exploration tool for making conjectures and verifying relations between elements of geometrical objects. As in Kullberg and Sun above, the dependency relationships we want students to learn about are available to be learnt if students are presented with varied examples of them so that conjectures can be generated and tested, and the behaviour and domains of the relationship experienced. So far we have seen different domains of communication: visual, symbolic, dynamic, gestural and verbal variation and how these can combine to give access to dependency relationships that underlie surface variation in examples.

How Much Variation and Variation of What?

I now move to an example of the use of variation in pedagogy in which considerations of the dimensions and ranges of variation became central. Koichu and his colleagues draw on the idea of a *space of learning* to consider the relationship between the intended and enacted objects of learning as an area for pedagogic decision. Their study is "an application of variation theory to design of a task aimed at enhancing learners' awareness of mathematics as a connected field of study ... awareness of mathematics as a connected field of study was an intended object of learning" (Koichu, Zaslavsky, & Dolev, 2013, p. 461). Awareness here means the ability and disposition to discern, through and between different representations. They designed a sorting task with the twin aims of (a) completing the sorting and (b) undertaking analytical reasoning to do the sorting. There are several layers to this study: the task design as a tool for learning about similarities and differences; learners reflecting on the process to become aware of such similarities and differences in future; and the design process itself. Evidence from task outcomes, participants' comments in discussion, and records of their work gave insight into how they completed the task (53 subjects in three roughly equal cohorts). The design of the task was based on assumptions about the subjects' previous experience based on typical textbooks, and the need to control variations in sets of objects from which learners "might observe regularities and differences, develop expectations, make comparisons, have surprises, test, adapt and confirm their conjectures within the exercise" (Watson & Mason, 2006, p. 109).

Three types of controlled variation were introduced in the initial task design (Figure 5 shows 14 of the original 24 items to be sorted): mathematical objects to be sorted; representations including verbal descriptions and instructions; prior knowledge requirements to achieve the sorting. Although these variations appear to make pedagogical sense, and provide material for making important contrasts, at the design stage the critical aspects of the intended object of learning were not known.

With the first cohort, learners could achieve the desired sorting by focusing on algebraic manipulation and then classifying items by surface features instead of connecting different representations by using their underlying mathematical connections. The sorting had not been achieved by the analytical reasoning which would be evidence of the intended awareness. For the second cohort, items that had been treated algebraically were omitted and the cohort did not spend so much time on superficial similarities. However, surface features of the visual representations seemed to present obstacles in making sense of the verbal descriptions. From these observations it was decided that the third version should exclude the dimensions of variation that had hindered task completion, and focus on verbal descriptions of the main generating elements of each locus and other representations that had emerged as critical aspects in the earlier sortings (e.g. see items 4 and 13 in Figure 5).

The relationship between this task and variation theory is complex. The intended object of learning is 'awareness' and although learners' awareness can be discerned phenomenographically (Marton & Booth, 1997) it cannot be directly varied in the presented task, since it is a property of learners and not of the mathematical items. 'Awareness of ... a connected field ...' might suggest that the connections themselves be varied, but because mathematics *is* a connected field it is hard to imagine how connectivity as a concept could be varied. Yet awareness is a legitimate objective for

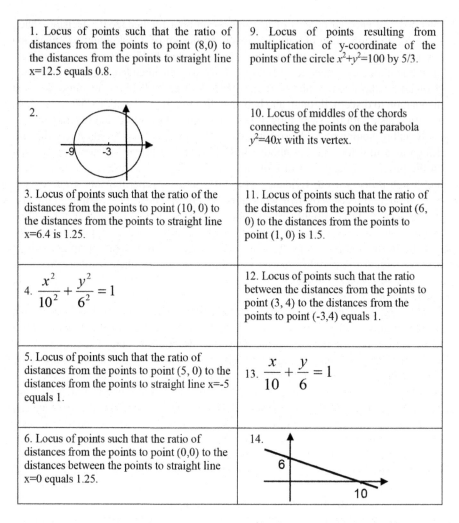

1. Locus of points such that the ratio of distances from the points to point (8,0) to the distances from the points to straight line x=12.5 equals 0.8.	9. Locus of points resulting from multiplication of y-coordinate of the points of the circle $x^2+y^2=100$ by 5/3.
2.	10. Locus of middles of the chords connecting the points on the parabola $y^2=40x$ with its vertex.
3. Locus of points such that the ratio of the distances from the points to point (10, 0) to the distances from the points to straight line x=6.4 is 1.25.	11. Locus of points such that the ratio of the distances from the points to point (6, 0) to the distances from the points to point (1, 0) is 1.5.
4. $\dfrac{x^2}{10^2}+\dfrac{y^2}{6^2}=1$	12. Locus of points such that the ratio between the distances from the points to point (3, 4) to the distances from the points to point (-3,4) equals 1.
5. Locus of points such that the ratio of distances from the points to point (5, 0) to the distances from the points to straight line x=-5 equals 1.	13. $\dfrac{x}{10}+\dfrac{y}{6}=1$
6. Locus of points such that the ratio of distances from the points to point (0,0) to the distances between the points to straight line x=0 equals 1.25.	14.

Figure 5. Part of Koichu et al.'s original sorting task (Koichu, Zaslavsky, & Dolev 2013)

the teaching of mathematics, indeed Leung identifies a 'progression of awareness' in his work connecting Marton's four types of variation to dragging modes (Leung, 2008, p. 153) finishing with fusion as the ultimate level of awareness. However, variation is a key component of Koichu et al.'s task design, since it has been used to generate the examples to be sorted, and their sorting is achieved through discerning similarities and differences in the set of examples. Furthermore, the designers reduced the set to one that contained only those features whose variation led to learners exhibiting the intended awareness of connectivity. It seems that variation in the parameters and conditions offered in the worded examples was enough to lead to the relevant awareness. Removal of distracting variations led to success. Koichu and his colleagues had hoped that learners would 'fuse' the understanding generated by algebraic forms, by graphs and by words during their sorting processes, but variation had to be successively limited towards variation *within* representations, rather than variation *of* representations, for the awareness of the embedded mathematics to be the lived experience of learning.

MATHEMATICS PEDAGOGY AND VARIATION THEORY

These reports have aired a range of issues that arise in the manifestation of variation theory in mathematics, and the use of variation in earlier texts. The decision to control deliberately the relationship between variation and invariance in a situation is pedagogic, and hence is in the realm of education rather than the mathematics itself, in which the variation relationships are inherent. The examples I have described above lead to some observations that extend variation theory in the context of mathematics education in ways that recognise the importance of dependency relations in mathematics:

- the intended object of learning is often an abstract relationship that can only be experienced through examples; it is by observing the relationship between two varying aspects that the invariant relationship can be experienced and understood. By 'relationship' I do not mean the contextual fusion of two variables merely because they co-exist, but a *dependency relation* in which a change in one variable causes a change in another, when one variation necessitates another variation. Examples include the invariant relation between addition and subtraction (Sun above) or the action of dragging to change characteristics of a shape (Leung above) or when divisor being <1 or >1 implies increase or decrease in a quantity (Kullberg above).
- characteristics of a relationship may vary in response to varied input, so the *behavior* of the relationship varies for different inputs, but the relationship itself does not change (Kullberg).
- learners' action may not be the reflective, deliberate, action that is intended if it is easier to apply intuitive habits of mind (Koichu).
- when the intended object of learning is *awareness* identifying suitable dimensions of variation is difficult because awareness is a characteristic of the learner, not of the examples (Koichu).
- variation of appropriate dimensions can sometimes be directly visible, such as through geometry or through page layout (explicit), but often requires meaningful interpretation of symbolic forms (implicit). All the examples so far demonstrate aspects of this distinction. Koichu et al.'s work demonstrates the value of limiting the dimensions of variation, in their case to variations within representations to focus on meaning.
- the role of the teacher, or some other method, in drawing attention to connections, similarities and differences in the given examples introduces other dimensions of variation in the enacted object of learning (Kullberg, Sun, Leung, Koichu).

I hope I have shown above that if the object of learning is a dependency relationship, revealed by manipulation of variables, then higher levels of generalization can be attained through pedagogic attention to variation and control of dimensions of variation. One possible criticism of the application of variation theory to mathematics pedagogy is that inductive reasoning cannot lead to a higher level of abstraction. Can students be scaffolded to work at a higher level of abstraction than can be provided by comparison and generalization from given examples? By 'abstraction' I mean something beyond generalization of mathematical relationships – I am not talking only of invariant background relationships here. 'Abstraction' in my use means that a dependency relationship itself becomes a kind of mathematical concept, so for example linear functions can be understood as dependency relations of a particular kind between two variables, or as objects in their own right with their own dimensions of variation, ranges of permissible change, operations, properties and so on (Watson & Mason, 2004). In general these levels of mathematical concept are only available to us through speech and mathematical symbolization. We cannot, for example, point to the concept of ratio; we can only point out situations in which ratio is the relationship between objects, and particular numerical instantiations of ratio, yet ratio as an idea has its own existence, definitions, variations and so on. Literature about this change of emphasis falls into two separate camps: the idea that cognitive change happens through processes of assimilation, accommodation and equilibration; or the idea that new objects can be brought into the communicable world through language and processes of enculturation. For me, variation theory provides part of an intellectual bridge to describe a combination of those processes, and also to inform design of learning environments. But the teaching of mathematics and presentation of near simultaneous examples that are constructed along the lines suggested in variation theory needs also appropriate forms of variance/invariant *language* and appropriate forms of variant/invariant *presentation*. We have already seen something of this in the examples so far, but now I shall demonstrate the importance of these considerations in achieving a shift to levels of higher abstraction.

Task Sequence Showing a Trajectory through Levels of Abstraction

In the following sequence of tasks, dimensions of variation are controlled in such a way that a hierarchy of relationships is achieved, first through generalization of dependency relations that have been exemplified, then through questioning which transforms the generalization into a new object. In workshops with students, teachers at all levels, and teacher educators I have found these tasks to be almost universally effective in giving learners an experience of becoming more powerful with ideas that previously were abstract, within a context that is not dependent on advanced school mathematics curriculum knowledge.

The first task is to create what is called a 'tetramino' chosen from the collection of all possible tetraminoes. An analysis of these shapes leads people to the correct definition – four congruent squares joined at edges. In Marton's words learners are providing for themselves the 'necessary conditions of learning', that is they are aware that other numbers of squares are possible, and other ways of joining them.

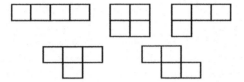

Participants are then given a number grid on which to place their tetramino (Figure 6), and asked to identify the relationships between the four numbers that they have covered. So far, therefore, there is variation in shape and variation in the numbers covered. These fulfill two different purposes: the first is pedagogic, so that students are not using the same shape and can have a conversation about the different ways in which they have to express generalities later and how these relate to the shapes themselves; the second is based on the theory that we learn from examples, and that variation in those examples serves to draw our attention to what they have in common, by comparing them and/or reasoning inductively from them.

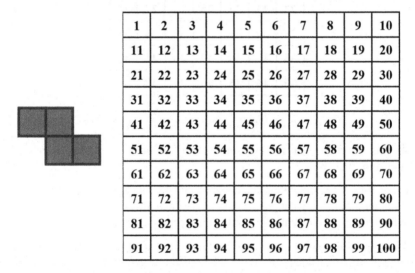

1	2	3	4	5	6	7	8	9	10
11	12	13	14	15	16	17	18	19	20
21	22	23	24	25	26	27	28	29	30
31	32	33	34	35	36	37	38	39	40
41	42	43	44	45	46	47	48	49	50
51	52	53	54	55	56	57	58	59	60
61	62	63	64	65	66	67	68	69	70
71	72	73	74	75	76	77	78	79	80
81	82	83	84	85	86	87	88	89	90
91	92	93	94	95	96	97	98	99	100

Figure 6. First grid and a chosen tetramino

They should then find that the *relationship* between the four numbers is the same, whatever position they have chosen on the grid for their tetramino, but different from the relations underneath other tetraminoes. This relationship can be expressed in general terms, such as: $n - 1$; n; $n + 10$; $n + 11$ using the tetramino shown next to the grid. The relationship depends on the shape and its position. However, the way we express the relationship can also vary. The same relationship can be expressed as n; $n + 1$; $n + 11$;

$n + 12$ by varying which cell is described as n. Students with the same shape can compare expressions; students with different shapes can compare relationships.

The grid content is then varied (Figure 7), but is mathematically similar in structure to the previous grid, i.e. consists of consecutive whole numbers. The task is repeated and the new relationship expressed, such as: $n - 1$; n; $n + 7$; $n + 8$. Participants begin to realise that some of the numbers they have to use in the relationship are dependent on the grid size. The grid size has been varied, but the shape remains the same and the structure of the relationship stays the same. The object of learning at this point is the relationship structure, which stays the same even when the grid size varies. This use of variation confirms that we do not learn only about varied aspects, but about underlying relationships by becoming aware of similar structures in varied examples, as Sun describes (above).

1	2	3	4	5	6	7
8	9	10	11	12	13	14
15	16	17	18	19	20	21
22	23	24	25	26	27	28
29	30	31	32	33	34	35
36	37	38	39	40	41	42
43	44	45	46	47	48	49

Figure 7. Varying the grid

At this point the teacher asks new forms of question which are about the relationship, such as:

On an 9-by-9 grid my tetramino covers 8 and 18. Guess my tetramino.
What tetramino, on what grid, would cover the numbers 25 and 32?
What tetramino, on what grid, could cover cells $(m - 1)$ and $(m + 7)$?

These questions could be tackled through the materials, but are also accessible through abstract consideration of the relationship through looking at the structures of different generalizations. They are not questions that can be easily answered by repeating the original actions with different inputs unless a process of trial-and-adjustment is successful. New forms of reasoning are triggered which draw attention to the relationship, away from the initial manifestation; the particular relationship varies but its structure does not. This approach can be varied to other kinds of grid, such as bivariate grids, which I shall not consider further here.

For each successive task I deliberately vary a dimension of variation that would then become itself a parameter (a structuring feature) for a new task, creating a relationship between grid and shape that we could call the 'grid-shape' object. This new object, which is an abstract connection between grid and shape, can then be talked about, and new kinds of question posed about it, thus scaffolding abstraction. The task sequence illustrates: variation as a generator of examples for selection, comparison and generalization; the use of the outcomes of generalization as new objects which can themselves be varied; the twin roles of presenting variation and asking new questions that require deductive reasoning about new objects.

I have presented this task sequence as an example of how attention to variation can provide pedagogic strategies and pathways towards understanding mathematical ideas at higher levels of abstraction, a role for variation which is as yet under-researched. It has been hinted at in Marton's idea of fusion, but the outcome of fusion than needs to be seen as an object with its own behavior and properties, and also in Leung's idea of level-2 invariance, but again the invariant idea has to become an object in itself.

CONCLUDING REMARKS

In this chapter I have brought together a wide range of mathematical tasks and reports that depend to some extent on implicit or explicit use of variation theory to generate learning and/or reveal the range of learners' understandings. In so doing I have included examples from textbooks to show that variation is an issue for textbook design as well as task design and pedagogy more broadly.

In all the examples I have given, there is more going on than merely asking learners to act on examples in which a critical aspect of an object of learning is varied. All examples address the harder problem of learning something about an underlying dependency relationship, which is very often the aim of mathematics teaching. This might be through: additional reflective tasks; contrasting behavior in examples; pedagogic talk and gesture; juxtaposition of OPMS, OPMC and MPOS examples; direct connections between actions, visual layout and the relationship; limiting dimensions of variation; and avoiding variations that can be treated superficially. The variations themselves can contribute to inductive reasoning. On its own this form of reasoning is unlikely to lead to higher levels of abstraction, and might lead to unexpected inductive generalizations, but might also lead to useful conjectures about dependency relationships. I have also given a demonstration that higher levels of abstraction can be achieved through controlled variation, when the relationships identified in one cycle of variation become themselves the variable objects for the next cycle. In all these observations, the invariant qualities are as important as the variations, either as background, or as limiting factors, or as the relations that are often the aim of learning mathematics.

REFERENCES

Al-Murani, T. (2006). Teachers' awareness of dimensions of variation: A mathematics intervention project. In J. Novotna (Ed.), *Proceedings of the 30th Conference of the International Group for the Psychology of Mathematics Education* (Vol. 2, pp. 25–32). Prague: Charles University.

Cai, J., & Nie, B. (2007). Problem solving in Chinese mathematics education: Research and practice. *ZDM-International Journal on Mathematics Education, 39*, 459–473.

Godfrey, C., & Siddons, A. W. (1915). *Elementary algebra volume Ll.* Cambridge: Cambridge University Press.

Gu, L., Huang, R., & Marton, F. (2004). Teaching with variation: An effective way of mathematics teaching in China. In L. Fan, N. Y. Wong, J. Cai, & S. Li (Eds.), *How Chinese learn mathematics: Perspectives from insiders* (pp. 309–348). Singapore: World Scientific.

Hewitt, D. (1998). Approaching arithmetic algebraically. *Mathematics Teaching, 163*, 19–29.

Huang, R., Mok, I., & Leung, F. (2006). Repetition or variation: Practising in the mathematics classrooms in China. In D. J. Clarke, C. Keitel, & Y. Shimizu (Eds.), *Mathematics classrooms in twelve countries: The insider's perspective* (pp. 263–274). Rotterdam: Sense Publishers.

Koichu, B. (2013). *Variation theory as a research tool for identifying learning in the design of tasks.* Retrieved August 8, 2014, from http://www.mathunion.org/icmi/digital-library/icmi-study-conferences/icmi-study-22-conference/

Koichu, B., Zaslavsky, O., & Dolev, L. (2013). Effects of variations in task design using different representations of mathematical objects on learning: A case of a sorting task. In C. Margolinas (Ed.), *Task design in mathematics education, Proceedings of the ICMI study 22* (pp. 467–476). Retrieved August 8, 2014, from http://hal.archives-ouvertes.fr/hal-00834054

Kullberg, A., Runesson, U., & Måtensson, P. (2013). The same task? – different learning possibilities. In C. Margolinas (Ed.), *Task design in mathematics education, Proceedings of the ICMI study 22* (pp. 615–622). Retrieved August 8, 2014, from http://hal.archives-ouvertes.fr/hal-00834054

Leung, A. (2008). Dragging in a dynamic geometry environment through the lens of variation. *International Journal of Computers for Mathematical Learning, 13*, 135–157.

Leung, A. (2011). An epistemic model of task design in dynamic geometry environment. *ZDM – The International Journal on Mathematics Education, 43*, 325–336.

Leung, A. (2013). *Thoughts on variation and mathematics task design.* Retrieved August 8, 2014, from http://www.mathunion.org/fileadmin/ICMI/files/Digital_Library/Studies/Thoughts_on_Variation_and_Mathematics_Pedagogy.pdf

Leung, A., & Lee, A. (2008, July). *Variational tasks in dynamic geometry environment.* Paper presented at the Topic Study Group 34: Research and development in task design and analysis ICME 11. Monterrey, Mexico.

Leung, A., Baccaglini-Frank, A., & Mariotti, M. A. (2013). Discernment in dynamic geometry environments. *Educational Studies in Mathematics, 84*, 439–460.

Margolinas, C. (Ed.). *Task design in mathematics education, Proceedings of the ICMI study 22.* Retrieved August 12, 2014, from http://hal.archives-ouvertes.fr/hal-00834054

Marton, F. (2015). *Necessary conditions of learning.* London: Routledge.

Marton, F., & Booth, S. A. (1997). *Learning and awareness.* London: Psychology Press.

Marton, F., & Pang, M. F. (2006). On some necessary conditions of learning. *The Journal of the Learning Science, 15*, 193–220.

Mason, J. (2000). Asking mathematical questions mathematically. *International Journal of Mathematical Education in Science and Technology, 31*(1), 97–111.

Mathematics Textbook Developer Group for Elementary School. (2005). *Mathematics.* Beijing: People's Education Press.

Michener, E. R. (1978). Understanding understanding mathematics. *Cognitive Science, 2*, 361–383.

MME, Midlands Mathematics Experiment. (1970). *CSE vol II part A.* London: Harrap.

Paterson, W. (1911). *School algebra.* Oxford: Clarendon Press.

Sun, X. (2011). Variation problems and their roles in the topic of fraction division in Chinese mathematics textbook examples. *Educational Studies in Mathematics, 76*, 65–85.

Sun, X. (2013). *The fundamental idea of mathematical tasks design in China: the origin and development.* Retrieved August 12, 2014, from http://www.mathunion.org/fileadmin/ICMI/files/chinese_variation_theory-final-short-final.pdf

Watson, A., & Mason, J. (2004). The exercise as mathematical object: Dimensions of possible variation in practice. In O. McNamara (Ed.), *Proceedings of 24th Conference of The British Society for Research into Learning Mathematics* (Vol. 2, pp. 107–112). London: British Society for Research into Learning Mathematics.

Watson, A., & Mason, J. (2006). Seeing an exercise as a single mathematical object: Using variation to structure sense-making. *Mathematical Thinking and Learning, 8*(2), 91–111.

Anne Watson
Department of Education
University of Oxford, UK

PART II

VARIATION AS A PEDAGOGICAL PERSPECTIVE FOR CLASSROOM INSTRUCTION IN CHINA

JOHN MASON

INTRODUCTION

Applying variation as an effective pedagogical tool can be traced back to a teaching experiment led by Gu in the 1980s in Shanghai, which was reported in the book *Learning to Teach* (Gu, 1991, see also Gu, 1994). Gu, Huang and Marton (2004) summarized a pedagogical theory of teaching with variation, distinguishing two types or uses of variation: *conceptual variation* and *procedural variation*. The essence of Gu's theory of teaching with variation is to "illustrate the essential features by demonstrating different forms of visual materials and instances or highlight the essence of a concept by varying the nonessential features" (Gu *et al.*, 2004, p. 315).

The chapters in this section provide examples of lessons involving topics in both algebra and geometry in order to illustrate and highlight different forms of variation, and different ways in which variation can inform pedagogical choices. In each case the authors set the lesson topic in a theoretical background drawing on both eastern and western sources. Each in their own way leads the reader to question whether distinctions between conceptual and procedural variation are useful theoretically, but most especially whether they are likely to be informative for teachers (see also Watson, 2017).

As I read and re-read these chapters, I became aware that variation in and of itself provides, in the words of Marton (2015), "what is available to be learned", but tells us nothing about what is actually learned. Several of the chapters are at pains to make connections between the pedagogic structure of the lesson and both learner proficiency and learner reflection on the lesson itself in order to demonstrate that students do in fact learn from the variation employed, whether in changing the context, the format, the representation, or significant mathematical parameters.

Beneath the surface of some of the reports, and partly explicitly in others, there lie subtle pedagogic choices, pedagogic actions to be enacted. Although these are strategies recognizable in many classrooms where effective teaching takes place, variation as an aide-memoir highlights their importance, and provides a frame for emphasizing them. I would like to call this *variation-pedagogy*.

Each of the chapters promotes particular distinctions, so it behooves the reader to use the examples provided to see if they recognize those distinctions in their own experience, and to consider whether there are useful pedagogic actions which might be associated with those distinctions so that recognizing such a distinction in the future, whether putatively when planning or in-the-moment while teaching, brings actions to the surface to be available to be enacted. This is an example of the use of

R. Huang & Y. Li (Eds.), Teaching and Learning Mathematics through Variation, 107–109.

the *discipline of noticing* (Mason 2002) through the education of awareness (Mason, 1998).

A significant feature worth attending to in these chapters is the habit of labeling things in order to aid discernment in multiple contexts. Teachers all over the world do it, but there is a particularly effective style of labeling and of making use of labels to direct attention which can be discerned in some of these chapters. The habit of labeling applies to pedagogical moves as well, as for example using the label *pudian* meaning foreshadowing and hence scaffolding. Labels assist by providing a vocabulary for discerning details and so sensitizing one to notice opportunities and possibilities, and for enabling meaningful discussion between colleagues, whether in a mathematical topic or in the pedagogical heart of a lesson (Mason, 1999).

In a preface such as this it is not appropriate to quote specific details from the different chapters, so instead I recommend to the reader, when reading the descriptions of variation-informed teaching in these chapters, to be on the look out for specific pedagogic moves or actions being enacted. I suggest that it is not enough to say "the teacher guided discussion", or "the teacher guided students to analyze", because these generalities miss the actual action and the lived experience of students, and it is in the lived experience of teachers and students that we will find actions that are supporting and exploiting the variation that is provided. I suggest that readers ask themselves questions such as

"What are students attending to at this point in the lesson?"

"How are they attending to it?" (see following questions)

"What is the teacher doing to direct student attention to this and directing students to attend in this way?"

"When is there time for students to dwell in gazing, in holding wholes, before being invited to shift their attention to details?"

"What are students being invited to discern at this point in the lesson?"

"What relationships are being recognized and stressed by the variation provided by the teacher at this point in the lesson?" (eg. relationships between (re)presentations, between varied examples or problems or exercises)

"What properties are students being invited to perceive as being instantiated at this point in the lesson?" (eg. what generalities are being called upon to be expressed and instantiated?)

"What properties are being called upon for acceptable reasoning in this part of the lesson?"

My questions are based on a framework that I find extremely useful when observing a lesson, whether as real-time observer or as researcher in working with video, audio or even field notes (Mason, 2003). Briefly, and in alignment both with van Hiele (van Hiele, 1986, see also van Hiele-Geldof, 1957), and with the SOLO taxonomy (Biggs & Collis, 1982), but unlike both in that levels are inappropriate because attention is like a humming bird. It can hover apparently stationary, and it can very quickly dart to a different place, taking a different form. It seems to me that attention can take various forms including holding wholes (gazing, before specific details are discerned); discerning details; recognizing relationships in a particular situation; perceiving properties as being instantiated in the particular; and reasoning on the basis of agreed properties. The idea is that if the teacher and students are not attending to the same 'thing', then communication between them is likely to be ineffective. But even when they are attending to the same aspect, they may be attending differently, and this too will make communication difficult.

In my commentary chapter I raise several questions about variation that might be worth pursuing so as to inform teachers' pedagogical choices and to enable detailed discussions between teachers. I then elaborate on the main thing which struck me in reading these chapters, namely that paying attention not only to what the teacher and students are attending to, but how they are attending to it could be helpful in elaborating pedagogic moves which may be necessary in order to exploit variation effectively in classrooms.

REFERENCES

Biggs, J., & Collis, K. (1982). *Evaluating the quality of learning: The SOLO taxonomy.* New York, NY: Academic Press.

Gu, L. (1991). *Xuehui Jiaoxue* [Learning to Teach]. Hubei: People's Press.

Gu, L. (1994). *Teaching experiment: Research on methodology and teaching principle in Qingpu experiment.* Beijing: Education Science Publisher.

Gu, L., Huang, R., & Marton, F. (2004). Teaching with variation: An effective way of mathematics teaching in China. In L. Fan, N. Y. Wong, J. Cai, & S. Li (Eds.), *How Chinese learn mathematics: Perspectives from insiders* (pp. 309–347). Singapore: World Scientific.

Marton, F. (2015). *Necessary conditions for learning.* Abingdon: Routledge.

Mason, J. (1998). Enabling teachers to be real teachers: Necessary levels of awareness and structure of attention. *Journal of Mathematics Teacher Education, 1,* 243–267.

Mason, J. (1999). The role of labels for experience in promoting learning from experience among teachers and students. In L. Burton (Ed.), *Learning mathematics: From hierarchies to networks* (pp. 187–208). London: Falmer.

Mason, J. (2002). *Researching your own practice: The discipline of noticing.* London: Routledge.

Mason, J. (2003). Structure of attention in the learning of mathematics. In J. Novotná (Ed.), *Proceedings of international symposium on elementary mathematics teaching* (pp. 9–16). Prague: Charles University.

van Hiele, P. (1986). *Structure and insight: A theory of mathematics education.* London, UK: Academic Press.

van Hiele-Geldof, D. (1957). The didactiques of geometry in the lowest class of secondary school. In D. Fuys, D. Geddes, & R. Tichler (Eds.), 1984. *English translation of selected writings of Dina van Hiele-Geldof and Pierre M. van Hiele.* Brooklyn, NY: National Science Foundation, Brooklyn College.

Watson, A. (2017). Variation: Analysing and designing tasks. *Mathematics Teaching, 252,* 13–17.

John Mason
Open University, UK

AIHUI PENG, JING LI, BIKAI NIE AND YANJIE LI

6. CHARACTERISTICS OF TEACHING
MATHEMATICAL PROBLEM SOLVING IN CHINA

Analysis of a Lesson from the Perspective of Variation

INTRODUCTION

Research over the past two decades has alluded that there are national patterns of mathematics teaching (Stigler & Hiebert, 1999). For example, Tweed and Lehman (2002) pointed out that there are distinctive features between Eastern and Western classrooms. Researchers have also found that there is evidence that teaching methods have evolved differently in particular countries. China appears to have developed a teaching approach that is different from Japan and Korea, though all three of them are rooted in the Confucian Heritage Culture (Givvin, Hiebert, Jacobs, Hollingsworth, & Gallimore, 2005; Park, 2006).

Recently, there has been increasing interest in uncovering the enigma of Chinese students' outstanding mathematics achievements in international studies (cf. OECD, 2010, 2013). Considerable research has focused on characteristics of mathematics education in China, and it is recognized that "teaching with variation" is a Chinese way of promoting effective mathematics learning (Gu, Huang, & Marton, 2004; Wong, 2014; Wong, Lam, Sun, & Chan, 2009). Teaching with variation has almost become the teaching routine for Chinese mathematics teachers (Marton, Runesson, & Tsui, 2004) and has been applied either consciously or intuitively for a long time in China (Li, Peng, & Song, 2011).

In addition, problem solving has long been a staple of school mathematics (Stanic & Kilpatrick, 1988). In China there is a long history of interest in integrating problem solving into school mathematics (Siu, 2004; Stanic & Kilpatrick, 1988), and this tradition extends to the present (Cai & Nie, 2007). The development of students' abilities to solve problems has remained one of the fundamental goals in school mathematics over the years. Problem solving is a distinctive mathematics activity from other mathematics learning areas such as mathematical concepts, algorithms, and theorems.

Researchers have identified some characteristics of teaching mathematical concepts from the pedagogy of variation in China. For instance, research shows that students are provided a series of problems in which essential features of mathematical concepts are kept unchanged, but the nonessential features of mathematical concepts are changed (Li et al., 2011). Huang and Leung (2004) found that teaching with

R. Huang & Y. Li (Eds.), Teaching and Learning Mathematics through Variation, 111–125.

variation helps learners acquire knowledge step-wise, progressively develop experience in problem solving, and form well-structured knowledge. However, it is not clear how problem solving is taught from the pedagogy of variation. Given the significance of problem solving in mathematics education, the lack of such studies will limit our understanding of the full picture of mathematics teaching in China. This chapter aims to fill in this gap and make such a contribution through analyzing a well-structured Chinese mathematics lesson on solving right triangles in ninth grade.

THEORETICAL FRAMEWORK

Gu (1994) stated that teaching with variation is an important method through which students can easily understand relevant mathematical concepts. Furthermore, it illustrates the essential features by using different forms of visual materials and sometimes highlighting the essence of a concept by changing the nonessential features. The aim of teaching with variation is to understand the essence of an object and to form a scientific concept by eliminating nonessential distractions. Based on a series of longitudinal mathematics teaching experiments in China, Gu (1994) systematically synthesized and analyzed the concepts of teaching with variation. He identified and illustrated the two forms of variation, namely "conceptual variation" and "procedural variation." Conceptual variation aims at providing students with multiple perspectives and experiences of mathematical concepts. Procedural variation aims to provide a process for the formation of concepts step-by-step so that students' experiences in solving problems are manifested by the richness of varying problems and the variety of transferring strategies (Gu et al., 2004).

In particular, Gu et al. (2004) identified the following three types of variation: (1) varying the conditions of a problem: extending the original problem by varying the conditions, changing the results, and generalization; (2) varying the processes of solving a problem: using different methods of solving a problem; and (3) varying the applications of a method: applying the same method to a group of similar problems. Likewise, Cai and Nie (2007) identified three types of variation problems in Chinese mathematics education practice: one problem with multiple solutions, multiple problems with one solution, and one problem with multiple changes.

More theoretically and fundamentally, the research from Marton and Pang (2006) and Marton and Tsui (2004) indicated the following points for the theory of variation: learning is a process in which learners develop a certain capability or a certain way of seeing or experiencing; in order to see something in a certain way, the learner must discern specific features of the object; and experiencing variation is essential for discernment and is thus significant for learning content. Marton et al. (2004) argued that it is important to attend to what varies and what is invariant in a learning situation.

Building on the ideas from Marton et al. (2004, 2006), Watson and Mason (2006) also argued that because some features of problems are invariant while others are changing, learners are able to see the general through the particular, to generalize,

112

and to experience the particular. As pointed out by Cai and Nie (2007), teaching with variation by presenting a series of interconnected problems could help students understand concepts and master problem-solving methods, thereby developing students' knowledge of mathematics.

In addition, Watson and Mason (2006) saw generalization as sensing the possible variation in a relationship and saw abstraction as shifting from seeing relationships as specific to the situation to seeing them as potential properties of similar situations.

In this study, we are going to analyze a lesson with the three key components of the theory of variation: invariant, varied, and discernment (Marton et al., 2004, 2006) and the three types of variations (Gu et al., 2004), as well as using "generalization" as a lens to check students' learning (Watson & Mason, 2006).

METHODS

The Considerations: Why This Study Chooses This Lesson

The data included in the current study is a videotaped lesson. The topic of the lesson is solving right triangles. It belongs to a chapter about trigonometric function of acute angles in ninth grade, which includes two sections. The first section presents the definitions of trigonometric functions of acute angles including sine, cosine, tangent, and the second section presents solving right triangles that are the main focus of the selected lesson. Prior to the lesson, students learned the Pythagorean theorem, the definition of trigonometric functions of acute angles, and the methods on how to find the side length or angles of right triangles.

The lesson chosen for this study is a typical Chinese lesson under the background of China's current mathematics curriculum reform. It includes six typical phases of the national pattern of teaching of a Chinese lesson (Peng, 2009). First, a context is set so as to lead to the mathematical problem that is going to be discussed in the lesson. Second, the new mathematical knowledge is introduced, on which the students are expected to collaboratively engage in inquiry-based learning. Third, a generalization is made. Fourth, students practice to enhance the new knowledge. Fifth, the students reflect what they have learned from the lesson. Sixthly, homework is assigned. The lesson lasts a total of forty-five minutes. Another reason to choose this lesson is that this lesson not only covers important content such as trigonometry, geometry, and algebra, but it also includes problem solving.

Data: The Lesson

The lesson was taught by Miss Li, a prospective teacher. She designed the lesson under the guidance of her teaching mentor in her university. She was in the last year of her 4-year bachelor degree program when she taught the lesson. It was enacted in a multimedia classroom with a projector, computer, and mathematical teaching materials including set squares and protractors. Teacher's lecturing, students' inquiry learning, and self-study form the main methods of teaching and learning during the lesson. Figure 1 shows the mathematics classroom where the teacher was discussing the problem with students.

Figure 1. The teacher was discussing solutions with students

Corresponding to the six phases, this lesson includes the following activities:

Activity 1: Introduction of the problem. The lesson began with an open question that asked, "How could you apply the knowledge of solving right triangles to solve real life problems?" Next, the teacher presented a real life problem situation on how to find the height of a broken tree (Figure 2), accompanied with five sets of

Data 1	the length between the treetop and tree root (4 meters)
Data 2	the angle between treetop and the ground (37°)
Data 3	the length between the treetop and tree root (4 meters)
	the length between the treetop and the ground (3 meters)
Data 4	the length between the treetop and tree root (4 meters)
	the angle between treetop and the ground (37°)
Data 5	the angle formed by the falling and the upright part (53°)
	the angle between treetop and the ground (37°)

Figure 2. A problem on how to find the length of a broken tree

different givens regarding the different components of the tree. This data consisted of the length between the treetop and tree root (4 meters), the angle between treetop (broken branch the tree) and the ground (37°), the length between the top of the broken tree (trunk) and the ground (3 meters), and the angle formed by the broken part and the upright part is 53 degrees. The question was: "Which set of data can be used to find the height of the broken tree?"

Activity 2: Analysis of the problem. The teacher guided students to analyze the problem and then introduced the topic of the lesson--"solving right triangles, the process of finding the unknown measurements by using given measurements in a right triangle." This analysis transferred the real life problem into a rigorous pure mathematical problem on how to solve a right triangle. The teacher re-stated the question: "Which of the five sets of data can be used to find the height of the broken tree?" The students were required to think about this question carefully and individually. After a while they were grouped to analyze the five sets of data under the knowledge framework of solving a right triangle and explored how to find the length of the tree by using the knowledge of solving right triangles. Figure 3 shows the visual representations of the five sets of data in right triangles, which were from students' group work. In the drawings 3a, 3b, and 3e, the three hypotenuses show students' different attempts. In Figure 3a, when only the length between the treetop and tree root (4 meters) is given, it is impossible to find original height of the broken tree. Corresponding to the situation in a right triangle, it means that, given the measure of one side, it is impossible to find the missing measurements. In Figure 3b, when only the angle between treetop and the ground (37°) is given, it is also impossible to find the length of the broken tree. Corresponding to the situation in a right triangle, it means that, given the measure of one angle, it is impossible to find the missing measurements. In Figure 3c, when both the length between the treetop and tree root (4 meters) and the length between the top of the broken tree and the ground (3 meters) are given, the length of the broken tree can be found. And it is $\sqrt{3^2 + 4^2} + 3 = 8$. Given the measures of two of the three sides, the missing measurements can be found using the Pythagorean theorem. In Figure 3d, when both the distance between the treetop and tree root (4 meters) and the angle between treetop and the ground (37°) are given, the length of the broken tree can be found: $\frac{4}{cos37°} + 4tan37° \approx 8$. Corresponding to the situation in a right triangle, it means that, given the measure of one side and one of the other two angles, the missing measurements can be found. In Figure 3e, when both the angle of the broken tree (53°) and the angle between treetop and the ground (37°) are given, it is impossible to find the length of the broken tree. Corresponding to the situation in a right triangle, it means that, given the measurements of two angles, it is impossible to find the missing measurements.

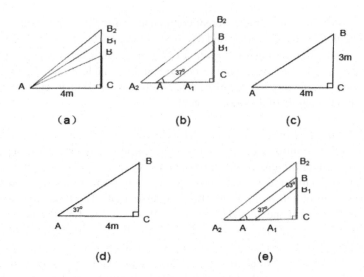

Figure 3. The visual representations of the five sets of data in right triangles

Activity 3: Generalization of problem solving. Students and the teacher generalized the conclusion about how to solve right triangles (Figure 4) together. The teacher stated: "One of the most important applications of trigonometry is to 'solve' a right triangle. By now, you should know that every right triangle has five measurements: the lengths of its three sides and the measures of its two acute angles. Solving a right triangle means to find the unknown measurements when some of them are given. You can use trigonometric functions to solve a right triangle if relevant information is provided. Is there anybody who wants to summarize which information is needed in order to solve a right triangle?" Students answered "the length of one side and the measure of one acute angle, or the lengths of two sides. Namely speaking, if we know the values of three out of the five elements of the right triangle (except the right angle, and at least one side must be included), we can find the values of the remaining elements using trigonometric ratios."

Activity 4: Application of learned knowledge to various situations related to the same problem. There are two examples of application of the problem. First is a pure mathematical problem on solving a right triangle as follows:

In *Rt*△ *ABC*, $\angle C = 90°$, if $a = \sqrt{6}$, $b = \sqrt{2}$, solve this right triangle.

The second example is based on the question posed by the teacher: "If the tree is not broken, how could you find the length of the tree?" Specifically, it states that Xiao Ming wants to know the length of a big tree, which grows vertically on the campus. He stands 10 meters away from a tree root, and the angle of elevation from his position to the tree top is 50° measured by goniometer. The distance between his eyes and the ground is 1.5 meters. The question is: can you find the height of the tree? Figure 4 illustrates the conditions of this problem. Students are divided into groups to discuss the problem and they reach an agreement that right triangles can be constructed in order to solve the problem. Students proposed some interesting solutions, which will be discussed in the next section on varying the methods of solving the problem.

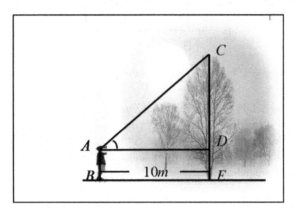

Figure 4. Visual representation of the second applied problem

The teacher encouraged students to find multiple ways to solve it. Below are two examples of students' strategies.

Student 1: "I draw a diagram according to the problem (as shown in Figure 5). And I find that there is a segment AD when point A and D are connected, and there is a right triangle ADC. Naturally, using the knowledge of solving a right triangle I can solve the problem."

In $Rt\triangle ADC$, $\angle CAD = 50°$, $AD = BF = 10m$.

Since $CD = AD \times tan50° \approx 10m \times 1.192 = 11.92m$, $AB = DF = 1.5m$,

We get the height of tree: $CF = DF + CD = 1.5m + 11.92m = 13.42m$.

Student 2: "We can construct right triangles to solve the problem. Extend segment CA and intersect the extension line of FB at point E, and there will be a triangle CEF. Since the length of segment AB is known, the right triangle AEB can be easily solved, and then the right triangle CEF can be solved (See Figure 5). In this way, the length of the tree can be found."

Here is the student's solution:

$$In\, Rt\triangle ABE,\, AB = 1.5m,\, \angle AEB = 50°,\, EB = \frac{AB}{tan50°} \approx \frac{1.5}{1.192} \approx 1.258$$

$$In\, Rt\triangle CEF,\, EF = EB + BF = 1.258 + 10 = 11.258.$$

$$CF = EF \cdot tan50° \approx 11.258 \times 1.192 \approx 13.419 \approx 13.42$$

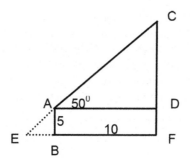

Figure 5. Student's drawing to the second applied problem

We get that the height of the tree is 13.42*m*.

Students then were divided into groups to discuss the multiple ways. With the teacher's guidance, the multiple ways are compared. And finally, the specific steps and key points on how to use the knowledge of solving a right triangle to solve applied problems are generalized.

Activity 5: Review the lesson and assign homework.   The teacher summarized the main contents of the lesson with the students. It included: (1) understanding what it means to solve a right triangle; (2) knowing that to solve a right triangle, at least one of the following two conditions are necessary: the length of one side and the measure of one acute angle, or the lengths of two sides; (3) using three tools for solving a right triangle: the trigonometric functions of acute angles, the Pythagorean Theorem, and the knowledge that the sum of the angles of a triangle is 180° (or the two acute angles are complementary, namely they add up to 90°); (4) being able to construct mathematical models and to solve simple practical problems by using knowledge regarding solving a right triangle.

Next, the teacher assigned two different types of tasks to the students. The first one is a basic task: In a right triangle ABC, angle A is 90°, solve the right triangle in terms of the given conditions as shown below:

1. if $a = 30$ and $b = 20$;
2. if angle B is 72° and b = 14.

The second one is an application task: Measure the height of the flagpole on campus with another classmate.

FINDINGS

By analyzing the activities implemented in this lesson, we have the following findings.

Varying the Conditions and Contexts of the Problems

As we see from the introduction and analysis of the problem from activities 1 and 2, the conditions of the problem are varied. In varying the different given measurements of right triangles, students understood the minimum conditions for solving right triangles, and thus understand the nature of solving right triangles. The visual representation of the five sets of data in right triangles drawn by students showed that students' mathematical reasoning contained higher order thinking skills and understanding of problem solving with close attention to angles between two segments and length between two points. By keeping the problem situation invariant while varying the given conditions and modeling with varying visual representations, the students could discern the object of learning. For different conditions in the case of the right triangle, the number of solutions could be zero, one, or multiple. Table 1 indicates the three components of the variations.

Table 1. Varying the conditions of the problem from activities 1 and 2

Invariant	Varied	Discernment
Context: the broken tree trunk	The types of conditions: side or angle	In what conditions, a right triangle is solvable
The quantities: the measures of sides and angles	The number of conditions	

From activity 4, we found that the teacher presented two examples by varying both the conditions and situations of the broken tree trunk problem. Table 2 shows the three components of the variations.

Table 2. Varying the conditions and situations of the problem

Invariant	Varied	Discernment
Right triangles	The conditions: sides and angles	Solving right triangles
	Contexts	

Generalization of Problem Solving

Generalization is the result or refinement of the discernment. In activity 3, by comparing what varied (different conditions provided by students) against what remains invariant (the same situation), the object of learning should be discerned. In a right triangle, different conditions (known sides or angles) resulted in different methods for solving the triangle (sometimes one solution, multiple solutions, or no solution). The students and the teacher generalized ideas about solving any right triangles in Figure 6:

a	b	c	$a^2+b^2=c^2$
$\angle A$	$\angle B$	$\angle C$	$\angle A+\angle B=90^\circ=\angle C$
$\sin A = \dfrac{a}{c}$ $\cos A = \dfrac{b}{c}$ $\tan A = \dfrac{a}{b}$	$\sin B = \dfrac{b}{c}$ $\cos B = \dfrac{a}{c}$ $\tan B = \dfrac{b}{a}$		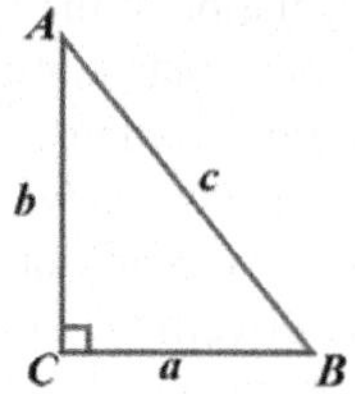 (right triangle ABC with right angle at C; sides b, c, a)

Figure 6. The summary and generalization of solving right triangles

Varying the Methods of Solving the Problem

In the studied lesson, the teacher adopted this form of variation to foster students' problem solving ability by varying the methods of solving a problem. The teacher encouraged students to find multiple ways to solve it. Specifically, two methods were used to solve the second application problem. Table 3 presents the three components of the variations.

Table 3. Varying the methods of solving the problem

Invariant	Varied	Discernment
Measures of sides or angles	Focused on different triangles by Constructing new triangles	The height of the tree
Tangent is used		The relationships between the quantities

DISCUSSION

Varying the Conditions and Contexts of the Problems

Varying the conditions of the given problem provides students with an opportunity to experience a way of mathematical thinking in which they investigate the cases from special to general, from which students can see and construct mathematical concepts (Watson & Mason, 2006). Varying the conditions of a given problem provides a systemic experience for students to understand why a problem could be solved with one or multiple solutions or a problem could be unsolvable (Gu et al., 2004).

By varying the conditions of the problem, the situation of the problem is simplified, structured, and made more precise so that the students would be able to easily understand the problem situation. This provides the foundational work for their problem solving (Gu et al., 2004).

Varying the context of problems means to change the contexts of problems while the mathematical essence of the problems remains similar. Gu et al. (2004) suggested that, during the process of solving problems, reorganizing separate but interrelated learning tasks as a group can provide a platform for learners to make connections between some interrelated concepts. In this sense, students are able to develop their experience in problem solving through "one problem with multiple changes" (Cai & Nie, 2007).

In the studied lesson, the teacher guided students to understand how to solve right triangles by creating related problems within different situations (both mathematical and contextual situations) and to apply the knowledge and strategies in different contexts.

From the application activities and the exercise assignment, we argue that varying the context of a problem can provide a scaffold for learners to make connections between relevant mathematical ideas; therefore, variation can enhance students' problem-solving ability. In this form of variation, it is the structure of the tasks as a whole that encourages mathematical sense making (Watson & Mason, 2006).

Generalization

In this study, the teacher guided students to summarize the general rules of solving right triangles. The actual solution will depend on the specific problem, but the three tools are always used: the trigonometric functions, the Pythagorean theorem, the theorem that the sum of the angles of a triangle is 180°. There is not necessarily a "right" way to solve a right triangle. One way that is usually "wrong," however, is solving for an angle or side in the first step, approximating that measurement, and then using that approximation to finish solving the triangle. This approximation will lead to inaccurate answers. As we can see from above, the varied conditions of the problem increases the complexity and cognitive requirements of problem solving, which helps students to understand the nature of solving a right triangle. Watson and Mason (2006) argued that generalizations created by students can become tools for developing more sophisticated mathematics and are a significant component of their mathematical progress.

Varying the Methods of Solving the Problem

Gu et al. (2004) stated that students' experience in solving problems is manifested by the variety of transferring strategies. In the studied lesson, the teacher adopted this form of variation by varying the method of solving the problem in order to foster students' problem solving ability.

The lesson was successful in the sense that students obtained good learning results with a high average score, 91 out of 100, on the test. The teacher designed the test to assess student understanding and application of solving right triangles. That showed they had reached the target learning objectives including basic knowledge and skills for solving a right triangle. The assessment teacher group in the school gave good evaluations, such as "the teaching activities aroused students' thinking" and "discussing the problems together was very helpful for students understanding and solving the problems."

Our data show that in teaching problem solving, this form of variation provides an illustration of the way in which multiple methods to approach the same task can promote deep understanding. In summary, this variation offers a structured approach to exposing underlying mathematical forms, which can enhance students' conceptual understanding of a series of related concepts (Lai & Murray, 2012).

FURTHER CONSIDERATIONS AND SUGGESTIONS

Characteristics of Teaching Problem Solving from a Variation Theoretical Perspective

From the perspective of variation, during the instruction of mathematical concepts students are provided a series of problems in which essential features of mathematical concepts are kept unchanged while the nonessential features of mathematical concepts are changed (Li et al., 2011). By doing this students are provided with multiple perspectives and experiences of mathematical concepts (Gu et al., 2004). Lesh and Zawojewski (2007) argued that problem solving is a learning activity that is more complex than the learning of mathematical concepts. It requires the problem solver to interpret a situation mathematically. The interpretation usually involves progression through iterative cycles of describing, testing, and revising ideas as well as identifying, integrating, modifying, or refining sets of mathematical concepts drawn from various sources. Through varying the conditions, contexts, and methods of solving the problem, the essential features of problem solving are highlighted. Students experience the process of problem solving, thus deepening their understanding and enhancing their ability.

Theoretically teaching with variation makes sense to foster students' learning and problem solving ability, but it lacks enough empirical studies to verify it (Cai & Nie, 2007). Though our current study is just a case-based study, the fine-grained analysis provides solid evidence to confirm, "students' experience in solving problems is manifested by the richness of varying problems and the variety of transferring strategies" (Gu et al., 2004, p. 322). Therefore the variations of problems help students make meaningful connections. Furthermore, our study has added new knowledge in this aspect by identifying the three types of variation for teaching mathematical problem solving and varying the conditions, contexts, and methods of solving the problem.

Researchers caution that teaching with variation does not necessarily lead to the development of basic skills. Sometimes, it can even limit the opportunities for fostering students' higher-order thinking skills. Thus, further research is needed to investigate ways to effectively teach with variation (Mok, Cai, & Fung, 2008).

Towards a Teaching of Problem Solving with a Balance of Content-Oriented and Contextualization Oriented Teaching

With an increasing emphasis being placed on the applications of mathematics in real-life situations, the priority of contextualization of problems in the interest of facilitating connections is generally recognized as the common trend in mathematics education in the West (Clarke, 2006; Sun, 2013). However, there are more mathematical problems in classrooms in Hong Kong, Japan, and Korea (high-achieving regions in mathematics), compared to counterparts in the West in TIMSS 1999 video study (Leung, 2005). This implies that emphasizing contextual problems in mathematics teaching alone does not necessarily lead to excellence in students' learning. One alternative may be making a balance between mathematical and contextual problems in mathematics teaching. To this end, teaching with variation may help us to make such a balance. As demonstrated in this study, the teacher presented variation problems with both contextual and mathematical situations for students to explore. This practice of teaching with variation in China may provide insights for mathematics educators in other cultures to reflect effective mathematics teaching.

CONCLUSIONS

Teaching with variation has been widely practiced in Chinese mathematics classrooms and is a teaching routine for Chinese mathematics teachers. The lesson featured in this study is a typical mathematics lesson in terms of teaching process and the use of variation. This study provides a vivid and concrete description of how teaching with variation was carried out in one type of lesson: teaching problem solving. Two types of variations are identified in our research, which may contribute to better understanding of teaching with variation in China. However, it is not our intent to generalize the findings to other lessons on problem solving in China.

ACKNOWLEDGEMENT

Research presented in this chapter was partially supported by funds from Chongqing Educational Research Institute and reciprocal learning in teacher education and school education between Canada and China (Grant 895-2012-1011).

REFERENCES

Cai, J., & Nie, B. (2007). Problem solving in Chinese mathematics education: Research and practice. *ZDM Mathematics Education, 39*, 459–475.

Clarke, D. J. (2006). Using international comparative research to contest prevalent positional dichotomies. *ZDM Mathematics Education, 38*, 376–387.

Givvin, K. B., Hiebert, J., Jacobs, J. K., Worth, H. H., & Gallimore, K. (2005). Are there national patterns of teaching? Evidence from the TIMSS 1999 Video Study. *Comparative Education Review, 49*(3), 311–343.

Gu, L. (1994). *Theory of teaching experiment: The methodology and teaching principle of Qinpu.* Beijing, China: Educational Science Press.

Gu, L., Huang, R., & Marton, F. (2004). Teaching with variation: A Chinese way of promoting effective mathematics learning. In L. Fan, N. Wong, J. Cai, & S. Li (Eds.), *How Chinese learn mathematics: Perspectives from insiders* (pp. 309–347). Mahwah, NJ: World Scientific.

Huang, R., & Leung, F. K. S. (2004). Cracking the paradox of the Chinese learners—Looking into the mathematics classrooms in Hong Kong and Shanghai. In L. Fan, N. Wong, J. Cai, & S. Li (Eds.), *How Chinese learn mathematics: Perspectives from insiders* (pp. 348–381). Mahwah, NJ: World Scientific.

Lai, M., & Murray, S. (2012, April). Teaching with procedural variation: A Chinese way of promoting deep understanding of mathematics. *International Journal for Mathematical Teaching and Learning,* 319–510.

Lesh, R., & Zawojewski, J. (2007). Problem solving and modeling. In F. K. Lester, Jr. (Ed.), *Second handbook of research on mathematics teaching and learning* (pp. 763–804). Charlotte, NC: Information Age Publishing.

Leung, F. K. S. (2005). Some characteristics of East Asian mathematics classrooms based on data from the TIMSS 1999 Video Study. *Educational Studies in Mathematics, 60*, 199–215.

Li, J., Peng, A., & Song, N. (2011). Teaching algebraic equations with variation in Chinese classroom. In J. Cai & E. Knuth (Eds.), *Early algebraization: A global dialogue from multiple perspectives* (pp. 529–556). New York, NY: Springer.

Marton, F., & Pang, M. (2006). On some necessary conditions of learning. *The Journal of the Learning Sciences, 15*, 193–220

Marton, F., Runesson, U., & Tsui, A. (2004). The space for learning. In F. Marton & A. Tsui (Eds.), *Classroom discourse and the space for learning* (pp. 3–40). Mahwah, NJ: Lawrence Erlbaum Associates Inc.

Mok, I. A. C., Cai, J., & Fung, A. F. (2008). Missing learning opportunities in classroom instruction: Evidence from an analysis of a well-structured lesson on comparing fractions. *The Mathematics Educator, 11*, 111–126.

OECD. (2010). *PISA 2009 results: Executive summary* Retrieved from http://www.oecd.org/pisa/pisaproducts/46619703.pdf

OECD. (2013). PISA 2012 results: *What students know and can do – Student performance in reading, mathematics and science* (Vol. I). Retrieved from https://www.oecd.org/pisa/keyfindings/pisa-2012-results-volume-i.htm

Park, K. (2006). Mathematics lessons in Korea: Teaching with systematic variation. *Tsukuba Journal of Educational Study in Mathematics, 25*, 151–167.

Peng, A. (2009). *Comparison of mathematics education in China and Sweden.* Presentation in the Umeå and Åbo Annual Seminar in Mathematics Education, Umeå, Sweden.

Siu, M. K. (2004). Official curriculum in mathematics in ancient China: How did candidates study for the examination? In L. Fan, N. –Y. Wong, J. Cai, & S. Li (Eds.), *How Chinese learn mathematics: Perspectives from insiders* (pp. 157–188). Mahwah, NJ: World Scientific.

Stanic, G. M. A., & Kilpatrick, J. (1988). Historical perspectives on problem solving in mathematics curriculum. In R. I. Charles & E. A. Silver (Eds.), *Research agenda for mathematics education: The teaching and assessing of mathematical problem solving* (pp. 1–22). Reston, VA: National Council of Teachers of Mathematics.

Stigler, J. W., & Hiebert, J. (1999). *The teaching gap: Best ideas from the world's teachers for improving in the classroom.* New York, NY: The Free Press.

Sun, X. (2013, February 6–10). *The structures, goals and pedagogies of "variation problems" in the topic of addition and subtraction of 0–9 in Chinese textbooks and reference books.* Paper presented at Eighth Congress of European Research in Mathematics Education, Analya, Turkey.

Tweed, R. G., & Lehman, D. R. (2002). Learning considered within a cultural context: Confucian and Socratic approaches. *American Psychologist, 57*(2), 89–99.

Watson, A., & Mason, J. (2006). Seeing an exercise as a single mathematical object: Using variation to structure sense-making. *Mathematical Thinking and Learning, 8*(2), 91–111.

Wong, N. Y., Lam, C. C., Sun, X., & Chan, A. M. Y. (2009). From "exploring the middle zone" to "constructing a bridge": Experimenting the spiral *bianshi* Mathematics curriculum. *International Journal of Science and Mathematics Education, 7,* 363–382.

Wong, Y. (2014). Teaching and learning mathematics in Chinese culture. In P. Andrews & T. Rowland (Eds.), *MasterClass in mathematics education: International perspectives on teaching and learning* (pp. 165–173). London: Bloomsbury Publishing.

Aihui Peng
Faculty of Education
Southwest University, China

Bikai Nie
Department of Mathematics
Texas State University, USA

Jing Li
School of Mathematics and Information
Langfang Teachers' College, China

Yanjie Li
New Century School
Handan, Hebei Province, China

CHUNXIA QI, RUILIN WANG, IDA AH CHEE MOK
AND DANTING HUANG

7. TEACHING THE FORMULA OF PERFECT SQUARE THROUGH *BIANSHI* TEACHING

INTRODUCTION

Pedagogy of variation has been in practice for a long time in China and can be dated back to Learning to Teach by Lingyuan Gu (Gu, 1994). Pedagogy of variation now has become a popular method in teaching mathematics in China. Many Chinese researchers have developed the application of the pedagogical model for different mathematical topics, and have provided enhancement for applying the pedagogical theory of variation in China. Therefore, it is fair to say that the Chinese Pedagogy of Variation[1] is an instructional model for designing a specific efficient learning path for students to understand a mathematical topic.

The objectives of this paper are: (i) to explain the Chinese Pedagogy of Variation via its application in the teaching of a lesson of the formula of perfect square; (ii) to provide empirical evidence of what students may have learned.

The study reported in this paper aimed to answer the question: Could an experimental lesson based on the application of the Chinese pedagogy of variation improve students' learning? We chose the topic of the formula of perfect square as the focus topic in the study. Why choose the formula of perfect square? Mathematical proposition, which comprises axioms, theorems, formulas etc., is very important in mathematics. Specifically, theorems and formulas are not only vital, but also challenging for students to learn. Some studies (Wu, 2006) have indicated that application of pedagogy of variations enables students to clarify the conditions and conclusions of theorems and formulas. Besides, pedagogy of variations provides assistance for students to understand the essence of theorems and formulas so that students' rigorous reasoning and computing abilities can be developed in mathematics learning (Yuan, 2006). Moreover, researchers have reported that eighth-grade students' intuitive understandings of multiplication are weaker than their understandings of addition (Dixon, Deets, & Bangert, 2001). The formula of perfect square, consisting of formula and multiplication of binomials, can be a difficult topic for students and is, therefore, a good platform for experimental teaching.

In the following sections of the chapter, we will first explain the Chinese pedagogy of variation to provide a theoretical background for the study, followed by research design of the study. Next, the analysis of the lesson and the students' learning

R. Huang & Y. Li (Eds.), Teaching and Learning Mathematics through Variation, 127–150.

outcomes will be reported. Finally, based on the findings of the experimental lesson, we argue that a successful mathematics lesson promoting mathematical thinking should go beyond a simple focus on variation and should make use of geometric intuition in exploration and problem solving, which strengthens the variation of mathematical thinking with an emphasis on the connection of knowledge.

LITERATURE AND THEORETICAL BACKGROUND

The Learning of Algebraic Expressions

Learning and teaching algebra has been under intensive research for decades and there are lots of literature reported (e.g., see Kieran, 1992, 2007). Kieran (2007) in a chapter in the Second Handbook of Research on Mathematics Teaching and Learning proposed four main sources of algebraic meaning. The focus of this chapter is about the teaching of an algebraic formula. Therefore, the discussion in this section will be based on two of the sources of meaning directly related to the topic, namely, the meaning from the algebraic structure involving the letter-symbolic form and the meaning from other mathematical representations.

A substantial part of activities in school algebra belongs to the category of "transformational activities" or "rule-based activities" including, for example, "collecting like terms, factoring, expanding, substituting one expression for another, exponentiation with polynomials, solving equations and inequalities, simplifying expressions, substituting numerical values into expressions, working with equivalent expressions and equations, and so on" (Kieran, 2007, p. 714). Despite the importance of these activities, some students inevitably find difficulties in the apprehension of their algebra classes (Kilpatrick, Swafford, & Findell, 2001) because there are five types of refocusing in developing students' algebraic thinking during the transition from arithmetic to algebra: a focus on relations instead of merely calculating a numerical answer, a focus on operations and the reverse operations, a focus on representing a problem in addition to solving it, a focus on number-letter expressions instead of numbers alone, and a refocus of the meaning of the equal sign (Kieran, 2004). Another important well-reported area is the difficulty in understanding algebraic expressions. In addition to the need for refocusing, there is the process-object dual meaning (Sfard, 1991), e.g., $x + 3$ can be an algebraic object of its own right as well as the process of adding 3 to the unknown x. Another obstacle is the parsing obstacle referring to reading an algebraic expression fully and in the right order, e.g., a student may make the mistake $12 - 5x = 7x$, $3 + x = 3x$ (Thomas & Tall, 2001). Common mistakes such as applying a rule to an inappropriate situation e.g., $(a + b)^2 = a^2 + b^2$ can sometimes be classified as inappropriate extrapolation (Matz, 1982; Mok, 2010).

One major competence in algebra relies on the fluency in manipulating the letter-symbolic forms or transforming an algebraic expression successfully into another algebraic expression that carries an equivalent meaning, for example,

$(a + b)^2 = (a + b)(a + b) = a^2 + 2ab + b^2$. An understanding of such transformation involves the understanding of the systemic meaning and the syntactic meaning of algebra expressions (Kieran, 1989). Systemic meaning refers to the algebraic properties governing the rules of the operations of addition and multiplication, e.g., the commutative property and the distributive property. Syntactic structure refers to correct rules of transforming the letter-symbolic strings between their equivalent forms. Specific to the latter, the appreciation of the equal sign and the meaning of equivalence are fundamental (Davis, 1975; Kieran, 1981; Linchevski & Vinner, 1990). Some researchers describe students' manipulation of algebraic expressions from the perspectives of perceptual recognition of forms. Kirshner (1987), while investigating elementary algebra errors, found that experts read the deep form when transforming an algebraic expression, e.g., $3x^2$ is interpreted as 3M[xE2] where M and E represent multiplication and exponentiation. Besides the difficulties in dealing with the syntax in formal algebra notations, Kaput (2007) argued that the lack of association between alternative representations such as tabular and graphical representations is another common student difficulty, hence promoting translations between mathematical representations for the purpose of building meaning (Kaput, 1989; Kieran, 2007).

Applying the Chinese Pedagogy of Variation to the Teaching of Formulas

The pedagogy of variation has been well used by many teachers for teaching mathematics since it was developed by Gu (Gu, 1994; Gu, Huang, & Marton, 2004). One of the major features in the pedagogy is to create experiences of variation of the mathematics objects so that students can learn the object in depth in an efficient way. According to Gu, Huang and Marton (2004), there are two important types of variation in application, namely the conceptual variation and procedural variation. Conceptual variation refers to understanding concepts from multiple perspectives, such as, using different visual and concrete examples, comparing with non-standard examples, and clarifying the connotation by non-concept variation. Procedural variation is progressively unfolding mathematics activities; that is, teaching process-oriented knowledge (how to do something) by enhancing the formation of concepts, experiencing (scaffolding) problem solving from simple problems to complicated problems, and establishing a system of mathematics experience so that the steps and strategies for transferring/exploring can be internalized. For the application of the pedagogy of variation in China, many variations in the types of problems have been developed (See Bao, Huang, Yi, & Gu, 2003a,b,c; Gu, Huang, & Marton, 2004, for details).

Specific to the teaching of formula, the authors of this chapter, based on the work of Gu, used two major categories of variation to help the teachers understand the application of theory of variation for the teaching of formula. They are explained below:

1. Variation in the style of examples or questions that includes:
   a. seeing the similarity in concrete examples (1a), and
   b. acquiring a deeper understanding in application (1b).
2. Variation in the way of recognizing the formula that includes:
   a. analyzing the relationship between formulas (2a), and
   b. recognizing the formula in multiple ways (2b).

When applying these concepts in the lesson design, there can be four types of variation:

1. contrast between examples and questions to see similarity and differences between the mathematical objects such as formula (type 1a);
2. applying the formula in a variety of problems and contexts to acquire a deeper understanding (type 1b);
3. analyzing different formulas to understand the relationship between formulas (type 2a);
4. recognizing the formula in multiple ways (type 2b).

Based on these ideas, 5 feasible learning steps were derived and applied in the planning the lesson (See figure 1). These steps were labeled as step 1 to step 5, noting that they do not need to be in a strict sequence.

- Step 1: contrast between examples and questions to see similarity and differences between the formula (type 1a);
- Step 2: analyze different formulas to understand the relationship between formulas (type 2a);

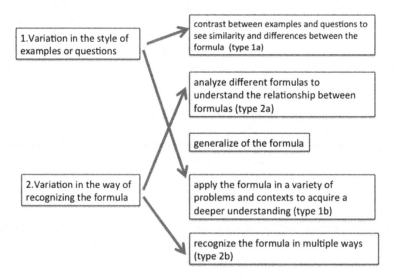

Figure 1. A framework for applying variation for the teaching of a formula

- Step 3: apply the formula in a variety of problems and contexts to acquire a deeper understanding (type 1b);
- Step 4: recognize the formula in multiple ways (type 2b);
- Step 5: generalize the formula.

Other Essential Factors in Planning an Effective Lesson

Furthermore, in the process of designing the experimental lesson, other important aspects were considered and they are as follows:

The nature of the mathematical content. The formula of perfect square is a topic for Numbers and Algebra and is about multiplication after the learning of multiplication of polynomials. Therefore, the students are expected to contrast the formula with the formula of the difference between two squares in order to derive the perfect square formula. The formula is a *Pudian*[2] for the learning of factorization in the future.

Analysis of the students' background includes the students' basic knowledge and the students' basic experience of activity in learning. With respect to basic knowledge, the students had already learned the concept of algebraic expression, addition and subtraction of algebraic expression, calculation involving indices, multiplication of algebraic expression, and the formula of difference between two squares. These topics provided the students with a foundation for the lesson. However, the students were anticipated to have difficulty in representing geometric figures and its area with algebra. In addition, though students might be good in perceptual recognition in applying the formula, some might make mistakes such as $(a + b)^2 = a^2 + b^2$ and $(a - b)^2 = a^2 - b^2$. They might have difficulty differentiating the meaning of sum and difference in the formulas. With respect to activity experience in learning, they had experienced activities of exploration and application for the topic of difference between two squares and should have a sense of the symbols and some ability to make generalizations.

The objectives of the lesson. The objectives of the lesson are (i) to deduce the formula of perfect square, to carry out calculation involving the formula, and to apply the formula for simple calculation and (ii) to advance the students' capacity of observing, comparing, discovering, and generalizing, and to experience the exploratory and creative nature of mathematics.

The analysis of the difficult parts and important parts of the topic. The important parts of the topic included: to deduce the formula of perfect square and to apply the formula for simple calculation. The difficult part was to understand the meaning of the letters in the formula.

Pedagogic strategy. Teaching would be carried by guiding questions. The lesson consisted of three phases: (i) discovering the formula; (ii) proving/justifying the formula; (iii) applying the formula. In addition, special reference to the application of geometric intuition was considered.

THE RESEARCH DESIGN

The experimental lessons took place in a middle school in Beijing. The chosen teacher had 14 years of teaching experience and was well informed by the pedagogy of variation. The teacher taught two 8th grade classes of different abilities. Class 1 had 38 students with average standard and Class 2 had 30 students with slightly poorer standard than Class 1.

Design of the Lesson

In the research experiment, the teaching design was based on the framework mentioned in a previous section. The research team has discussed the teaching design through three phases. The first phase focused on the nature of knowledge. The second phase focused on the Chinese pattern of variation. The last phase focused on the time arrangement. The researchers and the teacher cooperated closely on lesson preparation so that the intervention was carefully carried out. A summary of the lesson plan is given in Appendix 1.

Data Collection and Analysis

Collection of data. The researchers videotaped the two lessons in class 1 and class 2. At the end of the lessons, the students were invited to write their reflections and feedback, and they were asked to complete a 10-minute post-lesson test, which consisted of seven questions to assess students' understanding of the topic (See Appendix B).

Analysis of the data. The videotaped lessons were transcribed verbatim. The major features of the lesson are analyzed based on the framework (four types of variations). Students' work was analyzed in terms of the correctness and types of errors.

RESULTS

Analysis of the Lesson

The lesson includes three stages focusing on discovering, justifying, and applying the formula. The teacher implemented the variation pedagogy purposefully in this lesson. She guided students to grasp the formula step-by-step, making the students' experience the whole process. In order to show the variation process and students' responses, the analysis of the interaction between teacher (T) and students (S) is presented below into three parts according to the three stages in the lesson.

1. *Discovering the formula*

Episode 1:

[1] T – Earlier we learned polynomial multiplied by polynomial. Let's take a few practices and review.
1. $(m + n)(p + q)$
2. $(p + 1)^2$
3. $(m + 3)^2$
4. $(a + b)^2$

[2] S1 – Every term of the first polynomial multiplies each term of the second polynomial, and then add together.

(The students gave the expansion of the expressions orally. They obtained 4 equations:

$(m + n)(p + q) = mp + mq + np + nq$
$(p + 1)^2 = (p + 1)(p + 1) = p^2 + 2p + 1$
$(m + 3)^2 = (m + 3)(m + 3) = m^2 + 6m + 9$
$(a + b)^2 = (a + b)(a + b) = a^2 + 2ab + b^2)$

[3] T – Compare this observation with the characteristics of the four equations. Do you have any discoveries?

[4] T – If you want to classify, how many categories do you put the four equations into?

[5] S2 – Two.

[6] T – Question 1 is an ordinary polynomial multiplication, and followings are the multiplication of same polynomials, then we have a polynomial squared, is that right? OK, is that all?

[7] T – Well, the different left forms make differences in the results on the right side. Why do all the results consist of three terms?

(The students thought about it independently)

[8] T – This is an ordinary polynomial multiplication, so we got this result. Now according to the algorithm of polynomial multiplication rules: multiplying p by p, and multiplying 1 by 1 respectively, and we got p^2 and 1^2. Then, combining $p \times 1$ and $1 \times p$ will get…?

[9] S3 – collectively got 2p.

[10] T – Good, through this example we could consider the square of a polynomial as a special case of polynomial multiplication. Because of the special form on the left side, the result is special, too. They can be merged into three terms.

Analysis. In this episode, the teacher presented four problems in [1]. Students got familiar with the expansion and the forms of the formula step-by-step [1 to 2]. The teacher and students made a contrast between expressions/formulas with the form $(m + n)(p + q)$ and the form $(p + 1)^2$. By comparing the appearance, students easily discovered that there were 2 categories [3–5]. They were able to contrast between examples for observing similarities and differences between the formulas (type 1a variation). Next, with guidance from the teacher, students were asked to analyze the following two questions: "What are the differences among the four problems?" and "What causes these differences?" [6–7] The first question asked for "what" and the second question in fact asked for "why". These what-and-why questions were raised simultaneously, emphasizing the request for the explanation for the observed differences. These questions turned out to be the key elements in stimulating a deep approach in analyzing different formulas to understand the relationship between formulas (type 2a variation). In the teacher's explication and the student's response [8–9], the anticipated reason required the students to see the difference and the feasibility of collecting like terms in the expansions:

$$mp + mq + np + nq \text{ and } p^2 + p \times 1 + 1 \times p + 1$$

The episode ended with the teacher making a statement of generalization. [10]

Episode 2

[11] T – What's the result of $(a - b)^2$? How did you get this? What is the base on which the formula is derived?

[12] S4: It can be worked out the same way as the last one, it is $(a - b) \cdot (a - b)$ actually, so we can get it.

[13] S5: There is another way to get this. We can think of $(a - b)^2$ as $[a + (-b)]^2$, then use the result of No.4 example.

[14] T – Excellent! Although this is a small change, it reflects her (S5) understanding of the problem. We have replaced b with $-b$ so that we also have to replace b with $-b$ on the right side. Therefore $(-b)^2 = b^2$ and $+ 2ab$ changed to $-2ab$. Well done. That is a substitution. On the one hand, we can use the polynomial multiplication. On the other hand, we can consider $a - b$ as $a + (-b)$. These two ways make sure that we have got the correct answer. By the way, by multiplying two identical polynomials, the result can be solved directly. And this formula is called the Perfect Square Trinomials.

Analysis. In this segment of class discourse, the teacher again posed the questions containing the key elements (what-and-why) in guiding the students to observe, in a deep approach, the variation between examples:

$$(a + b)^2 \text{ and } (a - b)^2$$

Students discussed another form of the multiplication formula, $(a - b)^2$, and saw $(a + (-b))^2$ as an alternative form of $(a - b)^2$, and referred to two ways of getting the formula $(a - b)(a - b)$ an application of question 4, i.e. $(a + b)^2$. [12–13] Then the teacher drew the conclusion and generalized the idea of "Perfect Square Trinomials". [14] In fact, this exemplifies at least four of the five steps:

- analyzing different formulas $[(a + b)^2$ and $(a - b)^2]$ to understand the relationship between formulas (type 2a);
- applying the formula $(a - b)^2 = (a + (-b))^2$ in another case to acquire a deeper understanding (type 1b);
- recognizing the formula in two ways: $[(a - b)^2 = (a + (-b))^2$ and $(a - b)^2 = (a - b)(a - b)]$ (type 2b).
- generalizing the formula.

2. Justifying the formula

After discovering the formula of perfect square, the students are led to justify the formula from multiple perspectives.

Episode 3

[15] T – It is so general that we can directly apply this formula into the following calculation. $(a \pm b)^2 = a^2 \pm 2ab + b^2$ means that the square of sum or difference [of two terms] equals to sum of each term squared plus or minus 2 times of the product of the two terms.

[16] T – Since it is a special formula, we have to find out the characteristics of that. It is easy to see that the left side is a square of a polynomial. Can you find out the characteristics of the right side?

[17] S6 – There are 3 terms.

[18] S7 – It's quadratic trinomial.

[19] T – What degree is this polynomial? Here is the sum of a^2 and b^2, and here is two times the product of the terms. Which one is consistent with sign in front of the cross term (referring to 2ab)? It is the sign in front of b, isn't it?

[20] S8 – It is consistent with the sign in front of b.

[21] S9 – Look at $(a \pm b)^2 = a^2 \pm 2ab + b^2$, if the left sign is '+' there is '+2ab'. If not, there is '−2ab' then.

[22] T – Right! In order to memorize it easily, we can summarize it into simple way: [adding] first and last term squared, put 2 times product [of the terms] in the middle. According to Commutative Law of Addition, 2ab or −2ab also can put in any place.

[23] T – As a formula, it is general and representative. For example, I'm going to change a to x, b to 2y. It is $(x + 2y)^2$. Right now, can you orally answer it?

[24] S10 – $x^2 + 4xy + 4y^2$.

[25] T – a and b can represent numbers, monomials. Is there any other choice?

[26] S(all) – Polynomials.

[27] T – Correct. It can represent many things, such as integral expression and fraction. a and b are general and representative in the formula.

Analysis. In this episode, the teacher led students to observe the characteristics of the form of the formula $(a \pm b)^2 = a^2 \pm 2ab + b^2$. The characteristics included the three terms $(a^2, \pm 2ab, b^2)$ making a perfect square trinomial, the $\pm$ sign in front of ab. Apparently it seems to be observing and memorization. Nonetheless, mathematically $a^2 \pm 2ab + b^2$ represents two formulas $a^2 + 2ab + b^2$ and $a^2 - 2ab + b^2$, hence the students were comparing two formulas for the similarity to make a generalization and the generalization was justified or proved by the actual expansion of $(a \pm b)(a \pm b)$ [15–22]. The next example was an application of the formula by replacing a by x, b by 2y, forming $(x + 2y)^2$. [23–27] The example played a dual role. On the one hand, it was an application of the formula $(a \pm b)^2 = a^2 \pm 2ab + b^2$. On the other hand, the experience provided a contrast between $(a \pm b)^2 = a^2 \pm 2ab + b^2$ and $(x + 2y)^2 = x^2 + 4xy + 4y^2$, to provide a deeper understanding between formulas. Although it was only one single case of type 2a variation and was difficult to generalize, it could be seen as a kind of *Pudian* for phase 3 of the lesson which consisted of more applications.

Episode 4
[28] T – From the view of Algebra, we got two formulas according to the Law of the Polynomial Multiplication. Then we need to think about this: what did you recall in Geometry when you saw a^2, b^2 and $(a + b)^2$?
[29] S11 – is the area of a square with side a, and is the area of a square with side b.
[30] T – Let's try to explain the Perfect Square Trinomials from this point. Here we go. Please try to draw down it on paper.
(students' work for five minutes)
[31] S12 – I make a square whose length is $a + b$ with two small square and two congruent rectangle in it. Their areas are a^2, b^2 and ab. So the big square's area is $a^2 + b^2 + 2ab = (a + b)^2$.

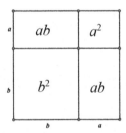

Figure 2. Decomposition of a square-method 1

[32] S13 – I've got a different way. The difference between these two ways is that the little squares and rectangles are located differently.
[33] S14 – Next, $(a - b)^2 = a^2 - 2ab + b^2$. (see Figure 4) I use a square with side $a - b$, $s_1 = s_2 = (a - b)b$. Then the big square's area is $a^2 = (a - b)^2 + b^2 + 2b(a - b)$. That is $(a - b)^2 = a^2 + b^2 + 2ab$.

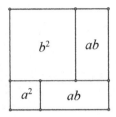

Figure 3. Decomposition of square – method 2

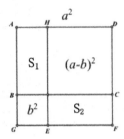

Figure 4. Decomposition of a square – method 3

[34] S15 – (see Figure 3). Since $S_{AGEH} = S_{BGFC} = ab$, then, the area of the middle square could be expressed as $a^2 - 2ab$ plus b^2 because when subtracting $2ab$, actually you subtract an extra b^2 which should be added back.

[35] T – Good. This way makes it easier. $(a - b)^2 + (S_1 + b^2) + (S_2 + b^2) - b^2 = a^2$. We have added b^2 twice so we should subtract it.

Analysis. In this episode, the teacher guided the students to explore the geometric representation of the formula, namely, the decomposition of a square to smaller squares with area a squared and b squared, and 2 rectangles of area ab. In this episode, the students participated in an activity to see whether they could recognize with justification the formula in the context of geometry [type 2b]. With a brief initial instruction [28–30], the students were given the opportunities to explore different ways to represent the formula with geometric figures, i.e., they could draw their own square with their own choice of partition (Figure 2 and Figure 3) and label the side of the square (Figure 2 and Figure 4). [31–35] Hence, in the context of geometric representation, the students explored different application of the formula to different figures (Figure 2 and Figure 3) and different formulas to the same figure (Figure 2 and Figure 4) [type 1b]. Reversely, the different partitions gave different ways of recognizing the formula with justification [type 2b].

Episode 5

[36] T – Let's go back to the formula, $(a - b)^2$ and $(a + b)^2$. We can change the sign of b, can we change the sign on a?

137

[37] S16 – $(-a - b)^2 = (a + b)^2$.

[38] S17 – $(-a + b)^2 = (b - a)^2$, same as $(a - b)^2$,

[39] S18 – $(-a + b)$ is the opposite of $(a - b)$. After squared the result is as same as $(a - b)$.

[40] T – Putting all this together, we can find out that because of the different combination of signs, there are four combinations. The way of transformation will depend on your understanding. Although they seem different, actually they are the same.

Analysis. In this episode, the teacher returned to the context of formula and put focus on the changing of the signs in front of a and b, hence, giving further experience of application of the formula [type 1b].

3. Applying the formulas
Episode 6

[41] T – Let's do some practice.

Case 1: use the Perfect Square Trinomials to calculate.

  1. $(4m + 3)^2$

[42] T – Which one is a? Which one is b?

Solution: According to $(a + b)^2 = a^2 + 2ab + b^2$,

$(4m + 3)^2 = (4m)^2 + 2 \times (4m) \times 3 + 3^2 = 16\,m^2 + 24m + 9$.

  2. $(x - 2y)^2$

[43] T – Which one is a? Which one is b?

Solution: According to $(a - b)^2 = a^2 - 2ab + b^2$,

$(x - 2y)^2 = x^2 - 2x(2y) + (2y)^2 = x^2 - 4xy + 4y^2$.

[44] Case 2: calculation.

  1. 102^2

  2. 99^2

(It's very easy for students to solve it.)

Solution:

  (1) $102^2 = (100 + 2)^2 = 10000 + 400 + 4 = 10404$.

  (2) $99^2 = (100 - 1)^2 = 10000 - 200 + 1 = 9801$.

[45] T – Sometimes use Perfect Square Trinomials can make certain operations simple.

[46] Case 3: calculation.

  1. $(4x + 5)^2$

  2. $(mn - a)^2$

  3. $(-2x - 3y)^2$

  4. $\left(x - \dfrac{1}{2}y^2\right)^2$

Solution:

$(4x + 5)^2 = 16x^2 + 40x + 25.$

$(mn - a)^2 = m^2n^2 - 2mna + a^2.$

$(-2x - 3y)^2 = 4x^2 + 12xy + 9y^2.$

[47] T – To avoid mistakes we can take as to calculate.

$$(x - \frac{1}{2}y^2)^2 = x^2 - 2x \times \frac{1}{2}y^2 + \left(\frac{1}{2}y^2\right)^2 = x^2 - xy + \frac{1}{4}y^4$$

[48] T – $\frac{1}{2}y^2$ is a one term in the polynomial and it replaces b in the Complete Square Formula.

[49] Case 4: calculation.

    1. $(a^2 + b^2)^2$

    2. $(a^n - b^n)^2$

    $(a^2 + b^2)^2 = a^4 + 2a^2b^2 + b^4.$

    $(a^n - b^n)^2 = a^{2n} - 2a^nb^n + b^{2n}.$

[50] T – The base becomes another form, but the key is to recognize which one is the "a".

[51] T – OK, let's move on. Everybody write two Perfect square trinomials on this paper and swap it. Then solve your partner's problems, and decide if it is right. Don't be too hard.

(students' seat work)

(Some students tried to construct difficult problems.)

[52] (two students show us)

$$\left(a^{100} + b^{100}\right)^2 = a^{200} + 2a^{100}b^{100} + b^{200}$$

$$\left(\frac{1}{4}m^n - \frac{1}{2}n^m\right)^2 = \frac{1}{16}m^{2n} - \frac{1}{4}m^nn^m + \frac{1}{4}n^{2m}$$

[53] T – a can be monomials or polynomials. That will generate a lot of questions, and we need pay attention to which one is a or b when we apply the formula. There is one case raised by someone, $(a + b - 3)^2$. Let's think about it, what will happen if it's a polynomial, and which one would you chose to become a polynomial between a and b?

[54] S19 – I combine a + b as a, 3 as b. $(a + b - 3)^2 = [(a + b) - 3]^2.$

[55] T – Let's do the addition one:

$[(a + b) + c]^2 = (a + b + c)^2 = (a + b)^2 + 2(a + b)c + c^2 = a^2 + 2ab + b^2 + 2ac$
$+ 2bc + c^2 = a^2 + b^2 + c^2 + 2ab + 2ac + 2bc$

This formula contains a sum of three squares and product of each two pairs from a, b, and c. Basic formula of Perfect Square Trinomials facilitate the calculation on this.

[56] T – We just explained Perfect Square Trinomials by the area of square visually. What about using the graph to represent it?

[56] S20 – [see Figure 5]

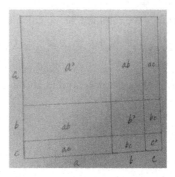

Figure 5. Expansion of the formula 1

[58] S21 – [see Figure 6]

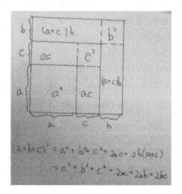

Figure 6. Expansion of the formula 2

[59] T – Can we conjecture the result of $(a + b + c + d)^2$? How to represent by graph? You can find it out after class.

Analysis.   This episode was about practicing application of the formula in different questions [type 1b]. It provided consolidation and deeper understanding of the formula via practice with different questions. The questions varied in complexity and difficulty depending on the use of ± sign, index, and fractions. The difficulty of the four problems increased gradually. The purpose of the first question [41] was to consolidate the formula. The second problem [44] was meant to apply the formula into simple calculation. In the third problem [46], letters in the formula can represent different monomials. The fourth

140

question [49] showed that the letters of formulas can express monomials with high index. Next, the teacher let students construct their own problems which can be solved by this formula, which aims at understanding that the letters in the formula can be replaced by monomials, polynomials etc. [51]. Then the teacher asked a further question: "in addition to representing numbers and monomials with lower or higher power and so on, can it also represent a polynomial [53]?" This leads to the question [54]. First, the teacher generalized the question to show the sum square of multiple items with letters [55]. Next the teacher modelled the idea just learned to understand the multiplication graphically [56]. Finally, further expansion was given [59]. Through these practices, the students were expected to learn more about the relationship between variations of the formula [type 2a], and applying and recognizing the formula in algebraic expressions of different complexity [type 1b and 2b]

What the Students Learned

The students' learning outcomes were analyzed in 2 parts: (i) the students' achievement based on their performance of the post-lesson test (appendix 2); (ii) the students' post-lesson written reflection.

Students' achievements
Students in class 1 and class 2 took a post-lesson test based on the objectives of the lesson. The test consisted of questions about the formula of perfect square.

The Question $(a + b)^2 - (a - b)^2$
In question 3, students needed to understand how to use the formula of perfect square trinomials and the formula of the difference of two squares. All the students in Class 1 gave the right answer and 76.7% students in Class 2 gave the right answer (see Table 1). Two students made errors on the formula of perfect square. Their answers are shown in Figure 7.

Table 1. Comparison between Class 1 and Class 2 for the question

Type	Class1		Class2	
	No. of students	%	No. of students	%
Right answer	38	100.0	23	76.7
Error occurred on expanding the bracket	0	0.0	2	6.7
Error occurred on the difference of two squares formula	0	0.0	1	3.3
Error occurred on formula of perfect square trinomials	0	0.0	2	3.3
Other error	0	0.0	2	10.0

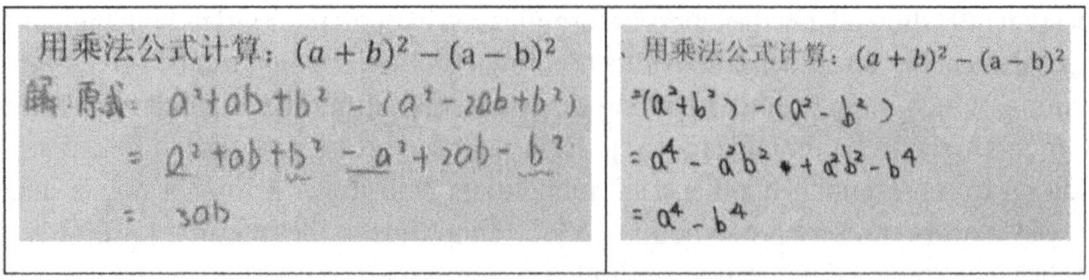

用乘法公式计算: $(a+b)^2 - (a-b)^2$
解 原式: $a^2+ab+b^2 - (a^2-2ab+b^2)$
$= a^2+ab+b^2 - a^2+2ab - b^2$
$= 3ab$

用乘法公式计算: $(a+b)^2 - (a-b)^2$
$= (a^2+b^2) - (a^2-b^2)$
$= a^4 - a^2b^2 + a^2b^2 - b^4$
$= a^4 - b^4$

Figure 7. Students' wrong answers in Class 2

The Question: Mary wrote $(a+b)^2 = a^2 + b^2$. Please use geometric figures to analyze whether her idea is correct or not?

The analysis of the students' performance is given in Table 2. For this question, the students in both classes sketched a graph to illustrate. Some of the students showed a correct geometric representation for the formula, such as in Figure 8, while a few students could not show a correct geometric representation, such as in Figure 9.

Table 2. Comparison between Class 1 and Class 2 for their performance for the question of analyzing with geometric figures

Type	Class 1		Class 2	
	No. of students	%	No. of students	%
Blank	0	0.0	2	6.7
Right answer	37	97.4	26	86.7
Error occurred on the formula	1	2.6	1	3.3
Error occurred on the diagram	0	0.0	1	3.3

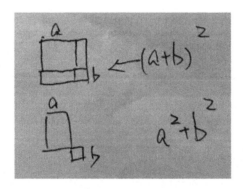

Figure 8. An example of a student's correct answer in Class 1

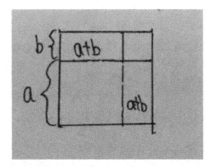

Figure 9. An example of a student's wrong answer in Class 2

Students' reflection on their learning. Analysis of the students' post-lesson written reflections shows that there were four themes:

1. Using geometric methods to prove the formula;
2. Other formulas were derived from perfect square trinomials;
3. The formula was easy to use for simplifying calculation;
4. Understanding from algebraic and geometric perspectives.

In class 1, 26.8% of the students mentioned the use of geometric methods to prove the formula; 22% of the students mentioned understanding from algebraic and geometric perspectives. Many students admitted that they were interested in the process of learning perfect square trinomials step-by-step. In their opinions, this lesson not only provided them opportunities to extend beyond the basics to become aware of the formula algebraically and geometrically and enrich their understanding, but it also broadened their horizon and enriched their knowledge of mathematics. Some examples of students' reflections are shown in figures 10 through 13. Figure 10 shows a student's reflection which consists two points: (i) "it is possible to justify the formulas by drawing geometric figures; (ii) a–b can be substituted by a + (–b), so the formula $(a - b)^2$ can be converted to $(a + b)^2$" (Theme 1). In Figure 11, the student emphasized the connections between formula of perfect square trinomials and several variations (Theme 2). In Figure 12, the student said that the formula could simplify the expression, saving a lot time for convenience (Theme 3). In Figure 13, the student described two ways of explaining a formula, the algebraic and geometric perspectives (Theme 4).

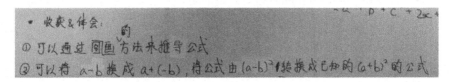

Figure 10. A student's reflection in Theme 1

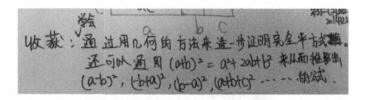

Figure 11. A student's reflection in Theme 2

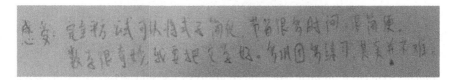

Figure 12. A student's reflection in Theme 3

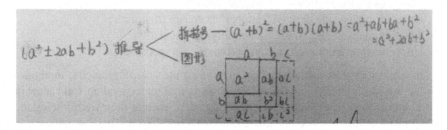

Figure 13. A student's reflection in Theme 4

CONCLUSION

The conclusion of the teaching experiment with respect to students' learning outcomes can be summarized below:

1. Students did well in applying formulas in calculation and demonstrated good computing skills.
2. Some students focused on memorizing the formulas but ignored the deduction and understanding of the formulas.
3. By constructing geometric figures, students demonstrated an alternative understanding of the formula of perfect square.
4. It's harder to explain $(a - b)^2 = a^2 - 2ab + b^2$ by graph than that of $(a + b)^2 = a^2 + 2ab + b^2$.
5. The test data shows that the lower achieving students have less comprehension on variation than higher academic performance students.

With respect to the pedagogy of variation for teaching the formula, the experiment has shown that skillful planning to use the four types of variation can bring about an effective lesson. This may also generalize to the teaching of other algebra topics of similar nature. The four types of variations are recapitulated here:

1. Contrast between examples and questions to see similarities and differences between the mathematical objects such as formulas (type 1a);
2. Apply the formula in a variety of problems and contexts to acquire a deeper understanding (type 1b);
3. Analyze different formulas to understand the relationship between formulas (type 2a);
4. Recognize the formula in multiple ways (type 2b).

DISCUSSION

In this chapter we reported a case of effective application of the Chinese Pedagogy of Variation in an experimental lesson of algebra. The experiment demonstrated an innovative application of the Chinese pedagogy of variation in tandem with a mathematical thinking model (discovering-justifying-applying), within the discovery phase, analysis showed specific examples of conceptual variation, whereas, the discovery, justifying, and applying phases demonstrated an innovative application of the procedural variation of unfolding the mathematical meaning of the formula through variation of activities. In addition, the experiment also provided evidence of student-learning outcomes for an effective lesson. While celebrating the success of the application of variation in teaching, it also shows that variation is not the only important element in planning a successful lesson, other elements are also important in the process of designing the lesson. They are:

1. the nature of the mathematical content;
2. analysis of the students' background;
3. the objectives of the lesson;
4. analysis of the difficult parts and important parts of the topic;
5. combined use of variation, geometric intuition and modelling of mathematical thinking, namely, discovering-justifying-applying.

Besides demonstrating a case of effective use of the Chinese pedagogy in the teaching of an algebraic formula, the experimental lesson also revealed two important features: making use of geometric intuition in exploration and problem solving; and strengthening the variation of mathematical thinking with an emphasis on the connection of knowledge. Specific to geometric representation, Curriculum Standard (MoE, 2011b) requires that students ought to know the geometric background of $(a \pm b)^2 = a^2 \pm 2ab + b^2$. Also, geometric intuition is one of the core ideas in Standard, which states, "Geometric intuition (MoE, 2011b) provides more assistance in simplifying complex problems and exploring the idea of solving problems. Geometric intuition helps students understand mathematics intuitively, playing an important role in mathematics learning" (p. 3). Therefore, while helping students understand an algebraic formula, teachers should assist students to explore the geometric meaning of the formula as well. During teaching, teachers could show students the quadrilateral figures as follows (Wei, 2013) to help them to present the algebra expressions using geometrical figures.

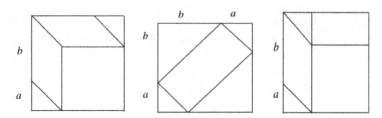

In addition to providing the variant figures of quadrilateral, teachers can try to show students triangles to analyze the connections among these geometric figures.

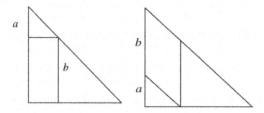

Students can strengthen their understanding of the meaning and application of formulas by the variation of these figures. There is an argument that "the more variations in graphing, the more conducive to students' learning." The answer should depend on appropriate variations (quality), not quantity. With respect to strengthening the variation of mathematical thinking with emphasis on the connection of knowledge, analysis of the lesson shows that the what-why questions and the application of the four types of variation created a strong connection of knowledge within each lesson episode and stimulated students' mathematical reasoning. The overall three stages of discovering, justifying, and applying created an essential experience of mathematical process. The Curriculum Standard (MoE, 2011c) considers mathematical thinking as experiencing the exploration of mathematical conclusions through plausible reasoning. Teachers should encourage students to explore the results from various aspects, which are related to real life, mathematical figures, and arithmetic expressions. From students' performances, we can see that students should make more efforts to explore and expand mathematical essence. Therefore, teachers should enhance the connection of knowledge in teaching and engage students in applying mathematical thinking in students' learning process.

NOTES

[1]   Rooted in Phenomenography, a theory of variation developed by Marton and his co-authors (Marton & Booth, 1997; Marton, 2014) also discusses variation. According to Marton's theory, the learner's experience and awareness of variation are essential for learning something (See chapter by Mok and chapter by Pang et al., same volume). To differentiate between the two theories, the pedagogy of variation discussed in this chapter is named as the Chinese Pedagogy of Variation.

[2]   *"Pudian"* is a Chinese term, literally means "bedding" or "foreshadowing", that is metaphorically referring to scaffolding in learning, see explanation in Gu, Huang, & Gu's chapter (this volume).

REFERENCES

Bao, J., Huang, R., Yi, L., & Gu, L. (2003a). Study in bianshi teaching [In Chinese]. *Mathematics Teaching* [Shuxue Jiaoxue], *1*, 11–12.

Bao, J., Huang, R., Yi, L., & Gu, L. (2003b). Study in bianshi teaching [In Chinese]. *Mathematics Teaching* [Shuxue Jiaoxue], *2*, 6–10.

Bao, J., Huang, R., Yi, L., & Gu, L. (2003c). Study in bianshi teaching [In Chinese]. *Mathematics Teaching* [Shuxue Jiaoxue], *3*, 6–12.

Davis, R. B. (1975). Cognitive processes involved in solving simple algebraic equations. *Journal of Children's Mathematical Behaviour*, *1*(3), 7–35.

Dixon, J. A., Deets, J. K., & Bangert, A. (2001). The representations of the arithmetic operations include functional relationships. *Memory & Cognition, 29*, 462–477.

Gu, L. (1994). *Theory of teaching experiment: The methodology and teaching principles of Qingpu* [In Chinese]. Beijing: Educational Science Press.

Gu, L., Huang, R., & Marton, F. (2004). Teaching with variation: An effective way of mathematics teaching in China. In L. Fan, N. Y. Wong, J. Cai, & S. Li (Eds.), *How Chinese learn mathematics: Perspectives from insiders* (pp. 309–348). Singapore: World Scientific.

Jupri, A., Drijvers, P., & van den Heuvel-Panhuizen, M. (2014). Student difficulties in solving equations from an operational and a structural perspective. *Mathematics Education, 9*(1), 39–55.

Kaput, J. J. (1989). Linking representations in the symbol systems of algebra. *Research Issues in the Learning and Teaching of Algebra, 4*, 167–194.

Kieran, C. (1981). Concepts associated with the equality symbol. *Educational Studies in Mathematics, 12*, 317–326.

Kieran, C. (1989). The early learning of algebra: A structural perspective. *Research Issues in the Learning and Teaching of Algebra, 4*, 33–56.

Kieran, C. (1992). The learning and teaching of algebra. In D. A. Grouws (Ed.), *Handbook of research on mathematics teaching and learning* (pp. 390–419). Reston, VA: National Council of Teachers of Mathematics.

Kieran, C. (2004). Algebraic thinking in the early grades: What is it. *The Mathematics Educator, 8*(1), 139–151.

Kieran, C. (2006). Research on the learning and teaching of algebra. In A. Gutiérrez & P. Boero (Eds.), *Handbook of research on the psychology of mathematics education: Past, present and future* (pp. 11–49). Rotterdam: Sense publishers.

Kieran, C. (2007). The learning and teaching of algebra. In F. K. Lester, Jr. (Ed.), *Second handbook of research on mathematics teaching and learning* (pp. 707–762). Reston, VA: National Council of Teachers of Mathematics.

Kilpatrick, J., Swafford, J., & Findell, B. (2001). *Adding it up*. Mathematics Learning Study Committee, Center for Education, Washington, DC: National Academy Press.

Kirshner, D. (1987). *The grammar of symbolic elementary algebra* (Doctoral dissertation). University of British Columbia, Vancouver.

Linchevski, L., & Vinner, S. (1990). Embedded figures and structures of algebraic expressions. In G. Booker, P. Cobb, & T. N. Mendicuti (Eds.), *Proceedings of the Fourteenth International Conference of the International Group for the Psychology of Mathematics Education* (Vol. 2, pp. 85–93). Mexico City, Mexico.

Luo, X. (2008). Introduction to variation in mathematics teaching. *Primary and Middle School Mathematics* (high school edition), *12*, 7–9.

Ma, F. (2012). *Mathematics textbooks for seventh grade* (pp. 23–27). Beijing: Beijing Normal University Press.

Marton, F. (2014). *Necessary conditions of learning.* New York, NY: Routledge.

Marton, F., & Booth, S. (1997). *Learning and awareness.* Mahwah, NJ: Lawrence Erlbaum.

Matz, M. (1982). Towards a process model for high school algebra errors. In D. Sleeman & J. S. Brown (Eds.), *Intelligent tutoring systems* (pp. 25–50). New York, NY & London: Academic Press.

Ministry of Education. (2011a). *Mathematics curriculum standard for compulsory education.* Beijing: Beijing Normal University press.

Ministry of Education. (2011b). *Mathematics curriculum standard for compulsory education.* Beijing: Beijing Normal University press.

Ministry of Education. (2011c). *Mathematics curriculum standard for compulsory education.* Beijing: Normal University press.

Mok, I. A. (2010). Students' algebra sense via their understanding of the distributive law. *Pedagogies: An International Journal, 5*, 251–263.

Sfard, A. (1991). On the dual nature of mathematical conceptions: Reflections on processes and objects as different sides of the same coin. *Educational Studies in Mathematics, 22*(1), 1–36.

Thomas, M., & Tall, D. (2001). The long-term cognitive development of symbolic algebra. In H. Chick, K. Stacey, J. Vincent, & J. Vincent (Eds.), *The future of the teaching and learning of algebra* (pp. 590–597). Australia: University of Melbourne.

Wei, M. (2013). Returning the math beautiful to student. *Middle School Mathematics Research, 5*, 24–26.

Wu, L., & Liu, B. (2006). The three point of variation pedagogy. *Mathematics Bulletin, 4*, 18–19.

Yuan, Q. (2006). The phycology analysis of variation pedagogy. *Mathematics Communication, 3*, 4–5.

Chunxia Qi
Faculty of Education
Beijing Normal University, China

Ruilin Wang
Faculty of Education
Beijing Capital Normal University, China

Ida Ah Chee Mok
Faculty of Education
The University of Hong Kong
Hong Kong SAR, China

Danting Huang
Beijing NO. 80 Middle School, China

APPENDIX 1
A SUMMARY OF THE LESSON PLAN BASED ON THREE PHRASES

The content of the lesson	*Remark:*
Stage 1: Discovering the formula Question 1: [Applying the pedagogy of variation] The teacher presented 6 algebra expressions and asked the students to find the pattern in the calculation. $(m + n)(p + q)$ $(2x + 3y)(a + b)$ $(a + 2)(a + 2)$ $(p + 1)^2 = (p + 1)(p + 1) = $ _____ $(m + 2)^2 = $ _____ $(2m - 2)^2 = $ _____ The teacher guided the students to observe the expressions on two sides of the equal sign, comparing the first two expressions with the later four expressions, pointing out the special cases in the later four. The students were then asked to discover the pattern and the teacher guided the students to think about the second question.	Step 1: contrast between examples and questions to see similarity and differences between the formula (type 1a); Step 2: analyze different formulas to understand the relationship between formulas (type 2a); Step 5: generalize the formula;
Question 2: Describe the pattern you find and explain how you find the pattern. [expecting the students to match the letters in the given expressions with "a" and "b" in the formula $(a + b)^2 = a^2 + 2 \cdot a \cdot b + b^2$] Question 3: How do you find the perfect square of $(a - b)$ from the perfect square of)? [expecting the students to see $(a - b)$ as $a + (-b)$]	
Stage 2: Proof/Justification of the formula Question 4: What are the patterns and characteristics of the perfect square formula? Explain in your own words. Remark: The teacher will guide the students to the idea that the perfect square formula is a special case of $(a + b)(p + q)$ when $a = p$ and $q = b$. [This was not implemented in the lesson.] Question 5: Can you derive the perfect square formula with other methods? The teacher may guide the students to use the method of drawing.	Step 3: apply the formula in a variety of problems and contexts to acquire a deeper understanding (type 1b). Step 4: recognize the formula in multiple ways (type 2b)

(Continued)

149

The content of the lesson	Remark:
Stage 3: Application of the formula The teacher will use a ppt to give the following examples: $(-a + b)^2$ $(2x - 3)^2$, $(4x + 5y)^2$, $(mn - a)^2$, $(a^2 + b^2)^2$ 102^2, 197^2 $(a + b + c)^2 = \cdots$, $(a - b + c)(a - b - c) =$ Question 6: Have you found the application of perfect square formula in daily life? Remark: The calculation of sum of area or difference of area is expected. Question 7: How do you understand the perfect square formula and its discovery? Remark: The teacher is expected to guide the students to give a summary for the lesson. [During implementation, there was not much interaction, the students were asked to put down their thoughts in writing.]	Step 3: apply the formula in a variety of problems and contexts to acquire a deeper understanding (type 1b); Step 4: recognize the formula in multiple ways (type 2b).

APPENDIX 2
THE POST-LESSON TEST FOR THE PERFECT SQUARE FORMULA

1. Calculate:
   (1) $(x - 1)^2$ (2) $(-x + 1)^2$
   (3) $(3a + 1)^2$ (4) $(-3a + 1)^2$
2. Apply the multiplication formula: $(x + 1)(x - 1)(x - 1)^2$
3. Apply the multiplication formula: $(a + b)^2 - (a - b)^2$
4. Mary wrote $(a + b)^2 = a^2 + b^2$. Please use geometric figures to analyze whether her idea is correct or not?

RONGJIN HUANG AND FREDERICK K. S. LEUNG

8. TEACHING GEOMETRICAL CONCEPTS THROUGH VARIATION

A Case Study of a Shanghai Lesson

INTRODUCTION

Chinese students' superior performance in mathematics in various international comparative studies (Fan & Zhu, 2004; OECD, 2010, 2014) has led to an increasing interest in exploring the characteristics of mathematics instruction in China (Fan, Wong, Cai, & Li, 2015; Li & Huang, 2013). Mathematics classroom instruction in China has been described as being conducted in large classes and teacher dominated, with students being portrayed as passive learners (Leung, 2005; Stevenson & Lee, 1995). On the other hand, Chinese classrooms have also been found to be polished (Paine, 1990), fluent and coherent (Chen & Li, 2010), with a focus on the development of important content, problem solving, and proving (Huang & Leung, 2004; Huang, Mok, & Leung, 2006; Leung, 2005). Gu, Huang and Marton (2004) and Gu, Huang and Gu (2017) developed a theory of teaching with variation and argued that it is an effective way to promote meaningful learning in mathematics in large class-size classrooms. Several examples in geometrical concepts and proofs have been used to illustrate the major features of teaching with variation (Gu, 1992; Gu et al., 2004), but there is a lack of investigation into how the principles of teaching with variation could be applied in teaching geometry that promote students' understanding of geometrical concepts. To this end, we aim to deepen understanding of mathematics teaching in China through examining how particular geometry concepts are taught from the perspective of variation.

LITERATURE REVIEW AND THEORETICAL CONSIDERATION

In this section, we first review the literature on the learning of geometrical concepts from a cognitive perspective. Then, variation pedagogy in general and learning geometry from a variation perspective in particular are discussed. Finally, a framework for this study is described.

Teaching Geometry: A Cognitive Perspective

According to Vinner (1991), a mathematical concept consists of two interconnected components: concept definition and concept image. It is important to introduce a

R. Huang & Y. Li (Eds.), Teaching and Learning Mathematics through Variation, 151–168.

concept by exploring carefully organized sets of examples and non-examples. Through comparing examples and non-examples, the discriminating properties of the concept can be identified. Based on this model, Hershkowitz (1990) proposed a sequence of activities for teaching geometrical concepts that include selecting the critical attributes of the concept that students should discover and the non-critical attributes that students often identify erroneously as an example or a non-example; providing an example and a non-example differing in each critical attribute and examples differing in each non-critical attribute. It was noticed that the prototypical images (such as the upright position of a right triangle, the (interior) altitude in a triangle) could be either a starting point of understanding the concept or a limitation on concept formation (Vinner & Hershkowitz, 1983; Vinner, 1981). Students and pre-service teachers tended to make their judgment based on prototypical examples resulting in incomplete concept images such as failing to draw an altitude when the base needs to be extended (Hershkowitz, 1990). Exploring various non-prototypical images could be used to develop analytical strategies that are based on definition and logical analysis. To process or operate figures in geometry, Duval (1996, 1999) highlighted the ways of reconfiguration, namely, dividing a given whole figure into parts of various shapes and then combing their parts in another whole figure or making new subfigures. For example, a parallelogram is changed into a rectangle, or can appear by combining triangles. Different operations with a figure give different insights into solving a problem.

In sum, from a cognitive perspective, it is essential to explore both prototypical and not-prototypical concept images, and compare concept examples and non-concept examples. In addition, developing the ability of reconfiguration within a given figure is critical for solving geometry problems.

Teaching Geometry: Perspectives from Variation Pedagogy

According to Marton and Tsui (2004), learning is a process in which learners develop a certain capability or a certain way of seeing or experiencing. In order to see something in a certain way the learner must discern certain features of that object. Experiencing variation is an essential experience for discernment, thus significant for learning. Marton and Pang (2006) further argued that it is important to pay attention to what varies and what is invariant in a learning situation. Objects of learning include a general and a specific aspect. The general aspect has to do with the nature of the capability such as remembering, interpreting and grasping. The specific aspect has to do with the subject on which these acts of learning are carried out, such as formulas and simultaneous equations. Teachers are often conscious of this object of learning and they may elaborate it in different degrees of detail. What teachers are striving for is the intended object of learning, which is an object of the teacher's awareness. However, what is more important is how the teacher structures the lessons so that it is possible for the object of learning to come to the fore of the students' awareness, which is called the enacted object of learning (Marton & Pang, 2006).

Interestingly, a theory of mathematics teaching/learning, called teaching with variation, has been developed based on a series longitudinal mathematics teaching experiments in China (Gu, 1994; Gu et al., 2004). According to this theory, meaningful learning enables learners to establish a substantial and non-arbitrary connection between the new knowledge and their previous knowledge (Ausubel, 1968). Classroom activities are developed to help students establish this kind of connection by experiencing certain dimensions of variation. Two types of variation are identified as important patterns of variation for meaningful learning: "conceptual variation" and "procedural variation" (Gu et al., 2004). Conceptual variation aims to provide students with multiple experiences from different perspectives. On the other hand, procedural variation is concerned with the process of forming a concept logically or historically, arriving at solutions to problems (scaffolding, transformation), and forming knowledge structures (relationship among different concepts) (Gu et al., 2004). With regard to teaching geometry, Gu (1994) identified specific patterns of variation. For example, to explore critical features of a geometrical concept, concept figures and non-concept figures have to be compared; and both prototypical and non-prototypical examples should be explored. These are *conceptual variations* serving for developing a deep understanding of concepts from multiple perspectives. To solve geometrical problems, *procedural variations* such as reconfiguring within a given complex figure; or transforming prototypical figures to a complex figure are needed (Gu et al., 2004, 2017).

A Framework for the Current Study

The description of variations in geometry by Gu et al. (2004) is supported by cognitive theories of geometry learning. In addition, Marton and Pang (2006)'s notions of objects of learning provide a lens for examining possible learning opportunities. Thus, both Gu et al.'s (2004) classification of variation and Marton's notions of enacted objects of learning are adopted to examine classroom teaching of geometrical concepts.

A CASE STUDY

Data Source

A videotaped seventh grade lesson used as evidence for the Excellent Young Teacher Award in Shanghai in 1999 constitutes the data source for this study. The lesson was taught by a young teacher (less than 5 years of teaching experience) to 56 students in a junior high school located in the countryside of Shanghai. This lesson is a typical and excellent lesson recommended by local teaching research specialists. The lesson was transcribed (in Chinese) verbatim. To ensure the validity of lesson analysis the video recording was referred to when needed. The lesson was analyzed based on Gu et al.'s (2004) classifications.

153

Description of the Lesson

The topic of the lesson is "Corresponding angles, alternate angles, and consecutive interior angles on the same side of the transversal". By and large, the lesson included the following stages: review, exploration of the new concept, examples and practices, and summary and assignment.

Reviewing and inducing. At the beginning of the lesson, the teacher drew two straight lines crossing each other (Figure 1(I)) on the blackboard, and asked students to use their previous knowledge (such as concepts of vertical angles and supplementary angles) to answer some review questions. After obtaining correct answers to those questions from the students, the teacher added one straight line to the previous figure (see Figure 1(II)) and asked students how many angles there are in the figure, and how many of them are vertical angles and supplementary angles. After that, the students were guided to explore the characteristics of a pair of angles from different vertices by being asked, "what relations are there between ∠1 and ∠5?", which actually is the new topic to be explored for this lesson.

Exploring new concepts. In order to examine the relationship between ∠1 and ∠5, a particular figure was isolated as shown in Figure 1(III). Through group discussion, the students found many features about these two angles, such as "∠1 and ∠5 are both on the right side of line 1, and above line a, and b". Based on the students' explanations, the teacher summarized and stated the definition of "corresponding angles". Then the students were asked to identify all the "corresponding angles" in Figure 1(II).

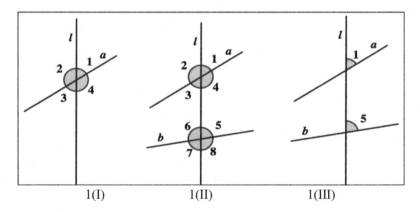

1(I)   1(II)   1(III)

Figure 1. Angle relationship in transversal figures

Similarly, another two concepts, "alternate angles and consecutive interior angles" were explored respectively.

Examples and exercise.　After introducing the three angle relationships, students were asked to identify them in different configurations. The problems are as follows:

Task 1: Find the "corresponding angles, alternate angles, and consecutive interior angles on the same side of transversal" in Figure 2:

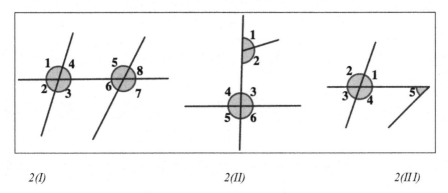

2(I)   2(II)   2(III)

Figure 2. Angle relationship within various transversals

Task 2: Find the "corresponding angles, alternate angles, and consecutive interior angles on the same side of transversal" in Figure 3(I).

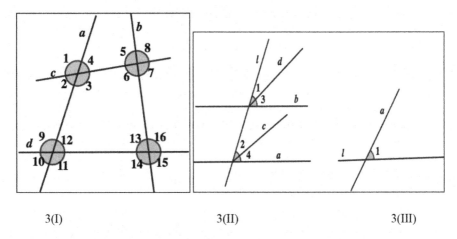

3(I)   3(II)   3(III)

Figure 3. Angle relationships in more complex situations

Task 3: In Figure 3(II), (1) Are ∠1 and ∠2 a pair of corresponding angles? (2) Are ∠3 and ∠4 a pair of corresponding angles?

Task 4: Given ∠1 is formed by line *l* and line *a* as shown in Figure 3(III). (1) Add one line b so that ∠2 formed by line l and line b, and ∠1 are a pair of corresponding angles. (2) Is it possible to construct such a line *b* so that ∠2 (formed by line *l* and line *b*) is equal to ∠1?

155

Summary and assignment. The teacher emphasized that these three types of relationship are related to two angles at different vertices. These angles are located in a "prototypical figure" which consists of two straight lines intersected by a third line. The key to judge these relationships within a complicated figure is to isolate a proper "prototypical figure" which includes these angles in question. Moreover, the teacher demonstrated how to remember these relationships by making use of different gestures as shown Figure 4 below.

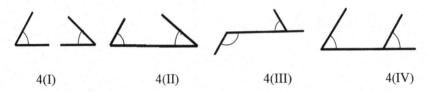

| 4(I) | 4(II) | 4(III) | 4(IV) |

Figure 4. Presenting angle relationship using finger gestures

Finally, some exercises from the textbook were assigned to students.

Enacted Objects of Learning

From the perspective of variation, and in order to examine what learning is made possible, we need to identify what dimensions of variation are constructed. Below we look at the lesson in greater detail from this particular theoretical perspective to identify the enacted object of learning and possible learning opportunities.

Procedural variation 1: Reviewing previous knowledge and bringing the new topic to the fore of students' awareness. At the first stage, *a variation*: varying from two intersecting straight lines to two straight lines intersected by a third one, was created by the teacher's demonstration and questioning. Through questioning students know how many angles there are in the new figures, and what relationships there are among those angles. A cognitive conflict with the previous knowledge reviewed about how to determine the relationship of angles at different vertices was then raised, which is the new topic to be explored in this lesson.

1. T: ... now, I've drawn one straight line b to the two intersecting straight line l (see Figure 1(II)), then how many angles are there in the figure?
2. S: Four angles [in unison]
3. T: Good. Increasing by four angles, then, how many angles are there in the figure: two lines intersected by a third line?
4. S: Eight angles [in unison]
5. T: Let's label the added angles as ∠5, ∠6, ∠7, ∠8. We call this figure as "straight line a and b intersected by a straight line l" [the teacher writes the part and highlights it with underline]. Then, there are eight angles. How

many vertical angles are there among them? How many supplementary angles are there among them? [The teacher repeated these questions]. Good, Pan Hong [nominating him]

6. Pan: There are four pairs of vertical angles, and eight pairs of supplementary angles.

7. T: Good! There are four pairs of vertical angles, and eight pairs of supplementary angles. Very good! Good, just now, I reviewed that all pairs of vertical angles and supplementary angles which are formed at the same point. Today, we are going to study the angle relationships among the angles formed at different vertices. For example, ∠1 and ∠5.

8. T: [Demonstrating by transparency as Figure 1(II)] How many angles are there in the figure: straight lines a and b intersected by straight line l?

9. S: Eight angles [in unison]

10. T: Good! Then, we study the positional relationship between two angles, which are at different vertices, such as ∠1 and ∠5. In order to make clear the positional relationship between ∠1 and ∠5, we isolate them from the figure, as showed in Figure 1(III) (demonstrating by transparency). Good! What are the positional features of ∠1 and ∠5.

In the above excerpt, the teacher guided students to construct a "prototypical figure" (e.g., transversal) and review previous knowledge (1~6), then the teacher drew students' attention to the angle relationship located at different points by contrasting with previous concepts: the angles at the same point (8). In order to examine the new relationship clearly, the teacher isolated the focused angles from the complex Figure 1(II), as shown in Figure 1(III). By isolating the focused sub-figure, the teacher tried to help students to clearly identify the characteristics of these angle relationships, and utilize a typical "isolation method", namely, isolating a focused subfigure from a complex figure in problem solving in geometry (Gu et al., 2004).

By opening with this variation (i.e., adding one new line while two intersecting lines remain the same), the relevant previous knowledge was reviewed and the new topic was introduced in a sequential and cognitively connected manner. Thus, this variation is a procedural variation.

At the introducing new concepts stage, two variations were created which are crucial for students to develop an understanding of the new concepts.

Conceptual Variation 1: descriptions of new concepts. During the process of forming the new concepts, expressions of the new concepts have been shifted among the following forms: rough description, intuitive description, definition, and schema. After a group discussion, the students were invited to present their observations, and the new concepts were built based on students' descriptions under the teacher's guidance as shown in the following excerpt.

1. T: ...good! What are the characteristics of the pairs of ∠1 and ∠5 in terms of their positions in the figure?" (Pointing to Figure 1(III) shown on the transparency). Please discuss this question in groups of 4-students [at once, the 4-student groups were organized: the students at the row in the front turn back so that the 4 students sit around a desk. Then students discuss actively and the teacher circulates around the classroom assisting students occasionally].

2. T: Good! Just now, students have an active discussion. I would like to ask one student to answer: What is the characteristics of the pair of ∠1 and ∠5 in terms of their position? [Pause] Fang Xiuting (who raised his hand), please.

3. Fang: ∠1 and ∠5 are on the right side, and...

4. T: ∠1 and ∠5 are on the right side. Please, explain [it] in more detail. For example, what is the relationship of ∠1 and ∠5 with regard to the straight line l in terms of their positions? Moreover, what is the relationship of them with regard to the straight lines a and b?

5. Fang: With regard to straight line l, ∠1 and ∠5 are on the right side of it. Regarding straight lines a and b, all the two angles are above the two straight lines respectively.

6. T: Good! Very good! Thus, we call the two parts of the plane divided by the line l as two sides of the straight line l [left side and right side], and call the two parts of the plane divided by lines of a and b as two sides of lines a or b [above and below]. Moreover, we define this pair of angles, which possess the previous characteristics as corresponding angles [In Chinese, the angles with the same position]. [Teacher writes down: corresponding angles: ∠1 and ∠5]. What kind of angles are ∠1 and ∠5 [called]?

7. S: Corresponding angles! [In unison]

8. T: Are there other corresponding angles in the figure [Figure 1(II)]? Cheng Dechong, please.

9. Cheng: ∠4 and ∠5 [hesitation for a moment]. No! No! It should be ∠4 and ∠8.

10. T: ∠4 and ∠8 [write down on blackboard], are there any more?

11. Cheng: ∠2 and ∠6.

12. T: ∠2 and ∠6[write down on blackboard], any more?

13. Cheng: No.

14. T: Very good!

In the above discussion, the representation of "corresponding angles" was transferred from the immature description by students (1~3) to a more precise description through the teacher's probing (4~5), then to a formal definition given by the teacher (6), and finally to a schema, which can be applied in simple situations (7~14). This variation of representation of the concept is a conceptual one.

Conceptual variation 2: Different orientations of "basic/standard/prototypical figure". Through questions and answers between the teacher and students, the concepts of three types of angle relationship were constituted in a "prototypical figure": two straight lines intersected by a third line (Figure 1(III)). After that, the teacher provided students with Task 1. By doing so, a new dimension of variation was opened for students to experience how to identify these angle relationships in different figures with various orientations. The teacher purposely varied the figures in terms of their positions and the number of angles in the figures.

1. T.... Next, I vary the picture (see Figure 2 (I)). Can you identify the corresponding angles, alternate angles, and consecutive interior angles on the same side of the transversal? [Present the problem by transparency]. How many angles are there in the picture?
2. S: 8 angles [in unison]
3. T: Then, what is the relationship between $\angle 4$ and $\angle 5$ in these 8 angles? Shi Chihong, please.
4. Shi: [it is a pair of] corresponding angles.
5. T: Now, I vary the picture again [show the picture by transparency like Figure 2 (II)]. Well, how many angles are there in this picture? [point to student S3]
6. S3: 6 angles.
7. T: 6 angles. Then, how many pairs of alternate angles, and consecutive interior angles on the same side of the transversal in the picture? Please [point the student S3].
8. S3: There are two pairs of corresponding angles.
9. T: Which two pairs are they?
10. S3: $\angle 3$ and $\angle 1$. $\angle 2$ and $\angle 6$

By providing students with these variations, the students were exposed to the concepts from different orientations of the figure. It may make student aware that these concepts are invariant although the orientations of the figure vary.

To consolidate the new concepts and develop a method of solving problems, the following procedural variations were constructed.

Procedural variation 2: Different contexts of "prototypical figures". After the students got a rich experience of these concepts in terms of their orientations of the prototypical figure, the teacher then deliberately provided a group of tasks in which "prototypical figures" were embedded in the complex contexts in Task 2 and Task 3. Through identifying the angle relationships in different contexts of the "prototypical figures", an invariant strategy of problem solving, i.e. identifying and isolating a proper "prototypical figure" (i.e., prototypical image) from a complex configuration. In general, isolating a proper sub-figure from a complex figure is a useful strategy of solving a geometric problem (Gu et al., 2004).

After highlighting the common features in the previous questions: identifying the "prototypical figure", the teacher presented a more complex picture [see Figure 3], and asked students to count the number of angles in the figure, and identify the three types of angle relationships in the figure.

1. T: Good. [There are] 16 angles in this figure. As we learned today, there are three types of angle relationships: corresponding angles, alternate angles, and consecutive interior angles on the same side of the transversal in a "prototypical figure" which consists of two straight lines intersected by a third line. In this picture, there are 4 lines. How can we identify these relationships among the angles? Can you identify these three types of angle relationships according to the given condition in this figure? Please, write down your answer on the worksheet [students think individually]. Please, have a close look at which two straight lines are intersected by which line. Which two straight lines are they in question (1)? [i.e., straight lines a and b intersected by straight line d, find all the corresponding angles, alternate angles, and the consecutive interior angles]

2. S: Straight lines a and b are intersected by line d. [in unison]

3. T: [The teacher demonstrates a transparency as shown in Figure 5(I). Students do seatwork individually, whiles the teacher circulated around the class, with occasional assisting of students] Are you ready?

4. S: Yes! [In unison]

5. T: Who would like to answer the question? Yang Ninao, please. How many pairs of corresponding angles are there?

6. Yang: [there are] 4 pairs of corresponding angles

7. T: What are they?

8. Yang: $\angle 9$ and $\angle 13$

9. T: $\angle 9$ and $\angle 13$ [pointing to the relevant angles]

10. Yang: $\angle 12$ and $\angle 13$.

11. T: $\angle 12$ and $\angle 13$ [pointing to the relevant angles]

    ...

After students selected the prototypical figure (1~2), they were asked to identify all three types of angle relationships one by one. The teacher confirmed students' answers by pointing out the relevant angles on the transparency (6~11).

Procedural variation 3: Different directions for applying the new concepts. As soon as the students answered the first question, the teacher posed a new challenging question: "conversely, if $\angle 1$ and $\angle 5$ are a pair of corresponding angles, which prototypical figure contains them?". After allowing individual students to think for a period of time, one student was called on to answer the question. The student gave a correct answer by saying that the prototypical figure is "straight lines a and b intersected by straight line c"(see Figure 5(II)). The teacher's effort to push students to identify the prototypical figure is evidenced by the following excerpt:

1. T: Think carefully! Which two straight lines intersected by a third line form ∠1 and ∠5, which are a pair of corresponding angles? Are you ready?
2. S: Yes![in unison]
3. T: You, please [point to one student]
4. S2: The straight lines a, b intersected by the straight line c.
5. T: ∠1 and ∠5 are formed by straight lines a, b intersected by line c. Is it right?
6. S: Right! [in unison]
7. T: So, which line in this figure has not been used?
8. S: [Straight line] d.
9. T: In other words, how do we deal with the straight-line d?
10. S: Cover it up!
11. T: [Remove the straight line d from the figure, and form a new figure, see Figure 5(II)]. Is it right?
12. S: Right! [in unison]
13. T: Moreover, if ∠3 and ∠12 are a pair of consecutive interior angles on the same side of the transversal, which two straight lines intersected by a third line form this pair of angles?

Similarly, by searching for a pair of consecutive interior angles on the same side of the transversal of ∠3 and ∠12, students identified a prototypical figure, "straight lines c, d intersected by straight line a" (see Figure 5(III)). Moreover, through identifying a pair of alternate angles ∠13 and ∠7, a prototypical figure, "straight lines c, d intersected by straight line b" was isolated (see Figure 5(IV)).

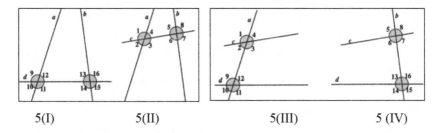

5(I)   5(II)   5(III)   5 (IV)

Figure 5. Identifying angle relationship through decomposing complex figures

After the students identified all the "basic" figures as shown in figure 5, and recognized the relevant angle relationships, the teacher summarized the key points for solving those problems, that is how to isolate a "prototypical figure", for instance, two straight lines *a, b* intersected by a third straight line d by deliberately "hiding" one line *c* from the original figure (see Figure 5(I)). Through identifying the three angle relationships within a given a prototypical figure or isolating a relevant 'prototypical figure' so that the given angle relationship is tenable, the students not only consolidated the relevant concepts, but more importantly, learned the *isolation method* of problem solving, i.e. isolating a basic sub-figure from a complex configuration.

Conceptual variation 3: Contrast and counter-example. After doing extensive exercises, the students might think that they had fully mastered the learned concepts. At this moment, the teacher posed *Task 3* (see Figure 3(II)) to assess whether students had truly mastered the concepts and methods of problem solving. Through isolating a prototypical figure shown in Figure 6(I), students concluded, "∠1 and ∠2 are corresponding angles". However, since students could only identify a figure as shown in figure 6(II), they denied that "∠3 and ∠4 are a pair of corresponding angles". Thus a new dimension of variation of experiencing corresponding angles was opened: example or counter-example of the visual judgment.

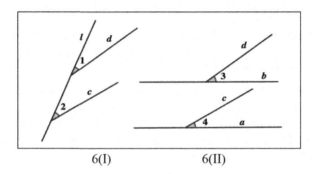

6(I)   6(II)

Figure 6. Contrast with counterexamples

Procedural variation 4: Creating a potential opportunity for learning a new topic. After solving the above problems through observation and demonstration, the teacher presented a manipulative Task 4. First, through playing with colored sticks, the first question was solved (see Figure 7(I), where *a* and *b* intersect). Then, based on drawing and reasoning, the second question was also figured out (see Figure 7(II), where *a* and *b* are parallel). During the process of problem solving, the students' thinking levels were shifted along the following forms: concrete operation (by playing with the colored sticks) (enactive); drawing (iconic); logical reasoning (abstract)

The following excerpt shows how students were guided to reason logically:

1. T: I repeat the question for you: what is the quantitative relationship between the two alternate angles [in Figure 7(b)]? Who will…?
2. S1: it is equal.
3. T: why?
4. S1: because these two angles are equal to 65 degree.

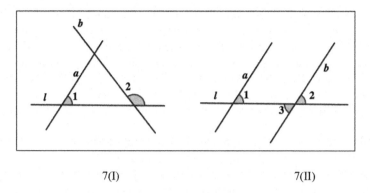

7(I)   7(II)

Figure 7. Exploring a new topic to be discussed in next class

5. T: Because they are equal to 65 degree! Good! Who would like to explain in more detail? [Pointing to student 6].
6. S2: Because ∠3 and ∠2 are a pair of vertical angles.
7. T: ∠3 and ∠2 are a pair of vertical angles.
8. S2: Vertical angles are equal.
9. T: Vertical angles are equal.
10. S2: And ∠1 is equal to ∠2 also;
11. T: Because ∠1 is equal to ∠2 also;
12. S2: So, ∠1 is equal to ∠3 in degrees.
13. T: ∠1 is equal to ∠3 in degree also. Good! Great! Furthermore, if we name the fourth angle as ∠4, what is the relationship between ∠1 and ∠4? Pleas, deal with the question after class.

Although the students found a solution by drawing, it is difficult to explain the solution. The previous dialogue demonstrates the teacher's intention to elicit a reasonable explanation. After the first student stated what he did (1~4), the student was probed for more details (5), and then another student gave a logical explanation by using previous knowledge (7~13). This exercise had two functions, on one hand, the "previous proposition: vertical angles are equal" was reviewed, on the other hand, "a further proposition: if the corresponding angles are equal, then the two lines are parallel" was operationally experienced. That means a potential space of learning was opened implicitly.

Conceptual variation 4: Consolidating and memorization of the concepts. As soon as the key points for identifying the three angle relationships in a variety of different situations were summarized, the teacher skillfully opened a new variation by making use of gestures to help students to memorize the three concepts. If the thumb and forefinger of the left hand form an angle, while the thumb and forefinger of the right hand form another angle, then all three angle relationships can be visually demonstrated by different gestures (see Figure 4) as follows:

1. T: In order to memorize the characteristics of the three angle relationships, I would like to introduce a gesture method. For example, this represents an angle [The thumb and forefinger in left hand form an angle], whilst that also represents another angle [The thumb and forefinger form an angle] (see Figure 4(I)). When the two thumbs are opposite each other, what is the relationship between the two angles? (see Figure 4(II))
2. S: Consecutive interior angles on the same side of the transversal![in unison]
3. T: Good! It is a pair of consecutive interior angles on the same side of the transversal. Then, how to represent alternate angles?
4. [Students try excitedly, some students have got the answer]
5. T: In fact, I just turn the forefinger over (see Figure 4(III)). How to represent corresponding angles? [Students actively take part in trying]
6. T: It is ok, if one angle is against the other one [see Figure 4(IV))

Thus, the students had experienced the three angle relationships in different representations: verbal, drawing, reasoning, and gesturing. These rich representations will benefit students' understanding, memorization and application of these concepts.

Summary

The lesson began with a review by questioning, and then moved forward inducing the new topic by varying an introductory task (procedural variation 1). Through several rounds of teacher-student interactions, the three concepts were built on students' answers (conceptual variation 1). These concepts were immediately applied in a simple situation. After that, the lesson moved to the stage of practice. By addressing a series of well-designed tasks presented by the teacher, the students had an extensive experience of identifying the three angle relationships in various complex situations and learned the isolation method of problem solving in geometry (conceptual variations 2, 3; procedural variations 2, 3). It is worthy mentioning that by solving the last problem, a new topic for further lessons was implicitly introduced (procedural variation 4). During the last stage, a climax of teaching was established by actively imitating the three angle relationships by means of hand gestures (Conceptual variation 4). These dimensions of variation were constructed purposefully to serve different learning goals (See Table 1).

Through exploring various dimensions of variation constructed by classroom interaction (mainly between the teacher and students), the students had been guided to develop and consolidate the concepts conceptually, and apply the concepts in different geometrical contexts, and implicitly explore the potential topics to learn. The lesson had a warm atmosphere with frequent teacher-student interactions and progressed in a coherent manner. The deliberate use of these variations seems to have ensured that the progress of the lesson was both smooth and coherent.

Table 1. Dimensions of variation, their functions, and enactment of objects of learning

Phases of the lesson	Dimensions of variation	Pedagogical effects of the variation	Enacted objects of learning
Reviewing and inducing	Procedural variation 1	Activating previous knowledge; Introducing the new topic	Developing the concepts
Exploring new concepts	Conceptual variations 1, 2	Forming, clarifying and consolidating the new concept	Defining, and consolidating the concepts
Examples and exercise	Conceptual variation 3	Deepening understanding of the new concept by contrasting non-examples;	Deepening the concepts
	Procedural variations 2, 3	Consolidating the new concept; Learning isolation method of problem solving	Consolidating and applying the concepts
Summary and assignment	Procedural variation 4	Creating a potential topic for further learning	Reinforcing the concept; exploring further learning
	Conceptual variation 4	Visualizing and memorizing the new concepts	topics

CONCLUSION AND DISCUSSION

According to the theoretical perspective, it is crucial to create certain dimensions of variation that enact the objects of learning. These objects of learning can be classified into two types. One is the content in question (such as concepts, propositions, formulae), another is the process (such as formation of concepts, or process or strategy of problem solving). In this particular lesson, the objects of learning include development of the concepts of three types of angle relationship involving a transversal (corresponding, alternative, and consecutive interior angles) and problem solving ability by applying these concepts. Two categories of variation, conceptual variation and procedural variation, have been strategically constituted to enact these objects of learning. It was demonstrated that the conceptual variations served the purpose of building and understanding the concept, while the procedural variations are used for activating previous knowledge, introducing the new topic, consolidating new knowledge, developing strategies for solving problems, and creating a topic for further learning.

From a perspective of pedagogy, this lesson was unfolded smoothly and consistently, and was guided by the teacher, which demonstrates the major features of mathematics classroom teaching in China (e.g., Huang & Leung, 2004; Leung, 2005). Yet, if looking at students' engagement and contribution to the generation of knowledge, namely, enacted objects of learning, we cannot say that students are passive learners. The analysis of this lesson indicates that the teacher can still encourage students to actively generate knowledge through strategically creating dimensions of variation. This observation echoes Huang's (2002, p. 237) description of the Chinese mathematics classroom:

> There are teacher, students and mathematics. The teacher presents mathematics and helps students engage in the process of exploring the mathematics by providing proper scaffoldings and asking a series of heuristic questions. The students are eager to listen and engage themselves in the process of learning.

From a perspective of learning geometry, the dimensions of conceptual variations which focus on contrasting concept images and non-concept images, juxtaposing prototypical figures and non-prototypical figures could help students develop a deep understanding of the concept (e.g., Vinner & Hershkowitz, 1983). Moreover, Duval's (1996, 1999) studies support that developing reconfiguration ability when processing geometrical figures is crucial for problem solving in geometry. The dimensions of procedural variation constructed in this Shanghai lesson demonstrate the teacher's competence in setting and implementing deliberate tasks for students' development of this figurative processing ability when applying the learned concepts. Thus, from a perspective of cognitive science, the two types of variation could help students to develop geometrical concepts and problem solving ability in geometry. This reinforces Huang, Miller and Tzur (2015, p. 104)'s assertion of "the power of teaching through variation to deepen and consolidate conceptual understanding and procedural fluency concurrently" based on a fine-grained analysis of 10 consecutive lessons.

In asserting the positive effects of appropriate application of the principles of teaching with variation, a caution of designing and implementing dimensions of variation has been mentioned (Gu et al., 2004, 2017). It is crucial to construct appropriate spaces of learning by exploring relevant dimensions of variation focusing on critical features of the objects of learning with regard to the contexts, reasoning and student learning trajectory (Gu et al., 2017).

REFERENCES

Ausubel, D. P. (1968). *Educational psychology: A cognitive view*. New York, NY: Holt, Rinehart & Winston.

Chen, X., & Li, Y. (2010). Instructional coherence in Chinese mathematics classroom – A case study of lessons on fraction division. *International Journal of Science and Mathematics Education, 8*, 711–735.

Duval, R. (1999, October 23–26). *Representation, vision and visualization: Cognitive functions in mathematical thinking. Basic issues for learning.* Proceedings of the Annual Meeting of the North American Chapter of the International group for the Psychology of Mathematics education, Morelos, Mexico.

Duval, R. (2006). A cognitive analysis of problems of comprehension in a learning of mathematics. *Educational Studies in Mathematics, 61*, 103–131.

Fan, L., & Zhu, Y. (2004). How have Chinese students performed in mathematics? A perspective from large-scale international comparisons. In L. Fan, N. Y. Wong, J. Cai, & S. Li (Eds.), *How Chinese learn mathematics: Perspectives from insiders* (pp. 3–26). Singapore: World Scientific.

Fan, L., Wong, N. Y., Cai, J., & Li, S. (2015). *How Chinese teach mathematics: Perspectives of insiders.* Singapore: World Scientific.

Fischbein, E. (1993). The theory of figural concepts. *Educational Studies in Mathematics, 24*(2), 139–162.

Gu, F., Huang, R., & Gu, L. (2017). Theory and development of teaching through variation in mathematics in China. In R. Huang & Y. Li (Eds.), *Teaching and learning mathematics through variation* (this volume). Rotterdam, The Netherlands: Sense Publishers.

Gu, L. (1994). *Theory of teaching experiment: The methodology and teaching principles of Qingpu* [In Chinese]. Beijing: Educational Science Press.

Gu, L., Huang, R., & Marton, F. (2004). Teaching with variation: An effective way of mathematics teaching in China. In L. Fan, N. Y. Wong, J. Cai, & S. Li (Eds.), *How Chinese learn mathematics: Perspectives from insiders* (pp. 309–347). Singapore: World Scientific.

Hershkowitz, R. (1990). Psychological aspects of learning geometry. In P. Nesher & J. Kilpatrick (Eds.), *Mathematics and cognition: A research synthesis by the International group for the psychology of mathematics education* (pp. 70–95). Cambridge: Cambridge University Press.

Hershkowitz, R., Bruckheimer, M., & Vinner, S. (1987). Activities with teachers based on cognitive research. In M. M. Lindquist (Ed.), *Learning and teaching geometry, K-12: 1987 Year book* (pp. 222–235). Reston, VA: National Council of Teachers of Mathematics.

Huang, R. (2002). *Mathematics teaching in Hong Kong and Shanghai: A classroom analysis from the perspective of variation* (Unpublished doctoral dissertation). The University of Hong Kong, Hong Kong.

Huang, R., & Leung, F. K. S. (2004). Cracking the paradox of the Chinese learners: Looking into the mathematics classrooms in Hong Kong and Shanghai. In L. Fan, N. Y. Wong, J. Cai, & S. Li (Eds.), *How Chinese learn mathematics: Perspectives from insiders* (pp. 348–381). Singapore: World Scientific.

Huang, R., & Leung, F. K. S. (2005). Deconstructing teacher-centeredness and student-centeredness dichotomy: A case study of a Shanghai mathematics lesson. *The Mathematics Educators, 15*(2), 35–41.

Huang, R., Miller, D., & Tzur, R. (2015). Mathematics teaching in Chinese classroom: A hybrid-model analysis of opportunities for students' learning. In L. Fan, N. Y. Wong, J. Cai, & S. Li (Eds.), *How Chinese teach mathematics: Perspectives from insiders* (pp. 73–110). Singapore: World Scientific.

Huang, R., Mok, I., & Leung, F. K. S. (2006). Repetition or variation: "Practice" in the mathematics classrooms in China. In D. J. Clarke, C. Keitel, & Y. Shimizu (Eds.), *Mathematics classrooms in twelve countries: The insider's perspective* (pp. 263–274). Rotterdam, The Netherlands: Sense Publishers.

Leung, F. K. S. (2005). Some characteristics of East Asian mathematics classrooms based on data from the TIMSS 1999 video study. *Educational Studies in Mathematics, 60*, 199–215.

Li, Y., & Huang, R. (2013). *How Chinese teach mathematics and improve teaching.* New York, NY: Routledge.

Marton, F., & Pang, M. F. (2006). On some necessary conditions of learning. *The Journal of the Learning Sciences, 15*, 193–220.

Marton, F., & Tsui, A. B. M. (2004). *Classroom discourse and the space of learning.* Mahwah, NJ: Erlbaum.

OECD. (2010). *PISA 2009 results: What students know and can do: Student performance in reading, mathematics and science* (Vol. I). Paris: OECD Publishing.

OECD. (2014). *PISA 2012 results in focus: What 15-year-olds know and what they can do with what they know.* Paris: OECD Publishing.

Paine, L. W. (1990). The teacher as virtuoso: A Chinese model for teaching. *Teachers College Record, 92*(1), 49–81.

Qingpu Experiment Group. (1991). *Learn to teaching* [In Chinese]. Beijing: Peoples' Education Press.

Stevenson, H. W., & Lee, S. (1995). The East Asian version of whole class teaching. *Educational Policy, 9*, 152–168.

Vinner, S. (1981). The nature of geometrical objects as conceived by teachers and prospective teachers. In Equipe De Recherche, Pédagogique (Eds.), *Proceedings of the 5 th PME international Conferences, 1*, 375–380.

Vinner, S. (1991). The role of definitions in the teaching and learning of mathematics. In D. Tall (Ed.), *Advanced mathematical thinking* (pp. 65–81). Dordrecht, Netherlands: Kluwer.

Vinner, S., & Hershkowitz, R. (1983). On concept formation in geometry. *ZDM-The International Journal on Mathematics Education, 83*(1), 20–25.

Rongjin Huang
Middle Tennessee State University, USA

Frederick K. S. Leung
The University of Hong Kong, China

XINGFENG HUANG, XINRONG YANG AND PINGPING ZHANG

9. TEACHING GEOMETRY REVIEW LESSON THROUGH VARIATION

A Case Study

BACKGROUND

In China, review lessons are quite common in mathematics teaching. After teaching a unit, a chapter, a book, or a course, teachers will arrange a lesson or several lessons to review what students have learned to help them consolidate what they have learned and therefore help them organize their knowledge systematically and improve their problem-solving ability. Another goal of review lessons is to help students prepare for examinations. In Chinese teaching culture, the result of examination is a critical evaluating indicator to students' learning outcomes and the teacher's teaching effectiveness as well. In primary and secondary schools, there are at least two school-unified examinations each semester: a midterm and a final. In fact, mathematics is a compulsory subject in these examinations. In particular, in order to help the students achieve higher scores on the entrance examinations, such as *Zhongkao (for entering high schools)* and *Gaokao (for entering colleges)*, mathematics teachers usually spend one to two semesters on systematically reviewing contents that have been taught before. In addition, there is also a clear distinction between a new content lesson and a review lesson. When teachers prepare for a new content lesson, they will design tasks, organize activities, and implement objectives based on a unified textbook. However, teachers do not have any standard reference materials to prepare for review lessons, except for *Zhongkao* and *Gaokao*. They have to rely on themselves or cooperate with colleagues to plan those lessons. It is a general challenge for every teacher to prepare review lesson. Therefore, the exploration of how to effectively teach review lessons attracts many mathematics teachers (Huang, 2003; Luang & Liang, 2011; Wei, 2008).

Teaching with variation is a widely used strategy for types of lessons. Patterns of variation include conceptual variation and procedural variation (Gu, 1981). Conceptual variation provides students with learning experiences for understanding concepts from multiple perspectives, while procedural variation can help promote the formation of conceptions, provide background knowledge for problem solving, and accumulate necessary learning experience (Gu, Huang, & Marton, 2004). It is quite common for teachers to design review lessons, particularly in geometry, from the

R. Huang & Y. Li (Eds.), Teaching and Learning Mathematics through Variation, 169–186.

perspective of procedural variation (Du, 2000; Tao & Xu, 2009; Zhang & Xu, 2013). First, this might be due to the fact that for teachers, geometric content provides more opportunities to design variation problems. Second, although literatures described lesson design using procedural variations from a teachers' perspective, it is largely unknown what should be paid attention to when teachers design and implement the procedural variation. Teachers usually believe that enlightening and exploring variation problems from easy to difficult can stimulate students' interests and guide students to think about problems in multiple ways. For this reason, teachers may believe it is a positive and desirable teaching strategy (Rui, 1998). However, there have been few appropriate empirical studies examining why and how we can use variation for effective teaching. Marton and his colleagues (1997, 2004) explained the necessity for students to learn concepts through exploring patterns of variation from general learning theory, and provided a theoretical support for teaching through variation, but their theories are not specific to learning mathematics. In this chapter, we examined the functions of using procedural variation in a geometry lesson and discussed its implementation from the perspective of students' mathematical cognition.

THEORETICAL FRAMEWORK

Nature of Geometric Figures

Geometric figures are abstracted from the real world, but they do not exist in reality. Zero-dimensional point, one-dimensional linear, and two-dimensional plane don't exist in the real world. Even a pillar made of stone or wood is just a model/ representation of a three-dimensional cylinder or prism. Therefore, geometric reasoning deals with the general, abstract geometric figures, rather than specific and concrete images (Fischbein, 1993). However, a geometric figure tends to be represented by a diagram. For example, we usually draw the diagram to represent a figure of triangle (Fischbein, 1993). Here comes a paradoxical phenomenon where the points and lines of the diagram construct a special triangle, but some of its properties don't appear in all triangles. In other words, a special diagram can't be used to represent a general geometric object (Fischbein, 1993; Herbst, 2004). In fact, properties of a figure are determined by its definition and axiom system. For example, we draw to represent square, then from the definition of square in an axiom system you can generalize many properties of squares (Fischbein, 1993). That is to say, only under the condition of a definition or some properties, a figure could represent an abstract geometric object, which is an abstract concept, such as triangle, square, circle, cube, or sphere. However, we usually understand a geometric concept and make logical reasoning based on its diagram. The complicated relation between them causes many cognitive difficulties in learning geometry for students (Duval, 1995).

170

Comprehension of Geometric Figures

Duval (1995, 1999) pointed out that students have different ways to understand a geometric figure. They may understand it intuitively and perceptually, where they identify properties of a geometric figure based on its shape and size. In this case, they think that diagrams and figures are equivalent. They may also understand a geometric figure in a discursive way, which is to understand properties of a geometric figure according to a definition or proposition. This kind of understanding might be the starting point of students' geometric proof. At the same time, in the process of constructing a geometric figure, students can understand it in a sequential way. Duval (1999) argued that construction can improve students' discursive understanding because they can't construct a figure just relying on visual perception. Constructions must be done based on the understanding of geometric properties. Operational understanding, which is to modify the existing geometric figure, is the most important way to understand a figure. This modification can be accomplished mentally or by drawing. Duval (2006) further pointed out that one of the most important ways to modify a geometric figure is reconfiguration. In order to solve a geometric problem, we usually decompose the complex geometric figure into several different parts, and then identify the sub-figures, or reconfigure the original figure into a new geometric figure in order to solve the original problem effectively. For example, we can reconfigure a parallelogram into a rectangle with the same area in order to calculate the area of the parallelogram (Duval, 2006).

When a figure only consists of simple figures, it is relatively easy to deal with the reconfiguration, such as a parallelogram being reconfigured into a rectangle, as mentioned above. But within a superimposed and staggered complex figure, it is harder to recognize hidden sub-figures. In addition, there are many different ways to reconfigure, so we should comprise, discriminate, and choose an appropriate reconfiguration in order to solve a problem effectively. This is very difficult for students due to two main factors of the cognitive difficulty. First, students do not have appropriate understanding of properties of a figure, because a deep understanding can help students to identify the hidden sub-figures, and then solve problems through configuration. Second, students may disconnect properties with diagrams, and observe and identify sub-figures based on visual perceptions. So they may overlook some configurations and not see the hidden sub-figures (Duval, 2006). In order to help students overcome these difficulties, Duval (1999) pointed out: "a true didactical approach requires to embrace the whole range of variations of the conditions of a problem and to bring out the various factors that make them clear" (p. 29). What he advocated is similar to what teaching through variation implies in China; specifically, these above notions correspond to what Gu described as procedural variation in his theory (Gu, 1981).

Procedural Variation

Reconfiguration of geometric figures. Gu (1994) argued that in some complex geometric figures, sub-geometric figures tend to be separated, broken, or staggered due to their background. Sometimes essential properties of the geometric objects/ elements are hidden within the backgrounds, which results in students' difficulties with understanding of the geometric objects/elements. To solve the problems, students have to learn how to identify geometric objects/elements from a complex background. This identification/discrimination not only relies on the complexity of the figure, but also relies on learners' prior knowledge and the problem to be solved. Gu's notions of teaching with variation are aligned with Duval's view about the understanding of geometric figures. In classroom teaching practice, Gu (1994) explored a teaching method named "transforming figure construction" (or in Chinese, it is called *Tuxing Yanbian*), where students were shown the process of transforming simple figures into complex figures by translation, rotation, and reflection. He believed that this process could help students understand how the geometric figures transform from simple to complex, from continuous to discontinuous, and from staggered to without staggering. This transformation can help students identify geometric objects from a complex background. Through transformation, it can build a bridge between the simple and complex figures, which can provide an opportunity for students to understand geometric figures in a sequential way. It can also promote further understanding of complex figures for students, thus helping them reconfigure the figures according to what is needed to solve the problem. For example, in Figure 1, a simple figure (triangle) can become a basic figure (sub-figure) through a transformation (rotation). Then by adding a line, we can get a complex figure (trapezoid). This process of transformation can help students reconfigure figures by identifying basic figures from background. Gu later coined this way of teaching as "procedural variation", and explored effective implementation in mathematics class in China. Now it has become one of the key characteristics of Chinese mathematics teaching (Gu et al., 2004).

Anchoring knowledge point and potential distance of knowledge. In the process of problem solving, procedural variation can be presented in three ways: (1) one problem with multiple change- changing the initial problem or expanding the initial problem by changing the conditions and conclusions; (2) one problem with multiple solutions- various solutions to a problem as variations and then connect the multiple solutions; (3) one solution with multiple use- use a same solution to solve similar problems (Gu et al., 2004). By this way of instruction, previous problem posing and solutions can set a necessary foundation for approaching and solving the subsequent problem. So the key point is how to design scaffoldings (in Chinese, it is called *Pudian*) for student learning, which can maintain an appropriate distance between the prior knowledge and new problem.

Gu (1994) put forward a hypothesis of "*Anchoring knowledge point*" and "potential distance of knowledge." The *anchoring knowledge point* means the prior knowledge serving as a foundation for new knowledge. The distance between a task to solve and the *anchoring knowledge point* is the potential distance. When the potential distance becomes larger, the task is more difficult. For example, in Figure 1, if we use the simple figure as the anchoring knowledge point to explore properties of the complex figure, which has a longer potential distance and more difficult than using the basic figure. Therefore, a teacher needs to design the necessary scaffoldings according to students' mathematics cognition and adjust the potential distance to achieve effective teaching results.

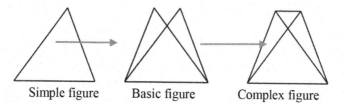

Simple figure   Basic figure   Complex figure

Figure 1. Potential distance between different figures

In this study, we adopt a combination of the perspectives from Gu and Duval mentioned before to analyze a lesson as a case to reflect on how the teacher enacted procedural variation in a review mathematics lesson.

METHODS

Participant and Context

Mr. Chou has been teaching middle school mathematics for 15 years and is currently a teacher and deputy director of academic affairs in a public middle school in W town. Mr. Chou was promoted as a senior secondary school teacher (See Huang et al., 2010 for detailed information about ranking system in China) in 2010, and has been selected as a young model teacher of the town and academic leader of the distinct. The lesson analyzed in the chapter is a public lesson taught by Mr. Chou in the spring of 2014. Nearly 30 mathematics teachers observed this lesson. We interviewed Mr. Chou about his teaching design and his perception of and reflection on the lesson after the lesson.

Data Collection

In this study, we collected data from a public lesson organized by a Master Teacher Workstation (MTW), which is a professional learning community consisting of a leader master teacher who is officially recognized and some key teachers (young and promising teachers). In May 2014, the MTW held the public lesson of *Fuxi Ke* (a type of lesson which reviews content from textbook unit learned in classroom). The public lesson development is similar to normal teaching research activity. Mr. Chou implemented public lessons first, and all members of the MTW observed the lessons. In the meeting after each lesson, the teacher explained his lesson plan and implementation briefly, then the leader of the MTW commented on the lesson and other observing teachers commented and discussed their questions. Collected materials included the lesson plan, the lesson video (about 45 minutes), and the meeting audio (about 120 minutes).

Description of the Lesson Plan

We identified two main teaching objectives of the lesson from the lesson plan: first, to facilitate students' understanding of congruent figures, Mr. Chou intended to connect congruency of triangles with geometry transformations, which would help students employ multiple solutions in problem solving. Second, Mr. Chou planned to design variation problems, trying to go through different tasks with a principle idea to help students understand the nature of the tasks during transformations.

The lesson plan included three major phases:

In the first section, Mr. Chou wanted to give each student a pair of cards of congruent right triangles (containing an angle of 30 degrees). Students were required to use the cards to form various basic figures by translation, reflection, and rotation, and were asked to draw the formed figures on the blackboard.

In the second section, Mr. Chou would pick three basic figures formed by translation, reflection and rotation from what the students draw on the blackboard (Figure 2), and then asked them to pose problems and solve them.

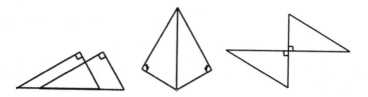

Figure 2. Basic figures formed by translation, reflection, and rotation

In the third section, on a basic figure by rotation (Figure 3), Mr. Chou would translate one of the triangles, and make the basic figure become a complex figure (Figure 4). When ΔAPN is congruent with ΔDCN, Mr. Chou required his students to prove ΔEPM is congruent with ΔBFM (Task 1). Then Mr. Chou keep translating the right triangle towards left along the common sides till point D overlaps with point B (Figure 5), connect AE, and take the midpoint G, students are asked to prove GF = GC (Task 2).

174

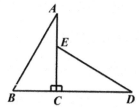

Figure 3. A basic figure by translation

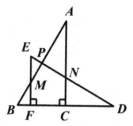

Figure 4. Two intersected triangles

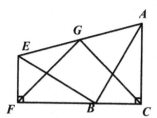

Figure 5. Nearly separated triangles

Research Presumption and Question

From the lesson design, it is evident that Mr. Chou planned to run through different tasks by the employment of variation in teaching design. First, he planned to ask students to form various basic figures (one figure with multiple changes) according to different geometric transformations, by which all kinds of basic figures of congruent triangles could be unified in geometric transformations. Then, he planned to pick three basic figures from the figures formed in the first section. He asked his students to pose different problems through adding some conditions by themselves, and prove different conclusions (one problem with multiple changes).

During this process, the teacher could review the basic knowledge of congruent triangles, while facilitating the students to compound understanding various properties of basic figures and help them accumulate learning experiences for recognizing sub-figures and re-configuring complex figures in the third section. What is worth noticing is that in his plan, all basic figures would be transformed once in the first two sections, while in the third section the two complex figures would be formed by two geometric transformations which are overlaid and intersected, including several sub-figures. This is anticipated to be more difficult for the students.

In the lesson design, Figure 4 would be obtained by a translation from Figure 3, which is a basic figure. When translating it, the teacher wanted to get Figure 5. It is a typical procedural variation where tasks were designed from a basic figure to complex figures by translation. Can the basic figures help the students shorten potential distance, or reduce their cognitive difficulties? Could solving Task 1 provide the students necessary scaffoldings for solving Task 2? We aim to answer these questions through examining students' behaviors and interaction between students and the teacher in the classroom.

LESSON OBSERVATION AND ANALYSIS

In this section, we break Mr. Chou's lesson into three phases: constructing basic figures, exploring properties of the basic figures, and solving complicated problems. The students' work and interactions between the students and the teacher from each phase are reported and analyzed.

Constructing Basic Figures

First of all, Mr. Chou asked each student to use the two right triangles cardboard to construct figures with transformations of translation, reflection, and rotation, and then draw these figures on the background. As a whole class, the students came up with three kinds of basic figures with translation (Figure 6), two kinds of symmetric figures (Figure 7), and four kinds of figures with rotation (Figure 8) on the blackboard.

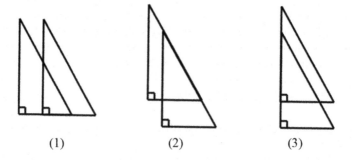

(1)   (2)   (3)

Figure 6. Basic figures with different translations

176

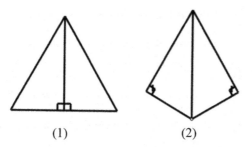

(1)   (2)

Figures 7. Different symmetric figures

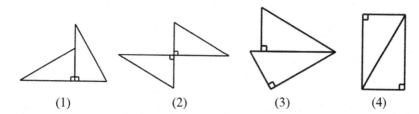

(1)   (2)   (3)   (4)

Figure 8. Basic figures with different rotations

Mr. Chou asked, "are there any other figures?" He found that a student constructed another different rotating figure and he showed it to the class (Figure 7(1)). The rotational center of this figure is same with Figure 8(3). By reducing the angle of rotation, the two right triangles were superimposed. Mr. Chou continued asking whether there were any other figures. When he walked around in the classroom, he found a new symmetric figure (Figure 9(2)) and raised the cardboard to demonstrate to the whole class. Mr. Chou looked for others that he had in mind, and asked for more figures again. As he returned to the podium, he found a new symmetric figure (Figure 9(3)) and drew this figure on the blackboard.

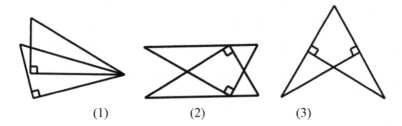

(1)   (2)   (3)

Figure 9. Three new-formed figures from students

According to Duval's view, the process of construction can help students understand geometric figures deductively. In other words, it can promote their

177

understanding of the properties of the figures (Duval 1995, 1999). In this lesson, although students did not construct figures with ruler and compass, their operations and drawings were under the guide of the geometric transformation, and followed the law of transformations. From this point of view, this strategy can further facilitate the students' understanding of the properties of figures. According to Gu's notion, transforming figure constructions can help students understand geometric figures in a dynamic manner, which allows students to identify geometric objects from a complicated background (Gu, 1994). In conclusion, according to the two scholars' view as mentioned above, the first section of Mr. Chou's lesson can help students understand basic figure properties, and it is conducive for them to reconfigure geometric figures. In terms of the teaching effect, students' performance in the section that follows.

Exploring Properties of the Basic Figures

Mr. Chou demonstrated a translation figure with a projector (Figure 10). This figure can be seen as a variation of the Figure 5(2), drawn by students on the blackboard. He asked the students to find conditions to make △ABC≅△DEF. The following hypotheses were made: (1) AD = CF, ∠B = ∠E, ∠A = ∠EDF; (2) ∠B = 90⁰, BC = DE, AC = DF, ∠BCA = ∠F; (3) ∠B = ∠E, ∠C = ∠F, AB = DE; (4) ∠B = ∠E = 90⁰, BC = EF, AD = CF.

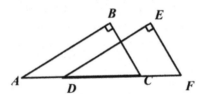

Figure 10. Adding conditions to make △ABC ≅ △DEF

Through translating the basic figure, Mr. Chou reviewed how to determine triangles' congruency. Meanwhile, it enhanced students' understanding of the properties of the basic figure by connecting the properties with triangle congruency and transformations.

The second basic figure Mr. Chou wanted the students to explore is in Figure 7(2). Here is an episode from the lesson.

Episode 1

[1] Mr. Chou: Can you use this figure to pose some problems? For convenience, we add some corresponding letter under the condition △ABC ≅ △ADC, ...who can try?

[2] Student 1: connect BD, so BD = AC (Figure 11(2)).

[3] Mr. Chou: why? ... We connect BD, and assume it intersects with AC on point O.

[4] Student 1: because $\triangle ABC \cong \triangle ADC$, so $\angle BAC = \angle BDC$, AB = AD, so BD is perpendicular to AC.

[5] Mr. Chou: why?

[6] Student 1: in an isosceles triangle, altitude, angular bisector, central line are the same.

[7] Mr. Chou: good, we can also prove it with congruent triangles. What else do you find?

[8] All the students: AC is perpendicular bisector of BD.

[9] Mr. Chou: well, if we take a point O on AC, Can you pose a problem? ......
(Figure 11(3))

[10] Student 2: BO=DO.

[11] Mr. Chou: Can you tell me why?

[12] Student2: because $\triangle ABO \cong \triangle ADO$.

[13] Mr. Chou: Do you all understand? As I just said ...... In fact this is a symmetric figure. If you fold it along its symmetrical axis, the two parts will coincide completely. ......If we take a point E on BC, and a point F on DC, then ......(Figure 11(4))

[14] All the students: AE = AF.

[15] Mr. Chou: what conditions do we need in order to ensure AE=AF?

[16] Student 3: BE = DF.

[17] Mr. Chou: why?

[18] Student 3: SAS.

[19] Mr. Chou: very good.

From the Episode 1, we can find in the Line [2], Student 1 conjectured that "connect BD, then BD = AC" and then completed its proof. Under the guidance of Mr. Chou, all the other students found "BO = DO" ([8]). Similarly, the other students also proved "BO = DO" ([9] ~ [12]), and "if BE = DF, then AE = AF" ([13]~[18]). This shows that Mr. Chou used a symmetric figure as an original figure and changed it during the communication with the students, which helped them to use this basic figure as an anchoring knowledge point. It shortened the potential distance to the explored problems and thus reduced the difficulty of the problem. In addition, it is also evident that the conclusions involved some properties of the isosceles triangle under the condition that the basic figure was treated as a symmetric figure. Through the proof of congruent triangles, students made connections between the triangle congruency and geometric transformations, which are the main learning goals of this lesson. On the other hand, through the exploration of these problems, the students utilized the symmetric properties upon the basic figures, so that the figure became a stronger anchoring knowledge point associated with abundant knowledge. According to Gu's (1994) view, it brings convenience to solve more complicated problems. The teacher-student interactions, in which the students made conjectures and proved by themselves, could promote their deductive reasoning related to the basic figure. When students have a deeper understanding of the basic figure, it will benefit them to reconfigure the complicated figures and solve more difficult problems (Duval, 2006).

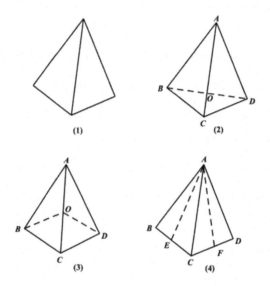

Figure 11. Exploring properties of a symmetric figure

Mr. Chou used the same strategy to discuss the third type of basic figure – a rotational figure (Figure 12(1)). The original figure is shown in Figure 8(2), which students drew on the blackboard in the first lesson section. There were three different variations: (1) drawing a line from point C which intersects with AB and DE on F and G, prove CF = CG (Figure 12(2)); (2) If connecting AE and BD, then AE = BD (Figure 12(3)); (3) if AF = DG, and connecting EF and BG, then EF = BG (Figure 12(4)).

At this point, the second section of the lesson was finished. It may be the scaffolding of the basic figures that made the potential distance of the problem relatively close and allowed students to solve the problem without any significant cognitive obstacles. Through exploring the three basic figures as described above, the students had a deeper understanding of the properties of the basic figures and learned more knowledge, which potentially improved their ability to identify sub-structures from complicated figures and reduce the difficulty of complicated problems.

It should be noticed that the figure Mr. Chou looked for and highlighted in the first section of the lesson was deliberate. According to what he claimed in the meeting, the figure was a key basic figure for students solving complex problems. However, if the figure is so important, why didn't he explore its properties with students in the class? In fact, according to Gu's view, this basic figure shows the interval of lines

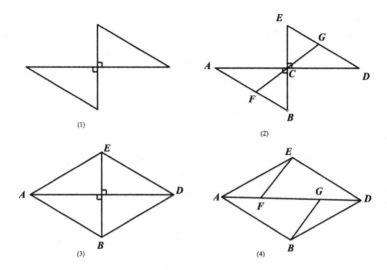

Figure 12. Exploring properties of rotational figures

and the stagger of triangles, so the positional relations of different lines and the measurement relations of line segments become more complicated (Gu, 1982). It may either be a missed teachable moment, or a deliberate choice of Mr. Chou, which was not clear without further elaboration from him.

Solving Complicated Problems

Encountering challenges/difficulties. Mr. Chou showed a rotational figure (Figure 3) on the projection, then translated RtΔECD to the left along the straight line CD, and asked, "What kind of positional relationship is maintained between ED and AB during the translation?" Students answered immediately that the two lines were perpendicular to each other. Then Mr. Chou asked a follow-up question, "if RtΔAPN is congruent with RtΔCDN, which triangles are congruent with each other (Figure 4)?" The students all answered that RtΔEPM would be congruent with RtΔBFM. Then the teacher asked them to prove it. After a few minutes, the teacher noticed that the students could not come up with any answer, so he suggested erasing some line segments to reduce the difficulty. Then a substructure as shown in Figure 13(1) was demonstrated on the blackboard. It was the figure (Figure 9) that the teacher found and drew on the blackboard in the first section. "If RtΔAPN is congruent with RtΔCDN, then which two triangles would be congruent with each other?" Mr. Chou asked. It was evident that the triangles were RtΔABC and RtΔBDP. A student volunteered to give a proof. Under the condition that RtΔAPN was congruent with RtΔCDN, the student got that AD = ND, PN = CN, and then AC = DP, so he successfully proved that RtABC was congruent with RtBDP.

Mr. Chou went back to the original figure and encouraged the student to make a conjecture, such as RtΔEPM was congruent with RtΔBFM. But the student only knew that ED = AB, as shown in Figure 4. Although Mr. Chou gave him an important hint that AB was equal to BD, the student still could not reason further. The teacher erased the line segments reluctantly, and went back to Figure 13(1), explaining that if RtΔABC was congruent with RtΔBDP, and then AB would be equal to BD. He returned to the original figure, erased other parts, and got a new substructure of Figure 13(2), which was still the basic figure as shown in Figure 13(1) with only the position changed. Mr. Chou said, "Can you prove that RtΔEPM is congruent with RtΔBFM?", in fact, in the figure, RtΔEFD is congruent with RtBPD because of ED = BD, so it is relatively easy to prove that RtΔEPM is congruent with RtΔ ABFM (EP = BF is evident, because of DP = DF and ED = BD).

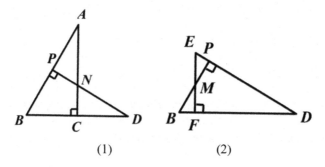

(1)   (2)

Figure 13. Two substructures in Task 1

From what we observed in the lesson, the students had difficulties solving the problem; at least, they were unable to complete their proof within a short amount of time. In other words, there was a long potential distance between the anchoring knowledge point to the problem they were exploring. The key to solving the problem is to identify the basic figure of symmetry in the complex background, and then reconfigure the original figure. However, the students demonstrated difficulties to accomplish it. In the lesson, although Mr. Chou had constructed the basic figure at the beginning of the lesson, he didn't lead the class to explore the figure's properties as doing with other figures in the later part of the class. It wasn't clear why Mr. Chou chose not to elaborate on these properties. It is plausible to conjecture that if the teacher could have done so, it may have provided more scaffolding for the students to identify the substructure, and possibly make the potential distance shorter to reach the solution.

The final variation problems. Mr. Chou kept translating the triangle towards the right where only a common point was shared, as shown in Figure 14(1).

Episode 2

[1] Mr. Chou: what would you find when we connect A and E (Figure 13(2))?

[2] Student 4: AB is perpendicular to EB, and AB = EB.

[22] Mr. Chou: that is to say ∆EBA is an isosceles right triangle. What would you come up with as you get the midpoint G of AE (Figure 14(3))?

[23] Student 5: BG is half of AE.

[24] Mr. Chou: when connect B and G (the teacher didn't do it on the figure), the median of the hypotenuse is half of it. If I connect F and G, and connect C and G, then what relation do the two segments have (Figure 14(4))?

[25] Student 6: FG is perpendicular with BG, and FG = BG.

[26] Mr. Chou: ∆FGB is also an isosceles right triangle. Please think about how to prove? (The teacher constructed the figure on the blackboard). Generally, if want to prove FG = BG, we should find two congruent triangles. Here we got ∆EFG, and here is FG. Which triangle do we put GC into?

[27] All: Into GBC, connect G and B.

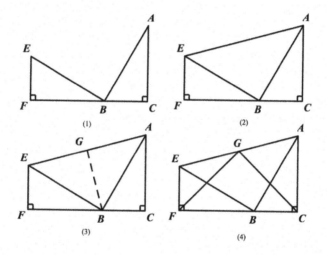

Figure 14. Variation figures in Task 2

From the Episode 2, we can see that Mr. Chou employed procedural variation and demonstrated the construction process of the figures from Figure 14(1) to Figure 14(4). This process was beneficial for the students to identify substructure of the complicated figure and reconfigure: at first, Mr. Chou connected A and E, asking his students to identify the shape of EBA ([20] ~ [22]), which scaffolded the students to recognize congruent triangles. When Mr. Chou took the midpoint G of AE ([22]), the students had an opportunity to mentally operate the figure and identify a basic figure with the median line of hypotenuse ([23]). It again scaffolded the students to successfully construct a new triangle in the figure ([27]). It might be because of the scaffolds from Mr. Chou that the students could prove this task smoothly.

In the lesson, the teacher made the figure in Task 2 based on a transformation from Task 1. When he prepared the lesson, Mr. Chou intended to make the two tasks into variation problems. A positive influence of the former task on the second was not evident in the observed episode. Mr. Chou's choice was plausible based on the result of the observation. A further look into the students' cognitive obstacles revealed missing opportunities of potential teachable moments, and that the specific scaffoldings provided by Mr. Chou might be beneficial to improve the effectiveness of the variation instruction.

CONCLUSION AND DISCUSSION

Summary

In the case study examined in this paper, Mr. Chou adopted procedural variations in his lesson design and implementation. At the beginning he structured multiple basic shapes through transforming triangles, and then explored three basic figures formed by the students. Based on the analysis of the teaching episode, the students solved the initial problems successfully possibly because the potential distance between these problems and the anchoring knowledge point of the students were close (needs evidence to support). Despite the fact that no cognitive obstacle was revealed during this phase, from a theoretical perspective, this instructional method can help students understand basic figures deeply and make necessary scaffoldings for students to identify basic figures from complicated figures.

However, Task 1 became more complicated and had many sub-constructions, which made it difficult for the students to reconfigure. This is plausible since the teacher did not conduct any exploration to the basic figure, which was required for the students to identify in the background. The potential distance between the anchoring knowledge point and the task explored was too far for the students to reach a further discussion. In addition, the teacher failed to give the students adequate time to explore and only provided two scaffolds. As a result, the students did not have enough opportunities to tackle the task. For Task 2, although the students solved it successfully, the teacher provided an exceedingly large amount of scaffolds by asking a series of questions. As a result, the students had limited space to explore on their own.

Conclusion

According to the literature, the amount of scaffolds made by teachers and explorations carried out by students distinguishes the difference between teacher-centered and student-centered instruction within a learning context. The more scaffolds a teacher provides, the less space is left for students to explore, and vice versa. The teacher in this case study tried to achieve a balance between the two, where he provided a certain amount of scaffolds to control the distance between the anchoring point and the task at hand, so that the students could have a manageable amount of space to explore the problem. Our findings showed that the distance varied throughout the episode, and different amounts of scaffolds were provided for different tasks. The decision-making moments for the control of the distances and the scaffolds are the most challenging parts for teachers to conduct procedural variation teaching (Gu, 1994).

Discussion

There was an extra task found in Mr. Chou's lesson plan (see Figure 15(1)), which was designed a year ago. Since he did not use this task in the observed lesson, we do not have data to elaborate on the students' cognitive obstacles on it. The task is shown in Figure 14(1): AC = BC, ∠ACB = 90°, BD is the bisector of ∠ABC, prove: AB = BC + CD.

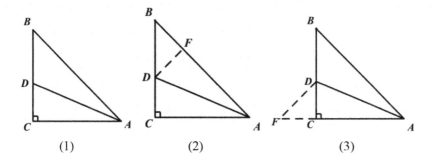

(1)   (2)   (3)

Figure 15. A task in the teacher's materials with different solutions

In the lesson plan, Mr. Chou planned to ask students to solve this problem with different methods. This task can be solved in at least two ways. First, students can use folding to reconfigure the figure (as shown in Figure 14(2)), which was explored in the second section of the lesson. Second, as shown in figure 14(3), students can use the properties of Figure 8(3), which can provide necessary scaffold for the solving of Task 2. The change of the lesson plan may have reflected difficulties of designing teaching with variations.

Many factors should be considered while designing teaching with variations, such as the limitation of teaching time, how deep the scaffolds should be made, and space for students to explore. Teachers need to reflect on their teaching moments in practice in order to design effective variations to tasks employed in teaching.

REFERENCES

Cheng, L., & Huang, X. (2003). Want to embarrass students but be puzzled by them. *Shanghai Research Education, 4*, 66–68.

Du, P. (2005). A case study on variation in review lessons. *School Mathematics 1*, 5–6.

Duval, R. (1995). Geometrical pictures: Kinds of representation and specific processes In R. Sutherland & J. Mason (Eds.), *Exploiting mental imagery with computers in mathematical education* (pp. 142–157). Berlin, Germany: Springer.

Duval, R. (1999). Representation, vision and visualization: Cognitive functions in mathematical thinking. *Basic Issues for Learning*. Retrieved from ERIC ED 466379.

Duval, R. (2006). A cognitive analysis of problems of comprehension in a learning of mathematics. *Educational Studies in Mathematics, 61*, 103–131.

Fischbein, E. (1993). The theory of figural concepts. *Educational Studies in Mathematics, 24*, 139–162.

Gu, L. (1982). The effective analysis on use figure variation to teach geometrical concept. *Education Research Communication, 5*, 34–37.

Gu, L. (1994). *Teaching experiment: Research on methodology and teaching principle in Qingpu Experiment*. Beijing: Education Science Publisher.

Gu, L., Huang, R., & Marton, F. (2004). Teaching with variation: A Chinese way of promoting effective mathematics learning. In L. Fan, N. Wong, J. Cai, & S. Li (Eds.), *How Chinese learn mathematics: Perspectives from insiders* (pp. 309–347). Mahwah, NJ: World Scientific.

Herbst, P. (2004). Interactions with diagrams and the making of reasoned conjectures in geometry. *ZDM – The International Journal on Mathematics Education, 36*, 129–139.

Huang, Y., & Liang, Y. (2011). Exploration on teaching design on junior school mathematics review lesson. *Elementary Education Research, 18*, 39–41.

Maton, F., & Booth, B. (1997). *Learning and awareness*. Mahwah, NJ: Laurence Erlbaum.

Maton, F., Runesson, U., & Tsui, A. B. M. (2004). The learning space. In F. Maton & A. B. M. Tsui (Eds.), *Classroom discourse and the learning space* (pp. 13–65). Mahwah, NJ: Laurence Eelbaum.

Rui, Z. (1998). Design and teaching on mathematics variation problems in junior school. *Middle School Mathematics Monthly, 4*, 7–10. [In Chinese]

Tao, Y., & Xu, W. (2009). Study on review lessons. *Theory and Practice of Education, 2*, 51–53.

Wei, G. (2008). Revolution on mathematics review lesson. *People's Education, 5*, 41–44.

Zhang, X., & Xu, X. (2012). Figure transformation: A case of rotation on two squares. *Mathematics Teaching in Middle Schools, 1*, 110–113.

Xingfeng Huang
Shanghai Normal University, China

Xinrong Yang
Southwest University, China

Pingping Zhang
Winona State University, USA

IDA AH CHEE MOK

10. TEACHING ALGEBRA THROUGH VARIATIONS

Contrast, Generalization, Fusion, and Separation

INTRODUCTION

Recent years have witnessed an increase in research focused on studying on the psychological and pedagogical perspectives of Chinese learners in the mathematics instructions. A main driver in these studies has been the sustained interest in cracking the phenomenon known as the "Paradox of Chinese Learners" (see for example Biggs, 1996; Mok et al., 2001; Leung, 2001; Huang & Leung, 2004; Watkins & Biggs, 2001) that highlights the apparent contradiction between the teaching methods and environments in East Asian and Western school, and the fact that East Asian students have regularly performed better than their Western counterparts in comparative studies, such as the Trends in International Mathematics and Science Study (TIMSS, Mullis, et al., 2012) and the Programme for International Student Assessment (OECD, 2010, 2014). Findings of these studies have contributed to a more comprehensive picture of Asian classrooms. In several studies, teaching with variation is identified to be an important feature of the Chinese ways for promoting effective learning in Chinese mathematics lessons (Fan, Wong, Cai, & Li, 2015; Gu, Huang, & Marton, 2004; Lim, 2007; Mok, 2006). The appreciation of variation as an important factor for effective learning is, indeed, not a culture specific feature. With the assumption that meaningful learning can only be achieved via discernment of the critical aspects, Marton and others developed the Variation Theory of Learning (Marton & Booth, 1997; Marton, Runesson, & Tsui, 2003; Marton & Pang, 2013; Marton, 2015; Pang & Marton, 2013). The aim of this paper is to provide an illustration of the Chinese teaching with variation via empirical examples found in algebra lessons of Hong Kong and Shanghai. The analytical tools developed in the Variation Theory of the phenomenography approach were used in the analysis to capture the examples. A brief summary of the Variation Theory for learning will be given in the next section, followed with a summary of studies of the Chinese way of teaching with variation. This theory is then used to analyze selected algebra lessons of Hong Kong and Shanghai taken from the Learner's Perspective Study (LPS) (Clarke et al., 2006).

R. Huang & Y. Li (Eds.), Teaching and Learning Mathematics through Variation, 187–205.

THE VARIATION THEORY FOR LEARNING

> Variation Theory is not a theory about how learning is organized but theory
> bout how the content of learning is organized. (Pang & Marton, 2013, p. 1066)

The Variation Theory finds its root in the work of phenomenography led by Marton and his co-researchers (Marton & Booth, 1997). The basic assumption is that learning is a kind of experience in which learners develop a way of seeing or experiencing (Marton et al., 2004). Referring to classroom learning, learning is centred on objects of learning and it is very important for the learners to discern the critical features of the object of learning. In this theory, learning is supported by an awareness of the critical aspects of the object of learning, where awareness depends on the experience of variation. In other words, via the experience of different patterns of variation, the learner makes sense of the "sameness" in different forms of the object of learning and the differences against a background of sameness (Marton & Pang, 2013; Marton, 2015). It is argued that the contrast between the variant and the invariant helps the learner experience the object of learning in a certain way. This is called discernment in the theory. The idea can be illustrated with an example of the concept of "green" (Marton, 2015). The color "green" can only be comprehended if people live in a world consisting of green color and the non-green color, and there are two patterns of variation and invariants for discerning what "green" is. Namely, different green objects (e.g., green ball, green cube, and green prism) and objects of different color (e.g., green ball, red ball, and blue ball). Furthermore, even though the learner may not see all these at the same time, the accumulated experiences of "green" and "color" will help the learner see a dimension of variation. For example, in this case, color is a dimension of variation in relation to green, red, and blue; green is a dimension of variation in relation to light green or dark green. Therefore, learning is promoted in an environment consisting of appropriate patterns of variation. Discernment is essential for meaningful learning to take place. Furthermore, discernment is made possible when variation concerning the critical aspects or features is created either in the design of the content (or the tasks) of the lesson or in the interaction between class participants (i.e., teacher and students, students and students). According to Marton, Runesson, and Tsui (2003), the teacher may have a specific object of learning and this may be elaborated in different degrees of detail. What teachers try to teach is the intended object of learning, which is an object of the teacher's awareness. However, what is more important is how the teacher structures the lessons so that it is possible for the object of learning to come to the forefront of the students' awareness. The researcher's description of the lesson from the point of view of a specific research interest, which describes how an object of learning appears in the lesson, is called the enacted object of learning. In other words, the enacted object of learning encompassing the content and the interaction between the learning tasks and the participants and between participants is depicted. Moreover, the enacted object of learning is compared with the intended object of learning created by the teacher's planning and the lived object of learning captured by an individual learner (e.g., Marton et al., 2003; Runnesson & Mok, 2005).

Variation can be created in different ways within a lesson. What patterns of variation may teachers have created in their lessons to enhance learning? Some examples are found in empirical studies of lessons. Marton and Tsui (2004) studied classroom discourse in lessons for different subjects (including language, mathematics, and science) and identified some patterns of variations, namely, contrast, generalization, separation, and fusion. Mok (2009), in her study of the lessons of a competent Hong Kong teacher, found patterns of variation such as contrast, separation, and fusion in the teaching of algebra. These concepts are briefly recapitulated here (for elaborate discussion, see Marton & Tsui, 2004; Marton, 2015):

Contrast. In order to experience something, a learner must experience something else to compare with, e.g. a comparison between what the object is and what it is not, such as, "three" (three balls) and "not three" (two balls, four balls).

Generalization. In order to understand what "threeness" is, one must see the meaning of "three" in three apples, three monkeys, three books, etc. These experiences are important for enabling the learner to grasp the idea of "threeness" and separate the focused aspect ("three") from the non-focused aspects (apples, monkeys, books). The pattern of generalization seems to be the same as that of induction but there is an important difference. In Marton's theory, contrast comes before generalization in the path of learning. For example, learners have discerned triangle as a feature by contrasting triangles, squares, and circles. Then by subsequently experiencing triangles of different sizes, different angles, and different rotational positions, learners may then generalize the geometric form of a triangle across size, angle, and rotational position.

Fusion. After discerning parts of an object of learning, the whole has to be put together. Fusion refers to learners' "putting together" the parts to constitute the whole through an experience of the variation of several critical aspects simultaneously. Fusion not only involves each case, all aspects being focused, but also deals with how these aspects are functionally or logically related to each other. For example, to learn a Chinese word with the correct sound, tone, and meaning; to recognize the meaning and equivalence of an equation when it is presented in apparently different forms, such as, $2x + 3y = 0$, $2x = -3y$. Referring to the path of learning, the stages necessarily occur in the sequence of contrast, generalization, and fusion.

Separation. Discernment implies separation. That is, when discerning an aspect of an object, one must separate the aspect from the other aspects via experiences of patterns of variant and invariant aspects of the object. For example, one cannot discern coefficients and unknowns without separating the coefficients ("2", "3") from the unknowns ("x", "y") in the equation $2x + 3y = 0$.

189

TEACHING WITH VARIATION: A CHINESE WAY FOR PROMOTING
EFFECTIVE LEARNING OF MATHEMATICS

Applying variation as an effective pedagogical tool can be traced back to the teaching experiment led by Gu in the 1980s in Shanghai, that was reported in the book Learning to Teach (Gu, 1991). Variation is also a component of Gu's model for structuring the lessons. Because of its positive impact on students' learning, teaching with variation, also known as *"Bianshi* Teaching" (Bao et al., 2003; Wong & Chan, 2013), has been widely adopted in China (Gu et al., 2004; Wong, Lam, & Chan, 2013). Gu, Huang and Marton (2004) summarized the pedagogical theory of teaching with variation with two concepts of variation: conceptual variation and procedural variation. The essence of Gu's theory of teaching with variation is to "illustrate the essential features by demonstrating different forms of visual materials and instances or highlight the essence of a concept by varying the nonessential features" (Gu et al., 2004, p. 315). Conceptual variation is concerned with understanding concepts from multiple perspectives, which can be achieved by varying visual and concrete instances, contrasting non-standard concept images figures. A kind of "procedural variation" is suggested to help students establish the concept progressively. For example, in writing the equation for the problem "James pays \$D 2 for buying three erasers and the seller gives him 2 coins in change (1/10 \$D). How much is each eraser?", three kinds of scaffolding can be introduced progressively: (1) representing the unknown by concrete things (e.g., 2D-♣♣♣=2C, presenting the question visually); (2) symbolizing the unknown (e.g., $20 - 3x = 2$, a concrete model of the equation); (3) replacing unknown x with the symbol of a box "□" ($20 - 3□=2$, a game for which □ represents a box for numbers). The purpose of the pedagogical model is to design a series of conceptual and procedural variation to create a system of experiences and strategies hierarchically and could be internalized into the cognitive structure (for details, see Gu et al., 2004, pp. 319–322).

THE USE OF VARIATION AS A CONCEPTUAL TOOL FOR
THE ANALYSIS OF MATHEMATICS LESSONS

There are now a significant number of research studies (e.g., Huang & Leung, 2004; Huang, Miller, & Tzur, 2015; Mok, 2004, 2009, 2013; Runesson & Mok, 2005) that have used variation as a conceptual tool to analyze mathematics lessons. Collectively, the findings contribute instances to support the contention that variation is an important feature in providing effective learning for mathematics in Chinese classrooms. In the context of algebra, Mok's (2006) analysis of mathematics lessons in Shanghai showed how variation played a role in the formation of concepts progressively while providing an experience for discerning the critical aspects of the relationship between the coefficients and the method of solving equations. Mok further argued that the Shanghai teacher had successfully developed a planned experience in exploring the intended object of learning and that the skillful use of variation brought about opportunities for students to experience the important aspects of the mathematics in the lessons, such as the coefficients of the equations, the contrast between the methods, and the relationship between procedural and conceptual aspects. Huang and co-researchers, studying lessons in Hong Kong and Shanghai, noted different patterns of variation in the pedagogy, for example, procedural variation for investigating the cases from special to general in mathematical proofs; implicit and explicit variation in the items for practice (Huang & Leung, 2004; Huang, Mok, & Leung, 2006). Also, on the study of instructional practice for algebra, Mok (2013) investigated the nature of instructional coherence in a sample of four consecutive Shanghai mathematics 7th grade lessons on the topic of systems of linear equations of two unknowns. In the findings five strategies supporting instructional coherence were identified and one strategy was the consolidation with variation in examples and exercises. Huang, Miller and Tzur (2015) developed a hybrid-model analysis of students' learning opportunities in Chinese classrooms that consisted of a tripartite theoretical lens, namely, reflection on activity-effect relationship, hypothetical learning trajectory, and teaching with bridging and variation. Via the lens of this model, the task sequence might serve the purposes of bridging, teaching intended ideas with variation, and elaboration with variation.

METHODS AND SOURCE OF DATA

The data used in this chapter is taken from the Hong Kong and Shanghai data set of the Learner's Perspective Study (LPS). The study recorded a sequence of at least ten consecutive lessons of each competent teacher in the study recommended by local researchers. The video recording used a three-camera setting: a teacher-camera, a student-camera on two focused students, and a class-camera on the whole class. The two focused students were invited for post-lesson interviews after each lesson and the teacher was interviewed three times during the data collection period. Stimulated recall method was employed; during the interview, the teacher chose one lesson video and elaborated his thinking, supporting the design and implementation of his lesson. The analysis of the lesson employed the learning perspectives with the essential elements of discernment and variation developed in the work of Marton and his co-authors. The main objective was to illustrate how useful patterns of variation may be created in algebra lessons, therefore, one Hong Kong lesson and one Shanghai lesson were chosen to be analyzed in detail. The lessons were chosen because they were potentially rich in patterns of variation and illustrative examples for how appropriate patterns of variation might be created. The Shanghai lesson took place in *Qingpu*, where the empirical origin of the pedagogy of variation was found and promoted. Therefore, the lesson could be seen as a typical application of the Chinese pedagogical model of variation. Unlike Shanghai, the pedagogy of variation was not a promoted pedagogy in the curriculum of Hong Kong; therefore, it was unlikely for Hong Kong teachers to use variation persistently in their design of lessons. The Hong Kong lesson was chosen because the teacher had reviewed the lesson in his interview, and he explained explicitly that he had employed the idea of variation in designing this lesson. It was expected that the contrast of the two lessons would enrich the understanding of how patterns of variation might be created.

RESULTS: SOME EXAMPLES IN THE ALGEBRA LESSONS OF
HONG KONG AND SHANGHAI

The Teaching of Factorization: Examples from a Hong Kong Lesson HK1

The lesson (HK1) was a grade-8 lesson on the topic: Factorization of polynomials. It was the first lesson within the topic sequence and the students had already learned multiplication of polynomials before the lesson. To help students develop a deeper understanding of factorization, the teacher used seven examples (Figure 1) in the class. The arrangement of the content and the use of dimensions of variation (contrast, separation, and fusion) are explained in the analysis here.

Q.1	$na + nb$
Q.2	$2a + 2b$
Q.3	$2na + 2nb$
Q.4	$-2na - 2nb$
Q.5	$-2na + 2nb$
Q.6	$2na + 2n^2b$
Q.7	$2na + 2n^2b^2$

Figure 1. The 7 examples used in the lesson (HK1) of "factorization"

Episode 1: "What is" and "What is not."   At the beginning of the lesson the teacher used an introductory example:

$m(a + b) = ma + mb.$

In the teacher-led whole class discussion, the teacher guided students to see the *contrast* of "what is factorization" and "what is not factorization." Taking into account the tradition that a mathematics statement should be read from left to right, that is s/he discussed the examples:

$ma + mb = m(a + b)$ is factorization. $m(a + b) = ma + mb$ is not factorization. (multiplication or expansion)

The intent of the examples was to establish that factorization involves the identification of the common factor of the terms and rewriting the statement in factor form. Hence, the introductory example provided a typical contrast between "what is" and "what is not."

Episode 2: The variant and invariant in the invariant form: common factors and highest common factor (HCF).   To carry out factorization successfully, the students need to discern the invariant form (*variant*)*a* + (*variant*)*b*, as well as the meaning of common factor and highest common factor in their experience of handling the algebraic expressions. While keeping the invariant form unchanged, the contrast between the examples (Q.1 to Q.3) creates an opportunity to discern the common factors, *n* in *na* + *nb*, 2 in 2*a* + 2*b*, 2*n* in 2*na* +2*nb*. Variation as such help students discern what is the common factor in the invariant form, separating the common factor from the variable in the expression, also generalizing the form (*variant*)*a* + (*variant*)*b*.

Zooming into the third example (Q.3), 2na + 2nb, the class discourse created another dimension of variation. The teacher drew the class' attention to this and initiated the student discussion by the following conversation:

T: Questions one and two are similar to Question three. It involves "two", and it involves "n." Is it confusing? Which one should we deal with first?

T: (after getting three answers 2(*na* + *nb*), *n*(2*a* + 2*b*), 2*n*(*a* + *b*) from the class) Okay! First of all, I would like to know, these three answers, are they the same as the original formula?

S: The same.

T: Then are all three answers correct?

S: No.

T: No? You said they are the same and now they are not all correct? How come? Discuss with your classmates and then tell me your conclusions!

The different possible common factors 2, *n*, and 2*n* create three factor forms in the class discourse:

$$2(na + nb)$$
$$n(2a + 2b)$$
$$2n(a + b)$$

The episode gives an example of *fusion* as the students had to consider multiple aspects together. In addition to the variation of factors 2, *n*, and 2*n* for the expression 2*na* + 2*nb*, the teacher intentionally recalled the students' experience of factorization of the number 12 ($12 = 4 \times 3$), hence, the meaning of factorization can be contrasted in the experiences between the factorization of a number and the factorization in an algebraic expression. The multiple instances of variation help the class to discern the idea of factors, highest common factor (HCF), the equivalence of different factor forms. The contrast between the three factor forms helps the realization of the "correct" answer using HCF in the process of factorization. Thus, knowing that 2*n*(*a* + *b*) is viewed as the correct answer in the convention, whereas the other two factor forms are not, was supported through the example choice.

Very often when an index is attached to a variable in an algebraic expression, the level of difficulties of the problem increases. Therefore, it is important to let students experience the variation of situations to develop a deeper awareness of implicit multiplication meaning in the embedded structure of the algebraic symbols (e.g, $2na + 2n^2b = 2 \times n \times a + 2 \times n \times n \times b$); and what should be selected as a factor in the process of factorization. The two questions (Q.6, $2na + 2n^2b$; Q.7, $2na + 2n^2b^2$) were embedded within a variation designed for raising awareness of the implicit meaning of multiplication between the symbols while also referencing the earlier idea of greatest common factor.

T: How do you check your answer?
LEO: Find the value by multiplication!
T: And? What is this? What's the relationship between them?
T: It is correct to multiply them, but it may not be the complete factorization. So, the relationship between this and the two terms must be?
S: Common factor.
T: What kind of common factor is it? One more word, what common factor?
S: The highest!
T: Bingo! The biggest common factor or the highest common factor!

To summarize, the teacher selected examples that provided the opportunity for the teacher to use multiple forms of variation—contrast, generalization, separation, and fusion—all of which served to help students discern variation at three levels while carrying out factorization:

- "what is factorization" and "what is not factorization",
- the different factors and the greatest common factor,
- the identification of factors and the embedded multiplication in the algebraic expressions.

*The Teaching of "a System of Equation": Examples from a
Shanghai Lesson (SH1)*

The lesson was a Grade-7 lesson on the topic, the meaning of a system of equations and its solution. The overall objectives of the lesson included: (1) the concept of a system of linear equations, (2) the concept of the solution(s) of a system of linear equations, and (3) the tabular method for solving a system of linear equations. This topic, in contrast to the aforementioned lesson of factorization, covered relatively much more content of mathematics examples and problems. Lessons with dense content are common within Chinese mathematics classrooms; however, the analysis here does not aim to compare the amount of content between lessons in different lessons, as mathematics is a subject rich in structure and relationship, and concept building relies a lot on scaffolding upon earlier concepts. Episodes in this lesson are chosen to illustrate how variation can be used to create a scaffolding path through different stages of the lesson. The beginning of the lesson was arranged through a set of 5 review tasks concerning the concept of a linear equation and the solution for a linear equation (Figure 2).

Task	Questions/ Description	Analysis
1	Identify whether the equations are in linear equations in two unknowns $\begin{cases} y = 3x^2 - 5 \\ \dfrac{2}{y} + 2x = 3 \end{cases}$	"What is a linear equation" and "What is not a linear equation"
2	Q: How many solutions for $2x + y = 10$?	Many solutions
3	Given $x + 3y = -4$, when x = 2, then y = ?	Finding a specific solution when x value is given. Applying the property of a solution.
4	If $x = -4$, $y = -5$ is one of the solutions of $2x + ay = 7$, then a = ?	Finding the unknown coefficient when a solution is given. Applying the property of a solution.
5	What is/are the solution(s) for $2x + y = 10$? What is/are the solution(s) for $x + 3y = -4$? a. $\begin{cases} x = 1 \\ y = 4 \end{cases}$ b. $\begin{cases} x = 0 \\ y = 10 \end{cases}$ c. $\begin{cases} x = 1 \\ y = -\frac{5}{3} \end{cases}$ d. $\begin{cases} x = -1 \\ y = 12 \end{cases}$	"What is a solution" and "What is not a solution"?

Figure 2. The five tasks for reviewing the concept of a linear equation and the solution of an equation

Analysis shows that in the review questions the following variations were utilized:

- "What is a linear equation" and "What is not" (Task 1)
- The multiple applications of the concept of solution (Tasks 3, 4, and 5): finding solutions when a linear equation is given; finding coefficients when a solution is given; testing a solution when equation is given, and which the meaning of solution remains invariant (the given values of x and y satisfy the equation)

For Task 1, the students were required to provide reasons to support their decision between "what is a linear equation" and "what is not." The conversation showed that they were expected to make a decision based on the critical aspect of "the index of the unknown." The task itself did not give any contrast between "what is" and "what is not" because both equations did not belong to the category of "linear equation." However, the style of questions suggested that the students were expected to be familiar with applying the skill of contrast to tell between "what is" and "what is not." In the class discourse, the student, Andrew, stated his reason for saying that the equation was not an equation. He said, "Both of them are not. It is because the index of the unknown is two." Obviously, the student was able to discern the unknown and the index of the unknown as the critical features for deciding whether the equation was linear or not. Therefore, while the question tag is asking for contrast, apparently, the given equations provided an experience of fusion of what the students had learned about linear equations, unknowns, and index of unknowns in earlier lessons.

For Tasks 3, 4 and 5 the students needed to apply the concept of "solution" to answer the questions. That is, putting the solution into the equation to test whether it satisfied the equation or not. There is a progressive variation between the questions to help the students develop an understanding of the concept of the solution:

- For Task 3, the equation, $x + 3y = -4$, when given a value of x, (a part of the solution), they put the value of x into the equation to find the other part, the value of y.
- For Task 4, the equation, $2x + ay = 7$, when given a solution ($x = -4, y = -5$), they put the solution into the equation and creating another equation for the letter a, then solved for a. In the process, the role of "a" changes from coefficient of y in $2x + ay = 7$ to the unknown variable in the new equation $2(-4) + a(-5) = 7$. In addition to a variation between the results of applying the concept of solution between Task 3 and Task 4, there is a change of roles of "a" in different equations. The variation of the role of "a" *creates* a separate focus for the coefficient "a" from the rest of the equation.
- For Task 5, the students may apply the concept by putting the given pair of x and y into the equation to decide whether the given pair is the solution or not. This provided an alternative way to apply the concept of solution for testing cases by discerning the variation between "what is" and "what is not."

To summarize, for the solution of a linear equation, the students might be expected to be familiar with the following dimensions of variation:

- "What is a solution" and "what is not" (Task 5),
- Change of the role of a letter symbol between equations while applying the concept of solution (Task 4),
- Applying the concept of solution in different problem situations (Tasks 3, 4 and 5).

Making these variations explicit in the beginning segment of the lesson created important ground work (*pudian*) for scaffolding in the later development for the learning of the concept of solution for a system of equations.

Episode 3: A Variation among the Text of the Concept, the Discourse, and Action of Applying the Concept

Task 6	In a group of 2 students, read the textbook about the system of linear equations in two unknowns and discuss the three questions (6a to 6c) after reading the textbook.
6a	Q1. What is "a system of equations"?
6b	Q2. How can you identify whether a system of equations is a system of linear equations in two unknowns?
6c	Q3. To identify whether the given is a system of linear equations in two unknowns. (Example given by teacher on the blackboard) (1) $\begin{cases} x + y = 3 \\ x - y = 1 \end{cases}$ (2) $\begin{cases} (x + y)^2 = 1 \\ x - y = 0 \end{cases}$ (3) $\begin{cases} x = 1 \\ y = 1 \end{cases}$ (4) $\begin{cases} \frac{x}{2} + \frac{y}{2} = 0 \\ x = y \end{cases}$ (5) $\begin{cases} xy = 2 \\ x = 1 \end{cases}$ (6) $\begin{cases} \frac{x+1}{y} = 1 \\ y = 2 \end{cases}$ (7) $u = v = 0$ (8) $\begin{cases} x + y = 4 \\ - \quad = \end{cases}$

Figure 3. Task 6 for the concept of a system of linear equations of two unknowns

The concept of a system of linear equations in two unknowns was taught via Task 6 (Figure 3). The task required students to read the definition in the textbook and discuss the three questions (6a, 6b, and 6c). The definition in the textbook is translated below:

> Several equations forming a system is called *a system of equations*. If the system of equations contains two unknowns and the indices of the unknowns are all one, then the system of equations is called *a system of linear equations of two unknowns*. (From the textbook, author's translation)

The analysis of the transcript of the episode is given in Figure 4. The class discourse contained three questions. The first two questions were based on the text definition: "What is a system of equations?" (6a); "How can you determine whether a system of equations is a system of linear equations in two unknowns?" or not (6b), while the two questions also serve the purpose of preparing the students to apply the concept to identify cases of a system of linear equations of two unknowns in (6c). At a superficial level, the questions (6a) and (6b) might appear to be aiming to check the students' comprehension of the text. However, the what-question is a recall question, whereas the teacher used the how-question to help students be aware of the

Transcript	Remarks
Angel: A system of equations is formed by a number of equations. T: Oh, what did she say? Angel: Formed by a number of equations. T: Oh, formed... by a number of equations. [teacher writing on the blackboard] Angel: Formed one pair of equations. T: What is formed? Angel: A pair of equations. T: A pair of equations. Angel: Called a system of equations.	(6a) • What is a system of equations? • Comprehension of the concept via the text. • Angel's answer is the same as the text book. (Recall, what is) • The teacher's questions drew focus onto the phrase "a number of equations".
T: What is the answer of the second question? ... anyone? That means how to identify? Aaron. Aaron: There are two unknowns in the equation and the indexes of the unknowns are one. This is called system of linear equations in two unknowns. ... T: Then, what have you to consider first when I ask you to identify whether they are system of linear equations in two unknowns? Bern. Bern: It should have two unknowns. T: It should have two unknowns. Bern: The indexes of the unknowns should be one. T: The indexes of the unknowns ... should be one. Sit down please. T: Can anyone make supplement on it? The index of each unknown is one. Okay, please talk about it. Bandson: And each term should be in a whole expression. T: And each term should be in a whole expression. Then each term... the index of the equation is ... one. T: If the index is one, then it should be ... in whole expression already. T: Ar ... this should be ... Bunney please talk about it. Bunney: The indexes of the unknowns. T: Ar, the indexes of the unknowns... they are ... one.	(6b) • How to identify whether a system of equations is a system of linear equations in two unknowns. • Comprehension of the concept via the text. • Aaron gave a definition (Recall, what is) • The teacher refrained from drawing conclusion and invited more students joined the conversation: The teacher continued to ask question, "What have you to consider first when I ask you to identify..." (Talking about action, talking about how to) – separation of the criteria from the text definition. • Expansion of the shared space: More students joined the conversation. Bern named two criteria, "2 unknowns", "the indexes of the unknowns should be one"; Bandson mentioned the criterion of "whole expression"; Bunney mentioned the indexes of unknowns

Figure 4. The analysis of the class discourse for questions (6a) and (6b)

	(6c)
T: Okay, these two points, oh, then, let us take a look at the following questions with these two points.	• Action: applying the concept to differentiate different cases of "what is" and "what is not".
T: Ar ... please take a look, come on, the first sub-question. Ok, please say.	• Contrast, separation and fusion
S: The first one is linear equation in two unknowns.	• Case 1, $+ y = 3, x - y = 1$: A case of "what is", the teacher made
T: The first one is linear equation in two unknowns. Ok, please sit down. Then, students, please look here.	sure that the class observed the two criteria.
T: The first problem, x and y ... there is two unknowns and the indexes are one.	• Case 2, $(x + y)^2 = 1, x - y = 0$: A case of "what is not", the
E: The index is one.	teacher made sure that the class
T: The index is one. The second equation, x minus y equals one, the indexes of the two unknowns x and y are one. Yes, it is a system of linear equations in two unknowns.	expanded the perfect square and saw the indexes were two.
	• Via the experiencing of different equations with different unknowns and different indexes, the students were given a chance
T: Then, let us look at the second question. Come on, you please.	to generalize the form of a system of linear equations across
Buss: They are not.	the variation of coefficients,
T: Oh, he said not. Why not?	indexes and unknowns.
Buss: Because in the equation, the index of the term is two.	
T: Oh, please look at this, x plus y bracket square what is the expanded form?	
E: (...) square root.	
T: Yep, the expanded form is x square plus two x y plus y square. You see, what is the index of the unknown x?	
E: Two.	
T: Good, what about the term xy?	
E: Two.	
T: Two. What about y? This is also two.	
E: Two.	
T: So, we can say although the two unknowns, x minus y, is with the index of one.	
T: We can't say the second equation is a linear equation when there are something on the upper side ... okay, then please look at the third question...oh, Bern please.	

Figure 5. The students attending to the critical aspects of unknowns and indexes while deciding between what-is and what-is-not cases

two critical aspects—that there are two unknowns and the index of the unknowns should be one. Importantly, the action of asking the two questions simultaneously with reference to the same piece of text in the textbook served to create a what-how dimension of variation for understanding the text.

We see below that the students had no difficulty in answering the what-question by recalling the definition from the textbook. The how-question (6b) and the way the teacher delayed making the summary which encouraged other students to join the conversation, supported the students to focus on the two criteria (the number of unknowns and the indexes of the unknowns). In other words, a separation of the criteria from the text definition. Furthermore, the shared space was expanded as more students (Bandson and Bunney) joined in the conversation contributing to what they saw as the key features (unknowns and the degree of the unknowns).

When the students tried to apply the concept to determine whether the given systems of equations were systems of linear equations of two unknowns or not (question 6c), the dimension of what-how was further extended to carrying out procedurally the contrast between "what is" and "what is not" (see Figure 5). The various examples in question 6c provided rich opportunities for students to attend to aspects such as the unknowns and the indexes and bring them together to determine whether the given was a system of linear equations in two unknowns or not. Therefore, contrast, generalization, separation, and fusion were enacted.

In working with Task 6, the students were provided with opportunities for experiencing the concept at three levels: the level of text, the level of discourse for talking about the concept, and the level of action for applying the concept (see Figure 6). This progressive variation is noteworthy as it explains the interaction between teacher-student-text in the enacted space of learning and it also delineates the variation of the concept from *the text of definition in the textbook*, to *discourse*

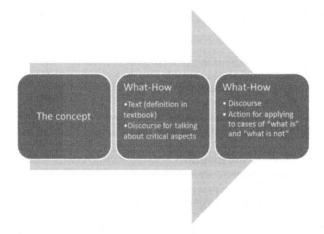

Figure 6. Experiencing the concept through the text-discourse variation and the discourse-action variation in Task 6

about the text, and *actions of applying the concept to problems,* then to the actual action of applying the concepts to solve a mathematics problem. Importantly, this arrangement of learning to help students develop their understanding through the *text-discourse-action* level is not by chance; rather it is a pedagogical strategy that the teacher tried to repeat skillfully. Immediately after this episode, the teacher applied the same instructional approach to teach the concept of solution for a system of equations (see Task 7 in Figure 7). In a similar way, the design of Task 7 provided a platform the students to experience the *text-discourse-action* variation for the meaning of "solution."

Task 7	In a group of 2 students, read the textbook and discuss the three questions (7a to 7c) after reading the book.
7a	Q1. What does "solution" mean in a system of equations?
7b	Q2. Why $\begin{cases} x=23 \\ y=12 \end{cases}$ is the solution of $\begin{cases} x+y=35 \\ 2x+4y=94 \end{cases}$?
7c	Q3. Is the solution(s) of equation $5x-3y=3$ must be the solution of $\begin{cases} 5x-3y=3 \\ x+2y=11 \end{cases}$? And vice versa?

Figure 7. Task 7 providing a platform for the text-discourse-action variation for experiencing the meaning of "solution"

Two Kinds of Content Scaffolding in the SH Lesson

In addition to the contrast-generalization-fusion-separation patterns of variation, the instructional approach depicted in the lesson utilized two kinds of content scaffolding (Figure 8).

- The first kind is the scaffolding occurred via the experience of similar patterns of variation in instructional approach of different contents. A mathematical object may often be presented in the what-how variation, answering the questions: *what is it* and *how to use it?* Whether it is a concept or a skill, it will have different forms of representations. In the consistent pedagogical arrangement in this lesson, the teacher guided a *text-discourse-action* variation from reading the definition in text, to a discussion of the concept in class, then to the action of applying the concept to demonstrate their discernment in a problem-solving context.
- The second kind is the scaffolding of knowledge according to the intrinsic hierarchy of mathematics topics, from linear equations, to a system of equations, then to a solution of a system of equations. There are different levels of embedding according to the hierarchical nature of the mathematics contents, i.e., "linear equations" is embedded in "system of equations"; "linear equations" and "system of equations" are embedded in "solutions of a system of equations." Embedding

in the different mathematical objects, linear equations and systems of linear equations are generalizations of the form of equations; and between the two kinds of systems of equations (a single equation and a system of equations), the concept of solution can be generalized. In addition, to discern the meaning of solution, the learner has to separate the meaning of solution in experiencing fusion of different features of the equation systems; and through the experience of the meaning solution of two kinds of systems (a single linear equation and a system of linear equations), the meaning of solution for an equation can be generalized. It is in the evolution of the second kind that students were empowered with a growing experience of the patterns of contrast, generalization, separation, and fusion.

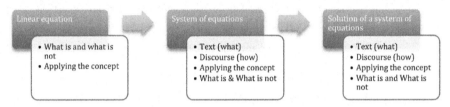

Figure 8. Two kind of scaffolding: A hierarchical arrangement of topics & text-discourse-action

DISCUSSION

What counts as an effective teaching strategy? Answers to this question depend very much on assumptions for meaningful learning based on psychological and epistemological grounds.

Variation Theory of Learning from a pedagogical perspective suggests a relationship between learning and the conditions of learning (Marton, 2015; Pang & Marton, 2013). Meaningful learning only happens when a learner discerns the critical aspects of the object of learning. For example, the common factors and greatest common factor in factorizing an algebraic expression, and the realization of the meaning of the greatest common factor can only happen after the learner has experienced cases with more than one common factor.

The learning of mathematics often involves the learning of a concept, which may appear as various forms in the process of learning. The learning of a concept to a certain extent is to experience the what-is question or to go through an experience of seeking an answer for the what-is question. For the example of "a system of linear equations in two unknowns", the students' experience of what-is in this study involved an experience going from the text form of the definition of the concept, to a shared space created in the class discourse for answering the what-is question, then to an action of applying the concept to solving mathematical problems. In this lesson, the experience involving the contrast between the what-is and what-is-not cases was supported through the creation of dimensions of variations. Specifically, the variation provided opportunities for learners to contrast between what-is and what-is-not, to separate the critical aspects from the non-critical, and to fuse (discerning different aspects and putting them together in a given context). The delineation depicted in dimensions of variation can be called the enacted space of learning. The enacted space is a dynamic one and there are no definite patterns of variation for the conditions for learning, and the arrangement of the learning contents may vary according to the teacher and the learners. The examples show a possible pattern of replicable pedagogical strategies employed by the teacher that helped the learners to experience an arrangement of the learning content scaffolding on the hierarchy of the intrinsic mathematical structure (from "linear equation", to "a system of equations", then to "the solution for a system of equations"), and a text-discourse-action pattern of variation in the process of learning.

A research framework of multiple perspectives enhances the understanding of the pedagogical approach. For example, in the work of Huang, Barlow, and Prince (2016), the hybrid framework of variation and task design made the comparison of lessons between two cultural systems possible. In this paper, the two lessons were from two different systems with very similar features such as large class size, a directive teaching tradition, examination-orientation, and competitiveness. However, any analytical framework may also delimit what the researchers can see through the theoretical lens provided. The two lessons depict two learning spaces of very different complexities. The contrast brings in the epistemological realm, showing the possibility of content scaffolding in the instructional approach in addition to the experience of the patterns of contrast, generalization, fusion, and separation. Although the patterns of variation appear to be of a finite number, the learning space experienced by the learners is by no means static. It is bound to be dynamic and develop into complexity as the learners are brought through a journey in the enacted space of learning.

ACKNOWLEDGEMENT

The project is funded by General Research Fund, Research Grants Council, Hong Kong SAR, China.

REFERENCES

Bao, J., Huang, R., Yi, L., & Gu, L. (2003). Study in *bianshi* teaching [in Chinese]. *Mathematics Teaching* [Shxue Jiaoxue], *1*, 11–12.

Biggs, J. B. (1996). Western misperceptions of the Confucian-heritage learning culture. In D. Watkins & J. Biggs (Eds.), *The Chinese learner: Cultural, psychological and contextual influences* (pp. 69–84). Hong Kong: CERC and ACER.

Experimenting Group of Teaching Reform in maths in Qingpu County, Shanghai. (1991). *Xuehui Jiaoxue* [Learning to Teach]. Beijing, China: People Education Publishers. (In Chinese)

Fan, L., Miao, Z., & Mok, I. A. C. (2015). How Chinese teachers teach mathematics and pursue professional development: Perspectives from contemporary international research. In L. Fan, N. Y. Wong, F. Cai, & S. Li (Eds.), *How Chinese teach mathematics: Perspectives from insiders* (pp. 43–70). Singapore: World Scientific.

Gu, L., Huang, R., & Marton, F. (2004). Teaching with variation: A Chinese way of promoting effective mathematics learning. In L. Fan, N. Y. Wong, J. Cai, & S. Li (Eds.), *How Chinese learn mathematics: Perspectives from insiders* (pp. 309–347). Singapore: World Scientific.

Huang, R., & Leung, F. K. S. (2004). Cracking the paradox of Chinese learners: Looking into mathematics classrooms in Hong Kong and Shanghai. In L. Fan, N-Y. Wong, J. Cai, & S. Li (Eds.), *How Chinese learn mathematics* (pp. 348–381). Singapore: World Scientific.

Huang, R., Mok, I. A. C., & Leung, F. K. S. (2006) Repetition or variation – "Practice" in the mathematics classrooms in China. In D. Clarke, C. Keitel, & Y. Shimizu (Eds.), *Mathematics classrooms in 12 countries: The insiders' perspective.* Rotterdam, The Netherland: Sense Publishers B.V.

Huang, R., Miller, L. D., & Tzur, R. (2015). Mathematics teaching in a Chinese classroom: A hybrid-model analysis of opportunities for students' learning. In L. Fan, N. Y. Wong, F. Cai, & S. Li (Eds.), *How Chinese teach mathematics: Perspectives from insiders* (pp. 73–110). Singapore: World Scientific.

Huang, R., Barlow, A. T., & Prince, K. (2016). The same tasks, different learning opportunities: An analysis of two exemplary lessons in China and the US from a perspective of variation. *The Journal of Mathematical Behavior, 41*, 141–158.

Ki, W. W., & Maton, F. (2003, August 26–30). *Learning Cantonese tones.* In EARLI 2003 Conference (European Association of Research in Learning and Instruction). Padova, Italy.

Leung, F. K. S. (2001). In search of an East Asian identity in mathematics education. *Educational Studies in Mathematics, 47*, 35–51.

Lim, C. S. (2007). Characteristics of mathematics teaching in Shanghai, China: Throughout the lens of a Malaysian. *Mathematics Education Research Journal, 19*(1), 77–89.

Marton, F. (2014). *Necessary conditions of learning.* New York, NY: Routledge.

Marton, F., & Booth, S. (1997). *Learning and awareness.* Mahwah, NJ: Lawrence Erlbaum.

Marton, F., & Pang, M. F. (2013). Meanings are acquired from experiencing differences against a background of sameness, rather than from experiencing sameness against a background of difference: Putting a conjecture to the test by embedding it in a pedagogical tool. *Frontline Learning Research, 1*(1), 24–41.

Marton, F., Runesson, U., & Tsui, A. B. M. (2003). The space of learning. In F. Marton, A. B. M. Tsui, P. Chik, P. Y. Ko, M. L. Lo, I. A. C. Mok, D. Ng, M. F. Pang, et al., (Eds.), *Classroom discourse and the space of learning* (pp. 3–40). Mahwah, NJ: Lawrence Erlbaum.

Marton, F., & Tsui, A. B. M. (Eds.). (2004). *Classroom discourse and the space of learning.* Mahwah, NJ: Lawrence Erlbaum.

Marton, F., Tse, S. K., & Cheung, W. M. (Eds.). (2010). *On the learning of Chinese.* Rotterdam, The Netherlands: Sense Publishers.

Mok, I. A. C. (2006). Shedding light on the East Asian learner paradox: Reconstructing student-centredness in a Shanghai classroom. *Asia Pacific Journal of Education, 26*(2), 131–142.

Mok, I. A. C. (2009). In search of an exemplary mathematics lesson in Hong Kong: An algebra lesson on factorization of polynomials. *ZDM Mathematics Education, 41*, 319–332.

Mok, I. A. C. (2013). Five strategies for coherence: Lessons from a Shanghai teacher. In Y. Li & R. Huang (Eds.), *How Chinese teach mathematics and improve teaching* (pp. 120–133). New York, NY: Routledge, Taylor and Francis Group.

Mullis, I. V., Martin, M. O., Foy, P., & Arora, A. (2012). *TIMSS 2011 international results in mathematics.* International Association for the Evaluation of Educational Achievement, Herengracht, Amsterdam, The Netherlands.

OECD. (2010). *PISA 2009 results: What students know and can do: Student performance in reading, mathematics and science* (Vol. I). Paris: OECD Publishing.

OECD. (2014). *PISA 2012 results in focus: What 15-year-olds know and what they can do with what they know.* Paris: OECD Publishing

Pang, M. F., & Marton, F. (2013). Interaction between the learners' initial grasp of the object of learning and the learning resource afforded. *Instructional Science, 41*, 1065–1082.

Runesson, U., & Mok, I. A. C. (2005). The teaching of fractions: A comparative study of a Swedish and a Hong Kong classroom. *Nordic Studies in Mathematics Education, 10*(2), 1–15.

Watkins, D. A., & Biggs, J. B. (Eds.). (2001). *Teaching the Chinese learner*. Hong Kong: Comparative Education Research Centre, The University of Hong Kong.

Ida Ah Chee Mok
Faculty of Education
University of Hong Kong
Hong Kong SAR, China

PART III

THE PEDAGOGICAL PERSPECTIVE OF VARIATIONS AS A PRINCIPLE FOR CURRICULUM DEVELOPMENT AND TEACHER PROFESSIONAL DEVELOPMENT IN CHINA

KONRAD KRAINER

INTRODUCTION

"The Lesson Plan Is Only the Teacher's Hypothesis of Students' Learning"

Chinese students' good performance in mathematics PISA 2012 (Programme for International Student Assessment [OECD], 2013) is a phenomenon that attracted increasing interest world-wide. The reasons for these good results are manifold and complex. Among others, they include sociocultural aspects (high societal importance dedicated to performance and effort, to collective thinking and enactment; high respect of mathematics), teacher education and recruitment (demanding selection, mathematics taught by mathematics teachers only), number of mathematics lessons taught at schools (higher than on PISA average), long tradition of bottom-up teacher movement aiming at self-determined quality assurance of teaching (teacher research groups, e.g. focusing on joint lesson planning), and sincere efforts to combine theoretical and practical dimensions of teaching (increasingly taking into account western theories and co-developing new theories like variation theory).

Two of the three following chapters directly refer to the good results regarding PISA. In one case, the authors stress that the consistent use of variation problems in textbooks and in classroom instruction provides strong support for students' learning that may provide further explanation of Chinese students' excellent performance. A second team of authors highlights that the success of pupils from Shanghai (ranked on first place in PISA 2012) made it important to understand how teacher learning takes place in Shanghai. All three chapters provide insightful cases showing how teaching and learning through variations can be used and implemented, with a particular focus on teacher professional development and curriculum development. In the following, all three chapters are described shortly, in each case supplemented by some reflections from a western mathematics education perspective.

The chapter by Zhang, Wang, Huang and Kimmins deals with the question how notions of variation pedagogy are adopted in *mathematics textbooks* in China. The authors stress that there are only sporadic studies on how variation tasks are used in Chinese textbooks. However, these few studies indicate that textbooks introduce new concepts and deepening understanding of concepts through use of variation tasks. In the chapter, six mathematics textbooks for grades 7, 8 and 9 are selected to identify the major characteristics of use of variation tasks. The authors sketch interesting examples, focusing on four features of use of variation tasks (building on Zhang, 2011): the use for learning of mathematical concepts (both conceptual and procedural), for discovering and understanding mathematical principals, for

R. Huang & Y. Li (Eds.), Teaching and Learning Mathematics through Variation, 209–212.

developing mathematical skills, and for developing mathematics thinking methods. From a western perspective, the positive connotation of textbooks (their importance in practice, their exemplary stance) are surprising, since in many western countries the impact of textbooks for teaching practice is not estimated that high and textbooks are analysed rather critically, highlighting both strengths and (and more often) weaknesses. In western countries, many textbooks are regarded as needy of theory, whereas the chapter here gives the impression of a good balance between (variation) theory and practice in the selected Chinese textbooks. The chapter gives a good insight into the (ideal) use of Chinese mathematics textbooks, the authors themselves stress the need for providing a comprehensive picture about the use of variation tasks in textbooks (going beyond the selected cases). Similar to most western countries is the high importance given to *teachers* (and their challenge to stimulate active student participation) and to *tasks* as a core means of planning mathematics teaching.

The chapter by Ding, Jones and Sikko analyses how an expert teacher supports the *professional learning of a junior teacher* focusing on mathematics teaching with variation and the interaction between the two teachers. The study uses teacher's teaching diary, reflection notes, lesson plans, video transcripts of interactions in the school-based teaching research group meetings, the textbook, and transcripts of a video-taped lesson. The Interconnected Model by Clarke and Hollingsworth (2002) and the Keli Model by Gu and Wang (2003) are used as a tool for categorizing the data and explaining the results. The chapter works out that the expert teacher guided the junior teacher in two sophisticated ways, namely through the use of teaching notions, and the use of teaching frameworks and language (that teachers commonly understand and practice in the country). The authors give a good insight into a junior mathematics teacher's reflections on her teaching and her learning for teaching with variation. From a western perspective, the use of a wide-spread and generally accepted teaching strategy is unique. The fact that teaching with variation has long been widely accepted by mathematics teachers in China defines a context, so far not (well) known in many western countries. One major advantage is the development of a common language which makes it easier to (jointly) plan teaching and to reflect on it. For many western countries, the direct guiding of the junior teacher by the expert teacher (e.g., stating "you did not really understand what should be done in each of the stages") is surprising. On the one hand, the clear way of communicating could be seen as a consequent guidance; on the other hand, when the expert teacher regards the students as self-determined learners, why not also (and even more justified) the junior teacher (helping her to realize critical issues herself)? However, this seems to be a cultural issue (in many western countries, teachers would not easily accept strong criticism by other teachers; surely, expert teachers might have a specific status in the Chinese teaching profession). The authors conclude that teachers' growth is not straightforward and continuous, in contrast, it is rather discrete and discontinuous. This is surely a shared view between eastern and western teachers and teacher educators.

The chapter by Han, Gong and Huang reports about a *designed lesson study* that integrates the concepts of *learning trajectory* (e.g. Simon, 1995) and teaching and learning through variations. The four participant teachers in the study were (voluntarily) engaged in the lesson study activity to design six lessons on the topic of division with fractions. They were supported by university mathematics education experts and district teaching specialists. The major data sources used in this study were students' post-lesson test, videotaped lessons and student interviews. The focus of the chapter is on the research lessons taught by one (experienced) teacher and the related teaching research activities. This teacher gradually shifted her instruction from teacher-dominated instruction to an instruction dominated by students' exploration and investigation, accompanied by several changes in the learning of her students. For many western countries, the clear statement that one approach (here, lesson study, see e.g., Huang & Shimizu, 2016) "makes schools become places where teachers, not just students learn" would be rather an innovation. Apart from some exceptions, such a long tradition of bottom-up teacher movement aiming at self-determined quality, is not developed in western countries like here in China (or going back even longer, in Japan). In particular, the wide-spread formation of teaching research groups is unique. This is apparently an outcome of a collectivist view on culture, education and society, whereas in many western countries teachers (and other citizens) are more regarded as individuals and the challenge is to foster joint action and reflection among teachers and to establish wide-spread collaborations between teachers and researchers.

One joint feature of all three chapters is the *strong role* given to *teachers*. They are regarded as practitioners and as experts (in teaching and students' learning) who investigate their own teaching in order to improve their own teaching (and that of their lesson study colleagues), and to contribute to the *generation of professional knowledge* (to be used by teachers but also by the scientific community). This means that teachers are regarded as *key stakeholders not only for mathematics teaching*, but also for *mathematics education research* (e.g., Krainer, 2011; Kieran, Krainer, & Shaughnessy, 2013). Regarding teachers as key stakeholders for mathematics education research implies taking the students as learners as the main focus. This cannot be better said then by teacher Yiji in the chapter by Ding, Jones and Sikko: "The lesson plan is only the teacher's hypothesis of students' learning."

REFERENCES

Clarke, D., & Hollingsworth, H. (2002). Elaborating a model of teacher professional growth. *Teaching and Teacher Education, 18*, 947–967.

Gu, L., & Wang, J. (2003). Teachers' development through education action: The use of 'Keli' as a means in the research of teacher education model. *Curriculum, Textbook & Pedagogy, I*, 9–15; *II*, 14–19.

Huang, R., & Shimizu, Y. (2016). Improving teaching, developing teachers and teacher educators, and linking theory and practice through lesson study in mathematics: An international perspective. *ZDM Mathematics Education, 48*, 393–409.

Kieran, C., Krainer, K., & Shaughnessy, J. M. (2013). Linking research to practice: Teachers as key stakeholders in mathematics education research. In M. A. Clements, A. J. Bishop, C. Keitel, J. Kilpatrick, & F. K. S. Leung (Eds.), *Third international handbook of mathematics education* (pp. 361–392). New York, NY: Springer.

Krainer, K. (2011). Teachers as stakeholders in mathematics education research. In B. Ubuz (Ed.), *Proceedings of the 35th conference of the international group for the psychology of mathematics education* (Vol. 1, pp. 47–62). Ankara, Turkey: PME Program Committee.

OECD. (2013). *PISA 2012 results: What students know and can do: Student performance in mathematics, reading and science* (Vol. 1). Paris: OECD.

Simon, M. A. (1995). Prospective elementary teachers' knowledge of division. *Journal for Research in Mathematics Education, 24*, 233–254.

Zhang, J. Y. (2011). *Theories of secondary mathematics curriculum* [In Chinese]. Beijing: Beijing Normal University Press.

Konrad Krainer
Department of Instructional and School Development
Faculty for Interdisciplinary Studies
Klagenfurt University, Austria

JIANYUE ZHANG, RONG WANG, RONGJIN HUANG
AND DOVIE KIMMINS

11. STRATEGIES FOR USING VARIATION TASKS IN SELECTED MATHEMATICS TEXTBOOKS IN CHINA

INTRODUCTION

In China, mathematics textbooks based on unified national "mathematics curriculum standards" (MOE, 2011) are major and core resources for teachers' teaching and students' learning. Mathematics textbooks in China generally emphasize the following aspects: making use of learning situations for which students are familiar; arranging mathematical tasks with variations step by step; guiding students to explore mathematics activities progressively; making contrast, analogy, induction, and generalization with varying learning situations to discover similarities and differences of learning objects and derive the mathematical essence of concrete instances; and finally developing profound understandings of mathematical knowledge. Through applying learned knowledge to a variety of contexts, students are expected to develop adaptive and flexible abilities in problem solving. Selection and arrangement of various mathematical tasks is one of the major considerations when compiling mathematics textbooks (Editorial Committee, 2005).

The structure and arrangement of mathematics content in textbooks are determined based on a coherent development of the material logically and on the development of student cognition and mathematics learning. The characteristics of textbooks have great impact on teachers' design of teaching, because textbooks in China are treated as mandatory documents that contain all essential knowledge students need to learn (Park & Leung, 2006). Each mathematics object in textbooks is presented according to the following rule: introducing learning contexts, defining concepts, deriving properties, building connections, and making applications. This sequence aims to illustrate the necessity of (1) introducing a new concept and abstracting the common features of the mathematics object from numerical and graphical perspectives, (2) defining the concepts explicating the mathematics object, (3) acquiring the properties of mathematics objects through exploring the relationships between different mathematical objects, (4) developing mathematics knowledge systems through building connections between relevant types of knowledge, and (5) deepening understanding of new knowledge through applying knowledge to

R. Huang & Y. Li (Eds.), Teaching and Learning Mathematics through Variation, 213–239.

solving mathematical and contextual problems (Zhang, 2014). This arrangement acknowledges the unity of mathematics knowledge structure and student cognitive development, the unity of learning mathematics knowledge and development of mathematical capacities, and formation of a systemic and developmental mathematical knowledge structure (Ding, 1992; Editorial Committee, 2005). To achieve this goal, one of the core tasks is to select and arrange mathematically rich tasks for exploring and developing relevant mathematical objects. The variation pedagogy that has been widely practiced in mathematics classrooms over decades (Gu, Huang, & Marton, 2004) has a great implication for selection and arrangement of learning tasks/activities (Zhang, 2011).

Induction and deduction are two complementary inquiry methods typically used to explore mathematics objects. On one hand mathematical objects are developed through the following inductive process: based on experiment and analysis of concrete instances, mathematical essence is induced; mathematics concepts are defined; and mathematics conjectures are made. On the other hand, through deductive reasoning, conjectures and mathematics propositions are proven or disproven, new mathematical discoveries justified or refuted, the connections and consistency of various concepts built, and finally, a coherent system of different mathematics objects developed (Xiang, 2015). Thus, student learning of mathematics knowledge generally goes through the following process: analysis of concrete instance, recognition of individual rules, abstraction of general principles, and formation of thinking and conception (Zhang, 2015). In mathematical textbooks, content is arranged to provide students with the experience of such a learning process. The selection and use of varying learning tasks is aimed to promote students' exploration and understanding of mathematics objects, and develop their capacities in flexible application of knowledge. Variation pedagogy that focuses on providing deliberate mathematical task selection and implementation in classroom instruction (Gu et al., 2014) has direct implications for compiling textbooks.

Thus, it is necessary to consider appropriate use of varying learning tasks/activities in textbooks regarding structure of mathematics knowledge and arrangement of mathematics content from a perspective of variation pedagogy. This chapter examines the methods of using varying learning tasks in a series of middle school mathematics textbooks published by People's Education Press (2012a, b; 2013a, b; 2014a, b).

THEORETICAL CONSIDERATIONS

This section includes four parts. First, literature on teaching mathematics through variations and the use of variation tasks in mathematics textbooks is briefly reviewed. Then, a brief historical review on the use of variation tasks in textbook development is provided. After that, a framework for categorizing mathematical knowledge is described. Finally, a framework for analyzing textbooks utilized in this study is presented.

Teaching through Variation: A Long-standing Tradition

Teaching through variation is an important teaching principle for developing students' understanding of concepts, and is described as follows:

> To illustrate essential features of a concept by demonstrating various visual materials and instances, or to highlight essential characteristics of a concept by varying non-essential features. The goal of using variation is to help students understand the essential features of a concept by differentiating them from non-essential features and further develop a scientific concept. (Gu, 1999, p. 186)

There has been a long tradition of implementing teaching through variation in mathematics education. In 1950s, some researchers explored how using multiple variations helps students distinguish the essential and nonessential features of a concept (Zhou, 1959). From a psychological perspective, Lu (1961) further examined the impact of experimental teaching of using "standard figures" and "varying figures" on student learning and found a positive role of using varying figures in geometry, namely, eliminating negative effects of non-essential features and improving middle grade students' capacities of problem solving. In 1980's, Gu (1994) first carried out systemic experimental studies and developed theoretical interpretations of teaching through variation in mathematics.

Since 2000, Gu and others have attempted to theorize the practice of teaching through variation (Gu et al., 2004; Wong, Lam, & Chan, 2009). Gu et al. (2004) systematically synthesized the basic principles of teaching with variation, and explained these principles using Western theories such as Dienes' (1973) variability principle, Marton's variation of pedagogy (Marton & Booth, 1997), and Brunner's (1985) scaffolding notion. According to Gu et al. (2004), *conceptual variation* includes two categories, concept variation and non-concept variation. Concept variation involves varying extensions of a concept; non-concept variation involves varying seemingly related but essentially relevant features of the extension of a concept, for instance, creating a counterexample. The goal of using these two types of variation is to gain understanding of a concept from multiple perspectives. They further clarified the meaning of *procedural variation* which mainly includes: progressing mathematics activities step by step, solving a big problem by breaking it down into sub-problems, gaining various activity experiences accumulatively during the process of instructional activities. There are three major functions of using "*procedural variation*": (1) Forming a concept, namely, helping students experience the process of forming a concept, and helping students understand the necessity of introducing the concept; (2) Problem solving, namely, transforming a unknown problem into a solved problem progressively, helping students clarify the process of solving the problem and understand the structure of problems, gaining activity experiences progressively, and advancing problem solving ability; and (3) Establishing a specific experience system through a series of variation (see Chapter 2 this volume for details). These variations mainly include creating different problems based on a given problem, using multiple methods to solve a problem, and using the same methods to solve different problems (Cai & Nie, 2007).

As discussed, several Western theories support why implementing teaching through variation appropriately could be effective for student learning of mathematics in a large classroom. In particular, Marton's (Marton & Booth, 1997) theory of variation provides an epistemological and conceptual foundation of the Chinese practice of teaching. Zheng (2006) argued that the core ideas of Marton's theory of variation are: (1) learning is to learn to discern [critical features of a learning object], (2) discernment relies on comparison (differences). Thus, it is important to provide students opportunities to explore appropriate *dimensions of variations* so as to broaden *learning space*. Gu et al. (2004) concluded that *conceptual variation* aims to construct a space of variation that focuses on critical aspects of the learning object, and to enhance students' understanding of essential aspects of the learning object. *Procedural variation* intends to scaffold students' learning to build substantive connections between the learning object and previous knowledge and promote students' development of mathematical concept and skills. They also cautioned that it is crucial to set appropriate potential distance between the learning object and existing knowledge. Thus, constructing an appropriate space of variation is essentially important for implementing effective mathematics teaching. If the potential distance is too short, it may constrain challenges and eliminate motion for critical thinking and exploration; if the space of variation is too small, it may provide students with incomplete learning conditions resulting in narrowness of understanding of the learning objects. Teachers' wisdom is needed to achieve a balance from the perspective of variation.

Use of Variation Tasks in Textbooks: An Emergent Area

There are sporadic studies on how variation tasks are used in textbooks (e.g. Sun, 2011; Wong et al., 2009). Yet, some of these studies indicated that mathematics textbooks in China emphasize introducing new concepts and deepening understanding of concepts through use of variation tasks. For example, in the textbook for "middle school algebra" (People's Education Press [PEP], 1963), eight examples were selected to illustrate the essential feature of an algebra equation: connecting two algebraic expressions by using equal sign, which belongs to conceptual variation (Figure 1). For another example, in the middle school geometry textbook (PEP, 1981), there is a set of practicing problems that is

$$a+b=b+a; \quad (1) \qquad (a+b)(a-b)=a^2-b^2; \quad (2)$$
$$x+x+x=3x; \quad (3) \qquad 6x^2 \div 3x = 2x; \qquad (4)$$
$$x+3=5; \qquad (5) \qquad 3y=1; \qquad (6)$$
$$x^2=4; \qquad (7) \qquad x+y=6. \qquad (8)$$

Figure 1. An example for conceptual variation

used to contrast concept and non-concept figures (Figure 2), and develop a deep understanding of vertical angles.

In the figures on the right, A, O, B are on a line and O, P are two points on line AB. Are ∠ 1 and ∠ 2 a pair of vertical angles? Why? Are ∠ 3 and ∠ 4 a pair of vertical angles? Why?

Figure 2. An example of non-concept figures

In fact, exercises and problems are usually compiled with purposeful variations in textbooks. Practice with variation problems is one of salient features of Chinese mathematics textbooks, which is intended to develop students' ability in learning by analogy (举一反三、触类旁通). Teaching through variations relies on intended variation tasks in textbooks. For example, in the 1990's, the *Journal of Secondary Mathematics Teaching References* included a specific column, called *variation problem collection in textbooks*. It was argued that "The problems included in university and high school entrance exams are crafted ingeniously. They look novel and unique. However, although there are a variety of variations with test problems, the test item creators have to follow a principle that is "rooting [test items] in textbook, not exceling (beyond) requirement of curriculum standards. Thus, many exam items can be found from their stereotype problems from the textbooks – either examples or exercises." (Ru, 1994, p. 26) It corresponds to the old Chinese saying that "changing embedment (of a problem) ten thousand times remains the same original essence or principle."(万变不离其宗)

Yet, few studies have been devoted to examination of the nature of using variation tasks in textbooks (Sun, 2011; Wong et al., 2009) in China. In her study, Sun (2011) classified problems in textbooks into two categories: problem variations with and without concept connections and problem variations with or without solution connections. It is argued that the roles of variation problems ("one problem multiple solutions" and "one problem multiple changes") used in Chinese textbooks aim to "provide opportunities for making connections, since comparison is considered the pre-condition to perceive the structures, dependencies, and relationships that may lead to mathematical abstraction" (p. 65). Furthermore, Wong and his colleagues (2009) developed a variation curriculum based on four types of *bianshi* problems: the inductive *bianshi*, the broadening *bianshi*, the deepening *bianshi*, and the applicative *bianshi*. An experiment with this curriculum with 21 sixth grade classes (a total of 686 students) revealed that "students using spiral *bianshi* teaching materials performed significantly better than their counterparts using standard textbook materials. However, no significant differences were detected among affective learning outcome variables despite the positive results on cognitive learning outcomes." (p. 363). This suggests that intentionally implementing curriculum with deliberate variation problems has the potential to result in high cognitive learning outcomes. However, these aforementioned two studies focused on elementary school mathematics topics (division of fraction, speed, and volume).

Since implementation of a new curriculum (MOE, 2011), the editors of textbooks have adapted research findings on teaching through variations in compiling textbooks to improve the selection and arrangement of mathematical activities, examples and exercises. However, no systemic analysis and theoretical reflection on the use of variation tasks in the standard-based textbooks has been carried out. This study aimed to extend our understanding of the use of variation tasks in textbooks by examining a set of popularly used mathematics textbooks in middle school in China (PEP, 2012a, b, 2013a, b; 2014a, b). In the sections that follow, we will illustrate a theoretical framework used for analyzing textbooks in this study.

Categorization of Knowledge

Textbooks provide comprehensive and systematic development and illustration of subject matter knowledge. The structures of textbooks indicate the organization of various components and elements of content（Liao & Tian, 2003), and imply instructional structures and methods. From a cognitive psychology perspective, the components of mathematics textbooks actually consist of various types of knowledge. Building on the taxonomy of Anderson et al. (2001), Zhang (2011) further illustrated four categories of knowledge. These include: *factual knowledge, conceptual knowledge, procedural and meta-cognitive knowledge.* Because textbooks consist of static and explicit mathematical teaching materials that have been purposefully presented by taking pedagogical principles and mathematical structure into consideration, we adopted the following categories of mathematical knowledge: (1) Mathematical concepts; (2) Mathematical principles including properties, rules, formulas and theorems; (3) Mathematical skills including operations by following certain procedures and steps, construction of figures, and data processing; and (4) Mathematical thinking methods underlying mathematical contents and skills. Mathematical concepts and principles are conceptual knowledge; mathematical skills are procedural knowledge; and mathematical thinking methods are strategic knowledge (part of metacognitive knowledge). Thus, we analyzed textbooks from four components: concepts, principles, skills, and thinking methods in mathematics. The material in textbooks is presented in three elements: introduction, major text, and exercise problems (Zhang, 2011): (1) The introduction focuses on illustrating the necessity of learning the new knowledge and explaining learning strategies. Use of variation materials aims to motivate students' learning. (2) The main text presents the mathematical knowledge structure that has been established historically. In addition to presenting basic thinking methods: observation and experimentation, induction and deduction, comparison and classification, analysis and synthesis, generalization and specialization, it also reflects basic models of how people approach problems such as conditions and conclusion, reasons and result, and problem solving methods. Use of variation tasks in main texts aims to promote students' understanding of concepts, principles, and thinking methods. (3) Exercise problems are designed to develop students' ability in applying learned knowledge to various situations. Practicing with variation problems aims to help students to apply knowledge in varying contexts and develop conceptual understanding and procedural proficiency in mathematics.

A Framework for Analyzing Use of Variation Tasks in Mathematics Textbooks

Based on mathematical knowledge categorization and types of variation, a framework is proposed to be used to analyze the features of the use of varying tasks in textbooks as shown in Table 1.

Table 1. A framework for analyzing use of variation tasks in textbooks

	Mathematical concept	Mathematical principles	Mathematical skills	Mathematics thinking methods
Conceptual variation (concept vs. non-concept)				
Procedural variation				

For each of the four types of knowledge, we analyzed how the two types of variation are used to develop content in textbooks when applicable.

METHODS

The six textbooks of mathematics for grade 7(A) and (B) (PEP, 2012a,b), mathematics for grade 8 (A) and (B) (PEP, 2013 a,b), and mathematics for grade 9 (A) and (B) (PEP, 2014 a, b) were selected to identify the major characteristics of use of variation tasks. We examined how mathematics tasks are selected and presented to develop four types of knowledge in different content areas. First, we listed all key mathematics objects (i.e., concepts, principles, skills, and mathematical thinking methods) across grades and examined the ways of presenting the key mathematical objects with respect to how mathematical tasks (conceptual variation (concept or non-concept), procedural variation, combination of the two types of variation or no variation at all) are used. The first and second authors developed a code table. Based on the identified mathematical objects, the third author individually developed a code table. The inter-rater agreement was about 75%. Then, the disagreements were resolved through discussions among authors. Based on comparing and contrasting the types and functions of variation, patterns of using variations emerged (See Table 2 below). After that, appropriate examples from the examined textbooks were selected to illustrate as shown in results.

THE MAJOR FEATURES OF USE VARIATION TASKS IN TEXTBOOKS

We first present the overall features of using variation tasks in developing the four types of knowledge. Then, relevant examples are used to illustrate the major characteristics of the use of variation tasks in textbooks.

Overall Features of Using Variation Tasks in Textbook

The frequencies of use variation tasks in textbooks are shown in Table 2.

Table 2. Frequency of variation tasks used to develop mathematical objects in textbooks

		Concept (49)	Principle (33)	Skill (15)	Thinking (14)	Total (N = 111)
Conceptual variation	Concept	23(47%)	11(33%)	3(20%)	0	38(34%)
	Non-concept	13(27%)	1	1	0	15(14%)
Procedural variation		17(36%)	29(88%)	12(80%)	14(100%)	72(65%)

Note. Since a mathematical object (i.e. concept, principle, skill, or thinking method) could be developed using more than one type of variation, the sum of percentages in a column is not necessarily equal to 100 percent.

The table shows overall features which include: (1) to support different types of concept learning, both conceptual variation (including concept variation (47%), non-concept variation (27%)) and procedural variation (36%) are used; (2) to discover and understand principles, both conceptual variation (33%) and procedural variation (88%) are used, but using procedural variation dominated; (3) to promote the transformation from mathematical knowledge and principles to problem solving abilities, mainly procedural variation (e.g., variation of problem situations and variation of problem type) is used; and (4) to develop mathematical thinking methods, solely, procedural variation (e.g., variation of problem situations and variation of problem types) is used. In the sections that follow, we will illustrate each of these features.

The Use of Variation Tasks for Learning Concepts

Learning a concept typically goes through the following phases: first, based on examining similarities among different instances, the common and essential features are abstracted and synthesized to define a concept; then, the newly developed concept is applied to similar situations. Finally, the concept is connected to a broad concept system and the knowledge structure is further strengthened (Cao & Zhang, 2014). Thus, how to help students classify concrete instances, synthesize key features of a concept through comparing and contrasting, and develop the ability to construct mathematical concepts is a key question needed to be addressed when compiling textbooks. Appropriate use of variation tasks is one of the important strategies.

Use of concept variation for forming a concept. Formation of concepts mainly uses concrete instances to abstract essential attributes/characteristics. Because essential attributes usually are recognized through comparing, the typicality and richness of variation tasks are critical. Typicality refers to the embedment (clear and explicit) of essential attributes in the variation tasks. Richness refers to the various representations of the essential attributes embedded in the variation tasks (Lin, 2011). Take the development of function concept for example.

Function is the most important concept in school mathematics. At the middle school level, the standards state that students should be able "to incorporate examples to know function concept and three representations, and provide examples of functions" (MOE, 2011, p. 29). The examples used in textbooks could be understood as concept variation, a type of conceptual variation. The textbook (PEP, 2013b, p. 71) provides the following questions for students to explore the ideas of a co-varying relationship between two variables in various contexts (such as speed and distance, income and number of products sold, and area of a circle and radius).

1. A car is driving at 60 km/h. If the distance traveled is denoted as s (km), the time traveled is denoted as t (h), fill in a table as follows. How does the change of s co-vary with t?
2. A theater was showing a movie with a ticket price of 10 CNY. If 150 tickets were sold for the first show; 205 tickets were sold for the second show; and 310 tickets were sold for the third show, how much income was gained from each show? If the total tickets sold for a show is x and the income gained is y, how does change of income y co-vary with the total tickets sold x?
3. A rectangular area is fenced using a 10m-long strip. When the length of one side x is 3 m, 3.5 m, 4 m, or 4.5m, how much is the other side y? Does the change of y co-vary with x?

Within different contexts, the same question is asked, "how does change of one variable co-vary with another variable?" This experience helps students synthesize the common feature: There is a relationship between two variables in a given situation: when one variable is given a value, this determines a unique corresponding value for the other variable. After that, the textbook provides more problem situations such as electrocardiogram using graphic representation (time vs. bio-electric current), and population in China in different years using tabular representation (year vs. population).

Based on experiencing the common feature with various contexts, the concept of function is introduced. This design reflects the idea of "conceptual variation", namely, examining the invariant relationship with various instances or context (from different perspectives). Through varying contexts and representations (expressions, diagrams and tables), the invariant characteristic of co-variation is discerned. This

221

exploration may help students move from individual quantitative changes to the co-variation relationship, the key idea of function concept.

Use of non-standard situation tasks for assimilation of concept. As discussed previously, the use of concept variation can highlight the connotation of a concept. However, after defining a concept, if activities (such as classification, assimilation, and decomposition) focus only on standard perception of the concept, it could cause an incomplete understanding of the concept. In a textbook, after using concept variation (various contextual situations) to explore the essential characteristics of the concept, non-standard variations can be used to discern essential features by contrasting non-essential ones, clarifying extension of the concept. Take the concept of altitude of a triangle as an example (PEP, 2013a).

An altitude is an important segment in a triangle, the concept of which includes two essential features: starting from a vertex and being perpendicular to the opposite side. The critical feature is perpendicularity. However, the typical perceived perpendicularity from daily life experience is "vertically perpendicular to horizontal ground", which is different from the concept of perpendicularity in geometry. Determining whether one line is perpendicular to another one relies on the relative positions of the lines (invariant 90 degrees of the angle formed by the two lines, with varying positions of two lines). At the beginning stage of learning geometry, students typically rely on their daily life experience and regard perpendicular to ground as the stereotype of "perpendicularity" (Cao, 1990).

In textbook PEP (2013a, p. 4), first of all, based on daily life perception of perpendicularity, a standard figure (Figure 3) is used to illustrate key features of altitude. In a triangle ABC, students are asked to draw a segment from vertex A perpendicular to opposite side BC, intersecting at D and instructed that the segment AD is called an altitude of side BC. Then, a new exploratory question is posed in a note box, "can you use the same method to draw other altitudes of other two sides?"

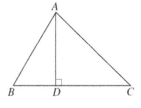

Figure 3

In order to eliminate the possible student misconception that an altitude must be vertical, various situations (particularly, the non-standard situations) with different orientations are provided for students to compare and contrast after introducing the concept. In the class exercise section, the textbook (PEP, 2013a, p. 5) provides a task inviting students to compare three different situations in a "standard figure" (see

Figure 4(a)). It aims to clarify the concept, eliminate irrelevant features, and develop a comprehensive understanding of the concept.

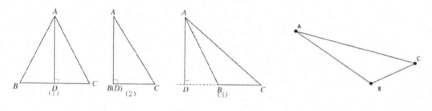

Figure 4 (a) (b)

Finally, in the post-lesson exercises, students are asked to draw three altitudes in a triangle as shown in Figure 4 (b), which is an obtuse triangle in a non-standard position (no horizontal sides).

Examining these non-standard variation figures aims to clarify the concept images of altitude. By varying types and positions of a triangle, the common invariant feature of altitude (mutually perpendicular to each other) is highlighted. This arrangement of tasks provides conditions for students to discern the essential features of altitude regardless of the type or position of triangles.

Use of variation tasks for building connections among relevant concepts. A common strategy in textbooks is to contrast closely related concepts using variation tasks to develop connections of different concepts. For example, after discussing the concept of altitude (as discussed previously), the textbook PEP provides problems for students to differentiate altitude from the relevant concepts of median and angle bisectors from a quantitative perspective. Specifically, in the section of "relevant segments in a triangle", the textbook (PEP, 2013a, p. 8) provides an exercise asking students to contrast the quantitative features of median, angle bisector and altitude from the same vertex in a triangle as shown in Figure 5.

In the figure (on the right below), in triangle △ ABC, AE is a median, AD is an angle bisector, and AF is an altitude, fill out the following blanks.

(1) $BE=$ _____ $=\dfrac{1}{2}$ _____;

(2) $\angle BAD=$ _____ $=\dfrac{1}{2}$ _____;

(3) $\angle AFB=$ _____ $=90°$;

(4) $S_{\triangle ABC}=$ _____.

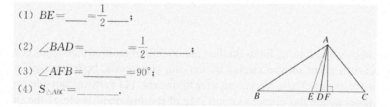

Figure 5

223

Use of variation tasks for elaborating concepts. For both concept formation and concept assimilation, it is necessary to provide practicing activities for clarifying and elaborating the concept (Wu, 2000). In textbooks, these activities normally vary systematically surrounding a concept. For example, the concept of inscribed angle of a circle is introduced by assimilating based on the concept of central angle (PEP, 2014a, p. 85). In a circle O, in addition to the central angle (∠ AOB), there is another type of angle such as ∠ ACB or ∠ ADB (the angle subtended at a point (C or D) on the circle by the two given points (A and B)) which is defined as inscribed angle.

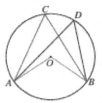

Figure 6

After that, the textbook (PEP, 2014a, p. 88) provides varying tasks for students to further clarify the concept of inscribed angles and examines the relationship between inscribed angles and central angles by presenting both concept and non-concept variation problems as shown in Figure 7.

Judge whether the angles in the following figures are inscribed angle or not, and explain your statement.

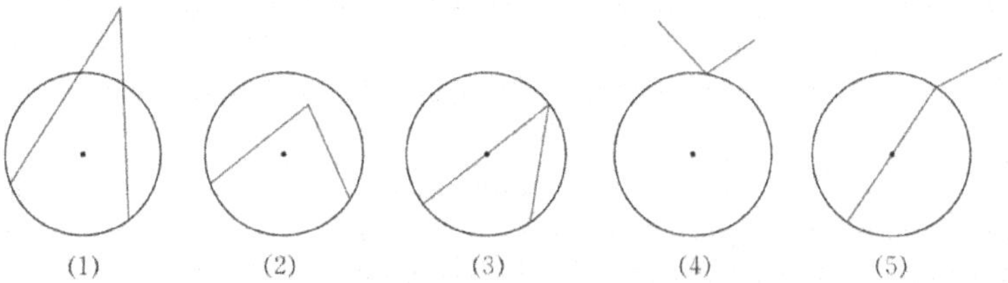

(1)　　　　(2)　　　　(3)　　　　(4)　　　　(5)

Figure 7

The above five figures focus on the connotation of an inscribed angle (two cords intersect at a point on the circle) by varying conditions, both *concept and non-concept* variations. These variations aim to discern: (1) vertexes outside the circle; (2) vertexes inside the circle; (3) one side of the inscribed angle as the diameter; (4) two sides without intersection with the circle (except the common vertex); and (5) only one side intersects the circle.

Use of Variation Tasks for Discovering and Understanding
Mathematical Principles

Mathematical principles, namely invariant patterns within varying contexts, include mathematical rules, formulas and properties. Similar to formation of a concept, the use of variation tasks could also be helpful for discovering invariant patterns. Ausubel (1968) suggests that the process of mastering knowledge includes three *phases of knowing, consolidating and applying. Regarding learning* of mathematical principles, we specify these three phases as forming a principle, building connections between relevant principles, and applying the principle flexibly.

Use of varying tasks for discovering principles. At the forming stage, the textbooks provide tasks/activities for motivating students, and providing concrete experiences which lays a foundation for discovering mathematical principles. There are multiple ways for students to discover mathematical principles (e.g., patterns in certain varying contexts). These include synthesis of common features of concrete instances, making conjecture through analogy, generalization or specialization, induction or deduction. The textbooks provide conceptual variation or/and procedural variation tasks depending on the characteristics of the content.

For example, to introduce various algebraic operation rules, textbooks usually adopt inductive reasoning based on concrete instances (from concrete to abstract, conceptual variations). Generally, textbooks first provide operation tasks with different concrete numbers and then ask students to see patterns of operation results; finally the patterns are analogous to algebra operations.

In textbook PEP (2013b, p. 6), the operation rules with square roots are introduced as follows:

First, students are provided exploration tasks to observe the patterns from the following operations with concrete numbers

1. $\sqrt{4} \times \sqrt{9} =$ _____ , $\sqrt{4 \times 9} =$ _____ ;
2. $\sqrt{16} \times \sqrt{25} =$ _____ , $\sqrt{16 \times 25} =$ _____ ;
3. $\sqrt{25} \times \sqrt{36} =$ _____ , $\sqrt{25 \times 36} =$ _____ ;

After that, algebraic operation rule for square roots is synthesized as:

1. $\sqrt{a} \times \sqrt{b} = \sqrt{a \times b}\,(a \geq 0, b \geq 0)$

In these three operation equations, the structure remains the same while the numbers change. Through computation and subsequent observation, students can find the invariant structure within the varying computation equations, and derive the algebra operation rule. The question such as "based on the observation of your computation results, what pattern do you find" leads students to thinking about general patterns based on concrete operations. The operation rule of square root

225

$\sqrt{a} \cdot \sqrt{b} = \sqrt{ab}$ is generalized from numbers to expressions with additional constraints of $a \geq 0$, $b \geq 0$. To draw students' attention to the constraint, the textbook provides an example as follows: simplify $\sqrt{4a^2b^3}$. If students do not notice the constraint, they will get $\sqrt{4a^2b^3} = 2ab\sqrt{b}$. If they notice the condition, then they have to consider the domain of a, b, and finally get the correct answer of $2|a| b\sqrt{b}$. Discussing this type of task (concept variation) could help students to understand the formula precisely.

Use variation problems for building connections between mathematical properties. Mathematical principles reflect the properties of mathematical objects and relationships between different elements of mathematical objects. Algebraic properties mainly focus on the invariant patterns of operations. Functional properties mainly reflect invariant patterns when variables change; geometric properties reflect invariant patterns when shapes, size and positions change. Thus, use of varying tasks can help students discover these properties. In textbooks, purposeful design of variation tasks aims to promote students' discovering and understanding of properties (Cao & Zhang, 2014).

For example, to explore the properties of parallelogram the textbook PEP presents the following sequence of exploratory tasks (2013b, p. 41–55). After introducing the definition of parallelogram the following task is presented:

Task 1: Draw a parallelogram based on its definition, observe the figure and explore any relationships between sides or angles of a parallelogram beyond the property of two opposite sides are parallel. Check your conjectures by measuring relevant elements.

After exploring basic properties about sides and angles, then the following is provided to help students discover properties related to diagonals.

Task 2: In the parallelogram ABCD (below), connect AC, BD intersecting at O. Are there any special relationships among OA, OB, OC, and OD? Justify your conjectures.

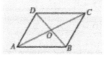

Figure 8

Further, tasks are provided to explore converse properties of parallelogram as follows:

Task 3: Based on previous exploration, we learned that in a parallelogram, the opposite sides are equal, opposite angles are equal, and diagonals bisect each other. Conversely if opposite sides are equal, or if opposite angles are equal, or if diagonals bisect each other in a quadrilateral, will the quadrilateral be parallelogram? That is to say, are the converse properties of parallelogram tenable?

Additionally, through specifying the angles and sides of a parallelogram, then, the specific parallelograms such as rectangle, rhombus, and square are explored.

Through the *procedural variation* problems, the properties of parallelograms are explored systematically. Based on the definition of parallelogram, through drawing, observing, measuring (variations in shape and size), the invariant relationships between sides and between angles in quadrilaterals are discerned. Then, through asking converse questions, "if two opposite sides are equal in a quadrilateral, will the quadrilateral be a parallelogram?" the theorems for determining a parallelogram are explored. Furthermore, through specifying, "an angle is right", or "a pair of adjacent sides are equal", or "an angle is right and a pair adjacent sides are equal", then, specific parallelograms of rectangle, rhombus and square are explored. Thus, the structure of the knowledge about parallelograms has been developed logically as shown in the chapter summary (Figure 9).

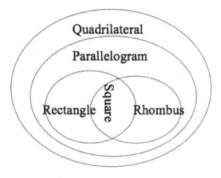

Figure 9

Use of variation tasks for developing multiple representations of a property. Profound understanding of concepts or principles depends on building interconnection among different types of knowledge (Zhang, 1995). In textbooks, multiple representations often are used to develop the connections among different types of knowledge and deepen understanding of mathematical principles. For example, the textbook PEP provides the following activities to develop the formula for the square of a sum (2013a, pp. 109–111):

Explore activity 1: Expand the following expressions. What patterns do you notice?

(1) $(p+1)^2 = (p+1)(p+1) = $ _____ ;

(2) $(m+2)^2 = $ _____ ;

(3) $(p-1)^2 = (p-1)(p-1) = $ _____ ;

(4) $(m-2)^2 = $ _____ .

Based on the computations for the expansion of the above sums, a common structure of expression is identified for $(a \pm b)^2$. Because

$$(a + b)^2 = (a + b)(a + b) = a^2 + ab + ba + b^2 = a^2 + 2ab + b^2$$

the following formulas for square of a sum and difference are derived:

$$(a + b)^2 = a^2 + 2ab + b^2$$
$$(a - b)^2 = a^2 - 2ab + b^2$$

In other words, the square of sum of two numbers (or difference) is equal to the sum of square of each number, plus (or minus) 2 times of the product of the two numbers (verbal representation). The textbook indicates the relationship between this square of sum formula and multiplication of polynomial expressions by saying that the formula is a special case of $(a+b)(p+q)$ when $p=a$ and $q=b$ in a note box. Finally, the textbook provides an exploratory task inviting students to find the algebraic formulas based on area relationships in each of the following figures (Figure 10).

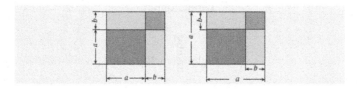

Figure 10

The algebraic formula has been discovered inductively by examining specific cases and then synthesizing the form of $(a \pm b)^2$ and by proving the formula by using multiplication of algebraic expressions. Moreover, the formula is represented in verbal, algebraic and graphic forms. Through the procedural variation of discovering the formula and conceptual variation of multiple representations, students can gain understanding of the formula adaptively.

Use of Variation Tasks for Developing Mathematical Skills

Mathematical skills include computation, construction and reasoning. Operation skills include numerical computations or algebraic transformations based on concepts, formulas and properties. Construction skills include drawing figures precisely based on given conditions. Reasoning skills refers to making logical arguments based on given conditions and by following certain procedures and steps (Ding, 1992).

Typical skills include operations with algebraic expressions, solving equations and inequalities, analyzing properties of functions, constructing geometric figures, and basic methods of logical reasoning. It is important to develop mathematical skills based on conceptual understanding through appropriate practicing. The process of acquiring mathematical skills includes the three phases of knowing, connecting and automatizing (Cao & Zhang, 2014).

1. Knowing phase: Students learn how to carry out procedures step by step, with a focus on sequence and results of each step.
2. Connecting phase: Students build connections between consequent steps (action and effect) so that taking each step becomes more smooth and effective.
3. Automatizing phase: The procedure becomes precise, natural, and automatic for the students.

Practicing with variations could play an important role in the process of developing mathematical skills. In textbooks, building on concepts, formulas and figures, the tasks are first presented in situations with which students are familiar. Then tasks are changed in different forms, and finally tasks are presented in novel contexts. Providing these variations (for example, changes in given conditions, or results, or contexts) aims to develop skills in applying mathematical concepts and principles to solve problems flexibly. These changes should be sequenced and systematic in alignment with the process of development of mathematics.

For instance, in geometry, various figures usually are derived from some stereotypical figures. Understanding these basic figures and relevant variations will help solve relevant problems effectively. Take one example from the chapter of "triangle" and "congruent triangle" to illustrate a stereotypical figure and its variations (PEP, 2013a). The figure is two triangles sharing a common side as shown in Figure 11.

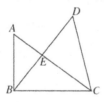

Figure 11

Based on this basic figure, there are a great number of derived figures appearing in 17 examples or exercises as displayed in Table 2.

Various ones of the seventeen variation figures in Table 2 are included in sections of the textbook dealing with the definition of triangle; basic properties of triangles; the altitudes, medians, and angle bisectors in a triangle; and congruent triangle. While the invariant feature of the figure was two triangles sharing a side, many things changed: (1) specific relationships between other two sides: equal, collinear, common point; (2) specific relationships between other angles: equal, right; (3) incorporating new concepts (Tasks 6 and 15); (4) transformations of the basic figure (translation, reflection, rotation) (Tasks 8, 9, 10, 14); and (5) substantial differences from the basic figure (Tasks 16 and 17).

Table 2. Variation figures derived from the same stereotype figure

Variation figures	Relevant tasks
	1. How many triangles are there in the figure? Label them.
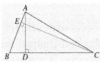	2. In triangle Δ ABC, AB = 2cm, BC = 4cm. AD and CE are altidudes. What is the ratio AD to CE? (hint: use the area formula of traingle)
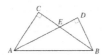	3. In the figure, ∠C = ∠D = 90°. AD, BC intersect at E. What relationships are there between ∠CAE and ∠DBE? Why?
	4. In the figure, D is on AB. E is on AC. BE and CD intersect at F. ∠A = 62°. ∠ACD = 35°. ∠ABE = 20°. Find ∠BDC and ∠BFD.
	5. In △ABC, BE and CF are angle bisectors of ∠B and ∠C respectively. BE and CF intersect at G. Prove: (1) ∠BGC = 180°–½ (∠ABC + ∠ACB); (2) ∠BGC = 90° + ½ ∠A
	6. In △ABC, AD is an altitude. AE and GF are angle bisectors and intersect at O. ∠BAC = 50°. ∠C = 70°. Find sizes of ∠DAC and ∠BOA
	7. In the figure, △AEC ≅ △ADB, and points E and D are corresponding points. (1) Find corrresponding sides and angles. (2) If ∠ = 50°, ∠ABD = 39° and ∠1 = ∠2, find the degree measure of ∠1.
	8. In the figure, points E, F are on BC. BE = CF. AB = DC. ∠C = ∠B. Show ∠A = ∠D.

Variation figures	*Relevant tasks*
	9. In the figure, $\triangle ABN \cong \triangle ACM$. $\angle B$ and $\angle C$ are corresponding angles. AB and AC are conrrespoding sides. Find other corresponding sides and angles.
	10. In the figure, $\triangle ABC \cong \triangle DEC$. CA and CD. CB and CE are corresponding sides. Are $\angle ACD$ and $\angle BCE$ equal? Why?
	11. In the figure, $AC \perp BC$. $BD \perp AD$. BD and AD intersect at C, and D respectively. $AC = BD$. Show $BC = AD$.
	12. In the figure, from point C, looking at A and B with an $\angle C$; the distances from C to A and B are equal, the distances from A to side BC is AD and the distance from B to side AC is BC. Are AD and BE equal? Why?
	13. In the figure, $AC \perp BC$. $BD \perp CB$. BD and AD intersect at C and B respectively. $AB = DC$. Show $\angle ABD = \angle ACD$.
	14. In the figure, points B, E, C, F are collinear. $AB = DE$. $AC = DF$. $BE = CF$. Show $\angle A = \angle D$.
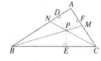	15. In the figure, BM and CN are the angle bisectors of $\triangle ABC$, and they intersect at P. Show: the distances between P and each of sides AB, BC, and CA are equal.
	16. In the figure, $\angle ACB = 90°$. $AC = BC$. $AD \perp CE$, $BE \perp CE$. BE and CD intersect at D and E, respectively. $AD = 2.4$ cm and $DE = 1.7$cm. Find the length of BE.
	17. In the figure, in $\triangle ABC$, AD is an angle bisector of $\angle A$. Show: Area of $\triangle ABD$: Area of $\triangle ACD = AB:AC$.

In textbooks, as the study of the triangle develops, these variation figures are arranged progressively in different sections. The basic figure is used for clarifying the definition of triangle and illustrating the structure of the figure. Variation figures in Tasks (2)–(5) are used for exploring basic properties of triangles, while the variation figure in Task (6) is closely related to the use of triangle properties. Variation figures in Tasks (7)–(15) are related to congruent triangles. Among them, the variation figure in Task (7) is a result by specifying sides, angles in an isosceles triangle. Variation figures in Tasks (8) and (9) are the result of specifying and translating, while figures in Task (10) are the result of rotation. Variation figures in Task (11)–(13) specify sides and angles.

In summary, the design of the problems in Table 2 aims to cultivate students' ability to discern the basic figure from various figures and then use the properties of the basic figure as a springboard for solving different problems.

Use of Variation Tasks for Developing Mathematics Thinking Methods

Mathematical thinking refers to essential understanding of mathematics objects, and fundamental opinions and ideas synthesized through the process of exploring mathematics knowledge (such as inductive and deductive reasoning thinking, equation thinking and so on) that have overarching guiding implications for doing mathematical activity (Cao & Zhang, 2014). Mathematical methods refer to the methods and strategies during mathematics activity (such as substitution methods, consideration of a special case, eliminating methods). Mathematics thinking and methods are closely related. Usually, overarching guiding thinking is deemed as mathematical thinking, while implementing process and strategies is referred to mathematical methods. Mathematical thinking and methods are about how to collect and process data, how to draw figures and make tables, how to select and design algorithms, and how to form and solve problems in contextual situations. These, related to how to think, belong to strategic knowledge (Cao & Zhang, 2014). It is necessary for students to explore more examples, practice with variation problems, and reflect on the process of problem solving.

Use of variation tasks for developing mathematical thinking in algebra. Mathematical textbooks present a logical system of mathematical content using mathematics language. Mathematical thinking methods are a type of knowledge about how to think about developing mathematical knowledge. Thus, mathematical textbooks have to reflect the integration of mathematical content and mathematics thinking methods. Variation tasks serve for uncovering the mathematical thinking methods embedded in different contents with different forms. It aims to highlight mathematical essence and help students' discover invariance within varying phenomena, while experiencing the process of mathematical discovering and thinking. The following is an example of introducing properties of inequalities in algebra using the *mathematical method of analogous reasoning.*

There is an introduction (PEP, 2012b, p. 116) as follows:

We know that adding to or subtracting from both sides of an equation the same number (expression), multiplying or dividing both sides of an equation by the same non-zero number, results in the equation remaining valid. Are there similar properties regarding inequalities?

In order to answer the question, students are asked to fill in following blanks using ">" or "<" and summarize the patterns:

(1) $5>3$, $5+2$____$3+2$, $5-2$____$3-2$;

(2) $-1<3$, $-1+2$____$3+2$, $-1-3$____$3-3$;

(3) $6>2$, 6×5____2×5, $6\times(-5)$____$2\times(-5)$;

(4) $-2<3$, $(-2)\times6$____3×6, $(-2)\times(-6)$____$3\times(-6)$.

Figure 12

Further, students are asked to fill in the following blanks based on their discoveries: when adding the same number to or subtracting the same number (positive or negative) from both sides, the direction of the inequality:____. When multiplying both sides by a positive number, the direction of the inequality: ____. When multiplying both sides by a negative number, the direction of the inequality: ____. In the note box, there is a suggestion on using other numbers to check these discoveries.

Using the *analogous reasoning* method, the textbook includes the task of exploring properties of inequalities. Then, four concrete examples are used to discover operation rules with inequalities (e.g., conceptual variations). After that, students are led to synthesize patterns by filling in blank tasks, and further using "note box" (using other number, verifying your conjectures) (e.g., procedural variations). In the textbook, the analogous method is used to put forward questions and make conjectures, then "invariability in operations" leads to discovering properties of inequalities. This arrangement reflects on how variation tasks could be used to develop mathematical thinking methods.

Use of variation tasks for developing mathematical thinking in Geometry. We consider another example involving proving the "theorem of sum of three interior angles" (PEP, 2013a, pp. 11–12) which allows us to reflect on the *mathematical thinking methods of inductive and deductive reasoning* using variation tasks.

Although in elementary school, students learned that the sum of interior angles of a triangle is equal to $180°$ through cutting and pasting, and measuring, students need to learn how to prove the property in middle school. From the textbook, four phases were used to discover and prove the property and help students move from manipulative activities (inductive reasoning) to iconic representations (i.e., segment figures), to final symbolic representations (deductive reasoning), and to multiple proofs.

Reviewing cutting activities and exploring proof. First, the textbook provides an exploratory activity (Draw a triangle, cut off three interior angles and put them together to form a straight angle. What do you find regarding proof the sum of interior angles of a triangle is 180°), allowing student to review what they did in elementary school.

Two of various samples of student work are presented in the textbook as follows:

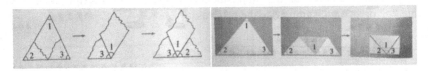

Figure 13

Based on this exploratory activity, students are asked to recall different ways to assemble three interior angles of a triangle forming a straight angle, which lays a foundation for discovering formal proof.

Selection of appropriate methods and construction of auxiliary line. How do we help students develop proving methods? Because the proposition that the sum of interior angles of any triangle is equal to 180° is equivalent to the statement that the three interior angles form a straight angle, namely, a line containing the vertex. The key to discovering a proof is to transform a "straight" angle into a straight line using the properties of parallel lines. Then, the problem is transformed to examine if there is an auxiliary line that contains a vertex and is parallel to one side of the triangle. The difficulty in making this transformation is the abstraction from physically cutting the figures to forming a geometric "figure". To help students make this transformation, the textbook provides two methods of assembling and highlights the "segment figures" as shown in Figure 14.

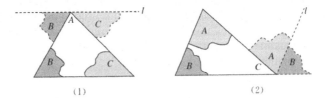

(1)   (2)

Figure 14

In Figure 14 (left figure), ∠A and ∠B are assembled around the vertex A (left and right sides without overlapping), and the three angles form a straight angle which forms a line *l* passing through A. The textbook provides probing questions in a note box such as "think about the relationship between *l* and the side BC of the triangle. Do you have any ideas about proving that the sum of interior angles is 180°?" The advancing questions are designed to lead students to observe the structure of the segment figure and discover line *l* passing through A, and focus their thinking on "the relationship between line *l* and side BC". Thus, the constructing an auxiliary line is the key to proving the property.

Developing deductive proof. Based on the previous exploration, the textbook provides a "pure" geometry figure (Figure 15) which includes triangles, parallel lines, and alternate angles. Meanwhile, the textbooks provide a complete, formal proving process.

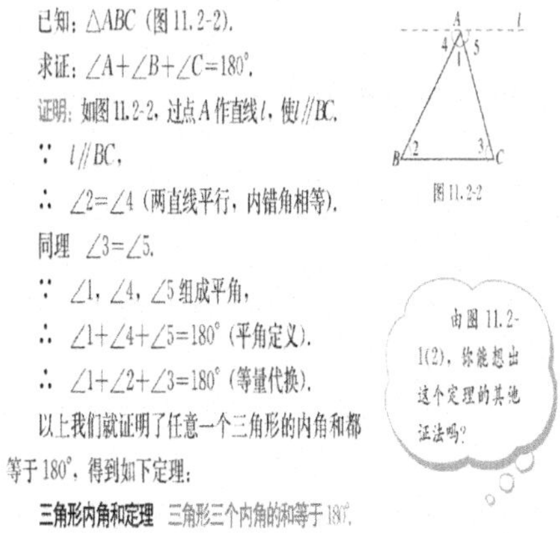

已知: △ABC (图 11.2-2).

求证: ∠A+∠B+∠C=180°.

证明: 如图 11.2-2, 过点 A 作直线 *l*, 使 *l*//BC.

∵ *l*//BC,

∴ ∠2=∠4 (两直线平行, 内错角相等).

同理 ∠3=∠5.

∵ ∠1、∠4、∠5 组成平角,

∴ ∠1+∠4+∠5=180° (平角定义).

∴ ∠1+∠2+∠3=180° (等量代换).

以上我们就证明了任意一个三角形的内角和都

等于 180°, 得到如下定理:

三角形内角和定理 三角形三个内角的和等于 180°.

图 11.2-2

由图 11.2-1(2), 你能想出这个定理的其他证法吗?

Given: the △ ABC (figure 11.2-2)

Prove: ∠A+∠B+∠C=180°

Proof: In figure 11.2.2, construct a line *l* containing A and parallel BC.

∵ *l*//BC,

∴ ∠2=∠4 (two line parallel, alternate angles are equal)

∠3=∠5 (The same reason as before)

∵ ∠1, ∠4, and ∠5 form a straight angle

∴ ∠1+∠4+∠5=180° (the definition of straight angle)

∴ ∠1+∠2+∠3=180° (equal quantity substitution)

Thus, the sum of interior angles of any triangle is 180°

Figure 15(a) (b)

So far, the textbook presents the entire process of proving as a transition from visual verification to abstract logical justification. The "segment figures" is the bridge between "physical manipulation" and "abstract geometry figure".

Multiple proofs. In a note box, students are encouraged to "think about making other proofs". Based on different figures (with different auxiliary lines), students are required to complete another poof.

The above example demonstrates how variation tasks (procedural variations) are used to promote student engagment in the process of discovering proofs from visual verification to deductive proof. Meanwhile, the mathematical thinking methods such as visual observation, conjecture making and conjecture justification could be experienced through these exploratory activities.

CONCLUSIONS AND DISCUSSIONS

Characteristics of the Use Variation Tasks in Mathematics Textbooks in China

Teaching through variation that relies on enlightening teaching principles and variation tasks in mathematics textbooks has been practiced over decades. Editors of mathematics textbooks have emphasized the use of variation tasks in textbooks historically, but little research has been devoted to the use of variation tasks in textbooks. To this end, the study focused on examples of how variation tasks (conceptual variation and procedural variation) are used to develop mathematical concepts, principles, skills and thinking methods in mathematics based on a set of the most widely used mathematics textbooks for middle schools in China. Based on a comprehensive analysis of the textbooks, we made the following observations:

Developing mathematical concepts. During the different phases of learning concepts, different variation tasks are used for different purposes: (1) When forming a concept, concept variation is used to explore the common features of different instances, and to synthesize the essential characteristics of a concept. (2) When assimilating a new concept, to avoid the distraction of non-critical features, non-concept variation tasks are used to clarify the critical features of the concept. (3) When consolidating and applying a concept, procedural variation tasks are used to help students build connections among different representations and different types of knowledge.

Developing mathematical principles. Regarding learning of principles, different variation tasks were used to develop principles at different phases. (1) To discover mathematics principles, multiple instances are used to identify the invariant features of different instances, and then generalization is made based on the exploration of the set of instances. The variation tasks are used to enable students to discover "invariant features" within variation tasks. Normally, *procedural variation* problems are the major strategies for discovering the invariant features within varying contexts. (2) To build connections among different principles, *procedural variation* tasks are used to discover proofs of the principles and build an interconnected knowledge network. (3) To apply principles, *procedural variation* tasks are used to discover the consistency of different representations, and build knowledge interconnections.

Developing mathematical skills. With respect to acquiring mathematical skills, practicing variation problems (procedural variation) is a necessary pathway to developing mathematical skills in applying mathematics concept and principles. Variation tasks are used to develop mathematical skills at different stages. These variation tasks build on basic concepts, formulas and figures and are presented progressively, from a situation with which students are familiar, via changing types of problems, finally to situations that are unfamiliar for students. Solving these variation problems could develop mathematical skills in applying concepts and principles within various situations.

Developing mathematical thinking methods. Mathematical thinking methods is a type of strategic knowledge that is implicit, generalizable, and enlightening. Textbooks adopted the design principle that "mathematical thinking methods should be reflected through mathematical content". Through variation and transformation in representation of mathematical content, mathematical thinking methods are introduced implicitly. The use of procedural variation tasks helps students discover and form problems, analyze and solve problems, and experience approaches to learning mathematics. In addition, variation problems provide students an opportunity to judge and make decisions based on different conditions.

DISCUSSION

This study shows that in the selected textbooks, systemic variation tasks (procedural and conceptual variations) are used to develop mathematical concepts, principles and mathematical skills and mathematical thinking methods. Both cognitive theory (Ausubel, 1968) and variation theory (Gu et al., 2004; Marton & Booth, 1997) argue the positive roles of these variations for students' meaningful learning. Teaching through variation is a long-standing and daily used teaching strategy, and Chinese teachers heavily rely on mathematics textbooks. Thus, the textbooks that include purposefully designed variation problems provide valuable and user-friendly materials for teachers to adapt. The consistent use of variation problems in textbooks and in classroom instruction provides strong support for students' learning that may provide further explanation of Chinese students' excellent performance of mathematics on international comparative assessment (OECD, 2012).

However, there is little empirical study on the relationship between use textbooks with variation problems and teaching through variation and student learning outcomes (Wong et al., 2009). More empirical studies in this area are needed. In addition, regarding compiling textbooks, there are several issues that need to be addressed. First, since there are substantial differences between algebra and geometry, how should design variation tasks be designed that reflects these differences? In geometry, the truthfulness of many propositions can be judged based on visual representations. However, in algebra, a proposition can only be justified based on algebra structure and formula. It is an inductive construction process. How can these differences be reflected in design of using variation tasks? Secondly, to what extent are the variation problems conducive to student learning? Less variation tasks may be not enough to explore critical features of a learning object, while too many variation problems may distract students' learning. So the appropriateness of design variation tasks is still a challenge when compiling textbooks.

FINAL REMARK

This study reveals some characteristics of the use of variation tasks in textbooks, which aims to develop mathematical concepts, principles, skills and mathematics thinking. The framework used in this study may provide a useful tool for further studies. More studies in this area are needed to provide a comprehensive picture about the use of variation tasks in textbooks. In addition, it will be interesting to examine the relationship between textbooks used and classroom instruction regarding use of variation problems and their effect on students' achievement.

REFERENCES

Anderson, L. W., Krathwohl, D. R., Airason, P. W., Cruikshank, K. A., Mayer, R. E., Pintrich, P. R., et al. (Eds.). (2001). *A taxonomy for learning, teaching, and assessing: A revision of Bloom's taxonomy of educational objectives.* Boston, MA (Pearson Education Group): Allyn & Bacon.

Ausubel, D. (1968). *Educational psychology: A cognitive view.* New York, NY: Holt, Rinehart & Winston.

Brunner, J. S. (1985). Vygotsky: A historical and conceptual perspective. In J. V. Wertsch (Ed.), *Culture, communication and cognition: Vygotsky perspective* (pp. 21–34). Cambridge, UK: Cambridge University Press.

Cao, C. (1990). *Instruction theory of teaching in secondary mathematics* [In Chinese]. Beijing: Beijing Normal University Press.

Cao, C., & Zhang, J. (2014). *Psychology of mathematics education* (3th) [In Chinese]. Beijing: Beijing Normal University Press.

Dienes, Z. P. (1973). A theory of mathematics learning. In F. J. Crosswhite, J. L. Highins, A. R. Ostorne, & R. J. Shunway (Eds.), *Teaching mathematics: Psychological foundations* (pp. 137–148). Ohio, OH: Charles A. Jones Publishing Company.

Ding, R. (1992). Review explanation for middle school mathematics teaching syllabus from grades 1–9 [In Chinese]. *Discipline Education, (5),* 2–8.

Editorial Committee. (2005). Study and compiling of mathematics textbooks for high school. *Curriculum, Textbook and Pedagogy, 25*(1), 45–50.

Gu, L., Huang, R., & Marton, F. (2004). Teaching with variation: An effective way of mathematics teaching in China. In L. Fan, N. Y. Wong, J. Cai, & S. Li (Eds.), *How Chinese learn mathematics: Perspectives from insiders* (pp. 309–348). Singapore: World Scientific.

Gu, L. Y. (1994). *Experimentation theories on instruction: Methodology of QinPu experiment and study on instruction principles* [In Chinese]. Beijing: Educational Science Press.

Gu, M. (1999). *Education directory* [In Chinese]. Shanghai: Shanghai Educational Press.

Liao, Z., & Tian, H. (2003). *Now theory of curriculum study* [In Chinese]. Beijing: Educational Science Press.

Lin, C. (2011). *Intelligence development and mathematics learning* [In Chinese]. Beijing: China Light Industry Press.

Lu, Z. (1961). Negative effect of standard figure in geometry [In Chinese]. *Journal of Psychology, 2,* 88–100.

Marton, F., & Booth, S. (1997). *Learning and awareness.* Mahwah, NJ: Lawrence Erlbaum Associates.

Ministry of Education, P. R. China [MOE]. (2011). *Mathematics curriculum standards for compulsory education* [In Chinese]. Beijing: Beijing Normal University.

OECD. (2012). *Programme for international student assessment PISA2000 technical report.* Paris: OECD.

OECD. (2013). *PISA 2012 results: What students know and can do: student performance in mathematics, reading and science* (Vol. 1). Paris: OECD.

Park, K., & Leung, F. K. S. (2006). A comparative study of the mathematics textbooks of China, England, Japan, Korea, and the United States. In F. K. S. Leung, K. D. Graf, & F. J. Lopez-Real (Eds.), *Mathematics education in different cultural traditions—A comparative study of East Asia and the West: The 13th ICMI study.* New York, NY: Springer.

People's Education Press [PEP]. (1963). *Middle school algebra.* Beijing: People's Education Press.

People's Education Press [PEP]. (1981). *Middle school geometry.* Beijing: People's Education Press.

People's Education Press [PEP]. (2012a). *Textbook for compulsory education- Mathematics 7A.* Beijing: People's Education Press.

People's Education Press [PEP]. (2012b). *Textbook for compulsory education-Mathematics 7B.* Beijing: People's Education Press.

People's Education Press [PEP]. (2013a). *Textbooks for compulsory education- Mathematics 8A*. Beijing: People's Education Press.

People's Education Press [PEP]. (2013b). *Textbooks for compulsory education- Mathematics 8B*. Beijing: People's Education Press.

People's Education Press [PEP]. (2014a). *Textbooks for compulsory education- Mathematics 9A*. Beijing: People's Education Press.

People's Education Press [PEP]. (2014b). *Textbooks for compulsory education- Mathematics 9A*. Beijing: People's Education Press.

Ru, Z. (1994). Variation problem and examination [In Chinese]. *Journal of Secondary Mathematics Reference, 1994*(7), cover 2.

Sun, X. (2011). Variation problems and their roles in the topic of fraction division in Chinese mathematics textbook examples. *Education Studies in Mathematics, 76*, 65–85.

Wong, N.-Y., Lam, C.-C., Sun, X., & Chan, A. M. Y. (2009). From "exploring the middle zone" to "constructing a bridge": Experimenting in the spiral Bianshi mathematics curriculum. *International Journal of Science and Mathematics Education, 7*, 363–382.

Wu, Q. (2000). *Cognitive psychology* [In Chinese]. Shanghai: Shanghai Science and Technology Press.

Xiang, W. Y. (2015, January 11). *Abstract thinking and simple logic: It roles in basic mathematics education*. Presentation at 10th Su Bu Qin mathematical education award, Beijing, China.

Zhang, J. Y. (2011). *Theories of secondary mathematics curriculum* [In Chinese]. Beijing: Beijing Normal University Press.

Zhang, J. Y. (2015). Mathematics learning and intelligence development. *Journal of Secondary Mathematics Teaching References, 2015*(7), 6–8.

Zhang, Y. (2014). Trends of mathematics education: Some excellent techniques. *Mathematics Bullet, 53*(10), 1–7 (and back page).

Zheng, Y. X. (2006). Development of variation theory. *Journal of Secondary Mathematics, 2006*(1), 1–3.

Zhou, H. (1959). Discussion about the psychological issue in middle school mathematics. *Journal of Hangzhou University, 1959*(4), 45–56.

Jianyue Zhang
People's Education Press
Beijing, China

Rong Wang
People's Education Press
Beijing, China

Rongjin Huang
Middle Tennessee State University
Murfreesobro, TN, USA

Dovie Kimmins
Middle Tennessee State University
Murfreesobro, TN, USA

LIPING DING, KEITH JONES AND SVEIN ARNE SIKKO

12. AN EXPERT TEACHER'S USE OF TEACHING WITH VARIATION TO SUPPORT A JUNIOR MATHEMATICS TEACHER'S PROFESSIONAL LEARNING

INTRODUCTION

Our study concerns an important issue raised by recent studies of teacher professional development (TPD); that of the process of teacher change. As long ago as 2002, Clarke and Hollingsworth pointed out that the key shift in TPD is "from programs that change teachers, to teachers as active learners shaping their professional growth through reflective participation in professional development programs and in practice" (2002, p. 948). More recently, Goldsmith, Doerr and Lewis (2014) have highlighted that in many existing TPD studies, teachers' learning has typically been treated as an indicator of the effectiveness of the TPD programme rather than the primary object of inquiry. Their research synthesis shows that, to date, few studies have focused on the processes or mechanisms of teachers' learning. Similarly, the latest report from The New Teacher Project (2015) suggests that despite considerable investment in TPD, the evidence base for what actually helps teachers improve remains very thin. Consequently, there is still much to learn about how teachers develop knowledge, beliefs, or instructional practices.

More particularly, the success of pupils from Shanghai, China, in the recent PISA (Programme for International Student Assessment) study has made it important to understand how teacher learning takes place in Shanghai. Our Lesson Design Study (LDS), which focuses on primary school mathematics teacher professional learning through school-based teaching research group activities on lesson design and action, is being conducted in Shanghai (see Ding et al., 2013, 2014, 2015). In this chapter, our research question focuses on how a Chinese expert teacher in Shanghai used the idea of teaching with variation (Gu, Huang, & Marton, 2004) to support a junior teacher (with three years of teaching experience) to develop certain ways of reflecting on her teaching.

LITERATURE BACKGROUND

Given our research question concerning the expert teacher's use of teaching with variation to support a junior teacher to improve her teaching, in this section we chiefly focus on two themes within the existing literature that are relevant to

R. Huang & Y. Li (Eds.), Teaching and Learning Mathematics through Variation, 241–266.

our study: one is teaching with variation; the other is teachers' learning through the social interaction processes within the professional community that leads to sustained learning, together with an understanding of the role of the mentor (or 'knowledgeable other').

Teaching with Variation

Teaching with variation (变式教学 *Bian Shi Jiao Xue* in Chinese) has long been widely practiced by mathematics teachers in China (e.g., Ding et al., 2015; Gu, Huang, & Marton, 2004; Huang, Mok, & Leung, 2006; Li, Peng, & Song, 2011; Sun, 2011). In Gu's early work (the 'Qingpu experiment study' led by Gu from 1977 to 1994 in collaboration with a number of teachers and researchers and focused on improving the effectiveness of teaching and learning of mathematics in the Qingpu district of Shanghai), Gu (1994) noted that the most effective mathematics teachers were those who were able intentionally to arrange what might best be called 'multiple layers of teaching and learning'. Accordingly, Gu, Huang and Marton (2004, p. 319) consider that mathematics teaching largely consists of two types of activities: teaching declarative knowledge (i.e., concepts) and teaching procedural knowledge (i.e., processes). They identify and illustrate two forms of teaching with variation adopted in the two types of mathematics teaching activity, namely *conceptual variation* and *procedural variation*. Within conceptual variation, there are two means of variation: (1) concept variation (i.e., varying connotation of a concept); (2) non-concept variation (i.e., giving counterexamples). Thus, conceptual variation emphasizes understanding concepts from multiple perspectives. In tandem, procedural variation highlights the formation of a hierarchical system of the learner's experiencing process in unfolding mathematics activities, which include steps and strategies for transferring/exploring. In the process of problem solving, for instance, there are three procedural variation approaches: (1) varying a problem; (2) multiple methods of solving a problem; (3) multiple applications of a method (for more details see Gu, Huang, & Marton, 2004, p. 324).

Gu (2014) further explains that it is the procedural variation that plays a key role as *Pudian* (铺垫); that is, in setting up a proper potential distance between previous and new knowledge in a student's learning. Akin to the notion of 'scaffolding', *Pudian* means to build up one or several layers so as to enable learners to complete tasks that they cannot complete independently. In this chapter we aim, in particular, to develop a deeper understanding of how the expert teacher's concrete ideas of teaching with variation were used in helping the junior teacher to develop a deep understanding of the teacher's role of setting up *Pudian* to engage all students in classroom learning.

Teachers' Individual Learning in the Professional Community

In the recent TPD studies there is a growing recognition of the dual nature (both individual and collaborative) of teachers' professional learning (e.g., Murray,

Ma & Mazur, 2009; Obara, 2010; Neuberger, 2012; Goos, 2014). Moreover, existing studies have noted that features of the individual teacher's learning, and of the collaborative community within which they work, can be culturally-dependent. In the years since Berliner (2001) noted that lesson study (or coached performance) was limited to some Asian countries, these forms of deliberate practice are now much more widespread (e.g., Hart et al., 2011). As we are interested in practice in China, here we chiefly refer to relevant studies of the concept of teacher professional development, the deliberate practice of particular kinds of school-based TPD models, and the notion and role of an expert teacher in China (e.g., Huang & Bao, 2006; Han, 2013; Li, Chen, & Kulm, 2009; Wong, 2012; Zhang, Xu, & Sun, 2014).

Zhang et al. (2014) point out that, in Shanghai, teacher professional development is defined as a process of continuous learning throughout a teacher's career. Commonly, in Chinese schools, each subject teacher belongs to two groups; a subject-based *teaching research group* and a subgroup of this, the *lesson preparation group* – the latter comprising all the teachers in the school who teach mathematics at the same grade level (Li et al., 2009). The school-based teaching research group (TRG) is the main professional community for teachers, as well as being the basic unit at the different levels (i.e., province, county and school levels) of the teaching research network within the country (Li et al., 2009; Yang, 2009).

Peng (2007) shows how 'lesson explaining', originally a 'bottom up' invention by teachers for their lesson study in the school-based TRG, has become an effective form of TPD particularly for developing teachers' mathematics subject knowledge and the professional community's shared pedagogical content knowledge. Peng illustrates how the fundamental feature of 'lesson explaining' – knowing both 'what' and 'why' in mathematics lesson design – leads individual teachers to reflect and develop their own subject matter knowledge (in Peng's case study on the topic of probability). Moreover, Peng reveals how the individual teacher gains a deeper understanding of mathematics, and develops their pedagogical content knowledge, from studying the textbook and through conversations with a mathematics expert teacher in the 'lesson explaining' community. Other teachers who participated in this form of professional activity also commented that they learnt and reflected on their own mathematics knowledge and pedagogical content knowledge from hearing other teachers articulating their thinking and reflection during the 'lesson explaining' activity.

Through a study of three lessons on the Pythagoras theorem, Yang (2009) analyses how a teacher changed the teaching behaviour during collaborative TRG teamwork: the first lesson emphasized applying the theorem, the second justifying the proposition, and the third producing propositions. Yang quotes from an interview with the teacher that illustrates the teacher's learning in the TRG:

> After the study of teaching, especially the discussion, I think the way of teaching is clearer than that in the textbooks. I have known it well. Where a question should be given to students and where an emphasis is arranged, and

the teaching details guided by master teacher in discussion, are more useful compared to my own lesson design. (Yang, 2009, p. 295; original translation)

Han (2013) notes that there are several shared forms of teacher mentoring in China, including observing and commenting on the mentees' lessons, inviting them to observe the teaching of the same lessons, and reviewing and revising lesson plan drafts through informal and formal discussions. Through the process of mentoring and deliberate practice of particular kinds, Han (2013) reports on how one teacher's skill in designing a good display on the classroom board was enhanced, while another teacher improved her skill in creating a clear sequence for the lesson that had a suitable structure to promote student learning, and approached instruction with variation.

Li, Huang and Yang (2011) highlight that 'expert teachers' in China are not just experienced teachers; they are part of the teaching culture in China and also play an important role in nurturing that culture. Moreover, Yang (2014) differentiates the multiple roles that an expert teacher plays in China: expert in teaching (i.e., organizing good teaching processes), in researching (i.e., conducting teaching research and publishing papers in professional and academic journals), in teacher education (i.e., mentoring non-expert teachers and facilitating non-expert teachers' professional development), in scholarship (i.e., having a profound knowledge base in mathematics and other areas), in examining (i.e., being able to pose examination problems), and in being an exemplary model for students and colleagues.

Huang, Gong and Han (in press) highlight the critical role played by 'knowledgeable others' (i.e., university professors, subject specialists, etc.) during the lesson study process. It is exactly the mechanisms of how these 'knowledgeable others' work with practicing teachers and develop the teachers' professional knowledge and skills through mentoring during lesson study that is the focus of this chapter.

THEORETICAL FRAMEWORK

There has been criticism that models of professional development oversimplify both teaching and teacher professional growth (e.g., Opfer & Pedder, 2011). We support Clarke and Hollingsworth's (2002) view that teachers' professional growth is more likely to proceed through a series of incremental changes than by a linear path from a single professional development experience via a change in practice to improvement of student outcomes.

We use Clarke and Hollingsworth's (2002) *Interconnected Model* as a tool for categorising the teacher change data we have accumulated in our study. Clarke and Hollingsworth's (2002) model conceptualises individual teacher change within four distinct domains: the personal domain (teacher knowledge, beliefs and attitudes), the domain of practice (professional experimentation), the domain of consequence (salient outcomes), and the external domain (sources of information, stimulus or support) (p. 950). The Interconnected Model particularly identifies the mediating processes of 'reflection' and 'enactment' as the mechanisms by which change in one domain leads to change in another. The term "change sequences" (p. 958) is employed when change in one domain leads to change in another, while the term "growth networks" (p. 958) is used to highlight the occurrence of change that is more lasting change, and thus signify professional growth.

While the Interconnected Model recognizes the multiple growth pathways among the domains, it does not suggest the specific ways of reflecting and enacting. Here we further refer to Gu and Wang's (2003) 'Action Education' Model (briefly named as the *Keli Model* in Huang & Bao, 2006), which enables us to examine the 'change sequences' and 'growth networks' (Clarke & Hollingsworth, 2002) of particular kinds through lesson study activities. The Keli Model emphasizes an exemplary lesson as a means of teacher's action (or enactment), and a whole process that includes three stages of teaching action and two main teacher's reflections between the three teaching stages. Huang and Bao (2006) illustrate the whole process of the Keli model as three stages.

For the first stage, called 'existing action' (or existing enactment), the individual teacher designs the lesson independently and delivers the lesson publicly to a class of students observed by all the Keli group members. After the lesson, the Keli members provide immediate feedback on the teacher's lesson in the first Keli meeting, with the aim to help the individual teacher to reflect and identify the gap between the existing experiences and the innovative design suggested by the curriculum and textbook.

During the second stage, called 'new design', the teacher revises the lesson design according to the Keli members' feedback and re-delivers (or re-enacts) the lesson in another class. The Keli members observe the teacher's second lesson enactment. After the second lesson, the Keli members' discussion with the teacher aims to help the teacher to develop a reflection on the gap between the new design and effective classroom practice (as suggested by the curriculum and textbook) and to improve the lesson design and enactment further. Through the third stage, called 'new action' (or new enactment), the teacher is helped to develop a deep understanding of how students learn in a new style and attain a high quality of learning that is consistent with the goals of the curriculum and textbook.

The Keli Model is also concerned with building up a collaboration that enables teachers and researchers to study theoretical ideas, design innovative learning situations, and reflect on the enactments of teaching and learning within the Keli community (Huang & Bao, 2006). As we have illustrated, we see a teacher's 'action' in the Keli Model as close to the term 'enaction' in the Interconnected Model of Clarke and Hollingsworth (2002, p. 951), in that the teacher's action represents the enactment of something that the teacher has experienced and learned in the Keli community.

In our lesson design study (LDS), we combine both the Interconnected Model (Clarke & Hollingsworth, 2002) and the Keli Model (Gu & Wang, 2003;

Huang & Bao, 2006) for examining teachers' potential change sequences and growth networks in our lesson design study activities. That is, during the lesson study process, we examine the mediating processes (teachers' enactments and reflections) that link the four domains: teacher's lesson design (personal domain), teacher's classroom action (domain of practice), the interactions in the TRG (external domain), and students' classroom learning (domain of consequence).

To illustrate the whole process of our LDS model we use junior teacher Jiyi's (all names are pseudonyms in this chapter) three main teaching cycles that we studied from September to December in 2013 (see L1, L2 & L3 in Figure 1). The first cycle (L1) includes Jiyi's initial stage of lesson design, lesson enactment and reflection. The second cycle (L2) represents the second stage of the re-designed (i.e., re-enacted) lesson of L1. The third cycle (L3) represents the re-redesigned (i.e., re-re-enacted) lesson of L1. Each stage (each cycle in Figure 1) includes a set of the school-based TRG activities, such as Jiyi's classroom teaching, lesson explaining (Peng, 2007) and our study members' observation and the mathematics TRG meetings. In our LDS model we use the term 'cycle' to address the nature of teaching as both comprehension and reasoning, and as transformation and reflection (Shulman, 1987). In Figure 1, T means teacher, LD1 means lesson design 1, action1 is teaching in lesson 1, reflection1 is teacher's reflection after lesson 1, TRG1 is school-based TRG meeting after lesson 1, and so on.

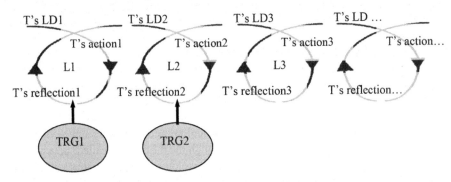

Figure 1. The three main cycles of the LDS model (including L1,L2 L3)

METHODOLOGY AND DATA

Our ongoing LDS study is being conducted through a school-based TRG in a local school located in the western suburb of Shanghai. The school is an international school (Grades 1-9, students age from 6 to 15 years old) funded by the China Welfare Institute with the key mission of launching innovative and laboratory educational classroom studies aimed at improving the quality of compulsory education for children in the country. The school consists of elementary (Grades 1-5) and lower secondary sections (Grades 6-9). Each section has two divisions; one is the domestic division, mainly for Chinese-speaking students; the other is the multi-culture division for both home and overseas students with English as the first language. Our study is conducted within the mathematics TRG in the elementary section. In total, in the elementary section there are 295 students in the domestic division, and 364 students in the multi-culture division. Each class has around 25 students. Students are mixed (both gender and academic attainment) in each class. There are seven mathematics teachers in the elementary section.

Teacher Jiyi had about three years elementary mathematics teaching experience at the time of our study. She was teaching mathematics to Grade 1 and 2 classes. All of her classes at the time of this study were in the domestic division. The class size ranged from 23 to 25 students. In general, students' learning attainment was above average for the school according to the school annual assessment.

Mei is an expert teacher invited by the school to support teachers in our study. The term 'expert teacher' in our study recognizes that Mei is not only an effective teacher of mathematics, but also that she plays the multiple roles that are described by Yang (2014, pp. 271–272). She has over 30 years teaching experience in elementary mathematics teaching in her school district. She has taken the leadership of the in-service elementary mathematics teachers TPD program at her school district level since 2009.

In reporting our findings, we present an analysis of the mediating processes (Jiyi's actions/enactments and reflections) that link Clarke and Hollingsworth's (2002) four domains through the LDS model (see teacher's lesson design, action, reflection and TRG meetings in Figure 1). To develop a deep understanding of individual teacher's learning and professional growth, our particular focus is to examine the interpretive acts and change phenomena that the teacher considered salient (Clarke & Hollingsworth, 2002). Thus, our analysis is primarily based on the following data sources: Jiyi's teaching diary; her reflection notes; her lesson plans (her own design and her redesigned versions); video transcripts of interactions in the TRG meetings; the mathematics textbook; and transcripts of the videoed lessons.

Our data analysis chiefly focused on the following two questions: How the expert teacher's main ideas of teaching with variation were used to create the conditions required to (i) stimulate change sequences, and (ii) foster the junior teacher to reflect on her teaching and changes (as learning) from certain perspectives towards the transformation into growth networks. In terms of the analysis of teaching with variation, we mostly focused on the type of *procedural variation*. We selected this focus because of our aim to understand more sufficiently why Mei emphasized the idea of 'not to lose the chain in learning mathematics' (Ding et al., 2015) in her guidance on lesson design that led Jiyi to make changes in her re-designed lesson and follow-up actions with her class.

Yang and Ricks (2012) argue that 'crucial teaching events' analysis (which is concerned with patterns of the interaction between the teachers and the students, and with the professional judgement of the teachers) is typical in TRG activities. We thus refer to two kinds of analysis of the 'critical incidents' in our analysis of the

L. DING ET AL.

interpretive acts and change phenomena that both Mei and Jiyi considered salient in the TRG meetings, specifically: (1) analysis of the 'three points' of the lesson plans, namely the lesson's 'key point' (重点 *Zhong Dian*) (content focus), 'difficult point' (难点 *Nan Dian*) (learning focus), and 'critical point' (关键点 *Guan Jian Dian*) (teaching focus) as these 'three points' are used by Chinese teachers when thinking about lesson preparation, lesson enactment, observation and reflection (in a typical lesson plan, the difficult point and the critical point can overlap); and (2) the identification, understanding, and resolution of 'crucial events' of the lesson implementation.

FINDINGS

In this section we present the key findings from the initial data analysis of our study. In the first part of this section, we focus on the first research question, namely how Mei's main ideas of teaching with variation were used to stimulate Jiyi's change sequences. In the second, we turn to the second research question, namely how the junior teacher was fostered to reflect on her teaching and changes (as learning) from certain perspectives towards the transformation into growth networks.

Mei's Use of Teaching with Variation to Guide Jiyi to Redesign L2

1. Using problem variation without consideration of instructional coherence and knowledge connections in Jiyi's lesson 1. In Jiyi's initial lesson plan and action (L1 in Figure 1), she tried the idea of teaching with variation by varying problems (see Tasks 1-4 in Figure 2). The four tasks were relevant to two learning goals of the lesson: (1) to make sense and understand division with remainder in hands-on operations (e.g., drawing, sharing candies); (2) to explore the relationship that a remainder is smaller than a divisor. Noticeably, in Jiyi's lesson plan these two goals were treated both as the key point and the difficult point of the lesson (here the difficult point overlapped with the critical point).

After Jiyi's action in the first lesson, the teaching research group meeting (TRG1) took place (illustrated in Figure 1). Based on the classroom observation of lesson 1, Mei considered that Jiyi's teaching in lesson 1 was likely to lead the students into rote learning. Mei explained that Jiyi did not really understand the role of problem variation in developing lesson coherence through multiple layers of teaching (Mei's own word 'teaching stage') for students' understanding and learning of mathematics. Using Mei's own words in the interaction with Jiyi in the TRG1 meeting, the problem variation through the four tasks did not help to develop students' understanding of the concept of 'division with remainder'—a 'crucial teaching event' (Yang & Ricks, 2012) of the lesson:

Mei: Generally speaking, your lesson (L1) can be seen through several stages (i.e., the four tasks in Figure 2). But you did not really understand what should be done in each of the stages. Thus, the lesson lacks coherence.

248

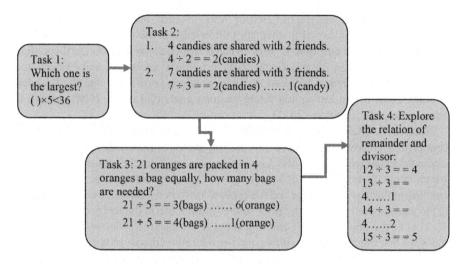

Figure 2. The main lesson structure of lesson 1 (L1)
[note that the six dots ..... indicates the remainder]

Students did not really understand what the 'six dots' (symbol of 'remainder', see Figure 2) meant on the blackboard. They just imitated what you did. This is a real example of rote learning. [All translations of Jiyi and Mei in this chapter were made by the author team.]

2. Mei's emphasis on 'the chain in learning mathematics' through teaching with variation. To help Jiyi develop a deep understanding of teaching with variation through intentional and systematic practice, Mei highlighted the 'crucial teaching event' (Yang & Ricks, 2012) – developing a deep understanding of the concept of 'division with remainder' through the instructional coherence and mathematics knowledge connections in the lesson; in Mei's own words, "not to lose the chain in learning mathematics" (Ding et al., 2015). Mei pointed out that the chain could be developed according to the teaching framework of three layers of knowledge, which is commonly shared by teachers in China. The specific teaching terms of the three layers of knowledge are (see Figure 3): (1) previously learned knowledge (旧知 *Jiu Zhi*); (2) key points of new learning goal of the lesson (新知识点 *Xin Zhi Shi Dian*; 教学目标 *JiaoXue MuBiao*); (3) future learning according to textbook and curriculum (后续学习 *Houxu Xuexi*; 教材 *JiaoCai*; 教学大纲 *JiaoXue DaGang*).

This teaching framework (illustrated in Figure 3) provided guidance for Jiyi to develop understanding of the connections of mathematics knowledge of two kinds; namely both declarative knowledge (in this case, concepts such as 'division with remainder', 'sharing', 'division', etc.) and procedural knowledge (in this case, the process of division operation) (Gu et al., 2004). Moreover, it enabled Jiyi intentionally to practice and reflect on teaching with variation at two specific levels: the first level was the question of 'how' to teach, namely to simultaneously set up the multiple layers of mathematics knowledge in the re-designed lesson; the second level was the question of 'why' to teach in such a way, namely the theoretical elements of teaching with variation such as 'procedural variation', and *Pudian*, 'the proper potential distance' between students' previous knowledge and the intended learning goals of the lesson and future learning goals (Gu et al., 2004; Gu, 2014; Ding, Jones, Mei, & Sikko, 2015).

Noticeably, Mei strongly helped Jiyi to develop a deep understanding of the connections between two aspects of students' previous knowledge: (1) to analyse students' actual learning (in Mei's own words, 'what have the students learned?'), which is the anchoring part of knowledge (i.e., previous knowledge underpinning learning of the new knowledge and the exploration of new problems, Gu et al., 2004); (2) to analyse the content order prior to the lesson topic in the textbook (see Figure 3). That is, the object of Jiyi's learning is not to critique the problem/task design in the ways that might be done with a poorly-produced textbook, or with questions the teacher has chosen themselves, but to build the coherence of a lesson around given topics in the textbook. This means that the purpose of the 'crucial teaching event' (Yang & Ricks, 2012) highlighted by Mei here is for Jiyi to understand, and exploit the potential for using, the problems/tasks given in the well-designed textbook with her students.

3. Teaching with procedural variation for establishing the chain of learning goals in Mei's guidance of lesson redesign. We use Figure 4 to show the chain of three key learning goals suggested by Mei (for Mei's own design of the same lesson topic, see Ding et al., 2015) – a concrete example for improving the lesson design of the 'crucial teaching event' (Yang & Ricks, 2012) that Mei discussed with Jiyi in TRG1. Noticeably, Mei pointed out that while the first two learning goals are the key points, the second and the third learning goals are the difficult points of the lesson (here the difficult points and critical points overlapped) (see Figure 4). Mei deliberately structured the lesson into three stages, in which each stage had its own learning goal but each progressively developed students' deep understanding of the connections between the concept and the operation of 'division with remainder' through mathematics activities. We consider this process of Mei's intentional, systematic, structured and effortful practice as teaching with procedural variation (Gu et al., 2004).

Figure 4 can be read together with Figure 2 so as to see the changes of learning goals through the multiple teaching stages that Jiyi later adopted in lesson 2 (as illustrated in Figure 1). For the purpose of developing a deep understanding of Jiyi's change sequences as learning in the later sections, in this section, we chiefly focus on Mei's ideas of "not to lose the chain in learning mathematics" (Ding et al., 2015), namely teaching with procedural variation (Gu et al., 2004) through the three tasks for the first learning goal. In a later section of our analysis of Jiyi's learning, we further trace the intentional practice with procedural variation from the first three

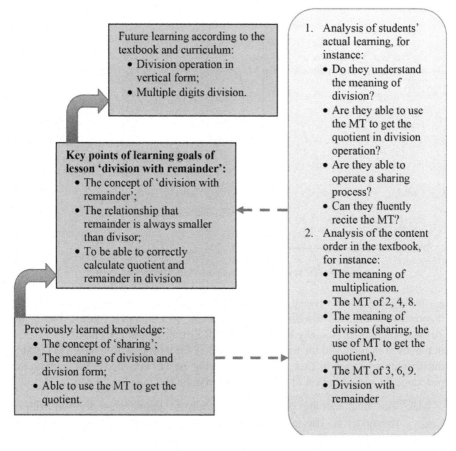

Figure 3. The teaching framework of three layers of knowledge
in Mei's guidance to Jiyi of redesigning L2
[MT = multiplication table]

tasks to the fourth task in the second learning goal, together with an explanation of the use of procedural variation to establish the chain for the third learning goal (see Figure 4).

Here we use two quotes from the interactions between Mei and Jiyi in TRG1 to show how Mei explained to Jiyi about the 'crucial teaching event' (Yang & Ricks, 2012), that of developing students' deep understanding of the connections between the concept and the operation of 'division with remainder' by deliberately setting up the multiple layers of teaching with procedural variation. In the first quote (about teaching Task 1 in Figure 4), Mei emphasized that the core teaching stage was to identify the 'anchoring' part of knowledge (Gu et al., 2004); in this instance, students' existing knowledge of the connections between the concepts of division

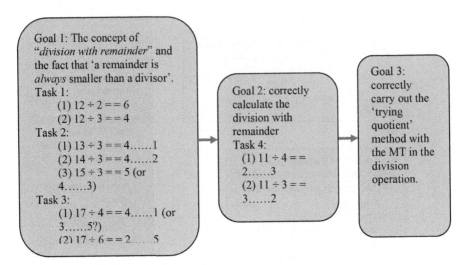

Figure 4. The key learning goals and tasks suggested by Mei

as sharing and as the reverse operation of multiplication. Using Gu et al.'s (2004) theoretical notion, the teaching focus was to set up Pudian (Gu et al., 2004; Gu, 2014) – students' previously learned knowledge of the meaning of numbers 12, 3, 4 in the division form and the use of the method of the multiplication table (MT) to try the division operation in Task 1 as the 'anchoring' part of knowledge for learning the new concept and operation of 'division with remainder' (see Figure 4).

Mei: The first learning goal is preliminarily to know what division with remainder is. The learning process can be divided into two stages. The first stage is of the concept of 'remainder', the other is of the fact that the remainder is smaller than the divisor. In Task 1, the problem is to share 12 peaches. Each monkey is to have 3 peaches. How many monkeys can there be? The purpose of this task is to lead students to review their previously learned knowledge. The teacher should ask students what the numbers 12, 3, 4 mean after they form the division for solving the problem. The second stage is to review how to use the method of the multiplication table to get the quotient [to see the relation of dividend, divisor and quotient in the multiplication operation]. Students should not recite each statement of the factor 3 [i.e., one three is three, two threes are six and so on; here Mei is suggesting that students should have learnt to see the relation of dividend, divisor and quotient in the multiplication table].

Noticeably, in the core of this lesson, Mei did not merely suggest a focus on the repeated subtraction or equal-sharing models (Gu & Wong, 2003) for making sense of the concepts of division and quotient, for this was the students' existing knowledge.

Rather, Mei's intention was focussed on using students' existing knowledge of a specific kind – the concept of division as sharing and as the reverse operation of multiplication – as the anchoring part of knowledge (*Pudian*) for developing a deep understanding of the connections of the new concept and the new operation of 'division with remainder' – this being the 'crucial teaching event' (Yang & Ricks, 2012) of the lesson. For Mei, the proper potential distance between previous and new knowledge in this lesson was for students to see the same kind of relationship between factors and products in the multiplication table and the dividend, divisor and quotient when varying in Task 2 (see Figure 4) and later in Task 4 at the second and the third stages (see the Goals 2 and 3 in Figure 4) of learning of the operation of division with remainder. The implicit *Pudian* (Gu, 2014) becomes evident when Mei addressed the use of students' such previous knowledge in her explanation of Task 4 for the second learning goal (Figure 4) (see the italics we highlight in the quote below).

> Mei: [referring to Task 4 in Figure 4] The second stage is to build up the connection of students' operation of sharing activity to mental calculation activity. Here, $11 \div 4$, while the class keeps drawing pictures to understand the quotient, some students would be able to use the multiplication table to try the quotient. Then, you [Jiyi] should ask the students how they did so. That is, how they think about the statements of 4 in the multiplication table. Two four is 8, but there is not 8. What to do then? To find a number that is smaller than 11, but closest to 11. In fact, the thinking method is the same as in the task of 'which one is the largest' [see Task 1 in Figure 2], but *we should use students' previous knowledge.* Next, $11 \div 3 = 3......2$. What does each number mean? How is the quotient obtained? Students should be trained to think so in the calculation procedure.

Identifying the Complexity of Jiyi's Learning Through the Change Sequences from Lesson 1 to Lesson 2

In this section, we show the complexity of Jiyi's learning through an analysis of three types of change sequences from lesson 1 to lesson 2 (as illustrated in Figure 1). Our data analysis of change sequences is based on Jiyi's teaching diary, the interactions of Jiyi with Mei in the teaching research group meeting after the second lesson (TRG2), and Jiyi's reflection notes throughout our study. The three types of change sequences we identified are: (1) changes within the teacher's personal domain; (2) changes from the personal domain to the practice domain; (3) a mixed picture of change sequences across the personal domain and the domain of practice.

1. Changes within the personal domain: Understanding the teaching terms of three layers of knowledge for teaching with variation. We found that Mei's guidance "not to lose the chain in learning mathematics" (Ding et al., 2015) in TRG1 first led

Jiyi to reflect on her analysis of the textbook and action in lesson 1, and consequently to make changes in the learning goals and the lesson structure in the lesson 2 plan. Here, we consider the teacher's lesson plan as an explicit realization of the teacher's personal domain (e.g., evidences of the teacher's implicit knowledge and beliefs of teaching and learning mathematics). We illustrate the change sequence within Jiyi's knowledge domain in Figure 5, where E = external domain; K = teacher's personal (knowledge) domain; P = practice domain; S = salient outcome; P-L1 = practice in L1; K-L2 = teacher's L2 lesson plan.

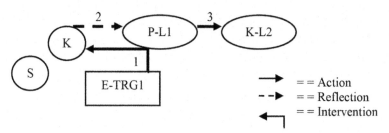

Figure 5. A change sequence made by Jiyi through L1 cycle (see Figure 1)

The first two steps in this change sequence (marked 1 and 2 in Figure 5) is of Jiyi's learning through her reflection on Mei's guidance of using the teaching framework with specific teaching terms of three layers of knowledge for analysing the textbook in the first teaching research group meeting (see TRG1 in Figure 1): (1) previously learned knowledge (旧知 Jiu Zhi); (2) key points of new learning goal of the lesson (新知识点 Xin Zhi Shi Dian; 教学目标 JiaoXue MuBiao); (3) future learning according to textbook and curriculum (后续学习 Houxu Xuexi; 教材 JiaoCai; 教学大纲 JiaoXue DaGang) (see Figure 3). In doing so, Jiyi focused on the 'crucial teaching event' (Yang & Ricks, 2012) of the lesson – developing students' deep understanding of the connections between the new concept and operation of 'division with remainder'. In her teaching diary, Jiyi wrote as follows:

> After an analysis of the textbook, *students have learned the following knowledge* before the lesson 'division with remainder': (1) multiplication of digits from 1 to 9; (2) the concept of 'sharing'; (3) division calculation. *The key points of knowledge of this lesson* (L2) are: (1) the concept of 'remainder'; (2) the meaning of each number in the form of division with remainder; (3) the relationship that remainder should be smaller than divisor; and (4) the calculation process of division with remainder. *Based on the previous knowledge*, students are *to learn the new knowledge*. *To build up the chain of these knowledge points*, I made considerably large changes in the lesson plan. [Italics used to highlight key phrases]

The phrases such as "students' learned knowledge", "the key points of knowledge of the lesson", "based on previous knowledge, to learn new knowledge", and "to build up the chain of these knowledge points" (highlighted in italic), illustrate that Mei's guidance on the use of the teaching framework of three layers of knowledge led Jiyi to develop a specific form of reflection on Mei's idea of teaching with variation, namely "not to lose the chain in learning mathematics".

Moreover, we noted that in her lesson 2 plan Jiyi adopted the three learning goals and the main teaching stages and tasks similar to Mei's guidance in TRG1 (see Figure 4). The third step in this change sequence (marked 3 in Figure 5) shows that changes in Jiyi's understanding of the teaching framework of three layers of knowledge (see Figure 3) for building up the coherence of knowledge chain in students' learning led her to change the learning goals of the lesson plan.

2. Changes from the personal domain to the practice domain: Learning precise teaching language and questioning strategy in teaching with procedural variation. To understand Jiyi's learning as an outcome from the first teaching cycle (illustrated as L1 in Figure 1), Mei suggested a 'lesson explanation' (Peng, 2007) activity (TRG2 in Figure 1) before Jiyi went on to teach the second lesson (L2). While there are considerable positive changes that took place in Jiyi's learning, here we focus on Jiyi's learning to use more precise teaching language and to focus on the learning goal underlying Mei's idea of teaching with procedural variation, namely "not to lose the chain in learning mathematics" (Ding et al., 2015).

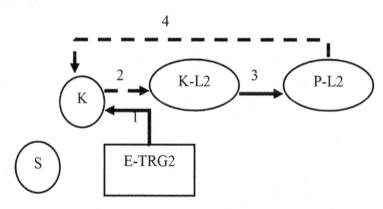

Figure 6. A change sequence made by Jiyi during L2 circle (see Figure 1)

The first two steps in this change sequence (marked as 1 and 2 in Figure 6) are an indication that Jiyi seemed to develop a specific way of reflection, or understanding, of teaching with procedural variation under Mei's support in the TRG2 meeting. That is, Jiyi learned to be more intentional and effortful in using precise teaching language when she explained how she was to teach Task 1 (see Task 1(1) 12 ÷ 2 = 6 in Figure 4). Here, we provide the key interactions between Jiyi and Mei of teaching Task 1 as follows (with italics used to highlight key parts):

Jiyi: Winter is coming; all animals are preparing food for the winter. Let's visit the rabbit family and take a look of what they are *doing*.

Mei: This is a nice start of the lesson. You may consider changing your word here. That is, not to ask students what the rabbit family is doing, but ask them how the rabbits are to *share* the carrots.

Jiyi: Rabbit mother brings 12 carrots to her two baby rabbits to share. I will ask students how many carrots each baby rabbit would have. Then I will ask who can give a mathematical formula and calculate it ($12 \div 2 = 6$). After students give answers, I will invite them to explain the meaning of the numbers 12, 2, and 6. For instance, 12 *represents* 12 carrots, and 2 *represents* 2 baby rabbits.

Mei: It's better not to say '12 *represents*', but to say '12 *means*.' [Note: In Chinese, the word 'represent' (代表 *Dai Biao*) does not request an explicit explanation or reasoning – for instance, a picture can 'represent' a meaning, however vague the meaning may be – while the word 'mean' (表示 *Biao Shi*) clearly requests an explicit explanation or reasoning.]

Mei's emphasis on the use of the precise teaching language such as share and means developed Jiyi's understanding of the important role of teacher's precise teaching language skills to enable students to focus on the key point of learning in the task, in this instance, the 'crucial teaching event' (Yang & Ricks, 2012) of the lesson— developing students' deep understanding of the connections between the new concept and operation of 'division with remainder'.

Next, Jiyi explained how she would teach when varying Task 1(2) (see Task 1(2), $12 \div 3 = 4$ in Figure 4). Mei's explanation intends to lead Jiyi not only to address the calculation procedure in teaching, but also deliberately to use the questioning strategy to encourage students to explain their calculation method, which was one of the key learning goals of the lesson. That is, not only to enable students to know 'how' to do so, but also to understand 'why' to do so in the division operation. A shift of the calculation method from students' previous knowledge to the new knowledge of the lesson is pinpointed by the teacher's questions of 'how' and 'why' through the teaching with procedural variation (from Task 1(1) to Task 1(2) in Figure 4) – a concrete teaching strategy for dealing with 'the proper potential distance' (Pudian) (Gu et al., 2004; Gu, 2014). Jiyi's clear statement of the term 'Pudian' in the following extract is evidence that she became aware of students' previous knowledge and learning experience as the anchoring part of knowledge in this lesson (with italics used to highlight key parts):

Jiyi: (Task 1: $12 \div 3 = 4$) Here, I will ask them *how* they get the quotient 4.

Mei: If you ask students "how they get the quotient 4", *how* would students respond in your class?

Jiyi: I will use '*Pudian*' by asking them a question about which statement of the multiplication table they will use [such as, for instance, one three is three, two threes are six, and so on in the multiplication table]. I expect them to respond by 'three fours are twelve'.

Mei: Did you emphasize this method in your previous lessons? If students do not know *how* the quotient 4 comes (that is, why $12 \div 3$ would get 4), it would be very difficult for you to teach today's topic. The new knowledge in today's lesson ought to be connected to students' previous knowledge.

Mei: $12 \div 3 = 4$. *How* the quotient 4 comes? Students should understand the [reasoning] method to get 4 here. That is, they need to understand the relationship between the divisor and quotient in the multiplication table (MT). If the divisor were 3, then they would think of the statement with 3 in the MT. *Why* to think of the statement with 3 in the MT? This is because it is students' previous knowledge. And, *why* would students think about the statement 'three four are twelve'? This is because of the relationship between divisor and dividend. Here the dividend is 12, so the statement 'three four are twelve' is considered.

We further identify that Jiyi adopted Mei's guidance of using precise language and the term 'Pudian' as discussed above and intentionally practiced in lesson 2 (see the third step in Figure 6). Jiyi's reflection on her effortful practice with the precise teaching language and proper questioning strategy in lesson 2 was also evident in her reflection note after lesson 2 as follows:

In lesson 2, I used more precise language, which was more vivid and more suitable for lower grade students [Grade 2 in her class]. Teaching should focus on students' thinking development, so the teacher should play the guiding role in students' learning. In teaching the calculation procedure of division with remainder, I encouraged students to explain their calculation process by questions such as "To think about which set of the statement in the MT (by looking at the divisor)?", "which statement is exactly related to the division?", "why it?", "how to get the remainder?", etc.

Significantly, we found that Jiyi particularly showed her willingness towards improving her teaching language skills in her reflection note after TRG2 (see the forth step in Figure 6). This can be considered as the teacher's commitment to the sustained learning which is a kind of teacher's potential 'growth network' (Clarke & Hollingsworth, 2002).

The teacher must be aware of using precise teaching language. Particularly to an experienced mathematics teacher, every word should be as precise as possible. Though I know that I am unable to be so precise in every word I say in my teaching, I am now improving my language towards this goal.

3. A mixed picture of change sequences across the personal domain and the domain of practice: The art of teaching with variation. Our data analysis shows a mixed picture of Jiyi's learning in her reflection and action on tackling the relationship between her leading role as teacher and the students' active learning through teaching with variation from lesson 1 (L1) to lesson 2 (L2), as captured in Figure 7.

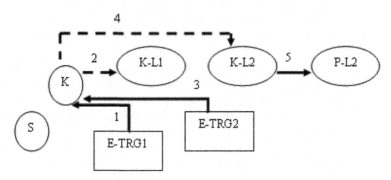

Figure 7. A mixed picture of change sequence made by Jiyi through L1 & L2 circles (see Figure 1)

Here, on the one hand, for the first two steps of the change sequence (labelled 1 and 2 in Figure 7) Mei's guidance of teaching with procedural variation in TRG1 led Jiyi to reflect carefully on the relationship of the three key elements in her initial lesson design (L1): textbook, teaching and learning. Jiyi wrote what she learned of 'the proper potential distance' (Pudian) (Gu et al., 2004; Gu, 2014) in her teaching diary as follows:

> Previously I planned lessons according to my understanding of the textbook content. I rarely thought about that I should deliberately connect what students already learned to what I was to teach in my lesson plan. Now, I think that it is very necessary to do so. Mei's guidance helped me to understand more that teaching should be based on students' existing learning, in order to help them to learn independently. That is, to teach students how to fish rather than giving them fish [an ancient Chinese saying]. So I should give students opportunities to explain what they see, do and think in the learning process.

Nevertheless, on the other hand, our data analysis of the lesson explanation meeting (TRG2 in Figure 1) shows that Jiyi had uncertainties in handling students' learning responses for independent learning, particularly when students' learning responses were not prepared in her lesson plan. Noticeably, it was Mei who helped Jiyi specifically to update her knowledge of *Pudian* by addressing the relationship of teaching and learning of two specific kinds (labelled 3 and 4 in Figure 7): one is to analyse students' potential learning problems and alternative ways of reasoning, which is related to Simon's (1995) notion of 'Hypothetical Learning Trajectory' (HLT); in Mei's own words 'knowing what students are likely to understand and respond' to the teacher's intentional teaching; the second is to improve teacher's teaching language and questioning skills (i.e., the teaching notion of '*follow their response by questioning*' (追问*Zhui Wen*), see the quote of Mei's exchange below) to enable students to focus on the learning goal of the mathematical reasoning development.

It was difficult for Jiyi to develop students' understanding through their independent learning of the division relationship that a remainder is always smaller than the divisor. When Jiyi added one more carrot into the picture for Task 2(1) in Figure 4, it was natural for students to see that the additional carrot in the picture could not be grouped and should remain as a single carrot. This is evident in the following exchange (with italics and bold text used to highlight key parts).

Mei: First, showing the problem [Task 2(1)] before providing a picture. Secondly, encouraging students to *guess* the result after they formed the formula (13 ÷ 3 = ?). After guessing, you can encourage them to *prove* their guess by grouping the carrots in the picture. You should *follow their response by questioning*; for instance, *why* the single carrot that is left cannot be grouped? This question is to encourage them to *prove* their claim. Thus, some students in the class would *explain* to others in the class that it is because each group has three carrots. The one remaining carrot is not enough to be counted as a group.

Jiyi: What shall I do then if some students do not give a clear explanation?

Mei: That is not a problem. You can invite other students to continue until they give a clear explanation. You have to adjust your questions to a *deeper level of teaching*. It is better to invite students to *guess* the result, rather than to *tell* them the result. If you asked them to *tell* the whole class their result, they may worry about giving a wrong answer. But if you encourage a *guess*, they would not worry about a wrong answer, as it is a guess anyway. *Teaching is an art.* Teacher's language plays a very important role in engaging students into deep learning interactions.

In analysing the interactions above, teaching with variation entails not only the precise teaching language for developing students' mathematical reasoning and understanding, but also an art of teaching language for engaging students into active and independent learning processes. On the one hand, as shown above, Mei's precise teaching language, like the words '*guess*', '*prove*', '*why*', and '*explain*' illustrate the important role of teacher's precise language in the development of students' mathematical reasoning and understanding. On the other hand, the teacher's questioning such as '*follow their response by questioning*', plays a significant role to enable students to play an active role in their own individual learning and the whole-class-shared mathematical reasoning. Mei's use of the two different kinds of teaching language shows a sophisticated level of teaching with variation.

The mixed picture of Jiyi's learning is further identified in her learning and reflection on the importance to '*follow their response by questioning*'. On the one hand, Jiyi's '*Oh, Yes!*' as learning is evident in the following interaction with Mei regarding *Task 2(3)* (with italics used to highlight key parts of Mei's response):

Jiyi: If all students can group 15 carrots into 5 groups and no one says 4 groups and 3 carrots left, what I should do?

Mei: Then you can *ask them why not.* Students would tell you that because the remaining 3 carrots can still be grouped. Then you should *follow up their response by questioning* "*why* in the last couple of examples, the remaining carrots were not grouped, but now the remaining ones can be grouped".

Jiyi: *Oh, yes*! This question is very important!

On the other hand, nevertheless, Jiyi confessed her difficulty in such questioning if students' learning responses were out of her lesson plan; that is, the questioning of 'follow their response by questioning' is used in the dynamic teaching process and requests a teacher's impromptu action in the authentic class. Jiyi wrote in her reflection note after TRG2 as follows:

The lesson plan is only the teacher's hypothesis of students' learning. But I am not sure of what to do if some learning situation out of my lesson plan happens in the class.

The fifth step in Figure 7 thus represents a mixed picture of Jiyi's changes and difficulties as we have illustrated above. She understands some specific ways of teaching with variation (e.g., learning of 'the proper potential distance', Pudian, Gu et al., 2004; Gu, 2014), yet she has difficulty making changes in action (e.g., teacher's language of two levels). As conveyed in Jiyi's teaching diary after L2, though she developed a considerable understanding of the teacher's leading role in the development of students' independent learning, it was difficult for her to do so in action.

During the process of redesigning the lesson, I found that the amount of content of this lesson is considerably large. After the lesson explanation meeting, I understand that I should guide students to explore by themselves the relationship that the remainder is smaller than the divisor. But I still find it difficult to do so to enable students to make correct conclusion from their own exploration.

DISCUSSION

We have identified three elements for our discussion of the expert teacher's use of the idea of teaching with variation to support a junior teacher's professional learning.

The first part examines the expert teacher's teaching notions that helped the junior teacher to learn the theoretical terms of teaching with variation. The second part of the discussion clarifies the special role that teaching language plays in setting up Pudian in the dynamic process of teaching with procedural variation. The final part highlights the complexity of teacher's professional learning.

The Expert Teacher's Use of Common Teaching Notions to Support the Junior Teacher's Learning of Teaching with Variation

As our data analysis in the foregoing section showed, the expert teacher (Mei) used teaching notions that teachers commonly share and understand in China to create the learning conditions for the junior teacher (Jiyi) to reflect and practice on the specific ways of teaching with variation. In Table 1 we highlight the key theoretical terms of teaching with variation (Gu et al., 2004) that the expert teacher Mei guided the junior teacher Jiyi to learn and to understand in lesson design and action. In Table 2 we summarize the uniqueness of the expert teacher's teaching notions that helped the junior teacher to develop an understanding of the relevant theoretical terms of teaching with variation (as shown in Table 1).

Table 1. *The theoretical terms of teaching with variation*

Theoretical terms (Gu et al., 2004)
Variation
Teaching with variation
Procedural variation
The proper potential distance and the anchoring part of knowledge
Pudian (akin to scaffolding)

The Complexity of Teaching with Procedural Variation: Building Up the Chain of Knowledge and Setting Up 'Pudian' in the Process of Dynamic Teaching

The expert teacher's teaching notions, summarised in Table 2, created learning opportunities for the junior teacher to understand the complexity of the theoretical notions of teaching with variation, in particular teaching with procedural variation (see Table 1). As pointed out by Gu et al. (2004), procedural variation plays a key role as Pudian in setting up a proper potential distance between previous and new knowledge in a student's learning. Akin to the notion of 'scaffolding', Pudian means to build up one or several layers so as to enable learners to complete tasks that they cannot complete independently. Our analysis in the foregoing sections shows that the complexity of teaching with Pudian requires a teacher intentionally and

Table 2. The expert teacher's teaching notions of teaching with variation

The expert teacher's teaching notions
Coherence
Not to lose the chain in learning
Multiple teaching layers/stages
Students' existing knowledge, the order of textbook content, students' potential learning difficulties/problems and alternative ways of reasoning
The teaching framework of previous knowledge, key points of learning goal, future learning

consciously to practice the following two parts as a whole: (1) building up the chain of knowledge embedded in mathematics textbooks and curriculum; (2) developing the dynamic teaching process with an emphasis on the relationship of the teacher's language and students' understanding and active learning.

To build up the chain of knowledge embedded in the mathematics textbook and curriculum, the notion of 'an anchoring part of knowledge" (Gu et al., 2004) was specifically emphasized through the teacher's analysis of student's existing knowledge and the order of learning content embedded in the textbooks and curriculum. Moreover, it was necessary for the teacher to develop a more sufficient understanding of students' potential learning difficulties/problems and alternative ways of reasoning, which makes resonance with an understanding of the notion of 'proper potential distance' (Gu et al., 2004).

To develop the dynamic teaching process with Pudian, expert Mei highlighted the significance of the teaching framework and teaching language/notions that teachers commonly understand in China as the key elements of effective classroom teaching and learning mathematics. The teaching framework is useful to guide the junior teacher to conduct the analysis of the textbook, to focus on the learning goals of the lesson, and to develop an understanding of students' existing knowledge and potential learning (see Figure 3). We wish to point out that a teacher's teaching language plays a special role in Pudian, apart from setting up the multiple layers of teaching and the well-designed tasks. Our data analysis identifies two levels of teacher language: (1) the preciseness of teacher language, which plays an important role in students' understanding and reasoning in mathematics; (2) the art of teacher language (i.e., 追 问 Zhui Wei questioning strategy – 'follow their response by questioning'), which leads students not only to develop active individual learning but also to develop a kind of shared-learning with one another in the whole class. These findings lead us to suggest that the term Pudian in teaching with procedural variation is more specific than the theoretical term 'scaffolding', because it tells new teachers more about how to achieve scaffolding in the authentic classroom.

The Complexity of Teacher's Professional Learning through Intentional, Systematic and Effortful Practice

In the foregoing data analysis section, we showed three types of teacher change sequences: (1) changes within the teacher's personal domain; (2) changes from the personal domain to the practice domain; (3) a mixed picture of change sequences across the personal domain and the domain of practice. We wish to point out that the expert teacher Mei played an important role in guiding the junior teacher to develop reflections in specific ways (i.e., labelled 1&2 in Figure 5; 1&2 in Figure 6; and 1&2, 3&4 in Figure 7). Consequently, the junior teacher Jiyi made change sequences according to her reflections (i.e., labelled 3 in Figure 5; 3 in Figure 6; and 5 in Figure 7). We consider these change sequences as intentional, systematic and effortful practice through professional learning.

Our data analysis also showed a complex picture of Jiyi's professional learning. On the one hand, we identified Jiyi's change sequences as learning and professional growth; on the other hand, we recognized Jiyi's difficulties in the professional learning process. Gu (2014) identifies three stages of teacher's professional learning through various kinds of TPD program: (1) listening [to 'knowledgeable others'] but not understanding; (2) listening and understanding, but not knowing immediately how to act; (3) listening, understanding, and acting. Gu notes that the transition from understanding to action takes a considerable amount of time. Our findings of three types of change sequences support Gu's observation. Our data analysis also leads us to suggest that while teachers' professional growth is more likely to proceed through a series of incremental changes (Clarke & Hollingsworth, 2002), such growth is not straightforward and continuous; rather it is discrete and discontinuous.

CONCLUSION

In this chapter, we sought to address the question of how an expert teacher used the idea of teaching with variation to support a junior teacher to develop certain ways of reflecting on her teaching, and as a result to make 'change sequences' (Clarke & Hollingsworth, 2002) as learning from her teaching enactment and reflection. We identified the expert teacher's significant guidance in the following two sophisticated ways: (1) the use of teaching notions that teachers commonly share and understand in China to understand the theoretical terms of teaching with variation; (2) the use of teaching frameworks and language that teachers commonly understand and practice in the country to understand an emphasis on the fundamental 'chains' in learning mathematics and the dynamic process of Pudian. Our study reveals how the detail of didactics and mathematics pedagogy can be zoomed in on when there is an understood structure within which to do this; in this case the teaching framework (see Figure 3), the lesson structure (see Figure 4) and common understandings of teaching notions and language about variation (see Table 2). Our study makes explicit the possible high-quality expert input in teacher education. It contrasts with other studies where the 'expert' teacher is a mentor or coach who focuses primarily on classroom behaviour and management.

Moreover, we wish to point out that what is also important is that there is a commonly understood structure – the school-based teaching research group (TRG) – in which teachers learn from 'knowledgeable others' for their professional development and network in China (e.g., Huang & Bao, 2006; Huang et al., in press; Peng, 2007; Yang, 2009; Li et al., 2011; Han, 2013).

In focusing on the junior teacher's professional learning through our lesson design study, we found that the teacher modified her lesson plans more than ten times from lesson 1 to lesson 2, according to data from Jiyi's teaching diary and reflection notes. Apart from the redesign of the lesson structure and the improvement of teaching language, there were other considerable changes that were related to our lesson design study, such as the design of number in the tasks (i.e., all numbers in the tasks in Figure 4 were deliberately designed), the amount of tasks, classroom interactions, and so on.

While understanding the 'black box' of teacher's professional learning is in its early stages, the contribution of our study is of the expert teacher's teaching notions (see Table 2) that expands knowledge of using the Chinese practitioner's ideas of teaching with variation to guide mathematics teacher preparation and teacher professional development.

REFERENCES

Berliner, D. C. (2001). Learning about and learning from expert teachers. *International Journal of Educational Research, 35*, 463–482.

Clarke, D., & Hollingsworth, H. (2002). Elaborating a model of teacher professional growth. *Teaching and Teacher Education, 18*(8), 947–967.

Ding, L., Jones, K., Mei, L., & Sikko, S. A. (2015). "Not to lose the chain in learning mathematics": Expert teaching with variation in Shanghai. In *Proceedings of the 39th Conference of the International Group for the Psychology of Mathematics Education, Vol 2* (pp. 209–216). Hobart, Australia: PME.

Ding, L., Jones, K., & Pepin, B. (2013, July). Task design through a school-based professional development programme. In *Proceedings of the ICMI study 22: Task design in mathematics education.* Oxford: University of Oxford.

Ding, L., Jones, K., Pepin, B., & Sikko, S. A. (2014). An expert teacher's local instruction theory underlying a lesson design study through school-based professional development. In *Proceedings of the 38th Conference of the International Group for the Psychology of Mathematics Education, Vol. 2* (pp. 401–408). Vancouver, Canada: PME.

Goldsmith, L. T., Doerr, H. M., & Lewis, C. C. (2014). Mathematics teachers' learning: A conceptual framework and synthesis of research. *Journal of Mathematics Teacher Education, 17*(1), 5–36.

Goos, M. (2014). Researcher-teacher relationships and models for teaching development in mathematics education. *ZDM: International Journal in Mathematics Education, 46*, 189–200.

Gu, L. (2014). *A statement of pedagogy reform: Regional experiment and research record.* Shanghai: Shanghai Education Press. [顾泠沅著. 口述教改－地区实验或研究纪事. 上海教育出版社]

Gu, L., Huang, R., & Marton, F. (2004). Teaching with variation: An effective way of mathematics teaching in China. In L. Fan, N. Y. Wong, J. Cai, & S. Li (Eds.), *How Chinese learn mathematics: Perspectives from insiders* (pp. 309–348). Singapore: World Scientific.

Gu, L., & Wang, J. (2003). Teachers' development through education action: The use of 'Keli' as a means in the research of teacher education model. *Curriculum, Textbook & Pedagogy, I,* 9–15; *II,* 14–19. [教师在教育行动中成长—以课例为载体的教师教育模式研究. *课程－教材－教法,* 2003, 第一期, 9–15; 第二期, 14–19.]

Han, X. (2013). Improving classroom instruction with apprenticeship practices and public lesson development as contexts. In Y. Li & R. Huang (Eds.), *How Chinese teach mathematics and improve teaching* (pp. 171–185). London: Routledge.

Hart, L. C., Alston, A., & Murata, A. (Eds.). (2011). *Lesson study research and practice in mathematics education: Learning together.* Berlin: Springer.

Huang, R., & Bao, J. (2006). Towards a model for teacher's professional development in China: Introducing Keli. *Journal of Mathematics Teacher Education, 9,* 279–298.

Huang, R., Mok, I., & Leung, F. (2006). Repetition or variation: Practising in the mathematics classroom in China. In D. Clarke, C. Keitel, & Y. Shimizu (Eds.), *Mathematics classrooms in twelve countries* (pp. 263–274). Rotterdam: Sense Publishers.

Huang, R., Su, H., & Xu, S. (2014). Developing teachers' and teaching researchers' professional competence in mathematics through Chinese Lesson Study. *ZDM: The International Journal on Mathematics Education, 46,* 239–251.

Huang, R., Gong, Z., & Han, X. (2016). Implementing mathematics teaching that promotes students' understanding through theory-driven lesson study. *ZDM: The International Journal on Mathematics Education 48,* 425–439.

Kaiser, G., & Li, Y. (2011). Reflections and future prospects. In Y. Li & G. Kaiser (Eds.), *Expertise in Mathematics instruction* (pp. 343–353). London: Springer.

Li, Y., Chen, X., & Kulm, G. (2009). Mathematics teachers' practices and thinking in lesson plan development: A case of teaching fraction division. *ZDM Mathematics education, 41,* 717–731.

Li, Y., Huang, R., & Yang, Y. (2011). Characterizing expert teaching in school mathematics in China: A prototype of expertise in teaching mathematics. In Y. Li & G. Kaiser (Eds.), *Expertise in mathematics instruction* (pp. 167–195). London: Springer.

Li, J., Peng, A., & Song, N. (2011) Teaching algebraic equations with variation in Chinese classroom. In J. Cai & E. Knuth (Eds.), *Early algebraization: A global dialogue from multiple perspectives* (pp. 529–556). New York, NY: Springer.

Murray, S., Ma, X., & Mazur, J. (2009). Effects of peer coaching on teachers' collaborative interactions and students' mathematics achievement. *Journal of Educational Research, 102,* 203–212.

Neuberger, J. (2012). Benefits of a teacher and coach collaboration: A case study. *Journal of Mathematical Behavior, 31*(2), 290–311.

Obara, S. (2010). Mathematics coaching: A new kind of professional development. *Teacher Development, 14,* 241–251.

Opfer, V. D., & Pedder, D. (2011). Conceptualizing teacher professional learning. *Review of Educational Research, 81*(3), 376–407.

Peng, A. (2007). Knowledge growth of mathematics teachers during professional activity based on the task of lesson explaining. *Journal of Mathematics Teacher Education, 10,* 289–299.

Shulman, L. (1987). Knowledge and teaching: Foundations of the new reform. *Harvard Educational Review, 57*(1), 1–22.

Simon, M. (1995). Reconstructing mathematics pedagogy from a constructivist perspective. *Journal for Research in Mathematics Education, 26,* 114–145.

Sun, X. (2011). 'Variation problems' and their roles in the topic of fraction division in Chinese mathematics textbook examples. *Education Studies in Mathematics, 76,* 65–85.

The New Teacher Project (TNTP). (2015). *The mirage: Confronting the hard truth about our quest for teacher development.* Washington, DC: TNTP.

Wong, J. L. N. (2012). How has recent curriculum reform in China influenced school-based teacher learning? An ethnographic study of two subject departments in Shanghai, China, Asia-Pacific. *Journal of Teacher Education, 40*(4), 347–361.

Yang, X. (2014). *Conception and characteristics of expert mathematics teachers in China.* Berlin: Springer.

265

Yang, Y. (2009). How a Chinese teacher improved classroom teaching in teaching research group: A case study on Pythagoras theorem teaching in Shanghai. *ZDM: The International Journal on Mathematics Education, 41*, 279–296.

Yang, Y., & Ricks, T. E. (2012). How crucial incidents analysis support Chinese lesson study. *International Journal for Lesson and Learning Studies, 1*(1), 41–48.

Zhang, M., Xu, J., & Sun, C. (2014). Effective teachers for successful schools and high performing students: The case of Shanghai. In S. K. Lee, W. O. Lee, & E. L. Low (Eds.), *Educational policy innovations* (pp. 143–161). London: Springer.

Liping Ding 丁莉萍
Faculty of Teacher and Interpreter Education
NTNU, The Norwegian University of Science and Technology, Norway

Keith Jones
Southampton School of Education
University of Southampton, UK

Svein Arne Sikko
Faculty of Teacher and Interpreter Education
NTNU, The Norwegian University of Science and Technology, Norway

XUE HAN, ZIKUN GONG AND RONGJIN HUANG

13. TEACHING AND LEARNING MATHEMATICS THROUGH VARIATION IN LESSON STUDY

INTRODUCTION

Since The Teaching Gap, authored by Stigler and Hiebert, was published in 1999, Japanese lesson study as a form of teacher development has been adapted by many teachers and school districts around the world (Huang & Shimizu, 2016). Lesson study challenged the traditional way of teacher professional development, most of which were snapshot workshops to tell teachers what to do on some designated days during a school year. In lesson study activities, teachers learn to teach through collaborative study on teaching a lesson, and examining what works and what does not with a focus on student learning (Hart, Alston, & Murata, 2011). Similarly, teachers in China also work together in teaching research groups to study how to teach more effectively.

Teachers in China learn to teach through conducting public lessons or exemplary lessons (known as Chinese lesson study hereafter) within a school or across schools (Han & Paine, 2010; Huang & Bao, 2006; Huang, Su, & Xu, 2014; Yang & Rick, 2013). Many studies (Borko, 2004; Franke, Kazemi, Shih, Biagetti, & Battey, 2005; Garet, Porter, Desimone, Birman, & Yoon, 2001; Grossman, Wineburg, & Woolworth, 2001; Little, 2002; McLaughlin & Talbert, 2001; Wilson & Berne, 1999) revealed that effective teacher learning is built into teachers' daily and weekly teaching practices that are school-based, curriculum-based, and student learning-centred. Lesson study turns schools into places where both students and teachers learn. Teaching is a public activity in China, which lends itself to collaborative research on lessons. Recently, lesson study in China has attempted to shift the focus from teaching performance to student learning. Teachers, teacher researchers, and educators in China have been modifying public lesson as deliberate practice (Han & Paine, 2010). In this study a group of sixth grade mathematics teachers in Eastern China developed lessons about the topic of dividing fractions, which was facilitated by university experts in math education and several district teaching research specialists. The group of teachers drew on two concepts to design lessons through Lesson Study. One concept is learning trajectory, and the other concept is teaching and learning math through variations. As a designed research study that integrated two theoretical concepts into the lesson study activities, this study attempted to answer two research questions: How did the designed lesson study activities change lessons? How did the designed lesson study activities influence student learning?

R. Huang & Y. Li (Eds.), Teaching and Learning Mathematics through Variation, 267–293.

CONCEPTUAL FRAMEWORK AND LITERATURE REVIEW

Learning Trajectory: Division of Fractions

Realistic Mathematics Education (Freudenthal, 1991) argued that mathematics instruction should give students a "guided" opportunity to discover mathematics. The guided opportunities existed in long-term learning and teaching trajectories that aimed at achieving certain learning goals (Van den Heuvel-Panhuizen, 2000). With the support and facilitation of university experts of mathematics instruction and the district teaching research specialists, the group of sixth grade teachers in an elementary school of Eastern China developed a learning trajectory for the topic of dividing fractions. The lesson study activities the group of teachers conducted was embedded with creating, designing, modifying, and testing the learning trajectory of dividing fractions.

Learning trajectories include sequences of tasks and activities aimed at the progressive development of mathematical thinking and skill (Clements & Sarama, 2004, 2007; Daro et al., 2011; Simon, 1995, 2014; Van den Heuvel-Panhuizen, 2008). A hypothetical learning trajectory is what teachers or researchers predict as to how student learning might develop regarding a certain mathematics topic. The theory of learning trajectory asks teachers to plan lessons based on how students might construct the new mathematical knowledge. Simon (1995) proposed three components of learning trajectory, including learning goals, learning activities, and learning process. All three aspects can be achieved through interactions among teachers, students, and curriculum in the classroom. The traditional way of deciding scopes and sequences of mathematics curriculum mainly considered the nature and structure of mathematics knowledge while the learning trajectories are "rooted in actual empirical study of the ways in which students' thinking grows in response to relatively well specified instructional experiences, as opposed to being grounded mostly in the disciplinary logic of mathematics and the conventional wisdom of practice" (Daro et al., 2011, p. 12).

Clements and Sarama (2004) further developed the theory of learning trajectory which described students' mathematical thinking and design as a series of learning tasks to promote students' developmental progression in their mathematical thinking. They suggested three stages to designing learning trajectories: identifying research-based models to depict students' knowledge construction, selecting and designing key mathematical tasks, and sequencing the tasks to compose the hypothetical learning trajectory. In this study the authors supported the group of teachers to design and modify the learning trajectory by following these three stages.

Division of fractions was often considered the most mechanical and least understood topic in elementary school (Carpenter et al., 1988; Fendel, 1987; Payne, 1976). The common mistakes students made reflected this observation. For example, many students inverted the dividend instead of the divisor, or they inverted both the dividend and the divisor before multiplying numerators and denominators

(Ashlock, 1990; Barash & Klein, 1996). Meanwhile, it has been challenging for teachers to teach division of fractions for understanding (Ball, 1990; Borko et al., 1992; Ma, 1999; Son & Crespo, 2009; Tirosh, 2000). Ma (1999) described difficulties American teachers had with contextualizing $1\frac{3}{4} \div \frac{1}{2}$ in a story context. In the study of Borko et al. (1992), a novice teacher stumbled with a conceptual explanation of division of fractions.

When designing the learning trajectory that was adapted for teachers and students in China, the university experts first drew on several versions of the Chinese textbooks and research on the topic of division of fractions (Ott, Snook, & Gibson, 1991; Sowder, Sowder, & Nickerson, 2010; Tirosh, 2000; Tirosh, Fischbein, Graeber, & Wilson, 1998). The team also referred to the Common Core State Standards for Mathematics (2010), which proposed a sequence for learning division of fractions. In the designed learning trajectory,[1] students were exposed to two ways of interpreting the meanings of division of fractions through visualization, story contexts, and proportional reasoning. When the expert team and the teachers agreed upon the learning trajectory, the teachers selected mathematical tasks for the lessons and sequenced those tasks in the lesson plans. The teachers were facilitated to use the theory of teaching and learning mathematics through variations for selecting math tasks and planning lessons.

Teaching and Learning through Variation

Teaching and learning through variation emphasizes the importance of using varied mathematics tasks to develop students' understanidng and support students in problem solving (Gu, Huang, & Marton, 2004; Lo & Marton, 2012; Marton & Pang, 2006; Marton & Tsui, 2004; Watson & Mason, 2006). Variation and invariance in mathematical tasks affect student learning through interactions between teachers, students, and learning objects. Ference Marton and his colleagues in Hong Kong and Sweden (Lo & Marton, 2012; Marton & Tsui, 2004; Marton & Pang, 2006) developed the variation theory of learning which argues that students construct new knowledge by identifying the critical features of the knowledge. Those critical features make the new learning objects differ from others. For example, when students learn the algorithms of division with fractions, they need to discern the relationship between the dividend and divisor in a specific problem situation and identify the appropriate visual representation of the relationship for conceptual understanding of the algorithm. Invariance is underlined in the variation theory, as learners need a background of invariance to recognize critical features of the new learning. Marton and Tsui (2004) proposed four types of variation and invariance patterns: separation, contrast, fusion, and generalization. The separation pattern of variation and invariance reveals one critical aspect of the new knowledge to students by holding the other aspects invariant. The pattern of contrast differentiates examples and non-examples that the new knowledge can be applied to. The variation and invariance pattern of fusion poses a higher cognitive demand level, as multiple critical aspects of the problem situation vary at the same time. The generalization pattern requires students to use the new knowledge (understanding the critical aspects) to solve problems in similar situations.

Similarly, Chinese researchers (Gu, 1991; Gu, Huang, & Marton, 2004) employed the theory of teaching mathematics through variation to discuss effective teaching practices in the mathematics classrooms of China. The theory of teaching mathematics through variation includes conceptual and procedural variations. Conceptual variation aims at revealing and highlighting the essential features of a concept (e.g., showing polygons and non-polygons to deepen students' understanding of the concept of polygon). Conceptual variation can be achieved in two ways: varying the connotation of a concept with various visual and concrete representations in a standard and non-standard context and offering counterexamples to delineate the boundary of the concept. Procedural variation helps students develop skills in problem solving, deriving from three aspects— solving extended problems, using multiple ways to solve problems, and applying solution methods to other similar problems (Gu et al., 2004). Lo and Marton (2012) argued that systematically varying certain aspects while keeping other aspects constant helps children discern the essential features of a new object. With the conceptual and procedural variations in mind, the group of teachers chose and modified mathematical tasks to develop the students' mathematical proficiency related to division with fractions.

Lesson Study, Teacher Learning, and Student Achievement

Lesson study is a collaborative activity done by a group of teachers who focus on student learning and the subject matter, integrate inquiry stance into their daily practice, and reflect upon their teaching practice for improvement. Lesson study has been argued to be an effective approach to teachers' professional development as it incorporates many key features of effective professional development programs identified in the literature (Borko, 2004; Cochran-Smith & Lytle, 1999; Darling-Hammond et al., 2009; Desimone, 2009; Franke, Kazemi, Shih, Biagetti, & Battey, 2005; Garet et al., 2001; Grossman, Wineburg, & Woolworth, 2001; Little, 2002; McLaughlin & Talbert, 2001; Porter et al., 2003; Wilson & Berne, 1999). The research literature reached a consensus on the key features of effective professional development: being focused on knowledge of the subject, the curriculum, and student learning; being ongoing, inquiry-based, and integrated into the daily work of teachers; providing opportunities for teachers to become actively engaged in the meaningful analysis of teaching and learning, and promoting coherence between teachers' professional development and other professional experiences; and engaging teachers in collaboratively doing mathematics, reflecting on teaching and learning mathematics, and refining practices in a community of learners.

In the past decade, more studies emerged in the literature to reveal the influences of lesson study on teaching, teacher learning, and student achievement (Hart, Alston, & Murata, 2011; Huang & Han, 2015; Leiws & Hurd, 2011; Lewis, Perry, Friedkin, & Roth, 2012; Perry & Leiws, 2011). These studies argued for the effectiveness of lesson study to improve teaching, teacher learning, and student knowledge. Among the emerging studies on lesson study in the US, experimental or longitudinal studies are rare. Lewis and the team (Perry & Lewis, 2011) conducted a longitudinal case study on the effects of school-based lesson study on teachers and students. Their studies revealed changes in teachers' instructional practice and increased standardized test scores of students in mathematics. Further studies done by the team (Perry, Lewis, Friedkin, & Baker, 2011; Perry & Lewis, 2011; Perry & Lewis, 2015) found that lesson study improved teachers' and students' mathematical knowledge. In more recent years, researchers (Han & Paine, 2010; Huang & Bao, 2006; Huang et al., 2014; Huang & Han, 2015) conducted several small scale qualitative studies to understand the influences of Chinese lesson study on teaching practices and teachers' learning. They argued the participant teachers improved the core aspects of instructional practices and identified the changes in their knowledge and beliefs. This study drew on the data of a small case study on one group of teachers' lesson study activity to investigate the effects of the theory-driven lesson study activity on teacher learning and student learning in the topic of division with fractions.

The participant teachers in the study were engaged in lesson study activities to design lessons on the topic of division with fractions. Their lesson study activities were supported and facilitated by university mathematics education experts and district teaching specialists. The teachers aimed at identifying the learning trajectory that was appropriate for student cognitive development in learning division with fractions, while producing effective instructional practices.

Conceptual Frameworks for This Study

Mathematics teachers have been teaching with variation consciously or unconsciously in their daily practices for decades (Gu et al., 2004). Chinese lesson study is a job-embedded, practice-based approach to professional development that has been in place for half a century (Yang, 2009).[2] However, researchers pointed out that the theory of teaching with variation and Chinese lesson study have paid great attention to improving teachers' performance, with less attention to students' learning (Chen & Fang, 2013; Gu & Gu, 2016; Huang et al., 2014), which is deviated from the recommendation in the new curriculum. To address this issue, the theory of learning trajectories was incorporated into the design of the lesson study activities that also adopted the variation theory. In the larger project, the researchers and the participant teachers employed both of the theories to guide the planning, teaching, reflection, and revision of research lessons throughout the lesson study (see Huang, Gong, & Han, 2016 for details).

271

RESEARCH METHODS

Research Setting

In an Eastern coastal large city of China, four elementary teachers formed a lesson study group on a voluntary basis. The second author, Dr. Gong, and two teaching research specialists, Mr. Sao and Mr. Ren, from the districts were involved in the lesson study activities as experts. They supported developing and modifying the learning trajectory for the topic of division of fractions as well as observing and debriefing research lessons. The four participant teachers were three experienced teachers, Ms. Shao, Ms. Han, and Ms. Tang, and a less experienced teacher, Ms. Lu, who had five years of teaching experience. Both Ms. Lu and Ms. Shao volunteered to teach the Research lessons in parallel lesson study activities,[3] but the current study chose to focus on the Research lessons taught by Ms. Shao and the related teaching research activities. Altogether, the lesson study group designed two lessons that reflected their collaborative work on the learning trajectory of division of fractions. Lesson One was about fractions divided by whole numbers and Lesson Two was about whole numbers divided by fractions. Ms. Shao taught each of the two topics to three different sixth grade classes in the same school. The average class size was about 30 students. Among the three classes, one class always received the first Research lessons, the second class received the second Research lessons, and the third class received the final public lesson. Table 1 shows the timeline and organization of the Research lessons.

Table 1. Timeline and organization of research lessons

Topic of research lessons	Rehearsal research lesson 1 Class: 605	Rehearsal research lesson 2 Class: 603	Final public lesson Class: 606
A fraction divided by a whole number	Date: 10-9-2014	Date: 10-10-2014	Date: 10-15-2014
A number divided by a fraction	Date: 10-11-2014	Date: 10-14-2014	Date: 10-17-2014

Data Collection

The study lasted about three months, from September to November 2014. The data sources of the study included three videotaped research lessons and debriefing meetings, audiotaped interviews with the participant teachers and some students, lesson plans, student worksheets, student quizzes, and the participant teachers' reflection journals. The post-lesson quiz had five word problems about division of fractions and asked the students to justify their solution methods with words, drawings, and symbols. The quiz was given right after each research lesson.

Each quiz was about 20 minutes. All completed quizzes were collected. The one-on-one interviews were conducted with all the participant teachers and 10 of the students on a voluntary basis at the end of the study. During the interviews, the students were asked about their understanding of the different solution methods of division with fractions. The major data sources used in this study were students' post-lesson test, videotaped lessons, and student interviews.

Data Analysis

The authors first read through each set of the following data sources: the lesson plans, transcribed debriefing meetings, transcribed lesson videos, and transcribed interviews with the teachers and district teaching research specialists. The authors coded the common terms that emerged from the data. With the labeled common terms, the authors examined the data across the different data sources to seek any emerging themes regarding conceptual variation and procedural variation. The triangulation of the data sources produced several themes, including (1) enriching visual representations, (2) revising story contexts, and (3) reorganizing student learning to allow free exploration that promoted conceptual and procedural variations.

Meanwhile, the authors read through all the students' post-tests to identify common understandings, mistakes, and misconceptions the students had regarding division with fractions. Employing the concept of mathematical proficiency, the authors thoroughly examined all the tests in the following dimensions: procedural fluency—having correct answers and setting up correct number sentences; conceptual understanding—using pictorial representations and using words to explain thinking; strategic competences—using different pictorial models to demonstrate solution methods. After examining all the tests after the first and last research lessons, we compared the results of each test in the aforementioned three dimensions to identify changes in student learning. The analysis of the student tests' data was triangulated with other data sources such as student interview data, transcribed lesson videos, debriefing meetings, and teacher interviews.

RESULTS

Improving Teaching through Constructing Appropriate Dimensions of Variation

The topic of division with fractions at 6th grade was broken into two sub-topics—fractions divided by whole numbers and whole numbers divided by fractions. Each sub-topic was taught to three different groups of students during the lesson study. The lesson study contained three full cycles of planning, teaching, and debriefing for each sub-topic. Examining the three lessons for each sub-topic, we identified the approaches the teachers employed to teach the topic through conceptual variation and procedural variation. Conceptual variation was created in the lessons mainly through enriched visual models. To support the students to understand the reasoning behind the algorithm of division with fractions, the teachers enriched the visual representations that aimed at making the critical aspects of the new knowledge noticeable to the students. Procedural variation was produced in several ways in the lessons, including revising how to activate the students' prior knowledge, modifying the numbers in the story contexts while keeping the background of the story contexts invariant, and encouraging and comparing multiple ways to solve the problems. Meanwhile, the teachers reorganized student learning to scaffold students in initiating conceptual and procedural variation.

Conceptual variation: Enriched visual representations. The major lesson objective was focused on understanding the standard algorithm of division with fractions. Traditionally, it was not difficult to calculate answers of division with fractions, but it was challenging to explain and understand why the algorithm works using pictures, words, and story contexts. The teachers in the lesson study group took on the challenge to design and revise the visual representations that were used to develop the students' conceptual understanding of the algorithm.

In the three lessons on fractions divided by whole numbers, the teachers worked on two critical aspects of understanding the algorithm. One was to recognize the partition division in the story context where several people equally shared a certain amount of juice. The amount of juice was expressed in fractions. The other critical aspect was seeing the relationship between multiplication and division with fractions. Dividing a whole number in the partition division situation is to multiply the reciprocal of the whole number, such as dividing $^4/_5$ by 2 that is to figure out half of $^4/_5$. The first critical aspect of understanding the algorithm seemed to not be challenging for the students, which was demonstrated and explained to the students through procedural variation. We will discuss this in the section of procedural variation. In the following paragraphs we describe and analyze how enriched visual models helped the students understand the second critical aspect.

Originally, the teachers planned to draw on area model to demonstrate the algorithm in the lessons of dividing fractions by whole numbers. After the first research lesson, Teacher Shao observed three difficulties her students had with using pictorial models to demonstrate and explain the standard algorithm. One difficulty was they did not know how to divide in the picture. The second difficulty was they did not realize they needed to partition the whole to show the answer. The last difficulty was some students skipped the division number sentence and wrote a multiplication number sentence based on the picture. At the debriefing meeting, the other teachers and the district experts pointed out another observation that some students were able to draw the picture, but they first calculated the answer and used the answer to guide their drawing. Instead of being an end, all the teachers agreed that using a visual model should be a means to help the students understand the algorithm. They decided Teacher Shao would encourage the students to diversify the visual models in order to deepen the students' conceptual understanding of the algorithm.

The advantage of the area model is that it clearly indicates the relative size of a part to a whole (Cramer, Wyberg, & Leavitt, 2008). For example, the students would easily see 4 parts out of 5 equal parts in a whole rectangle, which was used in the lessons – $^4/_5 \div 2$. The topic of dividing fractions by whole numbers is usually introduced and explained in the area model by drawing on the interpretation of division as partition division. In the lessons, the students could easily understand dividing fractions by whole numbers as equal sharing problems; however, it was challenging for the students to discern the reasoning for the standard algorithm in the visual models—why to multiply the reciprocal of divisor. For example, finding how 2 people can equally share $^4/_5$ of a liter of juice (Figure 1) is the same as finding half of $^4/_5$ of a liter of juice. Connecting with the interpretation of multiplication with fractions, to figure out half of $^4/_5$ of a liter, we multiply $^4/_5$ with ½. The teachers noticed that it was not easy for the students to make this conceptual connection between multiplication and division related to fractions.

Figure 1. Area model in the lesson on fractions divided by whole numbers

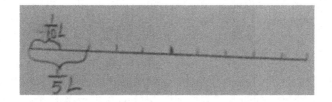

Figure 2. Length model in lesson on fractions divided by whole numbers

To further support the students to make the connection, starting from the second research lesson, the teachers decided to make use of the students' work that adopted the length model to demonstrate the partitive division (Figure 2). The length model is important in developing student understanding of fractions and other fraction concepts (Petit et al., 2010; Siegler et al., 2010). In this lesson, after the students discussed and shared their justification of the ways they divided $^4/_5$ by 2, Teacher Shao elicited a different model by asking, "Is there any different picture you drew? I remembered some of you drew a different model, but followed the same reasoning. Let's take a look at a different picture" (Lesson on Oct.10, 2014). One student presented his length model and explained what he did. "I divided the line segment into 5 equal part. I then took 4 equal parts to represent $^4/_5$. The 4 equal parts, $^4/_5$, was then split in half. One half of the 4 equal parts thus showed the answer $^2/_5$" (Lesson on Oct.14, 2014). Following the first example problem, the students solved the second example problem—$^1/_5$ of a liter of juice equally shared by 2 people. Teacher Shao purposefully called on one student to share her length model picture. The students first divided a line segment into five equal intervals, split $^1/_5$ interval into halves, and then labeled one half of $^1/_5$ as $^1/_{10}$ to display the answer. To clearly show the answer, Teacher Shao reminded the whole class of dividing the other four equal parts in half too, which would indicate the fractional part out of the whole. In the last research lesson, once again Teacher Shao chose both models produced by the students to present and share with the whole class.

As the teachers reflected at the second debriefing meeting, when Teacher Shao gave more opportunities to the students, the students came up with more visual models. Teacher Shao built upon her instruction on those visual models to scaffold the students in understanding the standard algorithm through the pictures. In the second research lesson Teacher Shao called on three groups to share their discussions after the students worked together in their small groups. One group of students shared their thoughts on making the connection between multiplication and division with fractions.

S1: To divide $^4/_5$ by 2 is to multiply it by ½.
T: Why did you think so? Let me see. Your group drew a similar picture. Can you (another student's name) explain why it is to multiply ½?
S2: Because we turned the division sign into a multiplication sign.
T: (pointing to Student 1) You said you understood it. Please share your understanding.
S2: Dividing by 2 is equal to half of it. That's to say, ½ is equal to half.
T: Do you understand what he said?
S: (all the students) No.
T: Please explain your thought one more time.
S1: To divide a number by 2 is to split that number into half. So ½ represents half of that number.

The district teaching specialist, Mr. Sao, pointed out some students were able to not only draw a visual model, but also explain what the drawing demonstrated after the second research lesson. In the last research lesson we noticed that the students quickly made sense of the connection when Teacher Shao invited one student to use his picture to explain it. The student stated, with his length model, "To divide $^4/_5$ by 2 is to find out its half. The reciprocal of 2 is ½. So $^4/_5$ divided by 2 is $^4/_5$ multiplying ½" (Lesson on Oct.15, 2014). The conceptual variation through diverse visual models produced by the students eventually made the critical aspect of the new knowledge, the relationship between multiplication and division with fractions, salient to the students.

Meanwhile, two different critical aspects of understanding the algorithm were emphasized in the lessons on whole numbers divided by fractions. First, the students were expected to understand the algorithm through the relationship of distance, time, and speed. When a person walked 5 kilometers within $^2/_3$ of an hour, finding the speed per hour was a division problem (distance ÷ time = speed), which was

$5 \div \frac{2}{3} =$ speed per hour. The second critical aspect of the new knowledge in the three lessons was to discern a multiplicative relationship among quantities in the problems and draw on proportional reasoning to explain and understand the standard algorithm. 5 kilometers within $\frac{2}{3}$ of an hour is in a proportional relationship with the distance within one hour that is the speed. In all three lessons, Teacher Shao immediately asked the students to identify the quantitative relationship once she displayed the first example problem. The students had no difficulty discerning the quantitative relationship as distance, time, and speed, and setting up the division number sentence, such as $3 \div \frac{1}{2}$, $5 \div \frac{2}{3}$, and $\frac{21}{8} \div \frac{3}{4}$ in the last research lesson. In what followed we focused on the analysis of drawing on the proportional relationship to understand the standard algorithm.

In the lessons on the topic of whole numbers divided by fractions the teachers solely relied on the length model by interpreting the division of whole numbers by fractions as special partitive division. The central problem the students worked around in the last research lesson was: *Xiaohua walked 3 kilometers within $\frac{1}{2}$ hour. Xiaoming Walked 5 kilometers within $\frac{2}{3}$ hours. Xiaohong walked $\frac{21}{8}$ kilometres within $\frac{3}{4}$ hours. How many kilometers did each of them walk in one hour?*

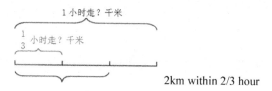

2km within 2/3 hour

Figure 3. Single line diagram

Originally, the teachers used one single line diagram to illustrate the problem (Figure 3). At the debriefing meeting after the first research lesson Teacher Shao and the district teaching research specialists realized the difficulty the students had when they tried to use one single line to demonstrate how to calculate the answer and how to explain the standard algorithm. There were two reasons Teacher Shao and the specialists decided to employ double line diagrams to represent the problem in the second research lesson. One line represented the distance the person walked within certain time, and the other line represented the speed per hour. The first reason was that Teacher Shao mentioned that the average and low students could not figure out how to show the time and the distance on one single line at the same time. For example, some students got stuck with showing $\frac{2}{3}$ hour and 2 km when a person walked 2 km within $\frac{2}{3}$ hour. They were not sure if the one single line should represent 2 km or $\frac{2}{3}$ hour. Or if they labeled the one single line to represent $\frac{2}{3}$ hour, they stumbled with expressing one hour on the line. The teacher and the specialists thought the original one line diagram in the textbook could be confusing for the students. They came out with double line diagrams to represent the given condition and the question. For example, in Figure 4 the top line diagram showed the distance of 2 km a person walked within ⅔ hour and the second line diagram indicated the distance a person walked in one hour that the students needed to seek an answer for. The double line diagrams were adopted in the second research lesson.

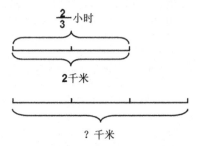

Figure 4. Double line diagram

The second reason was that they tried to find out a way that could support the students' understanding of the standard algorithm of division with fractions from the perspective of multiplicative relationship. At the debriefing meeting after the first research lesson Teacher Shao noticed there was only one girl in her class who touched on the idea of multiplicative relationship when the students were struggling with explaining the reason for multiplying by the reciprocal of the divisor $-2 \div ⅔ = 2 \times {}^3\!/_2$. The girl explained in her small group that if Xiaoming walked 2 km within ⅔ hour, he would walk ${}^3\!/_2$ times as many km per hour as the distance he walked within ⅔ hour. However, the rest of the class did not understand her idea. Teacher Shao commented that her students did not learn much from the lesson. Therefore, she proposed how she could revise the lesson to help the students make sense of the algorithm from the perspective of multiplicative relationship. The district teaching research specialists agreed with her and focused their discussions on the possible way that could best scaffold the students' understanding of the standard algorithm.

The district teaching research specialist, Mr. Ren, first suggested that a two line diagram should be used to represent the multiplicative relationship between the quantities. Anticipating the possible difficulty the students would have in understanding the standard algorithm as multiplicative relationships, Mr. Sao posed that they might need to consider keeping some conditions the same and varying others. For example, three different story contexts could be set up where a person, a dog, and a car travelled different distances within ¾ hour. As three dividends were divided by the same divisor, ¾, the students might be able to notice the pattern that dividing ¾ was to divide 3 and multiply 4 in all three problems. However, the other district teaching research specialists disagreed with Mr. Sao's idea. On one hand, they were afraid the students' attention on understanding multiplying the reciprocal would be distracted when they felt comfortable with dividing the numeration and then multiplying the denominator. On the other hand, they thought there would be inconsistency between the multiplicative relationship perspective and employing the associative property to identity the pattern $- 2 \div \frac{2}{3} = 2 \div 2 \times 3 = 2 \times \frac{1}{2} \times 3$. They finally reached the agreement that the second lesson would not connect the multiplicative thinking with the associative property and that was more for the purpose of calculation. Therefore, the second lesson would be centered on using the double line diagrams to demonstrate the multiplicative reasoning for making sense of the standard algorithm.

According to Thompson and Saldanha (2003), the development of multiplicative reasoning in division with fractions resulted from a network of meanings that demanded conceptualizations of fractions, multiplication, division, measurement, and proportionality. Vergnaud (1988) argued that proportions were the foundation of the multiplicative conceptual field that consisted of all situations related to proportions, multiplications, and divisions. A conceptualized measure has a ratio relationship. For example, what the teachers and the district teaching research specialists discussed entailed such a ratio relationship—one hour is $\frac{3}{2}$ times as much time as $\frac{2}{3}$ hour. Proportions are important for conceptualizing measured quantities. A single proportion, for example, a relationship between the distance and time, indicates one quantity (time, e.g., $\frac{2}{3}$) increases by a factor of s (e.g., $\frac{3}{2}$), then the measure of the other quantity (distance, e.g. 2km) will increase by the same factor of s ($\frac{3}{2}$) to keep the proportional relationship ($\frac{3}{2}$ times as many as). Linking the multiplicative reasoning and proportional relationship to division with fractions, Thompson and Saldanhe (2003) interpreted $a \div \frac{m}{n}$ as n times as large as $\frac{1}{m}$ of a because $a \div m$ could be explained as $\frac{1}{m}$ of a. Thus $a \div \frac{m}{n} = a \times (\frac{n}{m})$. In terms of relative size and multiplicative thinking, they thought employing the proportional relationship in division with fractions was a conceptual derivation of the standard algorithm of inverting and multiplying, and its interpretation should be straightforward. Obviously, instead of considering a conceptual derivation from the rule of 'invert and multiply", the teachers and the district teaching research specialists tried to adopt the proportional relationship as a conceptual path to develop the students' understanding of the standard algorithm. In the second lesson, Teacher Shao used the double line diagrams to support the students' conceptual development of seeing the proportional relationship in dividing whole numbers by fractions.

Procedural variation. Procedural variation is concerned with arriving at solutions to problems, using multiple methods to solve problems, and applying the knowledge to other problem contexts. In the six research lessons, the teachers activated procedural variation in three ways: reviewing prior knowledge to relate to the new knowledge closely, modifying the numbers in the story contexts while keeping the background of the contexts invariant, and sharing and comparing multiple ways to solve the problems.

Reviewing prior knowledge can activate students' prior knowledge and get them ready for new knowledge in a lesson. The teachers in the lesson study designed and revised the tasks for the purpose of making the connection between the students' prior knowledge and the current critical aspects of the new knowledge in the lessons.

279

They created two tasks in the three research lessons on fractions divided by whole numbers. Task One was "Two people equally shared 2 liters of juice. How much did each person get?" Task Two was "Two people equally shared 1 liter of juice. How much did each person get?" As we mentioned above, the first critical aspects of understanding the standard algorithm in a story context was to discern the partition division in that context. The two tasks in the review section of the lesson aimed at linking partition division with whole numbers to partition division with fractions. The teachers expected the students to recognize the same interpretation of partition division both with whole numbers and fractions. The students had learned the meaning of division as equal sharing and been able to identify the story contexts of partition division with whole numbers. Making the connection, the students could efficiently transfer their prior knowledge of partition division to the new knowledge in the lessons. Following the review of the two tasks, Teacher Shao showed the first example problem—How much each person got when two people equally shared $^4/_5$ of a liter of juice. Throughout the three research lessons, the students had no difficulty with discerning the partition division context and setting up a correct division number sentence. This procedural variation held the story context invariant while changing the numbers from whole numbers to fractions, which successfully connected division with whole numbers and division with fractions in a partitive context.

In the three lessons on whole numbers divided by fractions, the teachers revised how to review the students' prior knowledge. In the first lesson, Teacher Shao simply reviewed the reciprocals of five numbers. When the teachers realized the first lesson did not achieve the objectives, they discussed how the review should be revised at the debriefing meeting. Reviewing reciprocals did not help the students understand the algorithm from the perspective of proportional relationship. Teacher Shao wanted to start with reviewing how many ½ hour, ⅓ hour, $^1/_5$ hour, and $^1/_{10}$ hour are in one hour, which would prepare the students' conceptual understanding of multiplicative relationship in division with fractions. Ms. Han followed with her idea that the students would be able to realize the distance changed at the same rate as time changed. In other words, the quantities of distance and time had the same multiplicative relationship, such as the time changing from ⅔ to one hour at the rate of $^3/_2$ times, while the distance changed at the same rate from 2 km to $^3/_2$ times 2km.

In the second research lesson, Teacher Shao reviewed the reciprocals of five numbers and then posed the question of how many ½ hour, ⅓ hour, $^1/_5$ hour and $^1/_{10}$ hour are in one hour, respectively. After the second research lesson the teachers decided to remove the review of reciprocals of five numbers. They did not want to give the students an excessive hint to multiply the reciprocal of a divisor in the standard algorithm. Instead, they expected the students to focus on the conceptual understanding of the algorithm from the perspective of proportional relationship. To achieve that goal, the teachers revised the numbers in the tasks and added three more questions to the review tasks in the final research lesson. The final review tasks were how many $\frac{1}{3}$ hour in $\frac{2}{3}$ hour, how many $\frac{1}{4}$ hour in $\frac{3}{4}$ hour, how many $\frac{1}{3}$ hour in one hour, how many $\frac{1}{5}$ hour in one hour, and how many $\frac{1}{10}$ hour in one hour. The new numbers – $\frac{2}{3}$ and $\frac{3}{4}$ in the review tasks were aligned with the numbers in the example problem that followed in the final lesson. Meanwhile, Teacher Shao asked the students three new questions: how many times bigger one hour is than $\frac{1}{3}$ hour, how many times bigger one hour is than $\frac{1}{5}$ hour, and how many times bigger one hour is than $\frac{1}{10}$ hour.

T: I can also express in this way- how many times bigger is one hour than $\frac{1}{3}$ hour.

S: Three times.

T: Next problem.

S: There are five copies of $\frac{1}{5}$ hour in one hour.

T: How can you express this relationship in a different way?

S: One hour is five times $\frac{1}{5}$ hour.

T: How about $\frac{1}{10}$ hour? How many $\frac{1}{10}$ hour are there in one hour?

S: Ten.

T: Express it in another way? Let's say it together.

S: One hour is ten times of $\frac{1}{10}$ hour. (Lesson on Oct.17, 2014)

Through changing the review task from reviewing reciprocals to thinking about the multiplicative relationship between $\frac{1}{3}$ and $\frac{2}{3}$, $\frac{1}{4}$ and $\frac{3}{4}$, $\frac{1}{3}$ and one, $\frac{1}{5}$ and one, and $\frac{1}{10}$ and one, the teachers established links with the example problem. The prior knowledge of multiplicative relationship was activated, which prepared students for exploring the conceptual understanding of the standard algorithm through proportional relationship in pictures and words. This procedural variation played an important role in making sense of the critical aspect of the standard algorithm in a special partition division context. The story contexts that asked for a unit rate (e.g, speed/hour, price/pound, etc.) represented a special partition division situation. Compared with the measurement interpretation of division when a number is divided by a fraction, story contexts of seeking a unit rate are more challenging for students to understand.

In the three research lessons on fractions divided by whole numbers, the teachers modified the numbers in the problems to focus the students' attention on the reasoning behind the algorithm. Following Example Problem One – $\frac{4}{5}$ liter of juice is equally shared by 2 people, the teachers added Example Problem Two that changed $\frac{4}{5}$ liter to $\frac{1}{5}$ liter in the second and the final lessons. Example Problem Two was "$\frac{1}{5}$ liter of juice is equally shared by 3 people. How much does each person get?" In the first lesson, the students came up with the method of $\frac{4}{5} \div 2 = \frac{(4 \div 2)}{5} = 2/5$. Similarly, we also noticed the teachers changed the numbers in the three lessons on whole numbers divided by fractions, e.g., from $2 \div \frac{1}{2}$ to $3 \div \frac{1}{2}$ in the example problem, etc. The second example problem was added with the intent to provide a context where the students could realize the limit of applying this method to solve similar problems, such as $\frac{1}{5} \div 2$. When the students went beyond this method, they would consider why the standard algorithm worked in every problem of division with fractions. At the same time, it was seen that the teachers designed a consistent story context throughout the three lessons on each of the two sub-topics. In the three lessons the example problems were about equally sharing juice and had the background of walking some distance within a period of time. Though the teachers designed different numbers and modified the numbers in the example problems, the background of those problems stayed invariant. The consistent backgrounds with different numbers helped the students focus on their quantitative relationships and thus understand the algorithm.

The third kind of procedural variation throughout all six lessons was encouraging, sharing, and connecting different solution methods to problems. Though the major lesson objective was to understand the reasoning of the standard algorithm, the teachers did not constrain the students' thinking within the standard algorithm. They designed different ways to organize student learning, which opened the door for the students to produce various solution methods. In the lessons on fractions divided by whole numbers, the students came up with three other solution methods besides the standard algorithm. In the first lesson, one different method was shared – dividing numerators. In the second lesson after Teacher Shao had the students work in small groups, one group of students converted fractions into decimals and divided—$^4/_5 \div 2 = 0.8 \div 2 = 0.4 = ^2/_5$. In the final research lesson, the students came up with three different methods, including the standard algorithm, dividing numerators, and multiplying the reciprocal of the divisor to both numerator and denominator. One student explained, "I divided the whole into five parts and then took four parts. $^4/_5$ divided by 2 is to evenly split the four parts into two parts. So $^{(4 \div 2)}/_5 = ^2/_5$" (Lesson on Oct.10, 2014). Another student explained her method, "I used the property of division—the quotient will not change if we multiply both the dividend and divisor by the same number. The dividend $^4/_5$ times $^2/_1$ and the divisor times $^2/_1$ too. So the quotient does not change. Then 2 multiplying $^1/_2$ equals to 1. $^4/_5$ times $^1/_2$ gives me $^2/_5$. So $^2/_5 \div 1 = ^2/_5$" (Lesson on Oct.10, 2014).

Similarly, in the final research lesson on numbers divided by fractions, when Teacher Shao created an opportunity for the students to explore their own methods to solve the problems independently and collaboratively, the students brought about three different methods: multiplying both dividend and divisor by the reciprocal of the divisor, the standards algorithm, and dividing numerator and multiplying denominator (e.g. $5 \div ^2/_3 = 5 \div 2 \times 3$). Teacher Shao also attempted to connect the three different methods in the lesson. She invited students to think about if the method of multiplying by the reciprocal of the divisor was related to the method of multiplying both dividend and divisor by the reciprocal of the divisor. For example, $3 \div ^1/_2 = (3 \times ^2/_1) \div (^1/_2 \times ^2/_1) = 3 \times 2$, Teacher Shao asked the class, "3 times 2, $^1/_2$ times 2. What is he trying to explain? His method can demonstrate my answer is correct, isn't it? So let's find out if the two methods are related to each other. Aren't they? Why did he multiply 2? Is it because one hour is what of $^1/_2$ hour?" (Lesson on Oct.17, 2014). The whole class answered "two times $^1/_2$ hour". When discussing their methods to solve the problem—the speed of walking 5 kilometers within $\frac{2}{3}$ hour, one group of students elaborated on their reasoning of $5 \div \frac{2}{3} = 5 \div 2 \times 3$. "… we see $\frac{2}{3}$, which is these two parts (pointing to the picture), we need to figure out the time for one part. So $\frac{2}{3}$ divided by 2 is equal to $\frac{1}{3}$. Then the distance should be divided by 2 too. That is to divide 5 kilometers by 2. It is equal to 2.5 killometers" (Lesson on Oct.17, 2014). Teacher Shao guided the students to compare the three methods and identify that they all eventually arrived at multiplying the reciprocal of divisor, such as $5 \div \frac{2}{3} = 5 \times (\frac{3}{2})$. The procedural variation expanded the students' approaches to solving problems of whole numbers divided by fractions. Connecting the three methods from the perspective of multiplicative relationship consolidated the students' understanding of the standard algorithm.

Reorganizing student learning to initiate learning through variations. While observing and revising the lessons, Teacher Shao gradually shifted her instruction to the students' exploration and investigation from teacher-dominated instruction. When Teacher Shao made the shift, she embraced openness, diversity, and complexity in the classroom. She created opportunities for the students to initiate multiple ways to solve the problems, apply their solution methods to similar problems, and reason about the algorithm, which promoted conceptual and procedural variations at the same time. In all six lessons, Teacher Shao spent more time on having students explore how to solve problems both independently and collaboratively. In each of the two last lessons on the two different topics, respectively, Teacher Shao did not present her way of solving the problem, including her visual models. Instead, she posed the problem and linked the meaning of division with fractions to that of division with whole numbers at the beginning. Then she had the students investigate the solution methods and explain their solution methods in number sentences, pictures, and words. Building upon the students' ideas, she guided the students to compare and discuss their different solution methods.

At the debriefing meeting after the second lesson on the topic of dividing fractions by whole numbers, Teacher Shao reflected that her students came up with multiple solutions methods and multiple visual models compared to the first lesson. She was surprised to see one group of students convert the fractions into decimals and divide, e.g., $\frac{1}{5} \div 2 = 0.2 \div 2 = 0.1$. This method was not proposed by the students in the first lesson when the teacher dominated the learning process of the students. In the second lesson, more students drew the length model to explain their solution methods, while there was only one student in the first lesson who used the length model. Several students used a different partition in the area model that was not seen in the first lesson either. As the district teaching specialist, Mr. Sao commented at the debriefing meeting, "… when a teacher gives students an opportunity to freely explore, the students' mind would be open and unbounded. Otherwise, in the first lesson the students' thinking was confined to one visual model and one solution method presented by the teacher" (The debriefing meeting on Oct. 10, 2014). Based on the observation data on student learning in the second lesson, several district

283

teaching research specialists suggested that Teacher Shao change her way of organizing the lesson in order to learn the first two example problems. In the second lesson, Teacher Shao focused her students' learning on the first problem – $\frac{1}{5}$ liter of juice equally shared by 2 people, for which she arranged independent thinking, small group discussion, and whole class discussion. However, the district specialists all pointed out the second example problem-$\frac{4}{5}$ liter of juice equally shared by 2 people, was a big leap in terms of student cognitive difficulty. They recommended that Teacher Shao organize the lesson to explore this second problem in small groups and to spend more time on discussing their solution methods to this problem and illustrating their understanding of the algorithm through the second problem.

Similarly, Teacher Shao revised her way of organizing student learning in the three lessons on dividing whole numbers by fractions in order to promote student thinking and reach the goal of understanding the standard algorithm through conceptual and procedural variations. As discussed above, at the debriefing meeting after the first lesson on this topic, the teachers and the district specialists came to an agreement that a double line diagram should be used to replace a single line diagram to represent the multiplicative relationship between quantities. In the second lesson, Teacher Shao adopted double line diagrams as visual models. However, the learning outcomes from the students were not positive. Ms. Tang pointed out she noticed that some students could not understand the relationship between the two lines. For example, some students first calculated the answer of $\frac{15}{8} \div \frac{3}{4}$ and then used the result $\frac{5}{2}$ to draw the length model that had a shorter line with two parts and a longer line with five parts. They did not understand why the double line diagram could help them illustrate and explain the algorithm at all. When discussing the reason for why the students could not understand the double line diagrams, the experts thought the double line diagrams separated the fractional parts and the whole, such as $\frac{1}{3}$ hour and one hour drawn in two different lines, which did not clearly show to students $\frac{1}{3}$ hour as one fractional part of one hour. In addition, the double line diagrams Teacher Shao modelled for the students funnelled their thinking to her method, which was evidenced in the interviews with some students after the lesson. All the interviewed students used no other ways than her way to illustrate their reasoning. The specialists speculated that the students would produce more ideas on how to model and explain their reasoning if Teacher Shao revised her way of organizing student learning to allow them investigate the topic on their own. It did not matter if the students drew single line diagrams or double line diagrams. What mattered was that they came up with their own ideas on visual models and explanations. In the final lesson, Teacher Shao did not demonstrate double line diagrams anymore. Instead, she built her instruction upon the students' thoughts.

Dr. Gong, the university expert in the lesson study, cited from Book of Rites on Learning, commented on Teacher Shao's second lesson on the topic of dividing whole numbers by fractions and stated that a teacher should help students understand why and inspire them to think independently. When a teacher funnels student thinking and tells them conclusions without their own thinking, students can not develop their reasoning and their thinking would be confined. Conceptual and procedural variations are not simply achieved through choosing, adapting, and revising mathematical tasks by teachers. When teachers create rich opportunities to learn for students and build instruction upon students' mathematical ideas, conceptual and procedural variations are produced in the classroom. The literature reveals that discussions can provide opportunities to learn for all students in the mathematics classrooms (Cirillo, 2013; Gearhart et al., 2014; Webb, Franke, Ing, Wong, & Fernandes, 2013). The lesson study, with designed learning trajectory and the lens of teaching through variation, showed that teaching through variation is not only a pedagogical lens or tool for teachers to teach, but also a result of students' investigation and thinking as well as a lens to examine student learning.

Changes in Student Learning

Drawing on the concept of mathematical proficiency, the authors analyzed and compared the post-tests after the first and last research lessons in the three dimensions: procedural fluency—having correct answers and setting up correct number sentences; conceptual understanding—using pictorial representations and using words to explain thinking; strategic competences—using different pictorial models to demonstrate solution methods.

After the first and last lessons on the topic of dividing fractions by whole numbers, a post-test[4] was administered to the students. On both tests there were 3 word problems and the students were directed to calculate answers and use multiple ways to explain their thinking, including number sentences, pictures, and words. The three problems were as below.

A rope that is $\frac{6}{7}$ meter long is cut into three equal parts. How long is one part?

A rope that is ½ meter long is cut into 3 equal parts. How long is one part?

A rope that is ⅔ meter long is cut into 5 equal parts. How long is one part?

Table 2 listed the numbers of students in the two tests who got correct answers, set up correct number sentences, drew completely correct or partially correct pictures, and used words, area model, and length model to explain their thinking.

From Table 2, it is clear that on both post-tests the students almost had no problem with calculating the correct answers, but nine of twenty-five students (36%) produced partially correct visual models on the first post-test compared to only four of twenty-eight (14%) on the third post-test. There were three students on the third post-test who did not draw visual models, but instead used words to explain their thinking correctly. The four students who employed the length model (single line diagram) on the first post-test all presented their models as the unit fractional part of the rope, such as showing $\frac{1}{5}$ of ⅔ on the single line. Only one student had difficulty partitioning the presented rope length into equal parts for the first and last problems. That student did not know how to divide the ⅔ out of the whole one into five equal parts and show the correct answer in the models. Though their length models could not illustrate the answers, they demonstrated the meaning of dividing fractions by

Table 2. Post-tests: Fractions divided by whole numbers

	First lesson (N = 25)	Third lesson (N = 28)		First lesson (N = 25)	Third lesson (N = 28)
Correct answers	24 (96%)	28 (100%)	Partially correct pictures	9 (36%)	4 (14%)
Correct number sentences	21 (84%)	28 (100%)	Area model	22 (88%)	23 (82%)
Verbal explanations	11 (44%)	8 (29%)	Length model	5 (20%)	8 (29%)
Correct pictures	16 (64%)	21 (75%)	Use both models	2 (8%)	5 (18%)

whole numbers as partition division, e.g., $\frac{2}{3} \div 5$ to partition $\frac{2}{3}$ into 5 equal parts. That was the same with the length models of the 7 students on the third post-test. We can see that on the third post-test, the visual models the students drew were slightly more diverse. More students tried to employ the length model to represent their thinking.

However, it was worth noting that the percentage of the students who chose to verbalize their thinking dropped from the first test to the third test. Almost half of the class on the first test tried to explain their thinking verbally, and 10 out of 11 students did it correctly. All 8 students showed their verbal explanations accurately on the third post-test, while six of the eight students used visual models. The reason for this issue could be that the students were not asked to write down their explanations in the lessons. Even though Teacher Shao and the district specialists encouraged them to talk about their thinking, they did not have a chance to practice jotting down their thinking in words on paper. From the debriefing meetings and interviews with the participant teachers, we can see writing down their verbalized thoughts on paper was not the focus of the lesson study.

It was not surprising to find out that on the third post-test more students used two or three ways to solve the problems. On the first post-test only 20% of the students (5 out of 25) used two different ways to solve the problems. As we discussed above, Teacher Shao and the district specialists decided to empower the students more in the last lesson. The students were organized to independently and collaboratively explore different solution methods and make sense of the standard algorithm. Thus 61% of the students (17 out of 28) on the last test calculated the answer in two or three different ways, including the standard algorithm, the method of dividing numerators (e.g., $\frac{6}{7} \div 3 = \frac{(6 \div 3)}{7} = \frac{2}{7}$), and the method of multiplying the reciprocal of divisor with both dividend and divisor (e.g., $\frac{6}{7} \div 3 = (\frac{6}{7} \times \frac{1}{3}) \div (3 \times \frac{1}{3})$). On the first post-test, the majority of the students used only the standard algorithm to solve the problems and no student solved the problems by using the method of multiplying the reciprocal of divisor with both dividend and divisor.

Following each of the first and last lessons on the topic of dividing whole numbers by fractions, a post-test was administered to the students. Both post-tests included the same set of five word problems. The five problems are presented below:

A person walks 3 km within $\frac{1}{5}$ hour. How many km does he walk in one hour?
A person walks 1 km within $\frac{2}{3}$ hour. How many km does he walk in one hour?
A person walks 3 km within $\frac{2}{3}$ hour. How many km does he walk in one hour?
A person walks $\frac{1}{3}$ km within $\frac{1}{5}$ hour. How many km does he walk in one hour?
A person walks $\frac{4}{5}$ km within $\frac{2}{3}$ hour. How many km does he walk in one hour?

Table 3 lists the number of students in the two tests who got correct answers, set up correct number sentences, drew completely correct or partially correct pictures, and used words, area model, and length model to explain their thinking.

Table 3. Post-tests: Numbers divided by fractions

	First lesson (N = 31)	Third lesson (N = 29)		First lesson (N = 31)	Third lesson (N = 29)
Correct answers	22 (71%)	27 (93%)	Partially correct pictures	13 (42%)	0
Correct number sentences	27 (93%)	28 (97%)	Area model	3 (10%)	1 (3%)
Verbal explanations	5 (16%)	9 (31%)	Length model	30 (97%)	26 (90%)
Correct pictures	18 (58%)	27 (93%)	Use both models	2 (6%)	0

As what was aforementioned, Teacher Shao and the district specialists had detailed discussions at the debriefing meeting after the first lesson on the approaches they should adopt to support the students' understanding of the standard algorithm. The test results of the first post-test reflected what they observed. 42% of the students on the first post-test did not accurately produce visual models to represent their thinking. Only five out of 31 students tried to explain their thinking in words. At the debriefing meeting the participant teachers seemed to agree on an idea that the students could develop their conceptual understanding of the algorithm from the perspective of multiplicative reasoning. Following the second debriefing meeting, Teacher Shao accepted the feedback from her colleagues and reorganized student learning by giving them more space to freely explore the topic. It was remarkable that 93% of the students on the third post-test drew correct visual models and 31% of the students made an attempt to spell out their ideas in words. Out of 9 students who verbalized their thinking, there were 6 students who clearly illustrated their thinking in the proportional relationship. For example, $\frac{2}{3}$ hour increases $\frac{3}{2}$ times to reach one hour, and so does 3 km to reach $\frac{9}{2}$ km. Those six students clearly used words and diagrams to illustrate the proportional relationship involved with the quantities in the problems. We can speculate that the teacher's revision of the approach to understanding and the way of organizing student learning boosted the production of verbal explanations on the third post-test.

In addition, comparing the solution methods the students adopted to solve the five word problems on the two post-tests, it was seen that there was a tremendous change in the number of students who drew on two or three ways to solve the problems. On the first post-test there were only two students (6%) who used two different solution methods. On the third post-test 18 students (62%) demonstrated two or three solution methods. Their multiple solution methods were similar to what we have described above: the standard algorithm, the method of dividing the numerator and multiplying the denominator of the divisor (e.g., $3 \div \frac{2}{3} = (3 \div 2) \times 3 = \frac{9}{2}$), and the method of multiplying the reciprocal of divisor with both dividend and divisor (e.g., $3 \div \frac{2}{3} = (3 \times \frac{3}{2}) \div (\frac{2}{3} \times \frac{3}{2})$).

DISCUSSIONS AND CONCLUSIONS

In this study, we drew on the multiple data sources to examine six research lessons on the topics of division with fractions. The participant teachers worked closely with the district teaching research specialists to design the learning trajectory and adopt the conceptual lens of teaching through variations to improve teaching and students' learning. We argued that the participant teachers made use of conceptual and procedural variations through enriching visual models and modifying story contexts. In addition, our analysis revealed that teaching through variation was not only a conceptual lens or tool for teachers to design and improve instruction, but also a conceptual lens to examine student learning. In other words, students could get ample opportunities to learn through experiencing the variations which focus on critical aspects of the object of learning when a teacher enacts appropriate dimensions of conceptual and procedural variations in the classroom. Therefore, it will promote conceptual development of student mathematical thinking.

Division of fractions has often been considered the most mechanical and least understood topic in elementary school (Borko et al., 1992; Carpenter et al., 1988; Fendel, 1987; Payne, 1976). For example, Borko et al (1992) documented the difficulty the student teacher and her students had with conceptual explanation for the standard algorithm of division with fractions. To promote the conceptual development of the algorithm of division with fractions, the Common Core State Standards for Mathematics (2010) proposed that students at 5th and 6th grade should understand division with fractions in various ways, including using visual models, story contexts, equation, and reverse relationship between multiplication and division. Similarly, in the current study, a conceptual explanation for the standard algorithm was also a challenge for both the teachers and the students. The participant teachers studied and explored different ways to help students reach a conceptual explanation. Parallel Lesson Study guided by the theories of learning trajectory and variations made it possible for the teachers to theorize their local instruction and produce their own new ways of teaching and learning division with fractions.

In order to scaffold the students to discern and understand the critical aspects of the new knowledge, especially the relationship of multiplication and division with fractions and the multiplicative reasoning, Teacher Shao and the district specialists implemented conceptual variation through diverse visual models. Various visual models became tools to develop conceptual variation in the lessons. In addition, they achieved procedural variation through changing numbers in the story contexts of partition division while keeping the background of the contexts invariant. Because there were two teachers who were teaching the same two topics at the same time in the large parallel lesson study, Teacher Shao taught all her six research lessons by interpreting division as partition, while the other teacher drew on the meaning of division as partition (fractions divided by whole numbers) and measurement (fractions divided by fractions) to teach another 6 research lessons. In the research lessons the teacher gradually shifted her instruction from teacher-dominated to student exploration, which engaged the students in yielding multiple methods of division with fractions. This change to the lesson helped promote conceptual and procedural variation.

Multiplicative reasoning in understanding the standard algorithm was another approach the participant teachers tried so hard to implement in the classroom. This way of understanding the standard algorithm of division with fractions had not been seen in the math textbooks the participant teachers used. This idea is rare in the mathematics classrooms in the US as well. Thompson and Saldanha (2003) mentioned that understanding of reciprocal relationship of relative size was very rare among the US students. They argued that this was a significant problem for mathematics education in the US and suggested investigating the reason why mathematical instruction failed to support its development among students. When teaching the topic of dividing whole numbers by fractions, the participant teachers redesigned the tasks and learning activities to scaffold student understanding of the proportional relationship[5] between the quantities in the problems. For example, "A person walks 5 km within ⅔ hour. How many km does this person walk in one hour?" To solve this problem and produce a conceptual explanation, the students needed to reason through the relationship between ⅔ hour and 1 hour. With the relationship, they needed to understand the distance within the two time units shared the same relationship. Both time and distance change at the same rate as they have a proportional relationship. Therefore, if we know ⅔ hour is $\frac{3}{2}$ times as many as 1 hour, we understand the unknown distance will be $\frac{3}{2}$ times as many as 5km. That leads to a conceptual explanation of $5 \div \frac{2}{3} = 5 \times \frac{3}{2}$. Actually, this method could be connected with the method of multiplying both dividend and divisor with the reciprocal of divisor as $5 \div \frac{2}{3} = (5 \times \frac{3}{2}) \div (\frac{2}{3} \times \frac{3}{2})$, both dividend and divisor increasing $\frac{3}{2}$ times so that we can figure out the distance within 1 hour.

A remarkable shift in the six lessons was a change of the participant teachers' discussions from teacher performance to student learning. In the past some studies revealed that teachers' comments and feedback used to focus on a teacher's performance in a lesson (Han & Paine, 2010). However, one of the notable features of lesson study is the focus on student learning. The elements of learning trajectory design and teaching through variations in the parallel lesson study altered the narrative. At the debriefing meetings, in the participant teachers' observations, and through the interviews with them, we can notice the meaningful shift. They focused more on how students learned, responded, and understood. The theoretical lens of teaching through variations led the teachers to recenter their discussions and reflections on supporting students' conceptual development, which helped the teachers revise the way to organize student learning in the classroom. Students' independent and collaborative exploration eventually initiated opportunities to learn through conceptual and procedural variations.

NOTES

[1] The details of the designed learning trajectory can been seen in Huang, Gong and Han (2016). Implementing mathematics teaching that promotes students' understanding through theory-driven lesson study. *ZDM Mathematics Education, 48*, 425–439.

[2] Chinese teachers usually work in a school-based teaching research group that is organized by subject, e.g., mathematics teaching research group. In the teaching research group teachers are involved in various activities, among which collaboratively conducting public lesson or exemplar lesson is a key approach to their professional development. The structure and procedure of conducting public lesson or exemplar lesson are similar to Japanese Lesson Study while some researchers argue Chinese lesson study has multiple purposes and traditionally focused more on teacher performance (Han & Paine, 2010; Yang & Ricks, 2013).

[3] The information about Parallel Lesson Study can be found out in Huang and Han (2015).

[4] The teachers did not score the post-tests. The tests were collected for analysing and understanding the students' learning.

[5] Students in China start learning proportional relationship at Grade 5.

REFERENCES

Ashlock, R. D. (1990). *Error patterns in computation*. New York, NY: Macmillan.

Ball, D. L. (1990). Prospective elementary and secondary teachers' understanding of division. *Journal for Research in Mathematics Education, 21*, 132–144.

Barash, A., & Klein, R. (1996). Seventh grades students' algorithmic, intuitive and formal knowledge of multiplication and division of non negative rational numbers. In L. Puig & A. Gutierrez (Eds.), *Proceedings of the 20th conference of the International Group for the Psychology of Mathematics Education* (Vol. 2, pp. 35–42). Valencia, Spain: University of Valencia.

Borko, H. (2004). Professional development and teacher learning: mapping the terrain. *Educational Researcher, 33*(8), 3–15.

Borko, H., Eisenhart, M., Brown, C.A., Underhill, R., Jones. D., & Agard, P. (1992). Learning to teach hard mathematics: Do novice teachers and their instructors give up too easily? *Journal for Research in Mathematics Education, 23*, 194–222.

Carpenter, T. C., Lindquist, M. M., Brown, C. A., Kouba, V. L., Silver, E. A., & Swafford, J. O. (1988). Results of the fourth NAEP assessment of mathematics: Trends and conclusions. *Arithmetic Teacher, 36*(4), 38–41.

Cirillo, M. (2013). *What does research say the benefits of discussion in mathematics class are?* (Research Brief No. 19). Reston, VA: National Council of Teachers of Mathematics. Retrieved from http://www.blockfest.org/research-brief-19-benefit-of-discussion.pdf

Clements, D., Sarama, J., Spitler, M., Lange, A., & Wolfe, C. B. (2011). Mathematics learned by young children in an intervention based on learning trajectories: A large-scale cluster randomized trial. *Journal for Research in Mathematics Education, 42,* 127–166.

Cochran-Smith, M., & Lytle, S. (1999). Relationships of knowledge and practice: Teacher learning community. *Review of Research in Education, 24,* 249–305.

Cramer, K., Wyberg, T., & Leavitt, S. (2008). The role of representations in fraction addition and subtraction. *Mathematics Teaching in the Middle School, 13,* 490–496.

Darling-Hammond, L., Wei, R. C., Andree, A., Richardson, N., & Orphanos, S. (2009). *Professional learning in the learning profession: A status report on teacher development in the United States and abroad.* Dallas, TX: National Staff Development Council. Retrieved from http://learningforward.org/docs/pdf/nsdcstudy2009.pdf

Daro, P., Mosher, F., & Corcoran, T. (2011). *Learning trajectories in mathematics* (Research Report No. 68). Madison, WI: Consortium for Policy Research in Education.

Fendel, D. M. (1987). *Understanding the structure of elementary school mathematics.* Newton, MA: Allyn and Bacon.

Franke, M., Kazemi, E., Shih, J., Biagetti, S., & Battey, D. (2005). Changing teachers' professional work in mathematics: One school's journey. In T. A. Romberg, T. P. Carpenter, & F. Dremock (Eds.), *Understanding mathematics and science matters* (pp. 209–229). Mahwah, NJ: Lawrence Erlbaum Associations.

Freudenthal, H. (1991). *Revisiting mathematics education. China lectures.* Dordrecht: Kluwer Academic Publishers.

Garet, M. S., Porter, A. C., Desimone, L., Birman, B. F., & Yoon, K. S. (2001). What makes professional development effective? Results from a national sample of teachers. *American Educational Research Journal, 38,* 915–945.

Gearhart, M., Leveille Buchanan, N., Collett, J., Diakow, R., Kang, B., Saxe, G. B., & McGee, A. (2014). *Identifying opportunities to learn in mathematics discussions in heterogeneous elementary classrooms* (Unpublished manuscript). University of California, Berkeley, CA. Retrieved from http://www.culturecognition.com/lmr/sites/default/files/Identifying%20opportunities%20LMR%20June2014.pdf

Gu, F., & Gu, L. (2016). Characterizing mathematics teaching research mentoring in the context of Chinese lesson study. *ZDM Mathematics Education, 48,* 441–454.

Gu, L., Huang, R., & Marton, F. (2004). Teaching with variation: An effective way of mathematics teaching in China. In L. Fan, N. Y. Wong, J. Cai, & S. Li (Eds.), *How Chinese learn mathematics: Perspectives from insiders* (pp. 309–348). Singapore: World Scientific.

Grossman, P. L., Wineburg, S. S., & Woolworth, S. (2001). Toward a theory of teacher community. *Teachers College Record, 103,* 942–1012.

Han, X., & Paine, L. (2010). Teaching mathematics as deliberate practice through public lessons. *The Elementary School Journal, 110,* 519–541.

Hart, L. C., Alston, A. S., & Murata, A. (2011). *Lesson study research and practice in mathematics education: Learning together.* New York, NY: Springer.

Huang, R., & Bao, J. (2006). Towards a model for teacher's professional development in China: Introducing keli. *Journal of Mathematics Teacher Education, 9,* 279–298.

Huang, R., & Han, X. (2015). Improving teaching and enhancing teachers' growth through parallel lessons development: A Chinese approach. *International Journal for Lesson and Learning Studies, 4,* 100–117.

Huang, R., & Shimizu, Y. (2016). Improving teaching and learning, developing teachers and teacher developers, and linking theory and practice through lesson study in mathematics: An international perspective. *ZDM Mathematics Education, 48,* 393–409.

291

Huang, R., Su, H., & Xu, S. (2014). Developing teachers' and teaching researchers' professional competence in mathematics through Chinese Lesson Study. *ZDM Mathematics Education, 46,* 239–251.

Lewis, C., & Hurd, J. (2011). *Lesson study step by step: How teacher learning communities improve instruction.* Portsmouth, NH: Heinemann.

Lewis, C., & Perry, R. (2015). A randomized trial of lesson study with mathematical resource kits: Analysis of impact on teachers' beliefs and learning community. In J. Middleton, J. Cai, & S. Hwang (Eds.), *Large-scale studies in mathematics education* (pp. 133–158). Switzerland: Springer International Publishing.

Lewis, C., Perry, R., Friedkin, S., & Roth, J. (2012). Improving teaching does improve teachers: Evidence from lesson study. *Journal of Teacher Education, 63,* 368–375.

Little, J. W. (2002). Locating learning in teachers' communities of practice: Opening up problems of analysis in records of everyday work. *Teaching and Teacher Education, 18,* 917–46.

Lo, M. L., & Marton, F. (2012) Towards a science of the art of teaching: Using variation theory as a guiding principle of pedagogical design. *International Journal for Lesson and Learning Studies, 1,* 7–22.

Ma, L. P. (1999). *Knowing and teaching elementary mathematics.* Mahwah, NJ: Lawrence Erlbaum.

Marton, F. (2015). *Necessary conditions of learning.* London: Routledge.

Marton, F., & Pang, M. F. (2006). On some necessary conditions of learning. *The Journal of the Learning Science, 15,* 193–220.

McLaughlin, M. W., & Talbert, J. E. (2001). *Professional communities and the work of high school teaching.* Chicago, IL: The University of Chicago Press.

National Governors Association Center for Best Practices, Council of Chief State School Officers. (2010). *Common core state standards for mathematics.* Washington, DC: National Governors Association Center for Best Practices, Council of Chief State School Officers.

Ott, J. M., Snook, D. L., & Gibson, D. L. (1991). Understanding partitive division of fractions. *The Arithmetic Teacher, 39,* 7–11.

Payne, J. N. (1976). Review of research on fractions. In R. Lesh (Ed.), *Number and measurement* (pp. 145–188). Athens, GA: University of Georgia.

Perry, R. R., & Lewis, C. C. (2011). *Improving the mathematical content base of lesson study summary of results.* Oakland, CA: Mills College Lesson Study Group. Retrieved from http://www.lessonresearch.net/IESAbstract10.pdf

Perry, R., Lewis, C., Friedkin, S., & Baker, E. K. (2011). *Improving the mathematical content base of lesson study: Interim summary of results.* Retrieved from http://www.lessonresearch.net/IES%20Abstract_01.03.11.pdf

Petit, M., Laird, R. E., & Marsden, E. L. (2010). *A focus on fractions: Bringing research to the classroom.* New York, NY: Taylor & Francis.

Porter, A. C., Garet, M. S., Desimone, L. M., & Birman, B. F. (2003). Providing effective professional development: Lessons from the Eisenhower program. *Science Educator, 12*(1), 23–40.

Siegler, R., Carpenter, T., Fennell, F., Geary, D., Lewis, J., Okamoto, Y., Thompson, L., & Wray, J. (2010). *Developing effective fractions instruction for kindergarten through 8th grade: A practice guide* (NCEE#2010-4039). Washington, DC: National Center for Education Evaluation and Regional Assistance, Institute of Education Sciences, U.S. Department of Education. Retrieved from https://ies.ed.gov/ncee/wwc/pdf/practice_guides/fractions_pg_093010.pdf

Simon, M. A. (1995). Prospective elementary teachers' knowledge of division. *Journal for Research in Mathematics Education, 24,* 233–254.

Son, J. W., & Crespo, S. (2009). Prospective teachers' reasoning and response to a student's non-traditional strategy when dividing fractions. *Journal of Mathematics Teacher Education, 12,* 235–261.

Sowder, J., Sowder, L., & Nickerson, S. (2010). *Reconceptualizing mathematics for elementary school teachers.* New York, NY: W. H. Freeman & Company.

Stigler, J. W., & Hiebert, J. (1999). *The teaching gap: Best ideas from the world's teachers for improving education in the classroom.* New York, NY: Free Press.

Thomspon, P. W., & Saldanha, L. A. (2003). Fractions and multiplicative reasoning. In J. Kilpatrick, G. Martin, & D. Schifter (Eds.), *Research companion to the principles and standards for school mathematics* (pp. 95–114). Reston, VA: National Council of Teachers of Mathematics.

Tirosh, D. (2000). Enhancing prospective teachers' knowledge of children's conceptions: The case of division of fractions. *Journal for Research in Mathematics Education, 31,* 5–25.

Tirosh, D., Fishbein, E., Graeber, A., & Wilson, J. W. (1998). *Prospective elementary teachers' conceptions of rational numbers.* Retrieved from http://jwilson.coe.uga.edu/texts.folder/tirosh /pros.el.tchrs.html.

Van den Heuvel-Panhuizen, M. (2000). *Mathematics education in the Netherlands: A guided tour. Freudenthal Institute Cd-rom for ICME9.* Utrecht: Utrecht University.

Vergnaud, G. (1988). Multiplicative structures. In J. Hiebert & M. Behr (Eds.), *Number concepts and operations in the middle grades* (pp. 141–161). Reston, VA, NCTM.

Watson, A., & Mason, J. (2006). Seeing an exercise as a single mathematical object: Using variation to structure sense making. *Mathematical Thinking and Learning, 8*(2), 91–111.

Webb, N. M., Franke, M. L., Ing, M., Wong, J., Fernandez, C. H., Shin, N., & Turrou, A. C. (2014). Engaging with others' mathematical ideas: Interrelationships among student participation, teachers' instructional practices, and learning. *International Journal of Educational Research, 63,* 79–93.

Wilson, S. M., & Berne, J. (1999). Teacher learning and the acquisition of professional knowledge: An examination of research on contemporary professional development. In A. Iran-Nejad & P. D. Pearson (Eds.), *Review of research in education* (Vol. 24, pp. 173–209). Washington, DC: AERA.

Yang, Y., & Ricks, T. E. (2013). Chinese lesson study: Developing classroom instruction through collaborations in school-based teaching research group activities. In Y. Li & R. Huang (Eds.), *How Chinese teach mathematics and improve teaching* (pp. 51–65). New York, NY: Routledge.

Xue Han
National Louis University, Chicago, USA

ZiKun Gong
Hangzhou Normal University, Hangzhou, China

Rongjin Huang
Middle Tennessee State University, Murfreesboro, USA

PART IV

USE OF THE PEDAGOGY OF VARIATION
AROUND THE WORLD

DAVID CLARKE

INTRODUCTION

Putting Variation Theory to Work

The chapters in this section offer accounts of the application of Variation Theory in different contexts and for different purposes. The overarching message is that Variation Theory offers such an intuitively universal perspective (see Runesson & Kullberg) that it can be applied usefully to any instructional situation with the expectation that insight will follow. This demonstrable effectiveness of Variation Theory as a tool for analyzing pedagogical approaches has at least three implications:

- Variation Theory systematizes a *natural* (possibly inevitable) pedagogical inclination to vary aspects of the object of learning.[1]
- The *systematic structure* of Variation Theory and the associated vocabulary provide a powerful tool for the analysis of instruction.
- The productive applicability of Variation Theory to the four very different educational purposes discussed in these four chapters provides evidence of the *general utility* of Variation Theory.

Indeed, the chapters themselves are so artfully varied that it seems legitimate to consider how effectively the variation between chapters supports the learning of the reader, where "Variation Theory" is the object of learning. I therefore posed the question to myself, "How does the variation provided in the chapters contribute to our understanding of Variation Theory?" What follows is my answer to this question.

THE INDIVIDUAL CHAPTERS

Consider the chapters as elucidating "Variation Theory" through its varied application in specific educational settings. Each chapter varies with respect to originating country/school system, mathematical content addressed, instructional context explored, and in the aspect of variation theory that is foregrounded. It is useful for me to make these specific variations explicit in reference to each chapter.

The chapter by Hino utilizes variation theory to examine the Japanese problem solving approach to mathematics teaching. This chapter connects the pedagogy of variation with what are perceived to be effective practices in the Japanese education system. Three particular viewpoints are presented: (1) presenting problems with

R. Huang & Y. Li (Eds.), Teaching and Learning Mathematics through Variation, 297–300.

variation, (2) providing opportunities for students to construct variation themselves, and (3) promoting student reflection on variation toward the intended object of learning. On the basis of the application of these viewpoints to two primary mathematics lessons, implications for teaching through variation are discussed. Hino's approach is to articulate the basic features of Japanese problem solving pedagogy and identify elements that can be interpreted in terms of variation theory. Having identified structural elements of variation within the iconic Japanese problem solving instructional prototype, Hino illustrates the presence of these elements within two lessons on the comparison of fractions in fifth-grade.

Hino legitimately concludes "a structured problem solving lesson can be viewed from the perspective of variation" (p. 17). She identifies specific resonances between the Japanese prioritization of mathematical thinking and instructional strategies, such as procedural variation, made visible by the variational analysis. The chapter is full of rich examples of aspects of Japanese pedagogy made visible by consideration from the perspective of variation.

The chapter by Barlow et al. takes as its curricular setting the U.S. literature on the development of algebraic reasoning and integrates considerations of variation theory in the instructional use of carefully sequenced mathematical tasks. The specific focus is on the recognition and generalization of mathematical patterns facilitated through the selective variation of a single task parameter at a time ("in order to adhere to variation theory"). A distinctive emphasis is the statement that "the enacted objects of learning are described through the patterns of variation and invariation that were actually co-constructed by the teacher and the students." Variation Theory emerges as a powerful vehicle by which "U.S. algebra instruction" might better facilitate student transition from arithmetic to algebraic thinking.

Runesson and Kullberg open with the characterization of variation as a "taken for granted" aspect of mathematics instruction. The authors cite Sun (2011) as suggesting that "the idea of variation is almost invisible to teachers." Swedish "learning study" provides the two cases discussed in this chapter. The content focus was 8th grade division with positive denominators less than 1. Emphasis in the first case is on the collaborative design of mathematical tasks to facilitate student learning about division. A second case examines an individual teacher's lessons on the same topic two years apart. Despite evident changes in sequence and patterns of variation, the teacher's discussion of his instruction, "did not talk about variation at all." The principal message of the chapter is that Swedish Learning Study, predicated on the principles of variation theory, provides a structure by which implicit teacher knowing can "become visible, reflected upon and developed."

The chapter by Peled and Leiken contrasts two instructional approaches, characterized by two task types: Multiple Solution Tasks (MSTs) and Modeling Tasks (MTs). Peled and Leiken employ "multiplicity" as a common dimension by which to connect and compare the two approaches. "Multiplicity of mathematical tasks at two levels (pedagogical approaches and solution methods)" becomes a surrogate for "Variation Theory", and insight arises from comparison of the "nature and goals of these two multiplicities." For the reader, seeking to understand Variation Theory, the two approaches can be seen as offering useful differences in perspective; demonstrating the benefits of within-task variation, while simultaneously making comparison between two variant applications of the general instructional principle of multiple solutions. As with the other chapters, the object of learning is, in fact, Variation Theory, about which more becomes known through its separate consideration in the contexts of MST and MT use.

SOME GENERAL REMARKS

I have argued elsewhere that comparison is fundamental to the act of research (Clarke, 2015) and perhaps a fundamental aspect of what it means to be human. It seems to me, given the evident universal utility of Variation Theory as a lens by which to interrogate both instruction and learning, that not only is the developing capacity to discern identical with learning (Marton & Booth, 1997), but also the promotion of that discernment is encrypted in almost every instructional act. Runesson and Kullberg's account of Mr B's instructional development suggests this. Hadamard is reputed to have said, "The purpose of mathematical proof is to legitimize the conquests of intuition." In the same way, Variation Theory may represent the formalization of something so fundamental to learning and instruction as to be both intuitive and invisible. The suggestion of the chapters in this section is that Variation Theory makes visible a fundamental aspect of learning, systematizes it, and renders it visible for reflection and instructional optimization. The diversity of contexts provided by the chapters and the different emphases employed by the authors provide a form of meta-validation of the effectiveness of variation in elaborating the object of learning: in this case, Variation Theory itself. The chapters are scholarly, lucid and purposeful. Their combination has a value that transcends even the sum of their individual worth. Of course, that is what Variation Theory would lead us to expect. I commend them to your careful consideration.

NOTE

[1] Instructional methods without variation might be classified as catechistic and associated with the verbatim memorisation of sacred or culturally significant text. Such memorisation can serve legitimate educational purposes and should not be dismissed as valueless. However, the educational purposes that motivate variation can be treated separately for the purpose of this discussion.

REFERENCES

Clarke, D. J. (2015). The role of comparison in the construction and deconstruction of boundaries. In K. Krainer & N. Vondrova (Eds.), *Proceedings of the Ninth Congress of the European Society for Research in Mathematics Education (CERME9)* (pp. 1702–1708). Prague, Czech Republic: Charles University (ISBN: 978-80-7290-844-8).

Marton, F., & Booth, S. (1997). *Learning and awareness*. Mahwah, NJ: Lawrence Erlbaum Associates.
Sun, X. (2011). "Variation problems" and their roles in the topic of fraction division in Chinese mathematics textbook examples. *Educational Studies in Mathematics, 76*(1), 65–85.

David Clarke
University of Melbourne, Australia

KEIKO HINO

14. IMPROVING TEACHING THROUGH VARIATION

A Japanese Perspective

INTRODUCTION

International comparisons of classroom practices promote the growth of research on the design of classroom tasks, principles for organizing lessons, and ways of structuring classroom discourse to support students' understanding and thinking (e.g., Clarke, Emanuelsson, Jablonka, & Mok, 2006; Clarke, Keitel, & Shimizu, 2006; Hiebert et al., 2003; Li & Shimizu, 2009; Shimizu & Kaur, 2013; Stigler & Hiebert, 1999; Watson & Ohtani, 2015). Teaching through variation is an increasingly prominent method that provides a framework for effective mathematics teaching and learning (e.g., Gu, Huang, & Marton, 2004; Watson & Mason, 2006; Wong, 2008; Wong, Lam, & Chan, 2013). The fundamental principle of teaching through variation is that the learners experience and discern the critical features of the intended object of learning through completing a series of tasks in which some parts vary while others do not (Runesson, 2005). In particular, this method has been used and studied vigorously in mathematics instruction in China (e.g., Gu, Huang, & Marton, 2004; Wong, 2008). This chapter connects the pedagogy of variation with what are perceived to be effective practices in one education system. Such an attempt will contribute to a systematic examination of the pedagogy of variations, which goes beyond what is valued in China and is one of the issues addressed in this book.

THE JAPANESE PROBLEM SOLVING APPROACH

Teaching Mathematics through Problem Solving

Teaching mathematics through problem solving is a widely preferred method within the community of mathematics educators in Japan. Generally, mathematics teaching is associated with solving mathematics problems (Hiebert et al., 2003), but quite often, solving problems is regarded as the application of knowledge acquired in a lesson. In Japan, having students solve problems is deeply connected with the goal of fostering mathematical thinking, which has been the goal of mathematics education for more than 50 years. Here solving problems is not only regarded as application of

R. Huang & Y. Li (Eds.), Teaching and Learning Mathematics through Variation, 301–320.

learned knowledge but also used as a vehicle for imparting new knowledge (Hino, 2007).

To effectively teach mathematics through problem solving in the classroom, it is crucial to provide students with worthwhile tasks and to engage them in active mathematical thinking. It is equally critical to organize the lessons in such a way that students can experience the problem solving process. These two facets continue to attract the interest of mathematics educators in Japan (Hino, 2007).

Investigation of mathematics problems that demand higher-order thinking as well as arouse student interest has been a major issue of *Kyozaikenkyu* (instructional materials research) in lesson study. In this regard, a well-known undertaking is the development of open-ended problems, or problems with multiple correct answers. This approach originated in the research on the evaluation of higher-order thinking conducted by Shimada and his colleagues at the beginning of the 1970s (Becker & Shimada, 1997). Their investigation encouraged mathematics educators to exploit a more varied range of teaching materials and ways of organizing lessons (e.g., Nohda, 1983; Takeuchi & Sawada, 1984). The idea of openness in teaching and evaluation has developed and expanded in various ways since then.

Investigations into effective lesson organization for the purpose of deepening students' understanding and fostering mathematical thinking were already prevalent in the 1960s (e.g., Sugita Elementary School, 1964). Mathematics educators studied the seminal works of Polya and Poincaré and sought to develop ways to help students discover new ideas and construct knowledge on their own. They incorporated Polya's four phases of problem solving (understanding the problem, devising a plan, carrying out the plan, and looking back) into the organization of mathematics lessons. Sugiyama and Ito (1990, p. 155) described the rationale for sequencing lessons in this way as follows:

> To have students experience problem solving means more than letting them solve the problem at hand. It means having them learn *how to think* and *how to overcome difficulty* and having them experience the desire, effort, struggle, joy, and so on in the process of solving the problem. In order to achieve this, it is important for teachers to help students:
>
> 1. Build confidence and experience the joy of being able to find a preliminary solution to the problem by fully drawing on their own knowledge, and
> 2. Appreciate more fully elaborated solution methods, and experience the joy of continuously searching for better ways. (emphasis in original)

For students to go through the intended process of problem solving, the teacher's role was considered crucial. With respect to teachers' questioning, Katagiri (1988) examined the mathematical thinking used in each stage of problem solving and developed a list of questions that would foster students' mathematical thinking in the classroom. Koto et al. (1992, 1998) suggested principles for organizing discussions after students found preliminary solutions by drawing on their own knowledge. They proposed three stages: *examination of the validity of each solution*, *examination of the relationship between solutions*, and *self-determination of better solutions*. Teachers were advised to organize discussions by thoughtfully considering the multiple types of solutions that the class should deal with to achieve the lesson objective (see also Hino, 2015).

Thus, mathematics educators in Japan generally believe that letting students experience the process of problem solving is an excellent way of fostering mathematical thinking and recognizing its value. They also acknowledge the crucial role of teachers to realize this goal in the classroom.

Features of Structured Problem Solving Approaches

The Japanese problem solving approach became widely known through the Trends in International Mathematics and Science Study (TIMSS) videotape studies on mathematics lessons. In their investigation of eighth-grade mathematics lessons in Germany, Japan, and the United States, Stigler and Hiebert (1999, pp. 79–80) described the Japanese lesson pattern as a sequence of five activities:

- Reviewing the previous lesson,
- Presenting the problem for the day,
- Students working individually or in groups,
- Discussing solution methods, and
- Highlighting and summarizing the major points.

A distinct feature of the Japanese lesson pattern, when compared with those of the other two countries, was that presenting a problem set the stage for students to work on developing solution procedures. Stigler and Hiebert (1999) called this pattern *structured problem solving*. In contrast, other students worked on problems only after the teacher demonstrated how to solve them (in the U.S.) or after the teacher directed students to develop procedures for solving the problem (in Germany). Stigler and Hiebert contended that these cultural scripts for teaching were grounded on beliefs about the nature of the subject, about how students learn, and about the role that a teacher should play, all of which served to maintain the stability of cultural systems (pp. 89–90).

Further comparative studies on mathematics classrooms across countries have clarified that Japanese classrooms are distinguished by teachers' intentional guidance of students through their multiple solutions to the mathematical task. In the Learner's Perspective Study (LPS) (Clarke, Keitel, & Shimizu, 2006), eighth-grade mathematics lessons taught by competent teachers from 16 participating countries were analyzed from various perspectives. The results in the three Japanese classrooms repeatedly showed the teachers offering intentional guidance in response to their students' multiple solutions, in the form of posing additional questions or summarizing the lesson (Koizumi, 2013; Shimizu, 2006). Funahashi and Hino (2014) further described the teacher's role in drawing out and extending students' thinking toward achieving the lesson's objectives through an interactional pattern called the *guided focusing pattern*.

Another feature, closely related to those explained above, is lesson coherence, which refers to the connectedness or relatedness of the mathematics within and across the lessons. Stigler and Hiebert (1999), in their three-country comparison study, used coherence as an indicator of mathematical content in lessons. One way in which they measured coherence was by whether the teacher explicitly pointed out connections among the ideas and activities. In this regard, only Japanese teachers were found to routinely link the parts of a lesson together. Moreover, they examined the mathematical connections between segments of lessons by delineating how a given segment was similar to, dependent on, or extended to the previous segment mathematically. Among 30 analyzed lessons in each country, they reported the percentage of lessons in which all segments were connected through at least one appropriate mathematical relationship as 45% in the U.S, 76% in Germany, and 92% in Japan. These were considered as the lessons that "told a single story" (Stigler & Hiebert, 1999, p. 64). Similar results were obtained by the TIMSS 1999 video study that compared lessons in seven countries (Hiebert et al., 2003).

Several Japanese researchers have explored the idea of a story or a drama as a metaphor for an excellent Japanese lesson. Shimizu (2009) pointed out that some key pedagogical terms shared by Japanese teachers have their roots in a story or a drama. One such term is *Yamaba*, or the climax of a lesson. Another is *Ki-Sho-Ten-Ketsu*, which describes the particular structure of a lesson's flow from the beginning (*Ki*) toward the end (*Ketsu* means a summary of the whole story). The implication of these terms is that a lesson should have a beginning, reach a climax during the whole-class discussion, and then arrive at a conclusion. Shimizu further pointed out that the highlight or climax should be based on students' active participation and that teachers guide students to process and reflect on the methods by which a problem is solved. He summarized these aspects by stating that "a coherence of the entire lesson composed of several segments, students' involvement in each part of the lesson, and the reflection of what they did are all to be noted for the quality instruction in Japanese classrooms" (p. 314).

Okazaki, Kimura, and Watanabe (2015) examined the coherence of mathematics lessons from the viewpoint of the genesis and development of students' learning goals. They inquired as to the generation of the coherent plot of a lesson, in which the students were the protagonists of the story. Four levels of student-established learning goals were set and used for the analysis of two mathematics lessons. The results showed that in both lessons, the initial learning goals emerged from the student and were then enhanced by the teachers during the activity of discussing solution methods. The authors concluded that "a lesson can become coherent when the students' learning goal gradually develops in terms of its level and when there are fruitful interactions for connecting and reflecting on ideas" (Okazaki et al., 2015, p. 407). Teachers and students collaboratively set and refine the learning goal by connecting and reflecting on their previous experiences.

THE JAPANESE PROBLEM SOLVING APPROACH VIEWED
FROM THE PERSPECTIVE OF VARIATION

Variation Theory

Variation theory accounts for differences in learning and provides a way to describe the conditions necessary for learning (Marton & Booth, 1997; Marton et al., 2004; Runesson, 2006). According to this theory, learning is defined as "a change in the way something is seen, experienced or understood" (Runesson, 2005, p. 70). What the learner experiences or sees in the situation is critical. The theory regards learning as being aware of critical aspects of the object (e.g., a situation or a problem). For learning to take place, the learner must develop the capability to discern certain aspects that are critical to a specific way of seeing the object. Therefore, the theory positions the *object of learning* as its center.

In classroom learning, three types of objects of learning are distinguished. The *intended object of learning* is the capabilities that the teacher wants students to develop. The *enacted object of learning* is the object that is co-constituted in the interaction among the class members and afforded to the learners. Finally, the *lived object of learning* denotes what the learner actually learned. Whereas the intended object of learning is a product of the teacher's awareness, the enacted object of learning is what the students encounter and defines "what it is possible to learn in the actual setting, from the point of view of the specific object of learning" (Marton & Tsui, 2004, p. 4). Therefore, even if the intended object of learning is the same in two instructional settings, differences in the enacted objects result in crucial differences in the opportunities for student learning.

With regard to the enacted object of learning, the theory is used to analyze what the student experiences in the process of learning. In other words, it examines what aspects or features come to the forefront of the student's attention and are discerned. It further examines how the student discriminates and differentiates the features, discerns certain aspects simultaneously, makes relations among them, and gains richer understanding. In order to discern certain aspects or features, variations that appear within the experience can play a central role. It is impossible to discern an aspect unless we experience a variation in that aspect. Therefore, for learning to take place, one necessary condition is to provide the students with the possibility of experiencing for themselves certain patterns of variation and invariance of these features in the critical aspects of the object (Lo & Marton, 2012).

The patterns and dimensions of variation and invariance discerned by the student form a space for learning. This term denotes the whole of what the student can possibly learn from the lesson (Marton et al., 2004). The space of learning is not the situation per se, but the "potential for learning offered in terms of variation and invariance opened in the situation" (Runesson, 2006, p. 403). It is not predetermined but created by the learner. Through his or her inquiry into the situation, the learner opens up a space for the dimensions of variation, which are different features critical for a particular learning.

Conceptual Variation and Procedural Variation

Variation theory underpins the Chinese mathematics teaching method called *teaching with variation*, which "intends to illustrate the essential features by demonstrating different forms of visual materials and instances or highlight the essence of a concept by varying the nonessential features" (Gu, 1999, cited by Gu, Huang, & Marton, 2004, p. 315). Teaching with variation has occurred for a long time in Chinese classrooms, either consciously or intuitively. For several decades, Chinese researchers have made explicit the principles of this method of teaching.

Gu et al. (2004) identified two types of variations that exist within the practice of teaching with variation. One is *conceptual variation*, which encompasses two ways of creating variation: "varying connotation of concept" and "varying instances which confuse the connotation of concept" (p. 315). For the former, in order to induce abstract mathematical concepts, variations are created in visual and concrete items, such as visual models experienced in daily life, or figures and diagrams. For the latter, to highlight the essential features of the concept, nonessential features are varied through providing non-standard figures or counterexamples. In this way, conceptual variation aims to help students understand concepts from multiple perspectives.

The other type of variation is *procedural variation*. Here, procedure means *process*, or dynamic knowledge of problem solving and meta-cognitive strategies (Gu et al., 2004, p. 319). According to Gu et al., this is the aspect that extends the concept of variation, helping students to arrive at solutions to a problem by forming different processes and connections between the known problem and unknown problems. Procedural variation aims at providing a process for formulating the concept stage by stage. Gu et al. stated that "the richness and effectiveness of the process system are important for upgrading cognitive structure" (2004, p. 324).

Gu et al. (2004) distinguished three dimensions of problem solving for the purpose of constructing student experience through procedural variations. The first dimension is *varying a problem*. This includes using the original problem as a basis for scaffolding, or extending the original problem by varying the conditions, changing the results, and making generalizations. The second dimension is *varying the process*, which involves producing multiple methods of solving a problem and associating them with each other. The third dimension is *varying the application* of a method by applying the same method to a group of similar problems.

Huang and Leung (2005) analyzed a well-taught Shanghai lesson by using this framework. The teacher was described as unfolding the lesson smoothly by following a deliberate design in a seemingly teacher-dominated manner. Both conceptual variation and procedural variation were demonstrated during the lesson. Conceptual variation was observed in the phases of forming new concepts and of consolidating and memorizing the concept. Procedural variation was observed in the phases of reviewing previous knowledge, introducing a new concept, consolidating the new concept, developing a method to solve problems with the new concept, and preparing for further learning. The researchers pointed out that the two types of variations were created alternatively for different purposes of experiencing the enacted object of learning.

Variation in Structured Problem Solving Lessons

As described in a previous section, problems used in the lesson and ways of organizing the lesson are two crucial facets of Japanese problem solving. Furthermore, the lesson pattern of structured problem solving constitutes a distinct feature of organizing the lesson. As described, high-quality mathematics instruction in Japan has several aspects that are connected with structured problem solving. Below, a quality mathematics lesson with structured problem solving is examined from the perspective of variation. Specifically, three viewpoints are presented to show how teachers use variations strategically to create a rich space for learning in the lesson.

The first viewpoint concerns *presenting problems with variation*. Developing rich problems aimed at lesson objectives is an important part of lesson construction. Here, teachers use variation in the problem and examine the affordance of learning by changing the nature of variations (Sekiguchi, 2008). For example, to introduce the method of composing or decomposing numbers into tens in addition with whole numbers, first-grade teachers carefully consider variation in numbers. When students are presented with the problem "9 + 4," they will be led more naturally to make 10 by adding 1 to the 9 than students who are presented with "8 + 6." In some cases, however, teachers may use "8 + 6" from the outset, if they want to encourage a range of student thinking by allowing the application of different strategies. As noted above, Gu et al. (2004) distinguished three dimensions of problem solving through procedural variation; a teacher considers his or her intention and decides how to manipulate each of these dimensions in the problems. In structured problem solving, usually a small number of problems is covered in a lesson. However, those problems are carefully developed and sequenced to realize rich paths of learning toward the intended object of learning.

The second viewpoint concerns *providing opportunities for students to construct variation themselves*. The deliberately chosen problems often take the form of open-ended questions. Students are first requested to approach the problem in their own way by drawing on their knowledge. This phase produces variations in students' ways of solving the problem, which may be idiosyncratic, unsophisticated, or even erroneous. These variations then become the object of attention in the discussion phase, during which students are asked to explain their thinking and the reasons behind it. Variations in students' explanations are indispensable in the process of refining the solutions and approaches to make them more sophisticated and integrated through extensive whole-class discussion (Shimizu, 1999). A teacher anticipates these variations when planning the sequence of problems. Involving students in the activity of constructing variations is vitally important in the structured problem solving lesson.

In a structured problem solving lesson, a teacher guides students toward the intended object of learning by promoting their reflection on the variations they have constructed. Therefore, the third viewpoint concerns *promoting students' reflection on variation toward the intended object of learning.* This viewpoint especially applies to the discussion phase, as students compare and contrast proposed variations in thinking and find ideas that integrate them, identify the relationship among them, or create and justify better ways (Hino, 2015; Koto et al., 1992). These discursive activities contain the act of reflection because they include critically examining the obtained solutions, drawing on self-knowledge for further inquiry, and constructing arguments, alternatives, or suggestions (Polya, 1985). The teacher plays an important role in guiding the students toward the intended object of learning through their reflection on variations. Funahashi and Hino (2014) pointed out the importance of the teacher controlling students' focus of attention by identifying important ideas on which to focus, proposing another focus when necessary, and modifying or improving students' focus.

Sekiguchi (2012) analyzed LPS data from three Japanese classrooms with respect to how they coordinated coherence and variation in their lessons. In the analysis, he identified different types of key questions to encourage students to reflect on their experiences of variations:

- Classifying or isolating (e.g., which ones look similar?)
- Noticing (e.g., what differences or similarities do you notice?)
- Comparing and contrasting (e.g., what is different?)
- Evaluating (e.g., which one is more efficient?)

These are conceived as key instructional actions to direct students' reflections toward the intended object of learning. Nevertheless, how to encourage students' discernment of a critical feature while they construct variation is an important theme of Japanese lesson study.

In summary, the three viewpoints—presenting problems with variation, providing opportunities for students to construct variation themselves, and promoting students' reflection on variation toward the intended object of learning—are highlighted when we look at a structured problem solving lesson from the perspective of variation. In the next section, these viewpoints are used to analyze mathematics lessons in a primary school classroom.

VARIATION IN MATHEMATICS CLASSROOMS: A CASE STUDY OF COMPARING THREE FRACTIONS

Outline of the Two Lessons

This case study comes from two consecutive fifth-grade lessons on comparing fractions. The lessons were taught by Mr. Taka (all the names used in this chapter are pseudonyms) in 2010 in a university-affiliated primary school in Tokyo. There were 38 students in the classroom. The duration of one primary school lesson in Japan is 45 minutes. The lessons were conducted as part of the Learner's Perspective Study—Primary (LPS-P) (Fujii, 2013; Shimizu, 2011). The lessons analyzed in this chapter are the first two in a series of 16 lessons on the topic of addition and subtraction with unlike denominators. Drawing on the methodology from the earlier LPS (Clarke, 2006), the LPS-P collected data from the lessons and from interviews with the teacher and four focus students.

The objectives of these two lessons were to understand that fractions can be compared if a common "unit fraction" is found and to understand the reasons for comparing fractions by finding a common denominator or numerator. In the teacher interview, Mr. Taka emphasized repeatedly the idea of finding a common unit fraction because once it is found, one can compare the fractions and add or subtract fractions in the same way as was previously learned with whole numbers. He said that these concepts connect with building students' understanding of fractions as numbers. In his teaching, Mr. Taka consistently focused on the "unit" or "unit fraction."

In these two lessons, a situation of comparing three quantities, 2/4L, 3/4L, and 2/3L, was given. Table 1 shows the implemented flow of the lessons. In Lesson 1, the students compared 2/4L and 3/4L first and then 2/4L and 2/3L. In Lesson 2, after reviewing Lesson 1, the students compared 3/4L and 2/3L.

Analysis of the Lessons from Variation Perspectives

Presenting problems with variation. Since these lessons served as an introduction to the topic of fractions with unlike denominators, Mr. Taka chose the three fractions carefully to represent three variations of fractions:

a. Different numerator, same denominator (2/4 and 3/4)
b. Same numerator, different denominator (2/4 and 2/3)
c. Different numerator, different denominator (3/4 and 2/3)

The students had learned to add and subtract fractions with like denominators in earlier grades. Therefore, they could compare fractions of type A easily. Type B is newer and would require additional thinking; Type C is completely new to the students. By presenting these variations of fraction comparisons, Mr. Taka attempted to connect students' previous knowledge and new knowledge. Mr. Taka began the lesson by writing 2/4L, 3/4L, and 2/3L on the blackboard and posed an open-ended question: "Which one is bigger? What do you notice at a glance?" He encouraged the students to speak up freely. A student responded that 2/4L < 3/4L (type A). After some discussion, another student said that 3/4 > 2/3 (type C). Mr. Taka postponed the student's thinking until Lesson 2 by stressing "at a glance" in his question. Therefore, quite naturally, the class proceeded to discuss type A and then type B in Lesson 1, and type C in Lesson 2. The variation of these problems is shown in Figure 1, in a similar way as the illustration of procedural variation as scaffolding for problem solving in Gu et al. (2004).

309

Table 1. The flow of the lesson on comparing three fractions

Activity	Phase	Content of activity
Lesson 1		
"Which one is bigger?" Looking at the fractions and finding explanations	Presenting the problem Discussing the solutions	The teacher wrote a problem on the blackboard, "Which one is bigger? 2/4L, 2/3L, or 3/4L." He asked the students to judge at a glance. Through interaction between the teacher and the students, they discussed 2/4 < 3/4 and 2/4 < 2/3 by proposing several explanations.
Explaining why we need 12 to compare 2/4 and 2/3	Focusing on the problem Working individually Discussing the multiple solutions	In one of the explanations, a student used "12" as the least common multiple of 3 and 4. The teacher posed a question regarding the reason for using 12. He made the students write the reason for using 12 in their notebooks so that everyone could fully understand it. Later, other students presented different explanations.
Summarizing what we found today	Summarizing the lesson	On the basis of the students' explanations above, the teacher summarized that we cannot compare the fractions unless the unit fractions are common between the two fractions.
Lesson 2		
Reviewing Lesson 1	Reviewing the previous lesson	The teacher and the students reviewed the reasons for 2/4 < 3/4 and 2/4 < 2/3.
Comparing 2/3 and 3/4	Discussing a solution	The class dealt with the comparison between 2/3 and 3/4, which had been postponed. One student presented 2/3 < 3/4 by noticing the difference between the fraction and 1. By proving her explanation, the class reached the consensus that they can compare fractions if either numerators or denominators are the same.

Activity	Phase	Content of activity
Comparing 2/3 and 3/4 by finding common numerator or denominator.	Presenting the problem Working individually Discussing solution methods	The teacher asked the students to compare 2/3 and 3/4 by the other methods, namely, by finding a common numerator or denominator. After working individually for about six minutes, two students presented their solutions. One student's solution of finding a common numerator was examined, and in the discussion, several students further explained its plausibility.
Summarizing today's lesson	Summarizing the lesson	On the basis of the students' explanations, the teacher summarized that in order to make two equivalent fractions, they need to multiply both numerator and denominator by the same number.

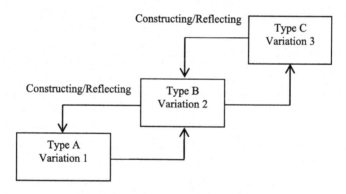

Figure 1. Variation in the lesson on comparing three pairs of fractions

The variations in the problems had specific intentions. Type A and type B comparisons were intended to promote students' awareness of the value of finding a common unit fraction when comparing two fractions. Here, awareness means that the students recognize what they have done in the act of comparing fractions, not that they are discovering some novel phenomenon. The purpose of type C comparison was to further promote the students' clearer understanding of this idea. In addition, Mr. Taka emphasized the connection between type C and the other two types by enlightening students' application of the idea to the type C comparison. In this way, type A and B comparisons were used as scaffolding for the type C comparison.

Providing opportunities for students to construct variation themselves. In the two lessons, Mr. Taka provided several opportunities for the students to construct variation. For types B and C, Mr. Taka requested the students to develop clear explanations of the reason for their judgments. Thus, multiple explanations using different representations were abundant in these lessons. Importantly, the students constructed alternative explanations by attempting to supplement or modify the previous explanations given by their peers.

In Lesson 1, two occasions arose in which the students proposed multiple explanations. The first was when they discussed the reasons why $2/4 < 2/3$. The other occasion resulted from focusing on one of the explanations given by a student, who explained her reasoning for $2/4 < 2/3$ by using 12, the least common multiple of 3 and 4. Mr. Taka posed his question regarding the reason for using 12 and requested the students to write down the reason. On these occasions, the students' various reasonings were refined toward more viable understandings with a clearer focus on the idea of finding a common unit fraction.

In Lesson 2, when the class engaged in the activity of comparing 2/3 and 3/4, there were two instances in which student solutions became the object of discussion. The students again improved their explanations, and this process contributed to clarifying the meaning of finding a common numerator or denominator.

Below, one occasion is presented in which the students constructed variations in their reasoning with regard to the comparison of two fractions. When the students and the teacher discussed the reason why $2/4 < 2/3$ in Lesson 1, one student explained, "The numerator is the same. If we compare two [parts] of what we divided into four and two [parts] of what we divided into three, 2/3 is larger." At this point, Mr. Taka asked the students if anyone could give additional detail. Then five students proposed explanations by way of attempting to make the reasoning clearer and more detailed:

C1: The one that is divided into three [is larger], because the area of one part is larger, so we know 2/3L is larger.

C2: I used a figure. (C2 represented 2/4 and 2/3 visually by drawing two cups on the blackboard.) Two of four equal parts are this part, and … 2/3L means, well, divide this into three equal parts, and take two of them, they are here. (Mr. Taka added lines and made Figure 2.)

C3: (when asked to explain the relationship between C2 and C1's explanations): Well, the area of one part is this part. (She colored the 1/4 part red as shown in Figure 2.) For this one, this is the part. (She colored the 1/3 part red in the same way.) (Mr. Taka asked C1 if this was what she had intended to say.)

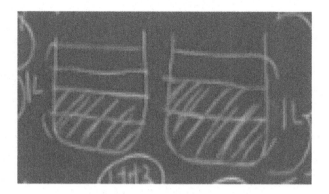

Figure 2. A figure by C2

C4: Mine is easier to know the difference than C2's figure. (Mr. Taka drew Figure 3 on the blackboard by looking at C4's notebook.) The least common multiple between 3 and 4 is 12. So, I divided a rectangle into 12. I connected 12 blocks. This is one block (pointing to 1/12 part). (Mr. Taka marked it with red chalk and wrote "a block.") For 2/4, I divided the blocks into 4 chunks, and 1, 2, well, I marked here (pointing at the area of 2/4 in Figure 3). (She explained 2/3 in the same way.) Then we know that 2/3 is larger by the difference of 2 blocks. (Mr. Taka drew a dotted line.)

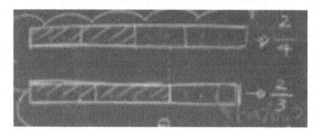

Figure 3. A figure by C4

C5: (drawing two circles on the blackboard): These are the same size. (C5 showed 2/4 and 3/4 in the circles.) ... C1 said the area of one part; 2/4 is two of four divided parts (marking the parts in yellow as shown in Figure 4); 2/3 is two of three-divided parts (marking the parts). C1's area of one part is here and here (marking the area). For 2/3, the shape of area of one part is larger, so we know 2/3 is larger. I can use this method for other fractions such as 2/4 or 3/4.

The students' utterances show that C1 stated the words "area of one part" to make the previous explanation clearer. Then C2 explained the "area of one part" by

313

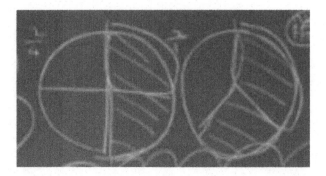

Figure 4. A figure by C5

drawing two cups, and C3 emphasized it by using red chalk. C4 supplemented the previous discussion by proposing a different new perspective. Finally, C5 further clarified the "area of one part" by drawing another representation. The student drew a circle because he thought that a circle showed the difference of two areas more clearly than a cup. With some prompts for clarification by Mr. Taka, the students proposed multiple explanations one after another.

Promoting students' reflection on variation toward the intended object of learning. The students' reflection on the varied reasoning was intimately linked to their activity of construction. As illustrated in the episode above, this is because the students constructed alternative explanations by attempting to supplement or modify the previous explanations given by their peers. Mr. Taka also played an important role in guiding their process of refining their explanations. He checked the chain of reasoning, sometimes negotiated it, and occasionally summarized what they had reached as a consensus.

Through the students' active involvement in constructing and reflecting on explanations of the reasons for their judgments, they were provided with ample opportunity to discern critical features of the intended object of learning. Nevertheless, Mr. Taka was consistently checking whether the students made sense of the idea of finding common unit fractions when comparing two fractions. He was especially sensitive to whether the students paid attention to the meaning.

For example, in Lesson 1, after the discussion of $2/4 < 2/3$, Mr. Taka questioned C4's use of 12: "I really don't understand why this 12 comes out." He took time to write their explanations as to the reason for the necessity of 12. When the students presented their reasons, one said, "We must make the denominators the same number. Twelve is the number that divides both three and four evenly. So I used 12." Mr. Taka asked for clarification: "Why must you make the denominators the same?" and the discussion continued. In the teacher interview conducted after the lesson, Mr. Taka described his dissatisfaction with the students' superficial understanding when they simply made calculations without thinking much about their meaning. He also said that he wanted the students to verbalize that they need to divide the whole into 12 equal parts to "make the areas of one part the same size."

Similar opportunity for discussion was observed in Lesson 2. When a student explained the method of finding the common numerator to compare 2/3 and 3/4, she said that 2/3 and 4/6 are in a proportional relationship. Mr. Taka posed a question: "Is it a proportional relationship? Why do you need to multiply the denominator by two if you multiply the numerator by two?" He requested the students to clarify this point by using figures. In this way, Mr. Taka grasped the quality of students' reasoning from their verbal and written expressions, and he reacted in various ways to improve their reasoning, such as questioning, probing, clarifying, or asking for additional alternative expressions or elaboration.

Mr. Taka also guided the students toward the intended object of learning by encouraging connections with the previous activity and learning. When comparing 2/3 and 3/4, a student proposed her method of finding the difference between each fraction and 1. After the explanation, Mr. Taka asked the students whether this method was different from the method of finding a common denominator or numerator that they had been using. At first the students did not notice the relationship between the two ways. One of them replied, "I think this has nothing to do with that. The other method is an easy one because the numerator or denominator is the same, but this one is about the difference." Mr. Taka gave a prompt, "Yes, but after that the method compares 1/4 and 1/3, doesn't it? [It compares] which result is larger. So it compares the remaining amount, 1/4 and 1/3." Then several students came to recognize the similarity between the two ways. A student said, "1/4 and 1/3. Yeah, I think it probably has something to do with … ." Then another student gave a clearer reason: "1/4 and 1/3 have the same numerator. So it has a relationship with the fact that we can compare fractions if either the numerator or the denominator is common."

Rich and consistent connections between the tasks and the activities were an invariable feature of Mr. Taka's lessons. Mr. Taka said in the interview that, for him, a good lesson involved the process of elaborating incomplete solutions into the complete one by adding different opinions. This feature was also heard in the student perspectives. In the interviews conducted after each lesson, four students were asked about their significant learning events as they reviewed a video of the lesson. They primarily chose moments when they were listening to their peers' comments. At these points, they were relating their classmates' solutions and reasons with their own, as also exhibited by the eighth-grade students in Hino's (2015) study. The students also chose moments when their peers remembered and used the ideas that they had learned some time ago. For example, Katsu said, "He said 'proportional relationship.' That is a word that we learned in the first semester, a long time ago. He made use of it in today's lesson. I thought, 'Oh, that's great,' because he used what we had learned before." Moreover, all four students described, as part of their experience, their positive expectation of connections within the lesson and between the lessons:

Nami: This is the way we do mathematics in the classroom. Someone proposes an idea, then everyone else adds to the idea, and we connect one after another.

Koma: I like the lessons in which everyone proposes ideas, connects them, and derives conclusions. In today's lesson, we have not yet reached a good conclusion, but everyone proposed ideas, so I think today's lesson was good.

Katsu: (when asked about connections): For example, if the ideas [expressed] today will connect to the solutions we will use in the next semester ... if we connect different types of thinking and think more, then the solutions in the previous lessons are helpful.

Fuji: When I was thinking of comparing 3/4L and 2/3L, I looked at my notebook and reviewed the methods we used in the previous lesson. Then I thought that C2's way of using cups and C5's way of using circles are good because they can be used everywhere.

The students made positive comments on the rich connectivity realized with their peers through the support of their classroom teacher.

DISCUSSION AND CONCLUSIONS

The research question of this chapter referred to exploring types of variation that teachers use strategically in structured problem solving lessons. To answer this question, three viewpoints were developed by synthesizing Japanese problem solving with the variation theory and teaching with variation. The three viewpoints were presenting problems with variation, providing opportunities for students to construct variation themselves, and promoting students' reflection on variation toward the intended object of learning. The viewpoints highlight how the teacher and the students collaboratively enacted objects of learning in the lesson by experiencing and discerning the critical features of the intended object of learning.

These viewpoints were applied to two primary mathematics lessons conducted by an experienced Japanese teacher. To achieve the lesson objectives, the teacher incorporated variation into the problems. Although the number of problems was small, he chose a specific problem as a representative of a group of problems and also incorporated open-endedness into the question. He placed each variation in the context of the entire lesson and planned a sequence of variations. In the lesson, the teacher provided opportunities for the students to construct variations through their reasoning and explanations. Moreover, the teacher promoted and regulated the students' reflection on the variations by making different reactions such as questioning, probing, or asking for elaboration. These forms of feedback exhibit the teacher's critical role in enabling the students to discern invariance, that is, the key idea of finding a common unit fraction in order to compare fractions.

The three viewpoints as applied to the lesson analysis show that a structured problem solving lesson can be viewed from the perspective of variation. The results obtained in this chapter will contribute to the examination of the pedagogy of variation, because structured problem solving has unique features as described in a previous section.

An implication of this chapter on teaching with variation is that some types of variation will promote students' mathematical thinking and problem solving ability. Huang and Leung (2005) described a lesson in terms of conceptual variation and procedural variation and pointed out that both were created alternatively for different purposes in experiencing the enacted object of learning. Both types of variations were also observed in the lessons analyzed in this chapter. Procedural variation was especially rich, as the teacher emphasized *process*. To foster autonomous thinking, he incorporated variation as the scaffolding for problem solving. In this regard, the dimensions of variation of problem solving identified by Gu et al. (2004) were used strategically. The observed conceptual and procedural variations, especially the rich opportunity for procedural variation, can be said to reflect the emphasis on mathematical thinking in Japanese problem solving. The analyzed lessons were conducted with the objective of introducing new mathematical content. Such an objective would also have an influence on the salience of certain features of variation. On the other hand, in the literature on teaching with variation, there are many studies and practices examining Chinese lessons that aim to consolidate new knowledge. Needless to say, the types of variation to be presented will differ according to the lesson's aim. It would be useful to further clarify the aspects of variation for different objectives of learning.

Another implication of this chapter is that students' autonomy in the activity of variation is an important condition for learning. In elucidating this point, the chapter further clarified the critical role of the teacher in directing students' reflection on variation. Marton and Booth (1997) identified a *surface approach* and a *deep approach* to learning. In the analyzed classroom, we have observed the students' superficial attention to the object of learning. Catching students' surface approaches and offering various and flexible forms of feedback and intervention are how the teacher can change the students' ways of seeing, experiencing, or understanding the critical features. A crucial observation is the close relationship between construction of and reflection on the variation. By letting the students construct and reflect on variation in their reasoning and explanations, the teacher involved them in the activity of changing their ways of seeing and experiencing the critical features. Lo and Marton (2012) recommended a teaching sequence of "fusion, contrast, generalization, fusion" for effective teaching with variation. The pedagogical actions observed in the teacher described in this chapter will offer important information on how to provide students with *natural but necessary transitions* between the stages in realizing the teaching sequence.

Lastly, the three viewpoints and the lesson analysis call attention to the importance of examining the students' actual experience of and engagement in variation with their peers and the teacher. This study implies that both *teaching with variation* and *learning with variation* need to be explored. In particular, we need further inquiry into the steps of providing opportunities for students to construct variation themselves and promoting students' reflection on variation toward the intended object of learning, because, as shown in the analysis, students' paths and reactions are divergent and subtle. It is also interesting to look at the enacted object of learning from the perspective of the students' lived object of learning. The interviews revealed that the focus students were impressed by their peers' reasonings and benefited from the connections that their teacher and their peers made between multiple solutions and explanations in the lessons. Considering that their lived object of learning was deep, their comments in the interviews may suggest important information on raising the quality of the enacted object of learning. One such insight is that the teacher should routinely demonstrate a deep approach to learning in his or her interaction with students.

REFERENCES

Becker, J. P., & Shimada, S. (Eds.). (1997). *The open-ended approach: A new proposal for teaching mathematics*. Reston, VA: NCTM. (Original work published 1977)

Clarke, D. (2006). The LPS research design. In D. Clarke, C. Keitel, & Y. Shimizu (Eds.), *Mathematics classrooms in twelve countries: The insider's perspective* (pp. 15–36). Rotterdam, The Netherlands: Sense Publishers.

Clarke, D., Keitel, C., & Shimizu, Y. (Eds.). (2006). *Mathematics classrooms in twelve countries: The insider's perspective*. Rotterdam, The Netherlands: Sense Publishers.

Clarke, D. J., Emanuelsson, J., Jablonka, E., & Mok, I. A. C. (Eds.). (2006). *Making connections: Comparing mathematics classrooms around the world* (pp. 127–145). Rotterdam, The Netherlands: Sense Publishers.

Fujii, T. (2013). *Cross-cultural studies on "collective thinking" in mathematics "lesson study" among U.S., Australia and Japan*. Research Report of Grants-in-Aid for Scientific Research by Japan Society for the Promotion of Science (No. 20243039), Tokyo Gakugei University (In Japanese).

Funahashi, Y., & Hino, K. (2014). The teacher's role in guiding children's mathematical ideas toward meeting lesson objectives. *ZDM—The International Journal on Mathematics Education, 46*, 423–436.

Gu, L., Huang, R., & Marton, F. (2004). Teaching with variation: An effective way of mathematics teaching in China. In L. Fan, N. W. J. Cai, & S. Li (Eds.), *How Chinese learn mathematics: Perspectives from insiders* (pp. 309–347). Singapore: World Scientific.

Hiebert, J., Gallimore, R., Garnier, H., Givvin, K. B., Hollingsworth, H., Jacobs, J., Chiu, A. M.-Y., Wearne, D., Smith, M., Kersting, N., Manaster, A., Tseng, E., Etterbeek, W., Manaster, C., Gonzales, P., & Stigler, J. (2003). *Teaching mathematics in seven countries: Results from the TIMSS 1999 Video Study*. Washington, DC: U.S. Department of Education , National Center for Education Statistics.

Hino, K. (2007). Toward the problem-centered classroom: Trends in mathematical problem solving in Japan. *ZDM-The International Journal on Mathematics Education, 39*, 503–514.

Hino, K. (2015). Comparing multiple solutions in the structured problem solving: Deconstructing Japanese lessons from learner's perspective. *Educational Studies in Mathematics, 90*, 121–141.

Huang, R., & Leung, F. K. S. (2005). Deconstructing teacher-centeredness and student-centeredness dichotomy: A case study of a Shanghai mathematics lesson. *The Mathematics Educator, 15*(2), 35–41.

Katagiri, S. (1988). *Mondai kaiketsu katei to hatsumon bunseki* [Problem solving processes and analysis of teacher's questioning]. Tokyo: Meiji Tosho.

Koizumi, Y. (2013). Similarities and differences in teachers' questioning in German and Japanese mathematics classrooms. *ZDM—The International Journal on Mathematics Education, 45*, 47–59.

Koto, S., & Niigata-ken-sansu-kyoiku-kenkyukai. (Eds.). (1992). *Sansuka tayo na kangae no ikashikata matomekata* [Ways of utilizing and summarizing various ways of thinking in elementary mathematics class]. Tokyo: Toyokan.

Koto, S., & Niigata-ken-sansu-kyoiku-kenkyukai. (Eds.). (1998). *Communication de tsukuru atarashii sansu gakushu* [New mathematics learning created by communication: How to utilize and summarize various ways of thinking]. Tokyo: Toyokan.

Li, Y., & Shimizu, Y. (2009). Exemplary mathematics instruction and its development in selected education systems in East Asia. *ZDM—The International Journal on Mathematics Education, 41*, 257–262.

Lo, M. L., & Marton, F. (2012). Towards a science of the art of teaching: Using variation theory as a guiding principle of pedagogical design. *International Journal for Lesson and Learning Studies, 1*(1), 7–22.

Marton, F., & Booth, S. (1997). *Learning and awareness.* Mahwah, NJ: Lawrence Erlbaum Associates.

Marton, F., Tsui, A. B. M., Chik, P. P. M., Ko, P. Y., Lo, M. L., Mok, I. A. C., Ng, D. F. P., Pang, M. F., Pong, W. Y., & Runesson, U. (2004). *Classroom discourse and the space of learning.* Mahwah, NJ: Lawrence Erlbaum Associates.

Nohda, N. (1983). *Sansu/sugakuka open approach ni yoru sidou no kenkyu* [A study of "open-approach" strategy in school mathematics teaching]. Tokyo: Toyokan.

Okazaki, M., Kimura, K., & Watanabe, K. (2015). Examining the coherence of mathematics lessons in terms of the genesis and development of students' learning goals. In C. Vistro-Yu (Ed.), *In pursuit of quality mathematics education for all: Proceedings of the 7th ICMI-East Asia Regional Conference on Mathematics Education* (pp. 401–408). Quezon City: Philippine Council of Mathematics Teacher Educators, Inc.

Polya, G. (1985). *How to solve it: A new aspect of mathematical method* (2nd ed.). Princeton, NJ & Oxford: Princeton University Press. (Original work published 1945)

Runesson, U. (2005). Beyond discourse and interaction. Variation: A critical aspect for teaching and learning mathematics. *Cambridge Journal of Education, 35*(1), 69–87.

Runesson, U. (2006). What is it possible to learn? On variation as a necessary condition for learning. *Scandinavian Journal of Educational Research, 50*(4), 397–410.

Sekiguchi, Y. (2008). Sugaku kyoiku ni okeru variation riron no igi to tenbo [Meaning and prospect of variation theory in mathematics education: Inquiry into "affordance" in learning]. *Proceedings of the 42th annual Meeting of Japan Society in Mathematical Education*, 733–738.

Sekiguchi, Y. (2012). An analysis of coherence and variation in Japanese mathematics classrooms. *Proceedings of the 12th International Congress on Mathematical Education* (pp. 4332–4340). Seoul, Korea.

Shimizu, Y. (2006). How do you conclude today's lesson?: The form and functions of 'Matome' in mathematics lessons. In D. Clarke, J. Emanuelsson, E. Jablonka, & I. A. C. Mok (Eds.), *Making connections: Comparing mathematics classrooms around the world* (pp. 127–145). Rotterdam: Sense Publishers.

Shimizu, Y. (2009). Characterizing exemplary mathematics instruction in Japanese classrooms from the learner's perspective. *ZDM—The International Journal on Mathematics Education, 41*, 311–318.

Shimizu, Y. (Ed.). (2011). *Cross-cultural studies of mathematics classrooms from the learners' perspective.* Research Report of Grants-in-Aid for Scientific Research by Japan Society for the Promotion of Science (No. 19330196), University of Tsukuba (In Japanese).

Shimizu, Y., & Kaur, B. (2013). Learning from similarities and differences: A reflection on the potentials and constraints of cross-national studies in mathematics. *ZDM—The International Journal on Mathematics Education, 45*, 1–5.

Stigler, J. W., & Hiebert, J. (1999). *The teaching gap.* New York, NY: Free Press.

Sugita Elementary School. (1964). *Kangaeru chikara wo nobasu tameno hatsumon to jogen* [Teacher's questioning and suggestions for the purpose of fostering the students' ability of thinking]. Yokohama, Japan: Author.

Sugiyama, Y., & Ito, S. (Eds.). (1990). *Shogakko sansuka jyugyo kenkyu* [Lesson study in elementary mathematics]. Tokyo: Kyoiku Shuppan.

Takeuchi, Y., & Sawada, T. (Eds.). (1984). *Mondai kara mondai e* [From problem to problem]. Tokyo: Toyokan.

Watson, A., & Mason, J. (2006). Seeing an exercise as a single mathematical object: Using variation to structure sense-making. *Mathematical Thinking and Learning, 8*(2), 91–111.

Watson, A., & Ohtani, M. (Eds.). (2015). *Task design in mathematics education: An ICMI study 22.* London: Springer.

Wong, N. Y. (2008). Confucian heritage culture learner's phenomenon: From "exploring the middle zone" to "constructing a bridge." *ZDM-The International Journal on Mathematics Education.* doi:10.1007/x11858-008-0140-x

Wong, N. Y., Lam, C. C., & Chan, A. M. Y. (2013). Teaching with variation: Bianshi mathematics teaching. In Y. Li & R. Huang (Eds.), *How Chinese teach mathematics and improve teaching* (pp. 105–119). New York, NY: Routledge.

Keiko Hino
Graduate School of Education
Utsunomiya University, Japan

ANGELA T. BARLOW, KYLE M. PRINCE, ALYSON E. LISCHKA
AND MATTHEW D. DUNCAN

15. DEVELOPING ALGEBRAIC REASONING THROUGH VARIATION IN THE U.S.

INTRODUCTION

Historically, algebra in the U.S. has been viewed "as a gatekeeper to a college education and the careers such education affords" (Kilpatrick & Izsák, 2008, p. 11). As such, current curriculum documents emphasize the need to support *all* students in learning algebra (Common Core State Standards Initiative [CCSSI], 2010; National Council of Teachers of Mathematics [NCTM], 1989, 2000). To do so, however, requires a reconceptualization of the preparation students receive for the formal study of algebra (Kilpatrick & Izsák, 2008). In considering this preparation, scholars have indicated that students need opportunities to engage in algebraic reasoning (Blanton & Kaput, 2005; Earnest, 2014; Hunter, 2014; Kaput, 2008; Kilpatrick & Izsák, 2008). Different perspectives exist, though, with regard to the core aspects of algebraic reasoning.

Kaput (2008) characterized algebra in two ways. First, he described algebra as an inherited subject or cultural artifact. Second, Kaput portrayed it as a human activity that requires humans for it to exist. In our work, we focus on the latter and explore Kaput's (2008) view that "the heart of algebraic reasoning is comprised of complex symbolization processes that serve purposeful generalization and reasoning with generalizations" (p. 9).

Within this view of algebra, Kaput (2008) described a core aspect of algebraic reasoning as involving "algebra as systematically symbolizing generalizations of regularities and constraints" (p. 11). Although this core aspect appears in some form across all strands of algebra, we are particularly interested in algebraic reasoning as it supports generalizing a pattern through argumentation for the purpose of building towards functions (Kaput, 1999; Warren & Cooper, 2008). This view of algebraic reasoning has permeated recent international curriculum documents (e.g., Ministry of Education, 2007; Ontario Ministry of Education, 2005) as well as U.S. curriculum documents for over two decades. Table 1 provides an overview of the algebraic presence in U.S. curriculum documents, including *Curriculum and Evaluation Standards* (*CES*, NCTM, 1989), *Principles and Standards for School Mathematics* (*PSSM*, NCTM, 2000), and *Common Core State Standards for Mathematics* (*CCSSM*, CCSSI, 2010).

R. Huang & Y. Li (Eds.), Teaching and Learning Mathematics through Variation, 321–339.
© 2017 Sense Publishers. All rights reserved.

The inclusion of algebraic reasoning in U.S. standards is informed, in part, by a literature base that supports a need to develop algebraic reasoning in middle school students (Blanton, 2008; Carraher & Schliemann, 2007; Lins & Kaput, 2004; Soares, Blanton, & Kaput, 2005). Note that we define middle school students as those in grades five through eight, approximately 11 through 14 years old. Additionally, algebraic reasoning is described as the process of building general mathematical relationships and expressing those relationships in increasingly sophisticated ways (Ontario Ministry of Education, 2005; Soares et al., 2005; Warren & Cooper, 2008). Furthermore, Carraher and Schliemann (2007) stated that the role of functions was *the* link between learning algebra from the middle school level through college. Thus, implementing this view of algebraic reasoning in middle grades is substantiated and of "great relevance for mathematics education because it provides a special opportunity to foster a particular kind of generality" (Lins & Kaput, 2004, p. 47) in students' thinking.

Table 1. Algebraic reasoning in U.S. documents

Understanding patterns	
CES	Analyze tables and graphs to identify relationships (Grades 5–8)
PSSM	Generalize a variety of patterns with tables, graphs, and words (Grades 6–8)
CCSSM	Analyze patterns and relationships (Grade 5)
Representing mathematical situations	
CES	Represent situations with tables, graphs, and equations (Grades 5–8)
PSSM	Use symbolic algebra to represent situations and to solve problems (Grades 6–8)
CCSSM	Represent and analyze quantitative relationships (Grade 6)
Generalizing to functions	
CES	Generalize number patterns to represent physical patterns (Grades 5–8)
PSSM	Identify functions and contrast their properties between quantities and contrast their properties from tables (Grades 6–8)
CCSSM	Use functions to model relationships (Grade 8)

Despite the importance of algebraic reasoning demonstrated in both the curriculum documents and the literature, U.S. and international classrooms have fallen short in providing an opportunity for this type of learning (cf. Carraher & Schliemann, 2007; Stacey & Chick, 2004). To address this issue, Blanton (2008) developed curricular materials aimed at supporting teachers as they introduce algebraic reasoning in elementary and middle grades. In these materials, Blanton (2008) described algebraic reasoning as a habit of mind that students acquire through instruction that gives opportunities to "think about, describe, and justify general relationships" (p. 93).

This focus allows for students to engage in algebraic reasoning, a process that is supported by the following teacher practices:

- helping students learn to use a variety of representations, to understand how these representations are connected, and to be systematic and organized when representing their ideas;
- listening to student's thinking and using this to find ways to build more algebraic reasoning into instruction; and
- helping students build generalizations through exploring, conjecturing, and testing mathematical relationships (Blanton, 2008, pp. 119–120).

Through these practices, algebraic reasoning can focus on functional thinking via arithmetic tasks that are transformed into opportunities for generalizing mathematical patterns and relationships (Blanton, 2008; Ontario Ministry of Education, 2005). One way that this can be accomplished is through varying a single task parameter (Blanton, 2008; Blanton & Kaput, 2003, 2005; Ontario Ministry of Education, n.d.; Soares et al., 2006).

Varying a "parameter allows you to build a task that looks for a functional relationship between two quantities" (Blanton, 2008, p. 58) and "can shift the focus from arithmetic thinking to algebraic thinking" (Ontario Ministry of Education, n.d., p. 19). This emphasis on varying a parameter suggests that applying a theory of variation to the design of instruction may be an important means for providing middle school students with an opportunity to engage in algebraic reasoning. Therefore, the purpose of this chapter is to present a case that describes a series of tasks whose development was informed by a theory of variation. Collectively, the tasks align with the vision established in the U.S. curriculum documents and aim to support the development of algebraic reasoning in sixth grade students. In the subsequent sections, a theory of variation will be presented, followed by a description of a four-task sequence, including its implementation in a sixth grade classroom. Finally, a discussion and reflection on the role of variation in the task sequence will be provided.

THEORY OF VARIATION

According to Marton, Runesson, and Tsui (2004), learning is a process in which students acquire a particular capability or way of seeing and experiencing. In order to see something in a certain way, students must discern critical features of an object. This is known as the theory of variation (Leung, 2012; Marton & Pang, 2006; Marton et al., 2004). The theory of variation can aid teachers in developing students' algebraic reasoning skills by providing students with opportunities to discern critical aspects of what is to be learned, also known as the object of learning (Ling, 2012). While teachers cannot guarantee the lived objects of learning experienced by the students, they can focus students' attention on critical features by providing contrasting experiences that allow students to develop and test conjectures. After all, students can only begin to understand the object of learning once they have seen it in various situations and with varying dimensions (Marton et al., 2004). Therefore, it is imperative that students discern the patterns of what varies and what is invariant in a learning situation (Leung, 2012). It is the main objective of the teacher to reveal these patterns to support students in powerful ways of *seeing* the intended object of learning, which leads to powerful ways of acting (Marton et al., 2004).

There are two features of the object of learning: "the direct and the indirect objects of learning" (Marton & Pang, 2006, p. 194). The direct object of learning is defined in terms of content, such as evaluating algebraic expressions. In contrast, the indirect object of learning refers to "the kind of capability that the students are supposed to develop such as being able to give examples, being able to discern critical aspects of novel situations" (Marton et al., 2004, p. 4). In the paragraphs that follow, we apply this theory of variation to the design and implementation of a four-task lesson sequence that aimed to support the development of algebraic reasoning. We include descriptions of both the direct and indirect objects of learning as evidenced in the design and enactment of the task sequence.

TASK SEQUENCE

Design

Defined as what the teacher aims for the students to learn, the intended direct objects of learning during this task sequence were for students to be able to generalize a linear pattern given a series of geometric figures, give the generalization as an expression involving one variable (i.e., $an + b$ where a and b are integers), and justify the generalization based on the geometric pattern. This objective supports standard 6.EE.9 from the *CCSSM* (CCSSI, 2010), which states:

> Use variables to represent two quantities in a real-world problem that change in relationship to one another; write an equation to express one quantity, thought of as the dependent variable, in terms of the other quantity, thought of as the independent variable. Analyze the relationship between the dependent and independent variables using graphs and tables, and relate these to the equation. (p. 44)

The intended indirect objects of learning, or capabilities to be developed, during the lessons included seeing the grouping structures within the geometric figures (a), relating these groups to the corresponding figure number (n), and recognizing the constant as what appears each time in the figure but is not in a group (b), where a, n, and b represent integers in the generalization $an + b$.

The students in these lessons needed to see linear patterns in different circumstances, with certain aspects varying in dimension. Research posits, "The most powerful strategy is to let the learners discern one at a time, before they encounter simultaneous variation of the features" (Lo & Marton, 2012, p. 11). This idea was

324

considered when developing the sequence of tasks. Table 2 provides an overview of the lesson sequence, including the geometric patterns featured in each lesson. In each task, a series of figures is presented and the student is expected to develop a means for determining the number of segments needed to produce the figure, based on the figure's position in the pattern.

Table 2. Overview of lesson sequence

Task	Fig. 1	Fig. 2	Fig. 4	Generalization
1	(figure)	(figure)	(figure)	$3n + 1$
2	(figure)	(figure)	(figure)	$4n + 1$
3	(figure)	(figure)	(figure)	$4n + 4$
4	Students are given a generalization and are expected to create a geometric pattern.			___ $n + 4$

Task 1. The purpose of this task was to introduce the process of generalizing the pattern. The intent was for Task 1 to provide a common experience on which to build for the students. This included introducing common vocabulary, such as *generalization*, and a particular way of looking for a relationship between the figure number and its corresponding figure. In this lesson, the intent was for students to experience variation with the number of segments in the figure (referred to as fence panels in the problem context and represented by toothpicks) given the number of squares (referred to as corrals in the problem context). Although the corresponding algebraic expression for *n* corrals is $3n + 1$, the goal for this lesson did not necessarily include representing the pattern algebraically, only verbally. The variation in Task 1 was limited to only variation found within the pattern, as students examined Figures 1, 2, and 4 separately. Therefore, there was no *contrast* or anything with which to compare it, perhaps making it difficult to discern what aspects caused the general expression to be $3n + 1$.

Task 2. In order for the learners to discern the critical features of the object of learning, Task 1 focused on introducing the idea of finding a generalized pattern. In contrast, Task 2 introduced a different pattern that allowed students to experience the variation of one dimension of the object of learning – the number found in each group. The new pattern held the constant invariant, while the group value changed, leading to the corresponding expression $4n + 1$. In this way, students had the opportunity to see the object of learning under different circumstances and test the validity of any conjectures that they had, seeking to understand the new figures by trying to discern what was critical and what was not (Ling, 2012). Moreover, this task provided students with the opportunity to be aware of the two situations at the same time in order to compare and contrast them, what is known as "diachronic simultaneity" (Marton et al., 2004, p. 17). Based on what the students had experienced before and what they were experiencing in this task, there was the potential for them to develop "separation" (Marton et al., 2004, p. 16) with the group feature and be able to discern it from other features. It was also important that this first variation be situated within a similar situation so that everything else was invariant, making it clear what was affecting change.

Task 3. Task 3 was similar to Task 2 in two ways. First, the grouping structure (i.e., the house shapes in the pattern), and thus the coefficient (*a*), remained the same. Second, variation of one dimension of the object of learning was present. However, in this scenario, it was the constant value that was *separated* so that students could experience how the invariant structure within the pattern affects the general expression. The teacher intended to keep the grouping structure the same so that this effect would be clearer. According to Marton et al. (2004), students need to experience the following related to the object of learning: contrast instances, make generalizations from varying appearances, separate each individual aspect, and fuse them together simultaneously (Leung, 2012). In this task, students are separating the last aspect of the object of learning. As a result, they should be able to discern between the two aspects of the object of learning and have a basic understanding of how varying dimensions of those aspects alter the general expression.

Task 4. The purpose of this final task was to further develop students "professional seeing" (Marton et al., 2004, p. 11) of generalizing patterns by providing them with the opportunity to experience the object of learning from a novel perspective. In this task, students are asked to create a geometric pattern that satisfies __ $n + 4$. In order to build a corresponding geometrical pattern, students must experience the grouping structure and constant simultaneously and understand how each aspect affects their pattern. Afterward, students are able to compare and contrast solutions, recognize different grouping structures, and see multiple representations of the same algebraic formula.

Summary. This sequence of tasks should allow students to become aware of the critical features of the object of learning through carefully selected experiences directed by the theory of variation. Through sequences of contrast, generalization, and separation (Marton et al., 2004), students should be able to enhance their "seeing" (Marton et al., 2004, p. 11) of the intended objects of learning. However, what matters most is what the learner actually encounters and what is possible to learn in the context of the lesson, what is known as the enacted objects of learning

(Marton et al., 2004). In the section to follow, the enacted objects of learning are described through the patterns of variation and invariance that were actually co-constructed by the teacher and the students.

Implementation

In this section, we present a summary of the four-task lesson sequence (see Table 2), or enacted objects of learning, that was implemented in a sixth-grade class in a suburban school district located in the southeastern United States. The class had 20 students and met for 55 minutes each day. The first author was the instructor for the lessons. In her role as a university professor, she spends a considerable amount of time teaching demonstration lessons in local schools and has been recognized for her expertise and experience in implementing reform-oriented lessons. The four-task lesson sequence was videoed for the purpose of developing a multimedia case to support teachers' understanding of reform-oriented instruction.

Lesson 1.   To begin the lesson, the teacher described a problem scenario designed to support the students in understanding the task at hand.

> I have some land that I just bought and I am going to build corrals on the land. We will use toothpicks to represent the corrals. *(Displays a square-shaped corral made with four toothpicks).* That will be one corral. How many panels does it take to build one corral? *(Students respond with four.)* I can build more than one corral but they will be built lengthwise. Now, I am cheap and I do not like to spend money. When I build the second corral, I do not double up on fence panels. *(Displays two corrals made of toothpicks.)* How many fence panels have I used? *(Students respond with seven.)* So here is our problem. I want to build as many corrals as possible on my land but I do not know how long the land is or how many fence panels I will need. This *(pointing to Figure 2)* is two corrals, and it takes seven fence panels. Predict how many fence panels we need for four corrals. Do you have your number? Build your corrals and see if your prediction is correct. *(Students build four corrals with toothpicks.)* How many panels did you need? *(Students respond with 13.)* So here's our task: If I tell you the number of corrals I can build on my land, I need you to tell me how many fence panels I will need.

After supporting students in thinking about the problem scenario, the teacher asked questions aimed to support students' recognition of the structure of the corral pattern.

> T: When you built the corral and then counted the fence panels, how did you count? Think about how you could describe how you counted the fence panels. Jot down how you counted and we will share our strategies in just a moment. *(Students take approximately one minute to write their strategies.)* Let's start with Ben.

S1: I counted the first pen with four and then I added three three times.

T: Do you all understand what Ben said? I am going to ask Candy to repeat Ben's idea.

S2: He counted the first pen with four and then he counted threes.

T: Larry, how did you count?

S3: I counted the left toothpick, then the top toothpick, then the bottom toothpick, then the right toothpick, like all in one box. *(The student illustrates how he counted the remaining toothpicks: top, bottom, right, top, bottom, right, top, bottom, right.)*

T: Did someone count differently?

S4: I counted the ones in the middle, then the ones on the top, then the ones on the bottom.

S5: I counted the top and bottom and then the middle.

Following this exchange, each student was given a number of corrals (i.e., 6, 7, 9, 10, 12) for which they were to figure out the corresponding number of fence panels. After students in their small groups checked each other's work, the teacher asked the students to look across the different problems and identify two or three things that they noticed. The following exchange occurred.

T: What is something that you or your partner noticed?

S1: The number of panels is the number of corrals times three and then you add one.

T: I think I heard a lot of different groups saying something like this. I want you to talk about this – why would this be true? If you didn't see this, check it with your problem. Check it – why would this be true?

S2: We thought because of the four and the rest was three. We didn't have to add any more because the first one was whole.

S3: If we are counting the first four and we take off one and add all the rest together that would bring us to, say nine times three is twenty-seven, and then you add back on the one you took off.

S4: Wouldn't that "three times the number of corrals plus one" – would that be a formula for the problem?

T: I'm going to write that over here. Remember that I do not know how big the land is. What are some other observations?

S5: We noticed that you should make sure that you counted all the panels.

S6: That the number of corrals had an impact on the number of panels.

S7: If you use a simple pattern and you lay it out the long way, it is easier to complete. It is simple to complete.

T: So you are thinking about how you can see the patterns in there. Remember that I do not know how big the land is. They are going to call me up and say, "Hey, we think you could have 200 corrals on there," and I need to be able to immediately say how many panels I need. Which of our observations is going to help me with that? Talk to your partner about that.

S8: The first one because it would be 200 times three which would be 600 plus one making it 601.

T: Thumbs up if you agree that the first observation is going to be most useful for solving our problem. Ok. Thumbs up if you agree that for 200 corrals we will need 601 fence panels. Wow! I am going to have to challenge you now. Remember this word *formula*. How could you use symbols and a variable to represent this first observation? Talk with your partner.

Students eagerly talked with their partner about how to represent the observation (i.e., the number of panels is the number of corrals times three and then you add one) with symbols. The following expressions were offered: $C \times 3 + 1$; $3n + 1$; $(C*3) + 1$; $3c + 1$. Next, the teacher linked the students' use of the word *formula* to the words *expression* and *generalization*. After some discussion regarding why the generalization was useful for the problem, the teacher asked how many corrals could be built if there were 61 fence panels. The class ended with a discussion of the solution to this problem.

Lesson 2. For their homework, students revisited the corral task and responded to the following prompt: *When Sarah looked at the corrals, she said that she saw groups of 3. What do you think she meant by that?* To start the second lesson, the teacher asked the students to take out their homework sheet and compare their responses to this prompt. Then, the following exchange occurred.

T: I would like to have three people share with us what they have written. Alice?

S1: I thought that she started with the first corral and she took out the first toothpick so it would have groups of three toothpicks.

S2: After you have the first set of four toothpicks, you have sets of three toothpicks.

S3: She was thinking about three corrals.

T: My question is: We see how Sarah is thinking about these groups of three. Right? Alice said that toothpick is gone and we have these groups of three. And then Larry said we have this group of four and then we have these threes. And then Alden is talking about these corrals of threes. And so my question that I want you to think about inside your head for just a minute is: How did Sarah's groups of three help us to think about the pattern? *(The students discuss their thoughts in small groups.)* Let's start with Callie.

S4: Take out one toothpick and then there will be threes and then you add the one back.

T: How is this helping you?

S4: Then you can figure out how many toothpicks?

S5: Every time you are going to times it by three and then – take that one panel off then times it and then add the one back.

S6: I thought maybe you could take one out and add three each time.

T: So you take the one out and add three each time. And repeatedly adding the threes is multiplying. *(Teacher points at the multiplication symbol in the generalizations recorded from the previous day.)*

S7: She said that she saw groups, meaning there was more than one group of three. So when you did the formula and taking one out, you would just multiply the number of fence panels times the number of corrals that you have the number of fence panels that you need for all of them.

T: So from this what we are beginning to see is this idea of groups - when we are trying to figure out our generalization it is helpful to think about groups.

Following this exchange, the teacher introduced the task for the day by telling a story, similar to the one from the previous day and using a new shape for the figures, which the students called a house. After asking students to share what they noticed about the pattern, the teacher asked students to think about how this new pattern was different from the pattern explored on the previous day.

S1: Instead of the three in the pattern, we are going to have a four.

T: So you are thinking about multiplying by four. Someone else?

S2: Instead of adding three we are adding four.

T: Good. Another idea?

S3: Houses use four toothpicks.

T: Do you all understand what he is saying? Where are the groups in this pattern? Remember in the homework, Sarah said something about the groups. Where do we see groups in this pattern? Write your ideas down on the paper.

S4: I see groups of four.

T: Will you come up and show us where you see groups of four? *(The student demonstrates at the front of the class the groups of four that she sees.)* Do you all see the same groups?

S5: Each one would have a group of four toothpicks, except for that first one.

T: How can we use our strategies to figure out how many toothpicks are needed for a certain number of houses?

Following this exchange, each student was given a number of houses (i.e., 8, 9, 10, 11, 12, 15) for which they were to figure out the corresponding number of toothpicks. After students in their small groups checked each other's work, the teacher used their number pairs (i.e., number of houses and number of toothpicks) to create a function table. In the function table, she recorded an n in the input column and asked the students to think about the corresponding generalization to record in the output table. After time for small group discussion, the students offered the following generalizations: n x 4 + 1; 4n +1; 4h +1; 4 * n + 1. The lesson concluded by finding the output for an input of 50 and finding the input for an output of 81.

Lesson 3. On this day, the opening of school was delayed by two hours due to inclement weather. As a result, the original lesson was modified to fit within a 30-minute timeframe. To begin the lesson, the teacher distributed a paper that contained representations of the new pattern. Students noted that a garage had been added to the houses. The teacher asked them to create a function table for the pattern. After several minutes of working, the teacher asked one student to display her work for the class to examine.

S1: I took the one house – it was five toothpicks. And then I added another three for the garage. Then for the second one, I did the two houses, which was nine toothpicks and added three for the garage. Then I saw a pattern – add four each time so that's 8, 12, 16, 20, 24.

T: Tammy, can I stop you a second? Will you all take a look at Tammy's outputs and see if you agree with those? *(Students compare their charts with Tammy's work.)* Ok, so keep going, Tammy.

S1: I did the same thing and then the formula would be *n* times four plus one plus three or to simplify that it would be *n* times four plus four.

T: Tammy, can you tell us again how it is that you figured out the formula or the generalization?

S1: I took the formula that we did yesterday, *n* times four plus one, and I noticed that the garage was just another three sides so all I did was just add three to the formula.

T: And I noticed that some of the other groups did the same thing. They had the plus one and then the plus three, which simplified to 4*n* plus four. So the generalization that she is offering to us is *n* times four plus one plus three or *n* times four plus four. So I want you to do two things in your groups. First, take this generalization and check it. Take an input value, substitute it into the generalization, and see if it produces the correct output. And then second, I want you to think about *why* are we multiplying by four and then why today are we *adding* four when we were adding one yesterday? Talk to your partners. *(Students work in their groups for several minutes, writing down their ideas.)* Let's share out whole group what we are thinking.

S2: I was thinking you would remove this square – the garage- and then you count the pieces of the houses and you get four and you multiply by the number of houses you have and then you add the four back on.

S3: You have four sides on each of the pentagon houses and then you add on the square and that puts the side back on the house.

T: Remember how Sarah saw groups in our problem the other day. Talk to your neighbor about the groups that you see.

S4: She saw groups of four. *(Student outlines the house, missing one side.)*

T: It happens that there is a group of four here in the garage too. This four is different. This number sitting out there by itself is called the constant. So we are looking at what comes in groups and we are looking at the constant – what is sitting here.

With only a few minutes remaining in class, the teacher asked the different pairs of students to develop a pattern for a pre-selected generalization. All generalizations were of the form ___ $n + 4$, where the coefficient of n differed for each group. Students were not able to make much progress, however, as class ended.

Lesson 4. Following some discussion of a homework problem, the teacher began class by asking students to look back across the three patterns developed during the previous three lessons. She reminded them of the groups and the constants that had been discussed previously. Then, students began working to develop their own geometric pattern that could be represented by the generalization that was assigned to them. Two groups were asked to present their work to the class. The dialogue from one discussion, which focused on the pattern shown in Figure 1, is featured here.

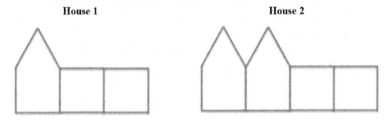

Figure 1. Pattern presented by students

T: Lets give our attention to this group and think about their work.

S1: We got four n plus seven. We thought about a house with two garages. In figure number one, you remove the two garages and count the four panels and then put the garages back on; that is the plus seven.

T: Can you show us where your groups of four are?

S1: The groups of four are right there (outlines part of the house).

T: And where is the constant seven?

S1: It would be here in the garage.

Following the two presentations, students were asked to reflect on the ideas learned over the past four lessons. Students' ideas included: the meaning of the word generalization; it can be hard to find figures given the generalization; the constant; the input/output table.

THE PRESENCE OF VARIATION IN THE LESSON SEQUENCE

The intended objects of learning for this sequence of lessons were for students to be able to generalize a linear pattern given a series of geometric figures, give the generalization as an expression involving one variable (i.e., $an + b$ where a and b are integers), and justify the generalization based on the geometric pattern. Employing the theory of variation allowed for the intended object of learning to be made accessible to the learners in the classroom. In this section, we present a discussion of the intended objects of learning, the enacted objects of learning, and the lived objects of learning.

Intended Objects of Learning.

The planned sequence of lessons, as represented in Table 3, demonstrates the intentional use of variation to bring attention to the features of linear functions. In the first lesson of the sequence, a toothpick pattern of corrals was introduced in order to provide a starting point for the discussion of linear functions. Then, within the first lesson, only the number of corrals was varied, bringing awareness to the relationship between an input and an output in a linear function. This use of variation established a common experience on which to build understanding of the process of generalization.

Table 3. Dimensions of variation by task

Task	Dimension	Variant	Invariant	Object of learning
1	Corrals	Number of corrals (1 to n)	Group size (3) and constant (1)	How the number of corrals relates to the number of fence panels needed
2	Groups	Group size (3 to 4)	Constant (1)	How the number within each group alters the general expression
3	Constant	Constant (1 to 4)	Group size (4)	How the additional fence panels alters the general expression
4	Direction	Given expression instead of picture, group size (4 to __)	Constant (4)	Create a geometric figure given a general expression
Day 2 Homework	Type of Pattern	Counting shapes instead of sides	Generalization (3n+1)	Transferability

The subsequent lessons then proceeded to vary one feature of linear functions at a time so as to bring attention to the characteristics of the parts of a linear function.

The second lesson focused on a new toothpick pattern in which the number in each group varied from the corral pattern of the first day. Then the third lesson presented a third toothpick pattern in which the constant was varied. In order to adhere to variation theory, the explored pattern for each day was of the same style (i.e., envisioned as built out of toothpicks), therefore allowing this aspect of the discussion to remain invariant. In addition, only the position in each sequence (or input) was varied within the main activity in each lesson. By keeping these portions invariant, the lessons drew attention to the varied feature, allowing students to separate these features.

Homework was assigned on days two and three in which the visually presented pattern was of a different form than the in-class toothpick models. This variation was intended to provide students an opportunity to extend their thinking about linear patterns into different visual images while maintaining the same generalization that had been explored in class. For example, the homework pattern on the second day was an equilateral triangle with squares built on each side of the triangle (see Figure 2). In counting the number of shapes (i.e., squares and triangles) used to create each "Y," the generalization was $3n + 1$, where n represents the position of the figure in the pattern. This problem required students to count shapes rather than segments but utilized the same generalization that students explored in class on the first day.

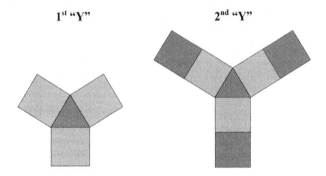

1ˢᵗ "Y"   2ⁿᵈ "Y"

Figure 2. Homework task pattern for Day 2

The intention for including a different style of pattern in the homework was to vary the type of pattern with which students interacted while keeping the generalization of the pattern invariant, bringing awareness to the transferability of the concepts of generalizations of linear functions.

Enacted objects of learning. Throughout the four lessons in the sequence, the instructor focused student attention on the object of learning with clear questions. In the first lesson, the instructor asked, "When you built the corral and then counted the fence panels, how did you count?" This question encouraged students to consider the different ways in which the panels could be counted and set in motion the possibility for a wide variety of generalizations. In the next phase of this lesson, however, the first student offered that he noticed, "The number of panels is the number of corrals times three and then you add one." This student statement seemed to constrain the ways in which other students later considered the generalization of the relationship. Rather than offering a rich variety of generalizations for the pattern, the generalizations were limited to similar expressions (i.e., $C \times 3 + 1$, $3n + 1$, $(C*3) + 1$, $3c + 1$). Although the generalizations were limited, the experience allowed students to focus on the pieces within a linear function and begin to operationalize the ideas of groups and constants as related to them.

At the start of the second lesson, the instructor focused student discussions on the homework by asking, "How did Sarah's groups of three help us to think about the pattern?" This focusing question constrained student thinking to consideration of the groups rather than consideration of the entire linear function. We see the impact of this constraint in the responses of the students during the class discussion as students connected the groups of four in the day two lesson to the groups of three in the day one lesson. Student responses in the class discussion incorporated the language as they said, "I see groups of four," and, "Each one would have a group of four toothpicks except for that first one."

Having established the idea of the role of groups in linear functions during the first two lessons, the planned lessons varied the constant on the third day and held the number of groups invariant. After students generated the function for a new pattern, the instructor asked a focusing question: "Why today are we *adding* four when we were adding one yesterday?" Because the duration of the lesson on this day was shortened (due to weather delays), students did not have enough time to grapple with the idea of the constant and returned to discussion of the groups in their conversation. However, in their presentations on the last day of the lesson sequence, students clearly identified the role of the groups and the constant.

From observations of the enacted lessons, it appears that students were beginning to make sense of the concepts of the role of groups and the role of the constant in linear functions. The choice to use only toothpick structures during the lessons seemed to allow students access to learning about the concepts separately. In a continuation of these lessons, variation concerning the physical structure of the patterns may provide opportunities for students to generalize more broadly.

Lived objects of learning. On each day of the lessons, students were assigned homework. We can glean some insight into the lived objects of learning by examining the student work, looking for patterns in learning. On the first homework assignment, students were asked, "When Sarah looked at the corrals, she said that she saw groups of three. What do you think she meant by that?" Student responses to this question varied. Within one group of students who were seated together in class, the responses included: "She saw three even groups of toothpicks;" "That there is a group of four and groups of three connected to it;" "That after you have one set of four toothpicks you have sets of three toothpicks;" and "She saw three panels with three groups." It is clear that there were still a variety of levels of understanding of the concept present in the class.

Homework assigned on the second day required students to draw figures related to the pattern presented in Figure 2 and then generalize the pattern. In most cases, students were able to draw the fourth and tenth figure in the patterns. However, various correct and incorrect generalizations of the pattern were suggested. Provided generalizations included: $3n + 1$ (a correct generalization); $4n$; $n \times n + 1$; $n + 7$; and $4n + 1$. Of the 14 students who submitted the assignment, six of them provided a correct generalization. Of the eight who had incorrect generalizations, three provided responses that did not represent generalizations (i.e., 35 or 4).

Homework assigned on the third day included the following problem:

> Joseph made a pattern using squares. The first figure of Joseph's pattern is pictured below along with his function table. Draw the next two figures in the pattern so that the pattern matches the function table. Then, generalize the pattern.

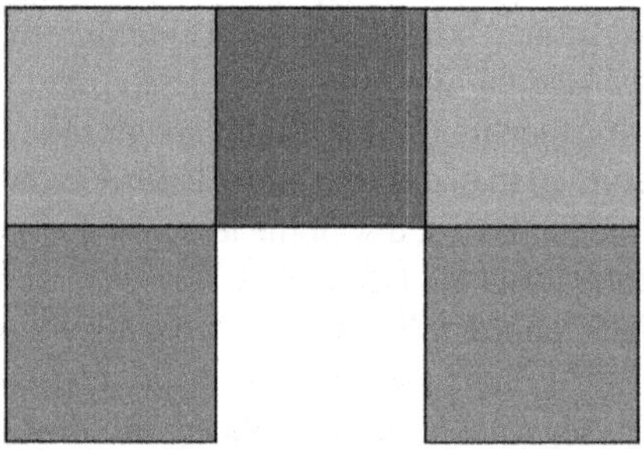

Input (Shape Number)	Output (Number of Squares)
1	5
2	7
3	9
4	____
.	.
.	.
.	.
10	____
.	.
.	.
.	.
n	____

Figure 3. Homework task for Day 3

On this assignment, half of the students provided a correct generalization. In other words, more students were attending to the nature of the role of groups and constants in generalizations of linear patterns. In addition, students were asked to create their own patterns and provide a generalization. Although many students still chose to work with toothpick models, there was more variation in the arrangement of the toothpicks and some students even chose to create a model other than a toothpick model.

Across the assignments and in-class work, gains in understanding were found. Through variation on the object of learning, the students were afforded the opportunities to consider features of linear functions. The lived objects of learning indicate that most students were beginning to make sense of the concepts of linear functions.

CONCLUSION

Informed by the theory of variation and U.S. perspectives on developing algebraic reasoning in middle grades learners (Blanton, 2008; Blanton & Kaput, 2003, 2005; Kaput, 1999), the sequence of tasks presented in this chapter transformed student noticing into powerful ways of seeing. These tasks provided rich opportunities for students to learn by strategically varying features of the geometric figures being represented. By analyzing what varied and what was invariant, evidence was found of the development of the indirect objects of learning, as students were able to recognize patterns and discern the critical features of the object of learning, (i.e., the aspects and structure of generalized linear relationships). This process utilized variation as a means of building on concepts of pattern and generality, which are typically developed as a path to algebraic reasoning in Western English-speaking countries (APPA Group, 2004).

Moreover, the teacher incorporated questions during the lessons that elicited various strategies for counting the fence panels in order to support students' "professional seeing" (Marton et al., 2004, p. 11). Focusing on different ways of counting provided students the tools by which they could count the fence panels without actually counting them one-by-one. The use of questioning in this way is an example of one of the pedagogical tools suggested as a means for extending knowledge of "numerical concepts to algebraic reasoning" (Hunter, 2014, p. 280). The incorporation of variation in the planning of the lesson tasks allowed for specific areas in which the instructor could press students to make public their thinking about the direct objects of learning (i.e., generalizations of linear patterns), which engaged students at a high level of cognitive function (Hunter, 2014; Kazemi, 1998).

Constructing these generalizations led students to be able to begin to transfer their understanding in order to build linear functions to represent the various geometrical figures. As a result, the series of tasks presented in this chapter collectively align with the vision and aim to support the development of algebraic reasoning in sixth grade students. From a theoretical perspective, careful analysis of the intended, enacted, and lived objects of learning found in this task sequence provides a clear picture of teaching through variation in the U.S. Further, this chapter provides an example that can potentially move U.S. algebra instruction away from a state in which schools do "not adequately prepare students to successfully navigate the significant transition from the concrete, arithmetic reasoning of elementary school to the increasingly complex, abstract algebraic reasoning required for middle school and beyond" (Blanton et al., 2015, p. 76).

337

REFERENCES

APPA Group (led by Sutherland, R.). (2004). A toolkit for analyzing approaches to algebra. In K. Stacey, H. Chick, & M. Kendal (Eds.), *The future of the teaching and learning of algebra* (pp. 73–96). Dordrecht: Kluwer.

Blanton, M. L. (2008). *Algebra and the elementary classroom: Transforming thinking, transforming practice*. Portsmouth, NH: Heinemann

Blanton, M. L., & Kaput, J. J. (2003). Developing elementary teachers': "Algebra eyes and ears." *Teaching Children Mathematics, 10*, 70–77.

Blanton, M., & Kaput, J. J. (2005). Characterizing a classroom practice that promotes algebraic reasoning. *Journal for Research in Mathematics Education, 36*, 412–446.

Blanton, M., Stephens, A., Knuth, E. Gardiner, A. M., Isler, I., & Kim, J. S. (2015). The development of children's algebraic thinking: The impact of a comprehensive early algebra intervention in third grade. *Journal for Research in Mathematics Education, 46*, 39–87.

Carraher, D. W., & Schliemann, A. D. (2007). Early algebra and algebraic reasoning. In F. K. Lester, Jr. (Ed.), *Second handbook of research on mathematics teaching and learning* (pp. 669–705). Reston, VA: National Council of Teachers of Mathematics.

Common Core State Standards Initiative. (2010). *Common core state standards for mathematics*. Washington, DC: National Governors Association Center for Best Practices and Council of Chief State School Officers. Retrieved from http://www.corestandards.org

Earnest, D. (2014). Exploring functions in elementary school: Leveraging the representational context. In K. Karp (Ed.), *Annual perspectives in mathematics education: Using research to improve instruction* (pp. 171–179). Reston, VA: National Council of Teachers of Mathematics.

Hunter, J. (2014). Developing learning environments which support early algebraic reasoning: A case from a New Zealand primary school. *Mathematics Education Research Journal, 26*, 659–682.

Kaput, J. J. (2008). What is algebra? What is algebraic reasoning? In J. J. Kaput, D. W. Carraher, & M. L. Blanton (Eds.), *Algebra in the early grades* (pp. 5–17). Reston, VA: National Council of Teachers of Mathematics.

Kazemi, E. (1998). Discourse that promotes conceptual understanding. *Teaching Children Mathematics, 4*, 410–414.

Kilpatrick, J., & Izsák, A. (2008). A history of algebra in the school curriculum. In C. E. Greenes (Ed.), *Algebra and algebraic thinking in school mathematics: Seventieth yearbook* (pp. 3–18). Reston, VA: National Council of Teachers of Mathematics.

Leung, A. (2012). Variation and mathematics pedagogy. In J. Dindyal, L. P. Cheng, & S. F. Ng (Eds.), *Proceedings of the 35th Annual Conference of the Mathematics Education Research Group of Australasia* (pp. 433–440). Singapore: MERGA.

Ling, M. L. (2012). *Variation theory and the improvement of teaching and learning*. Gothenburg, Sweden: Acta Universitatis Gothoburgensis.

Lins, R., & Kaput, J. J. (2004). The early development of algebraic reasoning: The current state of the field. In K. Stacey, H. Chick, & M. Kendal (Eds.), *The future of teaching and learning of algebra: The 12th ICMI study* (pp. 45–70). Boston, MA: Kluwer Academic Publishers.

Lo, M. L., & Marton, F. (2012). Towards a science of the art of teaching: Using variation theory as a guiding principle of pedagogical design. *International Journal for Lesson and Learning Studies, 1*, 7–22.

Marton, F., & Pang, M. F. (2006). On some necessary conditions of learning. *The Journal of the Learning Science, 15*, 193–220.

Marton, F., Runesson, U., & Tsui, A. B. M. (2004). The space of learning. In F. Marton & A. B. M. Tsui (Eds.), *Classroom discourse and the space of learning* (pp. 3–36). Mahwah, NJ: Lawrence Erlbaum Associates.

Ministry of Education. (2007). *The New Zealand curriculum*. Wellington: Learning Media.

National Council of Teachers of Mathematics. (1989). *Curriculum and evaluation standards*. Reston, VA: Author.

National Council of Teachers of Mathematics. (2000). *Principles and standards for school mathematics*. Reston, VA: Author.

Ontario Ministry of Education. (2005). *The Ontario curriculum: Grades 1–8 mathematics*. Toronto, ON: Queen's Printer for Ontario.

Ontario Ministry of Education. (n.d.). *Paying attention to algebraic reasoning*. Retrieved from http://edu.gov.on.ca/eng/literacynumeracy/PayingAttentiontoAlgebra.pdf

Soares, J., Blanton, M. L., & Kaput, J. J. (2005). Thinking algebraically across the elementary school curriculum. *Teaching Children Mathematics, 12,* 228–235.

Stacey, K., & Chick, H. (2004). Solving the problem with algebra. In K. Stacey, H. Chick, & M. Kendal (Eds.), *The future of the teaching and learning of algebra* (pp. 1–20). Dordrecht: Kluwer.

Warren, E., & Cooper, T. (2008). Generalising the pattern rule for visual growth patterns: Actions that support 8 year olds' thinking. *Educational Studies in Mathematics, 67,* 171–185.

Angela T. Barlow
Department of Mathematical Sciences
Middle Tennessee State University, USA

Kyle M. Prince
Central Magnet School in Murfreesboro
Tennessee, USA

Alyson E. Lischka
Department of Mathematical Sciences
Middle Tennessee State University, USA

Matthew D. Duncan
Department of University Studies
Middle Tennessee State University, USA

IRIT PELED AND ROZA LEIKIN

16. USING VARIATION OF MULTIPLICITY IN HIGHLIGHTING CRITICAL ASPECTS OF MULTIPLE SOLUTION TASKS AND MODELING TASKS

INTRODUCTION

Let us consider the following two problems.

Problem 1:

The Flower Patch Problem: A square piece of land, with a length of 10 meters on each side, is divided into 4 sections as described in the figure. Flowers are planted in the 2 dark areas and grass in the two white areas. What should be the length of the square at the bottom right so the flower area will be minimal?

Problem 2:

The Lemonade Stand Problem: During the County Fair, Patricia and Max put up a lemonade stand. Max bought disposable cups for $5 and Patricia bought some concentrated juice for $10. These were all their expenses. They sold lemonade for a total of $300. Help Patricia and Max figure out how to split the money.

We urge the reader to solve these problems before reading the paper. Then we suggest that the reader asks himself whether there is a different route or a different analysis of the given situation that leads to a different solution to any of the problems.

These two problems represent the kind of problems each of the article's authors uses in their didactical approaches and research tools: a Multiple Solution Task approach and a Modeling approach. Each of us has her own specific way and yet we feel that there is also a lot in common. Using the terms of variation theory, we were trying to identify or discern the nature and critical aspects of our learning (or teaching) objects. In this article we show how variation theory has offered us a relevant direction of analysis, and how its principles can be borrowed to help us achieve our goal, leading us to learn more about our own instruction.

Variation theory suggests that learning is always directed at changing one's view of the object of learning that has some critical features that the learner

R. Huang & Y. Li (Eds.), Teaching and Learning Mathematics through Variation, 341–353.

is expected to discern from among other possible features (Lo & Marton, 2012; Marton & Booth, 1997). The change can be associated with a mathematical or meta-mathematical concept, for example, a geometric figure such as a triangle (Lo & Marton, 2012), a set of numbers such as fractions, or the concept of proof.

Watson and Mason (2006) took the definition of the object of learning a step further and "use it to mean a thing on which a learner focuses and acts intelligently and mathematically by observing, analyzing, exploring, questioning, transforming, and so on. Thus an object could be a symbol, some text, a diagram, a theorem...." (p. 101). As explicated later, in this paper we consider variations in learning objects of two levels: the first is a didactical approach to teaching mathematical problems solving as function of a type of mathematical task presented to learners and the second object comprises the nature and meaning of a solution.

The main point of variation theory is that in order to discern critical features of the learning object one should have the opportunity to experience such a feature together and in comparison with other [non critical] features in the same dimension. That is, the learner must experience potential alternatives (Marton & Pang, 2006).

While variation theory focuses on learning, we borrow its ideas to identify features of our instruction. Using its principles about learning we can say that in implementing our approaches we have something specific towards which we direct our instruction, and want our students to learn as a result. As mathematics educators we are interested in being more aware of the nature of our object of instruction (and our students' object of learning).

In our case variation theory suggests that in order to discern critical features of each of our approaches, it would be helpful for us to make comparisons within a dimension that is common to the two approaches. Since both approaches create opportunities for students to investigate and discuss different solutions, the common dimension is identified as the dimension of multiplicity. That is, we compare the two approaches as two cases on this dimension by analyzing the nature and goals of these two multiplicities.

It is interesting to note that variation is present in this article in two levels: Didactical approaches (solutions within an approach), and concept constructs and meanings within a task. The first level involves viewing our approaches as alternatives in a space of approaches that promotes multiplicity, the second level is manifested within each approach, where students are encouraged to offer alternative solutions and engage in discussions about these variations.

The two approaches are compared using the two problem examples introduced above. Problem 1 will be discussed as an example of a Multiple Solution Task (MST) and Problem 2 as an example of a Multiple Model Task (MT). We will analyze the differences and similarities in the goals and learning mechanisms associated with MSTs and MTs, highlighting critical features that emerge from this comparison. We will then argue that both types of problems, together with each problem's didactic contract, encourage flexibility in different ways and aspects and yet similarly (and complementarily) lead to the development of mathematical thinking and creativity.

MULTIPLE SOLUTION TASKS (MSTs)

MSTs are tasks in which a student is explicitly required to solve a mathematical problem in different ways (e.g., Leikin, 2009). The problem may be solved using tools from different branches of mathematics (e.g., solving maxima-minima problems with tools from Euclidian or transformational geometry), or different tools from the same branch of mathematics (e.g., different representations of functions).

In a comparative analysis of mathematics lessons in the United States, Germany, and Japan, Stigler and Hiebert (1999) found that encouraging the idea that there may be multiple solutions to a problem enhanced the quality of the lessons. Solving problems in different ways is an effective instrument for developing connectedness of mathematical knowledge (Leikin, 2003, 2007; NCTM, 2000; Polya, 1981; Schoenfeld, 1985; Silver, 1997). It supports the construction of mathematical knowledge by encouraging students to shift between representations, compare strategies, and connect different concepts and ideas (Fennema & Romberg, 1999). Put differently, it supports the development of creativity and flexibility. Mathematical creativity—sometimes thought to be the province of advanced research mathematicians—is evaluated in school pupils with reference to their previous experience and to the performance of other students who have a similar educational history (Leikin, 2009; Liljedahl & Sriraman, 2006). Liljedahl and Sriraman (2006) defined mathematical creativity at the school level as a process that results in original (insightful) solutions to a given problem and/or approaches to an old problem from a new perspective (Liljedahl & Sriraman, 2006). Many researchers have shown that MSTs nurture such mathematical creativity and flexibility in students (e.g., Elia et al., 2009; Ervynck, 1991; Kwon, Park, & Park, 2006; Leikin, 2009; Silver, 1997; Star & Newton, 2009; Torbeyns, De Smedt, Ghesquière, & Verschaffel, 2009).

In the classroom, MSTs have other advantages as well. For instance, awareness of the possibility that a problem may be solved in different ways helps students persist in searching for the solution. Also, the existence of two solutions to a given problem provides solvers with two strategies in their mathematical practice, each one available when needed (Schoenfeld, 1988).

When the instructions for solving Problem 1 include a requirement to find many solutions to the problem, as depicted in Figure 1, the problem becomes an MST problem. In a class setting, the implementation of such a problem is designed to help the teacher create an atmosphere of inquiry, where the goal is not simply to solve a given problem. Ultimately, the teacher (or the teacher educator) working with students (or teachers) can create a didactic contract that promotes the habit of solving problems in as many ways as possible. While at first students are specifically required to find many possible solutions, the creation of classroom norms can make doing this a habit, even when there is no explicit request for multiple solutions.

Example 1: Towards Flexibility and Connections

Problem 1 was presented to teachers, and following their own experience with MSTs, the teachers presented the problem as an MST in their classes. In one of the classes, students worked with Problem 1 in small groups of three or four and each group was directed towards one of the solutions. After reaching the required solution, the students were encouraged to think about additional explanations for the solution or additional ways of solving the problem. When the work in small groups was completed, students from the different groups presented their solutions to the whole class.

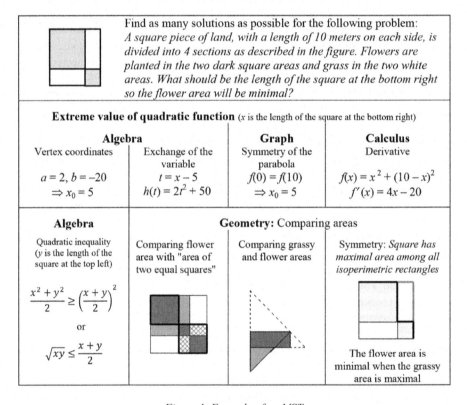

Figure 1. Example of an MST

The nature of students' work is an additional expression and another use of variation theory in this article. As detailed above, the problem was held constant while the students discussed and compared alternative solutions. This type of variation is described by Ryve et al. (2012), who offer some ideas for establishing mathematics for teaching through the introduction of variation. As further discussed, this variation enabled the discovery of critical features and facilitated interesting insights.

The following excerpts demonstrate that the MST format was used by the teacher (Miki) to encourage a flexible problem-solving process. The teacher encouraged students to provide varied explanations and solutions, and thereby opened opportunities for the students to draw connections themselves.

Miki: Is there any *additional explanation*? [The student in this group (who worked with a table-of-values card) determined the domain $0 < x < 10$ and calculated the area for various x-s.]

After the student answered the question, Miki asked for a more rigorous explanation:

Miki: O.K. They say that x is between 0 and 10. First the values increase and then decrease [she draws a parabola starting at $(0, 0)$ and ending at $(10, 0)$], and *now what do you say*?

Student: It [the maximal point] is exactly in the middle... between the smallest and the biggest x. ... as long as it is a parabola *it must be symmetrical.*

When three solutions to the problem were presented, Miki asked students about *additional solutions.*

Miki: Is there an *additional solution*?

Student: It is possible *to combine* the second and third ways. ...*The vertex* [of the parabola] is the extreme point [at which the derivative equals 0]. ...[We got the vertex] *using symmetry*. I take the two intersection points with the x axis and find the middle.

When discussing this episode, Miki reported:

Miki: Without my guidance, the *students had drawn connections between table-based and parabola-based solutions.* This was really surprising... The connection to symmetry made *by the students* was simply astonishing!

Following presentation of the solutions, Miki directed students toward a discussion in which they compared the different proofs, identified their differences and similarities, and looked at their difficulty and their beauty. Such comparisons lead to the development of both critical thinking and rigorous use of mathematical language. While some differences are obvious ("since the picture looks different"), others are less trivial. Moreover, by comparing similarities between obviously different solutions, learners construct connections between different mathematical concepts and theorems (e.g., median and midline, circle radius, and hypotenuse of a right triangle) and thus deepen their mathematical understanding. In short, such

345

discussions can help students look at performed proofs through a new lens, and can raise the level of the mathematical discussion or even move the discussion to new mathematical territory.

MODELING TASKS (MTs)

While MSTs (as presented above) are directed at promoting creativity and expertise in problem solving, researchers in recent years have drawn attention to tasks that involve problem solving of a different nature, with different goals (Blum & Niss, 1991; Lesh & Doerr, 2003; Lesh & Zawojewski, 2007). This type of task often involves complex word problems that present a realistic situation and obey special design principles (Lesh et al., 2000).

A central part of the task entails organizing the situation and making decisions with regard to mathematizing the situation (i.e., by using some mathematical model or integrating different models). This process of fitting mathematical models to situations is termed modeling, and the problem solver is expected to go through a modeling cycle described by Blum and Leiß (2007). Researchers have shown that students (and teachers) need to work on a sequence of modeling problems in order to develop modeling competencies (Maaβ, 2006) and go through the whole cycle successfully. These problems are different from traditional problems, and it takes students some time and practice to realize that the didactic contract has changed and that they need to adjust their problem solving habits to the new contract.

In addition, as suggested by Peled and Bassan (2005) and Peled and Ballacheff (2011), the promotion of modeling tasks should also aim at helping students better understand what it means to fit mathematical models to situations. This involves a new understanding of the roles of mathematical tools and an understanding of the (differing) degrees of freedom the problem solver has in mathematizing different problem situations.

Example 2 below is presented as a part of an instructional sequence. Unlike common school problems, where the solver is expected to use one specific mathematical model (a model that the problem composer had in mind), in this case the didactic contract allows and encourages the solver to consider other models.

Because this problem is similar to familiar investment problems, there is some tendency to solve it by fitting a ratio model and using the purchase ratio to split the profits. Still, other mathematical models are possible, with each model leading to a different solution. Figure 2 shows three examples from the space of possible models and solutions.

Example 2: Towards an Epistemological Understanding

Peled and Balacheff (2011) detailed a discussion evoked by this problem in a group of elementary school teachers, who came up with the three solutions shown in

Figure 2. In reacting to the teacher educator's question about whether one of the solutions can be considered better than the others, one responded (p. 313):

Anna: The answer that uses proportion is the correct answer. The other two answers can be correct only in a social-studies class. In a mathematics class I expect a mathematical solution.

| **The Lemonade Stand Problem:** |
| During the County Fair, Patricia and Max put up a lemonade stand. Max bought disposable cups for \$5 and Patricia bought some concentrated juice for \$10. These were all their expenses. They sold lemonade for a total of \$300. Help Patricia and Max figure out how to split the money. |
| 1. Reimburse expenses and split the rest evenly. The total amount spent on expenses is 5 + 10, leaving 300 − 15 to be evenly split. Thus, Max would get \$5 + \$ ((300 - 15) / 2) = 147.5 and Patricia would get \$10 + ((300 − 15) / 2) = 152.5. |
| 2. Regard expenses as investments or risks. Divide the total earnings proportionally using the investment (expenses) ratio 5:10 (1:2). In this case Max gets \$100 and Patricia gets \$200. |
| 3. Split the earnings evenly. In this case Max and Patricia get \$150 each. |

Figure 2. Example of an MT with alternative solutions

The teacher educator (TE) asked Anna to try and convince the group that they should use proportion. Turning to the whole class, the TE asked them to think about the question: *Who determines the mathematical model we should use, and how do we know that proportion is the right model here?*

Leora: I think that in the other two solutions, half-half and reimburse and split, we made some assumptions on the basis of which the solution was given.

TE: And what about the proportion solution – did we make no assumption there?

Leora: No. There was no assumption there. This is given in the problem: This is the investment and this is the income.

Molly (turns to Leora abruptly):

Who said so?! It isn't written here (in the problem) "please split the income using the investment ratio."

As this episode shows, while one of the teachers was absolutely sure that the problem calls for proportion, another teacher realized that there is no information in the problem that dictates the use of proportion. The choice of proportion as *the one* correct model is often made in such cases despite the fact there is no relevant information in the problem to support it.

The discussion of alternative answers creates an "insight" moment that helps teachers (as learners) break away from the habit of using proportion intuitively, without much deliberation about the situation or about why proportion is used, just because the problem seems to belong to a familiar type of proportion problems.

Indeed, this problem was designed precisely to serve as an example of a situation where the participants (in the situation) or the problem solvers could have chosen from a variety of mathematical models. On the one hand, the problem has a structure similar to the structure of a proportion problem. On the other hand, it is not a familiar textbook problem, and so solvers might use their personal experience to suggest another solution. In this latter case, they are likely to suggest another mathematical model (e.g., reimburse and split).

Thus, as in the case of the MST approach, variation is exhibited here through alternative solutions to the same modeling problem. This multiplicity is, again, a good trigger for argumentation that leads to insight and promotes the development of a metacognitive perspective of the meaning of mathematizing a given situation.

As mentioned earlier, modeling competencies and modeling perspectives involve a new type of problems that have to be experienced gradually. Thus, as detailed by Peled and Balacheff (2011), the Lemonade Stand Problem is not an isolated problem solving experience. It is presented within a problem sequence, the purpose of which is to change teacher or student modeling conceptions and competencies.

DISCERNING CRITICAL ASPECTS

The didactic contracts associated with MSTs and MTs include mathematical assignments that lead to the transformation of relatively standard problems into problems that promote mental flexibility through the request to generate and discuss different solution alternatives.

Still, there are many differences between the components of the learning process when tasks of these two types are employed. The focus on comparing student or teacher behavior in the two problems facilitated the identification of relevant features and resulted in the analysis presented in Figure 3.

Although both problems serve as examples of multiplicity and flexibility, their multiplicities are of an entirely different nature. MSTs are problems that essentially have one solution, and their multiplicity is exhibited in the different ways of reaching this result. These different ways often involve a description of a certain mathematical structure by using different mathematical tools. The different views of the structure create analogical expressions that suggest interesting connections between, for example, geometry and algebra, and might lead to the construction of more general structure schemes.

	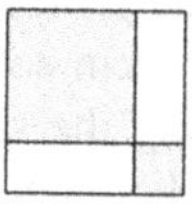 MSTs	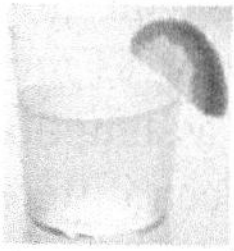 MTs
MAP of multiplicity	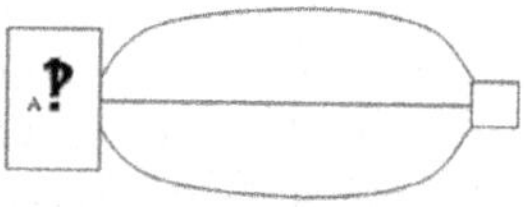 The problem has one solution (result), but there are multiple ways to get to this solution.	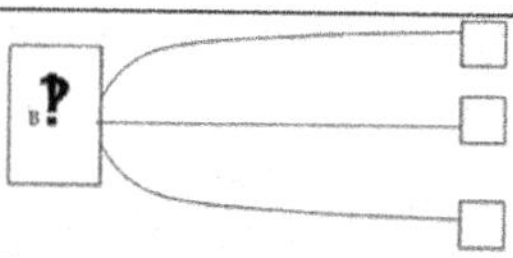 The problem might* have multiple models fitted to the given problem situation, each leading to a different solution (result). *some MTs have multiple routes leading to the same result, as in MSTs.
The goal	Developing mathematical connections and intra-task flexibility by using different mathematical tools. Developing mathematical and cognitive meta-knowledge: Awareness of the possibility of using different mathematical tools.	Developing modeling skills (skills involved in decision making in fitting mathematical models to given situations). Developing epistemological and cognitive meta-knowledge: Awareness of the freedom to choose different models depending on problem context.
Production of multiple solutions	Each student produces multiple solutions. Student initiated or teacher guided. Implementation of different tools to one problem by a student.	Each student produces one solution. If different solutions are not produced, then the students are presented with (prepared) "children's solutions." Different mathematical models are chosen by different students.
Habits of mind	Production of multiple solutions, search for mathematical connections and elegant solutions.	A shift from automatic application of conventional schemes towards analysis of the situation in context.
The role of reality	The use of the situation is artificial. A mathematical problem dressed as a real-world problem.	An authentic situation with a genuine need for a solution. Demonstrates the role mathematics plays in helping us cope with everyday situations.

Figure 3. Comparison of two types of Tasks

In contrast, the multiplicity in MTs, especially those involving a social-moral situation, involves multiple structures. The problem solver might have the choice of different assumptions and ways of organizing the situation, which results in a choice between different kinds of models. Each student might suggest a different mathematical model leading to a different result, and the class discussion would lead to an understanding of the legitimacy of these multiple structures and results.

Thus, the way in which we open "closed" problems has to do with the goals that can be attained in each case. MSTs usually lead to proving a specific mathematical property or finding a specific numerical answer, whereas MTs lead to different, sometimes, controversial results. MSTs nurture mental flexibility and connectedness of mathematical knowledge, while MTs develop modeling skills and an awareness of the possibility of applying multiple mathematical structures to a particular problem. MSTs develop freedom in choosing solution routes, and MTs develop awareness of the potential for freedom in choosing a mathematical model. In both cases students advance their specific problem-solving skills along with their understanding of the structure and nature of the problem-solving process.

DISCUSSION

In this article, we demonstrate the contribution of variation theory in two different cases or levels. First we view a didactical approach as an object of learning, placing two didactical approaches on the same dimension where they can be compared to discern their critical aspects. Another use involves variation within each of the approaches. Now the object of learning is a solution and the goal is to understand the meaning of a solution. Within a given approach a problem is kept constant and alternative solutions in the dimension of different routes or the dimension of different structures are encouraged and compared.

The first use involves a comparison of two approaches involving multiplicity. One approach (MSTs) involves the explicit challenge (that might later become implicit) to find multiple mathematical tools that can be used in its solutions. The other (MTs) calls on solvers to (1) question whether a mathematical model that is usually applied is justified and (2) apply considerations of "social justice" to the situation given in a problem and then to apply mathematical models that fit those considerations.

In an effort to better understand the nature of each of these approaches we follow principles of variation theory. The theory suggests that critical features of each of these two approaches would emerge when an approach, viewed as a learning object, is compared to another learning object. Such a comparison is helpful, especially when the objects can be placed in a common dimension. In this case, both approaches could be situated in the dimension of multiplicity. This enables us to investigate similar and different features of the two multiplicities.

Our comparison resulted in discerning several critical features where the learning objects varied with respect to these aspects. The main difference involved the nature of "what" varies within a given multiplicity. MSTs focus on multiple strategies to the same solution that are based on different properties/theorems of the same mathematical concept, whereas MTs focus on problem structure. That is, different realistic considerations or assumptions might lead to organizing a given situation using different mathematical models (e.g., an additive structure versus a multiplicative structure). The different structures, i.e., mathematical models that fit the situation, might lead to different results.

A close question to "what varies" is "who offers multiple solutions." MSTs require that each of the problem solvers comes up with many solutions, and, in fact, individual's creativity and mathematical connections are determined by observing the number and quality of the solutions. MTs, in contrast, encourage group work where each group makes its own assumptions, and the variety of solutions comes up later in class discussion. It should be noted, however, that the didactical contract in MTs encourages students to consider and analyze the situation rather than impose a certain structure almost automatically.

Another critical feature is the nature of using reality. The focus of MSTs is basically mathematical, i.e., to afford the use of different mathematical concepts and experience connections between them (e.g., a geometric solution and an algebraic solution). In MTs, on the other hand, the focus is on developing modeling skills, i.e., to learn to analyze and organize a situation. Correspondingly, reality does not play a "real" role in MSTs. It serves more as an ornament or motivation, or an excuse for constructing a mathematical model. Once this model is constructed there is no genuine interest in the result. In MTs, on the other hand, the dilemma is genuine and "someone" in the story is interested in getting a real-world answer.

The second use of variation is exhibited in the article within each of the approaches. In each case, the students are encouraged to construct or discuss alternative solutions. In the MST example, students constructed different solution routes using, for example, algebra, geometry, or a qualitative analysis. In their discussion they mapped solutions, made connections, and discovered special features such as symmetry, and thus acquired new insights from the opportunity to experience variation.

In the MT example teachers were given a problem that was designed to elicit several different mathematical models resulting from making different assumptions about the realistic situation. The discussion involved argumentation that challenged existing habits leading to a new meta-perspective on the meaning of mathematizing a situation.

Our experience demonstrates that after a period of systematic (teacher-initiated) engagement with MSTs and MTs, students search for different solutions on their own initiative. However, the didactic situations created by the two types of problems are different: When coping with MSTs, each student is required to find several means of reaching the solution, and then students take part in a critical and comparative discussion of the collective solution space. When coping with MTs, the solution process starts with a discussion of different (non-mathematical) considerations that can be applied to the situation, and then the students are encouraged to fit to each

351

of the considerations a different mathematical model. This stage can be performed collectively or individually according to the instructor's decision.

Our analysis of MSTs and MTs shows that in spite of the different ways in which these problems encourage multiple solutions, the openness in both cases has a good potential to develop learners' critical reasoning, thinking about the meaning of mathematical solutions, and an ability to search for alternative explanations and interpretations of mathematical situations.

We hope that the openness created by these multiplicities will lead to a more general opening of minds. Hopefully, students who get used to facing one of these problem types will also start questioning conventions related to the other type. For example, students who have developed the habit of searching for non-conventional solutions may behave less automatically when applying mathematical structures to situations. Perhaps we should facilitate this flexibility by having each of us discuss her colleague's approach with students just as we have discussed and compared the approaches in this article. That is, introduce variation of approaches in class.

The idea is to develop a problem solver who will not let conventions make decisions for him, but will take responsibility during all steps of the problem-solving process. For this problem solver, flexibility and self decision-making become "the name of the game."

REFERENCES

Blum, M., & Leiβ, D. (2007). How do students and teachers deal with modelling problems? In C. Haines, P. Galbraith, W. Blum, & S. Khan (Eds.), *Mathematical Modeling (ICTMA 12): Education, engineering and economics* (pp. 222–231). Chichester: Horwood Publishing.

Blum, V., & Niss, M. (1991). Applied mathematical problem solving, modeling, applications, and links to other subjects – State, trends and issues in mathematics instruction. *Educational Studies in Mathematics, 22*, 37–68.

Elia, I., Van den Heuvel-Panhuizen, M., & Kolovou A. (2009). Exploring strategy use and strategy flexibility in non-routine problem solving by primary school high achievers in mathematics. *ZDM Mathematics Education, 41*, 605–618.

Ervynck, G. (1991). Mathematical creativity. In D. Tall (Ed.), *Advanced mathematical thinking* (pp. 42–53). Dordrecht, The Netherlands: Kluwer.

Fennema, E., & Romberg, T. A. (Eds.). (1999). *Classrooms that promote mathematical understanding.* Mahwah, NJ: Erlbaum.

House, P. A., & Coxford, A.F. (1995). *Connecting mathematics across the curriculum: 1995 Yearbook.* Reston, VA: NCTM.

Kwon, O. N., Park, J. S., & Park, J. H. (2006). Cultivating divergent thinking in mathematics through an open-ended approach. *Asia Pacific Education Review, 7*, 51–61.

Leikin, R. (2003). Problem-solving preferences of mathematics teachers: Focusing on symmetry. *Journal of Mathematics Teacher Education, 6*, 297–329.

Leikin, R. (2007). Habits of mind associated with advanced mathematical thinking and solution spaces of mathematical tasks. In D. Pitta-Pantazi & G. Philippo (Eds.), *Proceeding of The Fifth Conference of the European Society for Research in Mathematics Education – CERME-5* (pp. 2330–2339) (CD-ROM and On-line). Retrieved June 2, 2016, from http://ermeweb.free.fr/Cerme5.pdf

Leikin, R. (2009). Exploring mathematical creativity using multiple solution tasks. In R. Leikin, A. Berman, & B. Koichu (Eds.), *Creativity in mathematics and the education of gifted students* (pp. 129–145). Rotterdam, The Netherlands: Sense Publishers.

Lesh, R., & Doerr, H. M. (2003). *Beyond constructivism: A model and modeling perspective on teaching, learning, and problem solving in mathematics education*. Mahwah, NJ: Lawrence Erlbaum.

Lesh, R., Hoover, M., Hole, B., Kelly, A., & Post, T. (2000). Principles for developing thought-revealing activities for students and teachers. In A. Kelly & R. A. Lesh (Eds.), *Handbook of research design in mathematics and science education* (pp. 591–645). Mahwah, NJ: Lawrence Erlbaum.

Liljedahl, P., & Sriraman, B. (2006). Musings on mathematical creativity. *For the Learning of Mathematics, 26*, 20–23.

Lo, M. L., & Marton, F. (2012). Toward a science of the art of teaching: Using variation theory as a guiding principle of pedagogical design. *International Journal for Lesson and Learning Studies, 1*(1), 7–22.

Marton, F., & Booth, S. (1997). *Learning and awareness*. Mahwah, NJ: Erlbaum.

Marton, F., & Pang, M. F. (2006). On some necessary conditions of learning. *The Journal of the Learning Science, 15*, 193–220.

Maaβ, K. (2006). What are modelling competencies? *ZDM Mathematics Education, 38*, 113–142.

National Council of Teachers of Mathematics (NCTM). (2000). *Principles and standards for school mathematics*. Reston, VA: Author.

Peled, I., & Balacheff, N. (2011). Beyond realistic considerations: Modeling conceptions and controls in task examples with simple word problems. *ZDM Mathematics Education, 43*, 307–315.

Peled, I., & Bassan-Cincenatus, R. (2005). Degrees of freedom in modeling: Taking certainty out of proportion. In H. L. Chick & J. L. Vincent (Eds.), *Proceedings of the 29th International Conference for the Psychology of Mathematics Education, 4*, 57–64.

Polya, G. (1981). *Mathematical discovery: On understanding, learning and teaching problem solving*. New York, NY: Wiley.

Ryve, A., Nilsson, P., & Mason, J. (2012). Establishing mathematics for teaching within classroom interactions in teacher education. *Educational Studies in Mathematics, 81*, 1–14.

Schoenfeld, A. H. (1994). What do we know about mathematics curricula? *Journal of Mathematical Behaviour, 13*, 55–80.

Silver, E. A. (1997). Fostering creativity through instruction rich in mathematical problem solving and problem posing. *ZDM Mathematics Education, 3*, 75–80.

Star, J. R., & Newton, k. J. (2009). The nature and development of experts' strategy flexibility for solving equations. *ZDM Mathematics Education, 41*, 557–567.

Stigler J. W., & Hiebert J. (1999). *The teaching gap: Best ideas from the world's teachers for improving education in the classroom*. New York, NY: The Free Press.

Torbeyns, J. De Smedt, B. Ghesquiere, P., & Verschaffel, L. (2009). Jump or compensate? Strategy flexibility in the number domain up to 100. *ZDM Mathematics Education, 41*, 581–590.

Watson, A., & Mason, J. (2006). Seeing an exercise as a single mathematical object: Using variation to structure sense-making. *Mathematical Thinking and Learning, 8*, 91–111.

Irit Peled

Mathematics Education

Faculty of Education, University of Haifa, Israel

Roza Leikin

Mathematics Education, Gifted Education

RANGE center

Faculty of Education, University of Haifa, Israel

ULLA RUNESSON AND ANGELIKA KULLBERG

17. LEARNING TO TEACH WITH VARIATION

Experiences from Learning Study in Sweden

TEACHING WITH VARIATION: A TAKEN FOR GRANTED DIMENSION?

Let us imagine two different grade 6 classrooms where the aim of the lesson is the same; to calculate examples such as ¾ of 12 = 9. When introducing this, in one of the classrooms, the teacher demonstrates a method for computing; "divide the integer (12) by the denominator (4) and multiply the quotient (3) by the numerator (3)." This method is then applied to three different problems; ⅔ of 90, $\frac{1}{5}$ of 40 and $\frac{3}{5}$ of 60. In the other classroom, the teacher gives the learners a problem to solve: "mark $\frac{3}{7}$ of a 7 by 8 squared rectangle." After having worked out the problem in pairs, they present their solutions. It was found that some learners had divided the small squares into eight groups of seven and marked three of them. Others had divided the small squares into eight groups of seven and marked three out of seven squares in each group (cf., Behr, Harel, Post, & Lesh, 1992). These differences in how the same topic was handled in the two classrooms could, on a general level, be described as; in the first lesson the same method was applied to different examples, whereas in the second, different methods were applied to the same example. Or put differently, in one of the lessons the method was invariant and the examples varied, in the other lesson it was the opposite. Thus, that which was varied and that which was invariant—the pattern of variation—was different in the two lessons (Runesson, 1999).

It might be the case that how variation appears in teaching materials and is used by teachers is so familiar that it is almost invisible (Sun, 2011). This seems to be the case for these teachers too. When studied in action they demonstrate an ability to use variation and invariance when they focus on aspects of the topic taught. However, when they talked about their lesson plan in the interview before the lesson and were directly asked how to teach to enhance students' learning of fractions as operator (e.g., ¾ of 12), they did not mention the use of variation at all. Instead, they talked about the organization and arrangements of the lesson. For instance, they emphasized 'interaction' as an important means for the learners to discuss and reflect. The importance of using manipulatives was also mentioned, as one of the teachers said, "it must be tangible, [they will be] cutting strings, folding paper [in the lesson]" (Runesson, 1999, p. 164). From this we would ask: Is it possible to make such taken-for-granted principles visible to teachers and can they learn how to create patterns of variation more purposefully and systematically? In this chapter we will

R. Huang & Y. Li (Eds.), Teaching and Learning Mathematics through Variation, 355–372.

use two cases to illustrate, (1) how a group of Swedish teachers can learn to make use of principles of variation and invariance, and (2) how that seems to affect their ways of handling the topic over time. These teachers had participated in a form of professional learning community, called learning study (described below), where a theory of learning—variation theory—was used as a guiding principle.

VARIATION—A NECESSARY CONDITION OF LEARNING

Does a difference in the enacted pattern of variation, such as the ones described above, matter for learning? This can be answered by studying how teaching and learning are related. However, there are indeed problems with this. Learning can hardly be predicted and there is no simple cause and effect relationship between teaching and learning. Still, there is a need to know how teachers' actions affect student learning. Particularly, teachers themselves need to be aware of this. For that purpose, they need a theory that can guide them to evaluate and plan a lesson that would lead to better learning (Nuthall, 2004, 2005). Variation theory (Marton, 2015; Marton & Booth, 1997) has been implemented with that purpose in mind and with promising results.

Variation theory explains learning failures in a specific way and spells out the conditions of learning; when learners fail to learn what was intended, they have not discerned aspects necessary to discern. So, the very core idea of variation theory is that discernment is a necessary condition of learning. The point of departure is that our awareness has a structure. We do not attend to all aspects of an object. Neither do we attend to them in the same way or simultaneously. However, what aspects we attend to or discern is of decisive significance for how we understand or experience the object. So if that which seems to be 'the same thing' (e.g. ¾ of 12) is experienced differently, this has to do with differences in discernment of aspects of 'the same thing.'

Discernment cannot happen without experiencing variation, however. So for example, it is more likely that the relational aspect ¾ of 12 is discerned, if different relationships are possible to experience at the same time. If the relationship ¾ of 12 is opened up as a dimension of variation, (e.g., by juxtaposing and comparing dividing a 3 × 4 rectangle into three groups of four then marking three of the groups, with the same rectangle divided into three groups of four with three small squares marked within each group), it is likely discerned that ¾ of 12 represents relationship. Thus, it is a premise of variation theory that discernment presupposes variation; we learn from seeing differences and making distinctions (cf., Gibson & Gibson, 1955) prior to seeing similarities.

Variation theory states that learning is a function of discernment and discernment comes from experiencing variation and making distinctions. Therefore, on a theoretical ground it could be argued that the pattern of variation and invariance matters. When comparing two lessons where the same topic was taught and arranged similarly, several studies have demonstrated that differences in the pattern of variation seemed to have a significant role for student learning. These studies suggest that ideas about variation and invariance are powerful principles of pedagogical design that maximize student learning (Cheng & Lo, 2013).

Furthermore, variation theory states that the variation must concern the aspects we want to draw the learners' attention to. Teachers must be aware of (1) what aspects the learners must attend to, and (2) make these aspects learnable by means of variation. In learning study (described in detail below) teachers can become aware of how the use of variation can focus learners' attention to aspects of the object of learning.

VARIATION THEORY AS A GUIDING PRINCIPLE IN LEARNING STUDY

When Lesson study (Lewis, 2002; Yoshida & Fernandez, 2004) was introduced in the West, it was suggested that this collaborative learning and teacher development model contributed greatly to the high quality learning of the Japanese students. In the reflective and iterative process, teachers can observe the lesson and gain insights into teaching and learning; insights that are shared and are the basis for revision and refinement of the lesson. The potential of Lesson study arrangement for teacher professional development was picked up by a group of researchers in Hong Kong around 2000 in a project aiming at developing teachers' capabilities to deal with diversity in the classroom. They took Lesson study as a point of departure, but introduced variation theory as a basis for their work. They anticipated that an explicit theory of learning would add value to Lesson study by focusing on what is learned (the object of learning), what the necessary conditions for learning might be, and how to make them discernable in class. In this way variation theory was put to the test as a pedagogical theory used by teachers in their everyday practice.

Furthermore, they added a diagnostic pre- and post-test as well as a more systematic approach to the observation of the lessons, and named it 'learning study' (since learning, rather than lesson, was the focus) (Marton & Pang, 2003). Thus, learning study became a research-like version of Lesson study "with the double aim of boosting the participating teachers' ability to help their students to learn, on the one hand, and to produce new insights into learning and teaching that can also be shared with teachers who do not participate in the study, on the other hand" (Marton & Runesson, 2015, p. 104).

LEARNING STUDY

Variation theory focuses on *what* is learned prior to *how* it is learned. For every object of learning there are certain aspects of that object that must be learned. Some students master these, others do not. Those aspects that are not (yet) discerned, but are necessary to discern, are called 'critical aspects.' These aspects must be identified for every object of learning and for every group of learners. Furthermore, what is critical for learning cannot be derived either from variation theory or from

357

mathematics *alone*, but must be identified by studying and relating the learners' learning and how the object of learning is handled in the lesson. By comparing the learning outcomes from the diagnostic test before and after the lesson and carefully analyzing the lesson, differences in student learning can be related to features of the lesson. If the learners do not improve on the post-test, questions about the necessary conditions—what they might be—and whether they were made possible to discern in the lesson can be addressed.

When the critical aspects are identified, principles from variation theory (e.g., what we want the students to notice must vary) are used to design the lesson in terms of how to handle the content.

In learning study teachers can become aware of how the use of variation can focus learners' attention towards aspects of the object of learning. They can also put to the test and explore how a deliberately designed pattern of variation affects student learning (Elliott, 2012; Kullberg, 2010).

In the Swedish landscape, learning study has been used as an approach for research (Holmqvist, 2011; Kullberg & Runesson, 2013; Marton & Pang, 2013; Vikstrom, 2014) and as an arrangement for teacher professional development. It is well known and has engaged thousands of teachers and their students from pre-school to upper secondary level and university level in various subjects. It has been promoted as an effective model for school development and collaborative learning by The Swedish National Agency of Education.

USING VARIATION PRINCIPLES TO COLLECTIVELY DESIGN AND REVISE A TASK

The first example we will use to illustrate teachers' learning to teach with variation describes how a group of teachers collectively tried to enhance grade 8 students' learning of division with denominators <1 but >0 by exploring how variation between examples affected students' learning.

The idea that it is possible to design a task based on a systematic and conscious use of variation has been suggested by Watson and Mason (2006). They argue that "Constructing tasks that use variation and change optimally is a design project in which reflection about learner response leads to further refinement and precision of example choice and sequence" (p. 100). Furthermore, the notion that an inbuilt pattern of variation between examples, where only one or few variable changes at a time and in a systematic way, can draw learners' attention to essential structures and make learners aware of relationships of numbers has been shown (e.g., Runesson, 2005).

The learning study with division was conducted with three teachers at the same school in collaboration with a researcher (see Kullberg, Runesson, & Mårtensson, 2014 for further details). The group met regularly for approximately three months to design and revise the lesson based on analysis of video-recordings from the lessons and learning outcomes of the pre- and post-test. They were all experienced mathematics teachers (8–20 years of teaching experience) and participated on a voluntary basis.

Our analysis is mainly based on transcripts of video-recorded lessons, but complemented with analysis of transcripts of pre- and post-lesson meetings. Our rational for studying teacher learning in class when enacting the lesson, and not from analyzing interviews or self-reports for example, comes from Ryle (1949/2002) who conceived knowing as a disposition to act, and Schön's (1983) notion of 'knowing-in-action.' What we count as teacher learning is the enacted learning in the classroom and furthermore, what is enacted, we see as significant since that is what the learners encounter and have possibilities to experience.

From the teacher designed diagnostic pre-test the group found that some students answered in a way that could be interpreted as: 'when dividing with a decimal number (e.g., $4 \div 0.2$, $4 \div 0.02$, or $4 \div 0.002$) the quotient is less than the quotient in divisions with whole numbers, e.g. $4 \div 2$ (cf. Bell, Swan, & Taylor, 1981; Bell, Fischbein, & Greer, 1984; Bell, Greer, Grimison, & Mangan, 1989; Fischbein, Deri, Nello, & Marino, 1885; Okazaki, & Koyama, 2005). To overcome these difficulties among the students and change their ways of understanding, the teachers designed the lesson to achieve what they thought must be the learning goal: that the students should understand why the quotient sometimes becomes greater than the numerator in a division (Mårtensson, 2015).

The teachers designed some tasks they thought would enhance students' learning. One of these tasks, comprising a set of examples, is illustrated in Figure 1. The set of examples demonstrates variation and invariance. Taking a closer look at the variation between the examples in the two columns, there is a *variation in operations* (multiplication and division, 6 examples of each). There is also *variation between the examples in each column*. The numbers in the denominator (and in one factor), consist of numbers both greater and less than 1, with 20 being the biggest and 0.1 the smallest. Comparing the examples in the two columns, the factor/quotient 100 is invariant and the same numbers in the denominator/factor are used in both columns.

Thus, the variation between the examples (within and between the columns) creates opportunities for students to experience differences and similarities of various kinds.

However, the inherent pattern of variation needs to be presented in class in a way that brings out the aspects that teachers intend learners to notice. What is made possible to see in terms of similarities and differences is due to what differences and similarities between the examples are pointed to. So, even if teachers might have the skill to design a set of examples based on principles of variation, they might not have the skill to implement it in a way that brings the intended pattern of variation (and thus, the critical aspect) to the fore of attention. In the following section we will show how the above set of examples was successively implemented and re-designed during the iterative process of observing and revising the lesson. This, we interpret, led to a more efficient use of the inherent pattern of variation in terms of how the anticipated critical aspects were brought out.

$$100 \cdot 20 = 2000 \qquad \frac{100}{20} = 5$$

$$100 \cdot 4 = 400 \qquad \frac{100}{4} = 25$$

$$100 \cdot 2 = 200 \qquad \frac{100}{2} = 50$$

$$100 \cdot 1 = 100 \qquad \frac{100}{1} = 100$$

$$100 \cdot 0.5 = 50 \qquad \frac{100}{0.5} = 200$$

$$100 \cdot 0.1 = 10 \qquad \frac{100}{0.1} = 1000$$

Figure 1. The set of multiplication and division examples designed by the teachers

Lesson 1

Although the teachers had designed the task to make it possible for the students to see why the quotient sometimes can be greater than the numerator, this was not made possible to experience in lesson 1. In lesson 1, the examples were sequenced and discussed in a way that mostly emphasized the multiplication – division relationship. The numbers (1) to (3) in Figure 2 show the order in which the examples were introduced in the discussion. First, in sequence, (1) two multiplication examples were solved ($100 \cdot 20$, $100 \cdot 4$), followed by two division examples ($100 \div 20$, $100 \div 4$). The teacher emphasized that the same numbers were used in the calculations, but did not point out any relationship at that time. In (1) the operations varied, whereas the numbers 100, 4, and 20 were invariant. Thereafter, the examples in (2) and (3) were calculated.

After the calculation of the examples, the teacher directed the students' attention towards the division column and inverse relationship between multiplication and division. She pointed out that the quotient multiplied by the denominator is equal to the numerator ($5 \cdot 20 = 100$, $25 \cdot 4 = 100$, $50 \cdot 2 = 100$, etc.). She concluded, "So one can connect these two operations (multiplication and division)." The analysis of the similarities and differences that were explicitly pointed out suggests that the planned variation inherent in the task was not fully used. Although the teacher at one point said that "the answers get greater the further down (in the division column) one gets", this did not address *why* the quotient sometimes is greater than the numerator. Instead the implemented variation, in terms of similarities and differences between and within the examples, brought the inverse relationship between division and multiplication to the fore.

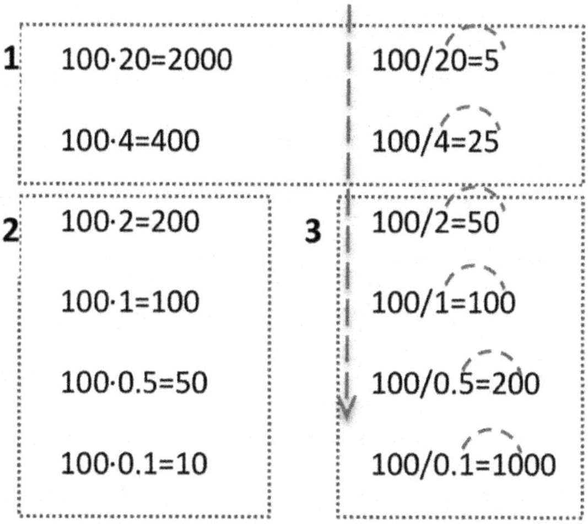

1	$100 \cdot 20 = 2000$		$100/20 = 5$
	$100 \cdot 4 = 400$		$100/4 = 25$
2	$100 \cdot 2 = 200$	3	$100/2 = 50$
	$100 \cdot 1 = 100$		$100/1 = 100$
	$100 \cdot 0.5 = 50$		$100/0.5 = 200$
	$100 \cdot 0.1 = 10$		$100/0.1 = 1000$

Figure 2. The sequence of the examples enacted in lesson 1, see (1 to 3). The arrows show what the teacher directed students' attention to, in this case inverse relationship between multiplication and division, and that the further down in the column, the greater 'the answer'

Lesson 2

During the post-lesson meeting after lesson 1, the teachers realized that the way the task was enacted did not help the learners to see what was targeted: why the quotient in a division with a denominator <1 but >0 is greater than the numerator. This insight led to another way of enacting the task in lesson 2 (with a new group of students). Now the teacher directed the students' attention towards (1) the patterns in the multiplication and the division column in terms of the relationship between the size of the product/quotient the multiplicand/the denominator successively changes into a smaller number, and (2) the difference between examples of divisions with denominators < 1 and >1, (3) 'the turning point', i.e., the multiplicand/denominator =1, and (4) the internal relationship between the quotient, numerator, and denominator.

As is seen in Figure 3, the examples in each column were calculated separately; first the multiplication column (1) and next the division column (2). Thereafter the teacher asked if the students could identify any patterns in terms of similarities and differences between the examples. One difference found by the students was concluded by the teacher as: "the less number multiplied with (pointing at 20, 4, 2, 1, 0.5, 0.1, i.e., the multiplicands in the multiplication column), the less the product" (2000, 400, 200, 100, 50, 10), and thereafter, in the same way, while pointing to the division column: "the less number divided with, the greater the quotient").

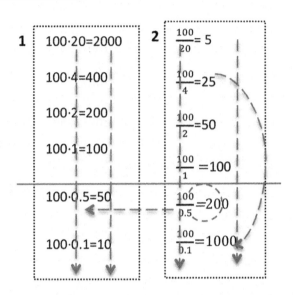

Figure 3. The sequence of the examples enacted in lesson 2 (1 and 2). The arrows show what the teacher directed students' attention to, e.g., that the quotient becomes greater than the numerator when dividing with a number less than 1, and 'the turning point ('1')'

Next, the teacher pointed out how some of the examples in the division column 'break the pattern.' He pointed to the two examples, 100÷20 = 5 and 100÷4 = 25 and said, "Here the quotient is less than the numerator, is it always like that?" The class came to the conclusion that the examples with denominators <1 was different. To emphasize this difference the teacher drew a line between the divisions (and multiplications) with numbers < 1, and division with numbers ≥ 1 to illustrate this 'turning point.' Division examples with denominators <1 were contrasted with the two division examples with denominators >1. The teacher said, "Around 1, do you agree with me that something happens here (draws a line under 100÷1), do you agree with me … ?" The teacher pointed to the denominator 1 and then to the denominator 0.5, and said, "When the denominator is less than 1 the quotient (pointed to the quotient 200) is greater than the numerator (pointed to the numerator 100). Next, the teacher made a contrast with multiplication: "But what about multiplication?" (see Figure 3). By comparing multiplication with division (100·0.5 = 50, 100 ÷ 0.5 = 200), it was pointed out that the quotient is greater and the product less, when the denominator or one of the factors is less than 1. So, it could be concluded that in lesson 2 the set of examples was utilized in a way that came closer to the intended goal. The pattern of variation and invariance, in terms of what was compared, brought out significant features of division with denominators >0 but <1 and how this is different from multiplication (multiplicands <1).

Lesson 3

In the post-lesson meeting, the teachers interpreted lesson 2 to better realize the learning target. However, they made some small changes in the set of examples that they thought would improve the enactment of the task in lesson 3 with a new group of students. First, in some of the examples the multiplicands/denominators were exchanged. Instead of dividing/multiplying 100 by 20 and 4 as was the case in lesson 2 (see Figure 3), *in the revised two first examples* in each column 100 was divided/multiplied by 50 and 5 (see Figure 4). This they thought would put less emphasis on the calculation. They anticipated that the learners would just 'know the answers' and thus, more directly see the pattern. This change implied that the variation between the examples in each column changed. Another difference in the set of examples in this lesson was that the two last examples ($100 \cdot 0.1 = 10$ and $100 \div 0.1$) were not on the board from the beginning, but presented after the other examples in each column had been discussed (Figure 4 (3)). In many ways this lesson was enacted in a similar way as lesson 2. The teacher first directed the students' attention towards the multiplication column (1) and asked for similarities and differences:

T: Look at the multiplication columns first. Do you see any pattern? Anything that is the same or different?
S: The smaller number [we calculate with] the less zeros there are [in the product]
T: Yeah, but what answer do we usually get in multiplication?
S: A larger number.
T: Is it always like that? When do we get a larger number?
S: After one.

The teacher challenged the idea she knew was common among the learners by asking, "What answer do we usually get when we calculate a multiplication?" The teacher continued and challenged the students' by asking if that is always the case. One student seemed to see the exception; s/he answered "After one."

Next, the teacher pointed at the multiplier 0.5 and the product 50 (in the example $100 \cdot 0.5 = 50$), and again at the product 50 and 100 to show that the product in this case was less than the multiplicand (100). By introducing a new example $100 \cdot 0.1 = 10$ (See Figure 4 (3)) and thus varying the multiplicand between the examples (from 0.5 to 0.1), it was demonstrated that this is true for other instances as well: the product is less than the multiplicand even in that example.

After, the teacher directed the students' attention to the division column (2) and, just as she did for multiplication, challenged the idea of the relationship between the numbers (in this case dividend, divisor, and quotient). She asked, "What answer do we usually get when we calculate a division?" The teacher then asked the students if it is always like that and continued. "Do you see where it turns? Here we get a greater answer (quotient) (100 ÷ 0.5 = 200), when do we *not* get a larger number (quotient)?" After answers from the students, the teacher continued, "Is this true for all decimals?" Just as in the discussion about multiplication, she introduced a new division example with a divisor <1 but >0: 100 ÷ 0.1 = 1000 in order to demonstrate and generalize the 'rule' (3).

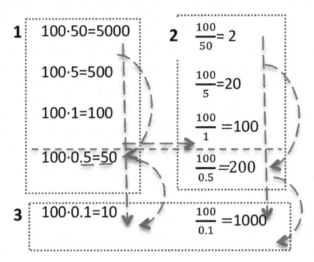

Figure 4. The sequence of the examples enacted in lesson 3 (1 to 3). The arrows show what the teacher directed students' attention to e.g., that the quotient becomes greater than the numerator when dividing with a number less than 1 and 'the turning point'

This example illustrates that the teachers were able to design a set of instructional examples based on the idea that variation and invariance within and between examples must appear in a systematic way to make aspects discernible to the learners. We have also shown that they could refine the task and its implementation from the analysis of the lessons and their students' learning just as Watson and Mason (2006) have suggested. The first lesson they did not find successful regarding what they wanted to accomplish. They came to realize that the way the examples were sequenced and hence, the pattern of variation that was brought out in the lesson, emphasized other relationships than those targeted. This was mainly due to that the inverse relationship between division and multiplication was highlighted by the enacted variation. Whereas, in the second lesson, when the set of examples was slightly changed and other patterns of variation and invariance were brought to the fore of attention, the teachers were more satisfied and other distinctions were made visible. Our analysis indicates that the teaching in lesson 2 and 3 more explicitly (although perhaps not fully) directed the students' attention to the relationship that the teachers wanted the students to discern.

Here we have only demonstrated one task from one of the learning studies. Other tasks were designed, implemented, and revised guided by the principles from variation theory in a total of 12 lessons in three learning studies. Analysis of these lessons, of pre- and post-lesson meetings and student learning out-comes demonstrated similarities to what we have shown here; the teachers could successively make use of ideas of variation in their teaching in a way that enhanced learners' possibilities to learn what was targeted (Mårtensson, 2015).

LEARNING TO TEACH WITH VARIATION—EFFECTS OVER TIME?

In the example above, the teachers inquired and tested how principles of variation and invariance can be used as a tool for designing tasks and planning the lesson to enhance learning. This was a collective process, with possibilities to discuss different options together but, first and foremost, to study the effects of various patterns of variation in class. However, do those experiences have any impact on their daily work? Considering that learning study is time consuming and takes a lot of effort for the participating teachers, we found it essential to find out if their experiences had any long-term effects. Twelve mathematics and science teachers' teaching before and after having participated in three learning studies, were studied by examining how the same topic (of their own choice) was taught before and after participating in learning study, with two years in between (Kullberg, Runesson, Marton, Vikström, Nilsson, Mårtensson, & Häggström, 2016). As in the previous example we followed the rational inspired by Ryle (1949/2002) and Schön (1983) to study aspects of what the teachers had learned by examining transcripts of the video-recordings of their actions in the classroom. It was found that 10 of the 12 teachers changed their way of handling the topic in a way that reflects principles of variation theory. One striking difference was found among all teachers' teaching after the intervention: both the mathematics and science teachers structured the content taught in another way after the intervention and thus, the enacted pattern of variation was different. In the following section we will give one example of how two mathematics lessons differed in terms of structure of the topic and the pattern of variation enacted before and after the teacher's participation in learning study and his experience with variation theory.

Changes in the Enacted Patterns of Variation

The teacher we will report on, Mr. B, taught grade 8 and the content taught on the two occasions was units of measurements and how to convert within units, e.g., 1 dm^2 to 100cm^2.

Lesson 1. Phase 1 in the first lesson started with a definition of 1 dm^2: a 1 dm × 1 dm square. How the unit cm^2 is related to the unit dm^2 was demonstrated next by

365

showing a 1 dm² square divided into 100 cm² and concluding that 1dm² = 100cm² (written on the board). Two examples of converting area units, from dm² into cm² and the reverse, were given to the class to solve (6 dm² = 600 cm²; 40 cm² = 0.4dm²). Next, the relationship between length units was discussed, and on the board the students could read: 1m = 10dm = 100cm. Finally, the relationship between different area units was the topic. It was stated and written on the board that 1m² = 100 dm² = 10000 cm².

Next, a worksheet with similar examples of converting area units from dm² into cm² and the reverse were practiced individually. When the tasks were corrected in public, the teacher gave 'a rule': "going from m² into dm² you add two zeros, going from dm² to cm² you add two zeros, or you multiply with 100", however, no explanation was provided. Thus, in this section, the area units and their relationship was the main topic.

In phase 2 volume and volume units were introduced by showing a 1dm × 1dm × 1dm cube. 'Volume' was defined as length × breadth × height and written on the board together with '1 dm × 1 dm × 1 dm = 1 dm³.' Here the notion 'dimension' was mentioned, "height is the third dimension". He further explained that the '3' in dm³ indicated three dimensions. Similarly, he explained the '2' in dm² as related to the two dimensions of area. Next, the relationship between cm³, dm³, and m³ was summarized on the board: 1 m³ = 1000 dm³ = 1000000 cm³. This was followed by individual worksheet work with examples of converting volume units. During the last five minutes of the lesson the tasks were jointly corrected and students were reminded of the rule, "Remember; add three zeros, multiply by 1000."

Section of the lesson/ activity	Section 1 plenary	Worksheet 1 individually	Section 2 plenary	Worksheet 2 individually
Topic	Area units relationships 1 m² = 100 dm² = 10000 cm²; 6 dm² = 600 cm²; 40 cm² = 0.4dm² Length units relationships 1 m = 10 dm = 100 cm	Converting area units (e.g., 3 dm² = 300 cm² and the reverse)	Volume units relationships 1 m³ = 1000 dm³ = 1000000 cm³	Converting volume units (e.g., 3 m³ = 3000 dm³, and the reverse)
Pattern of variation	Area/length invariant, variation within one unit (area/ length)	Area invariant, variation within one unit (m², dm², cm²)	Volume invariant, variation within one unit (m³, dm³, cm³)	Volume invariant, variation within one unit (m³, dm³, cm³)

Figure 5. Sequence of lesson 1 and the identified patterns of variation

Figure 5 gives an overview of the lesson and how the topic taught was sequenced. The analysis suggests that the *relationship within each unit (length, area, volume)* was taught *one at a time*, first in whole class and then practiced individually. In terms of patterns of variation enacted, the lesson could be described as consecutively opening up the relationship between units *within* area, length, and volume respectively.

Lesson 2. Two years later the teacher taught the same topic to the same grade (although not the same students). In contrast to the previous lesson, the teacher introduced all units (length, area, volume) from the start. Notes of length units, area units, and volume units were simultaneously on the board from the beginning of the lesson and the notion 'dimension' was presented right from the start. First, 1 dm (a line on the board) was compared to 1 dm^2 (a square) and 1 dm^3 (a cube) and 1 dm^3 was defined as 1 dm × 1 dm × 1 dm = 1 dm^3. The relationship *within* each unit and *between* length, area, and volume was simultaneously visible on the board and pointed out by the teacher: 1 dm = 10 cm; 1 dm^2 = 100 cm^2; 1 dm^3 = 1000cm^3. Thereafter, the following was written on the board:

Length	Area	Volume
1 dm	1 dm^2	1 dm^3
10 cm	100 cm^2	1000 cm^3
100 mm	10000 mm^2	1000000 mm^3

Figure 6. The white board in lesson 2. The three units of length, area, and volume are present at the same time

Throughout the lesson, the teacher compared the units. The relationship between length, area, and volume was made visible. For example, the teacher pointed to the three columns with different units. He said:

T: Do you experience or see any patterns? … Length units (points to the column and makes a vertical gesture), area units (points to the column and makes a vertical gesture), and volume units (points to the column and makes a vertical gesture)?
S: It's always bigger.
T: Definitely, if you go in this direction (makes a *vertical* gesture and points to the columns within length, area and volume, one at a time) and the same if we go in that direction (makes a *horizontal* gesture and points to length, area and volume).
T: Can you see something else?
S: You add the same amount of zeros as there is after decimeter.
T: Could you hear what Mary said?
Ss: No!
T: Say it again, Mary.
S: You add the same amount of zero as there is after decimeter.

We interpret her answer "after decimeter" as referring to the '2' in dm^2. That is, there is a 'two' after dm and this tells us how many zeros to add.

The teacher did not rephrase her comments, but directed students' attention to the different amount of zeros in each column and to the number of dimensions. He said:

T: Yeah, I have talked about dimensions. Look here, one dimension, length (a unit segment), decimeter to centimeter add one zero, centimeter to millimeter add one zeros, area (a unit square) decimeter it says 1 dm^2, when we go from dm^2 to cm^2 add two zeros, from cm^2 to mm^2 add additional two, two dimensions, area is two dimensions, three dimensions; volume (a unit cube) … dm^3, from dm^3 till cm^3 three dimensions add three zeros, if we go from cm^3 till mm^3 add three (zeros).

Here 'dimensions' were used to explain the number of zeros you can add when converting, for instance, dm to cm and dm^2 to cm^2. The 'rule' was explained and the rational for 'adding different numbers of zeros' was given. Next, the students worked with a worksheet with items about converting all three units, for example, from dm to m, dm^2, to cm^2 and from cm^3 to dm^3. Finally, students double-checked their answers on worksheets based on the answers provided by the teacher at the end of the lesson.

Our analysis suggests that this lesson was different from the previous one in terms of sequence and patterns of variation. In contrast to the first lesson, in lesson 2 all the units were dealt with simultaneously without interrupting with students practicing work. This we interpret as an indication of that the teacher wanted to deal with the three units as a whole. However, having all units on the board at the same time and dealing with them in relation does not imply that everything varied at the same time. Instead we found systematics in the way variation was used. Variation theory is based on the idea that seeing differences rather than similarities is the foundation for learning, and that generalization must be proceeded by experiencing how things differ—a contrast (Marton, 2015). A closer look at lesson 2 indicates a sequence of this kind. First, a contrast was made between length and area (1) in terms of number of dimension (one in contrast with two) and (2) units (1 dm = 10 cm in contrast with 1 dm^2 = 100 cm^2), followed by a similar contrast between length, area and volume (1, 2, 3 dimensions and units; 1 dm = 10 cm, 1 dm^2 = 1000 cm^2, 1 dm^3 = 10000 cm^3). Next, this relationship, between dm-cm, dm^2-cm^2, dm^3-cm^3, and numbers of dimensions (one dimension; adding one zero, two dimensions adding two zeros, three dimensions adding three zeros), was generalized to mm, mm^2, and mm^3 (the teacher asked whether the students could see a pattern see Figure 6).

Having length, area, and volume visible on the board at the same time, allowed for comparison *between* the three geometrical objects (length, area, and volume) and their corresponding units as well as *within* each object. In terms of variation, the lesson could be described as a *simultaneous opening of variation between and within units.* In lesson 1, we also find systematics of variation, however, of another character. In lesson 1 there was an opening of variation *within* each unit (length, area, and volume) before variation *between* units were opened. Although the identified difference between the lessons may seem subtle, we would argue that the relationship between length, area, and volume that was made explicit by the simultaneous handling in lesson 2, will likely give different learning possibilities when compared to lesson 1. Instead of taking one unit at a time (as in lesson 1), the three units were presented at the same time and systematically dealt with through contrast and generalization. So, when compared to lesson 1, lesson 2 enhanced the possibility to experience other connections.

SHIFTS IN THE WAY OF TEACHING WITH VARIATION

Teaching without accomplishing a pattern of variation is hardly possible. However, the pattern of variation—what is varied and what is kept invariant—could be spontaneously created and more or less systematic (cf., Runesson, 1999). We believe that it is not uncommon (at least not in Sweden) for teachers to present a set of examples on the board without having reflected on, for instance, what numbers to use and how to vary them between the examples in a systematic way. This may imply that too many things vary between the examples and consequently, that what we want the learners to notice will not come to the fore of their attention. It is not unusual that 'taking one thing at a time' and letting the learners practice before something 'new' is introduced to be conceived as facilitating learning, and that taking too many things at a time would make it more complicated and would risk learners 'mixing things up.' However, variation theory goes against such beliefs and states that the aspects of the object of learning that we want the learners to connect or see relationally must be possible to experience simultaneously. Further, to know what something is, requires to know what it is not, thus two things (at least) need to be contrasted in order to distinguish them. We also believe that this might have consequences for what is made possible to learn and for what is actually learned, as has been demonstrated in several studies (See Marton, 2015 for more details).

In this paper we have given two scenarios of teachers learning to make use of variation theory. In the first one, we described how a group of teachers in the collective and iterative inquiry process with the object of learning and students' learning in focus applied variation theory and improved their teaching skills when designing an instructional task. Our results suggest that they managed to design a set of examples when planning the lesson but did not manage to fully make use of and enact the potential of the designed task in their first trial. However, when reflecting on the lesson afterwards and how the set of examples was used, they came to realize what differences and what distinctions they must bring to the fore of learners' attention in order to promote the intended learning. In the iterative process, they were allowed to 'experiment' in the classroom. So, learning study became a platform that provided opportunities for exploring, testing, and further development of teaching the task.

The second scenario points to that the change and improvement of teachers' teaching skills that might be seen even if the lesson is not collectively planned. The teacher, Mr. B, was one of the teachers in the Learning study group reported on in example 1. The topic taught in the Learning study lessons was not the same as in example 2. Furthermore, the lessons were individually planned by Mr. B in the two occasions. Our main interest in the study reported (see Kullberg et al., in press) was to trace changes of teachers' ways of dealing with the same content in the classroom before and after participating in Learning study. When studying what teachers learn from teacher professional development it is common to involve interviews and various forms of self-reports from teachers. In our study, teachers' reflections on their own learning was not our main interest; we were not primarily interested in what the teachers said about their own experiences. We were more interested in what the learners encountered in class before and after the teachers' participation in Learning study. Therefore, the main data for our study was video recordings of the classroom. It is important to note that the teachers talked about the lesson with the researcher before the lesson was recorded. However, these interviews did not focus on their experiences of Learning study or how they made use of variation when planning the lesson. The teachers were asked to tell the interviewer about their objectives and plans for the lesson. Interestingly, it was found that Mr. B did not talk about using variation at all, neither in the first nor in the second interview. So, we cannot draw any conclusions of his learning of variation theory from these interviews.

Yet, the analysis of the two lessons showed that Mr. B rather radically – and on a concrete level – changed his way of handling the specific content of the lessons. We cannot exclude that these changes are influenced by other experiences Mr. B has had during the previous two years. They might even be quite accidental. What cannot be disregarded, however, is that the changes we have identified, to a great extent, reflect principles of variation theory (cf. Kullberg, et al., 2016, for the other eleven teachers in the study). Variation theory is a general theory of learning. It cannot be concluded from the theory what to vary or keep invariant for a particular object of learning. This must be decided in each and every case. What can be drawn from the theory, however, is that, the particular aspect we want to draw the learners' attention to should be opened up as a dimension of variation. This we can see happened in lesson 2. For instance, in lesson 2, attention was drawn to the number of dimensions as indicating dm, dm^2, dm^3 and the adding of numbers of zeros in the corresponding units (when converting from e.g., dm to dm^2) by opening up a variation in this respect right from the start. Actually Mr. B talks about this in the interview. He says:

I want them to see the logic, to me it's logical, and hopefully they will see this pattern too. Yes, from dm to cm, add one zero, from cm to mm, another zero. One dimension, one zero, are, two dimensions, two zeros are added in each step. And similarly, volume, three dimensions, three zeros are added in each step.

Our analysis suggests that this way of dealing with the content reflects principles we know the teacher has experienced when participation in three Learning studies.

When Sun (2011) talks about how the idea of variation is almost invisible to teachers, we interpret this as the knowledge of how to create patterns of variation when presenting the content to the learner, designing examples and so on, is unreflected but also 'knowing in action' (Schön, 1983). What has been reported here suggests that one of the strengths of Learning study is that such knowing can become visible, reflected upon and developed.

REFERENCES

Bell, A., Swan, M., & Taylor, G. (1981). Choice of operations in verbal problems with decimal numbers. *Educational Studies in Mathematics, 12*(4), 399–420.

Bell, A., Fischbein, E., & Greer, B. (1984). Choice of operation in verbal arithmetic problems: The effects of number size, problem structure and context. *Educational Studies in Mathematics, 15*, 129–147.

Bell, A., Greer, B., Grimison, L., & Mangan, C. (1989). Children's performance of multiplicative word problems: Elements of a descriptive theory. *Journal for Research in Mathematics Education, 20*(5), 434–449.

Behr, M., Harel, G., Post, T., & Lesh, R. (1993). Rational numbers: Toward a semantic analysis – Emphasis on the operator construct. In T. P. Carpenter, E. Fennema, & T. Romberg (Eds.), *Rational numbers. An integration of research* (pp. 13–48). Hillsdale, NJ: Erlbaum.

Cheng, E. C., & Lo, M. L. (2013). *Learning study: Its origins, operationalization, and implications* (OECD Education Working Papers No. 94). Paris: OECD Publishing. Retrieved from http://dx.doi.org/10.1787/5k3wjp0s959p-en

Elliott, J. (2012). Developing a science of teaching through lesson study. *International Journal for Lesson and Learning studies, 1*(2), 108–125.

Fischbein, E., Deri, M., Nello, M. S., & Marino, M. S. (1985). The role of implicit models in solving verbal problems in multiplication and division. *Journal for Research in Mathematics Education, 16*(1), 3–17.

Gibson, J. J., & Gibson, E. J. (1955). Perceptual learning: Differentiation – or enrichment? *Psychological Review, 62*(1), 32–41.

Holmqvist, M. (2011). Teachers' learning in a learning study. *Instructional Science, 39*(4), 497–511.

Kullberg, A. (2010). *What is taught and what is learned. Professional insights gained and shared by teachers of mathematics.* Göteborg: Acta Universitatis Gothoburgensis.

Kullberg, A., & Runesson, U. (2013). Learning about the numerator and denominator in teacher-designed lessons. *Mathematics Education Research Journal, 25*(4), 547–567.

Kullberg, A., Runesson, U., & Mårtensson, P. (2014). Different possibilities to learn from the same task. *PNA, 8*(4), 139–150.

Kullberg, A., Runesson, U., Marton, F., Vikström, A., Nilsson, P., Mårtensson, P., & Häggström, J. (2016). Teaching one thing at a time or several things together? – Teachers changing their way of handling the object of learning by being engaged in a theory-based professional learning community in mathematics and science. *Teachers, Teaching, Theory and Practice, 22*(6), 745–759.

Lewis, C. (2002). *Lesson study: A handbook of teacher-led instructional change.* Philadelphia, PA: Research for better schools inc.

Marton, F. (2015). *Necessary conditions of learning.* New York, NY: Routledge.

Marton, F., & Booth, S. (1997). *Learning and awareness.* Mahwah, NJ: Lawrence Erlbaum.

Marton, F., & Pang, M. F. (2003). Beyond "Lesson study": Comparing two ways of facilitating the grasp of economic concepts. *Instructional Science, 31*(3), 175–194.

Marton, F., & Pang, M. F. (2013). Meanings are acquired from experiencing differences against a background of sameness, rather than from experiencing sameness against a background of difference:

Putting a conjecture to test by embedding it into a pedagogical tool. *Frontline Learning Research, 1*(1), 24–41.

Marton, F., & Runesson, U. (2015). The idea and practice of Learning study. In K. Wood & S. Sithampram (Eds.), *Realising learning. Teachers' professional development through lesson study and learning study* (pp. 103–121). New York, NY: Routledge.

Mårtensson, P. (2015). *Att få syn på avgörande skillnader: Lärares kunskap om lärandeobjektet* [Learning to see distinctions: Teachers' gaining knowledge of the object of learning]. Jonkoping, Sweden: School of Education and Communication, Jonkoping University.

Nuthall, G. (2004). Relating classroom teaching to student learning: A critical analysis of why research has failed to bridge the theory-practice gap. *Harvard Educational Review, 74*(3), 273–306.

Nuthall, G. (2005). The cultural myths and realities of classroom teaching and learning: A personal journey. *Teachers College Record, 107*(5), 895–934.

Okazaki, M., & Koyama, M. (2005). Characteristics of 5th graders' logical development through learning division with decimals. *Educational Studies in Mathematics, 60*(2), 217–251.

Runesson, U. (1999). *Variationens pedagogik. Skilda sätt att behandla ett matematiskt innehåll* [The pedagogy of variation. Different ways of handling a mathematical topic]. Göterborg: Acta Universitatis Gothoburgensis.

Runesson, U. (2005). Beyond discourse and interaction. Variation: A critical aspect for teaching and learning mathematics. *The Cambridge Journal of Education, 35*(1), 69–87.

Ryle, G. (1949/2002). *The concept of mind.* Chicago, IL: University of Chicago Press.

Schön, D. (1983). *The reflective practioner: How professionals think in actions.* New York, NY: Basic Books.

Sun, X. (2011). "Variation problems" and their roles in the topic of fraction division in Chinese mathematics textbook examples. *Educational Studies in Mathematics, 76*(1), 65–85.

Vikstrom, A. (2014). What makes the difference? Teachers explore what must be taught and what must be learned in order to understand the particular character of matter. *Journal of Science Teacher Education, 25*, 709–727.

Watson, A., & Mason, J. (2006). Seeing an exercise as a single mathematical object: Using variation to structure sense-making. *Mathematical Teaching and Learning, 8*(2), 91–111.

Yoshida, M., & Fernandez, C. (2004). *Lesson study. A Japanese approach to improving mathematics teaching and learning.* Mahwah, NJ: Lawrence Erlbaum Associates.

Ulla Runesson
School of Education and Communication
Jönköping University, Jönköping, Sweden
and
Wits School of Education
University of the Witwatersrand, Johannesburg, South Africa

Angelika Kullberg
Department of Pedagogical, curricular and professional studies
University of Gothenburg, Gothenburg, Sweden

PART V

COMMENTARY AND CONCLUSION

NGAI-YING WONG

18. TEACHING THROUGH VARIATION

An Asian Perspective – Is the Variation Theory of Learning Varying?

PROLOGUE

In 1997, I invited Ference[1] (Prof. Marton) for an academic visit to the Chinese University of Hong Kong, where I was serving. In a lecture, he said he would start with his personal encounter. He then talked about his cultural origin and how he immigrated to the West, and then got in touch later with the Eastern culture. Learning from him, I would also start with my personal encounter with the variation theory of learning as well as *bianshi* teaching.

Figure 1. The author (left) introduces Ference (right) in his lecture at the Chinese University of Hong Kong

In fact I knew Ference much earlier, towards the end of my Ph.D. study. At that time, my supervisor, Prof. David Watkins, inspired me to the fertile field of understanding mathematics (Wong, Ding, & Zhang, 2016). He introduced me to Ference, whom David described as an expert in understanding 'understanding.' After that, Ference and I met several times and finally came up with a Hong Kong Research Grant Council competitive earmarked grant on *Enhancement of students' mathematics problem solving abilities by the systematic introduction of variations* in 2001.

R. Huang & Y. Li (Eds.), Teaching and Learning Mathematics through Variation, 375–388.

The basic idea of the project was to broaden students' *lived space* (Wong, Marton, Wong, & Lam, 2002) via the systematic introduction of non-routine (including open) mathematics problems. That granted research did generate a number of publications (Wong, Chiu, Wong, & Lam, 2005; Wong, Kong, Lam, & Wong, 2010) but the results were not as sharp as expected. One of the issues we saw was that the introduction of non-routine problems was not systematic enough. Many participating teachers found the whole idea not easily executable. At that time, I got acquainted with Rongjin[2] (Prof. Huang, one of the co-editors of this book) and got in touch with *bianshi* teaching. I knew that Prof. L. Gu had done a lot in the area in particular. In a book which I edited, it could be the first time that these two key figures (Ference and Gu) co-authored a chapter, with the great help of Rongjin, on the topic.

I heard of Gu's name early in 1992 in ICME-7,[3] in which he reported his *Qingpu* experience (Gu, 1992). For some reason we did not meet. It was until 1998 when I was invited for a visit to Shanghai by my first Ph.D. student, Qiping (Prof. Kong), that we met as Gu came to my lecture.

I realized that empirical studies on both variation theory of learning and *bianshi* teaching were lacking. Thereafter, I ran into a number of investigations (some conducted by my M.Ed./Ph.D. students) on **what, how,** and **why** they work (please refer to Wong, Chiu, Wong, & Lam, 2005; Wong, Kong, Lam, & Wong, 2010; Wong, Lam, & Chan, 2012; Wong, Lam, Sun, & Chan, 2009; and Wong, Lam, Chan, & Wang, 2008 for more details).

HOW IT STARTED: CONCEPTIONS OF MATHEMATICS AND DOING MATHEMATICS

As mentioned above, the entire project (which began in 1996, one year after I got my Ph.D., and spanned more than a decade) started off with the conceptions of mathematics. The results of my initial investigations had it that students from Hong Kong and Changchun hold a relatively narrow conception of mathematics, and this attracted my attention. In brief, mathematics, in the eyes of these students, is identified by mathematical terminologies and students took mathematics as a subject of *calculables* (Wong, 2002a; Wong, Marton, Wong, & Lam, 2002). Surprisingly (or unsurprisingly), teachers' and students' conceptions of mathematics were in close resemblance.

Not only that, such conceptions of mathematics directly affected students' problem solving tactics and, in particular, their thoughts that came to mind when they faced a mathematics problem. How they approach a problem is crucial to successful problem solving. What we found among the students in our studies is that, when students faced a mathematics problem, they tried to identify the key words, the prototype of the problem, which chapter (in the textbook) the problem might be situated in, which formulas were discussed in the chapter, and tried to fit the numbers into the formulas in order to check if they could get the answer (Wong, Marton, Wong, & Lam, 2002).

Another study that I (and collaborators) conducted indicated that although students were exposed to a variety of problem types, most of the problems were abstract mathematics problems rather than real-life ones. Most of the problems posed required students to only apply rules and routine procedures (Wong, Lam, & Chan, 2002). It reflected that the narrow conceptions of mathematics and mathematics problem solving are probably the results of a confined space that students lived in. However, this lived space is constructed by teachers, so it is a reasonable conjecture that **teachers'** narrow conceptions of mathematics and of mathematics teaching lead to the confined *lived space*, which leads to **students'** narrow conception of mathematics (Figure 2) (Zhang & Wong, 2015). A number of studies evidenced this point (see, e.g. Wong, 2002b; Wong, Han, & Wong, 2005). More seriously, if students, holding a narrow conception of mathematics, one day become teachers, it is possible that such a narrow conception, if not narrower, will be passed down from generation to generation.

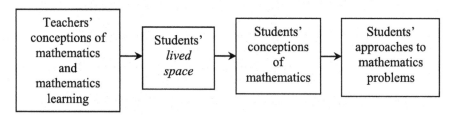

Figure 2. The lived space of mathematics learning

To reverse the vicious circle, as mentioned earlier, we tried to broaden the *lived space* by introducing non-routine mathematics problems. As we are all familiar with the theoretical basis is phenomenography, which I am not going to repeat. In brief, discernment is an essential element to learning, and variation is crucial to bringing about discernment. The lack of variation in the *lived space* of mathematics learning experienced by students would inevitably lead to a relatively narrow conception of mathematics. Furthermore, they would tend to hold a narrow conception of mathematics learning and would possess limited strategies when they are confronted with mathematical problems. In sum, less variation is associated with narrower ways of experiencing a phenomenon whereas more variation is associated with wider ways of experiencing that phenomenon. Thus, students' conceptions of mathematics would be broadened if their *lived space* of mathematics learning was widened by systematically introducing variation. They would become more capable problem-solvers as well (Wong, Chiu, Wong, & Lam, 2005; Wong, Kong, Lam, & Wong, 2010).

VARIATION THEORY OF LEARNING AND *BIANSHI* TEACHING: EAST OR WEST?

Besides the fact that we found our previous *lived space* project not easily executable, variation theory of learning deals with concept formation more than problem solving

(I do not mean the two are segregated). Problem solving is so essential in mathematics learning. It is so important that it was even asserted by the National Council of Supervisors of Mathematics as "the principal reason for studying mathematics" (1977, p. 2). Since one of our major goals was to enhance students' problem solving abilities, we turned to *bianshi* teaching, which has been practiced in the Chinese mainland for decades.

Figure 3. The author (middle) invited Gu (right) for an academic visit to the Chinese University of Hong Kong

After reviewing mathematics textbooks and papers concerned, we found that there are so many different *bianshis* in existence. *Bianshi* has been (or maybe still is) so popular in the Chinese mainland that every mathematics teacher labels his/her teaching a certain kind of *bianshi*! No doubt in a lecture that I invited Gu to deliver at the Chinese University of Hong Kong in 2005, he shocked the floor by saying that there is nothing particularly called *bianshi* way of teaching, it is simply a basic skill that every teacher should know!

Our sole aim was to develop a framework for (mini-) curriculum development in order to investigate the effectiveness of *bianshi* teaching. After some sorting and categorization, we came up with four basic *bianshis* that can be used to form the cornerstones of curriculum construction (Wong, Lam, Sun, & Chan, 2009). Figure 4 summarizes the four *bianshis* and their relationships. In brief, 'inductive *bianshi*' can be used to derive rules and concepts from the inspection of a number of realistic situations. These rules are consolidated by a systematic introduction of variation into mathematical tasks. Yet no new rules and concepts are introduced, and learners just broaden their scope through a variety of problems. This is the case in 'broadening *bianshi*.' At a certain point, by further varying the types of the mathematical tasks, learners are opened up to more mathematics. This is 'deepening *bianshi*.'

Mathematics is then applied to a greater variety of realistic problems, and this is 'applying *bianshi*' (Wong, Lam, Sun, & Chan, 2009).

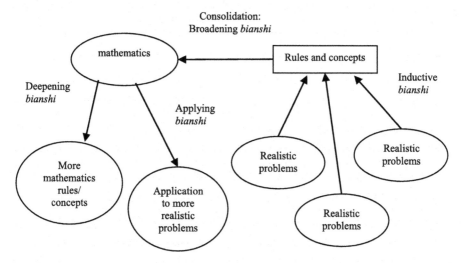

Figure 4. The bianshi *curriculum framework*

One may query whether these are the only *bianshis*. We suppose that this is not an issue. Different scholars can come up with their own particular *bianshis* for their own particular purposes. To us, these four are sufficient to develop our curriculum for further research. Not only that, the framework is in line with the process of mathematization and the nature of mathematics learning (National Council of Teachers of Mathematics, 1989).

As mentioned above, our main target was to investigate the effectiveness of *bianshi* teaching. In that sense, the framework was just a stepping stone. We must develop a curriculum for teaching experiment before we can test it. Division of fractions, which is perceived as the most difficult topic in primary mathematics, was chosen as our first trial. When it came to the actual process of curriculum construction, analysis of existing textbooks was taken as the first step to identify *difficult points* 難點. *Bianshi* can then provide scaffoldings to help students cross these hurdles. Ideally, diagnoses with students (through clinical interviews and/or analyses with their works) would provide more information for curriculum development (which we did in later projects). This may be similar to 'V1' in the Learning Study Approach, in which the following variations were identified (Cheng & Lo, 2013):

- V1. Variation in the students' understanding of the object of learning
- V2. Variation in the teachers' own ways of understanding and dealing with this object of learning in the past
- V3. Variation as a guiding principle of pedagogical design

Thereafter, we experimented in various topics, including Division of Fractions, Speed, Volume, Circumference, Bar Charts, and Use of Trigonometry to solve 3-dimensional Problems (please refer to Wong, Lam, & Chan, 2012; Wong, Lam, Chan, & Wang, 2008; Wong, Lam, Sun, & Chan, 2009 for the designs of some of these topics).

EFFECTIVENESS: IN WHAT SENSE?

As previously stated, our sole aim was to not just repeat the idea in different topics but to gather more empirical data to evaluate the effectiveness of the use of variations, whether variation theory of learning or *bianshi* teaching. Such empirical studies were so lacking then. But when we talk about effectiveness, we have to check whether (expected) learning outcomes are achieved. Learning does not only involve behavioural change but conceptual change. Thus, conceptual formation is naturally one of the major concerns.

There was an interesting discussion at the International Workshop on Updating Phenomenography, which was held in 2000. A participant reported his research result that, among the students, besides 'conventional' dimensions of cardinality and ordinality, there are other dimensions of number concepts, such as color and emotion (to some students, certain numbers are 'beautiful', while some are 'dull.' Or 'I hate the number 17', etc.). Whether these dimensions can be called part of the conceptions of mathematics (or of the concepts of numbers) aroused some debate. Apparently, to most mathematicians, the answer is negative. But if you take 'conception of X' as 'how one (student) conceives/perceives X', obviously we have to accept that these are dimensions that we actually found among the students. The issue boils down to whether they are **desirable** learning outcomes or not. Such a desirability is not defined solely by mathematicians or the curriculum documents but whether these dimensions can have sustainable development in higher mathematics or not (or so called esoteric mathematics: Cooper & Dunne, 1998).

There is yet another issue that we should not overlook. When we talk about learning, we have to realize that there are many aspects of learning. Let's ponder about the followings:

- Understand Newtonian mechanics
- Construct a wooden cart with low center of gravity that will not easily topple
- Comprehend a Shakespeare's piece
- Learn how to write a poem
- Learn how to play a musical instrument
- Learn Chinese kungfu and apply such skills in combat
- Learn how to swim
- Learn yoga or even meditation (the art of non-thinking)

...

380

It needs no further explanation that these require vastly different skills and ways to acquire each of the above. Even if we confine ourselves to mathematics, we have the following different aspects of learning outcomes:

- formulate and solve a realistic problem that concerns the maximization of the area of a rectangle
- factorise a cubic polynomial, knowing factor theorem
- solve a trigonometric equation
- construct the perpendicular bisector of a line segment
- construct a dodecahedron by cutting and folding papers
- explore geometry properties using DGS (**dynamic geometry system**)
- explain to others the strategies one used in solving a mathematics problem

...

(and which of the above are **means** and what are **ends**?) I do not want to run hastily into the recent hot topic of procedural and conceptual knowledge (deep procedures and reciprocal acquisition), put it in simplistic terms, having a clear concept may not directly lead to successful problem solving, and vice versa. So when one reads papers reporting the effectiveness of *bianshi*, one needs to clarify what sense of effectiveness these papers refer to.

In our empirical studies (Wong, Lam, Sun, & Chan, 2009), we did not only check the effectiveness through conventional test scores. We also included mathematics problem solving tests and affective measures (like attitude and motivation). We also checked the possible changes in the conceptions of mathematics: how students **see** and **do** mathematics differently – this is our most wanted aspect right from the start. In our later studies, we also incorporated clinical interviews to see whether or not their approaches to mathematics problem changed. Under the above conceptualization of the *lived space*, with the broadening of it, students should get hold of a wider range of approaches and strategies to approach mathematical problems, non-routine ones in particular.

DOES VARIATION/*BIANSHI* HAVE A 'NATIONAL/CULTURAL' IDENTITY? DO WE NEED ONE?

As we went along with the endeavor, several ideological issues came up. First, whether the 'Western' variation theory of learning and the 'Chinese' *bianshi* teaching are the same or difference. In Gu, Huang, and Marton (2004) the similarities between variation theory of learning and *bianshi* teaching were highlighted. Yet there are arguments whether they represent different perspectives (e.g., Pang, Bao, & Ki, 2017). My opinion is, even teaching methods bearing the same name could have differences (**variations!**) in their practices, if we take 'systematic introduction of variations' in the broad sense, undoubtedly the two belong to the same family.

Along this line, there were queries about whether our *bianshi* curriculum framework Chinese, Western, or a hybrid. To us, we did not go for *bianshi* for *bianshi*'s sake. As Shakespeare said, "What is in a name? A rose by any other name would smell as sweet."[4] Whether the designed curriculum belongs to Western or Eastern style of teaching (if there is anything as such) is unimportant. Mathematics learning, to some extent, has its universality. As said, our curriculum framework aligns with the nature of mathematics and mathematics learning. This is what ultimately matters.

For the betterment of mathematics learning, we look for ('good') practices from various cultures and utilize them without bothering whether they are labelled East or West (Wong, 2006).

In this book, we can see that teaching through variation exists in various cultures (Barlow, Prince, Lischka, & Duncan, 2017; Hino, 2017; Pang, Bao, & Ki, 2017; Runesson & Kullberg, 2017). Therefore, it is difficult to claim that variation belongs to a particular culture. Even for *bianshi*, one can say that it has Chinese origins, but it could be a bit far reaching to say that it has Chinese cultural roots. In addition, inevitably, some components of these different kinds of variations are common with other pedagogical ideas. For instance, 'offer problems with variations – providing opportunity for students to construct variations themselves' as mentioned in Hino (2017) could have similarities with the 'open problem – problem posing' cycle (Silver, 1994). Furthermore, among the four strategic means (see Leung, 2017), contrast, generalization, fusion, and separation, some of them might have similarities with progressive differentiation, integrative reconciliation that were proposed by the advance organizer of Ausubel (1990).

The theory of variation is itself changing (**bian!**[5]) too (which is quite natural). In *Learning and Awareness* (Marton & Booth, 1997), the phenomenon of learning was thoroughly analyzed (phenomenography). The analysis inspired teaching and learning. Almost at the same time, Ulla (Runesson) developed her pedagogy of variation (1999). When Ference visited us in 1997, he emphasized that phenomenography is (was?) not a research methodology but a research tradition. The positioning was changed again during the International Workshop on Updating Phenomenography (2000), the Education Bureau commissioned project, 'Catering for Individual Differences, Building on Variation' (2000), and then in the Learner Study. The whole thing gradually developed from 'analysis of learning' to 'means to enhance learning'[6] and to 'teaching method', though undoubtedly they are inter-related.

Do we really need to label a teaching method Chinese, British, Swedish, Western, or Eastern? Rather, when one talks about variation (the same for *bianshi*), it is important to know which version of variation we are talking about.

'CHINESE CULTURAL ROOT': WHERE IS THE CHINESE-NESS?

Some years ago, a colleague of mine invited me to give a talk on the Buddhist view of education in her class. However, she held a Western philosophy of education.

I told her, why not? If Buddhist had not come from the West, we wouldn't have had the novel *Journey to the West*.[7] East, West, Chinese, non-Chinese are sometimes just labels that we use in casual conversations. In academic discourses, particular care may be needed when these terms are coined.

It is often claimed that *bianshi* has Chinese cultural origins. It is possible that such discussions fall into common misconceptions about Chinese culture. Before making assertions like these, we may ask ourselves questions like:

- China comprises 23 provinces, 4 municipalities, 5 autonomous regions, and 2 Special Administrative Regions. It has 56 ethnic groups. If we talk about China, which part of China are we referring to?
- Even if we confine ourselves to the 'Middle Kingdom' 中原, what does it mean by Chinese culture?
- Is Confucianism mainstream 'traditional' Chinese culture? How do we see the influences of other schools like Daoism (some also mixed up Daoism 道家 and the Dao religion 道教), Buddhism, Mohism and Legalism?
- There had been changes in Confucianism (institutionalization, revitalization, …) in history, when we talk about Confucianism, which Confucianism are we referring to?
- With different waves of Westernization at the turn of the 20th century, in which 'down with the Confucian Mansion' was the refrain, how much 'Chinese' is contemporary China?
- Is (traditional) Chinese mathematics taught in Chinese regions (including Taiwan and Hong Kong)? Are they practicing traditional Chinese pedagogy?
- How much is mathematics treasured throughout the history of China? (some even claimed that Confucianism suppresses discursive reasoning and was a hindrance to the development of mathematics in China)

We won't run into details of these. Wong, Wong, and Wong (2012) could provide a good starting point for further discussions.

MY (ASIAN?) PERSPECTIVE: TEACHER-CENTREDNESS,
LEARNER-CENTREDNESS, LEARNING- CENTREDNESS

In this book, I was asked to write from an Asian perspective. Following the above line of discussion, if there is no so-called (unified) Chinese perspective, it is even more impossible to have an Asian one (Wong, 2013)! However, we can look at the whole thing from another angle.

It was argued that although Asian (Chinese in particular) classrooms have a large class size and students seem to be passive learners, classroom teaching is still effective (Gu, Huang, & Gu, 2017). A number of reasons were offered (for more details, see, e.g. Watkins & Biggs, 1996, 2001; Wong, 2004). In particular, Gao and Watkins (2001) pointed out that teachers and students establish a mentor-mentee relationship, teachers show personal concern for their students, the learning process in fact goes for a 'whole class teaching + after class mentoring' model. Furthermore, teaching is teacher-led yet student-centred (see, e.g., Wong, 2009; Wong, Ding, & Zhang, 2016). The learner is first led to 'enter the *way*', then gradually led to 'transcend the *way*' (Wong, 2006). If we regard this scenario as Asian (or Chinese at least), variation or *bianshi* has a prominent role to play.

In other words, the 'Chinese' (so-to-speak for the time being) mathematics classroom does not go for free discovery (we do not comment whether it is desirable or not) right from start. Students learn the basics ('entering the *way*') via the guidance of teachers. And through variations (or *bianshis*) precisely designed by teachers, students are enlightened to a higher level of understanding ('transcending the *way*').

There are vastly different methods to actualize 'transcending the *way*' (Wong, 2006). However, there could be a general impression that variation/*bianshi* only deals with the basics. Such an impression may be imposed by earlier studies that dealt with average students. We do think variation/*bianshi* have a lot of potential in enhancing higher order thinking skills. The above argument of broadening problem solving strategies and their flexible use provide evidence for this. This can be facilitated by the use of non-routine problems, open problems (Peled & Leikin, 2017), and new problems (Gu, Huang, & Gu, 2017). I think much should be explored to this end.

This book contains an abundance of good practices with variation and *bianshi*. To deepen the discourse, I think many more research studies are needed that go beyond textbook/classroom analysis, analysis of lesson plans, and classroom observation. More studies employing systematic curriculum evaluation methodologies are called for. As mentioned above, some research agendas could be concerned with how students attain various learning outcomes (cognitive, affective, psychosocial, conceptions, and approaches to mathematics problems), how the *lived space* is shaped by teachers' teaching behaviour, and how these behaviours were affected by teachers' conceptions[8] and knowledge (Figure 5).

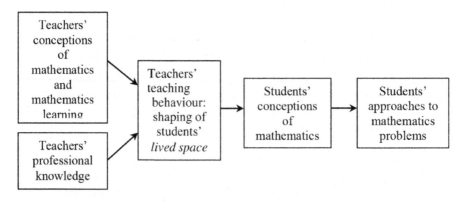

Figure 5. Teacher-student interaction in the lived space of mathematics learning

384

A final remark: as a teacher (and teacher educator), undoubtedly, we target to teach with solid grounds. We want to have the lessons well planned and organized (Runesson & Kullberg, 2017). Yet all these efforts were paid for the betterment of mathematics learning among **students**. The curriculum (as well as teaching methods), in a sense, is just a hardware that naturally has its limitations. The utopic imagination that students would automatically learn well once we have a good teacher delivering a well-designed curriculum is far from reality. Curriculum fidelity is not the only option. Perhaps (if we still have the teacher in the classroom – teacher-led yet student-centred), the teacher also needs to proceed from 'entering the *way*' to 'transcending the *way*' too, moving from having a script to having none (Wong, 2009; Wong, Zhang, & Li, 2013).

To finish, I would like to end this chapter with a little story in Chan (zen) Buddhism. Please notice how the master skillfully **changed** his topic spontaneously, according to the reactions of the monk during the dialogue.

At that time, several monks paid a visit (to Big Jewel) and said, "I wish to ask a question, will you still respond[9]?" The Master [Big Jewel] said, "Like the moon shadows in a deep pond, you can explore it at will (i.e., he is open to take questions)." (One of the monks) asked: "What is the Buddha?" The Master said, "Opposite to the clear pond,[10] who else is besides the Buddha?" Everybody got stunned. After quite a while, the monk asked again, "Master, what way[11] do you use to liberate others?" The Master said, "I don't have a way to liberate others!" The monk (spoke among themselves), "Chan masters are all like this." The Master asked rhetorically, "Venerable one, then what way do you use to liberate others?" (The monk) Replied, "I preach the *Diamond Sutra*". The Master asked, "How many sessions?" (The monk) Replied, "Twenty or so." The Master asked, "Who spoke that sutra?" The Monk raised his voice and replied, "The Master is kidding, isn't it spoken by the Buddha?" The Master said, "If one says that the Buddha uttered something, it is blasphemy against the Buddha, this is precisely the meaning (stated in the *Diamond Sutra*) of what the Buddha said, 'people don't understand my words'[12]; but if one says that is not spoken by the Buddha, it is blasphemy against the Sutra (accusing that the Sutra is a fake one). Venerable one, what is your take?" The monk got no responses. After a short while, the Master asked again, "In the Sutra [the *Diamond Sutra*], it was said that 'if someone sees me in forms, searches me in voices, one is on the wrong path and cannot see the Buddha.' Venerable one, please tell me then, who is the Buddha?" The Monk said, "At this point, I am lost." The Master said, "You have never realized, how can you get lost?"

時有法師數人來謁曰。擬伸一問。師還對否。師曰。深潭月影任意撮摩。問如何是佛。師曰。清潭對面非佛而誰。眾皆茫然。良久其僧又問。師說何法度人。師曰貧道未曾有一法度人。曰禪師家渾如此。師卻問曰。大德說何法度人。曰講金剛般若經。師曰。講幾坐來。曰二十餘坐。師曰。此經是阿誰說。僧抗聲曰。禪師相弄。豈不知是佛說耶。師

曰。若言如來有所說法。則為謗佛。是人不解我所說義。若言此經不是
佛說。則是謗經。請大德說看。無對。師少頃又問。經云。若以色見
我。以音聲求我。是人行邪道。不能見如來。大德且道。阿那箇是如
來。曰某甲到此卻迷去。師曰。從來未悟說什麼卻迷。

Record of Lineage Transmission in the Years of Jin-De景德傳燈錄 (Volume 6).

ACKNOWLEDGEMENT

The author would like to express his thanks to Miss Carrie Cheung for her assistance in polishing the language of the chapter.

NOTES

[1] I am used to calling him Ference. To maintain this personal touch, I address him as 'Ference' throughout this chapter.

[2] Chinese seldom call others by names, except for very close friends or juniors – difference between Chinese and Western culture! Due to my close relationship with Rongjin, I address him as 'Rongjin' throughout this chapter. And since Gu is a senior, I address him as 'Gu'.

[3] The Seventh International Congress on Mathematics Education, Quebec.

[4] Romeo and Juliet.

[5] The literal meaning of *bian* (the root of *bianshi*) is change.

[6] The above incident 'I hate the number 17' precisely shows the difference between analyses of phenomenon and a means to enhance learning.

[7] A legendary novel which depicts the journey of a monk from the Tang dynasty who travelled to the West (India: West of China) with his disciples to acquire Buddhist scriptures there.

[8] There have been discussions about whether beliefs, conceptions, etc. should be regarded as cognitive or affective. We choose to treat these terms loosely.

[9] Big Jewel refused to respond to any question for some time, claiming that he actually does not know Chan.

[10] There is a possibility that Master Big Jewel is making a pun, 'clear pond' has the same pronunciation with 'free chats' 清談, i.e. the one (Master Big Jewel himself) you are chatting with, if not the Buddha, who else?

[11] Dharma, may refer to a doctrine or a scripture.

[12] In a sense, the Buddha does not utter a word. Just like what Confucius said, the Nature does not speak a word.

REFERENCES

Ausubel, D. P. (1960). The use of advance organizers in the learning and retention of meaningful verbal material. *Journal of Educational Psychology, 51*(5), 267–272.

Barlow, A. T., Prince, K., Lischka, A. E., & Duncan, M. D. (2017). Teaching algebraic reasoning through variation in the US. In R. Huang & Y. Li. (Eds.), *Teaching and learning mathematics through variations* (this volume).

Cheng, E. C., & Lo, M. L. (2013). *Learning study: Its origins, operationalisation, and Implications* (OECD Education Working Papers No. 94). Paris, France: OECD Publishing.

Cooper, B., & Dunne, M. (1998). Anyone for tennis? Social class differences in children's responses to National Curriculum Mathematics Testing. *The Sociological Review, 46*(1), 115–148.

Gao, L., & Watkins, D. A. (2001). Towards a model of teaching conceptions of Chinese secondary school teachers of physics. In D. A. Watkins & J. B. Biggs (Eds.), *Teaching the Chinese learner:*

Psychological and pedagogical perspectives (pp. 27–45). Hong Kong: Comparative Education Research Centre, The University of Hong Kong.

Gu, F., Huang, R., & Gu, L. (2017). Theory and development of teaching with variation in mathematics in China. In R. Huang & Y. Li. (Eds.), *Teaching and learning mathematics through variations* (this volume).

Gu, L. (1992). *The Qingpu experience.* Paper presented at the 7th International Congress of Mathematics Education, Quebec, Canada.

Gu, L., Huang, R., & Marton, F. (2004). Teaching with variation: A Chinese way of promoting effective mathematics learning. In L. Fan, N. Y. Wong, J. Cai, & S. Li (Eds.), *How Chinese learn mathematics: Perspectives from insiders* (pp. 309–347). Singapore: World Scientific.

Hino, K. (2017). Improving teaching through variation: A Japanese perspective. In R. Huang & Y. Li. (Eds.), *Teaching and learning mathematics through variations* (this volume).

Leung, A. (2017). Variation in tool-based mathematics pedagogy: The case of dynamic virtual tool. In R. Huang & Y. Li. (Eds.), *Teaching and learning mathematics through variations* (this volume).

Marton, F., & Booth, S. (1997). *Learning and awareness.* Mahwah, NJ: Lawrence Erlbaum Associates.

National Council of Supervisors of Mathematics, U.S.A. (1977). *Position paper on basic mathematical skills.* Washington, DC: National Institute of Education.

National Council of Teachers of Mathematics. (1989). *Curriculum and evaluation standards for school mathematics.* Reston, VA: Author.

Pang, M. F., Bao, J., & Ki, W. W. (2017). "Bianshi" and the variation theory of learning: Illustrating two frameworks variation and invariance in the teaching of mathematics. In R. Huang & Y. Li. (Eds.), *Teaching and learning mathematics through variations* (this volume).

Peled, I., & Leikin, R. (2017). Openness in the eye of the problem solver: Choice in solving problems in Israel. In R. Huang & Y. Li. (Eds.), *Teaching and learning mathematics through variations* (this volume).

Runesson, U. (1999). *Variationens pedagogik: Skilda sätt att behandla ett matematiskt innehåll* [The pedagogy of variation: Different ways of handling a mathematical topic] (In Swedish). Göteborg: Acta Universitatis Gothoburgensis. Retrieved from http://www.ped.gu.se/biorn/phgraph/civil/graphica/diss.su/runesson.html

Runesson, U., & Kullberg, A. (2017). Learning to teach with variation: Experiences from learning study in Sweden. In R. Huang & Y. Li. (Eds.), *Teaching and learning mathematics through variations* (this volume).

Silver, E. A. (1994). On mathematical problem posing. *For the Learning of Mathematics, 14*(1), 19–28.

Watkins, D. A., & Biggs, J. B. (Eds.). (1996). *The Chinese learner: Cultural, psychological and contextual influences.* Hong Kong: Comparative Education Research Centre.

Watkins, D. A., & Biggs, J. B. (Eds.). (2001). *Teaching the Chinese learner: Psychological and contextual perspectives.* Hong Kong: Comparative Education Research Centre.

Wong, N. Y. (2002a). A review of research on conceptions of mathematics (數學觀研究綜述) [in Chinese]. *Journal of Mathematics Education, 11*(1), 1–8.

Wong, N. Y. (2002b). Conceptions of doing and learning mathematics among Chinese. *Journal of Intercultural Studies, 23*(2), 211–229.

Wong, N. Y. (2004). The CHC learner's phenomenon: Its implications on mathematics education. In L. Fan, N. Y. Wong, J. Cai, & S. Li (Eds.), *How Chinese learn mathematics: Perspectives from insiders* (pp. 503–534). Singapore: World Scientific.

Wong, N. Y. (2006). From "entering the way" to "exiting the way": In search of a bridge to span "basic skills" and "process abilities". In F. K. S. Leung, G.-D. Graf, & F. J. Lopez-Real (Eds.), *Mathematics education in different cultural traditions: The 13th ICMI Study* (pp. 111–128). New York, NY: Springer.

Wong, N. Y. (2009). Exemplary mathematics lessons: What lessons we can learn from them? *ZDM Mathematics Education, 41*, 379–384.

Wong, N. Y. (2013). The Chinese learner, the Japanese learner, the Asian learner – inspiration for the (mathematics) learner. *Scientiae Mathematicae Japonicae, 76*(2), 376–384.

Wong, N. Y., Marton, F., Wong, K. M., & Lam, C. C. (2002). The lived space of mathematics learning. *Journal of Mathematical Behavior, 21*, 25–47.

Wong, N. Y., Han, J. W., & Wong, Q. T. (2005). Conceptions of mathematics and mathematics education (數學觀與數學教育) [in Chinese]. In N. Y. Wong (Ed.), *Revisiting mathematics education in Hong Kong for the new millennium – Festschrift for Prof. M. K. Siu's retirement* (pp. 77–99). Hong Kong: Hong Kong Association for Mathematics Education.

Wong, N. Y., Chiu, M. M., Wong, K. M., & Lam, C. C. (2005). The lived space of mathematics learning: An attempt for change. *Journal of the Korea Society of Mathematical Education Series D: Research in Mathematical Education, 9*(1), 25–45.

Wong, N. Y., Lam, C. C., Chan, A. M. Y., & Wang, Y. (2008). The design of spiral *bianshi* curriculum: Using three primary mathematics topics as examples (數學變式課程設計——以小學三個課題爲例) [in Chinese]. *Education Journal, 35*(2), 1–28.

Wong, N. Y., Lam, C. C., Sun, X., & Chan, A. M. Y. (2009). From "exploring the middle zone" to "constructing a bridge": Experimenting the spiral bianshi mathematics curriculum. *International Journal of Science and Mathematics Education, 7*(2), 363–382.

Wong, N. Y., Kong, C. K., Lam, C. C., & Wong, K. M. P. (2010). Changing students' conceptions of mathematics through the introduction of variation. *Korea Society of Mathematical Education Series D: Research in Mathematical Education, 14*(4), 361–380.

Wong, N. Y., Lam, C. C., & Chan, A. M. Y. (2012). Teaching with variation: Bianshi mathematics teaching. In Y. Li & R. Huang (Eds.), *How Chinese teach Mathematics and improve teaching* (pp. 105–119). New York, NY: Routledge.

Wong, N. Y., Wong, W. Y., & Wong, E. W. Y. (2012). What do Chinese value in (mathematics) education? *ZDM Mathematics Education, 44*(1), 9–19.

Wong, N. Y., Zhang, Q., & Li, X. Q. (2013). (Mathematics) curriculum, teaching and learning. In Y. Li, & G. Lappan (Eds.), *Mathematics curriculum in school education* (pp. 607–620). Dordrecht, The Netherlands: Springer.

Wong, N. Y., Ding, R., & Zhang, Q. P. (2016). From classroom environment to conception of mathematics. In R. B. King & A. B. I. Bernardo (Eds.), *The psychology of Asian learners* (pp. 541–557). Singapore: Springer.

Zhang, Q. P., & Wong, N. Y. (2015). Beliefs, knowledge and teaching: A series of studies among Chinese mathematics teachers. In L. Fan, N. Y. Wong, J. Cai, & S. Li (Eds.), *How Chinese teach mathematics: Perspectives from insiders* (pp. 457–492). Singapore: World Scientific.

Ngai-Ying Wong
The Education University of Hong Kong
Hong Kong SAR, China

FERENCE MARTON AND JOHAN HÄGGSTRÖM

19. TEACHING THROUGH VARIATION

A European Perspective

INTRODUCTION

This book is about variation and invariance in the teaching of mathematics, that is, about what instances, examples, tasks are used and in which order, to make it possible for students to make concepts, principles, methods their own. Although we can find cases of individual teachers and individual textbook authors paying special attention to such aspects of the teaching of mathematics in different places in the world and at different points in time, such focused attention on the pattern of similarities and differences-especially on the latter-between tasks, instances, examples seems have been particularly common in China for a long time. Moreover, this character of Chinese practice of teaching mathematics has been made explicit by Gu (1991) who called it *Bianshi* (i.e. teaching with variation) and who tried to relate it to theoretical and empirical research on the learning and teaching of mathematics (in the following the acronym "BS" is used to widely refer to the Chinese tradition of systematically using variation and invariance in the teaching of mathematics). This is the major impetus of most chapters of the present book.

We also find another influence, not quite comparable in importance, with the former. It is our own research specialization, called the *Variation theory of learning*. This research specialization originates from a phenomenological interest in differences in how various phenomena appear to people, i.e., an interest in which different meanings the same phenomenon might have for different people. The reason for this interest is the assumption that people act in relation to things as they appear to them. Hence learning to handle situations in powerful ways takes learning to see them in powerful ways. As one particular contrast between *Bianshi* (BS) and the Variation theory of learning (VTL) is our focus in the present chapter, and as the former is elaborated in other chapters, we will deal with the latter at some length in the present chapter. There are shorter, but by no means less accurate, introductions to the theory in other chapters. First, when we have established the contrasts between BS and VTL, will we use it very briefly in the very last section as a perspective on the previous chapters. Doing so may appear odd, unconventional, and even disappointing. We have, however, found a problem that – we believe – has to be addressed for the field (the teaching of mathematics through variation) to move

R. Huang & Y. Li (Eds.), Teaching and Learning Mathematics through Variation, 389–406.

forward. Being the authors of one of the last chapters of the book, we were eager to make it pertinent beyond itself.

THE VARIATION THEORY OF LEARNING

What something looks like to someone is a function of what features of that phenomenon the person discerns and focuses on simultaneously. A feature is "[…] any discriminable attribute of a phenomenon that is susceptible of some discriminable variation from phenomenon to phenomenon" (c.f., Bruner, Goodnow & Austin, 1986, p. 28). Features have names and the most frequent form of adults helping children to learn is the learning of what the names refer to, i.e., learning the meaning of words, e.g., what does "green" (or "three" or "virtue" etc.) refer to, what does it mean? Interestingly, there is no agreed upon understanding of how this most frequent form of human learning takes place or how it can be made possible to take place. But can we not just say the word "green", at the same time pointing to a green thing or saying the word "circle", at the same time pointing to a circle, i.e., making use of what is called "direct reference" (Quine, 1960)? "Green" is certainly a feature of what we are pointing to, and so is "circle", but so is its size, its color, its appearance on a computer screen, its location on that screen, its movement across the screen (given that it is moving, of course), the speed of its movement, and many, many (actually an unlimited number of) other features. So how can the child possibly know what we have in mind? By knowing the meaning of the word "green" or "circle", of course, but this is exactly what she does not know and what we are trying to help her to learn.

We must then enable her to see some difference between the focused feature (the one that we have in mind) and other features. The widely accepted solution of this problem is to let the learner engage with instances of the focused feature, in which that feature is invariant (i.e., is the same), while other features vary (i.e., are different). In our two examples, the learner would encounter green things that vary in size and form or circles that vary in color and size perhaps. The learner is then supposed to see the invariant feature, which is the meaning of the word exposed (green or circle). This is called "induction" and is the only method we have for acquiring novel meanings, according to the American philosopher, Jerry Fodor (1980). Moreover, Fodor claims that the method does not work at all. The focused aspect is one that the learner has not yet acquired, this is why she has to learn it. Hence, she cannot possibly see what instances of the focused feature have in common. Novel meanings (concepts) cannot be acquired, Fodor concludes. They are innate.

Nonetheless, induction is the preferred way of teaching novel meanings. The teacher tells the student the novel meaning (concept, principle, method) followed by a great number of positive examples from which the students are expected to discern the focused feature. *Bianshi* (BS) is also frequently described in such terms. The essential meaning of the mathematical entities is supposed to be appropriated by the students through engaging with instances that have the focused feature in common, but differ otherwise.

But if we accept the thesis that novel meanings cannot be acquired through induction, without accepting the thesis that all meanings are innate, we are forced to come up with another explanation of how novel meanings are acquired. The Variation theory of learning (VTL) is based on a conjecture that affords such an alternative explanation. According to this conjecture, "[...] novel meanings are acquired from experiencing differences against a background of sameness, rather than from experiencing sameness against a background of difference" (Marton & Pang, 2013; see also Pang et al., 2017; Watson, 2017; Mok, 2017; Barlow et al., 2017). Or to put it in a more straightforward way: *Novel meanings are acquired through contrast and not through induction.* The former is the reversal of the latter: The focused feature varies while other features are invariant, instead of the focused feature being invariant while other features vary. In our example, in order to see a circle as a geometric figure, it has to be contrasted to another geometric figure, or to other geometric figures, such as an ellipse, a square, an octagon, etc. of the same size and of the same color. If we want to show what blue color is instead, we can use a blue circle juxtaposed to another circle of the same size, but of different color. Will we draw the learner's attention to its size ("small", for instance), we have to contrast it to a bigger circle of the same color.

According to this line of reasoning, a feature appears through a difference between two or more mutually exclusive features. Those mutually exclusive features define a dimension of variation, in which the features are "values". The dimension of variation is also called "aspect". We cannot experience an aspect without experiencing features that define it, nor can we experience a feature without experiencing the aspect to which it belongs. Two or more features must be experienced simultaneously. Thus, the aspect that is defined by the differences between the mutually exclusive features, is experienced simultaneously as well. In other words: By juxtaposing two or more mutually exclusive features, a dimension of variation is opened up. A dimension of variation being opened up for someone amounts to that person being able to see a relevant phenomenon in terms of that dimension of variation (thus, being aware of it).

Hence, there are two kinds of meanings: features and aspects. In order to acquire a novel meaning of any of those two kinds, the learner must simultaneously acquire (become aware of) a corresponding meaning of the other kind. Thus, acquiring a novel meaning amounts to discerning – or separating it – from that which the novel meaning is a meaning of, for instance discerning – or separating – the meaning "small", "blue", or "circle" from a small, blue circle. Upon encountering such features, the learner will be able to discern – or separate – them from instances of those features as long as she is aware of them and of the dimensions of variation to which they belong.

Contrast

So, novel meanings are acquired through discernment – separation – of features and aspects simultaneously. But new meanings (in the sense of new features) can also be acquired if the corresponding dimension of variation is already opened up in the learner's awareness. For instance, if she encounters a new geometric form after having encountered other geometric forms earlier and the dimension of variation "geometric form" is opened up already. Similarly, it is easier for a child to learn a new color if she is already aware of the dimension of variation "color". If it is necessary for the learner to be aware of a specific feature, or of a specific aspect (dimension of variation), in order to achieve a particular educational objective and she is not already aware of it, we call that specific feature or aspect *critical feature* or *critical aspect*. They are learned and used through *contrast*, i.e., by simultaneously experiencing two or more features in the same dimension of variation. By comparing geometric figures of the same size and same color (unfocused features are invariant), the (varying focused) features that define the differences between them, are highlighted. This is the way in which critical features and critical aspects are appropriated. We might mention in passing that this pattern of variation and invariance, which is of key importance in VTL, is not highlighted in BS.

Generalization

But there are features that the learner may assume make a difference and she therefore takes them to be defining or necessary features. Students may be used to seeing triangles with their base-line parallel to the short-side of their textbook with the vertex pointing upwards. The students might then have to open up for the dimension of variation "rotational position", which is a critical aspect (not a necessary or defining aspect, but an aspect that is necessary to separate from the necessary aspects, such as "three sides") to realize that a triangle can be in any position, and it still remains a triangle. In this case the focused feature is invariant and the unfocused features vary. This is basically the same pattern of variation and invariance as in induction, mentioned above, but in this case the learner is not supposed to discover a novel meaning ("triangle" in this case) but, instead, generalize a restricted meaning (triangle only in one specific rotational position) to a generalized meaning (triangle in any rotational position). This kind of change in meaning is called *generalization* ("contrasting with non-standard figures" in *Bianshi* belongs to this category).

Fusion

The point of departure of the present line of reasoning is that learning to a substantial extent is learning to see, and learning to see entails learning to discern and separate various features and dimensions of variation. Such learning can be made possible by letting certain features vary while others remain invariant. The combination of features in the environment itself makes it possible to discover certain features (meanings) and does not make it possible to discover other features. By allowing all kinds of combinations of features in practice for learning, learners get prepared to handle all kinds of combinations of features. This is the third pattern of variation and invariance that we might make use of in order to facilitate learning. It is called *fusion* and many features may vary simultaneously in this case.

Induction and Generalization

As we have stated above, according to the received wisdom, new meanings are arrived at by keeping the focused feature invariant, while other features vary. We have also argued that this arrangement cannot work and suggested contrast as an alternative, powerful way of making novel meanings our own. Questioning induction and suggesting contrast are key principles of VTL. When studying various accounts of BS, we might get the impression that it rests on the assumption of induction as the chief mechanism of the learning of novel meanings:

> To illustrate essential features of a concept by demonstrating various visual materials and instances, or to highlight essential characteristics of a concept by varying non-essential features. The goal of using variation is to help students understand the essential features of a concept by differentiating them from non-essential features and further develop a scientific concept. (Gu, 1999, p. 186)

These lines are quoted in other places in this book (Peng et al., 2017; Zhang et al., 2017). We can also find other, similar formulations, such as "[…] essential features of mathematical concepts are kept unchanged, but the non-essential features of the mathematical concepts are changed" (Peng et al., 2017).

The above quote from Gu (1999) and the other, similar, formulations make the impression of being in conflict with the basic principle of VTL, stating that novel meanings cannot be grasped by keeping the aimed at meaning (feature) invariant. We can write it as

$$\underline{x} \quad \underline{y}$$
$$i \quad v$$

where x is a focused feature, y is an unfocused feature, "i" stands for "invariant" and "v" for "varies." The pattern of symbols represents induction. According to the VTL, we cannot acquire novel meanings through induction, however, according to the BS, it seems we can. This potential contradiction is actually the focal point of our chapter. We consider the question so important for the development of the research field dealt with in this book, that we are using the space given for our comments to illuminate this – in our judgement – very important problem. BS does not, however, necessarily suggest that we can acquire novel meanings through induction. If we return to the paragraph on Generalization, we can see that it can be represented in exactly the same way as Induction. The VTL indeed suggests that in order to grasp a novel meaning, the focused feature needs to vary against the background of invariant unfocused features (contrast). But it also suggests that in order to separate focused and unfocused features, the focused feature needs to be kept invariant against the background of varying unfocused features (generalization), given that a necessary contrast has been made and the learner is already aware of the focused feature, even if it has not yet been sufficiently separated from other features. Gu's words may apply to any of the two (induction or generalization). This ambiguity calls for studying the practice of BS empirically. But there is still another reason for doing so. While Gu and other authors are explicit about the pattern "focused feature invariant, others vary" (implying induction or generalization), they do not mention the pattern "focused feature varies, others invariant" (implying contrast, the key to the acquisition of novel meanings according to the VTL). A highly relevant observation was made by Pang et al. (2017). After having made a comparison between teaching the same topic (adding three-digit numbers) in accordance with principles of BS in one class in Shanghai and in accordance with the VTL in another class in Hong Kong, the theoretical underpinnings of the two practices could not be differentiated. We are now going to look at a study in which the same topic (systems of linear equations in two unknowns) was taught in some classes in China and Sweden. In at least one of the classes in Shanghai, the teaching clearly followed the principles of BS. Interestingly, one of the lessons in that class was also analyzed by Mok (2017) in Chapter 10 of the present book. In particular, we want to find out in what sense the principle advocated by Gu in the quote above, was realized in that class. Could it really be the case that students acquired novel meanings through induction and that the basic assumption of the VTL (telling us that novel meanings cannot be acquired through induction) is simply wrong? Or did the particular pattern of variation (focused feature invariant, unfocused features vary) refer to generalization (i.e., the separation of already acquired novel meaning of focused feature and unfocused feature)? How was the novel meaning acquired in that case? And does contrast, the only path to novel meaning according to the VTL, occur at all in the practice of BS?

TEACHING OF SIMULTANEOUS EQUATIONS

In this section the introduction of the same content, systems of linear equations in two unknowns, in two classrooms is analyzed. The two classrooms were video-recorded in the Learner's Perspective Study (Clarke, 2000) and the data has previously been used in a larger study where Häggström (2008) analyzed and compared the teaching of 16 lessons in 6 classrooms. These lessons covered three topics: (1) the concept of systems of linear equations in two unknowns, (2) the solution to a system of linear equations in two unknowns, and (3) the method of substitution for solving a system of linear equations in two unknowns. Häggström's study focused on how the mathematical content was handled and what was made possible for students to learn. The analysis was founded in the VTL and made use of the concept "dimension of variation". In the analysis, a dimension of variation was considered opened if there were at least two different features of an aspect present simultaneously, or very close in time, which provides students with an opportunity to experience the difference. The study showed significant differences regarding what dimensions of variation were opened in the 6 classrooms (see Häggström, 2008). The largest number of dimensions of variation was opened in one of the classrooms from Shanghai (SH1) and the fewest were opened in the Swedish classroom (SW2). In the paragraphs that follow, we will take a new look at the classroom from Shanghai and compare it to the teaching in the Swedish classroom.

Table 1. Spaces of learning for systems of linear equations in two unknowns

Dimension of variation	Features	SW2	SH1
1. Number of equations	1a. Two equations, not one	x	x
	1b. More than one equation		x
2. Number of unknowns	2a. Two unknowns not one	x	
	2b. Two unknowns not three		x
3. Type of equations	3a. xy is not first degree		x
	3b. x^2, $(x + y)^2$, is not first degree		x
	3c. $1/y$ is not first degree		x
4. An unknown represents the same number in both equations	4a. "Unknowns are the same" is not taken for granted		x
5. Constants and coefficients can be different types of numbers	5a. Rational numbers not just natural	x	x
	5b. Negative numbers not just natural	x	x
	5c. Parameters not just specified numbers		x
6. Different letters may be used	6a. The letters x, y are not taken for granted		x
7. A system of equations can be in different formats	7a. Format of individual equations varies	x	x
	7b. One expression		x
	7c. Both unknowns not present in both equations	x	x

In Häggström's study, the patterns of variation in the 6 classrooms were studied without consideration of the character of the dimension of variation opened. That means, no discrimination was made between *contrast* or *generalization*. The result of Häggström's analysis for the first of the three topics in the two selected classrooms is shown in Table 1. The table shows that during the analyzed lessons, seven different dimensions of variation regarding the concept of systems of linear equations in two unknowns were opened ("x" means that the pattern of variation was found in the analyzed lesson). Further, a dimension could be opened in different ways, i.e., different features could open a dimension. For example, in the Swedish classroom they solve the same problem, first by means of *one* unknown, directly followed by the use of *two* unknowns. When two alternatives are provided in this way, the dimension of variation regarding the number of unknowns is opened – the potential experience of the difference between one and two unknowns makes it possible to become aware of this aspect of a system of equations. In SH1 the same dimension of variation – the number of unknowns – was also opened, but in a slightly different way. Here, examples of systems of equations with *two* and *three* unknowns provided students with the opportunity to become aware of this aspect.

Table 1 shows that all seven dimensions of variation were opened in the Shanghai classroom (SH1), and that it was done in several different ways. In contrast, just four of the dimensions of variations were opened in the Swedish classroom (SW2). From Häggström's study, it can be concluded that the use of variation was much more frequent in the Chinese classroom than in the Swedish and that the teaching in SH1 can be considered as following the BS tradition.

In the following re-analysis of the teaching in the two classrooms, the focus will be on the topic "systems of linear equations in two unknowns" only. Further, the analysis will go beyond just noting what dimensions of variation were opened and focus on how the students were provided with opportunities to become aware of *novel* aspects of the content.

Setting the Scene

The Swedish class, labelled SW2, is a high-ability mathematics class with 24 students from four regular classes. This formation is used exclusively for mathematics instruction. The students are in 9th grade and cover more topics than could be considered compulsory – system of linear equations in two unknowns is not mentioned in the Swedish syllabus. In the 12th recorded lesson (of a total of 14), the concept of systems of linear equations in two unknowns is introduced. During the 8 previous lessons, the class has worked with equations in one unknown, and more specifically solved problems by forming and solving linear equations in one unknown. The concept of system of equations is introduced as an alternative way to represent a problem – the same problem was solved in lesson 11 by means of one equation in one unknown. From the data available, it might be assumed that (most of) the students had not been exposed to equations with more than one unknown and had not handled more than one equation at a time by the time of the introduction of systems of linear equations in two unknowns.

The class in Shanghai (SH1) was different in many respects. It is a grade 8 class consisting of 50 students, roughly twice the number in SW2. Even though it was a grade 8 class, the level of mathematical proficiency of the students was no doubt much higher and the students previous experience was more advanced compared to the students in SW2. In SH1 the concept of systems of linear equations was introduced in the 5th recorded lesson. In the preceding 4 recorded lessons the class had worked with (single) linear equations in two unknowns, the coordinate plane, and graphs of linear equations in two unknowns. When the concept of systems of linear equations in two unknowns was introduced, the students in SH1 had already encountered equations with both one and two unknowns.

Contrast or Generalisation

Being interested in characterizing the patterns of variation in SH1 related to novel aspects as either contrast or generalisation, we need to establish what aspects of the mathematical content can be considered as novel to the students. Before the actual introduction of the new concept – systems of linear equations in two unknowns – in the Shanghai lesson (SH1-5), they revise previously covered topics. The revision was made with five questions posed to the students (see Figure 1).

1. Linear equations in two unknowns, or not?

   a) $y = 3x^2 - 5$

   b) $\frac{2}{y} + 2x = 3$

2. How many solutions have, $2x + y = 10$?
3. $x + 3y = -4$, when $x = 2$, $y = ?$
4. If $x = -4$, $y = -5$ is a solution for $2x + ay = 7$, then $a = ?$
5. $2x + y = 10$, $x + 3y = -4$, what are the solutions for each equation?

   a) $x = 1, y = 4$ b) $x = 0, y = 10$

   c) $x = 1, y = -5/3$ d) $x = -1, y = 12$

Figure 1. Overhead transparency – revision of previously covered topics in SH1-5

The revision revealed a number of things regarding the mathematical proficiency of the students in this class. At the time of the introduction, at the most three of the seven dimensions of variation in Table 1 could be regarded as novel to the students in this class. From the content of the revision questions, it is clear that aspects such as, "there can be more than one unknown" and "there are equations of different degrees" were not new to these students. However, what might be novel was to consider two equations simultaneously and that "an unknown represents the same number in both equations" – the fourth dimension of variation in Table 1. The third new aspect was the format of a system of equations, the seventh dimension of variation in Table 1.

After the revision (it lasted only a couple of minutes), the new concept was introduced. The teacher showed a new slide with three questions (Figure 2) and told the students to read a section in the textbook and discuss the questions in pairs.

1 What is a "system of equations"?

2 How can you tell whether a system of equations is a system of linear equations in two unknowns?

3 Identify whether the given is a system of linear equations in two unknowns.

1) $\begin{cases} x+y=3 \\ x-y=1 \end{cases}$ 2) $\begin{cases} (x+y)^2=1 \\ x-y=0 \end{cases}$ 3) $\begin{cases} x=1 \\ y=1 \end{cases}$

4) $\begin{cases} x/2+y/2=0 \\ x=y \end{cases}$ 5) $\begin{cases} xy=2 \\ x=1 \end{cases}$ 6) $\begin{cases} x+1/y=1 \\ y=2 \end{cases}$

7) $u=v=0$ 8) $\begin{cases} x+y=4 \\ x-m=1 \end{cases}$

Figure 2. Overhead transparency – introducing questions in SH1-5

After a couple of minutes, students answered the first two questions and two points were noted on the board:

1. the two equations should have two unknowns
2. the indexes of the unknowns should be one

The two points were repeated a number of times before they moved on to the third question.

Transcript, question 1 and 2, SH1-5

S: A system of equations is formed by a number of equations [question 1]
   [...]
S: There are two unknowns in the equations and the indexes of the unknowns are one. This is called system of linear equations in two unknowns [question 1]
T: Oh, sit down please. He has just mentioned the definition of system of linear equations in two unknowns
   [...]
T: ... let me summarise [...] the first point [...] these two equations should have two unknowns. The second point, the second, a classmate has just mentioned, the indexes of the unknowns ... should be one

Even though the aspects, "number of unknowns" and "type of equations" seemed to be emphasized, it may be considered that students *could* experience the difference in the aspect "number of equations". There was a contrast created between the concept of *one* linear equation in two unknowns, from the introductory revision, and systems of equations with more than one equation, in question one and two. This contrast opened the corresponding dimension of variation, thus enabling students to become aware of this novel aspect. Thus, even if the two aspects "number of unknowns" and "type of equations" were regarded as the "essential features of the mathematical concept" and were intended, following BS practice, to be kept invariant, the consequence of the pattern of variation that emerged was that a contrast between one and more equations were created. In our opinion this contrast opened up an important dimension of variation giving students the opportunity to discern a novel aspect regarding the new concept.

The eight items in question 3 generate a rich pattern of variation. The selection of items is an indication of the teacher's knowledge and experience of common student errors. It follows the BS practice of using *standard examples, non-standard examples,* and *non-examples* to generate variation in many different aspects. They were discussed in whole class, one at a time, and arguments for or against them meeting the necessary requirements were given. See an example below.

Transcript, question 3–2, SH1-5

Question 3-2 $\begin{cases} (x+y)^2 = 1 \\ x - y = 0 \end{cases}$

S: They are not linear equation in two unknowns
T: Oh, he said not. Why not?
S: Because in this system of equation, the index of the term is two

The two "essential" points noted on the board – "number of unknowns" and "type of equations" – were used in the argumentation. In one sense they were kept invariant, as the yardsticks to use when determining whether the items were systems of linear equations in two unknowns, or not. However, the eight items provided contrasts between two and three unknowns, as well as between linear and non-linear equations, and in that way, these two aspects were not kept invariant. During this episode, a number of dimensions of variations were opened (see Häggström, 2008), and we will particularly point to the novel aspect, "a system of equations can be in different formats" (see Table 1). The contrasts created by item 3 and 7, in particular, opened this dimension. The dimension of variation – an unknown represents the same number in both equations (the third novel aspect) – was not opened during the introduction (but was in following lessons).

As a comparison, we will outline the introduction of systems of equation in the Swedish classroom. In this classroom it was much more obvious that the "essential aspects" of the concept were varied, even though the teacher in question is by no means influenced by the VTL. As mentioned before, it can be assumed that to students in this class "equations with more than one unknown" and "more than one equation at a time" were novel aspects at the time of the introduction of systems of linear equations in two unknowns. The introduction was made in two steps. First the dimension of variation – "number of unknowns" was opened, followed by an episode where the dimension "number of equations" was opened.

In previous lessons, some students in the class had worked on a problem involving a number of dogs and cats. The problem can be solved by forming one equation in one unknown, but some students tried to use two unknowns. In the beginning of the lesson in question, the teacher connected to this idea and the number of cats and dogs were expressed both with one and two unknowns. During this episode the problem was kept invariant. The number of unknowns used is what varied. A contrast was made between the use of one and two unknowns, thus opening this dimension of variation and providing students with an opportunity to experience the number of unknowns as an (essential) aspect of equations.

The teacher then aimed to illustrate the need of two conditions (equations) in order to determine the values of two unknowns. He let one student "think of a number" and then he himself "thought of another number" [The student Joel overheard Tony's number, which probably was a miscalculation by the teacher. This is probably the reason why the points the teachers tried to make became less clear].

Transcript, think of a number-1, SW2-12

T: Tony, think of a number … tell me, but no one else [writes on the board] […]

T: I think of another number … I know that … [writes "$x + y = 60$" on the board]

T: Those two numbers together are 60 … and then, the big question is – which are the numbers? […] Which are the numbers? … Any suggestions? … Joel.

S: 56 and 4

T: Alright. Why is that?

S: It's 60.

[Teacher writes "$56 + 4 = 60$" on the board.]

T: Are there any other possibilities? … Yes, of course there are … Now, I know this is correct because you have seen through me here, but … is it enough to know the sum of two numbers is 60 in order to find the answer? Michael?

S: No

T: No it isn't

S: (…) it could be 40 and 20

[Teacher wrote this and a third possible pair of numbers on the board (Figure 3).]

Think of a number: x

Think of another number: y

$x + y = 60$

$56 + 4 = 60$
$40 + 20 = 60$
$35 + 25 = 60$
$\vdots$ $\vdots$

Figure 3. The board, SW2-12

The class came to a conclusion that there was not enough information to determine the two numbers. The teacher then added a second condition regarding the two numbers and completed the system of equations on the board (Figure 4).

Transcript, think of a number-2, SW2-12

T: Thus, it's not enough to know one condition
   [...]
T: Your [Tony's] number is 14 times my number
   [Teacher writes on the board]
T: Now, we already know the answers, it's a little ... no good, but anyhow ... now I have two conditions and two unknowns. Now we can easily calculate ... the whole, so let's do it

$$\begin{cases} x + y = 60 \\ x = 14 \cdot y \end{cases}$$

Figure 4. The board showing the systems of equations, SW2-12

In this second episode the two "unknown" numbers were kept invariant, while the number of equations were changed from one to two in order to determine the numbers. The teacher, most likely, had intended to clearly show the distinction between two cases: (1) with two unknown numbers and one condition (equation) there are many possible solutions, and (2) with two unknown numbers you need two conditions (equations) to obtain one solution. This intention is however not fulfilled due to the fact that the numbers, unintentionally, became known to the students beforehand.

This introduction indicates two patterns of variation, where the novel aspects – "number of unknowns" and "number of equations" – were made possible for students to experience by means of contrast.

In the next episode the teacher demonstrated how the value of the number y could be obtained by the method of substitution. The students then worked with (solved) systems of equations from the textbook (see Figure 5) and two of them were put on the board and discussed in whole class. For one of the systems of equations, the solution was verified by substitution into the two original equations.

920a) $\begin{cases} y = x + 2 \\ 3x + y = 6 \end{cases}$
b) $\begin{cases} y = 2x{-}1 \\ x + y = 5 \end{cases}$
c) $\begin{cases} y = 4x{-}3 \\ 2x + y = 6 \end{cases}$

921a) $\begin{cases} y = 2x \\ 9x{-}2y = 15 \end{cases}$
b) $\begin{cases} y = x + 1 \\ x + 2y = 11 \end{cases}$
c) $\begin{cases} y = 3x{-}2 \\ 2y{-}5x = 0 \end{cases}$

922a) $\begin{cases} y = 3x \\ 4x{-}y = 1 \end{cases}$
b) $\begin{cases} y = 5x{-}3 \\ 7x{-}y = 6 \end{cases}$
c) $\begin{cases} y = 4{-}x \\ 5x{-}y = 5 \end{cases}$

923a) $\begin{cases} y = x + 4 \\ 5x{-}2y = 1 \end{cases}$
b) $\begin{cases} y = 2{-}x \\ 4x{-}3y = 8 \end{cases}$
c) $\begin{cases} y = 2x + 5 \\ 6x{-}2y = 5 \end{cases}$

924a) $\begin{cases} y = 7 \\ 8x{-}3y = -1 \end{cases}$
b) $\begin{cases} y = 2, 5x{-}4 \\ 6x{-}2y = 12 \end{cases}$
c) $\begin{cases} 16x{-}2y = 9 \\ y = 7x{-}2 \end{cases}$

925a) $\begin{cases} x = 4y{-}2 \\ 3x{-}10y = 3 \end{cases}$
b) $\begin{cases} x = 9{-}2y \\ 5y{-}3x = 6 \end{cases}$
c) $\begin{cases} x = 0, 5y + 10 \\ 2y{-}x = 5 \end{cases}$

Figure 5. The tasks in the textbook, SW2–12

The tasks in the students' textbook are very similar, e.g., only x and y are used. Only one task (924a) is slightly different, perhaps even considered *non-standard*. The first equation in this task is the only one where not both unknowns are present (only y). The items in the Swedish textbook are, when compared to the items from SH1 (Figure 2), strikingly similar to each other. The use of variation seemed to be a lot less pronounced when it came to the tasks students worked with.

COMPARISONS OF THE TWO LESSONS

The use of contrast to provide students with opportunities to discern novel aspects of the mathematical content can be found in both classrooms, or to put it slightly differently: To the extent novel aspects of the object of learning were introduced, they were introduced by means of contrast, just as VTL predicts. This was the case in spite of the fact that BS does not point out this pattern of variation and invariance explicitly, and neither the Chinese nor the Swedish teacher had ever come across the

VTL. The reason is that nobody can teach mathematics without using *some* pattern of variation and invariance, although it can be done more or less systematically and with more or less awareness. BS is an explicit systematization of a certain teaching practice. VTL also captures a certain practice, although less explicitly. A difference between the two lessons is, however, that the pattern of variation in SW2 was much more limited as well as less complex. There were two distinct aspects ("number of unknowns" and "number of equations"), which were varied one at time and thus opening up dimensions of variation. In SH1, aspects already known by the students appeared to be emphasized, but even still, the patterns of variation created contrasts that opened up dimensions of variation, which were novel to the students. Overall, there were much more elaborated patterns of variation in SH1 than in SW2 and the awareness of the significance of varying mathematical content seemed to be greater in SH1. This was not the least evident when comparing the selection of items students work with in the two classrooms. Another striking difference was the little time spent on the new concept in SW2; after no more than 15 minutes of introduction, students were starting to solve a number of systems of equations. In SH1 the whole introductory lesson was spent on getting acquainted to the new concept and the method of substitution was not introduced until the following lesson.

SOME COMMENTS ON PREVIOUS CHAPTERS AND CONCLUSIONS

To the extent the teaching in the class in Shanghai can be considered representing the Chinese tradition of the systematic use of variation and invariance in the teaching of mathematics, Häggström's (2008) study implied at least some tentative answers to the questions about the practice of BS. First of all, we have to conclude that the description of the lessons was done in terms of the dimensions of variation opened up, or rather: in terms of dimensions of variation made possible to open up. This means that lessons were characterized in terms of patterns of variation and invariance, i.e., in terms of what was made possible to learn. All three patterns of variation and invariance defined above (contrast, generalization, and fusion) could be found in the lessons analyzed. The pattern with the focused feature varying and unfocused features being invariant (contrast) opened up (or rather, made it possible to open up) the dimensions of variation of necessary (essential) features. In accordance with the VTL, novel meanings were never acquired through induction, and this was in fact never attempted (the teacher never tried to help students acquire a new meaning by offering examples that had that meaning in common but differed otherwise). When the pattern of variation characteristic for both induction and generalization was used, it seemed to serve the latter. Contrast was indeed frequently used.

These observations support Pang et al.'s (2017) thesis that even if the description of the intended practice implied by BS and of the intended practice implied by the VTL differ, the enacted practices might look very much the same if described by the same framework (see also Chapter 3 where Pang et al., 2017, are demonstrating that the same practice looks different if described in different frameworks). Although the distinctions super-imposed by the two frameworks differ, they are commensurable: they can be mapped into each other.

But what about the idea that mathematical concepts are invariant and that we learn them by separating them from that which is not invariant? In Chapter 4, Leung (2017) is emphasizing the invariant nature of mathematical concepts and presents four principles of "the acquisition of invariance" that are supposed to be complementary to the four patterns of variation and invariance in the VTL. In Chapter 5, Watson (2017) argues that in mathematics the object of learning is often an abstract relation that can only be experienced through examples. She calls such an object of learning a dependency relation, in which one variable causes a change in another (when one variation necessitates another variation). Mathematical concepts and dependency relations are invariant, indeed, but we can never grasp their invariant form. They can only be grasped through their infinitely varying appearances (as Huang et al., 2017, claim in Chapter 9). In that sense, we can only perceive the invariance through variation, just as Gu Lingyan argues (see Chapter 2). VTL and BS frameworks agree on the principle that novel and essential aspects of the object of learning in mathematics can only be appropriated by the learners by means of separating those essential aspects from non-essential aspects. To the extent the origin of novel mathematical meanings is dealt with in the other chapters, this principle is expressed and followed in one way or another. The difference between the two frameworks boils down to this: According to BS, in order to separate essential and non-essential aspects, the former has to be kept invariant, while letting the latter vary. To the extent the question is raised at all, it is in this way that the principle is formulated in all the mainly BS inspired chapters. According to VTL, it is just the other way around: In order to separate essential and non-essential aspects, we must let the former vary, while keeping the latter invariant. To the extent the question is raised at all, it is in this way that the principle is formulated in all the chapters inspired mainly by VTL. But in every chapter, whether it builds on BS or on VTL, to the extent there are examples of how learners appropriate essential (and novel) aspects of the object of learning in mathematics, the essential (and novel) aspect varies (through contrast) while the non-essential aspects remain invariant *in practice*. Our conclusion, as far as the focal point of the chapter is concerned, is thus that the potential contradiction between BS and VTL seems illusory and mainly rhetorical.

As this chapter is written from the perspective of VTL, the above observations were easiest to make in chapters that had the same point of departure or one of their points of departure. What we have in mind are Chapters 3 (dual perspectives), 4, 5 (dual perspectives), 8 (dual perspective), 10, 15, 16, and 17. Chapter 1 is an introduction to the whole book and Chapter 2 describes the BS framework (just as this chapter is mostly about the VTL framework). Chapter 14 by Hino (2017) represents the Japanese framework for variation in the teaching of mathematics. We find an interesting idea well worth to be developed further: Helping students to explore and nurture their own use of variation. The remaining chapters reflect the BS tradition. Most of the students and teachers who have participated in the empirical studies are Chinese, many of them from Shanghai and Hong Kong.

This book represents an important step in establishing a new research specialization: Learning and teaching mathematics through variation (and invariance). This field is, to a considerable extent, built on a long and successful Chinese pedagogical tradition. But, as was mentioned in several contributions, there is quite a bit of research going on in different places in the world, in which the effect of various patterns of variation and invariance on learning is studied. We should try to develop connections and make this new research specialization truly international and visible as a genuine field of scientific enquiry.

REFERENCES

Bruner, J. S., Goodnow, J., & Austin, G. A. (1986). *A study of thinking*. New Brunswick, NJ: Transaction Publishers.

Chunxia, Q., Wang, R., Mok, I. A. C., & Huang, D. (2017). Teaching proposition based on variation principles: A case of teaching formula of perfect square trinomials. In R. Huang & Y. Li (Eds.), *Teaching and learning mathematics through variations*. [Chapter 7 in this book]

Clarke, D. (2000). The learner's perspective study. In D. Clarke, C. Keitel, & Y. Shimizu (Eds.), *Mathematics classrooms in twelve countries: The insider's perspective* (pp. 1–14). Rotterdam: Sense Publishers.

Ding, L., Jones, K., & Sikko, S. A. (2017). An expert teacher's use of teaching with variation to support a junior mathematics teacher's professional learning in Shanghai. In R. Huang & Y. Li (Eds.), *Teaching and learning mathematics through variations*. [Chapter 12 in this book]

Fodor, J. (1980). On the impossibility of acquiring "more powerful" structures. In M. Piatelli-Palmarini (Ed.), *Language and learning: The debate between Jean Piaget and Noam Chomsky* (pp. 142–162). London: Routledge.

Gu, F., Huang, R., & Gu, L. (2017). Theory and development of teaching with variation in mathematics in China. In R. Huang & Y. Li (Eds.), *Teaching and learning mathematics through variations*. [Chapter 2 in this book]

Gu, L. Y. (1991). *Xuehui jiaoxue* [Learning to teach]. Beijing: People's Educational Press.

Gu, L. Y., Huang, R., & Marton, F. (2004). Teaching with variation: A Chinese way of promoting effective mathematics learning. In L. H. Fan, Y. Wong, J. E. Cai, & S. Q. Li (Eds.), *How Chinese learn mathematics: Perspectives from insiders* (pp. 309–347). Singapore: World Scientific.

Gu, M. Y. (1999). *Education directory*. Shanghai: Shanghai Education Press.

Häggström, J. (2008). *Teaching systems of linear equations in Sweden and China: What is made possible to learn?* Gothenburg: Acta Universitatis Gothoburgensis

Hino, K. (2017). Improving teaching through variation: A Japanese perspective. In R. Huang & Y. Li (Eds.), *Teaching and learning mathematics through variations*. [Chapter 14 in this book]

Huang, X., Yang, X., & Zhang, P. (2017). Teaching mathematics review lesson: Practice and reflection from a perspective of variation. In R. Huang & Y. Li (Eds.), *Teaching and learning mathematics through variations*. [Chapter 9 in this book]

Leung, A. (2017). Variation in tool-based mathematics pedagogy: The case of dynamic virtual tool. In R. Huang & Y. Li (Eds.), *Teaching and learning mathematics through variations*. [Chapter 5 in this book]

Marton, F., & Pang, M. F. (2013). Meanings are acquired from experiencing differences against a background of sameness, rather than fro experiencing sameness against the background of difference. *Frontline Learning Research, 1*, 24–41.

Pang, M. F., Marton, F., Bao, J. -S., & Ki, W. W. (2017). Teaching to add three-digit numbers in Hong Kong and Shanghai: Illustration of differences in the systematic use of variation and invariance. *ZDM, Mathematics Education, 48*, 1–16. doi:10.1007/s11858-016-0790-z

Pang, M. F., Bao, J., & Ki, W. W. (2017). "Bianshi" and the variation theory of learning: Illustrating two frameworks variation and invariance in the teaching of mathematics. In R. Huang & Y. Li (Eds.), *Teaching and learning mathematics through variations*. [Chapter 3 in this book]

Peled, I., & Leikin, R. (2017). Openness in the eye of the problem solver: Choice in solving problems in Israel. In R. Huang & Y. Li (Eds.), *Teaching and learning mathematics through variations*. [Chapter 16 in this book]

Peng, A., Li, J., Nie, B., & Li, Y. (2017). Characteristic of teaching mathematical problem solving in China: Analysis of a lesson from the perspective of variation. In R. Huang & Y. Li (Eds.), *Teaching and learning mathematics through variations*. [Chapter 6 in this book]

Quine, W. V. O. (1960). *Word and object*. Cambridge: MIT Press.

Watson, A. (2017). Pedagogy of variations: Synthesis of various notions of pedagogy of variation. In R. Huang & Y. Li (Eds.), *Teaching and learning mathematics through variations*. [Chapter 5 in this book]

Zhang, J., Wang, R., Huang, R., & Kimmins, D. (2017). Strategies for using variation tasks in selected mathematics textbooks in China. In R. Huang & Y. Li (Eds.), *Teaching and learning mathematics through variations*. [Chapter 11 in this book]

Ference Marton
Department of Pedagogical, Curricular and Professional Studies
University of Gothenburg, Sweden

Johan Häggström
Department of Pedagogical, Curricular and Professional Studies &
National Centre for Mathematics Education
University of Gothenburg, Sweden

JOHN MASON

20. ISSUES IN VARIATION THEORY AND HOW IT COULD INFORM PEDAGOGICAL CHOICES

INTRODUCTION

This chapter is both a response to and a development from the preceding lucid and inspiring chapters in this book. It is a response because there are some clear issues arising from the examples of variation that have been provided, and I wish to elaborate on these. It is a development because my own thinking about the role of variation has been augmented and amplified by reading those chapters, through being stimulated to relate the various uses of variation to the nature and role of attention. I want to suggest that with a firm commitment to variation, it is possible to overlook other insights available in the preceding chapters, which suggest to me that variation is a significant stepping stone towards a more complex appreciation of what is available to be learned, and under what conditions that learning might actually be induced to take place. For example, it is important pedagogically not only to be aware of what needs to be varied, but when, and to consider how much variation, over what range, and over what period of time. These considerations are likely to lead to choices which are highly dependent on how novel the topic or procedure is to learners, and whether they are meeting it for the first time, after a brief or lengthy absence, or as revision or exploration.

In developing the notion of variation I find myself called upon to make use of a more complex view of the human psyche than the traditional *enction, affect* and *cognition,* by including *attention, will* and *witness* as well. Being committed to the lived experience of thinking mathematically, of learning and doing mathematics, I have chosen to illustrate my questions and conjectures using a single mathematical topic, the notion of *angle,* augmented with a few other examples where necessary. I begin by elaborating briefly on my theoretical framework.

ROOTS AND ESSENCE OF VARIATION THEORY

Several authors in this book (see for example Mok, Chapter 10 this book) indicate that the explicit articulation of variation as a principle on which to base lessons in mathematics in China derives from the work of Gu (1994) in *Qingpu* county Shanghai in the 1980s. However Sun (2011, p. 68) suggests that variation, being an integral part of Confucianism and Daoism, as manifested for example in the *I Ching,*

R. Huang & Y. Li (Eds.), Teaching and Learning Mathematics through Variation, 407–438.

the *Book of Changes* (Wilhelm, 1967), has underpinned Chinese pedagogic practices for many centuries, and is a basic principle of Confucian Heritage educational practices. For example, there is a Chinese maxim quoted by Gu, Huang and Gu (Chapter 2, in this book): "Only by comparing can one distinguish".

As several authors point out in their chapters, variation as an educational principle derives from the fact that the functioning of human beings is based on constant change. Thus sensation of any kind, whether visual, aural, touch, taste or smell depend on detecting change. For example, saccadic movement of the eyes is necessary in order to refresh the stimulation of receptors in the eye. The same applies to more abstract perception, and hence to conception as well. This has been expressed in many different ways at different times, for example, in the *I Ching* as "abstracting invariant concepts from a varied situation" (quoted in Sun, 2011, p. 68); in the adage attributed to Heraclitus that "you cannot walk into the same stream twice"; in the stressing of *mutabilitie* both in nature and in politics by Edmund Spencer (Zitner, 1968); in identifying disturbance as the basis for intellectual development by Heidegger (1927/1949); and in modern manifestations such as *cognitive dissonance* as the trigger for learning (Festinger, 1957), *cognitive conflict* (Tall, 1977a, 1977b), and *variation theory* as the necessary conditions for learning (Marton & Booth, 1997; Marton & Pang, 2006; Marton, 2015). But dissonance and conflict, originating as disturbance, can both originate in, and have consequences for, affect, enaction and cognition, not to say attention, will and witness.

The notion of experiences in the material world as being dominated by change finds resonance in mathematics. For example, in order to formulate mathematical models of material world phenomena it is often only possible to begin by expressing how things change. The calculus was developed in order to convert expressions of how things change into expressions that would predict their actual values. In addition, one of the major and pervasive themes of modern mathematics is the study of invariance in the midst of change, from cardinality of sets when order is changed, through properties of classes of geometric figures, to fundamental groups of manifolds, and beyond.

As Pang, Bao and Ki (Chapter 3) and Watson (Chapter 4) both observe, even change itself is only discernible in relation to something else, whether invariant or changing differently or less quickly. Two or more things may be changing together because they are linked, but seen against a relatively invariant background. Their co-variational relationship may be the object of learning, rather than simply the individual change in each.

Marton (2015) has always been very clear that his focus and interest lies in what is available to be learned. All of the authors of the chapters are clearly concerned in addition with whether what is available is actually accessed, whether opportunities afforded are actually experienced, and whether this experience is sufficiently marked so as to bring about learning of what is intended. To be of practical use, teachers need suitable pedagogical actions for exploiting variation, and some of these are either implied or described in the chapters in this book.

Anne Watson and I (Watson & Mason, 2002, 2005) found it useful to augment the notion of *dimensions of variation* by introducing *dimensions of possible variation*, in order to draw attention to the fact that although the teacher may be aware of aspects or dimensions that can vary, learners may not. The word 'possible' is intended to act as reminder of this. In order to keep in mind the fact that things that can vary may not be able to vary completely independently, that there may be constraints on how things can vary, we also introduced the phrase *range of permissible change*. Thus for example, the coefficients of a quadratic expression with integer coefficients which factors over the integers cannot all vary independently: there are structural relationships which govern their co-variation.

A SIX-FOLD HUMAN PSYCHE

I conjecture that when preparing to teach and when actually interacting with learners it would be extremely helpful to be thinking always in terms of all six aspects of the human psyche: attention, will and witness, as well as enaction, affect and cognition.

Traditionally, Western psychology has conceived of the human psyche as three-fold: *enaction* or *behavior*, usually associated with the body; *affect* or *emotion*, often associated in ancient psychology with the heart; and *cognition* or intellect, usually associated with the head. These appear to have been derived from ancient sources such as the Upanishads, and it is only comparatively recently in the West that attempts have been made to integrate them, despite the fact that our experience is a complex interweaving of these three strands and more. In the Baghavad Gita a similar trio of strands are the *purusha* (Ravindra, 2009) delineated by the *Gunas: rajas* (initiative, action), *tamas* (receptivity) and *sattva* (mediation, independence). The Upanishads (Rhadakrishnan, 1953, p. 623) offer a more complex image of the human psyche as a chariot drawn by horses, which was modernized by Gurdjieff (1950, pp. 1193–1199, see also Mason & Metz, in press). Additional complexity was identified by Ouspensky (1950) who proposed the metaphor of the head, heart and body as three centres, each of which has its own tripartite inner structure, again related to head, heart and body. To connect this with dual systems theory as trumpeted by Kahneman (2012) requires, in addition to *System 1* (reaction) and *System 2* (considered response) a *System 1.5* (emotional disposition which is the source or wellspring of most energy) and a *System 3* which is the source of creative energy, accessed by letting go, by indwelling without distraction, parallel to a meditative or contemplative state, much of which may be subconscious (Hadamard, 1945).

In addition to the standard three components, human will is a critical feature of human psyche. It is *will* that makes teaching an art as much as a science, because learners and teachers are not machines, however much they operate in machine-like modes out of habit (Ouspensky, 1950; Gurdjieff, 1950). People can and do exercise will to resist what is imposed on them, even though on the surface they may appear to be compliant. They can also mean to act in certain ways and yet fail to do so, as reported in Pang, Bao and Ki (Chapter 3 in this book).

And yet, learning can also take place even when people are not aware of it, as when we pick up stock phrases (like 'bottom line') without being consciously aware. This raises issues about the relation between variation and conscious awareness which will be developed in the next section. Several authors in this book have acknowledged the need for initiative to lie with learners some of the time, partly as a general desire, and as a will to learn, but more specifically to be willing to play any of the roles of initiating, responding and mediating (corresponding to the three *gunas*) in the various modes of interaction between teacher, learner and mathematics (Mason, 1979, 2008, see also Mason & Johnston-Wilder, 2004a, 2004b).

The inner *Witness* is generally overlooked but nevertheless a vital aspect of the psyche. It is signaled in the fourth phase of problem solving, *looking back* identified by Pólya (1962), and it is aligned with the second bird in a stanza from the Rg Veda (See Mason, 2002). It is also referred to as the *executive* (Schoenfeld, 1992), the *observer* (Ouspensky, 1950), and the *monitor* (Mason, Burton, & Stacey, 2010). This is the little voice that asks "why are we doing this?" when the going gets tough, or "isn't there a better way?". It observes but does not participate. The witness is one way in which System 2 (cognitively considered response) of Dual Systems theory is brought into play before System 1 (habitual reaction) can automatically initiate an action. Minsky (1975, 1986) uses the notion of *frames* as in 'frames of mind' to describe how actions are enacted as soon as necessary parameters for a frame receive values, often by default rather than through cognitive choice.

Actions in the moment relate centrally to assumptions we make about people and how the behavior they display is enacted. If learners and teachers are seen as acting intentionally through cognitive control and intentional initiative, their behavior may seem at odds with their articulations and their claims; if they are seen as sometimes acting spontaneously out of habit, or driven by certain emotional dispositions, then their behavior may be somewhat more construable. Norretranders (1998) captures this beautifully in his title *The User Illusion* which provides neuro-scientific evidence for what has been known in Eastern psychology for centuries concerning how actions are enacted and where initiative usually lies.

Attention, which William James (1890) considered, but which fell out of favor until relatively recently (see for example Gallagher, 2009), is turning out to be an extremely important strand of the psyche, a vital component of learning, and hence of teaching. In a sense, teaching is about directing learner attention appropriately. Attention has a rich substructure operating at meta, meso and micro levels, as is developed in the next subsection.

Structure or Forms of Attention

Of course we all see through our own lenses, through frameworks of distinctions that we have found fruitful. In my case, while reading and thinking about the chapters in this book I have found myself more and more convinced that one fruitful way of discerning details of pedagogic moves being used in the lessons being reported, and of appreciating what students are making of the lesson, is through a study of attention: what the teacher is attending to, what the teacher is inviting and directing students to attend to, and what the students are actually attending to. Furthermore, it is not simply what people are attending to that matters, the key ideas, but how they are attending to them.

There is a common cliché that "you are where your attention is", because attention is what, or perhaps *how* we have experience of which we are aware. We can only be *present* in what we are attending to, though that attention can be so diffuse that we are not really present to it at all. We dwell in what and how we are attending. We may be present *to* what we are attending to if the witness is awake, but we may be caught up in a flow of attention, the 'stream of consciousness' of James (1890). Notice though that attention can be split between several foci, and that the inner witness is not the same as attention.

At a meta level, attention can be experienced as having a locus (do you feel you are inside or outside of your body; is the seat of your attention dominantly from your head, heart or solar plexus? Is it front, side or back?). Attention can be single or multiple, like one or several searchlights illuminating the sky, so that you can actually attend to several things at once (or perhaps in rapid succession). Attention can also be diffuse, narrowly focused or somewhere in between. These are the locus, focus and scope of attention.

At a meso level, attention can be dominated by one or more concerns. For example, adolescents are commonly concerned about social relationships generally, and sex in particular; young teachers are often dominated by concerns centred around nest-building and starting a family; researchers by career prospects.

My interest in this chapter is particularly with the micro structure (Mason, 1988, 2003), which, although similar to van Hiele levels (van Hiele, 1986; see also van Hiele-Geldof, 1957), and to the SOLO taxonomy (Biggs & Collis, 1982), acknowledges that attention is skitterish. It is more like a humming bird than a staircase of levels: it can hover apparently stationary, and it can very quickly dart to a different place, taking a different form. It seems to me that attention can take various forms including *holding wholes* (gazing, before specific details are discerned, but including gazing at already discerned detail); *discerning details*; *recognizing relationships* in a particular situation; *perceiving properties* as being instantiated in the particular; and *reasoning* on the basis of agreed properties. The idea is that if the teacher and students are not attending to the same 'thing', then communication between them is likely to be ineffective. Even when they are attending to the same aspect or detail, they may be attending differently, and this too will make communication difficult. It behoves a teacher to be sensitive to how learners are attending so as to provide sufficient time for them to make appropriate shifts, and this is, I think, what is going on in the pedagogic moves described in the chapters in this book.

Immediate connections with distinctions made concerning types of variation can be found. For example, the need to separate out different dimensions of (possible)

411

variation corresponds to shifting from gazing, or holding wholes, to discerning details: identifying 'this not that' or 'what it is and what it is not' (Mok: Chapter 10 of this book). Leung (Chapter 5 in this book) calls this the *different and same principle*. Treating discerned details as wholes to be held or gazed at corresponds to Leung's *sieving principle*. Fusion between two or more dimensions of possible variation corresponds to recognizing relationships present in a situation, in the particular. In Leung this is the *co-variation principle* when it is in-the-moment, and the *shifts principle* when it is across time. Generalizing is the shift from recognizing relationships in the particular to perceiving them as instantiations of (general) properties. It comes about by stressing some features and consequently ignoring others (Gattegno, 1970), by 'becoming aware of the general through the particular', and this is what well-structured variation achieves. Perceiving properties as being instantiated, and more generally, as being available to be instantiated is an instance of 'seeing the particular in the general', as instances of a generality (Mason & Pimm, 1984).

Awareness

The term *awareness* is often used to mean *consciousness*, as in "I became aware of a fly buzzing at the window". Marton and Booth (1997) use it this way in their discussion about what can be learned. However I find it more convenient to use it in the sense of Gattegno (1987, see also Young & Messum, 2012) to mean 'that which enables action'. Thus, my awareness of the fly means that some or all of my conscious attention is directed to the fly, and this has brought to the surface various actions I could take, such as opening the window, seeking out something to act as a fly swatter, or simply ignoring it. These actions were always available, in some sense, since they have been internalized, but they become closer to being enacted, or they become available to be enacted through awareness, which may be somewhere on a spectrum from unconscious to conscious. Gattegno noticed that there are many actions that we carry out unconsciously, particularly in the somatic domain. Our bodies change which nostril is doing most of the breathing while the other one rests; they alter our rate of breathing, our heart rate, the openness of pores on the skin, and so on. These are all actions which as neonates we had to educate in ourselves (Gattegno, 1973, 1988).

One consequence of Gattegno's sense of awareness is contained in the memorable adage that he coined: "Only awareness is educable" (Gattegno, 1970). This implies that 'learning' is about gaining facility with, integrating and internalizing actions which have triggers in affect and resonances in cognition. Something in a situation then triggers or resonates (or both) those actions to make them available in the moment. Our cognition refers to this as 'our awareness'. Inspired by the image of the human being as a chariot drawn by horses as found in the Upanishads, I augmented Gattegno's assertion with 'only behavior is trainable' and 'only emotion is harnessable'. The extended view of the psyche might lead to proposals that 'only attention is directable', 'only will can initiate', and 'only witness can observe impartially'. As Maturana (1988) put it, "everything said is said by an observer". The cogency and impartiality of this observing is important so as not to be caught up in a stream of automaticity and habit.

Variation theory can be seen as awakening teacher awareness (in the common sense of consciousness) of the sorts of experiences that will make possibilities for learning most efficient, and awakening teacher awareness (in the sense of Gattegno) through making relevant pedagogical actions available to be enacted. Put another way, variation theory awakens practitioners and researchers to the need to discern (whether explicitly or implicitly) actions and their effects: this is the *action-effect* relation of Simon and Tzur (2004). A really important contribution of the chapters in this book is to begin to probe beneath the surface of lesson descriptions so as to enable teachers to 'educate their awareness' regarding variation-pedagogy choices.

ISSUES ABOUT VARIATION

There are a number of issues that arise in connection with what is to be varied, how, when and by whom, whether systematically or unsystematically, whether implicitly or explicitly, and the role of non-examples, so as to make the critical aspects of a concept or procedure as sharply discernible as possible. These overlap with pedagogical concerns about how to maximize the opportunity for learners to encounter, appreciate and comprehend concepts, procedures and techniques. Teachers and learners are both centrally concerned with what it is possible to vary (without changing the concept, or the procedure), and over what range or subject to what constraints that change is permitted to take place.

Since the issues and ways that people deal with them overlap and intertwine, I begin with an example concerning the notion of angle (in two dimensions) and how it is measured, since this traverses both primary and secondary school. I then use this example to raise and comment on various issues, calling upon a few extra examples along the way.

Angles and Their Measures

Take for example the notion of angle (in two dimensions). In Figure 1 the first angle diagram displays some variation of some irrelevant features, while the second displays variation of some relevant features.

Experience with both diagrams appears to be necessary in order to appreciate and comprehend the notion of angle. But what exactly is invariant amongst these figures? Irrelevant features include the orientation and lengths of the arms, and the position of the arrow; critical features include an indication of direction and an amount of turn. Once the notion of angle and how angles are presented has been firmly established, it might be desirable to move on to a procedural aspect of angle, namely measurement. However measurement of angles depends on another

413

Figure 1. Two examples of variation

construct, which is that ratios of lengths are invariant under scaling. Thus to make sense of measure using a protractor requires awareness that a 'larger protractor' will give the same measurement. When this is firmly established, Thales theorem about ratios of lengths in triangles being invariant under scaling is a special case, which then gives access to using ratios of sides of triangles to measure angles, known as trigonometry. Another aspect of angle, not treated here, is identification of angles which must be equal, and consequences of this.

Issues arising. Various issues arise not only from this one example but from many of the chapters in this book:

- When does something need to be varied?

  When the term *angle* is going to be formalized, variation has a major role to play. The diagrams are part of the iconic presentation of angle and its formalization, and would necessarily have followed physical experience of turning, and discerning the difference between 'pointy' or 'sharp' and 'blunt' parts of objects. Rotations through $0°$, $±90°$, $±180°$ etc. will have already been experienced and named.

- What needs to be varied: is attention to be on what is varied or what is invariant?

  Features of angles such as length of arms, orientation, direction of implied rotation need to be varied so that attention can be directed to what is invariant or common to all examples. Varying the 'size' of the angle is necessary so that attention can be directed to the range of permissible change (see also When). The two diagrams are in contrast, with the first varying the features that are irrelevant to what invariant that is common, and the second, mostly, varying what matters so as be aware of the range of permissible change of phenomena to which the concept *angle* applies. The aim is to identify angles in complex situations.

- How extensively to vary?

  Following the lead of the teacher whose lesson is described in Huang and Leung (Chapter 8 in this book), a teacher might choose to begin with two and then three line segments and get learners to investigate all the ways the

414

segments can interact. Situations which form one or more angles could then be identified. Subsequently, learners can be invited to locate angles in more complex diagrams. This variation places the concept in a more general context.

The first diagram has no angles opening downwards. The second diagram has no examples of obtuse angles, nor of any angles whose measure is greater than 360°. The relative sizes of the angles is not uniformly distributed, and the diagram avoids the issue of every angle being accompanied by its 360° complement by rotating the second arm to the first so as to make up a full rotation.

• What are the roles of both systematic and unsystematic variation?

Using dynamic geometry, or two sticks, perhaps hinged at their ends or elsewhere, the notion of an angle could be presented and encountered systematically as starting from 0° and varying until it makes a full revolution (or indeed more). The two diagrams are in some sense unsystematic in their choice of angle, arm length, orientation and so on, yet they are systematic in that each of the intended features has been varied.

The second diagram could keep the angle arms constant in length, but this might undermine experience and assumptions from the first diagram concerning the irrelevance of the length of the arms. Is it sensible to assume that a previously varied feature will be kept in mind as possibly variable?

• Who does the varying?

Here the author has done the varying, but pedagogically it is desirable if learners then try to find other instances and non-instances for themselves, so that they have direct experience of the variation and of the invariance. Asking learners to consider all ways that two or three segments could interact would leave much of the initiative to learners.

• What role is played by non-examples?

As mentioned above, non-examples, perhaps involving non-intersecting segments could help place the concept in a more general context rather than suddenly being imposed. Learner experience of 'angles', which is prior variation although not localized in time and space, could also be drawn upon. Note the common use of "at an angle" to refer to two possibly non-intersecting segments extended so as to intersect. There is also an issue concerning the angle between parallel lines, and other instances of an angle of 0°.

• How is variation experienced when the invariance is not directly experienced?

You cannot actually point to angle itself, only to aspects which demarcate or signify angle. So what are learners actually experiencing? Other examples will be given in the elaboration to follow.

415

- When is it sufficient to leave variation as implicit, and when is it necessary to be explicit?

  If learners are already familiar with what to do when encountering variation in diagrams, then they may not need to have their attention directed to what is varying and what is (relatively) invariant. However other learners, and perhaps in some circumstances, all learners, may need to have their attention directed explicitly.

  It is unlikely that either diagram alone, or even both together would be sufficient for all learners to absorb all of the features which are permitted to change, and to appreciate and comprehend what is invariant, without explicit attention being drawn to them. The diagrams themselves are, after all, only ink on paper. They do not 'contain' mathematical ideas or awarenesses.

As many of the chapters in this book indicate, when reporting actual lessons the pedagogic choices made by the teacher concerning length of time to dwell on varied and invariant aspects is what is really critical: the length of time taken to gaze at the whole; to discern details; to gaze at discerned parts; to recognize relationships that are invariant against the variation indicated in a diagram or manifested in an animation; to perceive more general properties as being instantiated; and to appreciate the scope and range of the suggested variation that constitutes those properties. Only then does it make sense to reason about and with those properties, for example to consider how an angle might be measured and how their measures might be compared, because this depends on a confident sense of 'what is and what is not' (Mok, Chapter 10 in this book) to be measured.

ISSUES CONCERNING VARIATION AND VARIATION-PEDAGOGY

One of the things that emerges for me from the chapters in this book is the critical role of pedagogical choices made by teachers when informed by the principle of variation. I find the notion of *variation-pedagogy* helpful, not because the use of variation requires special pedagogy, but because of the way that the principle of variation can lead to pedagogical thinking. Some of the chapters in this book provide glimpses of such pedagogical thinking, or pedagogical awareness, while others skim over the surface. I am convinced that further progress is required in delineating the ways in which variation can inform pedagogical choices, and that one way to do this will be by being awake and alert to teacher and learner attention, as described earlier. Many of the issues developed in this section arise not because of variation alone, but because of what they are supposed to achieve pedagogically.

What to Vary?

Is it the aspects that are varied that are important, or the aspects that remain invariant? On first encountering variation theory it is tempting think that it is obvious what to vary, and how, but for me it is not at all obvious. The two angle diagrams in Figure 1 highlight this contrast, and a sensible conclusion is that both are necessary, perhaps at different times, because both contribute to appreciation and comprehension of a concept, indeed of a procedure as well. What will matter most will be the pedagogical choices so that attention is directed appropriately.

The use of the adjective 'possible', as in *dimensions of possible variation* can be useful as a reminder that there are choices to be made, but it is important to probe deeply into the origins in experience of the distinctions to be made in the use of a concept, or in the aims and methods of a procedure. An *a priori* epistemological analysis, drawing on research as well as experience, serves to identify some potentially critical aspects. These will depend on known epistemological obstacles (Bachelard, 1938/1980) derived from structural underpinnings of the topic itself and found in the research literature, and the known pedagogically induced obstacles that students are seduced into encountering because of their previous experience, again often indicated in the research literature but more contextually dependent. Other critical aspects are based in the particular learners, their past and recent experience, their current dispositions and their willingness to take initiative, to 'assert' (make and test conjectures) rather than simply 'assent' to what the teacher says and does (Mason, 2009). The 'onlys' mentioned earlier provide one framework for taking all aspects of the human psyche into account in considering the essence of a topic (Mason & Johnston-Wilder, 2004a, 2004b).

Even focusing on critical aspects as those to be varied is not sufficiently definitive: different people recognize different aspects as critical, and this may be as much a reflection of their mathematical or pedagogical awareness as it is of their sensitivity to their particular learners. For example, Huang, Barlow and Prince (2016) report a difference between dimensions of (possible) variation activated in a Chinese lesson as compared to an apparently similar lesson in the USA.

My experience of mathematics has led me to a more balanced position on the roles of variation and invariance than is implied in the original formulation by Marton (see Marton & Booth, 1997; Marton, 2015). In Watson and Mason (2005) we showed some situations in which what strikes the viewer is the invariance, and other situations in which what strikes the viewer is the variation. For example, when shown a family of straight lines through the origin in quick succession, attention may be attracted to what is changing (the lines) rather than to what is invariant (the common point), whereas in the static picture (see first diagram in Figure 2) attention is drawn to the invariant point, for Gestalt-based reasons. The second diagram indicates a single frame of a dynamic version of the first diagram, and how as a static image there can be an ambiguity between whether attention is drawn to what is varying or to what is invariant. When shown a family of straight lines enveloping a curve as in the third diagram in Figure 2, attention is naturally drawn to the virtual curve which is invariant. Attention may be drawn to what is changing against a relatively invariant backdrop, or attention may be drawn to what is invariant in the midst of great changes.

417

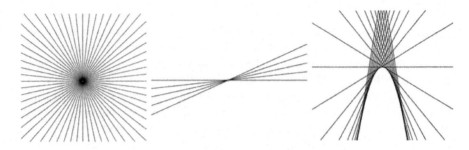

Figure 2. Three families: all at once; a few in sequence; all at once
What strikes you: variation or invariance?

Leung (Chapter 5 in this book) considers five principles for realizing (in its fullest sense) invariance in the midst of change and the range of permissible change of those dimensions. They are related to shifts of attention, as described earlier, concerning recognizing relationships and perceiving properties as being instantiated. But what happens when the mathematical ideas leave the world of the tangible? If the relationships really have become properties which are familiar and confidence inspiring, then they may become 'as-if' tangible, but it may require the learner to do the varying in order to get a sense of a further new invariance.

Although Lakoff and Nunez (2000) claim that mathematical ideas are developments from physical sensory experience, most mathematical concepts beyond the primary school involve relationships between ideas which are not easily presentable as perceptual 'things' and so cannot so easily be pointed to or embodied in physical action with material objects. In the case of 'angle', it's subtly intangible nature is masked by the various signs and signifiers used to denote and to indicate the presence of an angle. As another example, Thompson (2002) has studied co-variation extensively, and highlighted many of the difficulties students have in appreciating co-variation, largely because it is hard to 'see' named-ratios such as speed and density.

As yet another example, consider the first diagram in Figure 3 below. Dragging points A, B or C around makes no change in the ratios; moving points D, E or F on their respective lines changes individual ratios but leaves the overall equality relationship invariant.

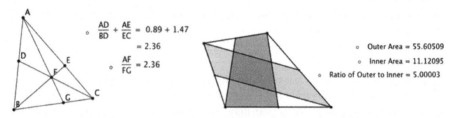

Figure 3. A hidden invariant relationship and a mistaken invariant relationship

I cannot see how to detect or present the equality relationship visually, nor arrange for it to be sensed physically, even when a dynamic version is experienced. Only with the inclusion of measurements can an invariance be observed, but by proxy, and although that may be convincing cognitively, it is less than convincing enactively. Consequently it has a reduced affective impact. It is not at all clear to me how greater enactive, and hence affective impact could be managed. However, after a period of immersion in and use of the invariance, the diagram itself can come to embody the relationship (sum of ratios) and so can be used as a signal to locate the algebraic statement whenever the diagram appears in a more complex configuration, and vice versa. To appreciate and comprehend mathematics requires mathematical thinking, in which what was previously abstract becomes sufficiently familiar and confidence inspiring to be experienced 'as-if' it were concrete (Mason 1980; Mason & Johnston-Wilder 2004a) drawing on the notion of 'acting as if' of William James (1890).

A further difficulty with virtual enaction is presented in the second diagram, where the divisions on the quadrilateral edges are midpoints. To two decimal places it appears that the ratio of the area of the whole to the area of the inner overlap quadrilateral is 5:1, but in fact it is a minimum of exactly 5 when the inner quadrilateral is a trapezium. If measurements are only taken to a few decimal places, something that is not invariant may appear to be.

Sometimes what is invariant and what is permitted to change can be obscure when even two aspects are varying at the same time, while at other times it is perfectly possible and even desirable to deal with more. Indeed, a task in which there are several different dimensions that could be varied opens up the possibility for learners to experience the need and effectiveness of choosing to fix some aspects while varying others in order to locate structural relationships for themselves, mindful of the potential dangers of reductionism. This is an action they might come to internalise (an educated awareness) so as to be able to initiate it for themselves in the future. For example, imagine an animation of two points each traversing their own circle, and a point P on the line segment joining them with its path being traced, with variations in the radii of the circles, the distance between their centres, the directions and speeds of travel around their circles, and the position of P on the line segment.

Figure 4. Two-circles configuration

These several dimensions open up many possibilities which can for most students only be dealt with by selecting some aspects to vary while fixing the others, then changing what is fixed and what is varied so as to uncover underlying structural relationships involving all or many of the dimensions of possible variation.

What reading this book has reinforced for me is that thinking in terms of what students are likely to attend to, informed by both what the teacher is aware of as needing attention and what the teacher is aware of in terms of the form of that attention, is one way of addressing the issue of what to vary. To become aware of the process of discerning details (separating), and recognising relationships in the particular situation, so as to come to (some authors say 'discover') properties which are being instantiated (fusing) is itself a process, akin to what Gattegno called educating 'awareness of awareness' (see Mason, 1998).

The Tetrad of Activity

Several authors in the preceding chapters have made use of the notion of a distance between what learners already know, what Gu, Huang and Gu (Chapter 2 in this book) refer to as the *anchoring point*, and the intended object of learning, and how important it is that both the tasks and the resources called upon from the learners themselves and from images and material embodiments, are appropriate for bridging that gap. Bennett (1993) incorporated this notion in his Systematics schema for activity, which unlike the Vygotskian triad, is based on a tetrad. It is formed from two axes, one concerning motivation or intention and the other concerning means (Figure 5).

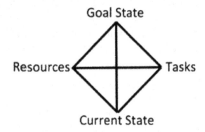

Figure 5. The tetrad of activity

The activity is maximally effective when each of the four triads comprising the tetrad in any particular instance are appropriately balanced. The motivational axis corresponds to the distance between *anchoring point* and *new knowledge* used by Gu et al. (Chapter 2 in this book) to gauge the appropriateness of the challenge being offered to learners. Ding (Chapter 4 in this book) makes reference to *Pudian* as the distance between previous knowledge and intended goals, which is the vertical axis of the tetrad of activity. Other authors use *Pudian* to refer to presaging something implicitly before addressing it explicitly, and relate this to a shift from *scaffolding* to *fading* (Seeley Brown, Collins, & Duguid, 1989) or from *directed* through *prompted* to *spontaneous* use by learners themselves (Love & Mason, 1992).

Pang, Bao and Ki (Chapter 4 in this book) draw a distinction between *Pudian* from one task to another or one situation to another, and *Pudian* related to differences within a task or situation. They see these as 'orthogonal' forms of variation. The first is to make the proximal distance or learner 'gap' manageable by learners, and the second is to make dimensions of possible variation discernible be learners through choice of tasks and resources called upon.

Sometimes authors recommend varying the essential features so that learners become aware of them as worthy of attention, which is the essence of Marton's claim that what is available to be learned is what is varied. Sometimes authors recommend varying the inessential features so that learners recognise that what is invariant is what is important (see for example, Gu et al., Chapter 2 in this book). Sometimes learners need to discern, that is separate out, what can be changed while still something else remains invariant and at other times they need to be not only aware of but actually disposed to ignore features irrelevant to a concept or procedure (Watson chapter 4 this book; see also Koichu, Zaslavsk, & Dolev, 2013), because as Gattegno (1970, 1987) points out, stressing with consequent ignoring is the basis of generalization, of shifting from recognizing specific relationships in a situation to perceiving these as instantiations of more general properties.

When to Vary?

When introducing a concept or the ideas behind a technique, structured variation has a clear, perhaps even essential role to play, especially if the teaching and learning are to be as efficient and effective as possible, as is illustrated throughout this book. Similarly, intentional variation is useful when exploring, when posing and resolving novel problems, whether set by someone else or by yourself, because this is the process of specializing and generalizing promoted by Pólya (1962) among many others. It is vital that learners internalize the use of systematic variation for themselves.

It is perhaps not so clear whether structured and systematic variation is helpful when students are reviewing a topic. A teacher might employ variation if, during revision, learners appear not to be attending in expected ways. Intentional variation can be used to bring concepts and procedures back to mind, but is not in itself likely to promote integration or internalization of actions by learners. The *one problem many contexts, one problem many solutions,* and *many problems one method of solution* forms of variation all need to be experienced. If learners are trying to gain facility, then random problems are probably a good idea, as found in many English and American mathematics texts in the 18th and 19th centuries, with sections headed *promiscuous problems,* where the challenge is to have an appropriate action become available as the problems contexts and types change. This too can be seen as a form of variation, mostly unsystematic, of all the dimensions associated with a particular course of study.

Revision itself can take the form of learners constructing examples which display possible dimensions of variation, and which therefore indicate the scope and richness of their appreciation and comprehension of a concept or a procedure

(Watson & Mason, 2005). Exploration and investigation, during which learners may extend the richness of what they notice, discern and relate, will often depend on learners having learned to make use of systematic variation for themselves. Wallis (1682) called this "my method of investigation" and although castigated by Fermat among others (Stedall, 2002, p. 169), it often proves very effective. Pólya (1962) called it specialising and the purpose was to detect underlying relationships which might turn out to be instantiated properties (Mason et al., 2010).

The whole point of experiencing variation is to enrich your sense of a concept or procedure through enriching the space of examples and example-construction techniques that you can access. It is unlikely that any single pedagogic recipe will be useful, because effective teaching depends very much on the students and the situation, and on their past and recent experience and expectations as to what might be appropriate.

The distinction between conceptual and procedural variation pointed to by Gu, Huang and Marton (2004) is to my mind simply pointing to differences in when to use variation. To get learners to attend to something not previously noticed or discerned, variation, in some form or other is absolutely essential. When some ideas or actions are going to be extended or developed, it is vital to bring previous experiences to the fore, such as previously discerned details, recognizable relationships and perceivable properties, before extending or developing these in some way. This is the *anchor points* notion of Gu et al. (Chapter 2 in this book) and so part of the tetrad of activity. It is notable in many of the chapters how reports of lessons include teachers spending time doing exactly this, rather than rushing straight into the new extensions and developments. To move to extensions and developments assumes that learners will have distinctions, relationships and properties immediately to hand. This seems to me to be the basis for the Western interpretations of Shanghai 'mastery-teaching', in which all learners make progress and actually learn something.

How Extensively to Vary?

Deciding how much variation, over what range, and how systematic to make the variation is part of the art of teaching, for it depends entirely on how quickly and effectively students show that they are attending to what is intended, and in the intended manner. Once learners have had multiple experiences of the act of generalization, which involves seeing one or more aspects as being variable, one 'good' example can often suffice to provide insight into what happens in general. A typical Chinese take on this is that "good learners can grasp the whole category from typical examples; [teachers] don't need to teach them all in detail" (Song, 2006). There is a remarkable resonance with Colburn (1829) in the USA who initiated the 'inductive method' of teaching in his textbooks. His version was

As the purpose is to give the learner a knowledge of the principles, it is necessary to have the variety of examples under each principle as great as possible. ... when the principles are well understood, very few subjects will require a particular rule, and if the pupil is properly introduced to them [s]he will understand them better without a rule than with one.

One general maxim to be observed with pupils of every age, is never to tell them directly how to perform any example. If a pupil is unable to perform an example, it is generally because [s]he does not fully comprehend the object of it. [Colburn 1829 preface]

His sets of exercises use unsystematic variation of numbers in a variety of contexts, but all involving the same operation.

Having been exposed to the notion of variation, in the form of the role of parameters which are temporarily constant but can be varied, it is often the case for me that a single object triggers generalization: a consideration of aspects that could be allowed to vary opening up the possibility of investigating the range of permissible change, the structural constraints governing that change, and what remains invariant. It is an opportunity for creativity in mathematics. For example, consider an elementary task such as

If Anne gives John 3 marbles, they will then have the same number of marbles.

How many more marbles does Anne have than John?

For me this is one instance in a whole space of 'marble tasks', through spontaneously wanting to vary the number of marbles given away; the effect of giving away marbles (eg. ending up with 3 times as many, 4 fewer, or 5 more than John, etc.); the number of people involved and who gives what to whom with what effect; the details of what to give or exchange (eg. Anne giving two of her red marbles for each 3 of John's blue ones). And of course the marbles themselves are of no concern: they might as well be counters or teddy bears, movements on a number line or people queuing at a bus stop.

Learners would benefit if they became encultured into seeing dimensions of possible variation for themselves, because this is what is required to do well on an examination: to recognize the 'type' of each task and to have an appropriate action become ready to enact. So studying for an examination involves recognizing dimensions of possible variation and rehearsing the action which is common to all, which is invariant, and which solves them all. Constructing your own particular cases so as to get a sense of the general, is well worth acquiring as a personal propensity. As Gu (1999, p. 186, quoted in Gu et al., in Chapter 2 in this book) points out, in China examinations have often been based on prototypical problems already familiar to students, which induces teachers to focus on prototypes in training their students. It makes sense in these circumstances to use variation to build up from the simple to the complex, and to vary the context so that students learn to recognize underlying structural relationships (*many problems one solution* and *one problem many contexts*). But as mentioned earlier, if students only ever encounter 'typical' problems, they are unlikely to learn what to do when they meet something fresh and novel. By sometimes posing complex unfamiliar challenging problems, and then collectively simplifying and specializing until something tractable is reached, then building back up to the complex through generalizing and varying for themselves, learners may begin to internalize not simply the procedures, but how to think mathematically (Pólya, 1962; Mason et al., 2010, among many others).

Locally and Globally Systematic Variation

The angles example already points the way to roles for both systematic variation, and for unsystematic variation, or more accurately, for globally systematic but locally unsystematic variation. Chinese lesson study involves recognizing opportunities to use systematic variation within variation (Huang et al., 2016, p. 10). To explore the possibilities of varying two dimensions of possible variation in concert or separately, I developed a collection of *structured variation grids* (Mason website). But it is not only a matter of what aspects to vary, but also in what order to vary them. There may not be a universal answer to this as it is likely to depend on the teacher's awareness, and on the learners' disposition, initiative and preparation.

An important example arises in early algebra. For years I was content to construct tasks in which learners were given the first few terms of a sequence. The objects might have been pictures or numbers. Mindful that mathematically there has to be some underlying rule or structural relationship which determines the sequence, I would first ask people to decide how they would extend the sequence and to articulate a rule for continuing the sequence indefinitely. Then, and only then was it appropriate to ask for a generalization, a formula, to count the number of components in the nth object, usually a picture (Mason, Johnston-Wilder, & Graham, 2005). However, I became aware that my invariant task structure of providing the first few terms in sequence was generating learner dependency and also inducing them to focus on term-by-term extension rather than looking for a general formula. Since the intended object of learning was experience in expressing generality, my systematicity was actually getting in the way, and so I moved to being much less systematic when presenting sequences for generalization.

The three forms of variation identified by Sun (2011), *One Problem Multiple Solutions*; *Multiple Problems One Solution*; and *One Problem Multiple Changes* are, like the angles example, amenable to locally unsystematic variation of the parameters but globally systematic variation of what needs to be varied, that is, of the *dimensions of possible variation*. Again I conjecture that there is no rule, no 'best practice', but rather, that variation can remind teachers to be sensitive to these various issues and so inform their pedagogical choices.

How many different dimensions can be varied at the same time is uncertain, but pedagogically significant. Too many things varying at once might put learners off, but too few might be considered condescending and rule-bound, as if learners are being 'led by the nose'. It is certainly tempting, once latching onto variation as a principle, to use it mechanically and strictly, rather than creatively when appropriate.

Furthermore, what it means to say 'varied at the same time' is unclear, since student attention is more likely to be consecutive rather than simultaneous. For example, Lo and Marton (2012) argue "when learners need to discern more than two … critical features, the most powerful strategy is to let the learners discern them one at a time, before they encounter simultaneous variation of the features" (p. 11). Pang and Ki (2016) and other authors use the term *separation* when one critical aspect varies while the other aspects are kept invariant, because what is varied is separated out. When two or more dimensions are varied simultaneously, usually subsequently, the term *fusion* is used.

But the situation is not so clear to me. In the following task, more than one thing is varying at once, but it is the joint co-variation between the numbers that are varying that is of interest. It provides an opportunity for learners to do some separating for themselves, detecting a single feature and trying examples of that for themselves.

Observe that:

$$45 \times 37 - 47 \times 35 = 20 = (4 - 3) \times (7 - 5) \times 10 \qquad 46 \times 38 - 48 \times 36 = 20 = (4 - 3) \times (8 - 6) \times 10$$
$$55 \times 47 - 57 \times 45 = 20 = (5 - 4) \times (7 - 5) \times 10 \qquad 56 \times 48 - 58 \times 46 = 20 = (5 - 4) \times (8 - 6) \times 10$$
$$45 \times 26 - 46 \times 25 = 20 = (4 - 2) \times (6 - 5) \times 10 \qquad 93 \times 74 - 94 \times 73 = 20 = (9 - 7) \times (4 - 3) \times 10$$

Figure 6. Some arithmetic facts

Looking across rows might reveal one relationship; looking down columns might reveal another. What is available is fusion of both and to this end it may help to read each statement out loud, placing emphasis on a particular digit (Brown & Walter, 1983). If done several times, varying the chosen digit, relationships may be recognized and articulated as properties being instantiated.

Here there is systematic variation but it has to be detected by directing attention to relationships between digits in the two digit numbers. The implicit invitation is to express a generality as a conjecture and then to check its validity. The concept involved is that the difference in the products when the units digits are switched must be divisible by 10 and can be calculated from the differences in the digits of the original numbers. This then could be seen as a procedure for multiplying two-digit numbers so as to simplify calculation. An underlying principle is that the product of two numbers is increased by making the two numbers closer to their mean. It can also be seen as a step towards generalizing to three digit numbers.

Two more examples are shown in Figure 7. On the left is Sundaram's Grid (Honsberger, 1970; Ramaswami Aiyar, 1934; see also Mason website). The relationship being instantiated is bilinear, so two dimensions changing together are essential, although the layout means that attention can at times be directed to a single dimension by focusing on a single row or column. Ultimately the claim requires an integration of both dimensions of possible variation simultaneously, whether encountered simultaneously from the start, or independently for some time with along the way. The same applies to the arithmetic equalities in Figure 6: whether a single dimension is separated out is a pedagogic choice with no definitive 'best approach', as it is likely to depend on the learners and their recent experience.

Claim: A number appears in this grid if and only if one more than double it is a composite number.

Remove the parentheses, and combine

...	...	...	...	...	...	...	
25	42	59	76	93	110	127	...
22	37	52	67	82	97	112	...
19	32	45	58	71	84	97	...
16	27	38	49	60	71	82	...
13	22	31	40	49	58	67	...
10	17	24	31	38	45	52	...
7	12	17	22	27	32	37	...
4	7	10	13	16	19	22	...

1. $9 + (3 + 2)$.
2. $9 + (3 - 2)$.
3. $7 + (5 + 1)$.
4. $7 + (5 - 1)$.
5. $6 + (4 + 3)$.
6. $6 + (4 - 3)$.
7. $3 + (8 - 2)$.

8. $9 - (8 - 6)$.
9. $10 - (9 - 5)$.
10. $9 - (6 - 1)$.
11. $8 - (3 + 2)$.
12. $7 - (3 - 2)$.
13. $9 - (4 + 3)$.
14. $9 - (4 - 3)$.

15. $7 - (5 - 2)$.
16. $7 - (7 - 3)$.
17. $(8 - 6) - 1$.
18. $(3 - 2) - (1 - 1)$.
19. $(7 - 3) - (3 - 2)$.
20. $(8 - 2) - (5 - 3)$.
21. $15 - (10 - 3 - 2)$.

Figure 7. Two examples of near-simultaneous variation

The set of exercises on the right in Figure 7 are the first actual tasks in *First Steps in Algebra* (Wentworth, 1894, p. 10) following a verbal introduction to indices and parentheses and many other technical terms. Notice the local variations suggesting dimensions of possible variation and hence indicating generality. Ex 13 and 14 offer a matched pair similar to Ex 1 & 2, but would students notice? Even if they did, would they be inclined to pause and construct a story about what was happening? The last exercise offers a single new variation which could be extended by the learner to a new dimension of possible variation, but which might also be ignored. Note that negative numbers are not introduced until a later chapter, which explains some dimensions not varied here. The numbers used are small enough to make it easy to check the result by evaluating the parentheses mentally, but the negative side of this is that students might be tempted simply to write down the answer.

Although not invoking 'variation' explicitly as a pedagogic strategy, quite complex variation is present. Because all of Wentworth's papers disappeared in a fire we know little of his pedagogic principles apart from analyzing his textbooks, but his many books sold millions of copies and were used over many years in the United States, so they must have been considered to be successful.

In all of these situations (and in the angle diagrams earlier), the variation could be said to be simultaneous since several or all of the examples are displayed at once. But human attention tends to work sequentially. After gazing for a while at the whole, details are discerned and relationships recognized within and between these details, which themselves may be gazed at as wholes for a time. Experience with invoking learners' powers to detect patterns suggests that presenting instances sequentially, pausing to allow processing time can be much more effective than simply moving on quickly, and this accords with the lesson descriptions in various chapters in this book.

Who Does the Varying?

People calling upon variation theory often assume that it is the teacher or author who provides the variation, yet it is clear that when someone varies different aspects for themselves, and experiences these as dimensions of either possible or inappropriate dimensions of variation, even more robust learning is likely. For example, young children learning to crawl, walk, run and speak introduce their own variations. Mathematical exploration and meaning-making almost require learners to take the initiative to vary just enough for them to appreciate both the dimensions of possible variation available and the ranges of permissible change within those. Extreme positions (always the teacher or always the learner) are unlikely to be helpful. Sometimes it is the teacher's awareness of dimensions of possible variation that the learner might not think of varying that is crucial, for that is at the heart of the role of the teacher: the teacher can do for the learners what the learners cannot yet do for themselves. This is the essence of the notion of *zone of proximal development* (Vygotsky, 1978; see also van der Veer & Valsiner, 1991). At other times teacher initiated variation may lead to learners depending on the teacher (or textbook) to do the varying for them.

When two or more dimensions are crucial to recognizing and underlying structural relationship, there is a pedagogical choice to be made as to whether to plan a careful staircase of development, so that the learners perhaps encounter increasing complexity with the gap between anchor point and intended learning carefully managed, or whether to expose learners to at least some complexity, and to engage them in choosing what to simplify so as to gain familiarity. It is very easy for a teacher to be tempted to simplify for learners rather than developing their confidence to simplify for themselves when necessary. (Stein, Grover, & Henningsen, 1996). Such a choice minimizes local disturbance, but ultimately disempowers learners.

Mathematics Education is plagued by an absence of theorems guaranteeing effects of actions. Yet this is precisely because education is about human beings who are capable of exercising will, of taking initiative. Exercising their will may include blocking what is being offered, shutting down in the face of challenge, or directing attention to other matters which may at the time seem much more important. Trying to control learner attention may result in training behavior, and may negatively influence any disposition to think mathematically. On the other hand, carefully constructed tasks in which attention is subtly and deliberately directed can be maximally efficient in bringing learners into contact with important awarenesses, what Gattegno (1987, 1988) called, controversially, "forcing awareness", leading to their experiencing effective actions that may then be internalised through further work. Furthermore, in order to respond creatively to unfamiliar challenges it is vital to develop a range of actions that the learner can initiate for themselves: actions such as specializing and generalizing, imagining and expressing, conjecturing and convincing (Pólya, 1962), Mason et al., 2010; Mason, 2008a).

Several chapters in this book make use of a pedagogic sequence of movement from 'concrete, through invariant methods, to applications' which sets a specific order for what to vary and when. Where learner behavior becomes dependent and reliant on previously trained behavior rather than calling upon or invoking internalized actions, creativity is likely to be restricted. I would counsel against rigidity since it fails to give learners experience of tackling the unfamiliar, making it familiar in order to make progress through learner use of their natural powers. Pedagogic rigidity is likely to lead to learners becoming dependent on the teacher-text rather than educating their awareness so as to be able to initiate use of these forms of variation for themselves. I conjecture that a truly effective Hypothetical Learning Trajectory (Simon & Tzur, 2004) affords opportunity for learners to use their own developing powers, not simply tread a staircase from simple to complex, from concrete to abstract, from particular to general. A range of pedagogical frameworks have been proposed to assist teachers in providing learners with such experience based on ideas of Bruner (1966): see for example Mok (Chapter 10 in this book); Mason and Johnston-Wilder (2004a, 2004b).

Variation can be thought of as a device for scaffolding (Huang et al., 2015, p. 11; Mok, Chapter 10 in this book) so that more variation ('simultaneous') can be introduced in line with growing confidence and facility. This is a form of 'fading' after initial scaffolding (Brown et al., 1989) or of making prompts less and less direct until learners can act spontaneously (Love & Mason, 1992). Judging when learners have recognized dimensions of possible variation, when they have internalized appropriate actions, and when they have access to triggers to initiate those actions, or put another way, have educated their awareness so as to enable actions (Gattegno, 1970) requires sensitivity and observation.

What Role Is Played by Non-Examples?

In order to discern what is important, it seems pedagogically desirable if not essential that learners experience for themselves non-examples so that they test the limits of the range of permissible change in addition to exploring the dimensions of possible variation. Furthermore, non-examples can provide a broader context in which a particular constraint can be imposed, as long as learners appreciate this is what they are experiencing. This aligns with the holist's desire to have an overview, a chance to *hold a whole*, before being immersed in detail.

Do non-examples always help? Bruner, Goodnow and Austin (1956) reported instances in which non-examples did not appear to assist learners in discerning the intended concept, whereas Gu et al. (Chapter 2 in this book), in line with Gagné (1977) and several others (see for example Cohen and Carpenter 1983) suggest that non-examples ought to, and even do in some circumstances, contribute to appreciation of the scope of instances of a concept. For example, Huang and Leung (Chapter 8 in this book) report how the teacher began with two intersecting lines, drawing attention to what was already familiar in terms of related angles, then introduced a third line intersecting one of the original lines, thus setting a context of intersecting lines, and worked on pairs of related angles for some time before moving to parallelism and equality of angles. Similarly, Gu, Huang and Gu (Chapter 2 in this book) report on a teacher inviting learners to consider all possible ways in which two circles of different sizes might interact, described in terms of the distance between the centers in relation to the radii, before moving to the same problem but with line segments on the same line.

It is most likely that it is not the presence or absence of non-examples alone that contributes to appreciation and comprehension of a concept, but the teacher's awareness, learner disposition and initiative, the pedagogic milieu, and the ways in which attention is directed, which can make the presence of non-examples effective or ineffective. Another factor could be the structure and systematicity of the implicit variation.

Implicit and Explicit Variation

When is it sufficient to leave variation as implicit, and when is it necessary to be explicit? Pedagogical reliance on implicit variation assumes that the presentation of variation is sufficient in order for learners to learn what is intended, whereas explicit variation (through using pedagogical actions such as Say What You See, Same and Different, What It Is and What It Isn't, etc.) incorporates some degree of explicitness, of explicitly directed attention, in the interaction between teacher and student. While systematic variation may make something available to be learned, it by no means ensures that it will be learned. Consequently, attempts to validate variation theory must take into account the scope of the teacher's awareness of the concept or procedure together with the variations that comprise it and the range of pedagogic strategies available to be enacted, as well as the pedagogical ethos or milieu of the situation, and the disposition, initiative and preparation of learners.

In terms of teaching, variation is always implicit until a teacher draws attention to it (Mok, Chapter 10 in this book). However a learner may or may not become aware (consciously) of variation or its implications, even when the teacher tries to draw attention to it. Note that as mentioned earlier, awareness of variation enables students to enact actions associated with variation, such as turning their attention to other dimensions of possible variation as well as to ranges of permissible variation, and this in turn is likely to shift attention to recognizing underlying structural relationships and to perceiving properties as being instantiated.

Fischbein (1987, 1993) pointed to the way in which learners make assumptions about what is important in a figure, often implicitly and because it is invariant in the examples they encounter, without realizing that they are doing it. He called these *figural concepts*. One classic example is of triangles always being presented with a 'base' parallel to the bottom of the page, with the implication that an altitude is always perpendicular to the base. Another classic example is the way that cubes

429

are presented on a page, leading to learner assumptions that this is the only way of depicting a cube. It is useful to extend the notion of *figural concepts* to apply to any concept in which unintended dimensions of possible variation are taken to be invariant and necessary. One example is the use of fractions as operators on figures in which the whole of the figure as presented is always the whole on which the fraction acts, leading to learners overlooking the possibility of selecting what part of a diagram is to be acted upon, and that what really matters with fractions is to be explicit (and hence flexible) about the whole that is to be operated on.

So an extremely important question to ask when variation is being used, is "what figural concepts might be adduced by learners unintentionally?". This is a vital pedagogic question that is essential whenever variation is planned, but not one that can be addressed by theoretical constructs or by invariant rules or principles. It requires mathematical and pedagogical experience.

Variation in Task Structure and Presentation

Having selected a task, there are many dimension of possible variation in how the task is presented. It can be presented on paper, on a screen or on a board. It can be presented statically and complete, or dynamically as an unfolding sequence, either by animation or by the teacher judging and varying the pace. It can be presented in silence, with commentary, or interactively. It can be used with strategies such as Say What You See, with or without small group discussion. Learners can be invited or prompted to make their own copies, to make another example, and to try to articulate some or all of the structural relationships (Mason & Johnston-Wilder, 2004a). Seeing these choices as pedagogic variation could enrich teacher choices by reminding them of pedagogic strategies and little variations according to their reading of the situation unfolding in the classroom.

VARIATION-PEDAGOGY AND PEDAGOGIC VARIATION

Although many of the chapters in this book focus on how variation can be used as a focus for analyzing lessons, and hence for planning lessons, they reveal more, namely that there are subtle pedagogic moves which both depend upon and exploit the variation. I use the term *variation-pedagogy* to refer to pedagogic actions used to exploit variation. I suggest that they can be informed by being aware of the relationship between what the teacher is attending to, and how, and what learners are attending to, and how. What is important is that pedagogic actions do not become solidified, that they do not form a rigid and constant sequence. Rather, they too are subject to variation in various dimensions, and that the art of teaching lies in the flexibility and variation of pedagogic choices.

The whole purpose of variation as a theory and as a practice is to make learning efficient by drawing upon the psyche of the learners, including their natural powers. While it is certainly the case that textbooks constructed along variation principles, used by teachers who appreciate and comprehend these principles, can make an important contribution, texts are themselves only ink on paper. They are not, I suggest, sufficient in and of themselves (*cf.* Zhang et al., Chapter 14 in this book). It requires a person to make sense of them, to seek and find their own coherence. An incoherent text may make this difficult for many readers, but a coherent text cannot in and of itself ensure coherence in the meanings constructed by teachers or by learners. The extra ingredients required include the will (initiative) of learners and the pedagogic choices made by teachers. Where the pedagogy is in alignment with learners' psyche, effective learning can be expected.

Some Specific Pedagogical Actions

Variation as an informing principle can open up opportunity to use pedagogic actions which might otherwise not be effective. For example, Huang and Leung (Chapter 8 in this book) describe a lesson in which great care has been taken in getting students to attend to relationships between angles. During work on 'applications', when the students do not detect an important sub-configuration, the teacher recommends the action of removing lines from complex diagrams. This action could develop into learning to ignore (without deleting) through stressing other lines. In the language of forms of attention, learners are given time to educate their awareness by internalizing the strategy of stressing some features and consequently ignoring others in seeking to discern details as wholes which can be held. These discerned wholes can then be exploited through relevant internalized actions associated with those sub-configurations, and experienced as perceiving properties being instantiated. All this is made possible by the previous work on becoming familiar with discerning pairs of related angles.

Overall, this process of working on discerning and exploiting familiar sub-configurations is referred to in Huang and Leung as *opening a space of learning*. However, without access to relevant pedagogic moves to achieve desired shifts of attention and educating of awareness, 'opening a space of learning' is liable to go the way of other summarizing labels, like 'zone of proximal development' and 'discovery learning' which, without specific details, are too vague to lead to effective action, being open to multiple interpretations.

An effective way to direct learner attention is through getting them to stress something, and consequently ignore other things. Brown and Walter (1983) articulated a strategy which achieves this. Different people are invited to read out a task or theorem or definition by placing particular emphasis or stress on just one of the words. The effect is to invite the question "why that word; how might that be varied?". Stressing one word, number or symbol can be sufficient to open it up as a dimensions of possible variation.

Several chapters in this book stress the importance of precise language, and make use of what seems to be a Chinese propensity to label things: both types of mathematical objects and pedagogic moves. Even so, as Ding et al. (Chapter 12 in this book) acknowledges, it can be difficult for teachers to change well established habits, and so difficult for professional development to be effective. It was for this very reason that the Discipline of Noticing was articulated (Mason, 2002) as a collection of methods to assist in replacing habits with fresh actions. It is possible that variation itself could be used to inform professional development practices.

A case has been made in the examples used to illustrate various issues concerning variation that pedagogic intervention can often be helpful, if not vital, and the analyses of the various lessons in chapters of this book underpin the fact that a great deal depends on the institutional and mathematical milieu (Brousseau, 1997), as well as on the teacher's sensitivity to learners' experiences both past and present. But pedagogical choices need to be subtle, not prescriptive, and so variation plays a role here too. Koichu, Zaslavsky, and Dolev (2013, p. 461), quoted in Watson (Chapter 5 this book) make a similar point through their use of the term *space of learning* which connects intended, enacted and experienced learning as a domain of pedagogic choice.

Pedagogic Variation

In parallel with 'what is available to be learned by students?' from one or more tasks, there is a corresponding pedagogic question: 'what is available to be enacted by a teacher?'. Not only is this a pedagogic form of variation, encompassing a range of pedagogic actions that can be used to initiate activity and interaction with learners, but it has associated dimensions of possible variation and ranges of effective change.

For a particular pedagogic action (for example, Talking in Pairs, Say What You See, Learners Writing on Boards, What It Is and What It Is not, or What is the Same and What is Different about ...) there are features of the principal action which can be varied, but only if the teacher is awake to them as possibilities. For example, in Talking in Pairs, the teacher can set a specific question to be addressed, or can invite learners to try to articulate something they have been working on; in Say What You See, learners can be in small groups, or in plenary and the teacher can make sure everyone has the opportunity to say something or can take a few contributions; they can choose to have students work individually, in small otherwise unstructured groups or in groups with specific tasks or specific roles or in plenary; Learners Writing on Boards, can be done individually, in small groups, or with movement between boards promoted so that there is collaboration both within a group and between groups.

The notion of *range of effective change* draws attention to limits to the scope of variation associated with a pedagogic action. For example, 'talking in pairs', or indeed any pedagogic activity, can be very effective at first, but if allowed to go on beyond the point where the energy in the room has dissipated and declined, it can turn into opportunity for learners to chat amongst themselves, permitting them to drift off task. Action initiated by the teacher may prove effective for a while (for example getting learners to evaluate their effort at the end of a lesson: see Baird and Northfield (1992); or getting learners to construct an easy, a hard and a novel or general example (see for example Bills, 1996; Watson & Mason, 2002). However, any pedagogic strategy will lose its potency if repeated too often or too frequently. If the action is one that learners could usefully integrate into their own functioning, then some process of scaffolding and fading (Brown et al., 1989) may be appropriate, in which initially direct prompts to action become increasingly indirect ("what did you do last time in this situation?") until learners spontaneously initiate it for themselves (Love & Mason, 1992). So not only the choice of action to initiate, but also the length of time the action is allowed to continue depends on the sensitivities of the teacher to what the learners are actually doing, and what the teacher hopes the learners will experience through the activity.

Withdrawing from an action in order to consider whether the action appears to be effective, and if so, when else it might be similarly effective, can help strengthen the *witness,* drawing attention to dimensions of possible variation of that action, and is a useful contribution to the 'something else' that is required in order to learn from experience. Prompting students to construct their own narratives, trying to articulate what sense they have made is clearly present in several if not most of the lessons reported in the chapters in this book. The same applies to teachers.

Pedagogic preparation for teaching a lesson includes bringing some appropriate pedagogic actions to the fore: imagining oneself as vividly as possible carrying them out mentally so that they are available to be enacted when needed. This is a form of *educating pedagogic awareness* following Gattegno (1970; see also Young & Messum, 2011). In these terms, one can see 'teaching' as creating conditions in which and experiences through which learners can 'educate their awareness', that is in which learners are led to integrate into their functioning not only the carrying out of procedures and the construction of examples but sensitivities to notice situations in which those actions could be useful. The Discipline of Noticing (Mason, 2002) can be seen as a collection practices directed to this end.

Ding et al. (Chapter 4 in this book) studied the way In which variation principles were addressed during teacher professional development, concentrating on gaps between pedagogic actions initiated by the teacher and suggestions made in the textbook. An obvious question arises as to whether variation principles could also inform the ways in which professional development is constructed and carried out. There is a lot to be gained by working with teachers in a manner consistent with how they are intended or expected to work with their students.

CONCLUSIONS

Variation as a principle informing what is available to be learned is consistent with the way human beings function. It follows that variation as a principle to inform both teaching and teacher education, including teacher professional development, is likely to be powerful. What the chapters in this book demonstrate is that variation alone is not going to guarantee that learning actually takes place. For learning to take place, that is for integration and internalization of mathematical actions, it is not usually enough to have experienced variation. "One thing we don't seem to learn from experience, is that we don't often learn from experience alone. Something more is required" (Mason, 1998). Worse "a succession of experiences does not add up to an experience of succession" (Mason & Davis, 1989). This turns out to be a version of an assertion by James (1892, p. 628) that "a succession of feelings does not add up to a feeling of succession". In other words, more is required than simply a succession of experiences of variation if we are going to learn from them.

Appropriate pedagogical moves are required to maximise the possibility that the variation provided will influence learners, and are themselves informed by awareness of dimensions of possible variation associated with each pedagogical action, and familiarity with appropriate ranges of effective change in those dimensions. These constitute *variation-pedagogy*. But in my view there is no recipe, no 'best sequence'. What is required is sensitivity to the topic, to the students and their past and current experiences. One way to develop this sensitivity is to pay particular attention to both what needs to be attended to, and how. This calls upon the teacher to be aware of their awarenesses, in the sense of Gattegno (1970; 1987 see also Mason, 1998), concerning both what they themselves are attending to, and how, with access to pedagogic moves that encourage and promote such shifts of attention.

Variation is something to be sensitized to, not a programme or a sequence of pre-determined pedagogical acts to enact. The chapters in this book all point to the artistry of variation-pedagogy rather than to a mechanical process to ensure learning takes place. Ensuring learning, attractive as it may seem to policy makers, is simply impossible because, as Confucius observed, self-motivation, the taking of initiative by learners, acting upon their recent and past experiences as they undertake tasks they are offered, is essential and not under teacher control. Will is a key part of the human psyche. Of course the teacher can create conditions which make learner participation more likely, and many of the pedagogic actions mentioned in chapters in this book are designed to assist with this, whether by maintaining a reasonable but neither excessive nor miniscule challenge, by providing time for learner attention to encounter and make sense of what is being offered as foci of attention, or time for personal construal and narrative building through discussion with peers and in the presence of the teacher. The same applies to teachers making sense of a lesson.

Several of the chapters in this book suggest or imply that it is very difficult to disentangle conceptual and procedural variation. For example, one of the effects of the pedagogic moves underpinning the examples in Peng, Li, Nie and Li (Chapter 6 in this book) is that variation, in their case changing conditions constituting the data, is really providing access to the conceptual underpinnings of the procedures for solving right triangles. In other words, making distinctions between conceptual variation and procedural variation is not as straightforward as it seems on the surface. I wonder whether it will prove to be helpful for teachers.

In terms of attention, lesson descriptions in this book indicate that variation-informed pedagogic actions devote time to a thorough exposure to *discerning*

434

relevant *details* and *recognizing* significant *relationships*, aiming for a fusion of awareness that might otherwise be skipped over superficially from a desire to 'get to the nub'. One of the lessons from variation theory is that the 'nub' is not the 'doing of exercises', valuable as that might be, but rather lies in appreciating and comprehending the critical features, the *details* that need to be *discerned* in order that structural *relationships* can be *recognized*, so that student attention can shift to *perceiving properties* as being instantiated. It is evident that time spent on 'student narratives', on students articulating and rephrasing for themselves the core ideas of the lesson is a significant part of learner experience when the teaching is informed by variation principles. In this way students experience contrast, generalization, separation and fusion. The whole point about making distinctions or discerning details is not to dwell in those distinctions themselves, but rather to have access to them, to have recourse to associated actions, when in the midst of an unfamiliar situation in the future. This is what *problem solving* is really about.

One of the features emerging from many of the chapters in this book is the value of being sensitive to learner experience, and this aligns well with the 'teaching-triad' of Jaworski (1994; see also Despari & Jaworski, 2002) which highlights sensitivity to learners, appropriate challenge, and management of learning. For example, taking time to make sure that everyone has time to gaze at a diagram or exercise before rushing to enact the first action that becomes available. In the language of attention this is holding wholes and applies not only to a 'whole' but to a discerned aspect or part. It is more efficient to make sure that learners are discerning details that the teacher knows are important than to rush on to seeking our relationships or perceiving properties as being instantiated too quickly. 'Stressing and consequently ignoring', is how generalization takes place, how learner attention shifts from recognizing a relationship in a particular situation to perceiving a property as being instantiated in the particular. Seeing the general through the particular, and the particular in the general are fundamental acts of attention which need to be invoked, supported, promoted, and internalized if learners are going to internalize actions (procedures) and appreciate and comprehend both concepts and procedures.

REFERENCES

Bachelard, G. (1938, reprinted 1980). *La Formation de l'Esprit scientifique*. Paris: J. Vrin.
Baird, J., & Northfield, F. (1992). *Learning from the peel experience*. Melbourne: Monash University.
Bennett, J. (1993). *Elementary systematics: A tool for understanding wholes*. Santa Fe: Bennett Books.
Biggs, J., & Collis, K. (1982). *Evaluating the quality of learning: The SOLO taxonomy*. New York, NY: Academic Press.
Bills, L. (1996). The use of examples in the teaching and learning of mathematics. In L. Puig & A. Gutierrez (Eds.), *Proceedings of the 20th Conference of the International Group for the Psychology of Mathematics Education* (Vol. 2, pp. 81–88). Valencia: Universitat de València.
Brousseau, G. (1997). *Theory of didactical situations in mathematics: didactiques des mathématiques, 1970–1990* (N. Balacheff, M. Cooper, R. Sutherland, & V. Warfield, Trans.). Dordrecht: Kluwer.
Brown S., Collins A., & Duguid P. (1989). Situated cognition and the culture of learning. *Educational Researcher, 18*(1), 32–41.

435

Brown, S., & Walter, M. (1983). *The art of problem posing*. Philadelphia, PA: Franklin Press.

Bruner, J. (1966). *Towards a theory of instruction*. Cambridge, MA: Harvard University Press.

Bruner, J., Goodnow, J., & Austin, G. (1956). *A study of thinking*. New York, NY: Wiley.

Cohen, M., & Carpenter, J. (1983). The effects of non-examples in geometrical concept acquisition. *International Journal of Mathematics Education, Science and Technology, 11*, 259–263.

Colburn, W, (1829). *Arithmetic upon the inductive method of instruction, being a sequel to Intellectual Arithmetic*. Boston, MA: Hilliard, Gray, Little & Wilkins.

Festinger, L. (1957). *A theory of cognitive dissonance*. Stanford, CA: Stanford University Press.

Fischbein, E. (1987). *Intuition in science and mathematics: An educational approach*. Dordrecht: Reidel.

Fischbein, E. (1993). The theory of figural concepts. *Educational Studies in Mathematics, 24*, 139–162.

Gagné, R. (1977). *The conditions of learning*. New York, NY: Holt, Rinehart, & Winston.

Gallagher, W. (2009). *Rapt: Attention and the focused life*. New York, NY: Penguin Press.

Gattegno, C. (1970). *What we owe children: The subordination of teaching to learning*. London: Routledge & Kegan Paul.

Gattegno, C. (1973). *In the beginning there were no words: The universe of babies*. New York, NY: Educational Solutions.

Gattegno, C. (1987). *The science of education part 1: Theoretical considerations*. New York, NY: Educational Solutions.

Gattegno, C. (1988). *The mind teaches the brain* (2nd ed.). New York, NY: Educational Solutions.

Gu, L. (1994). *Theory of teaching experiment: The methodology and teaching principles of Qingpu* [In Chinese]. Beijing: Educational Science Press.

Hadamard, J. (1945). *An essay on the psychology of invention in the mathematical field*. Princeton, NJ: Princeton University Press.

Heidegger, M. (1927/1949). *Existence & being* (W. Brock, Trans.). London: Vision Press.

Honsberger, R. (1970). *Ingenuity in mathematics* (New Mathematical Library #23). Washington, DC: Mathematical Association of America.

Huang, R., Barlow, A., & Prince, K. (2016). The same tasks, different learning opportunities: An analysis of two exemplary lessons in China and the U.S. from a perspective of variation. *Journal of Mathematical Behavior, 41*, 141–158.

Huang, R., Gong Z., & Han, X. (2016). Implementing mathematics teaching that promotes students' understanding through theory-driven lesson study. *ZDM-The International Journal on Mathematics Education, 48*, 425–439.

James, W. (1890 reprinted 1950). *Principles of psychology* (Vol. 1), New York, NY: Dover.

Jaworski, B. (1994). *Investigating mathematics teaching: A constructivist enquiry*. London: Falmer Press.

Kahneman, D. (2012). *Thinking fast, thinking slow*. London: Penguin.

Koichu, B., Zaslavsky, O., & Dolev, L. (2013). Effects of variations in task design using different representations of mathematical objects on learning: A case of a sorting task. In C. Margolinas (Ed.), *Task design in mathematics education, proceedings of the ICMI study 22* (pp. 467–476). Oxford.

Lakoff, G., & Nunez, R. (2000). *Where mathematics comes from: How the embodied mind brings mathematics into being*. New York, NY: Basic Books.

Lo, M., & Marton, F. (2012). Toward a science of the art of teaching: Using variation theory as a guiding principle of pedagogical design. *International Journal for Lesson and Learning Studies, 1*, 7–22.

Love, E., & Mason, J. (1992). *Teaching mathematics: Action and awareness*. Milton Keynes: Open University.

Marton, F. (2015). *Necessary conditions for learning*. Abingdon: Routledge.

Marton, F., & Booth, S. (1997). *Learning and awareness*. Hillsdale, NJ: Lawrence Erlbaum.

Marton, F., & Pang, M. (2006). On some necessary conditions of learning. *Journal of the Learning Sciences, 15*(2), 193–220.

Mason, J. (1979, February). Which medium, which message? *Visual Education*, 29–33.

Mason, J. (1980). When is a symbol symbolic? *For the Learning of Mathematics, 1*(2), 8–12.

Mason J. (1998). Enabling teachers to be real teachers: Necessary levels of awareness and structure of attention. *Journal of Mathematics Teacher Education, 1*, 243–267.

Mason, J. (2002). *Researching your own practice: The discipline of noticing*. London: RoutledgeFalmer.

Mason, J. (2003). Structure of attention in the learning of mathematics. In J. Novotná (Ed.), *Proceedings, International symposium on elementary mathematics teaching* (pp. 9–16). Prague: Charles University.

Mason, J. (2008). From concept images to pedagogic structure for a mathematical topic. In C. Rasmussen & M. Carlson (Eds.), *Making the connection: Research into practice in undergraduate mathematics education* (pp. 253–272). Washington, DC: Mathematical Association of America.

Mason, J. (2008a). Making use of children's powers to produce algebraic thinking. In J. Kaput, D. Carraher, & M. Blanton (Eds.), *Algebra in the early grades* (pp. 57–94). New York, NY: Lawrence Erlbaum.

Mason, J. (2009). From assenting to asserting. In O. Skvovemose, P. Valero, & O. Christensen (Eds.), *University science and mathematics education in transition* (pp. 17–40). Berlin: Springer.

Mason, J. (2011). Explicit and implicit pedagogy: Variation as a case study. In J. Smith (Ed.) *Proceedings of BSRLM, 31*(2).

Mason, J. (Website accessed August 2016). Retrieved from www.pmtheta.com/sundaram-grids.html and www.pmtheta.com/structured-variation-grids.html

Mason, J., & Davis, J. (1989). The inner teacher, the didactic tension, and shifts of attention. In G. Vergnaud, J. Rogalski, & M. Artigue (Eds.) *Proceedings of PME XIII* (Vol. 2, pp. 274–281). Paris.

Mason, J., & Johnston-Wilder, S. (2004a). *Fundamental constructs in mathematics education*. London: Routledge Falmer.

Mason, J., & Johnston-Wilder, S. (2004b). *Designing and using mathematical tasks*. Milton Keynes, UK: Open University; (2006 reprint) St. Albans: QED.

Mason, J., & Metz, M. (in press). Digging beneath dual systems theory and the bicameral brain: Abductions about the human psyche from experience in mathematical problem solving. In U. Xolocotzin (Ed.), *Understanding emotions in mathematical thinking and learning*. San Diego, CA: Elsevier.

Mason, J., & Pimm, D. (1984). Generic examples: Seeing the general in the particular. *Educational Studies in Mathematics, 15*, 277–290.

Mason, J., Johnston-Wilder, S., & Graham, A. (2005). *Developing thinking in algebra*. London: Sage (Paul Chapman).

Mason, J., Burton, L., & Stacey, K. (2010). *Thinking mathematically* (Second Extended Edition). Harlow: Prentice Hall (Pearson).

Maturana, H. (1988). Reality: The search for objectivity or the quest for a compelling argument. *Irish Journal of Psychology, 9*(1), 25–82.

Minsky, M. (1975). A framework for representing knowledge. In P. Winston (Ed.), *The psychology of computer vision* (pp. 211–280). New York, NY: McGraw Hill.

Minsky, M. (1986). *The society of mind*. New York, NY: Simon and Schuster.

Norretranders, T. (1998). *The user illusion: Cutting consciousness down to size* (J. Sydenham Trans.). London: Allen Lane.

Ouspensky, P. (1950). *In search of the miraculous: Fragments of an unknown teaching*. London: Routledge & Kegan Paul.

Pólya, G. (1962). *Mathematical discovery: On understanding, learning, and teaching problem solving* (combined edition). New York, NY: Wiley.

Potari, D., & Jaworski, B. (2002).Tackling complexity in mathematics teaching development: Using the teaching triad as a tool for reflection and analysis. *Journal of Mathematics Teacher Education, 5*, 351–380.

Ramaswami Aiyar, V. (1934). Sundaram's sieve for prime numbers. *The Mathematics Student, 2*(2), 73.

Ravindra, R. (2009). *The wisdom of Patañjali's yoga sutras: A new translation and guide*. Sandpoint, ID: Morning Light Press.

Rhadakrishnan, S. (1953). *The principal Upanishads*. London: George Allen & Unwin.

Schoenfeld, A. H. (1992). Learning to think mathematically: Problem solving, metacognition, and sense-making in mathematics. In D. Grouws (Ed.), *Handbook for research on mathematics teaching and learning* (pp. 334–370). New York, NY: MacMillan.

Seeley Brown, J., Collins A., & Duguid, P. (1989). Situated cognition and the culture of learning. *Educational Researcher, 18*(1), 32–42.

Simon, M., & Tzur, R. (2004). Explicating the role of mathematical tasks in conceptual learning: An elaboration of the hypothetical learning trajectory. *Mathematical Thinking and Learning, 6*, 91–104.

Song, X. (2006). Confucian education thinking and the chinese mathematical education tradition [In Chinese]. *Journal of Gansu Normal College, 2*, 65–68.

St. Augustine, (389/1938). (Trans. G. Leckie). *De magistro*. Appleton-Century-Croft.

Stedall, J. (2002). *A discourse concerning algebra: English algebra to 1685*. Oxford: Oxford University Press.

Stein, M., Grover, B., & Henningsen, M. (1996). Building student capacity for mathematical thinking and reasoning: An analysis of mathematical tasks used in reform classrooms. *American Educational Research Journal, 33*, 455–488.

Sun, X. (2011). An insider's perspective: "variation problems" and their cultural grounds in Chinese curriculum practice. *Journal of Mathematics Education, 4*, 101–114.

Sun, X. (2011). "Variation problems" and their roles in the topic of fraction division in Chinese mathematics textbook examples. *Educational Studies in Mathematics, 76*, 65–85.

Tall, D. (1977a). *Cognitive conflict and the learning of mathematics*. Paper presented at the First Conference of The International Group for the Psychology of Mathematics Education. Utrecht, Netherlands. Retrieved June, 2016, from www.warwick.ac.uk/staff/David.Tall/pdfs/dot1977a-cog-confl-pme.pdf

Tall, D. (1977b). Conflict & catastrophes in the learning of mathematics. *Mathematical Education for Teaching, 2*(4).

Thompson, P. (2002). Didactic objects and didactic models in radical constructivism. In K. Gravemeijer, R. Lehrer, B. van Oers, & L. Verschaffel (Eds.), *Symbolizing, modeling, and tool use in mathematics education* (pp. 191–212). Dordrecht: Kluwer.

van der Veer, R., & Valsiner, J. (1991). *Understanding Vygotsky*. London: Blackwell.

van Hiele-Geldof, D. (1957). The Didactiques of geometry in the lowest class of secondary school. In D. Fuys, D. Geddes, & R. Tichler (Eds.), *1984, English translation of selected writings of Dina van Hiele-Geldof and Pierre M. van Hiele*. New York, NY: Brooklyn College, National Science Foundation.

van Hiele, P. (1986). *Structure and insight: A theory of mathematics education* (Developmental Psychology Series). London: Academic Press.

Vygotsky, L. (1978). *Mind in society: The development of the higher psychological processes*. London: Harvard University Press.

Wallis, J. (1682). *Treatise of algebra both historical and practical sewing the original progress, and advancement thereof, from time to time; and by what steps it hath attained to the height at which it now is*. London: Richard Davis.

Watson, A. (2016). Variation: Analysing and designing tasks. *Mathematics Teaching, 252*, 13–17.

Watson, A., & Mason, J. (2002). Student-generated examples in the learning of mathematics. *Canadian Journal of Science, Mathematics and Technology Education, 2*, 237–249.

Watson, A., & Mason, J. (2005). *Mathematics as a constructive activity: Learners generating examples*. Mahwah, NJ: Erlbaum.

Wentworth, G. (1894). *The first steps in algebra*. New York, NY: Ginn.

Wilhelm, R. (Trans.). (1967). *The I Ching or book of changes*. Princeton, NJ: Princeton University press for Bollingen Foundation.

Young, R., & Messum, P. (2011). *How we learn and how we should be taught: An introduction to the work of Caleb Gattegno*. London: Duo Flamina.

Zitner , S. (Ed.). (1968). *Spencer: The mutabilitie cantos*. London: Nelson.

John Mason
Open University, UK

ABOUT THE AUTHORS

Jill ADLER holds the SARChI Mathematics Education Chair at the University of the Witwatersrand, which focuses on research and development in secondary mathematics education. Jill has spearheaded several large-scale teacher development projects, the most recent, within the Chair ambit, began in 2009, is called the Wits Maths Connect Secondary project. This work builds on her research on teaching in multilingual classrooms, and teacher professional development. Jill is a Visiting Professor of Mathematics Education at King's College London, UK. She is the recipient of numerous awards, the most significant of which are the 2012 Academy of Science of South Africa (ASSAf) Gold Medal for Science in the Service of Society, and the 2015 Freudenthal Award.

Jiansheng BAO is a professor of mathematics education in the Department of Mathematics at East China Normal University, China. He was a high school mathematics teacher for 6 years and earned his Ph.D. in mathematics education at East China Normal University. He was a Professor of Mathematics Education in Soochow University and Chief-editor of Secondary Mathematics Monthly. He is now the member of expert group for the modification of new High School Mathematics Curriculum Standards in Mainland China and Chief-editor of *Mathematics Teaching and Learning*. His research interests include mathematics teacher education, psychology of mathematics education, and international comparison in mathematics education.

Angela T. BARLOW is a professor of mathematics education and the director of the Doctor of Philosophy program in Mathematics and Science Education at Middle Tennessee State University. Her primary teaching responsibilities include doctoral level coursework aimed at the scholarly development of mathematics and science educators. Her research interests involve a range of issues that focus on supporting the instructional change process in elementary mathematics classrooms. Recent work includes the influence of implicit theories on the professional development experiences of elementary mathematics teachers, the use of a theory of variation for analyzing the learning opportunities afforded during instruction, and modeling with mathematics.

David CLARKE is Professor and the Director of the International Centre for Classroom Research (ICCR) at the University of Melbourne. Over the last twenty years, his research activity has centered on capturing the complexity of classroom practice through a program of international video-based classroom research in more than 20 countries. Other significant research has addressed teacher professional

439

learning, metacognition, problem-based learning, assessment, multi-theoretic research designs, cross-cultural analyses, curricular alignment, and the challenge of research synthesis in education. Professor Clarke has written books on assessment and on classroom research and has published his research work in around 200 book chapters, journal articles, and conference proceedings. The establishment of the Science of Learning Research Classroom at the Melbourne Graduate School of Education in 2015 provides Professor Clarke with access to new levels of detail and experimental precision for his classroom research. His most recent work addresses the conditions for legitimate international comparative research (the validity-comparability compromise) and the role of comparison in constructing and crossing boundaries.

Liping DING is Associate Professor in Mathematics Education at NTNU, Norwegian University of Science and Technology. She was a middle school mathematics teacher in Shanghai from 1993 to 2002. She completed her Ph.D. in mathematics Education at the University of Southampton, UK in 2008. She then developed her expertise in comparative research of mathematics classroom through her Postdoctoral Fellowship at Massey University, New Zealand from 2008 to 2010. Her research interest and expertise in mathematics education includes mathematics teachers' professional development, lesson design study, students/teachers' affect in mathematics and the van Hiele theory of children's geometrical thinking development.

Matthew D. DUNCAN is a lecturer of mathematics and is pursuing his Ph.D. in mathematics education at Middle Tennessee State University. He teaches algebra and statistics for at-risk college students as well as statistics for distance learners. His early research interests and recent work focuses on formative assessment and supporting reform-oriented instruction in statistics classrooms at all levels.

Zikun GONG is a Professor at Hangzhou Normal University. He is currently the associate director of center for education research. His research interests include teaching and learning procedural knowledge, children' cognitive development such as children' cognitive development of probability and inference, learning trajectories of core math concepts, and teacher professional development. He has edited national compulsory course textbooks, such as primary school mathematics textbooks and middle school mathematics textbooks. Additionally, he also published books: *Teaching and Learning of Procedural Knowledge, Mathematics Teachers' Professional Competence, Mathematics Pedagogy,* and *Theory and Practice of Chinese 'Two Basic' Teaching and Learning.* Dr. Gong has conducted a number of national research projects such as 'The adaptability research of national mathematics curriculum standards in compulsory education' and 'the children's cognitive development research in probability concepts.' Dr. Gong received the second prize in national basic educational teaching achievement in 2014 and presented his research findings at ICME-13 meeting in Germany, 2016.

Feishi GU is currently a teaching research specialist in high school mathematics at Xuhui District Educational Institute in Shanghai and a Ph.D. candidate at East China Normal University. He has chaired several large-scale projects including "learning from doing" (A Sino-French collaborative project), which won the exemplary project in teaching reform by the Ministry of Education in China. His research interests include mathematics education, teaching with variation, and mathematics educators' education.

Lingyuan GU is a professor at East China Normal University. He was the president of Qingpu Teacher Education School and Associate Dean of Academy of Educational Research in Shanghai. He was a member of the committee of Educational Sciences in China and the committee of K-9 Basic Education, vice president of expert team of Second and Elementary Mathematics Teaching in China, and a member of standard committee for Assessing Curriculum and Textbook at K-12 in China. He won the highest award of model worker at national and city levels, and was named an Education Hero in Shanghai. A final report based on a Qingpu teaching reform experiment over more than 20 years won the first prize of Educational Sciences in China. The research achievement has also been popularized by Ministry of Education in China. Another influential research on exploring an innovative approach to in-service teacher professional development, known as "Action Education" has been popularized as teacher professional development model in China. The research on developing this model won the first prize of Curriculum Reform Achievement in China. This model has been internationally coined as Chinese lesson study. Dr. Gu has been invited to give presentations as a keynote speaker at many international conferences including International Conference on Mathematics Education (ICME), International Conference on Education, and The World Association of Lesson Studies International Conference.

Xue HAN is currently an Assistant Professor in the College of Education at National Louis University, USA. She received her doctoral degree from Michigan State University with a concentration on mathematics teacher learning and professional development. She was a faculty member at University of New Mexico and Dominican University. Her research interests include mathematics teacher learning and professional development, elementary and middle school mathematics instruction, and international comparative education. She has published articles in highly prestigious journals including *Elementary School Journal*.

Keiko HINO is a Professor of Mathematics Education at Utsunomiya University in Japan. She received her M.Ed. from Tsukuba University and Ph.D. in Education from Southern Illinois University. Her major scholarly interests are students' development of proportional reasoning and functional thinking through classroom teaching, international comparative study on teaching and learning mathematics, and mathematics teachers' professional development. She has published 2 books,

441

20 book chapters, and over 40 journal articles and presented at over 40 conferences, including the International Congress on Mathematics Education, the International Conference of Psychology of Mathematics Education, the East Asia Regional Conference on Mathematics Education, and annual meetings of the Japan Society of Mathematics Education and of Japan Society for Science Education. She is also involved in activities for improving mathematics education as an editor of *Japanese Primary and Lower Secondary School Mathematics Textbooks* and External-expert for Lesson Study in Mathematics.

Danting HUANG is a mathematics teacher in Beijing No. 80 High School. She graduated from Beijing Normal University. During her study, she focused on mathematical literacy and published articles about conceptual understanding that played a significant role in mathematics literacy. She is currently a teacher who teaches Pre-calculus, AP Calculus, and other international mathematics courses in English in high school.

Rongjin HUANG is an associate professor at Middle Tennessee State University, USA. His research interests include mathematics classroom research, mathematics teacher education, and comparative mathematics education. He has completed several research and professional development projects such as Learner's perspective study (2006), Implementing effective mathematics teaching for all students through Lesson Study (2014), and Understanding progressions, assessment and content knowledge in mathematics (2015). Dr. Huang has published numerous scholarly works including eight books, more than 100 articles and book chapters, and two special issues. His recently published books include *How Chinese Teach Mathematics and Improve Teaching* (Routledge, 2013), *Prospective Mathematics Teacher' Knowledge of Algebra: A Comparative Study in China and the United States of America* (Springer, 2014). Dr. Huang has served as a guest editor for ZDM *Mathematics Education* and *International Journal of Lesson and Learning Studies*. He has organized and chaired many sessions at various national and international professional conferences, such as AERA (2013, 2014), NCTM (2009, 2012), and ICME (2008, 2016).

Xingfeng HUANG is an associate professor at Shanghai Normal University. He received his Ph.D. in Mathematics Education from East China Normal University in 2008. He had previously taught secondary mathematics in school for ten years from 1995 to 2005. His research interests include pre-service elementary teacher preparation and in-service teacher professional development.

Johan HÄGGSTRÖM is a Senior Lecturer at the Department of Pedagogical, Curricular and Professional Studies and at the National Centre for Mathematics Education, at University of Gothenburg. He is editor of *Nordic Studies in Mathematics Education*.

Keith JONES is an Associate Professor in Mathematics Education at the University of Southampton, UK, where he is Deputy Head of the Mathematics and Science Education (MaSE) Research Centre. His expertise in mathematics education includes mathematics teacher education and professional development, as well as geometrical problem solving and reasoning and the use of technology in mathematics education. He has well-established research collaborations with educators in China and Japan and various parts of Europe. He is on the editorial board of several prominent international journals and taken part in several ICMI studies. He has published widely; his recent co-authored books include Key Ideas in Teaching Mathematics and Youngsters Solving Mathematical Problems with Technology.

Wing Wah KI is an Associate Professor at the Faculty of Education of The University of Hong Kong, in the areas of mathematics, technology and liberal studies education, and the use of information and communication technology for teacher collaborative learning. In recent years, his research has extended to multilingual and intercultural education development and the application of phenomenographic theory in learning.

Dovie KIMMINS is a Professor in the Department of Mathematical Sciences at Middle Tennessee State University. Dr. Kimmins primarily teaches content courses for preservice elementary, middle, and high school teachers as well as the general mathematics population, and has developed and taught new coursework for middle and secondary preservice teachers. Over the past twenty years, Dr. Kimmins has directed or co-directed 23 professional development projects for inservice elementary, middle, and high school teachers, six of these being multiyear projects, directly impacting 1300 mathematics teachers. Dr. Kimmins's research focuses on students' learning in specific contents such as fractions and probability and teachers' learning from their practice.

Konrad KRAINER is a Professor and Dean of the Faculty for Interdisciplinary Studies at the Alpen-Adria-University Klagenfurt (Austria). He worked several years as mathematics teacher and wrote his doctoral and habilitation theses in the field of mathematics education. Dr. Krainer was guest professor and visiting scholar at universities in Australia (Melbourne/Monash), the Czech Republic (Prague), Germany (Duisburg), and the USA (Athens and Iowa City). His recent research focuses on mathematics teacher education, school development and educational system development. He is co-editor of several books (e.g., one volume of the *International Handbook of Mathematics Teacher Education* and the Austrian Education Report, 2015) and leader of the nation-wide IMST project. Krainer was associate editor of *JMTE* and member of international scientific committees (e.g., ERME board, Education Committee of EMS, advisory board of DZLM and the board of trustees of the University College of Teacher Education Carinthia). He gave several plenary presentations at international conferences (including ICME and PME) and was the Chair of the IPC for CERME 9 (Prague, 2015).

443

Angelika KULLBERG is an Assistant Professor at the department of pedagogical, curricular and professional studies at the University of Gothenburg. Her research is focused on teaching and learning of mathematics in classrooms. She is executive committee member in the European Association of Research on Learning and Instruction (EARLI).

Roza LEIKIN is a Professor of Mathematics Education and Education of Gifted at the Faculty of Education, University of Haifa. Her research and practice embrace three interrelated areas: Mathematical creativity and ability; Mathematics teacher knowledge and professional development; Mathematical challenges in education. She is interested in advancing the contribution of neuro-cognitive research methodologies to the field of mathematics education. Dr. Leikin is the Director of the RANGE Center – the Interdisciplinary Center for the Research and Advancement of Giftedness and Co-chair of the Neuro-cognitive laboratory for the investigation of creativity, ability and giftedness in the University of Haifa. She is the Head of the National Advisory Council in Mathematics Education of the Israel Ministry of Education and the President of MCG – the International Group for Mathematical Creativity and Giftedness (affiliated with ICMI http://igmcg.org/). She edited 10 volumes related to research in mathematics education and the education of gifted, published about 150 papers in research journals, books, and refereed conference proceedings. For more details, see http://ps.edu.haifa.ac.il/roza-leikin.html

Allen LEUNG is currently an Associate Professor at Hong Kong Baptist University. He obtained his Ph.D. in Mathematics at University of Toronto, Canada. Before engaging in mathematics education research, he was a secondary school mathematics teacher in Hong Kong. Dr. Leung was an Assistant Professor at The University of Hong Kong and the Hong Kong Institute of Education. Dr. Leung's main research interests are dynamic geometry environment, development of mathematics pedagogy using variation, tool-based mathematics task design, proof and argumentation in mathematics education and lesson study. He has published in major international mathematics education journals, PME conference Proceedings and was involved in ICME 11, 12 and 13 as a Topic Study Group organizing member, a presenter of Regular Lecture and a member of a survey team. Dr. Leung made contributions to four ICMI Studies was an IPC member of the 22nd ICMI Study: Task Design in Mathematics Education.

Frederick Koon-Shing LEUNG is a Kintoy Professor in Mathematics Education at the University of Hong Kong. His research interests include comparative studies of mathematics education and the influence of culture on mathematics teaching and learning, mathematics education of children of ethnic minorities in China, and the influence of the Chinese and English languages on the learning of mathematics. He is principal investigator of the Hong Kong component of Trends in International Mathematics and Science Studies (TIMSS), TIMSS Video Study,

444

and the Learner's Perspective Study (LPS). Professor Leung was member of the Executive Committee of the International Commission on Mathematical Instruction from 2003 to 2009, and member of the Standing Committee of the International Association for the Evaluation of Academic Achievement between 2007 and 2010. Professor Leung is also one of the editors for the *Second and Third International Handbook on Mathematics Education*, published by Springer. He was appointed a Senior Fulbright Scholar in 2003, awarded the Hans Freudenthal Medal in 2013 by the International Commission on Mathematical Instruction, named a Changjiang Scholar by the Ministry of Education, China, in 2104, and he received the World Outstanding Chinese Award in 2015.

Jing LI is an Associate Professor at Langfang Teachers' College, China. His main research interest is teaching with variation.

Yanjie LI is a math teacher at New Century School in Handan city, Hebei province, China.

Yeping LI is a Professor of Mathematics Education at the Department of Teaching, Learning, and Culture at Texas A & M University, USA. He is also named by Shanghai Municipal Education Commission as an "Eastern Scholar" Chair Professor at Shanghai Normal University, China, in 2016. His research interests focus on issues related to mathematics curriculum and teacher education in various education systems and understanding how factors related to mathematics curriculum and teachers may shape effective classroom instruction. He is the editor-in-chief of the *International Journal of STEM Education* published by Springer, and is also the editor of a monograph series *Mathematics Teaching and Learning* published by Sense Publishers. In addition to co-editing over 10 books and special journal issues, he has published more than 100 articles that focus on mathematics curriculum and textbook studies, teachers and teacher education, and classroom instruction. He has also organized and chaired many group sessions at various national and international professional conferences, such as ICME-10 (2004), ICME-11 (2008), and ICME-12 (2012). He received his Ph.D. in Cognitive Studies in Education from the University of Pittsburgh, USA.

Alyson E. LISCHKA is an Assistant Professor of mathematics education at Middle Tennessee State University. She teaches both content and methods courses for prospective secondary mathematics teachers and works extensively with practicing teachers in professional development settings. Her research interests focus on the ways in which both practicing and prospective teachers develop ambitious practices in their teaching of mathematics. Current projects involve investigation of the influence of implicit theories on professional development experiences, examination of the ways in which prospective teachers learn to provide effective feedback, and dissemination of the findings from a national conference on mathematics methods courses.

Ference MARTON is a Senior Professor at the University of Gothenburg, where he earned his Ph.D. in 1970 and has served in different capacities since then. He became Professor of Education 1977. For shorter periods (6 months to 3 years) he was affiliated to various universities in the United Kingdom, the USA, Australia, and China. He has received Honorary doctorate from the University of Edinburgh (2000), the University of Helsinki (2003) and from the Hong Kong Institute of Education (2007). Dr. Marton has published more than 250 papers and books in Educational Psychology, in particular within specializations such as qualitative differences in learning, phenomenography and the variation theory of learning.

John MASON is a Professor at the Open University in the UK where he has spent forty years at writing distance teaching materials in mathematics and mathematics education. His work focuses on core elements of teaching and learning mathematics, such as attention, mental imagery, and problem solving. He develops apps for use in workshops which help him explore mathematical problems or which can be used to work on key ideas in mathematics at all levels from kindergarten to tertiary.

Ida Ah Chee MOK is an Associate Dean and Associate Professor in the Faculty of Education at the University of Hong Kong. She obtained her B.Sc. (Mathematics Major, First Class Honour) and M.Ed. from the University of Hong Kong, and her Ph.D. from King's College, the University of London. She has been awarded the Diamond Jubilee International Visiting Fellowship (2013-2016) at the University of Southampton. Since 1990, she has been a teacher educator active in both the Hong Kong local community and the international research arena of mathematics education. She has a broad research interest that includes mathematics education, technology in mathematics education, comparative studies in mathematics education, teaching and learning, teacher education, pedagogical content knowledge and lesson study. She is a co-chair of the 11th International Congress on Mathematical Education (ICME 11) Topic Study Group: Research on Classroom Practice; invited plenary panel member of the 13th International Congress on Mathematical Education (ICME 13) on "International Comparative Studies in Mathematics: Lessons for Improving Students' Learning"; co-editor of the book *Making Connections: Comparing Mathematics Classrooms around the World*; author of the book *Learning of Algebra: Inspiration from Students' Understanding of the Distributive Law*; and co-author of the book *Polynomials and Equations*.

Bikai NIE is a Lecturer in the Department of Mathematics at Texas State University, USA. His research interests include the preparation for pre-service math teachers, professional development for in-service mathematics teachers, mathematics curricula for K-16, problem solving, problem posing, and quantitative methods in mathematics education research.

Ming Fai PANG is Associate Professor at the Faculty of Education of The University of Hong Kong, with research interests focusing on learning, teaching, and teacher education. He specializes in phenomenography, variation theory, and lesson and learning studies. Recently, he extended his research interests to financial literacy and education for sustainable development. He was the coordinator of the Special Interest Group 'Phenomenography and Variation Theory' at the European Association for Research on Learning and Instruction (EARLI) from 2003 to 2007. He has been the Editor of the SSCI journal *Educational Research Review* since 2010, and Editorial Board Member of *Vocations and Learning*, *International Journal of Lesson and Learning Studies* and *International Review of Economics Education*.

Irit PELED is a Senior Lecturer in the Mathematics Education Department at the University of Haifa. She had earned her doctoral degree at the Technion, Israel Institute of Technology. She directed a ten-year long nationally funded in-service teacher project aimed at improving elementary school mathematics, and served as the chair of the Mathematics Education Department and the Teaching and Teacher Education Department. Her current research interests include modeling processes with a focus on children with difficulties in mathematics. She directed a research project funded by the Israeli Science Foundation on the design of modeling tasks aimed to change teacher conceptions of modeling and of the role of mathematics.

Aihui PENG is an Associate Professor at Southwest University, China. Her research interests include mathematical knowledge for teaching at the secondary school level and mathematics teaching and learning in different cultural contexts.

Kyle M. PRINCE teaches mathematics at Central Magnet School in Murfreesboro, Tennessee, where he has been teaching for seven years. He was named the 2015-2016 Middle Tennessee Teacher of the Year and selected as a finalist for the Presidential Award for Excellence in Science and Mathematics Teaching. In addition to teaching high school, he recently received his Ph.D. in mathematics education at Middle Tennessee State University. His interests include teaching through problem solving and adapting Chinese and Japanese lesson study models in the United States. In his dissertation, Prince explored lesson study as an aid in enhancing teachers' understandings, implementations, and perceptions of mathematics teaching practices.

Chunxia QI is a Professor and Deputy Head of the Institute of Curriculum and Pedagogy, Faculty of Education at Beijing Normal University, China. She is also an executive member of the Curriculum Sub-commission of Chinese society of Education. She was a Fulbright scholar at Teachers College, Columbia University from 2006–2007. Her research interests include school-based curriculum, mathematics curriculum comparison, reform, and development. She has published sixty articles (both in Chinese and in English). She is one of the key members on the National Research and Development Team for Mathematics Curriculum Standards at the Compulsory Education Stage, which is a key decision-making body at the national level for the latest mathematics curriculum reform in China. She is also a chief expert who is responsible for the national mathematics assessment for eighth grade students in China.

Ulla RUNESSON is a Professor of Education and Faculty Dean at Jönköping University, Sweden and visiting professor at Wits School of Education, University of the Witwatersrand, Johannesburg, South Africa. Her research interests include learning and teaching, particularly in mathematics and the teaching profession in general. Over the years she has been responsible for several research projects involving teachers as researchers, funded by the Swedish Research Council. Her Ph.D. was the first one where variation theory of learning was used as an analytical framework and has been engaged with the development of the theory since then. She has been involved in several international research projects studying and comparing classrooms in different countries.

Svein Arne SIKKO is an Associate Professor in Mathematics Education at NTNU, Norwegian University of Science and Technology. He has a doctor degree in pure mathematics within the field of representation theory of algebras. Since 1998, he has been working with mathematics teacher education. His main areas of research interest are teacher professional development, lesson studies, inquiry based learning, and transitional issues.

Rong WANG is currently an Editor of secondary mathematics textbooks for Peoples' Education Press. He has focused on compiling textbooks on functions, pre-calculus, inequality, and statistics and published more than 20 articles in refereed journals in China.

Ruilin WANG is a Lecturer in the college of education at Capital Normal University, China. She is a member of the first cohort of experts under National Teacher Training Program and an expert in School of Continuing Education and Teacher Training, Beijing Normal University. She won the first prize of National Education Professional Degree Teaching Achievement Award in 2015. Her main research areas are Mathematical Education and Teacher Education. She is lead author of *Case Study on Integrative and Practical Mathematics*, co-editor of *The Research of Mathematical Instruction in Secondary School*, co-editor of *Analysis of Mathematical Curriculum Standard and Content in Secondary School*, and the translator of *Key Ideas in Teaching Mathematics*. Beijing Social Science Foundation has supported her research projects.

Anne WATSON is Emeritus Professor at the University of Oxford. She taught mathematics in challenging schools for thirteen years before becoming a teacher educator and researcher. For most of those years she used a problem-based approach and heterogeneous groupings designed to enable more students to achieve in mathematics using enquiry and ad hoc methods. Coming to doubt whether such an approach was supporting more students to develop mathematical habits of mind, she became interested in how tasks could be designed that altered students' natural and situated ways of thinking, so that they became more capable of appreciating and handling abstract relationships. As well as exploring this direction in mathematics education from a theoretical standpoint she remained close to teaching and has published numerous books and articles for teachers. She is known for her focus on social justice through improving learning for young adolescents, always rooting her work in the practices of committed teachers. Her research interests include task design using variation theory, promoting mathematical thinking through interactive strategies, forms of questioning that enable relational understanding, raising achievement for low attaining students, the development of understanding functions concepts and the cognitive work of teaching mathematics.

Ngai-Ying WONG is currently an Honorary Professor at the Education University of Hong Kong. He received his B.A., M. Phil., and Ph.D. from the University of Hong Kong, and M.A. (Ed.) from the Chinese University of Hong Kong. He was Professor at the Chinese University of Hong Kong before his retirement in 2014. He is the founding president of the Hong Kong Association for Mathematics Education. His research interests include classroom learning environment, mathematics education, belief and value, *bianshi* teaching and Confucian Cultural Heritage Learner's phenomena.

Xinrong YANG is an Assistant Professor Southwest University in China. He obtained his Ph.D. from the University of Hong Kong. He has worked as postdoctoral research fellow at Umea University in Sweden from September 2012 to August 2013 and the Institute of Education and The University of London from November 2013 to October 2014 respectively. He is currently undertaking his post-doctoral research at the Hamburg University under the support of Marie Curie Individual Fellowship. He has been working on the topics related to mathematics teacher professional development, classroom learning environment and primary school students' algebraic thinking. He published a few peer-reviewed journal papers on these topics.

Jianyue ZHANG is a Senior Editor in People's Education Press and a scientist in Curriculum, Textbook research institute. His research interests include theories of curriculum textbook compiling educational psychology and mathematics classroom research. He has served as editor in chief in secondary and elementary mathematics and on editorial boards of mathematics bullet, curriculum, textbook, and teaching. Dr. Zhang has numerous publications including mathematics textbooks for middle and high schools. Dr. Zhang has developed a theory of three types of understanding (understanding mathematics, understanding of students, and teaching pedagogy).

Pingping ZHANG is an Assistant Professor of Mathematics Education in the Department of Mathematics and Statistics at Winona State University. She received her bachelor degrees in English and applied mathematics from Beihang University, China, and her master and doctoral degrees in secondary mathematics education from Ohio State University. She has been working with secondary (6th through 12th) students and pre-service/in-service mathematics teachers in the U.S. for seven years. Her research interest lies in mathematical problem solving, metacognition, and teacher education. She currently teaches content courses for elementary and secondary pre-service teachers, and methods courses for middle and secondary pre-service teachers.

SUBJECT INDEX

Lightning Source UK Ltd.
Milton Keynes UK
UKOW05f1524211216
290553UK00005B/195/P